Contemporary Directions in Psychopathology

TOWARD THE DSM-IV

Contemporary Directions in Psychopathology

TOWARD THE DSM-IV

EDITED BY

Theodore Millon

AND

Gerald L. Klerman

THE GUILFORD PRESS

New York   London

PRINTED IN THE UNITED STATES OF AMERICA

Library of Congress Cataloging in Publication Data

Main entry under title:

Contemporary directions in psychopathology.

   Includes bibliographies and index.
   1. Psychology, Pathological—Classification.
2. Mental illness—Diagnosis.   3. Diagnostic and
statistical manual of mental disorders.   I. Millon,
Theodore.   II. Klerman, Gerald L., 1928–   .
[DNLM: 1. Mental Disorders—classification.   2. Mental
Disorders—diagnosis.   WM 15 C761]
RC455.2.C4C66   1986   616.89′0012   85–30549
ISBN 0–89862–659–5

Contributors

Hagop S. Akiskal, MD. Department of Psychiatry, University of Tennessee College of Medicine, Memphis, Tennessee

George W. Albee, PhD. Department of Psychology, University of Vermont, Burlington, Vermont

Nancy C. Andreasen, MD. Department of Psychiatry, University of Iowa, Iowa City, Iowa

Jules R. Bemporad, MD. Department of Psychiatry, Harvard Medical School, Boston, Massachusetts

Lorna Smith Benjamin, PhD. Department of Psychiatry, University of Wisconsin Medical School, Madison, Wisconsin

Roger K. Blashfield, PhD. Department of Psychiatry, College of Medicine, University of Florida, Gainesville, Florida

Nancy Cantor, PhD. Department of Psychology, University of Michigan, Ann Arbor, Michigan

Dennis P. Cantwell, MD. Neuropsychiatric Institute, University of California, Los Angeles, Los Angeles, California

W. C. Corning, PhD. Department of Psychology, University of Waterloo, Waterloo, Ontario, Canada

George S. Everly, Jr., PhD. Psychophysiological and Health Psychology Laboratory, Loyola College, Baltimore, Maryland

H. J. Eysenck, PhD. Institute of Psychiatry, University of London, London, England

Allen Frances, MD. Department of Psychiatry, Cornell University Medical College, and Outpatient Department, Payne Whitney Clinic, New York, New York

Sol L. Garfield, PhD. Department of Psychology, Washington University, St. Louis, Missouri

Nancy Genero, PhD. Department of Psychiatry, University of Michigan, Ann Arbor, Michigan

William M. Grove, PhD. Department of Psychology, University of Minnesota, Minneapolis, Minnesota

Adolf Grünbaum, PhD. Departments of Philosophy and Psychiatry, University of Pittsburgh, Pittsburgh, Pennsylvania

Samuel B. Guze, MD. Department of Psychiatry, Washington University School of Medicine, St. Louis, Missouri

Craig N. Karson, MD. Neuropsychiatry Branch, National Institute of Mental Health, St. Elizabeths Hospital, Washington, D.C.

Philippe J. Khouri, MD. Department of Psychiatry, University of Tennessee College of Medicine, Memphis, Tennessee

Donald J. Kiesler, PhD. Department of Psychology, Virginia Commonwealth University, Richmond, Virginia

Joel E. Kleinman, MD. Neuropsychiatry Branch, National Institute of Mental Health, St. Elizabeths Hospital, Washington, D.C.

Gerald L. Klerman, MD. Department of Psychiatry, Cornell University Medical College, and Department of Psychiatry, New York Hospital, New York, New York

M. Lorr, PhD. Center for the Study of Youth Development, Catholic University of America, Washington, D.C.

Paul E. Meehl, PhD. University of Minnesota Medical School, Minneapolis, Minnesota

Theodore Millon, PhD. Departments of Psychology and Psychiatry, University of Miami, Coral Gables, Florida

Herbert C. Quay, PhD. Departments of Psychology and Pediatrics, University of Miami, Coral Gables, Florida

Esther D. Rothblum, PhD. Department of Psychology, University of Vermont, Burlington, Vermont

Eugene H. Rubin, MD. Department of Psychiatry, Washington University School of Medicine, St. Louis, Missouri

Kurt Salzinger, MD. Department of Social Sciences, Polytechnic Institute of New York, Brooklyn, New York, and New York State Psychiatric Institute, New York, New York

Thomas J. Scheff, PhD. Department of Sociology, University of California, Santa Barbara, Santa Barbara, California

Mary E. Schwab, MD. Children's Outpatient Services and Department of Psychiatry, Harvard Medical School, and McLean Hospital, Boston, Massachusetts

Harvey A. Skinner, PhD. Addiction Research Foundation, and Department of Preventive Medicine and Biostatistics, University of Toronto, Toronto, Ontario, Canada

Laura J. Solomon, PhD. Department of Psychology, University of Vermont, Burlington, Vermont

John S. Strauss, MD. Department of Psychiatry, Yale University Medical School, New Haven, Connecticut

H. J. Walton, MD. Department of Psychiatry, University of Edinburgh, Edinburgh, United Kingdom

Myrna M. Weissman, PhD. Depression Research Unit, Department of Psychiatry, Yale University Medical School, New Haven, Connecticut

Thomas A. Widiger, PhD. Department of Psychology, University of Kentucky, Lexington, Kentucky

Richard Jed Wyatt, MD. Neuropsychiatry Branch, National Institute of Mental Health, St Elizabeths Hospital, Washington, D.C.

Charles F. Zorumski, MD. Department of Psychiatry, Washington University School of Medicine, St. Louis, Missouri

Joseph Zubin, PhD. Veterans Administration Medical Center and University of Pittsburgh School of Medicine, Pittsburgh, Pennsylvania

Preface

A change in the character of psychopathology has begun to evolve in the past decade. Slow though progress may be, there are inexorable signs that the study of mental disorders has advanced beyond its earlier history as an oracular craft. No longer dependent on the intuitive artistry of brilliant clinicians and theoreticians who formulated dazzling but unfalsifiable insights, psychopathology has acquired a solid footing in the empirical methodologies and quantitative techniques that characterize mature sciences. Although the term "psychopathology" was used in the past as synonymous with descriptive symptomatology, it can now be justly employed to represent "the science of abnormal behavior and mental disorders." Its methods of study now comfortably encompass both clinical *and* experimental procedures.

Among the many indices of progress is the construction in recent years of psychometrically sound diagnostic tools that have wedded the quantitative and statistical precision that typify rigorous empirical disciplines with the salient and dynamic qualities that characterize the concerns of a clinical profession. Contributing to this precision is the introduction of specific diagnostic criteria for each mental disorder, an advance that not only enhances the clarity of clinical communication, but strengthens the reliability of research, contributing thereby to the possibility of reciprocal and cumulative data. Along similar lines are a variety of sophisticated multivariate methods which can furnish quantitative grounds for analyzing symptom covariances and for constructing an orderly taxonomy.

Theoretical formulations have also begun to take on a more logical and orderly structure. Whereas earlier propositions were presented almost invariabily in haphazard form, and where derivations were typically circular, and empirical consequences ambiguous or conflicting, contemporary theorists now specify explicit and precise criteria for their concepts, and seek to spell out objective procedures and methods to test their hypotheses. Moreover, theorists are less doctrinaire in their positions than formerly, that is, they no longer appear as religious disciples of "theological purity." A true "ecumenism" has emerged, an openmindedness and sharing of views that is much more consonant with disciplines that possess secure foundations; thus, there are erstwhile analysts who have shed their former dogmatisms and now readily incorporate findings such as those in the neurosciences and social psychology; similarly, once diehard behaviorists are jettisoning earlier biases and integrating cognitive processes fully into their principles. On many levels and from several perspectives, signs do point consistently in a direction that indicates that psychopathology is becoming a full-fledged science.

It was our intent in the present volume to draw attention to a number of elements that comprise this direction. Special attention has been given the place of the DSM-III. Not just another manual composed of subjective diagnostic and statistical guidelines, the DSM-III has played a signal role in that it both reflects significant aspects of the progression toward a scientific psychopathology and is, in itself, a crucial tool in furthering that progress.

Although the present volume was intended to be neither a comprehensive textbook, nor a manual to accompany the DSM-III, several of its chapters provide thoughtful pedagogic reviews and heuristic recommendations which may prove useful to future taxonomists. In this latter regard we very much favor current efforts to construct a rapprochement between the American DSM and the World Health Organization's ICD. Work toward both the DSM-IV and ICD-10 is under way and we believe that a successful accommodation will come from the combination of careful theoretical and conceptual analyses, and the parallel acquisition of empirical data from well-designed research. This book not only reflects the current state of psychopathology as a science, but should help identify the issues and methods that can foster this important reconciliation.

It is our hope that this volume will contribute to reactivating another alliance—the long and fruitful collaboration between the disciplines of psychology and psychiatry. Psychopathology needs "all the help it can get" if it is to fulfill its promise as a science. The best minds are not to be found in one school of thought or in one mental health profession. Different perspectives not only contribute to "rounding out" important areas of content and technique, but help spark fresh insights and ideas. As co-editors we have found our work together to be both stimulating and rewarding; we hope it will serve not only as a model of cooperation between our two fields, but as an invitation to biochemists, epidemiologists, psychometricians, geneticists, as well as those of other disciplines, to join us in this enterprise.

In closing, we should like to express our appreciation to the book's contributors. They comprise a distinguished group, including both well-respected and promising young scholars from psychology, psychiatry, philosophy and sociology. Although we might take exception to a point or two in one or another chapter, we are extremely pleased with the high quality and original thought that went into each of them.

Theodore Millon
Gerald L. Klerman

Contents

PART III
CONCEPTUAL ISSUES

PART I
HISTORICAL BACKGROUND

CHAPTER 1

Historical Perspectives on Contemporary Schools of Psychopathology

Gerald L. Klerman

Introduction

The academic and scientific status of psychopathology as a discipline has yet to be fully established in the United States. On one hand, psychopathology is a subject of considerable interest in many academic, scientific, and professional groups and among important segments of the lay public and policy-makers in governmental and private institutions. Research related to psychopathology is an active ingredient of psychology, anthropology, physiology, genetics, and many other scientific disciplines. All mental health professionals are strongly affected in their practice by their conceptualization and knowledge of advances in psychopathology.

Yet, psychopathology has yet to emerge as a separate academic discipline and independent scientific field. The concept of a science of psychopathology emerged in the United States in the first decades of the twentieth century. Important leaders in psychiatry and psychology—including William James, Morton Prince, Adolf Meyer, and others—conceived of a scientific study of abnormal behavior, and the choice of the term "psychopathology" had a clear parallel to the emerging medical specialty of neuropathology. A new organization, the American Psychopathologic Association, was formed in 1909 and for a number of years served as a scientific arena for the growing number of individuals from different disciplines interested in these phenomena. However, at the present time, rather than being a multidisciplinary scientific society for the broad study of psychopathology, the American Psychopatho-

Gerald L. Klerman. Department of Psychiatry, Cornell University Medical College, and Department of Psychiatry, New York Hospital, New York, New York.

logic Association has become an honorific association mainly of psychiatrists from academic centers in the Northeast. There does not exist a national or international association devoted to the science of psychopathology, nor does there exist a single journal focusing on this topic, although important aspects of psychopathology appear in many journals of psychiatry, clinical and consulting psychology, anthropology, social work, and medicine.

Why this state of affairs should exist is a matter of some interest. One important contribution lies in the competing professional groups in the mental health field. Psychiatry, psychology, social work, and nursing are rivals for public attention, quality students, governmental and foundation funds, and, most importantly, patient fees for treatment, whether paid by the individual or by third-party insurance.

While these interprofessional rivalries are important, we must also acknowledge the theoretical and conceptual differences. There is no unifying school of psychopathology, and in Kuhn's (1970) conception of the history of science, psychopathology is preparadigmatic in that, as will be discussed later, no one paradigm has emerged as dominant to provide a unified approach to the field. In the absence of a scientific consensus, divisions and rivalries persist.

There are some encouraging signs, particularly since the publication of the DSM-III. There is increasing acceptance of this diagnostic framework as the basis for teaching and research. Gradually this approach had diffused into clinical practice with many mental health professionals. Even where there is theoretical and empirical disagreement with the general approach of DSM-III or the specific criteria for individual disorders, almost all teachers and researchers in psychopathology have over a relatively brief period of time, 5–6 years, come to accept the DSM-III as the starting point for teaching and research in psychopathology, but clearly not as the final consensus.

Current Revival of Interest in Psychopathology

During the past one and a half decades, the American mental health field has experienced a major revival of interest in psychopathology and in diagnosis and nosology, culminating in the publication in 1980 of the third edition of the *Diagnostic and Statistical Manual of Mental Disorders* (DSM-III) (American Psychiatric Association [APA], 1980). This revival follows decades of neglect of these topics. From the early 1940s through the mid-1970s, diagnosis and classification were minor concerns of American mental health professionals. From World War II on, debates continued over the question, "Diagnosis and classification of what?" In the absence of persuasive theoretical and therapeutic answers, the American mental health community answered with skepticism, disinterest, and disregard.

One of the main sources of this attitude was the apparent lack of relevance of diagnosis for treatment decisions. This was particularly true when the most valued treatment available was dynamic psychotherapy. If all mental conditions were indications of psychotherapy, then diagnosis and differential treatment assignments were not necessary. Today, however, treatment decisions cannot be responsibly informed and implemented without a sound nosological base. As effective treatments for mental disorders become diverse, the need for a highly differentiated diagnostic system becomes clearer. Spitzer, who guided the development of DSM-III, has stated (Spitzer, Endicott, & Robins, 1978): "The purpose of a classification of medical disorders is to identify those conditions which, because of their negative consequences, implicitly have a call to action to the profession, the person with the condition, and society" (p. 774). The call to action on the part of the medical profession (and its allied professions) is to offer treatment for the condition, or a means to prevent its development, or, if knowledge is lacking, to conduct appropriate research.

DSM-III incorporates a number of developments from recent clinical experience and research advances. It incorporates five innovations:

1. It represents a reaffirmation of the concept of multiple, separate disorders.

2. For the first time in an official nomenclature, there are operational criteria, both for inclusion and exclusion.

3. These criteria are based, for the most part, on manifest descriptive psychopathology rather than inferences or criteria from presumed causation or etiology, whether this causation be psychodynamic, social, or biological. The exception to this is the category of organic disorders whose etiology is established as caused by central nervous system pathology. The choice of descriptive rather than etiologic criteria does not in itself represent an abandonment of the ideal of classification and diagnosis based on causation; rather, it represents a heuristic decision to deal with the reality that most of the disorders we currently encounter have no established etiologic or even pathophysiologic basis. For most disorders, there are many competing hypotheses, but none has been clearly established.

4. DSM-III is the first official nomenclature to be tested for reliability in a field test. Never before has a medical specialty involved its practitioners in a field study to test the reliability of a new nomenclature. Never before has statistical evidence been produced concerning the acceptance, reliability, feasibility, and utility of a diagnostic scheme.

5. A multiaxial system has been introduced to accommodate the multiplicity of aspects of patients' lives and experiences.

Implicit in the creation of DSM-III and the mode of its formation and promulgation has been a principle of change. Already there is a push for DSM-IV. Thus, we have a diagnostic system that is not static and one that provides the basis for the generation of evidence to resolve disputes and conflicts.

DSM-III has generated controversy both within the United States and between United States psychiatrists and those from other countries, most of whom follow the World Health Organization (WHO) International Classification of Diseases (ICD) (1977).

This chapter will examine the diversity of the contemporary American mental health scene and will be interpreted in terms of Kuhn's theory of scientific change. Given the existence of multiple competing schools, each with its own paradigm, the emergence of DSM-III represents a partial solution to a set of problems surrounding diagnostic reliability and the selection of patients for differential treatment prescription. The response to DSM-III suggests that some partial consensus has emerged among researchers and teachers of psychopathology and among professional mental health practitioners.

Schools of Contemporary American Psychopathology

The first American mental health professions in psychiatry began in the late eighteenth and early nineteenth centuries with the creation of mental hospitals. Their medical superintendents—the forerunners of today's psychiatrist—were concerned mainly with the institutional care of people afflicted with "insanity," conditions that today we would classify as "psychotic." The predecessor of today's American Psychiatric Association was the Association of Medical Superintendents of Asylums for the Insane, founded in 1844; its official publication, the *American Journal of Insanity*, later became the *American Journal of Psychiatry*.

With the beginning of the twentieth century, psychiatrists were involved in settings other than asylums; they became active in general hospitals, private practice, and the military services, and were invited to be consultants to schools, prisons, and other institutions. Clinical psychology and social work developed in the early decades of the twentieth century. With these changes in setting, professionals saw patients with nonpsychotic conditions, variously called neuroses and personality disorders. Confronted with nonpsychotic patients with diverse symptoms and behaviors, mental health professionals and researchers began to form schools to give understanding to psychopathology and to guide treatments.

Schools of American Psychopathology

It is important to recognize that at the present time in the United States, no school of thought is dominant (Millon, 1983). Psychopathology has multiple scientific sources. It draws on specialized knowledge ranging from psychoanalysis to psychobiology and draws from related disciplines—psychology, the neurosciences, and epidemiology. The diversity characterizing the professional scene has resulted in considerable ferment and rivalry among the alternative schools. The extent of this diversity has been described by Armor and Klerman (1968), Havens (1973), and Lazare (1979).

Observers of the American scene have catalogued the diversity in different ways. In their influential study of social class and mental illness, Hollingshead and Redlich (1958) divided the practitioner community in New Haven, Connecticut into two groups, which they referred to as "Analytic and Psychological" (A-P) and "Directive and Organic" (D-O). Subsequent researchers employed other groupings. In the early 1960s, Strauss and his associates (1964) in Chicago, using sociological survey methods, and Armor and Klerman (1968), studying a nationwide sample of psychiatrists working in hospitals, identified three psychiatric schools—a biological (or organic) school, a psychological/psychodynamic school, and what was then emerging as a social psychiatric school.

Table 1-1 identifies the five schools most relevant, in this writer's view, to the current American scene with regard to psychopathology.

Observers of the American scene will note that a number of influential groups of practitioners are not represented here. For example, the existential school, identified and described by Havens (1973), while influencing many modern literary and social thinkers and writers by extending tenets of existential philosophy into therapeutic theory, has had relatively little impact on research or practice. Similarly, many types of psychotherapy that have proliferated in recent decades (such as Gestalt therapy, humanistic psychology, and transactional analysis) have often been antithetical to the psychiatric "medical model" and its modes of diagnosis and classification. The community mental health movement also does not appear as a separate school because although it has effected major changes in the delivery of mental health services, the theoreticians and practitioners of community mental health are, in fact, critical at times of the medical model and are allied in an antidiagnostic stance with the "antipsychiatry movement."

As described in Table 1-1, there are five different schools of psychopathology.

The biological school is historically the oldest. It has its roots in nineteenth-century Continental schools of biology and medicine, particularly the French and German schools. The biological school went into disrepute in the period between World War I and World War II. Following the triumphs of the discovery of syphilitic origin of general paresis and the nutritional origin of pellagra, the quality of research in biological psychiatry and the efficacy of treatments decreased (Klerman, 1981). Since the 1950s, biological psychiatry has had a marked resurgence of intellectual vitality. In part, this is the consequence of the therapeutic success of psychopharmacologic agents. In part, it is also the increasing sophistication of the neurosciences and the hope that research in central nervous system (CNS) neuroscience will enhance the understanding of many forms of mental disorder.

Psychoanalytic influence in the United States first appeared in the decade before World War I. The visit by Freud, Jung, and their associates to

Table 1-1

Contemporary Schools of Psychopathology

School	Major U.S. proponents	Theoretical sources	Research emphases	Therapeutic emphases
Biological	Kety Winokur E. Robins Snyder	Nineteenth-century Continental schools of biology and medicine	Genetic studies, CNS research	Pharmacotherapy
Psychoanalytic	Erikson Mahler Kohut Kernberg	Freudian psychoanalytic concepts and American modifications, particularly ego psychology and self psychology	Personality disorders	Intensive, insight-oriented dynamic psychotherapy and psychoanalysis
Interpersonal	Sullivan Fromm-Reichmann Fromm Horney Arieti	G. H. Mead, C. H. Colley, and the Chicago school of symbolic interactionists	Adult relations on marriage, work, and community	Broadened psychotherapeutic framework to include family and group therapies Psychotherapy with ambulatory patients with schizophrenia, depression, and other severe conditions
Social	Meyer Leighton Lindemann Caplan	Conceptual and empirical frameworks derived from sociology, anthropology, and other social sciences	Epidemiologic studies and large-scale social analyses	Community mental health services
Behavioral-cognitive	Wolpe Eysenck Beck	Pavlovian and Skinnerian theory Cognitive psychology	Behavioral analysis of symptoms Learning theory	Behavior therapies Cognitive therapy

Clark University in Worcester, Massachusetts in 1909 resulted in a flurry of interest in psychoanalysis, particularly with the support of William James in psychology and Adolf Meyer in psychiatry (Hale, 1971). The influence of psychoanalysis in America was heightened in the late 1930s and early 1940s because of the migration of highly talented psychoanalysts from Europe following the Nazi-German conquest. Currently, psychoanalysis is on the intellectual and scientific defensive, although its influence on practitioners remains strong. The area of psychopathology is mainly concerned with the personality disorders represented on Axis-II of DSM-III, and in continued understanding of normal personality development through the life cycle and personality functioning at all ages.

The interpersonal school is the first distinctively American school. It emerged in the Washington/Baltimore area in the late 1930s and early 1940s. The influence of Adolf Meyer was strong, as was the strong influence from the Chicago school of symbolic interactionists in sociology and social psychology. The intellectual collaboration of Harry Stack Sullivan (1953) and Frieda Fromm-Reichmann (1960) at Chestnut Lodge created the theoretical base for interpersonal theory, and Fromm-Reichmann's writings on psychotherapy combined with the influence of the neo-Freudians, such as Fromm and Horney, and resulted in the rapid proliferation of interpersonal techniques. The interpersonal school spearheaded the broadening of psychotherapy to include family techniques and various forms of group therapy. In research on psychopathology, it focuses on the immediate face-to-face relationships of individuals, both in the developmental phase and in adult functioning, and looks for the origin of psychopathology in maladaptive aspects of these face-to-face relationships. The interpersonal school differs from the social school by virtue of the unit of society chosen as the focus of interest. The interpersonal school focuses on small group relationships in which the individual is involved in face-to-face relationships. The social school is concerned with larger social units, such as urban life, economic change, demographic trends, and the impact of industrialization and economic forces.

The social school emerged in the United States following the writings of Adolf Meyer, who provided the theoretical basis for both social psychiatry and community mental health. Currently, the social school influences are mainly seen in epidemiologic studies, studies of mental health economics, and in attempts to understand the relationship between mental health and the larger society. Insights from anthropology have contributed to cross-cultural studies and important theoretical questions arise as to the universality of psychopathology or the relativism of symptoms and syndromes arising in different cultures. At the therapeutic level, the large emphasis in community mental health services in the decades from 1965 to 1980, supported by the National Institute of Mental Health (NIMH) Community Mental Health Services Program, represents the application of insights from sociological, anthropological, and epidemiologic research.

The behavioral and cognitive approaches are currently most popular, particularly in psychology, and increasingly in psychiatry, Based on the theoretical approaches of Pavlov and Skinner, a number of research projects have undertaken to provide behavioral and cognitive interpretations of the psychogenesis of depression, phobias, and personality disorders. Applied to therapeutics, the growing number of behavior and cognitive therapies attest to the vigor of the behavioral and cognitive school.

Kuhn's Theory of Scientific Progress

The schools of American psychopathology differ markedly in their concepts of mental illness and in their concern with diagnostic reliability, validity, and appropriateness. The differences in attitude toward diagnosis among the schools encompass moral and ethical judgments; some schools, for example, regard diagnostic efforts as depersonalizing, antitherapeutic, and politically repressive. The force of these ideological elements has often influenced efforts at revision of diagnostic nomenclatures, as manifested in some of the debates and controversies attendant upon the creation and promulgation of DSM-III.

Kuhn has proposed that the history of a scientific field is punctuated by revolutions, the essence of a scientific revolution being the emergence of a new paradigm that enables a significant restructuring of the ways in which the scientific field defines its problems and orders its ways of looking at them. In the revised edition of *The Structure of Scientific Revolutions* (1970), Kuhn notes that a "paradigm" has two components—the cognitive and the communal.

The cognitive component refers to the theories, hypotheses, and ideas by which a scientific field is delineated and the rules it employs to conduct research and evaluate evidence. The communal component refers to the collectivity of scientists (or practitioners) who share the ideas and values and acknowledge the validity of a particular form of scientific "truth." Kuhn's theory has been the subject of much controversy. It has been criticized for using physical sciences as the basis for extrapolation to other sciences, for identifying subject matters too closely with scientific communities, and for overstating the allegiance of scientists to a specific paradigm. Nonetheless, it represents a broad framework for understanding historical change within a scientific field, particularly one as diverse as psychiatry where no school has yet provided the dominant and unifying paradigm.

Kuhn proposes that when a single paradigm emerges as dominant within a scientific field, the scientific status of the field becomes defined and disputes are resolved. Within this framework, two assessments of the scientific status are possible. First, each school may be regarded as paradigmatic. The current American scene would then be regarded as an arena of multiple, competing scientific paradigms, each with its own cognitive structure (theories and research methodologies) and its own community of investigators and practitioners. According to this assessment, the various paradigms are competing with each other for scientific dominance, for intellectual status and prestige, and for the allegiance of practitioners in the mental health fields, including psychiatry, psychology, social work, and nursing. Second, since the view that no one paradigm has yet emerged, psychopathology should be described as a "preparadigmatic" science. Seen from Kuhn's perspective, the mental health field is still prescientific; a single, dominant paradigm does not yet exist.

Kuhn's perspective seems inadequate to deal with fields such as psychiatry, where the range of problems that are dealt with and the important social consequences of its activities bring policy and health considerations into play along with purely scientific and intellectual considerations. Therefore, contemporary mental health involves multiple competing paradigms. It may be that one paradigm will emerge as dominant in the future.

The Development of DSM-III: Has a New Paradigm Emerged?

Anthropologists, historians, and students of cross-cultural psychopathology have observed that every society has its own view of health and illness and its own classification of diseases. Some of these views are consistent with those that have emerged in Western European scientific medicine; others are culturally unique.

Although descriptions of various syndromes and illnesses appear in ancient Egyptian, Greek, and Roman texts, particularly those codified by Hippocrates, the modern concepts of medical disease and nosology did not emerge in Western Europe until the late eighteenth century. The general development of scientific thinking and experimental investigation contributed to the concept of multiple discrete illnesses, each with its own signs, symptoms, and natural course, outcome, and prognosis. This concept was most clearly enunciated by Thomas Sydenham in England, who has been called the father of modern medical nosology.

In the nineteenth century these views of illness were afforded scientific support and intellectual acceptance by discoveries from the biological sciences. Two discoveries were particularly noteworthy:

1. The correlation of clinical syndromes with structural changes noted at autopsy, by either gross morbid anatomy or histopathology. Pathology emerged as a basic medical science in France, Germany, and Austria in the mid-nineteenth century, and its rationale was codified in the writings of Virchow.

2. The discovery of microorganisms by Pasteur, Koch, and others resulted in delineation of many clinical disorders associated with specific bacteria or other microorganisms. The spectacular success in control of many infectious diseases by treatment with antibiotics or their prevention by

sanitary measures or immunization offered the most powerful validation of the concept of discrete disorder.

Later advances in diagnostic radiology following the discovery of X rays and in biochemical tests such as determination of serum glucose provided independent biological confirmation in the living organism of pathological processes correlated with clinical signs and symptoms.

These advances in biology gave medicine a scientific basis and were rapidly applied to understanding mental conditions, particularly in France, Germany, and Austria. In the latter half of the nineteenth century, attempts were made to correlate various mental syndromes with autopsy and bacteriological findings. There were notable successes in these searches for biological causes of mental conditions. By 1895, clinical and epidemiologic studies had shown that infection with syphilis was associated with the syndrome of general paresis, and this association was confirmed by the development of the Wasserman Test in 1905 and the isolation of the spirochete in the brain by Noguchi in 1911. After World War I, Goldberger and his associates in the U. S. Public Health Service discovered the relationship between pellagra and vitamin B deficiency; in addition to elucidating the biological basis of the disorder, this discovery paved the way for effective treatment and ultimately prevention.

From the 1920s through the 1950s, there were few new discoveries of biological correlates of the functional psychoses and other clinical disorders of psychopathology. This situation was not true of mental retardation, however; the discovery of the various forms of chromosomal anomalies led to an understanding of Down's syndrome and other retarded states and the discovery of multiple forms of mental retardation.

The concept of discrete disorders and the medical model applied to psychopathology came under considerable criticism within the profession and from without. Four lines of criticism were debated during the 1960s and 1970s:

1. The most fundamental criticism was the challenge to the legitimacy of psychiatry as part of medicine. Led by Szasz (1961), the antipsychiatrists and the labeling theorists in sociology and psychology derided the basic premise of psychiatry that mental disorders, such as psychoses, neuroses, and personality disorders, are true illnesses. They argued that in the absence of anatomic or physiologic evidence of some biological abnormality, the application of the concept of illness to behavioral, emotional, and cognitive states served the need for social control of deviance rather than medical practice.

2. A second line of criticism focused on the low reliability of psychiatric diagnosis made by clinicians and researchers. The absence of agreement on diagnoses among clinicians, especially in dramatic court cases, undermined the credibility of the mental health profession.

3. A third line of criticism pointed to the adverse social and psychological consequences of psychiatric diagnosis. This view was expressed forcefully by Karl Menninger in his influential book, *The Vital Balance* (Menninger, Maymon, & Pruyser, 1963), in which he drew attention to the dehumanizing and depersonalizing manner in which psychiatric diagnoses were often employed. This unfortunate consequence of diagnostic practice was expanded upon by the labeling theorists, particularly Scheff and Lemere, who saw diagnosis as central to the social control function of psychiatry. Many labeling theorists went even further, denying the existence of any intrinsic differences between those people who later came to be "labeled" mentally ill and people with other forms of deviance. The most dramatic effort to document this view was reported by Rosenhan (1973) in his widely quoted paper, "On Being Sane in Insane Places."

4. The fourth line of criticism derived from within the research community, mainly from psychologists and statisticians experienced in multivariate statistical techniques. These critics did not challenge the existence of mental illness or the legitimacy of research in psychopathology, but they did question the categorical or typological nature of the traditional medically dominated diagnostic systems. They advocated using dimensional approaches, pointing out that there are no sharp boundaries between the normal and the abnormal and that many of the phenomena involved in diagnosis are extensions of normal phenomena, such as anxiety and depression. Lorr, Overall, and Eysenck in psychology and Strauss and others in psychiatry are among the researchers who have expounded this view.

Mental health professionals from developing countries and cultural anthropologists criticized the conventional diagnostic system as being rooted in Western European culture and not relevant or valid in other cultures. Anthropologic investigations indicated that various cultures had different concepts of mental illness and that the criteria for abnormality varied from culture to culture and with historical change. This form of historical and cultural relativism seemed to undermine the universality of any diagnostic system.

In the period after World War II, descriptive psychopathology was in disrepute. Dimensional approaches to personality were the most popular among the diagnostic approaches. In psychiatric epidemiology, community surveys such as the Midtown Manhattan study did not attempt to estimate rates of specific disorders such as depression or schizophrenia, but rather attempted estimates of degrees of mental impairment. Sociological forces, particularly the stress of living, were emphasized as the major causative factors. In clinical practice, attention to psychopathology and diagnosis was considered irrelevant for decision making and for treatment planning, particularly if the dominant mode of treatment in practice was dynamic psychotherapy.

Revival of Interest in Diagnosis and Classification

Confronted by these challenges, the research community responded vigorously. By the early 1960s there was a growing awareness among clinicians and researchers that the absence of an objective and reliable system for description of psychopathology and for diagnosis was limiting progress. In 1965, the Psychopharmacology Research Branch of the NIMH sponsored a conference on classification in psychiatry, noting the problems created by inadequate knowledge of diagnosis and classification.

In the early 1970s, Lehmann (1970), commenting on the long period of neglect of diagnosis, nosology, and classification in North American psychiatry, predicted a renaissance of interest. His words were prophetic: Within a few years the Washington University criteria for operational diagnosis were published, and soon afterward the Schedule for Affective Disorders and Schizophrenia (SADS) (Endicott & Spitzer, 1978) and Research Diagnostic Criteria (RDC) (Spitzer *et al.*, 1978) were developed by the NIMH Psychobiology of Depression Collaborative Study (Katz & Klerman, 1979).

A number of factors contributed to these developments. Three factors are of special note: (*a*) the advance of new therapeutic modalities, especially the new psychopharmacologic agents, but also new behavioral and brief psychotherapeutic methods; (*b*) the availablity of high-speed electronic computers allowing management of large-scale data sets and the application of multivariate statistics; and (*c*) the use of rating scales and other psychometric techniques for quantitative assessment of symptoms, behavior, and personality. By themselves, however, these factors could not have created the changes incorporated into DSM-III—they created the climate for change, but did not define the nature of the changes.

At this point it is useful to return to Kuhn's theory of scientific progress. To recapitulate, Kuhn suggests that scientific progress occurs when a new paradigm emerges to resolve an impasse or, in his terms, to solve a crisis (Kuhn, 1970).

A New Paradigm

The new paradigm that emerged in the early 1970s involved the use of operational criteria for making diagnostic judgments of a categorical, typological, or nosological nature.

Many rating scales and checklists had been developed in response to the need for a descriptive system. Self-report instruments, checklists, and even specific scales for depression and for anxiety were developed. The new advances in clinical psychopathology drew upon existing psychometric methodologies, particularly those for educational testing, and the growing body of new statistical techniques, specifically those involving multivariate methods.

Within psychopathology, the initial developments involved the quantification of symptoms and behavior as a means of assessing change during treatment. A large number of reliable and valid scales were developed in the late 1950s and the 1960s, first for psychotic patients and then for depressed and anxious patients. Lorr, McNair, and Lasky (1962), Hamilton (1960), Zung (1965), Beck (1969), and Overall and Gorham (1962) were major leaders in these developments. In this effort there was active interchange among psychiatrists, clinical psychologists, psychopathologists, and psychopharmacologists. They were able to draw upon the extensive knowledge in psychometrics initially developed in the assessment of intelligence and other forms of cognitive and social performance, but gradually applied to psychopathology and abnormal behavior in the late 1930s, and slowly during the 1940s and 1950s.

By the late 1960s, however, considerable difficulty was encountered because of the lack of standardized techniques for the assessment of descriptive psychopathology necessary for differential diagnosis. Psychiatrists and other clinicians had been relying heavily on categorical (typological) nosological approaches, in contrast to the dimensional methods employed in rating scales and personality inventories. There was considerable dissatisfaction with existing methods, both within clinical practice and among researchers, because of the mounting evidence of the unreliability of psychiatric diagnosis. In addition to the scientific issues, considerable social and political criticism was expressed in the many lawsuits brought by civil rights advocates, not to mention the continuing criticisms of psychiatric diagnosis and practice by Szasz and other antipsychiatrists and by the labeling theorists in sociology and social psychology.

The development of operational criteria served to resolve the "crisis." The operational criteria formulated by the Washington University–St. Louis group led by Robins and Guze and codified in the 1972 paper by Feighner *et al.* led the way for improved reliability and empirical tests of validity. Fleiss *et al.* (1972) developed the kappa technique for quantifying diagnostic reliability and categorical judgments, and this technique was applied by Spitzer and associates to a wide range of data on psychopathology.

In rapid succession numerous studies demonstrated the ability of the standardized interview technique to provide reliable estimates not only in clinical settings, but also in epidemiologic community surveys. These operational criteria and associated measures of reliability were incorporated in the third edition of the *Diagnostic and Statistical Manual of Mental Disorders* (DSM-III) (APA, 1980).

The Neo-Kraepelinians as Leaders of the New Paradigm

The development of operational criteria constituted the main innovation of the new paradigm that served to resolve the crisis of reliability and relevance that seemed to paralyze research on psychopathology and diagnosis and classification through the 1960s and 1970s. Since the leaders of the Washington University–St. Louis group often adopted a point of view at variance

with the main currents of American mental health, they aroused considerable discussion and controversy. In an attempt to understand this development, the concept of the neo-Kraepelinians has been discussed in debates
about an "invisible college" of investigators (Blashfield *et al.*, 1982; Klerman,
1978).

During the past decade, therefore, a small group of neo-Kraepelinians
has emerged and has had a major impact on research activity.

Although the neo-Kraepelinians in psychiatry tend to be most interested
in biological, especially genetic, explanations for mental illnesses, a focus on a
categorical, nosological approach is not, in my opinion, unique to the biological school of psychiatry. For example, Freud and many of his early followers,
such as Abraham and Glover, proposed a classification of mental illness
based on psychosexual stages of development. In current research and clinical practice, however, most neo-Kraepelinians emphasize the biological bases
of mental disorders and, as a group, are neutral, ambivalent, or at times
even hostile toward psychodynamic, interpersonal, or social psychiatric approaches.

The neo-Kraepelinian point of view was first articulated in the influential textbook by Meyer-Gross, Slater, and Roth (1954). Strongly critical of
psychoanalysis, psychotherapy, and social psychiatry, this book was an aggressive reaffirmation of the Kraepelinian approach. In the United States,
neo-Kraepelinian activity originated at Washington University, in St. Louis.
Its early spokespersons were Eli Robins, George Winokur, andd Sam Guze.
Lee Robins has been instrumental in developing new psychiatric epidemiologic methods; Winokur has been most active in familial-genetic studies of
affective disorder; and Guze is best known for his research on Briquets
syndrome and reformulation of the category "hysteria." Their junior associates have included Paula Clayton, Donald Goodwin, and Robert Woodruff.
The dispersal of several members of the Washington University group—
Winokur's move from St. Louis to Iowa City, where he is Chair of the
Psychiatry Department at the University of Iowa; Goodwin's move to Kansas City, where he is Chair of the Department of Psychiatry at the University of Missouri (Kansas City); and the move of Paula Clayton to Minneapolis as Chair of the Department of Psychiatry at the University of
Minnesota—demonstrates the spreading influence of this germinal Washington University psychiatric community. Other emerging neo-Kraepelinians include Akiskal in Tennessee, Taylor and Abrams in Chicago, and
Wender in Utah.

There is now also a strong locus of neo-Kraepelinian activity in New
York, centered particularly around the work of Donald Klein. Klein's view is
that psychiatrists cannot prescribe treatment effectively without a careful
description of patients' symptoms and syndromes. He maintains that the
diagnostic approach based on categorical nosology is the most appropriate
approach to research and practice in psychopharmacology, and his volume
(written in collaboration with colleagues) on diagnosis and drug treatment
(Klein & Davis, 1980) has become the most influential textbook of clinical

psychopharmacology in the United States. In addition, Klein has been active in the description of new syndromes, such as panic states and "hysteroid dysphoria," and in documenting the distinction between panic states and agoraphobia and other forms of phobia.

It is not clear whether the neo-Kraepelinians represented a distinct school. To the extent that they believe in discrete mental disorders and the primacy of psychiatry as a specialty within medicine, they follow the tradition of Kraepelin and nineteenth-century classic psychiatric thinking. But to the extent that they are tentative about the etiology of individual disorders and emphasize an empirical, perhaps at times an agnostic point of view, they are at variance with the central European Kraepelinian tradition, which has remained more theoretical than empirical.

At this point, it is instructive to quote from Kraepelin himself, who toward the end of his career wrote (1974):

> On the other hand, we must seriously consider how far the phenomena on which we normally base our diagnosis really do afford insight into the basic pathological process. While it may be admitted that this procedure is generally valuable there is a fairly extensive area in which such distinguishing criteria are lacking: either they are insufficiently well-marked or they are unreliable. This is understandable if we assume that the affective and schizophrenic forms of mental disorder do not represent the expression of particular pathological processes, but rather indicate the areas of our personality in which these processes unfold. (p. 107)

Although DSM-III embodies many, but not all of these ideas, and although the neo-Kraepelinians played a significant role in providing the research and conceptual background for many of its innovations, it would be a mistake to identify DSM-III entirely with the neo-Kraepelinian point of view. Spitzer has explicitly stated his desire not to be considered a member of that invisible college of neo-Kraepelinians, but rather identifies himself with a larger concern for data and empiricism (Spitzer, 1982).

Returning again to Kuhn's concepts, DSM-III potentially does embody a new paradigm for American psychiatry, blending basic medical concepts of separate disorders, an empirical attitude toward available evidence concerning the etiology or pathogenesis of individual disorders, heavy reliance on psychometric and quantitative approaches to psychopathology, and, most significantly, incorporation of operational criteria as a means of increasing reliability and facilitating validity.

Psychopathology in the Mid-1980s

Six years after the publication of DSM-III, we are now in a period of accelerated research in psychopathology. Following Kuhn's theory, it appears that the acceptance of DSM-III as the basis of teaching and research in psychopathology has led to a reduction of certain controversies and has ushered in a period Kuhn would call "normal science." A large number of studies are under way to validate various diagnostic sets or to propose revisions in DSM-III categories. New rating scales and diagnostic interviews have been devised for specific DSM-III categories. The separation of Axis II from Axis I disorders has proved a major catalyst to research on personality disorders, and empirical studies are being undertaken on borderline person-ality disorder, narcissistic personality disorder, and a variety of other Axis II conditions. In this respect, it is of note that a number of psychoanalysts, particularly Arnold Cooper, Paul Chodoff, and Allen Frances, have joined in the efforts to modify DSM-III.

In this context, it is now valuable to assess the situation with regard to the various American schools of psychopathology as outlined in Table 1–1, and following this, to assess how clinical practice and teaching and interpro-fessional relations have fared.

Impact of New Psychopathology: Paradigms on American Schools

With regard to biological psychopathology, there continues to be tension concerning the use of DSM-III diagnostic categories. Much biological re-search, while accepting the concept of mental disorders, is nevertheless dissatisfied with the current reliance on descriptive psychopathological cri-teria. A number of efforts are under way to supplement or even supplant symptomatic criteria with laboratory tests. The hope is that these tests will provide more "objective" means of defining patient groups and thus not only facilitate decisions in clinical practice, but promote understanding of patho-physiology and, perhaps, etiology. Currently, the most widely used test is the dexamethasone suppression test (DST). Many biological investigators feel that such biological markers will prove to have greater validity than the symptom diagnostic sets now available.

Within psychoanalytic psychopathology, there has been considerable controversy about the formulation of DSM-III. Much of this controversy has recently subsided. As discussed earlier, there is relatively little within the formal concepts of psychoanalysis that precludes an interest in separate diagnostic categories. In fact, Freud and many of his early associates accepted the distinctions between psychoses and neuroses. Freud himself was instru-mental in describing what later came to be the standard categories of neuroses—conversion hysteria, anxiety neurosis, phobia, and obsessive-com-plusive states.

During the 1930s and 1940s many attempts were made to relate a predisposition to adult forms of mental illness to particular experiences during childhood stages of psychosexual development. When these failed to be verified by clinical and research experience, diagnostic concern seemed to decline markedly in American psychoanalysis, and diagnosis and classifica-tion came under criticism, particularly in the writings of Karl Menninger

(Menninger et al., 1963). Many psychoanalysts have been disappointed because DSM-III does not have an axis devoted to psychoanalytic mechanisms of defense and ego functions. An attempt was made during the development of DSM-III to develop such an axis, but it received no support from the American Psychoanalytical Association and was abandoned. Currently, there is considerable interest among psychoanalysts and dynamic psychotherapists in developing such an additional axis for DSM-IIIR and future editions of the manual.

Within social psychiatry there has been noteworthy research in psychiatric epidemiology. The new studies, particularly the NIMH Epidemiologic Catchment Area Project (ECA) (Regier et al., 1984), promise to provide important knowledge about the incidence and prevalence of individual mental disorders and relevant risk factors.

The first use of a structured interview to make RDC diagnoses in a community study in the United States was reported by Weissman and Myers (1978). Having demonstrated the feasibility of diagnosis in communities, the NIMH undertook to develop a new structured interview, the Diagnostic Interview Schedule (DIS) (Robins, Helzer, Croughan, & Ratcliff, 1981), which yields diagnoses according to the Feighner system, DSM-III, and the RDC. Five large community studies are under way, each with samples of a minimum of 3,000 people, in New Haven, Baltimore, St. Louis, Raleigh, and Los Angeles. The first results indicate the feasibility of using a structured interview in large-scale community samples and the meaningfulness of the diagnostic prevalence rates that are revealed.

It is hard to discern any specific trend of change with respect to DSM-III within the interpersonal school. The interpersonal school in the United States has pioneered in the development of new forms of therapeutic intervention whose focus is the individual in relationship to his or her primary groups. Notable have been the advances in family therapy, often using a systems approach, and in group therapy. For the most part, the developers of these techniques have not moved to specify these therapies for particular disorders with anything like the degree of specification that has emerged in behavioral psychotherapeutic techniques.

Nevertheless, after an early flurry of claims for the efficacy of family interventions in schizophrenia, a more modest approach is now apparent, and it is likely that as systematic trials of family therapy get under way, the investigators will use as their selection criteria operational criteria such as those specified in DSM-III.

One exception to this general trend within interpersonal psychotherapy is the development of interpersonal therapy for depression by the Boston–New Haven Collaborative Group (Klerman & Weissman, 1982). Their version of interpersonal psychotherapy (IPT) for depression relies heavily on the ideas of Sullivan (1953) and Bowlby (1969) (see Chap. 21 of this volume).

Within the behavioral school, the impact of DSM-III can be best seen in stages. While DSM-III was being developed, many psychologists, including those with a behavioral orientation, expressed concern lest DSM-III be considered a "medical" document that precluded the role of nonmedical practitioners in the treatment of patients with mental disorders. This concern seems to have subsided considerably. Behavioral treatments have always claimed specificity, particularly behavioral and cognitive interventions being designed for phobias, obsessions, and various forms of sexual dysfunction. In the selection of patients for intervention trials, however, the emphasis has usually been on the presenting symptoms, often assessed by psychiatric techniques. Relatively less attention has been given to differential diagnosis.

This survey of the impact of DSM-III paradigms on various schools of psychiatry indicates that intellectually, the concept of separate syndromes, diagnosed by operational criteria and the multiaxial system, is in principle compatible with the various schools—behavioral, interpersonal, social, and psychoanalytic.

Impact on Professional Activities—Clinical Practice

Two features of DSM-III have had the most impact on clinical practice: the use of operational criteria and the multiaxial classification system.

The use of operational criteria has rapidly been incorporated into clinical practice, with a noticeable increase in the reliability of diagnostic judgments and facilitation of communication among mental health clinicians. DSM-III has been effective in responding to the challenge of diagnostic unreliability. One of the main arguments of the antipsychiatry movement was the apparently low reliability of psychiatric diagnosis and the lack of validity for the categories. In response to this criticism, successful efforts have been undertaken to better understand the sources of unreliability; as they have been located and analyzed, attempts have been made, and are continuing, to overcome obstacles to reliability.

For example, Fleiss and associates (1972) applied the statistic kappa (developed by Fleiss) to measure more accurately the degree of concordance among diagnosticians. In addition, training techniques using videotapes and case vignettes have been developed. The utilization of these techniques has resulted in improved reliability not only in research settings, but also in clinical practice, as demonstrated by the reasonably high reliability coefficients found in the field trials for DSM-III conducted among a large sample of practitioners.

The other area in which the new paradigm has facilitated clinical practice lies in the prescriptions of forms of treatment. As the numbers of psychopharmacologic agents grew in the late 1960s and the 1970s, efforts were undertaken to provide reliable and valid predictors of which types of patients were likely to respond to the various classes of drugs. There seems to be a strong correlation between patterns of response to classes of psychotherapeutic drugs and classic grouping of different categories of psychopathology.

Although responses overlap among classes of drugs, the pattern of response seems to follow the general separation of the major disorders as delineated by the generation of Kraepelin and Bleuler.

This therapeutic utility of diagnostic classification extends also to the selection of patients for psychotherapeutic techniques. The efficacy of differentiated behavioral techniques is closely correlated with distinction among simple phobias, agoraphobia, and obsessive–compulsive states (Marks, 1981). The development of various forms of brief interpersonal, psychodynamic, and cognitive techniques for ambulatory patients with depression, most often nonbipolar, nonmelancholic, and nonpsychotic, also indicates the value of careful diagnosis in the selection of appropriate psychotherapeutic techniques.

During the period when individual dynamic psychotherapy was the preferred form of treatment and was considered applicable to all forms of mental illness, differential diagnosis was not a major research or clinical task. This unitary view of treatment was dominant in American mental health in the late 1940s and early 1950s, but is no longer tenable. Confronted with multiple forms of drug therapy and a variety of psychotherapies, clinicians need guidance in their selection of the appropriate treatment for individual patients.

The other feature of DSM-III that has gained the most acceptance among clinicians is use of the multiaxial system. This has gone a long way toward alleviating the major discomforts that practitioners have felt with diagnostic systems. It is an attempt to resolve a long-standing dilemma that exists for all medicine: Whereas the unit of scientific interest is pathology (the disorder or disease), the unit of clinical practice is the individual patient. Put another way, "Medicine studies diseases but treats patients" (Klerman, 1977).

This dilemma has contributed to continuing controversy about the relevance of diagnostic systems for humane practice. Practitioners have long complained that traditional classifications of psychopathology had hindered patient care in at least two ways. First, they claim that diagnostic categories are inadequate for understanding the complexity of individual patients and for clinical decision making. For example, it is argued that in evaluating the need to hospitalize suicidal patients, in addition to knowing whether the patient is depressed or psychotic, it is also necessary to assess personality dynamics, such as the patient's impulsivity or degree of self-control, and to have an adequate understanding of that patient's life circumstances, particularly current stresses, family, income, and other social supports. Second, some clinicians have asserted that assigning patients to categories contributes to depersonalization and deindividualization of the doctor–patient relationship.

To deal with these objections and to refine diagnostic assignment, DSM-III has incorporated a multiaxial framework. This five-axis system consists of clinical psychiatric syndromes, entailing chronicity and periodic aspects as well as symptoms (Axis I); personality disorders of adults and development disorders of children and adolescents (Axis II); physical illness (Axis III); psychosocial stressors (Axis IV); and level of adaptive functioning (Axis V). The first three axes are typological, involving categories; the last two are dimensional (Mezzich, 1980).

With these changes, DSM-III has gone a long way toward meeting some of the hesitations and criticisms of clinicians with regard to diagnostic systems. It is likely that further axes will be proposed, particularly dealing with psychoanalytic defenses and ego functions. At some point, however, there will need to be some limitations on the number of axes because of practical considerations.

Research on Psychopathology

The impact of new paradigms on research in psychopathology is relatively easier to assess. Inasmuch as the use of operational criteria and emphasis on diagnostic groups arose primarily from within the research community, DSM-III has served mainly to codify existing practices among research groups in psychopathology. It has, however, contributed to an apparent increase in activity in psychopathology and nosology. Numerous efforts are under way to compare the relative reliability and validity of various diagnostic sets for schizophrenia, bipolar illness, and other Axis I diagnoses. Within child psychiatry, there is a noticeable increase in concern for descriptive psychopathology; attention is now being given to the syndromes of childhood depression (previously its existence was questioned) and to the reliability and validity of other techiques (Cantwell, 1980). Within research on therapeutics, DSM-III has served to further codify the importance of careful selection of homogeneous patient groups for therapeutic trials.

It is almost universally accepted that the most powerful evidence for the efficacy of various treatments derives from controlled studies, particularly randomized clinical trials. Prominent medical, psychiatric, and psychological journals regularly report results of randomized trials of new drugs, surgical procedures, radiation, and psychotherapy. Thus, the regulations and guidelines of the U.S. Food and Drug Administration (FDA) not only have contributed greatly to the acceptance of the randomized trial as the standard method for the evaluation of treatment, but also have been an important stimulus to the development of diagnostic assessment methods.

Randomized controlled trials of mental health treatments have rapidly generated information of high scientific quality and clinical relevance. They have made it possible to specify clinical conditions for which a particular therapy is effective and to identify those for which we do not have adequate evidence, either positive or negative, concerning efficacy, as is the case with many forms of personality disorder represented in DSM-III on Axis II.

Interprofessional Relations

While DSM-III was in its final stages of development, lively discussions developed in various professional groups, particularly the associations of psychologists and psychoanalysts, with a number of relevant articles appearing in the *American Psychologist*.

With the publication of DSM-III, however, the controversy seems to have rapidly subsided. Almost all new textbooks of psychology incorporate DSM-III, and in clinical practice, DSM-III seems to be increasingly accepted as the basis for teaching diagnoses to mental health professionals.

International Relations

The decision of the American Psychiatric Association to develop DSM-III, apart from the ICD, created considerable tension. In an effort to minimize some of this tension, the Alcohol, Drug Abuse, and Mental Health Administration (ADAMHA) and the WHO sponsored a number of projects to improve communication in this area. Commenting on this development, John Cooper (1982) noted in the *British Journal of Psychiatry*:

> The mere fact that such a conference and program were conceived and worked through, however, suggests that there is now a widespread and international realization that close collaboration and communication between psychiatrists is of fundamental importance, if psychiatry is to continue its progress towards being recognized as a scientifically based discipline. The twin subjects of diagnosis and classification are an essential part of the foundations that are needed for this progress. (p. 531)

As the time approaches for the development of ICD-10 and/or DSM-IV, it is expected that there will be increasing pressure to bridge the gap between the current WHO and United States efforts. It is likely that all future official nomenclatures—national or international—will include a multiaxial system and operational criteria. Also, formal field trials for feasibility and reliability will doubtless be undertaken. This may be one of the major impacts of new paradigms, namely, the influence it has not only on mental health in the United States, but on psychiatry and other mental health professions in other nations and at the international level.

Prospects for the Future: Toward DSM-IV and ICD-10

The contemporary United States mental health field is characterized by competing schools—biological, social, interpersonal, psychodynamic, and behavioral—each of which has proposed different theories concerning the nature and origin of mental illnesses and emphasized various modes of treatment. So intense are the loyalties and emotions manifested by the adherents of these various schools that the mental health field appears from the outside to be more like an arena of conflicting ideologic sets than a scientific discipline based on commonly shared theoretical concepts, methodological approaches, and incremental advances based on empirical knowledge.

Applying Kuhn's theory of the history of science, one may say that psychopathology seems to be characterized by multiple competing paradigms, each of which offers a different conception of the nature of mental illness and mental health and invokes different rules of methods and evidence.

For many years there appeared to be no way out of this unsatisfactory situation. There was no independent means by which the claims of various schools concerning the causation of mental illness and the efficacy of their treatment could be established as valid or dismissed as unproven and unsubstantiated by empirical evidence.

In the past two decades, however, this situation has changed dramatically, particularly in the United States, in other parts of North America, and in England. It may well be that a new paradigm, in Kuhn's sense, has emerged, emphasizing a broader concept of the nature of separate mental illnesses than was the case in nineteenth-century thinking, but rejecting the unidimensional view of a continuation of mental health and mental illness that emerged after World War II.

Methodologically, the emphasis on quantitative methods from psychometrics and the application of operational criteria have contributed greatly to resolving the crisis surrounding reliability that seemed to paralyze progress through the 1960s. New methods and systematic empirical investigations to test hypotheses have been developed in psychopathology research. In the case of therapeutics, the controlled clinical trial, using standardized diagnostic and assessment methods, with some form of randomization or matching of patients to treatment groups and use of appropriate controls, such as placebos, has emerged as the standard means by which the efficacy and safety of mental health treatments should be evaluated.

The empirical approaches within psychopathologic research have been related mainly to the emergence of a new paradigm. Its methods have been applied primarily to biological research and to the evaluation of drug and behavioral therapy. The association between individual schools and quantitative methodologies is, however, in my view, not intrinsic to the theoretical principles of the schools or their specialized research techniques. In many aspects, this paradigm relies heavily on empiricism and positivism in science. There is a powerful influence of the British empirical tradition in philosophy and in science—the tradition of Mills, Bentham, and the Webbs. To quote Wing (1980): "Empiricism is not, of course, an atheoretical philosophy but it does entail a critical stance toward theories which are seen solely as a source of ideas to be tested, in the hope (though not, it must be admitted, in the expectation) that they might turn out to be useful" (p. 560).

This new paradigm in psychopathology emphasizes two aspects of the modern philosophy of science: (a) that the essence of modern science is testing hypotheses through experimental and quasi-experimental methods in the laboratory and in the clinic; and (b) that quantification of phenomena—whether directly observable, as in behavior, or inferred, as with mental processes, conscious or unconscious—is necessary.

As we look to the future, it has been announced that DSM-IV and ICD-10 will be promulgated in the early 1990s. Work has already begun on the part of the WHO to provide the groundwork for ICD-10. In the United States, the American Psychiatric Association has established a working group to revise DSM-III as an intermediate step toward DSM-IV. It is hoped that there will be convergence of American and European views so that the ICD-10 and DSM-IV can be identical or at least more congruent than the DSM-III and ICD-9.

The most important contribution toward such international consensus lies in the development of further scientific knowledge. In the past, international nomenclatures have been mainly created by consensus-developing methods, often involving compromises between national theoretical schools.

With the development of operational criteria and the increasing use of standardized interview techniques and psychometric approaches, active research is now under way to confirm the reliability of various diagnostic categories and, more important, to establish their validity.

In principle, the problem of reliability has been solved. Techniques for interjudge reliability, test–retest reliability, and related aspects of reliability are increasingly accepted. With the use of standardized interview techniques and operational criteria, reliability estimates are increasingly being reported which are in the acceptable range.

However, reliability does not guarantee validity. While reliability is a necessary precursor to establishing the validity of psychopathologic classes, special efforts are required for validity research. Nevertheless, unreliability diminishes the capacity to demonstrate validity.

A major problem confronted by researchers in psychopathology lies in the absense of evidence about casuation and pathogenesis. Most previous diagnostic systems, including the DSM-I and DSM-II in the United States and also the WHO-ICD, have included categories for the functional disorders that were confounded by assumptions about causation. For example, both the DSM-II and ICD-7, -8, and -9 have defined neurosis in terms of presumed psychosocial causation and even have accepted psychoanalytic concepts that neurotic symptoms serve as defense against the unconscious anxiety related to unresolved intrapsychic conflict. The ICD distinguishes neuroses and psychoses on the presumption that the psychoses have biological or constitutional bases. Stengel, the major consultant to WHO in the 1950s, pointed out that this feature was one of the barriers to international cooperation and diagnosis and classification (Stengel, 1959). Although Stengel was himself a psychoanalyst and committed to psychological explanations of mental disorder, he argued that the contamination of descriptive and etiologic classification and the nomenclature caused confusion. This particularly is the case for disorders in which there is absence of conclusive evidence for establishing etiology, as in the case of most of the "functional" disorders.

The current effort in psychopathology is to define disorders on the basis of operational criteria, most often criteria involving descriptive psychopathology. This has, in my opinion, contributed to increased quality of research and avoided the premature closure so common in previous writings of psychopathology. For example, having defined bipolar affective disorder as an independent condition and providing operational criteria for its clinical diagnoses, researchers are now in a position to test hypotheses about etiology. Bipolar illness may be a genetically transmitted disorder, as is the most widely held view. But until further evidence is conclusive, the diagnostic system should not make family association one of the defining criteria for diagnosis.

To take another example, borderline personality disorder may be due to a failure of individuation–separation in early child development. This view, based on Mahler's (1952) theory of child development and ego functions, is widely held among clinicians and theorists from a psychoanalytic background. However, the current evidence has not established this relationship conclusively, and until such evidence is forthcoming, it is better to define the condition of borderline personality disorder by behavioral and descriptive manifestations.

As was stated earlier, the DSM-III has been widely accepted as the starting point for teaching and research in psychopathology. It is not the final consensus. As the quality of research improves, areas of consensus will grow, but new problems for research and theory will almost certainly continue.

ACKNOWLEDGMENTS

Portions of this chapter have appeared in previous publications. Appreciation is expressed to the *American Journal of Psychiatry* and the American Psychiatric Press for permission to reproduce sections of previous work.

REFERENCES

American Psychiatric Association (APA). (1980). *Diagnostic and statistical manual of mental disorders* (3rd ed.). Washington, DC: Author.

Armor, D., & Klerman, G. L. (1968). Psychiatric treatment orientations and professional ideology. *Journal of Health and Social Behavior, 9*, 243–255.

Beck, A. (1969). Measuring depression: The depression inventory. In M. M. Katz & J. A. Shields

(Eds.), *Recent advances in the psychology of depressive illness*. Washington, DC: U.S. Government Printing Office.

Blashfield, R., Feighner, J. *et al.* (1982). Invisible colleges and the Matthew effect. *Schizophrenia Bulletin, 8*, 1–6.

Bowlby, J. (1969). *Attachment*. New York: Basic Books.

Cantwell, D. P. (1980). Rediagnostic process and diagnostic classification in child psychiatry (DSM-III). *Journal of the American Academy of Child Psychiatry, 19*, 345–355.

Cooper, J. E. (1982). The last big one? (Comments). *British Journal of Psychiatry, 141*, 531.

Endicott, J., & Spitzer, R. L. (1978). A diagnostic interview. The schedule for affective disorders and schizophrenia. *Archives of General Psychiatry, 35*, 837–844.

Feighner, J., Robins, E., Guze, S. *et al.* (1972). Diagnostic criteria for use in psychiatric research. *Archives of General Psychiatry, 26*, 57–63.

Fleiss, J. L., Spitzer, R. L., Endicott, J. *et al.* (1972). Quantification of agreement in multiple psychiatric diagnosis. *Archives of General Psychiatry, 26*, 168–171.

Fromm-Reichmann, F. (1960). *Principles of intensive psychotherapy*. Chicago, IL: Phoenix Books.

Hale, N. (1971). *Freud and the Americans*. New York: Oxford University Press.

Hamilton, M. A. (1960). A rating scale for depression. *Journal of Neurological and Neurosurgical Psychiatry, 23*, 56.

Havens, L. (1973). *Approaches to the mind*. Boston, MA: Little, Brown.

Hollingshead, A., & Redlich, F. (1958). *Social class and mental illness*. New York: Wiley.

Katz, M., & Klerman, G. L. (1979). Introduction: Overview of the clinical studies program. *American Journal of Psychiatry, 136*, 49–51.

Klein, D. F., & Davis, J. M. (1980). *Diagnosis and drug treatment of psychiatric disorders: Adults and children* (2nd ed.). Baltimore, MD: Williams & Wilkins.

Klerman, G. L. (1977). Mental illness, the medical model, and psychiatry. *Journal of Medical Philosophy, 2*, 220–243.

Klerman, G. L. (1978). The evolution of a scientific nosology. In J. C. Shershow (Ed.), *Schizophrenia: Science and practice*. Cambridge, MA: Harvard University Press.

Klerman, G. L. (1981). Biological psychiatry research: A paradigm for the relationship between basic investigation and clinical applications. In S. Matthysee (Ed.), *Psychiatry and the biology of the human brain: A symposium dedicated to Seymour S. Kety*. Amsterdam: Elsevier/North-Holland.

Klerman, G. L., & Weissman, M. M. (1982). Interpersonal psychotherapy: Theory and research. In J. Rush (Ed.), *Short-term psychotherapies for depression*. New York: Guilford Press.

Kraepelin, E. (1974). Comparative psychiatry. In S. R. Hirsch & M. Shepherd (Eds.), *Themes and variations in European psychiatry*. Charlottesville: University Press of Virginia.

Kuhn, T. (1970). *The structure of scientific revolutions* (2nd ed., Vol. 2, No. 2). Chicago, IL: University of Chicago Press.

Lazare, A. (Ed.). (1979). *Outpatient psychiatry*. Baltimore, MD: Williams & Wilkins.

Lehmann, H. (1970). Epidemiology of depressive disorders. In R. R. Fieve (Ed.), *Depression in the 1970's*. New York: Excerpta Medica.

Lorr, M., McNair, D. M., & Lasky, J. J. (1962). *Inpatient multidimensional psychiatric scale (IMPS)*. CA: Consulting Psychologists Press.

Mahler, M. (1952). On child psychosis and schizophrenia. *Psychoanalytical Study of the Child, 8*, 286–306.

Marks, I. (1981). Review of behavioral psychotherapy. I. Obsessive-compulsive disorders. *American Journal of Psychiatry, 138*, 584–592.

Menninger, K., Mayman, M., & Pruyser, P. (1963). *The vital balance: The life process in mental health and illness*. New York: Viking Press.

Meyer-Gross, W., Slater, E., & Roth, M. (1954). *Clinical psychiatry*. Baltimore, MD: Williams & Wilkins.

Mezzich, J. (1980). Multiaxial systems in psychiatry. In A. M. Freeman & B. J. Sadock (Eds.), *Comprehensive textbook of psychiatry* (3rd ed., Vol. 1). Baltimore, MD: Williams & Wilkins.

Millon, T. (Ed.). (1983). *Theories of personality and psychopathology*. New York: Holt, Rinehart & Winston.

Overall, J. E., & Gorham, D. P. (1962). The brief psychiatric rating scale. *Psychological Report, 10,* 799.

Regier, D. A., Myers, J. K., Kramer, M., Robins, L. N., Blazer, D. G., Hough, R. L., Eaton, W. W., & Locke, B. Z. (1984). The NIMH catchment area program. *Archives of General Psychiatry, 41,* 934–941.

Robins, L. N., Helzer, J. E., Croughan, J., & Ratcliff, K. (1981). National Institute of Mental Health diagnostic interview schedule. *Archives of General Psychiatry, 38,* 381–389.

Rosenhan, D. L. (1973). On being sane in insane places. *Science, 179,* 250–258.

Spitzer, R. L. (1982). Letter to the editor. *Schizophrenia Bulletin, 8,* 592.

Spitzer, R. L., Endicott, J., & Robins, E. (1978). Research diagnostic criteria: Rationale and reliability. *Archives of General Psychiatry, 35,* 773–782.

Stengel, E. (1959). Classification of mental disorders. *Bulletin of the World Health Organization, 21,* 601–663.

Strauss, A., Schatzman, L., Bucher, R. *et al.* (Eds.). (1964). *Psychiatric ideologies and institutes.* New York: Free Press.

Sullivan, H. S. (1953). *The interpersonal theory of psychiatry.* New York: Norton.

Szasz, T. (1961). *The myth of mental illness.* New York: Harper & Row.

Weissman, M. M., & Myers, J. K. (1978). Affective disorders in a U.S. urban community. *Archives of General Psychiatry, 35,* 1304–1311.

Wing, J. (1980). Social psychiatry in the United Kingdom: The approach to schizophrenia. *Schizophrenia Bulletin, 6,* 556–565.

World Health Organization. (1977). *International classification of diseases* (9th rev.). Geneva: Author.

Zung, W. W. (1965). A self-rating depression scale. *Archives of General Psychiatry, 12,* 63.

CHAPTER 2

On the Past and Future of the DSM-III: Personal Recollections and Projections

Theodore Millon

This chapter must be introduced with an admission of partial responsibility, as well as a measure of pride for having been persistent in presenting arguments in the spring of 1974 to a distinguished colleague and good friend, Melvin Sabshin, in favor of a more innovative leadership for the American Psychiatric Association's Task Force on Nomenclature and Statistics. The combined efforts of clinicians and researchers from diverse orientations and interests "saved" the DSM-III (American Psychiatric Association, 1980) from becoming a minor variant of the DSM-II (American Psychiatric Association, 1968) and a mirror image of the current ICD-9 (World Health Organization, 1977). Together with other steps, Sabshin, soon to assume the Medical Directorship of the American Psychiatric Association, invited both myself and Robert Spitzer for an all-day three-person conference to discuss procedures the APA could follow to strengthen the scientific undergirding of our diagnostic nosology. Spitzer, a member of the DSM-II Task Force, noted that substantive advances would not be likely if those who then comprised that committee were asked to extend their responsibilities to the development of the DSM-III. With an essentially new membership, however, one composed of active researchers and innovative theoreticians who would study and debate ideas with the view of constructing an empirically grounded and functional classification system, it was believed that a scientifically sound and clinically useful instrument might be developed.

As I reflect on the ultimate product inspired in part by that 1974 conference with Sabshin and Spitzer, I feel a sense of real satisfaction over the small role I played in encouraging and facilitating the modernization of the DSM. I am reminded of a statement that Lagrange, the eminent eigh-

Theodore Millon. Departments of Psychology and Psychiatry, University of Miami, Coral Gables, Florida.

teenth-century mathematician, made prior to the planned reading of his paper that was to have proved Euclid's Fifth Postulate. Approaching the lectern, Lagrange stopped, looked upon the audience, paused for a moment, quietly said, "Gentlemen, I have changed my mind," and stepped from the rostrum. Devoid of such foresight, I can no longer change my mind about the wisdom of having sought a fresh and, it was hoped, more progressive Task Force. Hence, I have no alternative at this time but to look back and examine the fruits of that inspiration. Most assuredly, few anticipated the vigor and intelligence with which Spitzer and his associates carried out their assignment, moving our scientific conceptions of psychopathology much further along than could possibly have been expected.

The wide range of topics the Task Force encompassed makes it difficult to be comprehensive in coverage and to furnish a coherently organized or highly focused presentation. Foregoing such goals, I will instead concentrate on those features I judge as representing the DSM-III's most signal conceptual and substantive advances. Worthy of record also are clarifications of public controversies that arose during the committee's tenure, as well as several myths that were widely promulgated concerning the operation, no less the motivation of the Task Force. Shortcomings in the DSM-III, of which many are noteworthy, will be recorded, as will suggestions for nosological alternatives and refinements.

First, however, I would like to take the opportunity to review the history of official "mental disorder" classifications, both national and international. Next, I will attempt to trace my personal recollections concerning the almost chance-like sequence with which so powerful a committee as the DSM-III Task Force was formed and the impact these largely random events may now have, not only in shaping the course and character of a profession, but on the lives of the patients to whom it ministers; it may prove an illuminating example of the serendipitous manner with which knowledge comes to be institutionalized.

Official Classifications Prior to DSM-III

One of the major problems facing a field as inchoate and amorphous as psychopathology is its susceptibility to subjective values, cultural biases, and chance events. Were we a "hard" science, anchored solidly in readily verified empirical fact, progress would presumably derive from advances of an essentially tangible and objective nature. Rather sadly, this is not the case with the subject of personality and the behavior disorders. Hence, it is important that readers from the mental health professions be apprised, albeit too briefly, of the historical events that formed the language conventions and classification rules which guide their work. An effort, therefore, will be made in the following paragraphs to summarize the twentieth-century background that preceded the thinking and formation of the DSM-III.

Early American Classifications in Medicine

Not until the 1920s was there an effort made to develop a relatively uniform nomenclature and classification system for medical disease in the United States. Prior to the first of a series of National Conferences on Nomenclature of Diseases, held in 1928 at the New York Academy of Medicine, each of the major teaching hospitals and university medical centers in the nation developed and promulgated their own terminology and nosology. Although these reflected the idiosyncratic needs of their place of origin, many were transplanted to other settings, not as a function of their special logic or utility, but owing to the fact that former staff members and trainees simply were comfortable with the nomenclature to which they were accustomed and, consequently, which they recommended be instituted in their new clinical milieu. Rarely could such transplants be rooted in their entirety and, hence, they had to be modified to meet the particular needs of their newly adopted setting. These replantings proliferated even more diversity upon an already variegated babel of medical terms and categories. To say the least, effective communication among clinical centers, no less useful records for epidemiologic statistics and research, were seriously compromised.

To disentangle this web of obscure language and esoteric custom, the New York Academy of Medicine launched a series of conferences and trial studies designed to develop uniform nomenclatures and systematic taxonomies for each of the major medical specialties. This work resulted in the 1932 publication of what was to be the first official edition of the *Standard Classified Nomenclature of Disease*, subsequently revised several times until superseded by the *International Classification of Diseases*, originally conceived in 1900 and currently in its ninth revision (ICD-9).

Early American Psychiatric Taxonomies

Tracking back for a moment, the American Medico-Psychological Association, forerunner of the present APA, anticipated the need for uniform record keeping prior to medicine in general. Toward this end, the Association appointed a Committee on Statistics assigned the task of devising a classification and nomenclature that would facilitate the recording and comparison of both incidence and prevalence data for use primarily in mental hospitals (a fact, parenthetically, that accounts in great measure for psychiatry's and psychology's focus on the severe mental disorders as well as the primacy given in past texts on clinical psychiatry and abnormal psychology to the serious and hospitalized patient). Adopted in 1917, the American Medico-Psychological Association's classification was circulated vigorously as the standard to be used throughout the United States by the National Committee on Mental Hygiene. Originally titled the *Statistical Manual for the Use of Hospitals for Mental Diseases*, it went through several editions under the imprimatur of the Mental Hospital Service of the APA.

Having subsequently participated in the development of the then new and widely adopted nosological system of the general medical profession, the *Standard Classified Nomenclature of Disease*, first published in 1932, the APA decided to undertake a significant revision of the forthcoming eighth edition of their *Statistical Manual*, ultimately printed in 1935. Considerable work was required to make the two manuals congruent, since the *Standard* focused on nomenclature clarity and clinical specificity, whereas record keeping and epidemiologic classification was the chief function of the *Statistical*. Successfully modified and coordinated, the *Statistical* was incorporated into the next edition of the *Standard*, listed under the Meyerian label (Meyer, 1908, 1912) as the "Diseases of the Psychobiologic Unit." This section remained essentially intact, with but minor revisions, until problems arose concerning its scope and utility during the Second World War. Despite earlier concerns and innovative modifications introduced at several university-affiliated training centers, the "psychobiologic unit" segment of the *Standard* proved to be more than adequate for those who routinely depended on it, alienists employed in public mental hospitals.

Difficulties arose with the utility of the *Standard* at the selection, training, and combat phases of World War II. A wide variety of patients seen by military psychiatrists not only differed substantially from those typically admitted to public mental hospitals, but could not be assigned a label in accord with the *Standard*'s nomenclature. Not only was there no provision for the diversity of psychological disturbances that arose in combat, an understandable deficiency, but a surprisingly wide array of neurotic, personality, and psychosomatic disorders could either not be categorized at all or were grouped under such broadly undifferentiated classes as to be virtually useless.

To overcome these deficits as well as provide a schema more suitable to the cases they faced, the Navy Department introduced a series of nomenclature modifications in 1944. These alterations proved quite modest when compared to those proposed by the Army Department in 1945; here, the *Standard* was thoroughly overhauled and essentially replaced by an innovative nosology based on then current notions of the origins and structure of mental disorders. This army taxonomy proved highly attractive and was adopted shortly thereafter as the model for all of the armed forces. The Veterans Administration, though influenced by the new armed forces nomenclature, devised its own format in 1946. Complicating matters further, a substantial revision was undertaken in 1948 of the *International Statistical Classification*, (ICD-6) which, though similar in certain features to the armed forces taxonomy, differed in several significant respects from both it, the recently developed Veterans Administration system, as well as the nosology and nomenclature of the *Standard*.

The DSM-I

Classificatory confusion reigned in the late 1940s as clinicians found it necessary to employ different systems for different purposes, one nomenclature for hospitalized patients, another taxonomy for statistical reporting, a third for disability coverage, and so on. Compounding this polyglot were the idiosyncratic modifications and syntheses proposed by clinicians who had returned from their diverse military experiences, each seeking to persuade their equally enthusiastic colleagues of the validity of some new syndromal entity or the applicability of this or that innovative classification system.

So great a diversity as this necessitated action on the part of the APA. Accordingly, its Board of Trustees requested that their Committee on Nomenclature and Statistics review the utility of the major taxonomies then in use with the thought in mind of assessing these data for a revision of the "Diseases of the Psychobiologic Unit" section of the *Standard*. Practitioner members of the association were also extensively canvassed for their views concerning modifications. Disorders of personality, transient stress reactions, and organic brain disease were the realms in which primary deficits were noted. Further recommendations were obtained from leading university and hospital training centers as well as those who had been engaged in developing the armed forces and Veterans Administration nomenclatures.

The nomenclature committee prepared a first draft of their proposed revision in early 1950, distributing copies for evaluation and commentary to a representative sample of nearly 15% of the APA membership. Opinions diverged but, in the main, were commendatory. With suggestions and recommendations in hand, numerous modifications were considered and introduced to form a new version. This second draft was reviewed by the editors of the *Standard* to ensure its suitability and adherence in both format and coding to the *Standard*'s nosological schema. Found consonant in these matters, this second draft was submitted for approval to the Council of the American Psychiatric Association in late 1950. This timing enabled its inclusion as the "Diseases of the Psychobiologic Unit" section of the forthcoming 1951 edition of the *Standard*. So approved, the committee was further charged with the task of preparing a separate and new *Diagnostic and Statistical Manual, Mental Disorders*. First published in 1952, this manual has, retrospectively, been referred to as the DSM-I (APA, 1952).

The ICD-8

Having succeeded in identifying its terminology and classification (DSM-I) with that of the *Standard Nomenclature of Diseases and Operations*, American psychiatry's next task was that of coordinating and cross-coding the DSM-I with the 1948 edition of the *International Classification of Diseases* (ICD-6). This proved to be a most onerous task, owing once again to differences in the primary function of the two manuals, one being that of a statistical classification (ICD-6), the other providing a nomenclature for coordinating and defining clinical observations. Compromises were needed not only on these grounds, but as a consequence of substantial differences that existed in the rubrics available for coding a number of the major syndromes. Thus, as an interim step, modifications were introduced into the text of the ICD-6 so as to make the ICD nomenclature more consonant with the APA's recently developed DSM-I. Since the mental disorder section of the ICD-6 was not scheduled for updating in its next, the 1955 revision, known as the ICD-7, incompatibilities with the DSM-I were to remain in force, much to the chagrin not only of psychiatric nosologists in the United States, but to most official psychiatric organizations comprising the membership of the World Health Organization (WHO) (Stengel, 1959).

To optimize uniformity on the international scene, a collaborative effort was undertaken by WHO in 1960 to fashion a new ICD that would resolve cultural disparities and overcome the well-recognized shortcomings in scope and depth of the ICD-7. Participants were drawn from many nations, each forming a committee assigned the task of submitting recommendations to be presented at a WHO-sponsored *International Revision Conference* scheduled for 1965, that is, some 5 years in the future. Toward this end, a joint United States and United Kingdom committee was formed in 1962 with the goal of coordinating efforts toward a single classification proposal. Approved by their respective national governing bodies, a joint U.S.–U.K. taxonomy and nomenclature was submitted for review by WHO in the summer of 1963.

Ultimately, a total of eight alternate systems were proposed to the Executive Council of WHO in 1963. Most of the differences among them were readily resolved. Controversial issues centered on a few diagnostic classes, notably the nature of the antisocial personality, descriptive distinctions among the brain syndromes, and the validity of the concept of reactive psychoses. Following meetings to settle these and related matters, the Secretariat of WHO submitted an agreed upon version in late 1964 for review and debate at the *International Revision Conference* held in July, 1965. There it was endorsed and forwarded to the nineteenth World Health Assembly for approval in May 1966, where the international community's collaborative efforts were commended and the conference proposal authorized as the basis for an official international classification. Enriched further by various national glossaries, this final product of international deliberation and compromise became, in both essence and detail, *the* "Mental Disorders" chapter of the eighth revision of the *International Classification of Diseases* (ICD-8), published and instituted as the official system in 1968.

The DSM-II

The formal and intimate involvement of the APA in the construction of the ICD-8 was a potent factor in motivating the organization to refashion its own DSM in a manner fully compatible with the new international nosology. Hence, shortly following approval of what was to be the ICD-8 at the WHO *International Revision Conference* in 1965, the APA reactivated its Committee on Nomenclature and Statistics. Its tasks clearly defined, the committee was able to submit, as early as 1967, an initial draft of the new DSM-II for review and comment to a select group of 120 psychiatrists. Suggestions for revision were received, collated, and incorporated in a mid-1967 final draft manuscript. This proposal was submitted to the APA Executive Committee where it was approved in late 1967 and subsequently published in 1968 as the DSM-II.

Despite efforts to coordinate all aspects of the DSM-II with the ICD-8, several divergences proved either advisable or necessary. Most disparities were less a matter of theoretical or empirical dispute than a desire to select terminology and to arrange the DSM sequencing to conform more closely to well-established American customs. To illustrate, the mental retardation classification was located at the beginning rather than the end of the organizational sequence, and both psychotic and nonpsychotic organic brain syndromes were grouped in one category; each of these alterations merely followed customary practices in the United States. Additional recommendations were made not to utilize certain ICD-8 diagnoses, most notably the concept and label "reactive" as a descriptive adjective. The DSM-II was subdivided into 10 sections, expanding thereby on the ICD's three major categories. Further increments were made by adding 39 diagnostic classes, achieved primarily by subdividing the more broadly inclusive categories of the ICD-8; for example, hysterical neuroses were separated into dissociative and conversion types. Modifications in terminology were also introduced, again in efforts to correspond more precisely with standard American usage, but also to simplify or abbreviate language complexities. To accommodate additional categories and to achieve diagnostic refinements, the developers of the DSM-II affixed a fifth coding digit to the four indexed in the ICD-8. This latter step enabled clinicians to record several "qualifying phrases" beyond those possible in the more limited framework of the ICD. Qualifiers such as acute versus chronic, or mild, moderate, and severe could now be noted to furnish data relevant to patient assessment and treatment.

A paragraph or two comparing the DSM-I and the DSM-II may be useful as a precis for later discussions on both the character and the extensive changes introduced in the DSM-III. Notable among the conceptual innovations was the DSM-II committee's decision to avoid terms that implied acceptance of a particular theoretical viewpoint, especially with regard to syndromes where matters of causality were notably controversial. Although the principle of eschewing theory-based positions was both explicit and authentic, it does appear curious, to say the least, that the only major shift of this character was the consistent elimination in the DSM-II of the syndromal adjective "reaction" from a diverse group of diagnostic labels. This reflected an active decision to expunge the Meyerian "psychobiologic" perspective from the nosology (Meyer, 1908, 1912). Untouched, however, were equally doctrinaire concepts, such as neuroses and psychophysiologic disorders, which derive their logic from "psychoanalytic" formulations. Notable also were the labels selected to substitute for those requiring modification. To illustrate, the label "schizophrenic reaction" was supplanted by "schizophrenia," a choice in accord with a Kraepelinian rather than a Meyerian model, and one in which mental disorders are phrased as if they were tangible and distinct entities. These transformations may have merely reflected the lessened stature of the Meyerian perspective in American psychiatry; by contrast, the resilience of psychoanalytic concepts in the face of the incursions and growing hegemony of Kraepelinian disease model was most impressive. Issues surrounding contrasting viewpoints were not readily put to rest, as evidenced by their revival in debates associated with the construction of the DSM-III, a topic to which we will turn in later discussions.

Among other DSM-II modifications was the judgment to disband the obscure and functionally irrelevant distinction that had been drawn in the DSM-I between personality trait and personality pattern disturbances; both sets were now to be grouped under the heading of Personality Disorders. New personality syndromes were added to the list, while others were eliminated, most controversially that of sociopathic personality disturbance.

Although the DSM-I implicitly encouraged multiple diagnoses, the DSM-II provided unequivocal guidelines as to when and how such concurrent labeling could be made. Despite these explicit instructions, multiple diagnoses still failed to assume the status of a routine procedure during the DSM-II's tenure. The concept was raised anew and, it was hoped, more effectively implemented in the DSM-III with the introduction of the multiaxial format; more will be said concerning this innovation later.

Origins and Goals of the DSM-III

It is necessary at this point to digress from the impersonality of scholarly review to illustrate the largely serendipitous character of "progress" in science, be it hard or soft.

Prelude

In 1970, I wrote a formal memorandum to my university colleague, Melvin Sabshin, then serving as Chair of the APA's Council on Research and Development, under whose direction the work of the Task Force on Nomenclature and Statistics is carried out. At our regular meeting to discuss departmental and professional matters, I often expressed my dismay over the unimaginative character of the DSM-II. It was Sabshin's wish to explore formal ways in which he could facilitate a thoughtful reexamination of the current nosology that prompted his request that I prepare a brief memo reflecting my concerns and suggestions. That memo, reproduced here in its entirety, was addressed to Sabshin in his role as Council Chair in March, 1971.

For many in psychiatry the appearance of the DSM-II had been the most important single event of the past decade. As I view it, however, its publication signifies that we have been bequeathed another in that long series of modest excursions from Kraepelin's misguided paths. Those, such as I, who dismiss the revision with the epitath "old wine" may be too severe, but who in our profession cannot be saddened by the knowledge that an unexcelled opportunity has been missed to bring fresh perspectives to our archaic taxonomy. More distressing is the total lack of creative innovation in the DSM-II. Some glimmer of imaginative boldness could certainly have been evidenced despite the major constraint on the Task Force, that of coordinating American nosology with the WHO's ICD-8. It is this latter fact which is perhaps most lamentable of all since the committee's major task was seen to be that of cementing the international nosology to our Kraepelinian past.

The purpose of this impassioned missive, as is obvious, stems from a deep concern of mine that future editions will be compromised as was the DSM-II; efforts must be initiated now to ensure that this will not be the case. Your post as Chairman of the APA's Council on Research and Development provides you with a base from which the need to incorporate our growing store of classification research and theory in future DSMs can be stressed. May I suggest that you use your good office to propose the formation of a committee composed of members and consultants to both the Council and the Task Force on Nomenclature and Statistics, and charged with the responsibility of reviewing research data and coordinating theoretical proposals for the next DSM?

Given the depth of his own scholarship and genuine commitment to facilitate progress in his profession, it was not surprising that Sabshin succeeded in arranging the appointment of an Ad Hoc Committee to evaluate contemporary models of classification, one that would function in parallel with the established Task Force on Nomenclature and Statistics. The new committee was composed of several distinguished psychiatrists known for their innovativeness and precedent-setting proposals. Unfortunately, but not unexpectedly, the deliberations of this committee were seen as anathema to the official Task Force; more significantly, it had no means to implement its evolving proposals other than convincing the established Task Force of the "wisdom of its ways."

Revisions scheduled for the new ICD-9 were well on their way during the early 1970s. Representatives from the APA who were engaged in this international venture were the same persons who had been involved in both the construction of the DSM-II and in ensuring its compatability with the ICD-8. What seemed a reasonable deduction from the foregoing appeared, in fact, to be taking place; that is, all signs indicated that the updating of the "Mental Disorder" section of the ICD-9 would be cosmetic, essentially devoid of any of the recent conceptual and methodological advances in research, theory, and clinical practice. Moreover, the prospects that the established Task Force would approach their future DSM-III responsibilities in an innovative manner, no less deviate from the apparent superficial changes planned for the forthcoming ICD-9, were rather bleak indeed.

In January 1974, Sabshin accepted the post of Medical Director of the APA, a position he planned to assume officially that summer. In discussing his aspirations for this new venture, I implored him to continue the serious reexamination he initiated some years earlier of psychiatric taxonomy and diagnosis. More concretely, I proposed that he schedule a meeting prior to undertaking the demanding responsibilities of office so that steps might be planned to ensure that contemporary advances be introduced into the body of the DSM-III. Time was short and, in April 1974, Robert Spitzer, Melvin Sabshin, and I took the opportunity to devote a full day's discussion both to substance and strategy. Clearly, new blood was needed in the Task Force if it were to be revitalized. A recommendation was therefore made to the Council on Research and Development and to the incoming president of the APA that a substantially reconstituted Task Force on Nomenclature and Statistics be appointed, with Spitzer, already a Task Force member, selected as its new chairperson. These arrangements were successfully implemented and approved at the annual meeting of the APA in May 1974.

The Task Force

Implicit in Spitzer's charge was the expectancy that the new Task Force would revamp the DSM in a manner consonant with current empirical knowledge, theory, and practice. Also implicit was the assumption that the product would be viewed by allied mental health professions as having been cognizant of their diverse interests and orientations.

To meet this mandate, Spitzer asked five psychiatrists, two psychologists, and one biometrician to join him that September to serve as the core group of appointees of what was henceforth to be known as the DSM-III Task Force. In addition to Spitzer, the initial assemblage consisted of Nancy Andreasen, M.D., Ph.D., Jean Endicott, Ph.D., Donald F. Klein, M.D., Morton Kramer, Sc.D., Theodore Millon, Ph.D., Henry Pinsker, M.D., George Saslow, M.D., Ph.D., and Robert Woodruff, M.D. Most were well-recognized contributors to the research and theoretical literature; as a committee, they formed an unusual alliance, possessing a significant array of professional interests combined with a substantial diversity in theoretical orientations. New members were added in later years to further broaden the Task Force's perspectives and expertise, but the original nucleus worked intensely and productively as a single, unified committee for over a year, meeting frequently, debating issues vigorously, and establishing a firm foundation and structural framework for both the form and the function of the DSM-III. Important modifications continued to evolve, of course, but the basic conceptual schema and its distinctive innovative features were set well in place by the end of its first full year of deliberation; for example, the use of operational criteria, the multiaxial format that separated clinical (Axis I) from personality (Axis II) disorders, the systematic and comprehensive description of disorders, and the plan to implement extensive and formal field trials.

Having laid the groundwork for the structure and having selected the features that would set the DSM-III apart from earlier nomenclature systems, the Task Force took its major role to be that of a steering committee to guide and evaluate the ongoing work of the 14 substantive advisory committees it appointed. Although it is often valid to apply that well-worn chestnut, "a camel is a horse designed by a committee," the final product of the Task Force is a much more coherent package than would be expected given the awesome number and heterogeneity of its decision-making committees. Unquestionably the DSM-III lacks the tight-knit integration that only a single synthesist could have brought to it. Despite the diversity of its advisors, the DSM-III retained the deeply etched template stamped onto it by the small, original Task Force group, each member of which continued in his or her role as project overseer and advisory committee participant.

What proved especially gratifying as well as fruitful in achieving a strongly shared consensus was the open and equalitarian spirit that prevailed in the Task Force's early deliberations. Not that there was a paucity of vigorous disagreement, nor that impassioned polemics were invariably resolved, but these divergences and spirited controversies did not result in group discord, or traditional academic schisms or professional power struggles; for example, the psychologists on the Task Force not only had full voting rights—when votes were necessary—but they provided perhaps more than their share of ideas, disputations, and formal text drafts.

In addition to the framework they constructed to give shape and structure to the DSM-III, Task Force members shared a number of implicit values as well as explicit goals that guided their review of the text and criteria drafts submitted by the advisory committees. They recognized that no ideal classification was possible in clinical psychopathology, that all nosological systems would be imperfect, and, regardless of what advances were made in knowledge and theory, the substantive and professional character of mental health would be simply too multidimensional in structure and too multivariate in function ever to lend itself to a single, fully satisfactory system. It was acknowledged also that no consensus would ever be likely found among either psychiatrists or psychologists as to how a classification might be best organized (e.g., dimensions, categories, observables), no less what it should contain (e.g., eitology, prognosis, structure, severity).

In the light of the foregoing, the Task Force agreed to take an explicitly nondoctrinaire approach, evident not only by avoiding the introduction of particular theoretical biases concerning the nature and etiology of mental disorders, but by actively expunging them wherever they were found in the DSM-II, actions which evoked the ire of serveral, deeply mortified professional organizations. The Task Force was equally committed to the goal of syndromal inclusiveness. The intent here was to embrace as many conditions as are commonly seen by practicing clinicians, thereby maximizing the opportunity of future investigators to evaluate the character of each condition as a valid syndromal entity. Choosing the inclusive rather than the exclusive route was a position that stirred considerable dismay in a variety of quarters, but for highly divergent reasons. The initial requirement for a potentially new category was that its diagnostic criteria be outlined with specificity and relative distinctness from other syndromes. The ultimate inclusion test was whether the condition had been utilized with reasonable frequency, as well as drawing positive comments concerning its clarity, from a significant number of clinicians participating in the field trials.

In addition to the principles enunciated above, the Task Force was guided by the following considerations in its DSM-III plans: Expand the classification to maximize its utility for outpatient populations; differentiate levels of severity and course within syndromes; maintain compatibility, where feasible, with the ICD-9; rely on empirical data to establish the diagnostic criteria; be receptive to the concerns and critiques submitted by interested professional and patient representatives.

Progress Reviews

Having drawn the basic architectural design and many of the DSM-III's initial syndromal drafts, Task Force representatives spoke formally for the first time about their work at a special session during the Annual Meeting of the American Psychiatric Association in May 1975. Following this inaugural appearance, the Task Force turned the manual's elaboration and refinement phases over to 14 advisory committees, several of which contributed substantively to both the conception and writing of those drafts for which they were responsible. Additional consultants were invited periodically to contribute in areas of their expertise. The Task Force continued as a body to evaluate successive drafts submitted by the substantive area committees, appraising them with reference to the goals, rationale, and standards they had set earlier for the manuscript.

The classification model and syndromal criteria of the DSM-III were extensively and critically appraised at a major conference held in St. Louis in June, 1976. Entitled "DSM-III in Mid-Stream," it drew both the critiques and commendations of over 100 invited participants with backgrounds relevant to both the nosology and major diagnostic categories of the projected document. Serving as representatives of allied mental health organizations, only a handful of these "mid-stream" evaluators had a part in the development of the 1976 draft manual. The conference proved of considerable value in that it served to highlight several deficiencies and ambiguities, as well as providing reinforcement for the Task Force's commitments to both the multiaxial schema and the specification of what was subsequently termed the "diagnostic" rather than the "operational" criteria.

As a follow up to the mid-stream conference, a formal invitation was extended to a number of interested professional mental health societies, encouraging them to establish liaison committees to the Task Force. Among those which formed such groups were The Academy of Psychiatry and the Law, the American Academy of Child Psychiatry, the American Academy of Psychoanalysis, the American Association of Chairmen of Departments of Psychiatry, the American College Health Association, the American Orthopsychiatric Association, the American Psychoanalytic Association, and the American Psychological Association. Each liaison group received major drafts of the DSM-III and were invited both to relay their concerns and to provide suitable recommendations. Most liaison committees chose an essentially pro forma role, offering little commentary or feedback to the Task Force. By contrast, impassioned controversies were stirred among both the American Psychoanalytic and the American Psychological Associations. These disputations fostered new and troublesome misconceptions and extended dialogues and written interchanges, all of which ultimately brought forth reasoned and balanced solutions; more will be said concerning the issues surrounding these disputes later.

In April 1977, a comprehensive volume encompassing detailed diagnostic descriptions and criteria drafts of the DSM-III's major syndromal categories was printed for general distribution and critical review. Although preliminary field testing had already begun in December 1976, the timing of this comprehensive printed draft was designed to coincide with the beginning of a series of formal national "field trials" in the fall of 1977 under the aegis of the Task Force and the sponsorship of The National Institute of Mental Health (NIMH). As with other documents possessing long-term implications, it was wisely decided by the Task Force that the proposed manual be fully evaluated several times *during*, rather than following, its development. This would not only keep subsequent problems to a minimum, but also increase the likelihood that the final version would prove maximally acceptable to clinicians and researchers *prior* to official adoption.

The 2-year NIMH-sponsored project, conducted from September 1977 to September 1979, included several sequential drafts of the DSM-III; it not only solicited evaluations based on case history studies, but requested specific judgments concerning the more innovative aspects of the manual as well as recommendations on a number of knotty diagnostic problems. The responses of more than 800 clinicians, both from private settings and over 200 public facilities, were obtained based on data from some 12,000 patients. Noteworthy were the findings of a formal questionnaire which indicated that clinicians of widely diverse theoretical views appraised the penultimate DSM-III draft in a highly and uniformly positive fashion.

Despite efforts to maintain a reasonable level of compatibility with the ICD-9, the Task Force saw its primary duty to be substantive and innovative. For this and other reasons, notably the rather widespread dissatisfaction of several nonpsychiatric medical specialties with the ICD-9, significant disparities continue to exist between the two taxonomies and nomenclatures. To accommodate the areas of dissatisfaction, a so-called "clinical modification" of the standard ICD, termed the ICD-9-CM, was developed in 1978 for primary use in the United States. The major difference between the two ICDs is the addition of a fifth-digit code to the indexing system of the ICD-9-CM; for both psychiatric and other medical specialties, the added digit not only permits greater diagnostic latitude, but enables the introduction of more refined discriminations and qualifiers. Most relevantly, the ICD-9-CM can now encompass the entire range of syndromal categories that comprise the DSM-III. The converse is not true, however; that is, although all of the codes in the standard ICD are included in the ICD-9-CM, many of the standard ICD diagnoses have not been incorporated in the DSM-III.

Its work essentially completed, the Task Force submitted its final DSM-III document to the Council on Research and Development at the APA's annual meeting in May 1979. Here it was approved and forwarded to the organization's Board of Trustees, where it was formally endorsed as the officially authorized document to be scheduled for publication and implementation as the *Diagnostic and Statistical Manual of Mental Disorders*, 3rd Edition, in 1980.

Some Controversies and Myths

At almost the moment the DSM-III's first draft reached the public eye, a rash of criticisms—from mild to fevered—spread upon the scene at professional symposia (Dreger, 1977; Lorr, 1977; Millon, 1977; Salzinger, 1977; Willems, 1977) and in a wide variety of periodicals (Garmezy, 1978; McLemore & Benjamin, 1979; McReynolds, 1979; Schacht & Nathan, 1977; Zubin, 1978). Most troublesome was the fact that so inchoate a glimpse of what "might" be forthcoming—and how one might, in turn, be affected thereby—led so many otherwise cautious and reasonable judges to leap to premature conclusions that proved far from the final mark. "Philosophical" and "conceptual" positions were ascribed to the Task Force as if the committee were composed of clones that rubber stamped some higher authority, rather than being a highly diverse and outspoken collection of independently minded professionals with clearly disparate views. Troublesome also were the questionable, if not malicious motives attributed to the committee. Attacked as spokesman for an "imperialistic" assault by psychiatry designed to gain hegemony over the mental health service marketplace, the partially visible efforts of the Task Force were seen not merely as unsuitable for scientific progress or for the viability of one or another professional discipline, but were conceived by some as leading inevitably to the undoing of patients themselves, particularly children. Others used the occasion to criticize the document for having expanded its predecessors 10-fold, encompassing ostensible "problems of living" which do not qualify as mental disorders. Still others lamented the deletion of favorite syndromes, so sorely missed as to lead them to pursue all avenues which might undo approval of the manuscript by the Board of Trustees of the APA unless their cherished concepts were reinstated in the manual. That the taxonomy and nomenclature of the forthcoming DSM-III signified to some a dismaying reaffirmation of the medical model was, somewhat perversely, counterbalanced by the vehement denunciation of others that it had abandoned that very model. Many of these skirmishes and reprehensions were the mere ravings of a misinformed or misguided reader-ship. Others represented issues of genuine substance that transcended the usual professional bickering and theoretical hairsplitting.

Reviewing the critiques from the vantage point of having been an active Task Force participant, I was reminded repeatedly of the Rashomon tale—except that none of the dissenters were even at the scene. Although perhaps blinded by the very fact of being present, I did manage, however, to retain my "outsider" identity as a psychologist working in psychiatry's vineyards. More aptly, I felt like a historian who was witness to the drafting of a preliminary sketch for a future nonfiction study and, before either the details or the ending was worked out, stumbled across a series of critical reviews, not of the completed book, but of a novelized movie adaptation that was based tangentially on the early outlines. Little of what I heard or read corresponded to either the process of the DSM-III's evolution or the product that finally emerged.

Lest the reader think otherwise, let me assure you that I am no apologist for the DSM-III's shortcomings, nor do I have especially fond illusions concerning the altruism or the power and economic interests of mental health professions. Neither do I dismiss the troubling struggles that cur-rently exist between psychiatry and psychology. But I do believe that it would be a grievous error to displace upon the substantive character of the DSM-III whatever legitimate misgivings one may have about the nature of this disquieting professional rivalry. However wrongheaded or deficient the manual may be, it was, in fact, an outgrowth of scholarly debate and empirical test and not any real or imagined ventures of psychiatric imperial-ism. This is not the chapter for elaboration, but I can assert confidently, and contrary to the beliefs of many of my psychological brethren, that the changes wrought in the DSM-III are more consonant, first with the rigorous empiricism that characterizes psychology—witness the requirement of ad-herence to specified and explicit diagnostic *criteria*—and, second, that it sub-scribes to the contextual orientation that increasingly typifies psychological thought—witness the fact that diagnosis must set the presenting clinical syndrome (Axis I) within the framework of a longitudinal pattern of endur-ing personality traits (Axis II) as well as within a broad, cross-sectional context of situational or psychosocial precipitants (Axis IV).

It will be useful to turn next to a brief exposition of several of the more memorable public controversies that were stirred during the Task Force's 5-year tenure; the "facts" should help discredit some myths.

Controversies with Psychology: "Mental Disorders Are a Subset of Medical Disorders"

Few issues evoked so strong a professional outcry as the belief that the statement "mental disorders are a subset of medical disorders" would be promulgated as an official pronouncement in the DSM-III. How did this misguided phrase gain its coinage?

At a May 1975 meeting of the then small and close-knit Task Force, the issue was raised as to whether the forthcoming DSM should contain a definition of "mental disorders." It seemed a reasonable thesis at the time, and members of the Task Force were invited to draft proposals accordingly as well as to distribute them to other committee participants prior to a scheduled fall meeting. Only one member of the Task Force, Donald Klein, was courageous (foolish?) enough to take it upon himself to write a full-fledged essay on the rationale of what he believed would be an acceptable definition. Despite its commendable scholarly nature, this draft appeared overly abstruse and theoretical, lacking both the specificity and the concreteness with which the main DSM text was to be characterized. Spitzer was notably disquieted, despairing that the committee might subscribe by default to this solitary proposal; hence, he requested that an opportunity be given him and Jean Endicott, another Task Force appointee and long-time research colleague, to draft an alternate statement and definition. The proposal they prepared shortly thereafter included the phrase "mental disorders are a subset of medical disorders." It was presented for the first time publicly in a paper at the May 1976 APA meeting, having been discussed only cursorily, and assuredly *not* given official status or coinage as a formal statement by the Task Force, a point explicitly acknowledged subsequently by Spitzer and Endicott. Nevertheless, many, having either heard or having read it shortly thereafter (Spitzer, Sheehy, & Endicott, 1977), assumed incorrectly that their's was the official voice of the Task Force (parenthetically, as should be well known by now, when the statement was put forward to formal committee vote, it was rejected as a counterproductive concept).

Despite numerous memoranda from Spitzer and Endicott restating that their's was a *personal* and not a Task Force viewpoint, as well as publishing an explicit disclaimer in the literature to the effect that the phrase should not be construed as meaning that mental disorders were the exclusive province of the psychiatric profession, nor that this one discipline was the sole possessor of what requisite skills were needed for their amelioration (Spitzer *et al.*, 1977), a storm of both official and unofficial protest from psychologists ensued following its publication. Several of the articles published at the time reflected either the frightened voices or the provocative trumpeting of self-servers whose concerns were the protection of psychology's vested commercial interests; others were more reasoned and scholarly critiques that illuminated the remaining deficits of what they saw to be an anachronistic medical taxonomy and nomenclature. In the end, the uproar proved a tempest in a teapot. At no time would the Task Force have jeopardized acceptance of the substantive advances they had wrought in the DSM-III by including a statement so obviously provocative to one of the major mental health professions. Perhaps one or two Task Force members might have seen the fight worth making, but it would have been a Pyrrhic victory, at best. Fortunately, when the concept was put to the test of a Task Force vote in February 1978, it was soundly, and wisely, defeated.

A related issue of no small import was the accusation that the DSM-III conceived every syndrome as intrinsically organic, thereby reflecting a "power play" by psychiatry to preempt the mental health field. In response to this concern, a distinguished former president of the American Psychological Association (Albee, 1977) wrote that "to attribute marital conflict or delinquency . . . to a biological defect, to biochemical, nutritional, neurological, or other organic conditions . . . is to sell our psychological birthright for short term gain." That this assertion was notably in error can be seen by the following text the Task Force approved in April 1979 for insertion in its glossary as *the* definition of mental disorder (regrettably, this statement was subsequently modified at the editorial level *without* Task Force approval; substitute wording was inadvertently and unfortunately introduced):

> No precise definition is available that unambiguously defines the boundaries of this concept. (This is also true of such concepts as physical disorder or mental or physical health.) However, in the DSM-III each of the mental disorders is conceptualized as a clinically significant behavioral or psychological syndrome or pattern of an individual that is associated, by and large, with either a painful symptom (distress) or impairment in one or more important areas of functioning (disability).

Note should be made here of the phrase "each of the mental disorders is conceptualized as a clinically significant behavioral or psychological syndrome."

Controversies with Psychoanalysis: "Neurosis: Real or Artifact?"

Troubles brewed within psychiatry's house as well. Some background history may be useful here.

The chairman of the Task Force responsible for the DSM-II recorded in his foreword to the 1968 manual that his committee sought to eschew terms and taxonomic principles that might convey a doctrinaire position concerning either the character or the etiology of syndromes in which definitive knowledge concerning such matters were lacking in fact (Gruenberg, 1969). He recognized that by leaving issues of this nature unspecified or ambiguous, his committee would be inviting readers to attribute whatever meanings and interpretations they found congenial to their theoretical or clinical biases; he averred, however, that such interpretations would be wholly unjustified. In great measure, the DSM-II Task Force did achieve its goal of disclaiming pretensions to knowledge they lacked—except in the case of syndromes inspired and interpreted in accord with psychoanalytic concepts of etiology and dynamics, for example, neurosis, psychophysiologic disorders. Here, the committee's aspirations wavered badly, having submitted early in their consultations to the entreaties of a powerful analytic lobby.

Such deference and acquiescence, it was believed, would never prove the case with the DSM-III. Convinced that it would avoid the pitfalls of etiologic speculation and desiring to maintain an explicitly empirical orientation, the new Task Force set its sights clearly toward the goal of expunging principles that signified the favoring of one notion of psychogenesis over another. So adamant a position may have appeared unduly rigid and may, in fact, have been an unwise, if not incomprehensible, decision to some. But doubts such as these did not faze the committee after observing the theoretic polemics its own members displayed in their early dialogues. An empirically grounded manual that would alienate the smallest number of clinicians possible would be a more realistic and desirable goal, it was concluded, than the potentially more laudible, if less probable, outcome of achieving interpretive consensus.

The Task Force could hardly have anticipated the storm of protest that arose when it resolved to do away with the label "neurosis" and, perhaps more significantly, its synthesizing rationale in psychoanalytic theory. As a unifying theme for explicating and coordinating diverse syndromes, the "neurotic" concept had outlived its usefulness both as a nomenclature designation and as a classificatory principle (see Chapt. 9 of this volume). Not only was the term misbegotten and anachronistic, having evolved through a long and checkered history of misguided reinterpretations, but the exclusiveness of the analytic interpretive model could no longer be sustained in light of equally plausible explanatory and empirically demonstrable alternatives; for example, a "snake phobia" may stem from repressed conflicts in which residual anxieties are symbolically displaced; it may also reflect directly conditioned or generalized avoidant learning; also possible are constitutionally low biological thresholds for a highly prevalent "instinctive" response.

The furor and threats that ensued deserve public censure, for they were not mere idle posturings. A review of the agonizing events that followed will be instructive in that they illuminate the awesome power of unremitting "political" pressure designed to thwart a courageous and "scientific" effort to undo questionable tenets and conceptual presumptions that are unsupportable by usual empirical or clinical criteria.

As is well known, by late 1978 the public media picked up the "neurosis" story, taking what appears as some delight in exposing what should have been a dispassionate professional debate. Having been thrust into front-page notoriety, the psychoanalytic campaign to dissuade the Task Force from its appointed rounds delivered its first official broadside: Desist or we will develop our own nosology and terminology. This was responded to with suggestions that the Task Force could appoint a committee to draft a special DSM-III appendix for clinicians oriented to a psychodynamic viewpoint in which the official nomenclature would be explicated in terms more suitable to their theory. This proposal gained some adherents within the Task Force, but charmed few in official psychoanalytic quarters. The stakes rose sharply as psychoanalytic groups sought to bring pressure on official psychiatric bodies. By the spring of 1979, the Task Force received a letter signifying considerable success on their part. It stated:

At the meeting of the Area III Council (of the American Psychiatric Association) on March 10, 1979, the following motion was passed:
> MOVED: Area III is opposed to the elimination of "neurosis" as a diagnostic term in DSM-III.

In subsequent discussion it was determined that Area III would move at the assembly meeting in the Spring to not approve the adoption of DSM-III unless it included this diagnostic category.

Indications were that assembly representatives from all areas would coalesce and bring down the wrath of the analytic community by blocking acceptance of the DSM-III at the annual APA Board Meeting that May. This was no mundane crusade. Hence, to avoid what was anticipated to be a brutal and potentially destructive confrontation, the Task Force proposed that the issue be cleverly finessed by separating the concept "neurotic disorder" from that of "neurotic process." Neurotic "disorder," signifying mere descriptive properties, could then be introduced as a formal DSM-III designation without necessarily connoting the operation of a neurotic "process," that is, a sequence in which intrapsychic conflicts are resolved unconsciously via various defense mechanisms, as well as being expressed symbolically in symptomatic form. An approved statement recording this distinction and its ostensive rationale was recommended for insertion in the Introduction to the DSM-III; an additional brief note in the summary chart of the DSM-III hence reads:

> In order to facilitate the identification of the categories that in DSM-II were grouped together in a class of the neuroses, the DSM-III terms are included separately in parentheses after the corresponding categories.

Not all factions of the Task Force shared or were heartened by this last-minute solution. One refractory member, Donald Klein, expressed his ire and contempt for the compromise, as well as what he judged to be the Task Force's dereliction of duty, thusly:

> The political pressure to reinsert the term "neurosis" into the DSM-III stems from those who . . . are not objecting to the absence of the term . . . because American nosology would be deprived of a useful descriptive term: They wish it reinserted because they wish a covert affirmation of their psychogenic hypotheses. The attempts to supposedly clarify the issue by redefining the term "neurotic disorder" as a purely descriptive term is really an attempt to obfuscate the real impact of its reintroduction. . . .
>
> I think the role of Task Force should be to act as an advisory group of nosological experts. We should make our recommendations to the APA. If the APA, in its wisdom, sees fit to reject any or all of our recommendations, that is its business. We have done our job and they have done their job.
>
> To respond to this sort of unscientific and illogical, but psychologically understandable, pressure . . . is unworthy of scientists who are attempting to advance our field via clarification and reliable definition.

Controversies over Language: The Concept of Disorders

Carlo de Sanctis, a contemporary Italian child psychiatrist, recounted his thoughts while observing a group of adolescent girls learning to water ski. They would start their run, he noted, with their legs together tightly; as they moved forward their skis would gradually drift further apart until the young ladies would inevitably descend into the water ever so gracefully on their youthfully firm and attractively spaced buttocks. Commenting on his observation, de Sanctis said:

> I went to medical school before the terminological reforms of the Geneva Anatomical Convention. What are now known as the adductors of the thighs were then known as the *protectator virginitatis*.

Lemkau (1969), who recorded the above tale, notes that a major fault of nosological systems, which subsequent editions invariably seek to correct, is that of having imparted more than a mere designation in the names it assigned its subject matter. As noted in the charming vignette just sketched, the task of constructing a suitable terminology proves problematic even in so "tangible" a subject as physical anatomy. How much more susceptible are conceptual subjects such as psychopathology to the vagaries and errors of superfluous connotation. For this reason, the mission of devising a nomenclature devoid of misguided and value-free implications was judged one of no small proportion to the DSM-III Task Force. Its members applied a toothcomb of fine grading to winnow out all possible misconceptions and solecisms which might contaminate or misdirect the course of future clinical and research endeavors.

A linguistic principle employed by the Task Force was that labels be not only interpretable and modernized, but that they consist, where possible, of everyday language, that is, be composed of familiar English words that convey the behaviors they seek to represent simply and directly. This seemingly modest if not virtuous goal evoked greater resistance than anyone could have anticipated. For example, the term "catatonia" was defended vigorously and remains fixed in the nomenclature, although I venture that less than 1% of the DSM-III readership is aware of either its origins or translation. Fortunately, and by contrast, "hebephrenia" was successfully deleted, replaced by the commonplace descriptive word "disorganized." Similarly the label "histrionic" was chosen to supplant "hysteria" as an Axis II personality designation, as was "somatoform" selected to supersede it as an Axis I clinical syndrome. New terms such as "avoidant" and "narcissistic" were likewise adopted not only to personify the most salient feature to characterize their respective syndromes, but by virtue of being familiar words, readily understood in everyday parlance.

Akin to the foregoing, the standard syntax and language conventions employed in the DSM-III were framed such that designated labels would be construed to define the syndrome and not the person who exhibits it. Thus, people are never referred to as "schizophrenics" in the DSM-III, but as persons who portray a "schizophrenic disorder." Worthy of note in this regard also is the eradication of the medical term "patient" and the sweeping substitution of words such as "person" or "individual."

Lest the reader be led to believe the Task Force was invariably successful in holding to its principles or otherwise failed to regress from its "noble" aspirations, any brief skimming of the DSM-III nomenclature should disabuse the reader from such thoughts. Numerous derelictions can be readily exposed, for example, the choice of the obscure term "dysthymia" as the appellation for recurrent or mild depressions, or "factitious" for simulated disorders. Transgressions such as these were of minor import when compared to a concerted effort to rescind an earlier and signal linguistic decision to apply the label "disorder" consistently to all syndromes. As one of its guiding principles, the committee chose this term for all conditions lacking an empirically demonstrable etiology. The principle reflected the Task Force's decision to eschew all unsupportable theoretical or pathogenic implications. In addition, the Task Force sought to highlight the inherent diversity that characterizes most syndromes by phrasing the term in its plural form, for example, the new nomenclature lists the label as "schizophrenic disorders." Despite the firm commitment it made to this principle, the Task Force began to drift off course, to which the author responded with some alarm in a memo dated July 16, 1978, as follows:

> This memo is in response to the letter of July 10 suggesting a series of modifications in labeling the affective disorders. What prompts me is not any strong pro or con reaction to the substantive suggestions, but rather to a reported "decision" that was tucked away in the memo to the effect that, henceforth, the label "schizophrenia" will replace that of "schizophrenic disorders," thereby undoing a Task Force decision that was agreed upon in late 1974.
>
> I very much agree with the point that "we are obliged to coin terms that are simple as well as descriptive," and toward that end will support such suggestions as substituting "major depression" for "major depressive disorder," and those pertaining to deletions of the term "chronic" where it is redundant or noncontrasting. My concern, however, is that simplicity and symmetry not become overriding principles that may conflict and undo other goals such as clarity and accuracy.
>
> As some of you may recall, I argued strongly at an early Task Force meeting in St. Louis that we adopt the term "disorders" as a modifier for *each major* syndrome category. This was, in part, a response to the problems that arose as a consequence of etiological theses that were implied in both DSM-I and DSM-II, most prominently illustrated with the schizophrenic syndrome. To recall, the label "schizophrenic reaction" was employed in DSM-I and, in DSM-II, the label was "simplified" to "schizophrenia." The objections raised were that the former implied a syndrome elicited "in response to a situational stressor," whereas the latter implied the identification of a homogeneous "disease entity," a focal ailment within the patient akin to such medical disorders as tuberculosis or measles. Both of these etiological theses, though conveyed subtly and indirectly by their promulgators, proved to be misleading and empirically unsupportable. Today, we

believe that there are a variety of schizophrenic disorders, a spectrum, if you will; that is, a heterogeneous syndrome, etiologically biogenic in some cases, psychogenic in others, and most likely interactive in the majority.

Without belaboring the academics of the issue, I would like to ask the Task Force to review the principles that guide such decisions as when to use the "disorders" term and when not. For me, when a label is a commonplace and clearly *descriptive English term*, with no etiological implications or undertones, such as "depression," the modifier "disorder" or "disorders" may occasionally be dropped. However, where the key term in the label suggests properties beyond mere description, such as implying the identification of a homogeneous entity (e.g., schizophrenia, cyclothymia, and dysthymia), then I contend that by leaving them stand we are doing a disservice to the profession and undermining our own explicit commitment to "steer clear" of introducing dynamics or suggesting causalities in what is essentially a descriptive text.

I hate to convey my objections so strongly, particularly since I am probably the most disposed of the Task Force members to the attractions of symmetry and parallelism. However, the cost in creating misleading implications seems too great for the ostensible gains of simplicity and balance.

As evident in the final DSM-III text, the Task Force's early plan to uniformly apply the label "disorders" did remain firm.

Controversies over Homosexuality: Science or Politics?

Late in the tenure of the DSM-II, the Board of Trustees of the APA reevaluated the well-established diagnostic category of "homosexuality" and substituted in its stead a classification termed "sexual orientation disturbance." This new label reflected a compromise among opposing factions of the profession concerning whether homosexual behavior per se was or was not a valid mental disorder. The descriptive text of revised DSM-II syndrome stated that the condition applies to "individuals whose sexual interests are directed primarily toward people of the same sex and who are either disturbed by, in conflict with, or wish to change their sexual orientation." This reconciliation between contrary and often implacably held views was judged successful by the vast majority of practitioners, essentially those who were beholden to none of the more radical positions.

Despite the recency and apparent satisfactory character of the DSM-II reassessment, the place of homosexuality was questioned again upon news of a forthcoming DSM-III, much to the dismay of those Task Force members who recalled the intense, uncompromising, and often bitter debates which preceded the final DSM-II accommodation. The Task Force's Advisory Committee on Psychosexual Disorders was asked to carry the brunt of what proved to be a new and even more trying imbroglio. Several designations evolved during the committee's desultory journey to fashion a synthesis among contending viewpoints, among them: homodysphilia, dyshomophilia, homosexual conflict disorder, amorous relationship disorder (this latter proposal represented an effort to record sexual role conflicts experienced by heterosexual as well as homosexual individuals), and finally, ego-dystonic homosexuality.

As implied in the preceding, an argument advanced in favor of dismissing the ego-dystonic concept was the assertion that it was illogical to classify homosexual discontent if one were not to categorize similarly troubled heterosexuals. Also argued, with no small merit, was the observation that depressed feelings prompted by an inability to function heterosexually are no different than depressed feelings arising from other sources, which are routinely assigned the diagnostic rubric of depression. Further compounding the issue is the fact that most homosexuals experience no discomfort as a consequence of their sexual proclivities; why identify the very few, then, and select them out as the basis for a special diagnostic classification? Moreover, when homosexuals do feel dismay, it often reflects society's role expectations and discriminations rather than an intrinsic dissatisfaction of sexual preference. Needless to say, these contentions were challenged by clinicians who were no less convinced of the correctness of their beliefs; they noted evidence such as the nonnormative character of these behaviors, the presumptive pathological upbringing of homosexual patients, the ostensive constitutional defect that subserves the "disease," and so on.

After numerous text revisions, an avalanche of letters from distinguished professionals and public spokesmen, as well as the inability to achieve full consensus, the final responsibility of achieving a resolution was passed up from the advisory committee to the Task Force itself. Here, the recommendations of the majority faction of the advisory committee were appraised against several broad principles and criteria, including the consequences of one or another decision for both the public at large and the various professions of mental health. Since no ideal solution was possible, it was decided, in effect, to let the individual him or herself, and not the Task Force or the practitioner, establish whether there is or is not a disorder. Thus, the person involved must state that he or she desires to achieve heterosexual relationships *and* views his or her homosexual impulses to be both unwanted and distressing. Given the inchoate, yet entangled web of social values and scientific facts surrounding homosexual behavior, the only consensus that seemed both just and sensible would be one fashioned by the person who experienced the phenomenon him or herself. It was on that note that the Task Force put aside one of its more vexing, yet intriguing assignments.

Conceptual Advances and Failures

Perhaps the only realistic and significant question to be posed in appraising a new taxonomy and nomenclature is not whether they mirror the state of the science perfectly or whether they provide answers to all possible questions professionals within the discipline may ask, but whether they are advances over preceding nosological systems and whether they will be employed with greater clinical accuracy and facility by future practitioners and researchers. Our text turns next to these latter questions.

That the DSM-III has been responded to well is evident in both formal questionnaire responses and in the rather startling number of copies that have been sold to date, a figure that is best grasped by the fact that more orders were received in the first 6 months following its publication than in both previous DSM editions combined, including their 30-plus reprintings.

Comprehensive and Systematic Description

It is almost inevitable that more detail will be incorporated in a later form of a nosology than in earlier versions. Hence, though far from a comprehensive textbook, failing to encompass matters of theory, etiology, and treatment, the DSM-III is nevertheless substantially more extensive and thorough than both of its predecessors. Being exhaustive and inclusionary, however, required that information on each syndrome be ordered in a reasonably standardized and systematic format. The organizational sequence that was adopted proceeds with the following information: essential (necessary) features, associated (frequent) features, and, where reasonably reliable data are available, age of onset, course, impairment, complications, predisposing factors, sex ratio, familial pattern, and differential diagnosis. Both the scope and organizational structure given the descriptive text signify important advances in the DSM-III, for the schema not only provides a logical guide for clinicians seeking information, but it establishes a coherent framework within which the data of future studies can be systematically introduced.

Diagnostic Criteria

The comprehensive and systematic character of the DSM-III is of maximal utility to the clinician. The spelling out of diagnostic criteria is also beneficial to the practitioner in that it serves to highlight the specific inclusion and exclusion components that comprise the elements of a diagnostic decision. It is this very precision in articulating specific and uniform rules of definition, originally and significantly termed "operational" criteria, that makes the DSM-III so serviceable and potentially fruitful also as a research tool. Not only do the criteria delineate the components that will enable reasonably homogeneous group assignments, but its application as a standard national (and, it is hoped, international) gauge will ensure at least a modicum of reliability and comparability among studies undertaken at diverse research settings. To illustrate, the "borderline" pattern will no longer be characterized one way at Massachusetts General Hospital, another at the Menninger Clinic, a third at Michael Reese Hospital, and a fourth at Langley Porter

Institute; each setting would likely uncover distinctive, yet discrepant syndromal properties in the past, since each selected its study population using dissimilar diagnostic criteria. Although the painfully slow progress of verifiable empirical knowledge in mental health cannot be attributed solely to the paucity of replicable research, the joint use of uniform DSM-III criteria should help stem the tide of insubstantial, unreliable, or, at best, minimally generalizable data that have come to characterize publications in the field.

It is reasonable to assume that greater reliability and research comparability will flow from the use of standardized diagnostic criteria, but it should be recorded that increased reliability is no assurance of increased validity (see Chap. 10 of this volume), and that these criteria offer *no more than a promise* at this time. Some interjudge reliability data have been obtained in the DSM-III field trials, and these are encouraging, especially when compared to prior studies utilizing earlier classifications. However, most of the criteria lack empirical support (Morey & Blashfield, 1981). Moreover, some are inadequately explicit *or*, conversely, are overly concrete in their operational referents. Many are redundant both within and with other diagnostic classes. Others are insufficiently comprehensive in syndromal scope or display a lack of parallelism and symmetry among corresponding categories.

The formalism and specificity of the diagnostic schema—a mini Chinese menu of so many of these and so many of those—may impose a rigidity on the assessment process such that clinicians employ the DSM-III as a sacred, yet mechanical checklist. On the other hand, the detailing of overly precise criteria, set in Procrustean diagnostic beds, may not only have the effect of narrowing the range and diversity of cases that can properly be assigned, but may lead clinicians to handle ambiguities by "reconsidering their ill-fitting" observations so as to match the formal requirements of the system, thereby undoing the very purpose for which the criteria were established, that of enhancing reliability and reducing subjective biases.

At best, then, the diagnostic criteria of the DSM-III represent a significant *conceptual* step toward a future goal when clinical characteristics of appropriate specificity and breadth will provide both reliable and valid indices for identifying the major syndromal prototypes. Although this chapter has neither the space nor is the setting within which to elaborate the theme, it should be said that the categorical syndromes of the DSM-III are conceptual prototypes and not tangible entities. Hence, it would be not only specious, but paralogical to aspire to develop sophisticated discriminations such as criterion "weights." Given that these syndromes are, in the main, only theoretical constructs, it will more than suffice for both clinical and research purposes to employ what has been devised—a standardized, reliable, and internally coherent mosaic of criterion descriptors. To the extent that the DSM-III has provided this foundation of clinical prototypes, it can fairly be judged to have made an advance worthy of commendation.

Diagnostic Decision Trees

It is partly a consequence of the prototypical nature of psychopathological constructs that certain kinds of "scientific" effort, such as developing criterion weights, are intrinsically illusory. Among other "silk purse" endeavors explored by members of the Task Force was the "decision tree" method for facilitating differential diagnosis. Although the ostensive purpose of the decision tree appendix in the manual is to aid clinicians in understanding the organizational and hierarchical order of the classification schema, it was, at heart, a method to optimize the ruling in and ruling out of alternate diagnostic possibilities by a series of decision-point choices. Not only is the sequence of this branching procedure painstakingly formalized and, hence, cumbersome to pursue, but it rests on a number of philosophical and pragmatic assumptions that are either counterfactual or untenable.

First, the DSM-III decision tree method presumes the presence of a hierarchical ordering of categories such that diagnostic classes listed earlier in the nosology comprise symptoms which may be found in later classes, but where the reverse is not true. A prime consequence of so carefully fashioned a sequential chain of categories would be the fact that successive syndromes in the classification invariably are more specific and convey more precisely differentiated information than those that precede them. This increasing distinctness and exactitude, necessary ingredients in a successful decision tree or branching procedure, assures that each successive category possesses authentic clinical features not found in categories previously listed. A serial pattern of this nature would be a remarkable nosological achievement for the DSM-III were it so in fact. Not only is there no inherent structure to psychopathology that permits so rigorous an arrangement, but the DSM-III imposes only a modest degree of sequential rigor on its classificatory organization. For this and other reasons to be enumerated shortly, the decision tree concept has proved not to be one of the Task Force's more notable achievements.

Second, differential diagnosis assumes that psychopathological phenomena adhere to the classical model of discriminable "entities." However, the compositional structure of DSM-III diagnostic criteria derives from a prototypical model (Cantor, Smith, French, & Mezzich, 1980), that is, one that allows for syndromal heterogeneity, recognizes the inevitable covariation of diverse symptoms within single categories, and acknowledges that no one symptom or even pattern of symptoms is either necessary of sufficient to define the category. The problems of pursuing a method designed for purposes of differential diagnosis (Spitzer & Endicott, 1968; Wing, Cooper, & Sartorius, 1974) are compounded further by the fact that the DSM-III not only permits, but encourages multiple diagnoses, a problem aggravated further by the manual's standard multiaxial framework. Thus, not only does the decision tree goal of definitive diagnosis run hard against the prototypical character of DSM-III syndromes, but its formalism and sequential requirements would be undermined repeatedly by the multidiagnostic aims and intrinsic multiaxial schema of the DSM-III.

Third, the process of articulating clinical data in so formal and demanding a manner as required by the decision tree sequence may not be faulted as specious by some, but it does impose a procedural complexity upon an otherwise facile and expedient process. From a pragmatic view, then, it is likely to be considered an unnecessary encumbrance for routine diagnostic tasks, quite impractical for everyday decision making, and, perhaps most relevantly, abhorrent to clinicians accustomed to the diagnostic habit of "intuitive" synthesis. Should the method guarantee significantly greater diagnostic accuracy in the future or prove useful for deepening clinical understanding or aid in the selection of efficacious treatment modalities, then it might gain a sufficient following to override the inertia of traditional practice. Failing in these regards, as seems inevitable, it is likely to remain, as it has, a novel and essentially academic concept.

Multiaxial Format

The formal adoption of the multiaxial schema in the DSM-III signifies a reformulation of the task of psychodiagnoses that approaches the magnitude described by Kuhn (1962) as a paradigm shift. It represents a distinct turn from the traditional medical disease model where the clinician's job is to disentangle and clear away "distracting" symptoms and signs so as to pinpoint *the* underlying or "true" pathophysiologic state. By contrast, the multiaxial assessment model (Essen-Möller & Wohlfahrt, 1947; Mezzich, 1979; Rutter, Shaffer, & Sheperd, 1975; Stengel, 1959; Strauss, 1975) not only recognizes that "distracting" features such as course, etiology, social functioning, and personality traits are aspects worthy of attention, but records each of them on its own representative axis as part of an interactive complex of elements that, only in their entirety, *are* the pathologic state.

A brief review of the various classes of information that comprise the DSM-III multiaxial system may be useful as we proceed to comment on its strengths and weaknesses. Well known by now is the fact that the classification consists of five axes, the first three of which are required as the bases for an official diagnosis.

Axis I constitutes the more-or-less traditional mental disorders, those relatively circumscribed or distinct symptom states, labeled "clinical syndromes" in the DSM-III, which are often transient or florid in character. Also indexed on Axis I are a number of special categories, including those conditions that are not attributable to a mental disorder, but have nevertheless become the prime focus of the clinician's attention or treatment efforts.

Axis II is composed of two segments, one for children, the other for adults. The child section encompasses a variety of relatively specific, albeit questionable, developmental disorders, such as maturational delays in language or speech articulation. Conceptually more significant is the innovative segregation of the Personality Disorders in the adult section into a separate axis, isolating them thereby from the Clinical Syndromes which comprise the other axis. This bifurcation assures that the more enduring and often more prosaic styles of personality functioning are not overlooked when attention is given the frequently more urgent and behaviorally dramatic clinical syndromes. It also takes cognizance of the fact that the lifelong coping styles and emotional vulnerabilities that comprise personality can provide a context within which the more salient and usually transient clinical states are likely to arise and be understood. Although the DSM text notes that individuals *may* have disorders on both axes, the Task Force was more purposeful in recommending that both axes be routinely recorded wherever justified. Toward that end it encouraged the formal notation of all relevant personality "traits" on Axis II, even when a distinctive personality "disorder" was not in evidence.

Axis III provides for the recording of physical disorders which may be potentially important or relevant to the understanding or management of the patient. Separating health disorders into mental (Axes I and II) and physical (Axis III), though of questionable philosophical merit, acknowledges a tradition in which disturbances with primary behavioral or psychosocial manifestations are kept conceptually distinct from those whose manifestations are primarily somatic or physical. The justification for including a physical disorder axis in a taxonomy designed for mental disorders merely recognizes that information of this nature may, first, offer suggestive etiologic leads (e.g., soft neurological signs), second, identify physical ailments that may stem in part from the impact of psychological factors (e.g., ulcerative colitis), and, third, note facts that should be considered in planning therapeutic regimens (e.g., coronary artery disease).

Axis IV consists of judgments concerning the presence and severity of "psychosocial stressors." The official recognition that psychosocial environments play a role in the development and exacerbation of mental disorders, though patently obvious, is nevertheless an achievement of great import. Not only does it acknowledge the empirical fact that disturbances that arise in response to stressors have better prognoses than those that do not, but, more impressively, it signifies in an officially recorded fashion the realization that psychosocial factors establish a context within which disorders not only unfold, but are sustained and exacerbated. Psychosocial information is to be coded in two ways. First, a numerical rating is given to represent the "objectively judged" severity of all concurrent stressors impacting upon the individual, independent of his or her vulnerability or capacity to cope with them. Second, the specific nature of the stressors themselves are to be briefly described; the suggested categories include family issues, interpersonal problems, and occupational difficulties.

The presence in the DSM-III of Axis V, the "highest level of adaptive functioning" in the past year, reveals another signal achievement, the resolve that individuals who are seen clinically at the time of their greatest distress *not* be diagnosed and potentially "stigmatized" as if their present behaviors were fixed and constant. Not only does the recognition of the individual's recent level of adaptive functioning serve as a useful prognostic index, but it furnishes a longitudinal context within which to appraise a person's current functioning. Moreover, it addresses the "positive" attributes and strengths of the individual, so often overlooked in the clinician's understandable preoccupation with "negative" attitudes and troublesome behaviors.

Much to the chagrin of a number of Task Force members, both Axis IV and Axis V were made optional, ostensibly to avoid possible breaches of confidentiality in social and personal realms that were judged not essential to the treatment enterprise. Though vigorously denounced at a Task Force meeting, the decision was upheld on the advice of a committee on insurance and confidentiality.

Together, the inclusion in DSM-III of Axis II (personality), Axis IV (psychosocial stressors), and Axis V (highest adaptive functioning), even though not required at times, augurs well for a radical reconception of psychopathologic diagnosis. Henceforth, the official classification directs the clinician to address, not just the specific symptoms and signs which define the "disease entity," but an entire panorama of contextual dimensions, notably the person's overall style of psychological functioning, the qualities of his or her current situational environment, and his or her strengths and potentials for constructive and healthy coping.

It should be noted that it was not a failure to acknowledge axes beyond the five listed in the DSM-III that accounts for their absence. Dimensions such as "course" and "severity" were debated extensively in Task Force discussions. In both cases it was concluded that they lack universal applicability and, hence, should be coded selectively in syndromal categories where they would provide useful information. Unfortunately, the number of coded digits available for purposes such as these proved to be appreciably less than originally anticipated. Hence, "severity," though originally scheduled for use in several diagnostic classes, failed to survive in any category. The fate of "course" as an informational code was only slightly less sullied; it survived as a recorded datum in a few syndromal categories, notably as the fifth digit code in both schizophrenic and substance use groups.

Considerable attention was given also to two other potentially quite useful informational axes, those of "etiology" and of "treatment response." Although insufficient time was available for an empirical field trial or even a systematic review, the notion of devising an etiologic axis that would permit clinicians to formulate their thoughts on both the origins and development of a disorder was an appealing one to several Task Force members. The model proposed for review would enable the diagnostician to select and rank order from a diverse list of known or hypothesized causal agents such as genetic factors, interpersonal relations, situational stressors, and intrapsychic conflicts. Not only would a list of this nature furnish useful data concerning what clinicians conceive to be the primary elements of etiology in diverse disorders, but it would provide a basis for understanding what relationships exist between causal formulations and those of treatment choice. The data generated by an axis such as this might, of course, say more about the biases of clinicians than about the attributes of patients. Etiology failed to take hold as a visible axis because the Task Force judged our current state of knowledge to be flawed and skimpy, at best. More time for systematic analysis and field testing was required than available to piece together a reasonably coherent and informed schema.

A different fate, though one that also failed to achieve formal stature, lay in store for propositions favoring the inclusion of axes for either "treatment choice" or "treatment response." At the very first meetings of the Task Force, it was concluded that a system which indexed both treatment regimen *and* treatment effect would, were systematic data gathered over time, provide exceptionally valuable information connecting diagnosis and therapy. With the exception of psychopharmacologic agents, however, the state of the general therapeutic art was judged both too inchoate and too complex to have its component parts disentangled in a meaningfully discriminable fashion. A consequence of this judgment was a decision to invite a wide range of treatment-based professional organizations to systematize their knowlege and technology in a manner relevant to diagnoses. To be collected in a volume, officially entitled *DSM–III and Treatment Planning*, this venture was known in Task Force memos as "Project Flower," the latter designation signifying our adherence to Chairman Mao's philosophical dictum, "Let all flowers bloom." In accord with this precept, the Task Force encouraged clinicians of divergent therapeutic orientations to formulate a rationale and methodology for treating the heterogeneous syndromes comprising the DSM-III. Invited to contribute chapters were the American Psychoanalytic Association, the American Academy of Psychoanalysis, the Association for the Advancement of Behavior Therapy, the Society for Biological Psychiatry, the American Group Therapy Association, and the American Association of Marriage and Family Therapists; the perspectives of the American Psychological Association and the American Academy of Child Psychiatry were to be represented by members of these associations who participated in the several treatment-based groups. Several months passed before draft chapters were received by the Task Force. Kindness judges them as merely deficient. Most members thought it best that Project Flower be allowed simply to wilt; one primary reviewer was more blatantly sarcastic, recommending that it "be sprayed with a potent herbicide." Not only were most chapters written as self-serving documents, but they displayed, from the perspective of scholarship, qualities more suitable to sophomoric term papers. Moreover, they exposed the narrow and highly routinized technologies that each school of treatment conceived an optimal for highly dissimilar syndromes. The Task Force simply could not put its stamp of approval on such pretensions to therapeutic infallibility.

Additional proposals for this, that, or another axis were recommended to the Task Force, many of which were well-reasoned treatises. Perhaps at some point in the distant future, when substantive fact and coherent theory are more characteristic of the field than they are today, several of these suggestions may be usefully incorporated into later DSM versions. Until that time, as Donald Klein, an outspoken Task Force member, wrote in response to his concerns regarding "axis proliferation":

> It is not the purpose of the DSM-III to allow everybody with their own idiosyncratic beliefs a set of categories that they can refer to since such a list would be indefinitely long. . . .
> Let us assure everybody that we are in favor of free speech and the creative use of everyone's background and mentality. Therefore, if they wish to make annotations . . . concerning etiology . . . or coping styles, they are free to do so. They can write anything on their charts that they please. That's their privilege.

And so the Task Force closed its book on multiaxial dimensions—until the DSM-IV.

Personality Disorders

The most important fact concerning the DSM-III personality disorders is their partition from the main body of clinical syndromes and their placement in a separate axis. Clinicians in the past were often faced with the task of deciding whether a patient was best diagnosed as possessing a personality or a symptom syndrome; that choice is no longer necessary. Henceforth, clinicians may record not only the current clinical picture, but also those characteristics that typify the individual's behaviors over extended periods, both prior to and concurrent with the present complaint. The new multiaxial format enables practitioners to place the clinical syndromes of Axis I within the context of the individual's lifelong and pervasive style of functioning, recorded as Axis II.

The personality disorders of DSM-III have been grouped, somewhat arbitrarily, into three clusters, the first characterized by odd or eccentric behaviors, the second by dramatic, emotional, or erratic behaviors, and the third by the notable presence of anxiety or fear. These clusters were devised by staff associates working with the Task Force chairman, but were never affirmed by the committee as a whole to be either a relevant or a useful way to categorize the personality disorders. In fact, the author wrote the following as part of a more extensive memorandum to his Task Force colleagues in 1978 in response to having seen the suggested clustering format for the first time:

> I never understood the importance of those dimensions that led us to cluster personality disorders in the manner described. Any number of

different dimensions could have been selected to group the eleven personality disorders in any of an almost infinite arrangement of sets or combinations. Why the specific one suggested in the text was selected out of these is not clear to me. Does it have some prognostic significance, some etiological import, logic in terms of a deductive theoretical model?

My own preference would be either to drop the new grouping entirely and list them alphabetically or to group them in terms of their known prevalence or potential severity. The likely severity of pathology, such as the probability to which these syndromes succumb to severe versus mild disorders, strikes me as a useful distinction if we are to make any one at all among these disorders.

There are two classification systems that are in current use which pay special attention to criteria for differentiating personality disorders along the dimension of severity, those of Kernberg (1967, 1970) and of Millon (1969, 1981). The major distinction between Kernberg and Millon is not found in the clinical signs they include to gauge severity, but rather in the ones they choose to emphasize. For Kernberg, primary attention is given to the internal structural characteristics of the personality, whereas for Millon the *external* social system and interpersonal dynamics are given a status equal that of internal organization. A rationale for utilizing both intrapsychic and external dynamics as a basis for determining severity was outlined by Millon (1981) in the following:

> The logic for broadening the criteria of severity to include the interplay of both individual and social systems seems especially appropriate when considering personality syndromes. Not only do personality traits express themselves primarily within group and familial environments, but the patient's style of communication, interpersonal competency, and social skill will, in great measure, elicit reactions that feed back to shape the future course of whatever impairments the person may already have. Thus, the behavior and attitudes that individuals exhibit with others will evoke reciprocal reactions that influence whether their problems will improve, stabilize or intensify. Internal organization or structure is significant, of course, but the character or style of relating interpersonally may have as much to do with whether the sequence of social dynamics will prove rewarding or destructive. It is not only the structural ego capacity, therefore, but also the particular features of social and familial behavior that will dispose the patient to relate to others in a manner that will prove increasingly adaptive or maladaptive. (p. 65)

Utilizing this mixed intrapsychic and interpersonal system perspective led Millon to group the 11 personality disorders of the DSM-III into three broad categories. The first includes the Dependent, Histrionic, Narcissistic, and Antisocial personality disorders. The second group, that viewed at a moderate level of severity, numbers the Compulsive, Passive-Aggressive, Schizoid, and Avoidant personality. The third set, reflecting still less competent levels of functioning, comprises the Borderline, Paranoid, and Schizotypal disorders. An extended discussion of the rationale and clinical character-istics of these three levels of personality pathology is fully presented in Millon (1981). A more up-to-date extension of this theoretical model will be found in Chapters 30 and 31 of this volume.

Brief note should be made of a number of DSM-II personality disorders that are no longer part of the DSM-III group. Among them are the Asthenic and Inadequate personalities, both of which were discarded owing to the infrequency with which they were utilized. The Cyclothymic personality was transferred to the Affective disorders classification, a decision that raised some controversy among Task Force members. Similarly, the Explo-sive personality disorder was transferred from the personality classification to that of the Impulsive Disorders in light of its highly circumscribed and intermittent nature.

Among the new DSM-III categories are the Avoidant, Dependent, and Narcissistic personalities. The initial drafts for the personality disorder sec-tion were written by the author in his role as a Task Force appointee. In these texts, considerable attention was given to the contrast between the Avoidant and the Schizoid disorders. The Avoidant's detachment is based upon a strong desire for social acceptance combined with a fear of rejection; in the Schizoid the prime characteristic is a passively detached style of interper-sonal behavior owing to a presumed intrinsic deficit in the capacity for affective and social gratification. The Dependent personality disorder paral-lels earlier DSM-I descriptions and represents diminished self-confidence combined with a search for security-providing relationships. The Narcissistic personality draft by the author was not written within the framework of currently popular psychoanalytic authors, notably Kohut (1971) and Kern-berg (1975), but rather derived from a social-learning developmental model (Millon, 1969). The new Schizotypal and Borderline personality types were likewise written by the author from a perspective at variance from tradi-tional theoretical viewpoints. The Schizotypal was conceived largely as an advanced or more severely dysfunctional variant of the Schizoid and Avoid-ant personality and is characterized by intense social detachment and eccen-tric behaviors. To a parallel degree, the Borderline personality was formu-lated to be a disintegrated Dependent, Histrionic, and Passive-Aggressive mix in which the individual's personal cohesion and interpersonal compe-tence has insidiously deteriorated. Among the more controversial topics at Task Force meetings were discussions pertaining to the concept of an Antiso-cial personality disorder. The diagnostic criteria selected for this syndrome are more properly suited for what may be termed the "criminal personality"; despite serious objections from many quarters, the criteria were retained with only modest alterations. The historical forerunners of the Antisocial personality can be traced back some two to three centuries and provide an illuminating and fascinating tale of the role of medical misconceptions and cultural biases (Millon, 1981).

Toward the DSM-IV

Now that the DSM-III has been formally published and has become *the* standard nosology, it has begun to assume a life of its own and is utilized and interpreted in diverse ways by clinicians and researchers of all theoretical schools to suit whatever special purposes and orientations they may have. The rationale that led to the original concepts and terminology formulated by the Task Force now plays but a small part as DSM-III users increasingly transform the instrument to fit their own purposes. Few are satisfied with every aspect of the manual, and it is sufficiently broad in scope to permit almost any clinician, theoretician, or researcher to modify one or another segment because of his or her dissatisfactions. It is hoped that empirical research, theoretical evaluation, and constructive proposals will lead to a better DSM-IV by the early to mid-part of the next decade.

Although it is clear that the Task Force's efforts to compromise diverse clinical and research perspectives contributed to its failure to produce a thoroughly unified manual, it is nevertheless desirable, in this author's view, that an even broader base of perspectives be brought to bear in the construction of the DSM-IV. For example, although several psychologists played active roles in the formulation of DSM-III, the American Psychological Association and the National Association of Social Workers should be included as part of the official planning group for the next version. Had the Task Force included a more substantial representation of clinical psychologists and clinical social workers, several of the more knotty problems that arose would undoubtedly have been resolved more expeditiously. More importantly, their perspectives regarding the conceptual character and clinical relevance of the manual would have made the product both more "scientific" and more "professionally" useful. The following statement of Zigler and Phillips (1961), made in summarizing their review of the status of the field more than 20 years ago, is still applicable today: "At this stage of our investigation, the system employed should be open and expanding. . . . Systems of classification must be treated as tools for further discovery, not bases for polemic disputation" (p. 75).

With this viewpoint as an introduction, let us proceed to suggestions concerning features which, if added to those already instituted in the DSM-III, will increase the clarity and utility of DSM-IV.

Conceptualizing Syndromes as Prototypes

There is need to explicitly recognize the intrinsic heterogeneity of the syndromes comprising the DSM-III and thereby formalize the paradigm shift that has occurred from a "disease entity" to a "prototypical" diagnostic model. The Task Force moved implicitly in the direction of what Cronbach and Meehl (1955) have termed "bandwidth fidelity" in which a balance is struck between conceptual breadth and measurement or identification precision. Cantor *et al.* (1980) address this issue as follows:

> The recent revisions in the standard diagnostic manual have brought the system even closer to the prototype view than before. Diagnostic criteria are now presented as prototypes—larger sets of correlated features rather than selected defining ones: guidelines for diagnosis also emphasize the potential heterogeneity of the symptoms of like-diagnosed patients. Moreover, a potential for overlap in clinical features across different diagnostic categories is underscored. . . . They help to emphasize, rather than obscure, the probabilistic nature of diagnostic categorizations.
>
> The recent changes . . . represent a shift in beliefs similar to ones occurring in other domains, away from the classical view of categorization systems and toward the prototype view. (pp. 191–192)

Employing a Coherent and Quantifiable Theory

The DSM-III classification was not only derived intentionally in an atheoretical manner, but no coherent theoretical system was seriously explored to provide a consistent framework for coordinating the various syndromes (Millon, 1969, 1981). Such a conceptual schema would be helpful, even if the established nosology was reliably anchored to empirical research, which it is not. If all of the principal clinical syndromes or personality disorders could be logically derived from a systematic theoretical foundation, this would greatly facilitate an understanding of psychopathology, organize this knowledge in an orderly and consistent fashion, and connect the data it provides to other realms of psychological theory and research, where they could be subjected then to empirical verification or falsification (Hempel, 1952; Popper, 1972). In this manner, psychopathology might advance much in the way as has physics. In describing the features that have given physics much of its success as a scientific discipline, Meehl (1978) notes "The physicist's scientific power comes from two . . . sources, namely, the immense deductive fertility of the formalism and the accuracy of the measuring instruments" (p. 825).

In line with the preceding, Skinner (Chap. 15 of this volume) has proposed the development of classification frameworks based on theories supplemented by parallel "operational measures." Using as a guide the principles and methods of "construct validation," originally developed in the field of psychometrics, Skinner (1981) evaluates a number of clinical theory constructs that possess supporting quantifying instruments as possible bases for a new classification schema. Notable among those which fit the construct validation model he espouses is the "schizoid taxon concept" proposed by Meehl (1979; Chap. 10 of this volume), the "interpersonal system" devised by Benjamin (1979; Chap. 29 of this volume), and the "biosocial personality theory" of psychopathology formulated by Millon (1969, 1981; Chaps. 30 and 31 of this volume).

Specifying Relationships among Syndromes

Although the DSM-III provides a multiaxial schema in which relationships that exist among clinical categories can be noted, each syndrome is still organized as if it were a discrete entity of clustered clinical signs independent and distinct from other syndromes. A framework that would spell out the inevitable overlap occurring among diagnostic groups would enable the clinician to immediately identify the intrinsic covariations that do exist among clinical disorders. Especially valuable would be the illumination of relationships between personality vulnerabilities and coping styles, on the one hand, and specific clinical symptom disorders, on the other. What is likely to be needed to achieve this end is more than a format that merely organizes the fragmented nature of the current nosology, but one, as noted previously, that is based on theoretical principles which furnish the logic and point out the bases for commonalities and interconnections observed in the clinical world.

Comparability and Parallelism among Syndromes

Although it may be difficult to identify and "carve those joints" which meaningfully divide the raw behaviors and traits that comprise clinical symptoms, we should, at the very least, utilize similar units and intervals throughout the diagnostic criteria of the DSM. Inconsistencies in the clinical phenomena which embody the diagnostic criteria will result only in a lack of comparability and a lack of parallelism among clinical assessments. Certain commonalities must be routinely addressed to ensure that the different syndromes can be compared and differentiated. Although, for example, the dimensions which can be included to assess personality disorders may range across a very wide domain of clinical phenomena, it would make good scientific and practical sense if certain specific realms were consistently addressed, for example, affective response, style of cognitive functioning, pattern of interpersonal behaviors, and self-concept.

Construction of a Situational Taxonomy

It is an exceptional achievement that the DSM-III instituted even its rudimentary taxonomy of psychosocial stressors. This should be seen, however, only as a beginning, a preparatory step for future DSMs to recognize more fully that behaviors and settings interact in lawful, interdependent systems, and, most relevantly, that people do behave differently in different settings (Barker, 1966; Endler & Magnusson, 1976; Millon, 1975; Moos, 1972; Willems, 1977). Serious thought must be given to formulate a taxonomic schema that will provide a systematic framework for sampling clinically relevant psychosocial situations, both stressful and commonplace. As the author noted in an earlier paper:

A rose may be a rose, but it is a different rose if it is presented to your wife in a birthday bouquet than if seen in passing as one among many in a garden. . . . Behavioral signs cannot be abstracted from their psychological and situational context without leading to false equivalences. . . . Hallucination 1 is simply not the same as hallucination 2 if they are a part of different behavioral and situational configurations. It is precisely this patterned and multivariate cluster of behaviors, set within a comparably delineated situational context, that can best serve as a framework for developing new syndrome groupings. (1975, p. 461)

Providing an Interpersonal Orientation

Numerous writers have suggested that the interpersonal dimension provides a particularly useful conceptual foundation for developing a diagnostic schema (Benjamin, Kiesler, Chap. 29 of this volume; Leary & Coffey, 1955; McLemore & Benjamin, 1979; Millon, 1969, 1981; Wiggins, 1982). Similarly, other authors have indicated that interpersonal behaviors are of particular significance from the viewpoint of providing a useful prognostic index, contributing to understanding therapeutic interactions, and exposing significant aspects of etiology. Now that great attention has been directed toward the DSM-III personality disorders, the logic for strengthening the interpersonal dimension is further enhanced. This can best be illustrated by the fact that the interpersonal "style" an individual employs to achieve goals and to resolve conflicts with others invariably evokes counteractions that will directly influence whether his or her problems stabilize, improve, or lead to further distress and decompensation. It is with these considerations in mind that the next Task Force might do well to ensure that interpersonal aspects of behavior are further highlighted in the specification of future diagnostic criteria.

Need to Incorporate Research Data

It has been argued (McReynolds, 1979), and not without justification, that in most fields of scientific inquiry the advent of new concepts and categories reflects the emergence of new observations and insights. Such would be the case in psychopathology if there were fundamental technological advances or discoveries that led to an increased understanding and capacity to describe new clinical disorders and syndromes. Unfortunately, what few advances have taken place in either theory or methodology cannot account for the tremendous proliferation of new or refined DSM-III categories. With some notable exceptions, for example, changes in the criteria for schizophrenia and the addition of theoretically derived personality syndromes, most DSM-III syndromes adhere closely to those formulated by Kraepelin, Freud, and their followers some three-quarters of a century ago. Substantial empirical and theoretical advances have certainly taken place in recent decades, but few of these have influenced the overall framework and syndromal particulars of the DSM. For example, the careful studies of Lorr (1966) and Lorr, Klett, and McNair (1963) suggest numerous modifications that would increase both the distinctness and homogeneity of the more severe disorders, but these have played almost no role in rethinking the major syndromal groups. Most encouraging, however, is the introduction of diagnostic criteria and the realignment of categories into several data axes. These steps make the DSM-III a significantly more researchable instrument, one that both facilitates and is much more open to empirical evaluation than its predecessors. Hence, the Task Force failed to construct an instrument that reflected previous research, but it has developed one that encourages more precise and comparable studies in the future. It is hoped that future Task Forces will avail themselves of the research data that will be generated as a consequence of the heuristic framework provided by the DSM-III.

Inclusion of Etiologic Considerations

Classification based on etiology is well established in most fields of medicine and would be a notable achievement in psychopathology. However, this aspiration faces many difficulties given the complex network of subtle and almost random influences which give rise and shape to the mental disorders. The fact that the Task Force bypassed etiologic variables so as to minimize dispute and to facilitate acceptance of the DSM-III by clinicians of diverse orientations is no reason to abandon the search. The DSM-III criteria will facilitate etiologic as well as other research endeavors, and the data these bring forth should be considered in the reconstruction of syndrome categories. There is no intrinsic reason why etiologic variables cannot play as important a role in psychopathologic classification as do descriptive and inferred clinical properties. Along similar lines, there is need to include, where feasible, the continuity displayed in behavior through life and, more relevantly and specifically, the developmental progression that often exists between the individual's premorbid personality style and his subsequent clinical disorder.

Incorporation of Therapeutic Implications

It is unfortunate that classifications based on clinical description alone will often group patients who, upon more careful evaluation, react to life situations, including their response to treatment, in substantially different manners. Hence, given its centrality to the clinical enterprise, classification categories should be designed to embody whatever data are accessible concerning the therapeutic effects of various treatment modalities. With the minor exception of the psychopharmacologic agents, the DSM-III offers very little that is concrete in this regard, owing in great measure, of course, to the scanty evidence at hand for such purposes. Here, as noted previously, the empirically oriented framework and criteria of the DSM-III should facilitate future systematic research of this nature. It is hoped that studies that deal with both the prediction of therapeutic response and the matching of treatment to diagnosis will become increasingly available for consideration in classifying DSM-IV diagnostic syndromes.

DSM-III-R and ICD-10

The DSM-III Task Force served an important function in that it had the courage to break a mold that has been imposed on psychiatric nosology by classifications of the past. As a transition to DSM-IV, an interim DSM-III-R (revised) Work Group was formed in 1983 with the responsibility of refining and elaborating DSM-III; chaired by Spitzer and composed of eight psychiatrists, including Klerman, co-editor of this volume, it will soon publish its proposed revisions and recommendations. Concurrently, progress toward the ICD-10 is well under way. Under the aegis of WHO, the new international system will reflect many of the proposals implemented in DSM-III. Although Kendell (1975) noted in his analogy between ship convoys and international classification committees that progress is invariably dictated by the speed of its slowest member, it appears that the ICD-10 Committee has judged it a higher responsibility to develop a more empirically based and clinically functional nosology than to adhere to tradition-bound concepts.

With the DSM-III's "radical" departures safely ensconced on the shelves of perhaps every mental health professional around the globe, a new DSM-IV Task Force will likely retain those elements of value in DSM-III and DSM-III-R, while building bridges to future ICDs. Innovations of a fundamental nature—notably the implementation of a multiaxial schema, the introduction of explicit diagnostic criteria, and the enhanced role assigned the omnipresent personality disorders—appear to have gained considerable acceptance by the larger international community. Many of DSM-III's other features of format and detail are best viewed as provisional and fully open to international debate and cross-cultural test.

Concluding Comments

Reflecting on his labors while serving as chairman of the Task Force for the DSM-II, Gruenberg (1969) noted that the instability of mental health diagnostic schemas over the centuries led him to wonder whether the excitement concerning the appropriateness of one or another classification might not actually reflect a deep need on the part of its contributors to obscure their lack of knowledge. Engaging in fruitless and labored debates over new terms and clever categories may be a simple displacement of effort in which one pretends that "correct" labels and taxonomies are themselves the knowlege gaps that exist. Having participated over an intense 5-year period as a member of the DSM-III committee, I am considerably more charitable about the purposes and success with which this Task Force met its responsibilities. I have no illusions, however, that we completed the task. On the other hand, I am convinced that the DSM-III represents not only a significant step forward in and of itself, but that it also provides a solid foundation for further progress.

I am reminded in writing this final comment of a favorite story of mine concerning the newer, computerized diagnostic techniques, an assessment innovation in which I am deeply engrossed at present (Millon, 1982; Millon, Green, & Meagher, 1982a, 1982b). The story goes as follows: A computer diagnostician was quite enthused by a new software program he devised in which the computer could ostensibly answer any clinical or biographical question that was put to it *in precise form*. He invited a dubious colleague to his laboratory and suggested that the colleague type any question he wished on the terminal. Obliging, the colleague typed the questions, "Where is my father?" In no more than a second, the printer recorded its reply: "Your father is fishing off the coast of Florida." The colleague looked askance at his friend and noted sarcastically, "A lot good this program is; my father died more that 10 years ago." Momentarily puzzled, the computer diagnostician regained his poise quickly and noted that the computer often requires that questions be phrased in a somewhat unconventional way and, hence, suggested that his associate pose the same idea in a somewhat different form. Obliging once more, the colleague typed in, "Where is my mother's husband?" After but a moment's hesitation, the computer printed, "Your mother's husband died over 10 years ago." The printer did not stop at that point, however. It continued at first with a series of dots, then stopped and typed, "P.S., Your father is still fishing off the coast of Florida."

The moral of this story? The DSM-III is an important and useful advance in diagnostic instrumentation and accuracy. However, you must learn to ask the right questions of it.

REFERENCES

Albee, G. W. (1977). Letter to the editor. *APA Monitor, 8*(11), 1–2.
American Psychiatric Association (APA). (1952). *Diagnostic and statistical manual of mental disorders* (1st ed.). Washington, DC: Mental Hospitals Service.
American Psychiatric Association (APA). (1968). *Diagnostic and statistical manual of mental disorders* (2nd ed.). Washington, DC: Author.
American Psychiatric Association (APA). (1980). *Diagnosticc and statistical manual of mental disorders* (3rd ed.). Washington, DC: Author.
Barker, R. (1966). *The stream of behavior.* New York: Appleton-Century-Crofts.
Benjamin, L. S. (1979). Use of structural analyses of social behavior (SASB) and Markov chains to study dyadic interactions. *Journal of Abnormal Psychology, 88,* 303–319.
Cantor, N., Smith, E. E., French, R., & Mezzich, J. (1980). Psychiatric diagnoses as prototype categorization. *Journal of Abnormal Psychology, 89,* 181–193.
Cronbach, L. J., & Meehl, P. E. (1955). Construct validity in psychological tests. *Psychological Bulletin, 52,* 281–302.

Dreger, R. M. (1977). *Behavioral approaches.* Paper presented at the annual meeting of the American Psychological Association, San Francisco, CA.

Endler, N. S., & Magnusson, D. (1976). Toward an interactional psychology of personality. *Psychological Bulletin, 83,* 956–974.

Essen-Möller, E., & Wohfahrt, S. (1947). Suggestions for the amendment of the official Swedish classification of mental disorders. *Acta Psychiatrica Scandinavica, Supplementum, 47,* 551–555.

Garmezy, N. (1978). Never mind the psychologists: Is it good for the children? *Clinical Psychologist, 31*(3–4), 1–6.

Gruenberg, E. M. (1969). How can the new diagnostic manual help? *International Journal of Psychiatry, 7,* 368–374.

Hempel, C. G. (1952). *Fundamentals of concept formation in empirical science.* Chicago, IL: University of Chicago Press.

Kendell, R. E. (1975). *The role of diagnosis in psychiatry.* Oxford: Blackwell Scientific Publications.

Kernberg, O. F. (1967). Borderline personality organization. *Journal of the American Psychoanalytic Association, 15,* 641–685.

Kernberg, O. F. (1970). A psychoanalytic classification of character pathology. *Journal of the American Psychoanalytic Association, 18,* 800–822.

Kernberg, O. F. (1975). *Borderline conditions and pathological narcissism.* New York: Jason Aronson.

Kohut, H. (1971). *The analyses of self.* New York: International Universities Press.

Kuhn, T. S. (1962). *The structure of scientific revolutions.* Chicago, IL: University of Chicago Press.

Leary, T., & Coffey, H. S. (1955). Interpersonal diagnoses: Some problems of methodology and validation. *Journal of Abnormal and Social Psychology, 50,* 110–124.

Lemkau, P. V. (1969). The anatomy of a group of illnesses and states. *International Journal of Psychiatry, 7,* 412–413.

Lorr, M. (1966). *Explorations in typing psychotics.* Oxford: Pergamon Press.

Lorr, M. (1977). *Symptoms, syndromes, and situational settings.* Paper presented at the annual meeting of the American Psychological Association, San Francisco, CA.

Lorr, M., Klett, C. J., & McNair, D. M. (1963). *Syndromes of psychosis.* New York: Macmillan.

McLemore, C. W., & Benjamin, L. S. (1979). Whatever happened to interpersonal diagnosis? A psychological alternative to DSM-III. *American Psychologist, 34,* 17–34.

McReynolds, W. T. (1979). DSM-III and the future of applied social science. *Professional Psychology, 10,* 123–132.

Meehl, P. E. (1978). Theoretical risks and tabular risks: Sir Karl, Sir Ronald, and the slow progress of soft psychology. *Journal of Consulting and Clinical Psychology, 46,* 806–834.

Meehl, P. E. (1979). A funny thing happened to us on the way to the latent entities. *Journal of Personality Assessment, 43,* 364–580.

Meyer, A. (1908). The problem of mental reaction-types, mental causes and diseases. *Psychological Bulletin, 5,* 245–261.

Meyer, A. (1912). Remarks on habit disorganizations in the essential deteriorations. *Nervous and Mental Disease Monographs, 9,* 95–109.

Mezzich, J. (1979). Patterns and issues in multiaxial psychiatric diagnosis. *Psychological Medicine, 9,* 125–137.

Millon, T. (1969). *Modern psychopathology: A biosocial approach to maladaptive learning and functioning.* Philadelphia, PA: Saunders.

Millon, T. (1975). Reflections on Rosenhan's "On being sane in insane places." *Journal of Abnormal Psychology, 84,* 456–461.

Millon, T. (1977). *The present status of DSM-III.* Paper presented at the annual meeting of the American Psychological Association, San Francisco, CA.

Millon, T. (1981). *Disorders of personality: DSM-III, Axis II.* New York: Wiley.

Millon, T. (1982). *Millon clinical multiaxial inventory manual* (2nd ed.). Minneapolis, MN: National Computer Systems.

Millon, T., Green, C. J., & Meagher, R. B. (1982a). *Millon adolescent personality inventory manual.* Minneapolis, MN: National Computer Systems.

Millon, T., Green, C. J., & Meagher, R. B. (1982b). *Millon behavioral health inventory manual* (3rd ed.). Minneapolis, MN: National Computer Systems.

Moos, R. (1972). Assessment of the psychosocial environments of community-oriented psychiatric treatment programs. *Journal of Abnormal Psychology. 79*, 9–18.

Morey, L. C., & Blashfield, R. K. (1981). A symptom analysis of the DSM-III definition of schizophrenia. *Schizophrenia Bulletin, 7*, 258–268.

Popper, K. R. (1972). *The logic of scientific discovery*. London: Hutchinson.

Rutter, M., Shaffer, D., & Shepherd, M. (1975). *Multiaxial classification of child psychiatric disorders*. Geneva: World Health Organization.

Salzinger, K. (1977). *But is it good for patients?* Paper presented at the annual meeting of the American Psychological Association, San Francisco, CA.

Schacht, T., & Nathan, P. E. (1977). But is it good for the psychologists? Appraisal and status of DSM-III. *American Psychologist, 32*, 1017–1025.

Skinner, H. A. (1981). Toward the integration of classification theory and methods. *Journal of Abnormal Psychology, 90*, 68–87.

Spitzer, R. L., & Endicott, J. (1968). DIAGNO: A computer program for psychiatric diagnosis utilizing the differential diagnostic porcedure. *Archives of General Psychiatry, 125*(Suppl.), 12.

Spitzer, R. L., Sheehy, M., & Endicott, J. (1977). DSM-III: Guiding principles. In V. M. Rakoff, H. C. Stancer, & H. B. Kedward (Eds.), *Psychiatric diagnosis*. New York: Brunner/Mazel.

Stengel, E. (1959). Classification of mental disorders. *Bulletin of the World Health Organization, 21*, 601–663.

Strauss, J. S. (1975). A comprehensive approach to psychiatric diagnosis. *American Journal of Psychiatry, 132*, 1193–1197.

Wiggins, J. S. (1982). Circumplex models of interpersonal behavior in clinical psychology. In P. C. Kendall & J. N. Butcher (Eds.), *Handbook of research methods in clinical psychology*. New York: Wiley.

Willems, E. P. (1977). *Behavioral ecology and psychological taxonomy*. Paper presented at the annual meeting of the American Psychological Association, San Francisco, CA.

Wing, J. K., Cooper, J. E., & Sartorius, N. (1974). *Measurement and classification of psychiatric symptoms: An instruction manual for PSE and CATEGO programs*. London: Cambrige University Press.

World Health Organization. (1977). *Manual of the international statistical classification of diseases, injuries and causes of death* (9th rev.). Geneva: Author.

Zigler, E., & Phillips, L. (1961). Psychiatric diagnoses and symptomatology. *Journal of Abnormal and Social Psychology, 63*, 69–75.

Zubin, J. (1978). But is it good for science? *Clinical Psychologist, 31*(2), 1–7.

PART II

CLASSIFICATION AND THE DSM-III

CHAPTER 3

A Critique of Contemporary Classification and Diagnosis

H.J. Eysenck

Introduction

Psychiatry on the whole is in poor repute. Already 2000 years ago, Marcus Tullius Cicero said: "Why is it that for the care and maintenance of the body there has been devised an art which, because of its usefulness, has had its discovery attributed to the immortal gods, and is regarded as sacred, while on the other hand the need of an art of healing for the soul has not been felt so deeply before its discovery, has not been studied so closely after becoming known, and has not been welcomed with approval by the majority; indeed has been regarded by most with suspicion and hatred?" Modern psychiatry hardly fares any better. In medical circles, it is commonly regarded as being at the bottom on the totem pole, and in the popular imagination psychoanalysis, which is often taken as the central part of psychiatry, is regarded with derision and mainly welcomed as the source of rather sour jokes. Why is this so?

There are two fairly obvious reasons, both of which may be related to a common cause. In the first place, compared with surgery and general medicine, psychiatry is relatively powerless. Admittedly in recent years there have been advances both on the biological and the behavioral front, relating respectively to psychotic and neurotic disorders, but treatments based on these are not nearly as certain as many medical treatments of physical disorders appear to the man in the street, and the eternal vagaries of psychotherapy and psychoanalysis have not impressed many people by their success. As a curative part of medicine, psychiatry has certainly not covered

H. J. Eysenck. Institute of Psychiatry, University of London, London, England.

itself in laurels, and although the necessity of its existence is recognized, it is not regarded as very successful.

Related to this, but in many ways distinct, is the impression held not only by the man in the street but also by scientists in general, and medical people in particular, that the search for causal factors in neurosis and psychosis has been rather elusive in its findings. We still have theories, such as the Freudian, which show a high degree of imagination in their origin, but have never found any convincing proof; indeed, the request for such proof is regarded by many analysts as almost indecent. Thus, psychiatry deals with disorders of unknown origin, treated by different psychiatrists in different ways, but hardly ever with very much success. These facts alone would suffice to explain Cicero's statement and its continued applicability to modern conditions.

What links these two defects in modern psychiatry, in my submission, is the resolute determination of psychiatrists to treat all the major problems of classification, diagnosis, and treatment on a notional rather than a scientific basis, and indeed to eschew scientific evidence as if it were in some way contaminated. DSM-III, like its predecessors, is the outcome of large-scale committee work, designed not so much to ascertain facts and to arrive at the truth, but rather to reconcile different power groups and pacify semipolitical Tammany Hall-type organizations whose influences are incommensurate with their scientific status. As H. J. Eysenck, Wakefield, and Friedman (1983) have pointed out, "Research conducted during the development of the DSM-III was mostly concerned with the reliability of diagnosis and the acceptability of the proposed categories to clinicians" (p. 177). Research on fundamental points, to be discussed later, does not even seem to have been considered by the authors, let alone incorporated in their scheme. As H. J. Eysenck *et al.* (1983) concluded in their survey of the DSM-III.

> Our survey of the available evidence on the DSM-III leaves us with the impression that while an improvement on previous schedules, the new scheme is based on foundations so insecure, so lacking in scientific support, and so contrary to well-established fact that its use can only be justified in terms of social need. Psychologists may have to use the system because of social pressures of various kinds, but this should not blind them to the fundamental weaknesses of any such scheme based on democratic voting procedures rather than on scientific evidence. (p. 183).

Principles of Taxonomy

There is little likelihood that DSM-IV will show any improvement on the procedures which have led to the scientifically disastrous DSM-III, but it may be worthwhile to consider the desiderata for any acceptable scheme of classification and diagnosis in psychiatry. To do so will be the object of this chapter. Classification and diagnosis, typology and trait psychology are all aspects of taxonomy, and the taxonomic problems that afflict psychiatry have to be seen in the context of numerical taxonomy in general (Sokal & Sneath, 1963). As they point out in their classic book, *Principles of Numerical Taxonomy,*

> It is widely acknowledged that the science of taxonomy is one of the most neglected disciplines in biology. Although new developments are continually being made in techniques for studying living creatures, and finding new characters, in describing new organisms, and in revising the systematics of previously known organisms, little work has been directed towards the conceptual basis of classification—that is, taxonomy in the restricted sense of the theory of classification. (p. 3)

Classification, as they point out, is the ordering of organisms into groups (or sets) on the basis of their relationships, that is, of their associations by continuity, similarity, or both. The term "relationship" often causes difficulties; it may imply relationship by ancestry, or it may simply indicate the overall similarity as judged by the characters of the organisms without any implications as to their relationship by ancestry. It is the second of these means which is relevant to psychiatry, and Sokal and Sneath call it "phenetic relationship," using this term to indicate that relationship is judged from the phenotype of the organism and not from its phylogeny. Genetic relationships in psychiatry may throw important light on taxonomy, of course, and in that case "relationship by ancestry" would become relevant to a complete system of classification.

Given that in psychiatry we deal with phenetic relationships, we may follow one of two alternative routes which have been named by Sneath (1962) "polythetic" and "monothetic." The ruling idea of monothetic groups is that they are formed by rigid and successive logical divisions so that the position of a unique set of features is both sufficient and necessary for membership in the group thus defined. They are called monothetic because the defining set of features is unique. Any monothetic system, such as that of Maccacaro (1958) in biology or that of Williams and Lambert (1959) in ecology, will always carry the risk of serious misclassification if we wish to make natural phenetic groups. This is because an organism that happens to be aberrant in the feature used to make the primary division will inevitably be moved to a category far from the required position, even if it is identical with its natural congeners in every other feature. The disadvantage of monothetic groups is that they do not yield "natural" taxa except by lucky choice of the feature used for division.

Polythetic arrangements place together organisms that have their greatest number of shared features, and no single feature is essential to group membership or sufficient to make an organism a member of the group. This type of system was introduced by Adamson (1827–1906) into biology; he was the first to realize correctly that natural taxa are based on the concept of "affinity," which is measured by taking all characters into consideration, and that the taxa are separated from each other by means of correlated features.

What is the method adopted by biologists in carrying out classification by phenetic relationships? Sneath (1964) has set out the procedures followed according to these four steps:

1. The organisms are chosen, and their characters are recorded in a table.
2. Each organism is compared with every other and their overall resemblance is estimated as indicated by all the characters. This yields a new table, a table of similarities.
3. The organisms are now sorted into groups on the basis of their mutual similarities. Like organisms are brought next to like and separated from unlike, and these groups are *phenons* and are taken to represent the "natural" taxonomic groups whose relationships can be represented in numerical form.
4. The characters can now be reexamined to find those that are most constant within the groups that have emerged from the analysis, and can then be used as diagnostic characters in keys for identifying specimens.

Sokal and Sneath (1963) discuss in great detail the many theoretical problems that arise as well as the mathematical formulae useful in the estimation of taxonomic resemblances. In what follows, I have tried to translate their views and recommendations into a form applicable to psychiatry and relate it to the practice of psychometrics as currently practiced and understood in psychology.

Taxonomy in Psychiatry: Continuity

What are the units in psychiatry which lead us to some form of classification? They are essentially what Foulds (1971) has called symptoms or signs, that is, abnormal behaviors indicative of psychiatric illness such as hallucinations and phobic fears, or normal personality traits such as sociability (or its absence), fearfulness, and curiosity. The difference is a real one, although probably not as clear-cut or fundamental as Foulds suggests; ordinary traits of behavior can become indicative of abnormality when taken to extremes, and symptoms may be only the extreme form of quite ordinary types of behavior. The question clearly is an empirical one which cannot be decided on a priori grounds.

In addition to signs and symptoms, variables which are often taken into account are response to treatment, the general course of a given illness, signs and symptoms in close relatives, and the patient's response to drugs and psychological and physiological tests. All these overlap, of course, with the signs and symptoms mentioned above, but may be rather different from certain points of view.

What are the major questions that arise when looking at all these different characters that can be used in making up a systematic classification? The main question, fundamental to any proper analysis of the problem, is the question of *continuity*. It is possible to hold two antagonistic views on this problem, which would lead to entirely different types of classification. The first of these, derived from medical models of disease, may be called the diagnostic or the categorical model. Following this type of nosology, a patient, by diagnosis, is put into a category, either a hysteric, or a psychopath, or an obsessive–compulsive, or an anxiety state, or an obsessional. The arbitrariness of these categories and their failure to accord with reality is often admitted by the system of multiple diagnosis; thus, a patient may be declared to be an anxious hysteric with schizophrenic undertones, or a depressive obsessive–compulsive individual, with psychopathic tendencies. The question is seldom asked whether this slavish following of medical practice in a new and possibly entirely different field is reasonable and rational, and many psychiatrists and clinical psychologists seem unaware even of the very existence of a problem here.

Nevertheless, the problem is, of course, a very ancient one, and there is much evidence concerning it. When Galen wrote about his "four temperaments" in the second century A.D. and when Immanuel Kant translated these types into descriptive German in his *Anthropologie* 1500 years later, it was explicitly assumed that a person fell into one or the other of these four categories (sanguine, choleric, melancholic, or phlegmatic), but where no mixtures or admixtures were permissible. Wundt (1903) was the first to change this categorical system into a dimensional one by grouping together the emotional types (melancholic and choleric) as opposed to the unemotional ones (phlegmatic and sanguine), thus creating a dimension of emotionality. Similarly, he grouped together the changeable (extraverted) types (choleric and sanguine) as opposed to the unchangeable (introverted) types (melancholic and phlegmatic), thus creating a second, independent dimension, as shown in Figure 3–1, which also contains in the quadrants a personality description given by Kant and Galen.

Modern research has borne out the importance and the reality of these two dimensions (H. J. Eysenck & S. G. B. Eysenck, 1969) as well as the implicit distribution of individuals along these dimensions in the form of a normal bivariate surface; in the personality field, dimensionality, rather than categorical "type" groupings, has been uniformly accepted as nearer reality. We thus have a marked contrast between the psychologist's dimensional picture of human personality and the psychiatrist's categorical picture of neurotic and psychotic patients. Of course, it is possible that what is true of the normal person is not true of the patient and that psychiatric dysfunctions may indeed be separate illnesses which produce categorical divisions in the dimensional system. Szasz (1961) has argued against this view of neurotic

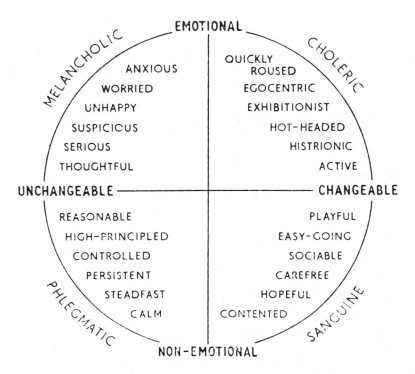

Figure 3-1. *Diagrammatic representation of the classical theory of the four temperaments in the dimensional form given by W. Wundt. From H. J. Eysenck (1970b).*

and psychotic disorders as "diseases," and the notion is indeed so alien to current psychiatric thinking that it need hardly be taken very seriously. The reasons for this rejection are not far to seek; there is complete absence of the specificity which is characteristic of physical illness, there is no separate etiology, and there are no obvious different types of treatment [Bannister, Salmon, and Lieberman (1964) have shown how little treatment is in fact related to diagnosis]. Nevertheless, so important a question cannot be answered by appeal to presumed facts or widely held views; clearly a more experimental course of enquiry is called for.

Aristotle had already suggested that the division between mental normality and mental abnormality was of a quantitative nature, being thus a precursor of the dimensional approach; this is the major alternative to the categorical diagnostic system widely accepted in psychiatry and incorporated in an absurdly detailed manner in DSM-III. It is interesting to note that the question itself (categorical or dimensional) is hardly ever seriously asked by psychiatrists, and that they show little interest in biometric methods designed to answer it, or the results of such studies. The medical model, although clearly inappropriate, still has a powerful grip in this field.

The Empirical Study of Continuity

The writer has suggested the method of criterion analysis to give a meaningful scientific answer to this important question (H. J. Eysenck, 1950). Shorn of its mathematical superstructure, the logical basis of the argument is quite a simple one. Let us consider two groups of people, equated for sex, educational status, and other relevant variables. One of these groups is made up of people considered psychiatrically "normal," the other of the people psychiatrically diagnosed as "psychotic." Let us now ask the question of whether these two groups are categorically distinct in the way that a person suffering from lung cancer is distinct from a person not suffering from lung cancer, or a person suffering from malaria is distinguished from a person not suffering from malaria, or is there a continuity between the two, such as that between a bright and dull person?

The first step in the argument is to select a number of objective psychological or physiological tests which clearly differentiate the two groups. Let these n tests be applied to the members of the two groups and arranged in such an order that the test giving the greatest difference between the two groups is called T_1, the test giving the second greatest difference is called T_2, and so on until we come to T_n, which gives the smallest difference between the two groups; each test gives a differentiation which is statistically significant at the 5% level or better. We may say that these n tests are relevant to the distinction between normal and psychotic, although it is not claimed that they embody all the possible distinctions between the two groups. It is important that the tests should be chosen from as widely different areas as possible in order to maximize the ground covered.

Let us now intercorrelate the scores on the n tests for each of the groups separately. On the assumption that the two groups are both placed on a continuum from normal to psychotic in such a way that the normals are clustered around one end, the psychotics around the other, we would be able to predict that the patterns of intercorrelations should be similar for the two groups, being produced by the differences in this continuum between the individuals making up each group. In other words, some normals are nearer the "normal" end of the continuum, others nearer the "psychotic" end of the continuum (although, of course, not as far in that direction as the actual psychotics!). Similarly, at the other end, some psychotics are more severely psychotic than others, thus differing with respect to the underlying variable which we may perhaps call "psychoticism." No such similarity of patterns of intercorrelation should appear if the two groups were categorically distinct from each other because there would nothing to associate scores on the tests for either group.

One obvious method of establishing similarity of patterning would be to carry out factor analyses separately for the two groups. On the continuity hypothesis it would be predicted that the first factor extracted from the normal group would be formally identified with the first factor extracted from the psychotic group. Furthermore, it would be predicted that the patterns of factor loadings for these two groups would be proportional to the differences between the groups produced by the tests. In other words, T_1, giving the greatest difference between normals and psychotics, should have the highest loading on this "psychoticism" factor, while T_n, giving the smallest differentiation between the two groups, should have the lowest loadings.

Such a study was carried out by H. J. Eysenck (1952a). There were 100 subjects in each of the normal and psychotic groups, and 20 tests were administered and used in the analysis. The pyschotic group consisted of 50 schizophrenics and 50 manic depressives. The between-groups comparison of covariances showed them to be very similar, and the respective correlations of the factors extracted from the normal and psychotic groups with the criterion column (i.e., the set of group differences from T_1, to T_n), were .90 and .95, respectively. The results indicated very strongly that psychoticism was a dimensional variable, not a categorical one, and that psychotics are not distinguished qualitatively from normals. Similar results have been reported when normals and neurotics were compared (H. J. Eysenck, 1950) showing that neurosis, too, gives rise to a dimensional and not a categorical differentiation, and that neurotics are not distinguished qualitatively from normals.

Provisionally, then, we may conclude that the evidence supports the dimensional framework and fails to support the categorical framework. Unfortunately, the problem does not seem to have attracted as much attention as it would seem to deserve from psychiatrists or clinical psychologists, and the studies mentioned are the only relevant ones which have come to the writer's notice. It will be clear that they do not suffice to establish such an important conclusion in any unequivocal manner. Neither the number of patients used nor the number and selection of tests employed can be said to have been sufficient to make any definitive conclusion feasible; at best, we have a suggestion as to the more likely direction in which a conclusion may be found. Nor is the method itself such as to guarantee success; it seems quite likely that more powerful methods will be suggested by others more competent in mathematical statistics. Nevertheless, the striking nature of the findings may be interpreted as indicating some interesting and possibly important regularity within nature which deserves to be followed up.

The Proportionality Method

This early work using the full criterion analysis method has been followed by later studies of psychoticism using a somewhat reduced form of it, which might be called the *"proportionality method."* H. J. Eysenck and Eysenck (1976) constructed a questionnaire (the *P* scale) for the measurement of psychoticism, independently of *N* (neuroticism) and *E* (extraversion–introversion); this is envisaged as providing a rough and ready indication of a person's position on this hypothetical dimension (Claridge, 1981). Given such a measure, we can now say that, on the basis of the dimensional theory, using any tests that significantly differentiate the normals from psychotics, normals with high P scores should have higher scores on this test than normals with low P scores, that psychotics with high P scores should show higher on this test than psychotics with low P scores, and that psychotics as a whole should score higher than normals on the whole. We can put this matter in the form of a proportionality equation:

$$P_{N+} \div P_{N-} = P_{P+} \div P_{P-} = \text{Psy} \div \text{Nor}$$

In this equation, P stands for psychoticism score, N+ and N− for high and low psychoticism scores of normals, and P+ and P− for high and low P scores of psychotic patients. Psy stands for psychotics, and Nor stands for normals.

As an example of the application of this principle, consider the human leukocyte antigen HLA-B27. McGuffin (1979) has reviewed the evidence to indicate that HLA-B27 is significantly more frequently present in psychotics than normals. It may therefore be used as a marker in a test of the proportionality hypothesis. Gattaz (1981) has shown that in a psychotic population, the presence of HLA-B27 is associated with high P scores and its absence with lower P scores at a high level of statistical significance. More recently he has shown that in a normal group the presence of HLA-B27 is also associated with high P scores, and its absence with low P scores. It will be difficult to explain these facts without recourse to a dimensional type of hypothesis.

As a second example, consider what Foulds would have called symptoms in relation to the P scale, which is essentially made up of "signs." Verma and Eysenck (1973) examined differences between psychotics scoring high and low on the P scale; the severity of the symptoms correlated significantly with psychoticism, as did various tests and ratings. Do such symptoms have a place in relation to normal subjects? Launay and Slade (1981) developed a 12-item questionnaire scale to measure hallucinatory predisposition, which included both pathological items and other items that appeared to represent subclinical forms of hallucinatory experience. With use of a nonpsychiatric sample of prisoners, a positive relationship was found in this normal group between hallucinations and high P scores. Such positive correlations between the P scale and the hallucination scale were found for both male and female prisoners separately as well as for the combined sample. The association between the P scale and the hallucination scale could not be accounted for in terms of either content contamination or similar response set bias. These findings suggest that the difference Foulds makes between signs and symptoms cannot readily be maintained, with such "symptoms" as hallucinatory experiences being found in normal groups, and in a quantitatively measurable manner.

As a third and rather more complex example, consider the theory advanced by Claridge (1967), which was based on the idea that psychosis may involve not a simple shift in such a variable as emotional arousal, but that it represents instead a much more complex "dissociation" of central nervous system (CNS) activity. He suggested that the schizophrenic nervous system is particular shows an uncoupling in CNS functions which are normally congruent in their activity. Two aspects of central nervous function were considered to be particularly involved in this uncoupling process, namely, emotional arousal, on the one hand, and a mechanism concerned with the regulation of sensory input, including variations in perceptual sensitivity and in broadening and narrowing of attention, on the other. Relative dissociation between these two systems might, he thought, progressively bring about a state of positive rather than normal negative feedback in the CNS, and might account for what seemed to be the core feature in schizophrenia as described by Bleuler, namely, the incongruous matching of affect to percept.

Venables (1963), Claridge (1972), and others have since collected data to indicate that predictions from this hypothesis can indeed be verified. To demonstrate what he calls the "phenomenon of reversed covariation," Claridge correlated with each other measures of tonic emotional arousal and measures of perceptual responsiveness which, according to conventional psychophysiological principles, should covary in a predictable way, but which in psychosis should show the opposite relationship, with the result that at any given level of tonic arousal, perceptual responsiveness is paradoxically greater or less that it should be. A review of this work is given by Claridge (1981), and no attempt will be made to repeat it here; what is important is the finding that when normal subjects are tested, those with high P scores show the same "phenomenon of reversed covariation" as do psychotics (Claridge & Birchall, 1978; Claridge & Chappa, 1973; Robinson & Zahn, 1979). Here again we have an application of the proportionality criterion in a field where no other hypothesis but that of continuity would be likely to make the predictions that were verified in the experimental work.

Much additional work is surveyed by H. J. Eysenck and Eysenck (1976) and by Claridge (1981); it is not my purpose here to go into any further detail. The point to be brought out is (a) that there are methods for tackling the question of continuity in a scientific manner, that is, by using the hypotheticodeductive method, and (b) that the results have been very favorable to the continuity hypothesis and correspondingly unfavorable to the categorical hypothesis. All this work is completely disregarded in modern psychiatric diagnostic practice and in the DSM-III; it does not seem exaggerated to feel that DSM-III has little reaction to scientific research and represents rather the power structure of contemporary feudal baronetcies.

One Dimension or Two?

Given that a proper model of psychiatric abnormality should be based on continuity rather than on categorical differences between diagnostic groups, we must next ask the second important question, namely, are we dealing with one dimension or two (or indeed more than two)? Freud's well-known view was that neurotic and psychotic disorders lie along one continuum such that the psychotic symptoms are indicative of a more deep-seated and severe disorder that the neurotic ones, but also such that with an increase in stress the latter can turn into the former. Opposed to this Freudian theory is the perhaps more orthodox psychiatric one according to which neuroses and psychoses are located along different and independent disorders. These two theories may be shown in diagrammatic form, the one-dimensional one in Figure3-2a, the two-dimensional one in Figure 3-2b. This clearly is a problem of fundamental importance. What statistical methods are open to us for its

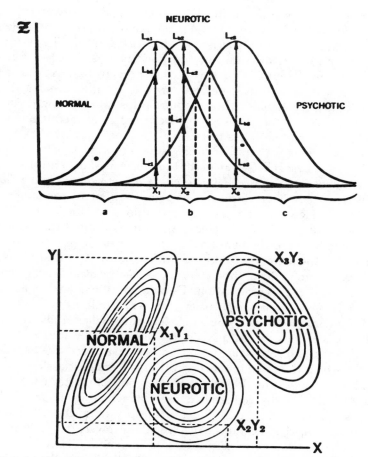

Figure 3-2. (a) *One-dimensional model of relation between normal, neurotic, and psychotic subjects.* (b) *Two-dimensional model of relation between normal, neurotic, and psychotic subjects. From H. J. Eysenck (1955).*

solution? I have suggested the use of discriminant function analysis for this purpose. In this method, n groups are tested or measured by means of m tests of a psychological or physiological kind, and the analysis discloses a number of significant latent roots which cannot exceed $n-1$ or $m-1$, whichever is the smaller, but which may not reach either value. Thus, if a neurotic, a psychotic, and a normal group are tested by means of at least three tests, the method may result in two, one, or no significant latent roots; this will correspond to a statement that the results require two or one dimensions or, of course, where none of the latent roots are significant, that the groups cannot be distinguished by means of the test chosen. This method is preferable in many ways to factor analysis, as fewer assumptions are made and more acceptable tests of significance are available (Slater, 1960).

A programmatics study of this kind used four dexterity tests from the general aptitude battery of the U.S. Employment Service on 50 normal, 50 psychotic, and 50 neurotic subjects (H. J. Eysenck, 1952a). The results were analyzed by means of discriminant function analysis, and two significant latent roots were found. The means of the three groups, as related to the two-dimensional space thus generated, are shown in Figure 3-3. The two variables jointly correlated with the criterion (psychiatric diagnosis) to the extent of .78; 71.3% of the subjects were correctly identified by these extremely simple and objective tests.

Two replications on a rather larger scale are available. In the first of these, S. B. G. Eysenck (1956) used 123 normals, 53 neurotics, and 51 psychotics; all of them were administered six objective tests, and a discriminant function analysis performed. Two significant latent roots were again discovered, and Figure 3-4 shows the distribution of scores on the two axes corresponding to these two variables. Again it was found that 71% of the subjects could be correctly identified on the basis of these tests, and it was suggested that the amount of misclassification shown in the study was due in large measure to faults in the criterion (psychiatric diagnosis), rather than in the tests and their combination. Devadasan (1964) has replicated Eysenck's study on an Indian population with very similar results.

H. J. Eysenck (1955) published a similar but smaller study in which 20 normals, 20 neurotics, and 20 psychotics were tested on four tests. Again, two significant latent roots were found, and the results are shown in detail in Figure 3-5. Much the same proportion of cases were misclassified, as in the two studies previously mentioned. It is interesting to note that two cases, marked A and B in the figure, had been classified as "neurotic" by the psychiatrists; their scores fell right into the psychotic cluster. Therefore, they count as misclassifications. Yet when they were readmitted to the hospital later on, the revised diagnosis was "psychotic." Here again, therefore, it may be suspected that much of the unreliability in the discriminant function analysis diagnosis is in fact due to unreliability in the criterion.

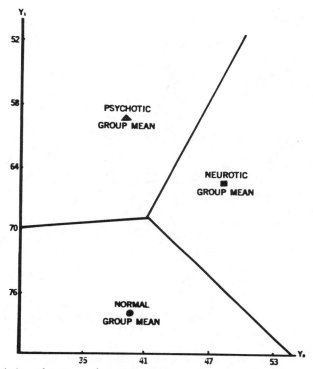

Figure 3-3. *Discriminant function analysis of performance on four tests of psychotics, neurotics, and normals. From H. J. Eysenck (1952a).*

Factor analysis has given similar results, as well, in the sense of requiring two rather than one dimension to accommodate neurotic and psychotic symptoms. Trouton and Maxwell (1956) used 45 rated items on a random sample of 819 patients at the Maudsley and Bethlem Royal Hospitals, intercorrelated these items, and factor analyzed the resulting matrix. Two clear-cut factors of neuroticism and psychoticism emerged; their nature can best be seen from Figure 3-6 (H. J. Eysenck, 1960). Table 3-1 and Figure 3-6 give the individual scores of 70 neurotic patients, 30 psychotics, and 20 normals, taken from the Trouton and Maxwell group (H. J. Eysenck, 1960). It is clear that the separation holds for persons as well as for signs and symptoms. There is one psychotic patient, marked B, whose score falls well into the neurotic group; on readmission he was rediagnosed "neurotic." There are two neurotics, labeled A in the diagram, whose scores fell well into the psychotic group; on readmission to the hospital these were rediagnosed as "psychotic."

It is clear from these factorial studies, as well as from the discriminant functions one, that we are dealing with two dimensions rather than one and

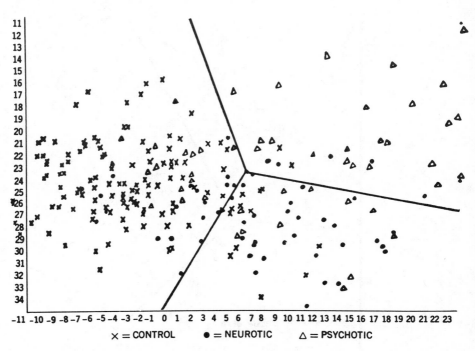

Figure 3-4. *Distribution of scores of 123 normals (x), 53 neurotics (●), and 51 psychotics (△) on two canonical variates. From S. B. G. Eysenck (1956).*

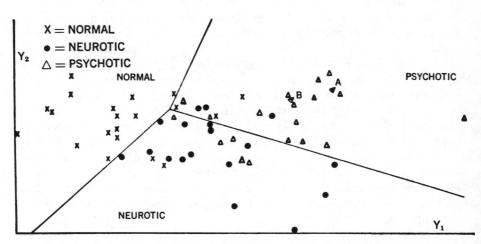

Figure 3-5. *Distribution of scores of 20 normals (x), 20 neurotics (●), and 20 psychotics (△) on two canonical variates. From H. J. Eysenck (1955).*

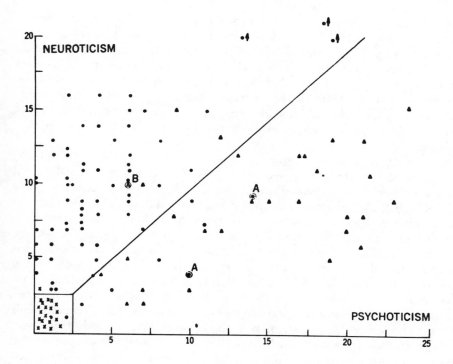

Figure 3-6. *Individual scores of 70 neurotics (●), 30 psychotics (Δ), and 20 normals (x). From H. J. Eysenck (1960).*

Table 3-1

Factor Scores of 20 Normals, 70 Neurotics, and 30 Psychotics, as Compared with Their Diagnoses[a]

Diagnosis	Normal	Neurotic	Psychotic	Total
Normal	19	1	0	20
Neurotic	2	60	8	70
Psychotic	0	4	26	30
	21	65	34	120

[a]From H. J. Eysenck (1960).

that neurotic and psychotic disorders are quite distinct. A similar conclusion was reached by Cattell (Cattell & Scheier, 1961) who concluded his survey of his own studies by saying, "Psychoticism has a direction of abnormality distinct from neuroticism . . . as a result, neurotic-contributory factors are not psychotic-contributory, that is, the neurotic-contributory factors discriminate between neurotics and normals, and between neurotics and psychotics, but they do not discriminate between psychotics and normals." (p. 157). Many other experiments supporting this view are cited in H. J. Eysenck (1973).

Another interesting approach is that via consanguinity. Cowie (1961) argued that if it is true that psychotic and neurotic disorders are orthogonal to each other, then we would expect that the children of psychotic parents should not show any greater degree of neuroticism than would the children of normal parents. Conversely, the unidemensional theory would have clear implications genetically regarding the high degree of neuroticism to be expected in the children of psychotic parents. In actual fact, the children were found, if anything, to be less neurotic than the children of normal parents—a finding which supports the two-dimensional hypothesis and which may also serve as a warning to those who would overstress the importance of environment in giving rise to neurotic disorders—it is difficult to imagine a more severe stress to a child than having a psychotic parent. The results are thus particularly important in that they give support to the two-dimensional theory in a direction quite different form those discussed thus far. Other genetic studies going in the same direction are reported by H. J. Eysenck and S. B. G. Eysenck (1976).

Subdivision of the Major Psychiatric Dimensions

It is not to be assumed that neuroses or psychoses are unidimensional, simply because when these disorders are contrasted as groups, they do occupy two orthogonal dimensions. It is possible to carry out similar dimensional analyses within either the neurotic or the psychotic group, and when this is done we again find quite reasonable dimensional systems. H. J. Eysenck (1970a) has reviewed a number of these studies, both factor analytic and discriminant function type, and only one or two of the major results will be mentioned here. Figure 3-7 shows the results of a factor analytic study of 700 neurotic patients (H. J. Eysenck, 1947), showing the breakdown of neurotic disorders into hysteric–psychopathic and dysthymic. A similar analysis from Cattell and Scheier (1961), using his rather different methods of measurement, comes to similar results.

These are factor analytic studies; Figure 3-8 shows results of a study by H. J. Eysenck and Claridge (1962) in which 60 normals, 60 hysterics, and 60

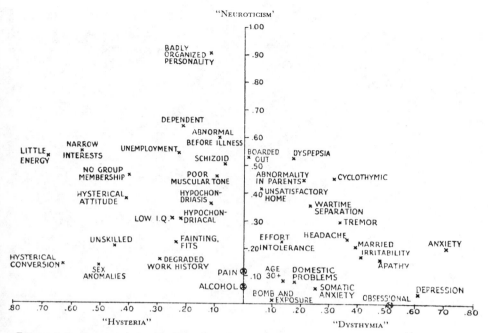

Figure 3-7. *Factor analytic study of 700 neurotic patients, showing the division of neurotic disorders into hysterical (extraverted) and dysthymic (introverted) symptoms. From H. J. Eysenck (1947).*

dysthymics were given a battery of tests, a discriminant function analysis was performed, and two major and significant latent roots extracted, corresponding to the two dimensions shown. These and many other studies thus suggest that extraversion–introversion, as a major dimension of personality, can, when superadded to the dimensions of neuroticism, give rise to meaningful dimensional subdivisions of the total population of neurotics.

When we turn to the subdivisions of the psychoses, the traditional system of Kraepelin, Breuler, and Kretschmer stresses the major grouping into schizophrenics and manic–depressives, with Kretschmer in particular advocating a continuum running from one exteme to the other (H. J. Eysenck, 1970b). When criterion analysis was applied to this division (H. J. Eysenck, 1952a), no factor corresponding to Kretscher's hypothetical schizophrenic–manic–depressive axis could be found, and a more inclusive review of the literature (H. J. Eysenck, 1970b) demonstrates no factors corresponding to these groupings, whether they are supposed to lie on a single continuum or not.

What we do find, instead, is rather that just as neurotics are divisible along a dimension of extraversion–introversion, so are psychotics (Verma & Eysenck, 1973); this corresponds quite well with subdivisions indicated by

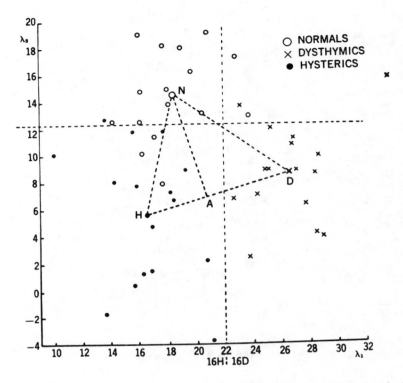

Figure 3-8. *Discriminant function analysis of 16 normals* (O), *16 hysterics* (●), *and 16 dysthymics* (x), *on basis of tests scores. From H. J. Eysenck and Claridge (1962).*

Wing (1978). It cannot be said that this hypothesis has been pursued resolutely enough to give definitive results; the obvious difficulties when working with psychotics, usually in institutions and with drugs, are too well known to require restatement. However, the possibility should not be ruled out that the psychotic realm, too, could be structured in line with such a dimension.

As the minimum set of descriptive dimensions structuring the psychiatric universe (leaving out, of course, nonfunctional disorders having a definite and recognized physical origin), we find that three major dimensions—psychoticism, neuroticism, and extraversion–introversion—are indicated; the possibility that further dimensions may be required cannot be ruled out and is subject to empirical enquiry. We thus arrive at a dimensional model as opposed to the traditional categorical or diagnostic model, and it may be interesting to see how the two differ in their application to psychiatric disorders.

DSM-III and Reliability of Diagnosis

DSM-III stands as a landmark of and a warning against the purely denotative and descriptive approach to this problem. It results in thousands of very small groupings based on no sound experimental or psychometric studies of any kind, failing to indicate relations (if any) with normal personality patterns, and generally incapable of being absorbed into any kind of theoretical and causal system which might be suggested.

It might be argued that reliabilities are higher using this scheme than they have been in the past, and that reliability is a prize so outstanding that any sacrifice may be worth making in order to achieve it. This would seem to be putting the cart before the horse. Reliability is desirable, but validity is far more important. Qualitative analysis has to precede quantitative analysis, and the fact that a scheme enables moderately reliable descriptions to be achieved says nothing about the correctness of the scheme (although the opposite is true—very unreliable data indicate grave faults in the theoretical scheme in question).

It is easy to achieve a high degree of agreement, and even unanimity, if we define "fish" as scaly things that swim in the water. There would be much agreement on this definition, but it would classify whales and porpoises, to take but one example, as fish rather than as mammals! Phenetic relationships have to be studied psychometrically and quantitatively in order to give relevant information on proper classificatory systems, and DSM-III is not based on any such approach. At best, we have very subjective ratings and descriptions strung together in a subjective manner and without any quantitative elaboration. This is not the way of science, and the fact that large committees have decreed that DSM-III represents an optimum description of psychiatric reality does not alter the fact that it is based on a fallacy, namely, the fallacy of categorical differences between groups. At times it is argued that differences in severity may supply the necessary quantitative element that leads to a dimensional system, but this is merely a sop to Cerberus, not a properly integrated element in the system.

By contrast, a dimensional system would not insist on diagnoses useful mainly for administrative rather than medical or scientific purposes. It would use established testing techniques, preferably of a laboratory nature and involving not only psychological but also physiological, hormonal, and other types of biochemical tests, followed by a working out of standard procedures to determine the position of the person on the three major dimensions (and any other dimensions which might appear well established and properly measurable.)

Each dimension might be measured on a 10-point scale, with 10 indicating the highest and 0 indicating the lowest mark. Thus, taking the three major dimensions in the order P, E, and N, a particular individual might be classified as 9, 7, 2, that is, being very high on psychoticism, very introverted, and with a dash of neuroticism. To anyone used to the system, this would give a better indication of the person's behavior and phenotype generally than would a categorical diagnosis. Furthermore, changes in his or her status could be traced, that is, by a reduction in the degree of psychoticism, an increase in extraversion, and so forth. Such would be the basis of a dimensional system, and the great advantage of such a system would be not only that it was in line with the facts outlined in the earlier part of this chapter, but also that the determination of a person's position on these three dimensions would be objective, and hence highly reliable. Something approaching such a dimensional analysis has, of course, been incorporated in the Minnesota Multiphasic Personality Inventory (MMPI), where categorical diagnoses are changed into quantitative variables and diagnostic profiles of a number of scales. However, the MMPI suffers from several major disadvantages, the most obvious being that it is entirely based on questionnarie responses, the second that the scales were made up in a rather arbitrary manner and without benefit of psychometric manipulation, and last, but not least, that it is based entirely on antiquated psychiatric formulations which it tries to follow as best it can.

Theory of Taxonomy: Neurosis

The main characteristic that springs to mind in reading DSM-III, apart from the unrealistic assumption of categorical diagnostic methodologies, is the complete absence of any theoretical considerations that might determine nomenclature and system. Of particular interest is the decision on the part of the authors to drop the term "neurosis," presumably on the grounds that the term is differentially used and that more specific subgroupings are more informative. There certainly is a dearth of proper scientific theories of neurosis (Gossop, 1981), but this is only so when we look at the large mass of purely subjective and a priori conceptions that pass for theories in this field. When we stop to look at a more rational and experimental approach, we find that there is considerable agreement on the definition of neurosis, and that, in addition, theory and diagnosis are closely integrated with treatment. A detailed outline of the neobehavioristic approach to neurosis is given elsewhere (H. J. Eysenck, 1982a), but the major ideas may be briefly outlined here.

Let us consider first of all the part that subjectivity and theory play in the hard sciences in making theory and observation agree. Heat can be measured by means of liquid-in-glass thermometers, but clearly not all liquids are equally good for this purpose. Water would not be a good liquid to use because it contracts from the ice point to the temperature of maximum density, thus giving an illusory decline in temperature when actually the temperature is increasing. In actual fact, the liquids most widely used (mercury and alcohol) were chosen in part because they fit in best with the kinetic theory of heat, which predicts that the final temperature of the fluid obtained by mixing two similar fluids of masses $m_1 m_2$, at the initial temperatures $t_1 t_2$, should be

$$t_f = \frac{(m_1 t_1 + m_2 t_2)}{(m_1 + m_2)}$$

The linseed oil thermometer was discarded because measurements made with the instrument did not tally with the predictions made by the kinetic theory; mercury and alcohol thermometers do tally. Thus, the choice of the measuring instrument is in part based on its agreement with theory; the same is true of psychological measurement and psychological concepts.

The neobehavioristic theory of neurosis says in essence that neurotic disorders are the products of Pavlovian conditioning and that they can be cured by the application of Pavlovian extinction methods. There are, of course, many qualifications and amplifications attending these statements; thus, the type of conditioning involved is Pavlovian B conditioning and not Pavlovian A conditioning. Furthermore, genetic factors linked with "preparedness" are also an important contributory element, and personality differences, both relating to the strength of emotional arousal (neuroticism) and the speed and strength of conditioning (extraversion–introversion), play an important part. However, this is not the place to exhibit the theory in detail, and we must take these various qualifications as read.

Using the example from the kinetic theory of heat as our guide, we would now be able to define neurosis as any kind of emotional disorder produced by Pavlovian B conditioning, following the general lines of the theory as stated by H. J. Eysenck (1982a). A necessary corollary would be that the disorder in question should yield to behavioristic methods of extinction, and the important recent work of Rachman and Hodgson (1980) indicates the degree to which neurotic disorders that previously appeared hopeless could be successfully treated by the use of behavior therapy extinction methods.

Rachman and Hodgson quote psychoanalytic writers admitting that there is no record that a single patient suffering from obsessive-compulsive handwashing was ever cured by psychoanalytic treatment, and our hospital records of hundreds of such patients do not disclose successful treatment by any psychotherapeutic method whatsoever, nor by any physical methods such as electroconvulsive therapy or leukotomy. Yet the application of the extinction methods of flooding plus response prevention produced very speedy and lasting cures in something like 90% of all patients involved. Facts such as these would justify us in including obsessive-compulsive behavior as part of neurosis, defined as a continuum rather than as a categorical description, of course.

In the same way it should be possible to go through the whole list of symptoms and groups of symptoms and ask the identical question: Did these disorders arise as a function of Pavlovian B conditioning, and do they respond to extinction-type treatment by behavior therapy? If they do, and if they fulfill the other demands of the paradigm in question, then they can be classified as neurotic disorders; if they do not, they cannot. Thus, we would use theory as a criterion for classification in a manner corresponding to that used in the hard sciences.

Theory and Paradigms in Psychiatry

It is not suggested here that our knowledge with respect to neurotic disorders or behavior therapy and the theory associated with it is anything like adequate to come to definitive conclusions or can claim to rank with the kinetic theory of heat and the experimental basis for that theory. But this fact should not close our eyes to the equally important consideration that in the neobehavioristic theory of neurosis we have a scientific paradigm, to use a term made popular by Kuhn (1970), which could form the basis of what he calls "ordinary science" puzzle-solving behavior, and could thus lead to a much better understanding of the concept "neurosis" and its relation to diagnosis and treatment. We already have here a much closer relationship between diagnosis and treatment than can be found in other areas of psychiatry, precisely because the theory defines not only the diagnosis and the origin of the disorder, but also its treatment. Obviously much more work will have to be done before we can be satisfied with the position, but what has already been done suffices to show that this model is superior to any alternative model on the market and hence deserves to be studied and experimented with in the future (Gossop, 1981). It is important, in evalutating the model, to look at its rate of success. Rachman and Wilson (1980) have reviewed the whole literature on the effects of psychological therapy and have quoted convincing evidence as to the superiority of behavioristic types of treatment as compared with all others. Theories that are supported by such convincing evidence of the effectiveness of methods of treatment based on them are in a different category to the vagaries commonly passing as psychiatric theories, which fail to be supported by such empirical success.

The important point to note here is not simply that the method of treatment based on the theory is outstandingly successful, but that it derives directly from the theory. Smith, Glass, and Miller (1980) have made claims for psychotherapy, suggesting not only that it is successful, but that it may be as successful as behavior therapy. Their own account belies this statement (Eysenck, 1983, in press), but what here is even more important is the fact that on their own showing the successes are quite unrelated to the theories in question. Any theory of psychoanalysis or psychotherapy would postulate that length of treatment was a crucial variable, and that the training of the therapist was an equally important variable. Smith *et al.*, on the other hand, find in their review of the existing literature that neither the amount of training received by the therapist nor the length of treatment bore any relation to the success of treatment! When we bear in mind the fact that on their own showing again placebo treatment was as successful as psychodynamic psychotherapy, it is becoming clear that they are not dealing with theory-derived treatment at all, but with what in truth are simply placebo effects of one kind or another.

By contrast, the neobehavioristic theory is able to explain not only the success of behavior therapy methods of treatment of neurotic disorders, but also such success as may be claimed for psychotherapy, psychoanalysis, and even spontaneous recovery. It is as part of such a wide-ranging and clearly successful theory that the classificatory model which is related to it assumes greater importance than it would otherwise do. We can say that it is not merely a convenient description of reality, however well supported by psychometric calculations and empirical investigations, but is part of successful general theory that the classificatory system here adopted must be seen.

It is possible, of course, to make the general theory here discussed more specific and relate it to what are traditionally called such diagnostic categories as psychopathy (H. J. Eysenck, 1980), hysteria (H. J. Eysenck, 1982b), and psychosomatic disorder (H. J. Eysenck, 1981). These more specific theories, in turn, suggest ways and means of measurement and improvement in classification along the dimensional scheme outlined above. It would take us too far afield to go into these details; they are given in the publications just listed.

All these suggestions made here and in previous publications may, of course, be mistaken, and the empirical investigations cited may be subject to alternative interpretation. This is true of all scientific endeavors, and it is only reasonable to admit weaknesses which are inevitable at an early stage of development of a system, and in particular a system which has not on the whole been discussed or criticized very much in psychiatric circles. Indeed, one of the points that arises from the historical development of the system is one that might have been anticipated from a reading of the history of science in general, that is, the failure of orthodoxy to pay any attention whatsoever to the facts and theories outlined. The juggernauts of the psychiatric establishment roll on regardless, disregarding facts and theories alike insofar as they do not fit in with the point of view regarded as orthodox at the time. DSM-III exemplifies this antiscientific and irrational approach to perfection; it does not discuss or argue, but lays down the law as if it were dealing with a paradigm which no rational person could quarrel with. The fact that such an approach and such an empty, atheoretical, and antiexperimental system can find acceptance in psychiatry says more about the nature of modern psychiatry than any critic, however hostile, might be able to say.

Of particular relevance for a consideration of DSM-III is the recent study by Fenton, Mosher, and Matthews (1981) in which they review data relevant to the evaluation for six systems for diagnosing schizophrenia. The systems tested are those of Schneider's first-rank symptoms, the Newhaven schizophrenia index, the flexible system, the Feighner criteria, research diagnostic criteria, and DSM-III. None of these, they maintain, has established construct validity, and all are, in a sense, arbitrary. "Choosing one over another cannot be data-based" (p. 452). They go on to advise caution and open-mindedness in the use of DSM-III, because the elevation of any one diagnostic system to an official status is thought to be premature, and they go on to say that "There is as yet no evidence that its criteria for schizophrenia are either less arbitrary or better (in identifying a group of "true" schizophrenics) than those of other systems" (p. 452). What is true of schizophrenia is equally or more true of the other diagnoses recommeded by DSM-III. In each case, the decisions made are arbitrary, not based on scientific evidence, and unlikely to agree with the kind of boundaries set by nature. As Sir Aubrey Lewis once said: "To set up sharp distinctions in the interests of academic accuracy, when the distinction is not found in nature, is no help to thought or action" (quoted in Mosher, 1978, p. 694). There comes a time in the history of any paradigm, as Kuhn (1970) pointed out, when the accumulation of anomalies, absurdities, and obvious falsities becomes too great to bear, and a revolution is required to rid the scientific world of a paradigm that has outlived its usefulness (if it ever had any usefulness!) (Barnes, 1982). DSM-III marks a time when this need is becoming desperate. There is no way of advance left for those accepting the premises and assumptions of DSM-III; it is not clear how, using the same or similar methodology as that adopted by the authors, any rational improvement will ever be possible. It is clearly necessary to throw out the whole approach, hook, line, and sinker, before anything better can take its place. DSM-IV, if ever such a misshapen fetus should experience a live birth, can only make confusion worse confounded and make the psychiatric approach to classification even less scientific than it is at the moment. What is needed is a complete rethinking of the whole approach, a consideration of the underlying problems, and an attempt to formulate experimental and psychometric approaches to these problems which may generate a universally agreed answer in due course. It is not suggested that the alternative system here outlined already provides such an answer; it is merely suggested that it may be an alternative approach which avoids some of the more obvious errors and absurdities of DSM-III. If the same amount of grant money and research endeavor were put into the new scheme as went into the old, it seems likely that a much better system of psychiatric classification could be produced than exists at the moment.

REFERENCES

Bannister, D., Salmon, P, & Lieberman, D.M. (1964). Diagnosis in treatment relationships in psychiatry—a statistical analysis. *British Journal of Psychiatry*, *110*, 726–732.
Barnes, B. (1982). *T. S. Kuhn and social science*. London: Macmillan.

Cattell, R. B., & Scheier, I.N. (1961). *The meaning and measurement of neuroticism and anxiety*. New York: Ronald Press.

Claridge, G. (1967). *Personality and arousal*. Oxford: Pergamon Press.

Claridge, G. (1972). The schizophrenics as nervous types. *British Journal of Psychiatry, 121*, 1–17.

Claridge, G. (1973). A nervous typological analysis of personality variation in normal twins. In G.S. Claridge (Ed.), *Personality differences and biological variations: A study of twins*. Oxford: Pergamon Press.

Claridge, G. (1981). Psychoticism. In R. Lynn (Ed.), *Dimensions of personality* (pp. 79–109). Oxford: Pergamon Press.

Claridge, G., & Birchall, P. (1978). Bishop, Eysenck, Block and psychoticism. *Journal of Abnormal Psychology, 87*, 664–668.

Claridge, G., & Chappa, H. (1973). Psychoticism: A study of its biological basis in normal subjects. *British Journal of Social and Clinical Psychology, 12*, 175–187.

Cowie, V. (1961). The incidence of neurosis in the children of psychotics. *Acta Psychiatrica Scandinavica, 37*, 37–87.

Devadasan, K. (1964). Cross-cultural validity of twelve clinical diagnostic tests. *Journal of the Indian Academy of Applied Psychology, 1*, 55–57.

Eysenck, H. J. (1947). *Dimensions of personality*. London: Routledge & Kegan Paul.

Eysenck, H. J. (1950). Criterion analysis: An application of the hypothetic–eductive method to factor analysis. *Psychological Review, 57*, 38–53.

Eysenck, H. J. (1952a). Schizothymia–cyclothymia as a dimension of personality. *Journal of Personality, 20*, 345–389.

Eysenck, H. J. (1952b). *The scientific study of personality*. London: Routledge & Kegan Paul.

Eysenck, H. J. (1955). Psychiatric diagnosis as a psychological and statistical problem. *Psychological Reports, 1*, 3–17.

Eysenck, H. J. (1960). Classification and the problem of diagnosis. In H. J. Eysenck (Ed.), *Handbook of abnormal psychology*. London: Pitman.

Eysenck, H. J. (1970a). A dimensional system of psychodiagnostics. In A. R. Mahrer (Ed.), *New approaches to personality classification* (pp. 169–207). New York: Columbia University Press.

Eysenck, H. J. (1970b). *The structure of human personality*. London: Methuen, 1970b.

Eysenck, H. J. (Ed.). (1973) *Handbook of abnormal psychology*. London: Pitman.

Eysenck, H. J. (1980). Psychopathie. In U. Baumann, H. Berbalk, & C. Seidenstucker (Eds.), *Klinische Psychologie* (Vol.3). Wein: Hans Huber.

Eysenck, H. J. (1981). Personality and psychosomatic diseases. *Activitas Nervosa Superior, 23*, 112–129.

Eysenck, H. J. (1982a) Neobehavioristic (S–R) theory of neurosis. In G. T. Wilson & C. M. Franks (Eds.), *Contemporary behavior therapy*. New York: Guilford Press.

Eysenck, H. J. (1982b). A psychological theory of hysteria. In A. Roy (Ed.), *Hysteria* (pp. 57–80). New York: Wiley.

Eysenck, H. J. (1983). The benefits of psychotherapy—a battlefield revisited. *Behaviour Research and Therapy, 21*, 315–320.

Eysenck, H. J. (in press) Meta-analysis: An abuse of research integration. *Journal of Special Education*.

Eysenck, H. J., & Claridge, G. (1962) The position of hysterics and dysthymics in a two-dimensional framework of personality description. *Journal of Abnormal and Social Psychology, 64*, 46–55.

Eysenck, H. J., & Eysenck, S. B. G. (1976). *Psychoticism as a dimension of personality*. London: Hodder & Stoughton.

Eysenck, H. J., Wakefield, J. A., & Friedman, A. F. (1983). Diagnosis and clinical assessment: The DSM-III. *Annual Review of Psychology, 34*, 167–193.

Eysenck, S. B. G. (1956). Neurosis and psychosis: An experimental analysis. *Journal of Mental Science, 102*, 517–529.

Fenton, W. S., Mosher, L. R., & Matthews, S. M. (1981). Diagnosis of schizophrenia: A critical review of current diagnostic systems. *Schizophrenia Bulletin, 7*, 452–476.

Foulds, G. A. (1971). Personality deviance and personal symptomatology. *Psychological Medicine,* 3, 222–233.

Gattaz, W. F. (1981). HLA-B27 as a possible genetic marker of psychoticism. *Personality and Individual Differences, 2,* 57–60.

Gossop, M. (1981). *Theories of neurosis.* New York: Springer.

Kuhn, T. S. (1970). *The structure of scientific revolution.* (2nd ed.). Chicago, IL: University of Chicago Press.

Launay, G., & Slade, P. (1981). The measurement of hallucinatory predispositions in male and female prisoners. *Personality and Individual Differences, 2,* 221–234.

Maccacaro, P. S. (1958). La misura della informazione countenta nei criteria di classificazione. *Annals of Microbiology, 8,* 231–239.

McGuffin, P. (1979). Is schizophrenia an HLA-associated disease? *Psychological Medicine, 9,* 721–728.

Mosher, L. R. (1978) Can diagnosis be nonpejorative? In L. C. Wynne, R. L. Cromwell, & S. Matthysse (Eds.), *The nature of schizophrenia: New approaches to research and treatment.* (pp. 690–697). New York: Wiley.

Rachman, S., & Hodgson, R. (1980). *Obsessions and compulsions.* Englewood, NJ: Prentice-Hall.

Rachman, S., & Wilson, G. T. (1980). *The effects of psychological therapy.* Oxford: Pergamon Press.

Robinson, T. N., & Zahn, T. P. (1979). Covariation of two-flash threshold and autonomic arousal for high and low scorers on a measure of psychoticism. *British Journal of Social and Clinical Psychology, 18,* 431–441.

Slater, P. (1960) Experiments in psychometrics. In H. J. Eysenck (Ed.), *Experiments in personality* (Vol. 2). London: Routledge & Kegan Paul.

Smith, M., Glass, G., & Miller, T. (1980). *The benefits of psychotherapy.* Baltimore, MD. Johns Hopkins Press.

Sneath, P. H. A. (1962). The construction of taxonomic groups. In *Microbiology classifications.* London: Cambridge University Press.

Sneath, P. H. A. (1964). Computers in bacterial classification. *Advancement of Science,* 572–582.

Sokal, R. R., & Sneath, P. H. A. (1963). *Principles of numerical taxonomy.* San Francisco, CA, Freeman.

Szasz, T. S. (1961). *The myth of mental illness.* New York: Harper (Hoeber).

Trouton, D. S., & Maxwell, A. E. (1956). The relation between neurosis and psychosis. *Journal of Mental Science, 102,* 1–21.

Venables, P. N. (1963). The relationship between level of skin potential and fusion of paired light flashes in schizophrenic and normal subjects. *Journal of Psychiatric Research, 1,* 279–287.

Verma, R. M., & Eysenck, H. J. (1973). Severity and type of psychotic illness as a function of personality. *British Journal of Psychiatry, 122,* 573–585.

Williams, W. T., & Lambert, J. M. (1959). Multivariate methods in plant ecology: Association-analysis in plant communities. *Journal of Ecology, 47,* 83–101.

Wing, J. K. (1978). *Reasoning and madness.* London: Oxford University Press.

Wundt, W. (1903). *Grundzuge der Physiologischen Psychologie.* Leipzig: Engelmann.

CHAPTER 4

Problems in Diagnostic Classification

Sol L. Garfield

There appears to be little question that methods of classification have potential utility. This holds for our everyday world as well as for science. Classification allows us to order a variety of phenomena and thus to bring them into some sort of meaningful relationship to each other. Such orderly systems also allow us to deal more economically with large amounts of data. Classification systems thus may have selective utility for a number of functions. At the same time, however, they may be inappropriate for some purposes, or some particular systems may be poorly designed and constructed, and thus of limited value.

The previous psychiatric classification system, DSM-II (American Psychiatric Association [APA], 1968) suffered from a number of weaknesses and a very serious attempt was made to improve it. Robert Spitzer and his colleagues were successful to some degree, and for this they deserve our appreciation. At the same time, the new classification manual (APA, 1980), as a result of both methodological limitations and apparent political-professional pressures, also has several important deficiencies. However, before focusing more specifically on DSM-III, some general comments on psychiatric classification are worthwhile.

Clinical Diagnosis

Psychiatry, as a specialty area within medicine, has, as might be expected, patterned itself after medicine and essentially utilized a diagnostic system based on diseases or types of illness. This system apparently has been

Sol L. Garfield. Department of Psychology, Washington University, St. Louis, Missouri.

moderately successful for medicine. Clinical medicine, with the aid of contributions from the basic sciences, has been able to categorize and describe a large number of medical disorders. Apart from descriptions of symptomatology, attention has been paid to the course of the illness, its incidence, prognosis, potential etiology, and possible treatments. Where the etiology of an illness is known, the application of preventative measures also becomes possible. In a similar way, where an effective treatment exists for a specific illness, the correct diagnosis is of definite importance in facilitating the recovery of the patient.

Whatever evaluation one makes of the medical model, it seems apparent that it has not worked particularly well for psychiatry. Many categories of mental illness have been defined and described by psychiatrists which do not appear to fit the illness model. During psychiatry's history, a number of designated mental illnesses have appeared in the various diagnostic classifications, only to recede later or to be replaced by new diseases or disorders. The most important mental disease when I was a graduate student, dementia praecox, has been replaced by schizophrenia. This, of course, does not mean that the disorder in question or the pathological behaviors have disappeared. Rather, it signifies a changed conceptualization and description of a segment or type of disordered behavior. In some cases this is due to an increase in our knowledge of psychopathology. In others, it is due to changing theories or views.

Psychiatric classification systems contain a listing and description of mental disorders which vary in important ways (Feinstein, 1977). This is as true of DSM-III as it is of its predecessors. Some of the disorders listed are organic or neurological disorders which resemble or are similar to nonpsychiatric illnesses. As a general rule, more is known about their etiology, course, and prognosis than is true of many other psychiatric disorders, and there tends to be greater reliability of diagnosis in such cases (Schmidt & Fonda, 1956). On the other hand, the diagnostic classification scheme contains disorders which really do not resemble traditional medical diseases. Apart from less certain knowledge concerning etiology and course of the disorder, the descriptions are largely behavioral or social in character, the symptomatology more general or diffuse, the diagnosis more uncertain, and the disorder more difficult to distinguish from problems of normal development. I shall have more to say about these problems a bit later. The point being made here, however, is that DSM-III includes a variety of diagnoses, perhaps greater in number than its two predecessors, and these disorders differ in many important respects. Some resemble traditional types of medical illnesses, some might turn out eventually to be of this type, and others seem to be quite different.

Although there appears to be little question that DSM-III has been more carefully considered, planned, and constructed than the earlier versions, and that the use of the multiaxial system was a positive attempt to include a broadened conception of diagnosis into psychiatric classification, the need to conform to a medical model of diagnosis leads to some problems. In addition, various groups within the American Psychiatric Association (APA) apparently had their own special concerns or interests to advocate for inclusion in the new classification system. As a result, the final product of necessity was something of a compromise. This may explain in part some of the heterogeneity evident in DSM-III. The system thus does not derive from any particular theoretical orientation or system and contains a listing and description of various psychiatric disorders based on varying critieria.

Reliability of Psychiatric Diagnosis

One of the serious problems encountered in the use of psychiatric diagnosis has been the reliability of the diagnoses obtained. This has been a problem for both clinical practice and research in the area of psychopathology. How well do different diagnosticians agree on matters of diagnosis? A number of studies were reported in the past which reflected poorly on the extent of agreement among the diagnosticians evaluated (Beck, Ward, Mendelson, Mock, & Erbaugh, 1962; Hunt, 1980; Hunt, Wittson, & Hunt, 1953; Kreitman, 1961; Schmidt & Fonda, 1956; Spitzer & Fleiss, 1974). Such problems in reliability were apparent not only in terms of very specific diagnoses or subtype diagnoses, but even in categorizing such broad and global designations as neurosis and psychosis.

Other evidences of diagnostic unreliability were apparent in observations of the diagnoses recorded in different wards of the same hospital or over different time periods. Anyone who has worked in a large clinical setting has probably noticed that there is no unanimity among the staff in diagnostic conferences. I have participated in staff conferences in which the final diagnosis was conclusively settled by an eight to seven vote of the staff members present! One may also note that some colleagues have their own preferred diagnoses which are offered with unusual frequency. In one study, for example, one of three psychiatrists in a hospital who worked with patients comparable to those of two other psychiatrists diagnosed over twice as many of his patients as schizophrenic as did the other two (Pasamanick, Dinitz, & Lefton, 1959).

It is also true that the rates for different diagnoses have varied over time and in terms of different national locales. Thus, the rate of first admission diagnoses of schizophrenia in state mental hospitals in the United States for the period from 1940 to 1960 varied by almost 50% (Kramer, 1965). One cannot state categorically whether such an increase represents an increase in the incidence of schizophrenia or reflects unreliability and variability in diagnostic performance. However, it does raise a question about the meaningfulness of such diagnoses and what they actually signify. Although, as we shall note later, the criteria for diagnoses in DSM-III are more clearly delineated and the rules are more strictly set down, problems still remain. An increase in reliability may be secured at the cost of some other considerations.

In any event, the unreliability of diagnosis has been a problem of some significance and still remains a problem in clinical work. The problem has been reduced somewhat in research studies involving particular diagnostic groups, since several types of criteria are used, interviewers and raters receive special training, and estimates of reliability of diagnosis are obtained. However, such procedures are not typical in nonresearch settings and, of course, problems of generalizing from the research situation to the various clinical settings remain. However, it is worth noting that diagnoses made by individual clinicians may be less reliable and more idiosyncratic than those which have been obtained in research investigations where attention is paid to the reliability of diagnosis.

DSM-III

As already indicated, the current diagnostic manual differs in a number of ways from the two earlier ones. Great efforts have been made to describe the diagnostic categories as clearly as possible and to list the specific criteria for making a diagnosis. It is also stated that as much as possible decisions were reached and controversies resolved on the basis of existing research findings. In these respects, the new diagnostic system is clearly superior to those that preceded it. Furthermore, besides much more extensive discussions, appraisal, and revision in the pre-final stages of development, the new system was field tested and evaluations of diagnostic reliability secured. The reliabilities secured by means of the kappa statistic for broad classifications such as schizophrenia or major affective disorders was generally good. However, the reliabilities for specific disorders and for some other general classifications tend to be lower and there is considerable variability. The reliability for diagnoses in the broad category of personality disorders is somewhat low ($\kappa = .56$) and the kappas for specific personality disorders are quite low.

As compared with DSM-I and DSM-II, DSM-III does appear to have higher reliability, although this was not the case in a study of childhood disorders (Mattison, Cantwell, Russell, & Will, 1979). Nevertheless, the reliabilities reported above are primarily for broad classes of diagnostic classification or for such categories as sexual disorders in which the behaviors or complaints tend to be more specific. Thus, the utility of the diagnostic system would depend somewhat on the uses to which it is put and the categories that would be emphasized. If one's purpose is met by diagnosing a patient as a case of schizophrenia, the use of DSM-III may lead to a reasonably reliable diagnosis. However, if the different types of schizophrenia are supposedly meaningful subclassifications and potentially useful for clinical purposes, then the more reliable but grosser diagnosis of schizophrenia would appear to be of lesser utility. In essence, does a diagnosis of paranoid schizophrenic carry different clinical implications for treatment and prognosis than a diagnosis of schizophrenia, catatonic type? If it does, then the reliability of subtype diagnosis is the important consideration and not the reliability of the overall diagnosis of schizophrenia. If such differentiation is of little importance, then conceivably clinicians should disregard such diagnoses and they should not be included in the diagnostic classification. It is interesting to note that the description of the catatonic type mentions that during "catatonic stupor or excitement the individual needs careful supervision to avoid hurting self or others, and medical care may be needed because of malnutrition, exhaustion, hyperpyrexia, or self-inflicted injury" (APA, 1980, pp. 190–191). This statement could be taken to signify that the diagnosis is a meaningful one because it alerts the nursing and medical staff to be particularly observant of the patient. If so, then the reliability and validity of the subtype diagnosis is an important consideration. Also of interest is the statement in DSM-III which immediately follows: "Although this type was very common several decades ago, it is now rare in Europe and North America" (APA, 1980, p. 191). What is the possible significance of this latter statement? Does it signify a real reduction in the incidence of schizophrenia, catatonic type? If it does, can we offer an adequate explanation for this apparent reduced occurrence of this type of mental illness? Or, is it possibly a result of improved hospital care or more careful or different approaches to psychiatric diagnosis? This is the same issue that was mentioned earlier in discussing variable rates in the hospitalization of diagnosed cases of schizophrenia over several decades. Unreliable diagnostic categories, unfortunately, do not allow one to draw reliable or valid conclusions.

Although the descriptions of the diagnostic categories and the stated criteria to be met for specific diagnoses are more clearly delineated than those used in the past, they present some problems of a different sort. This is particularly true if the new criteria are more stringent. The more stringent the criteria are, the greater the possibility of increased reliability, but reliability is secured at a cost. In this instance, fewer individuals receive a diagnosis and more are undiagnosed or excluded. Whether this is a desirable outcome or not is a matter of value judgment. However, problems are apparent if a large number of patients are essentially undiagnosed. Several studies have attempted to evaluate this issue and it is worth looking at their findings.

During the past few years, several diagnostic schemes were developed for greater diagnostic precision in research investigations, some of which had an influence on the development of DSM-III. Among them were the Feighner criteria (Feighner et al., 1972) and the Research Diagnostic Criteria (Spitzer, Endicott, & Robins, 1975). In one study of 166 patients who had received a clinical diagnosis of schizophrenia, these two diagnostic criteria along with four others were evaluated (Overall & Hollister, 1979). The various diagnostic criteria differed noticeably in terms of their agreement with the regular clinical diagnoses, "with the Feighner criteria accepting only 26%" (Overall & Hollister, 1979, p. 1198). Furthermore, the Feighner criteria and the Research Diagnostic Criteria disagreed 50% of the time. This kind of finding is quite disconcerting. In another study, 20 psychiatrists independently offered diagnoses on 24 cases of childhood psychiatric disorders based on actual case histories (Cantwell, Russell, Mattison, & Will, 1979). These diagnoses were then compared to the authors' consensus on the expected DSM-III diagnoses and the level of agreement did not quite reach 50%. Apart from the implications for clinical diagnosis where such exclusionary diagnoses are used, serious questions are raised about the generalizability of the results obtained from studies using the different diagnostic criteria. In fact, questions can be raised about the meaningfulness of a diagnosis of schizophrenia when it is based on some diagnostic criteria and not on others. Which diagnoses can be regarded as the most valid ones?

Other studies have also indicated the lack of agreement among different diagnostic systems and the fact that they consequently tend to select somewhat different samples of subjects (Endicott et al., 1982; Fenton, Mosher, & Matthews, 1981; Gift, Strauss, Ritzler, Kokes, & Harder, 1980; Singerman, Stoltzman, Robins, Helzer, & Croughan, 1981). One recent study compared the relationship between seven current diagnostic criteria for schizophrenia as well as comparing these diagnostic criteria with the dimensions of premorbid adjustment, paranoid symptomatology, and chronicity (Klein, 1982). These latter dimensions have been used rather widely in research on schizophrenia the past 35 years or so and have been correlated with a number of behavioral, prognostic, and treatment variables (Klorman, Strauss, & Kokes, 1977; Strauss, Kokes, Klorman, & Sacksteder, 1977). Thus, they are of some potential importance and an analysis of their relationship to different diagnostic criteria may be potentially informative concerning differences among the latter.

In the study by Klein (1982), a series of 46 cases of schizophrenia were selected from consecutive admissions to an acute inpatient ward. The patients had to meet three criteria: (a) a hospital diagnosis of schizophrenia based on DSM-II; (b) a score of four or more on the New Haven Schizophrenic Index (Astrachan et al., 1972), based on current symptomatology; and (c) be under 56 years of age and with no evidence of organic brain damage, toxic psychosis, alcohol or drug abuse, mental retardation, or recent electroconvulsive therapy. Within a week after admission, each patient was interviewed and diagnoses were secured based on the Schedule for the Affective Disorders and Schizophrenia (SADS) (Spitzer & Endicott, 1978) and hospital records. Several additional items were added to the SADS in order to provide information necessary for securing diagnoses based on the seven diagnostic criteria. The seven diagnostic criteria were: The Research Diagnostic Criteria (RDC) (Spitzer, Endicott, & Robins, 1978); the DSM-III; the Flexible System from the World Health Organization International Pilot Study of Schizophrenia (Carpenter, Strauss, & Bartko, 1973) using both the 5- and 6-point cutoffs (WHO 5 and WHO 6, respectively); the Feighner criteria

(Feighner *et al.*, 1972) as modified by Tsuang and Dempsey (1979); the criteria of Taylor, Greenspan, and Abrams (1979); and Schneider's first-rank symptoms (FRS) as defined by Carpenter and Strauss (1973). RDC and Feighner diagnoses considered to be at the probable as well as the definite level were used.

Descriptions of the measures used for indicating the dimensions of premorbid adjustment, paranoid symptomatology, and chronicity will be omitted here. Instead, let us proceed to a discussion of the results secured. The intercorrelations among the seven diagnostic systems ranged from −.21 to .89. Generally, the correlations were positive except for the FRS, which had low negative correlations with five of the other criteria. Not surprisingly, the DSM-III system correlated .89 with the Feighner criteria and .84 with the RDC, systems which served as models for it. Its correlations with the other four scales were much lower. The percentages of the sample that were diagnosed by the various systems varied from 24% for the Feighner criteria to 63% for the WHO 5. Use of DSM-III led to diagnosing 28% of the sample as cases of schizophrenia. The author of the study also noted the following: "The systems also differ in terms of which patients are diagnosed as schizophrenic, as indicated by the fact that only 4 of the 21 correlations . . . yielded kappa values greater than .51. The minimal overlap between criteria is further indicated by the fact that there were only nine patients (less than 20% of the sample) whom all seven systems diagnosed as being schizophrenia ($n = 3$) or nonschizophrenic ($n = 6$)" (Klein, 1982, p. 321).

With reference to the three specific dimensions studied, the results generally indicated only a weak trend among the diagnostic systems to pick out the chronic patients or those with poor premorbid adjustment. "The most striking aspect of these results, however, was the lack of significant relations among the seven diagnostic systems and the three subtyping dimensions" (Klein, 1982, p. 323). Our of 42 comparisons, only 5 were significant.

More could be said about the ways the different diagnostic criteria differ and what features each appear to emphasize. However, it does not appear necessary to provide such elaboration here. It is evident that there are important differences between them and that different numbers of patients will be diagnosed to be cases of schizophrenia by the different criteria. In the absence of a universally accepted definition or criteria of schizophrenia, it is impossible to decide which system is the most valid in diagnosing cases of schizophrenia. It is apparent, however, that such systems as the Feighner or DSM-III which have fairly stringent criteria tend to exclude many cases that would be diagnosed as schizophrenic by clinicians using other diagnostic criteria. This raises a serious question about the clinical usefulness of DSM-III or any of the other diagnostic systems. As has been mentioned before, increased reliability may be secured at the cost of excluding large numbers of patients from receiving a specified psychiatric diagnosis or of being given some other diagnosis as a result. Although, personally, I do not see any real harm in withholding a psychiatric diagnosis from a patient who has problems of a nonorganic nature, such arbitrary exclusion and classification of patients raises doubts about the efficacy of the classification procedure. Unless patients who receive a specific diagnosis can be shown to differ in significant ways from those who are excluded and who thereby require different treatment, the actual significance of attaching diagnostic labels can be seriously questioned. To put it bluntly, what purpose is served by such diagnostic practice? If the diagnosis is not linked in important respects to prognosis and treatment or to etiology, what good does it serve? In fact, in view of the influence of third-party payers, adherence to very strict diagnostic guidelines might lead to some peculiar practices. In order to be reimbursed, the clinician normally has to provide a diagnosis. If, for example, a patient has only four of the five necessary criteria for a specific diagnosis, he will have to be given a substitute diagnosis which may fit him less, but be more ambiguous in its stated criteria. In some instances, of course, the diagnostician might decide to overlook the fifth criterion and proceed with that diagnosis anyhow. Both of these possible practices could lead to a decrease in the meaningfulness of psychiatric diagnoses, which would be a sad outcome. All of this, of course, is conjectural and speculative, but it is at least within the realm of possibility.

Research Issues

Problems of clinical diagnosis have always loomed as important factors in research on psychopathology. In trying to understand more fully a certain type of psychopathology, investigators usually need to secure some sample of subjects which supposedly is representative of the type of psychopathology in question. Although one can learn a great deal from the intensive study of an individual case, there is always the question of how typical or representative any specific case is. Consequently, some sample of cases or subjects is required for a meaningful appraisal of exploratory hypotheses or for confirmation of previously held theoretical views. In the past, the problem which appeared to receive the greatest attention was the lack of reliability of psychiatric diagnoses. A sample of patients with a diagnosis of schizophrenia at one hospital diagnosed by one or more of the psychiatric staff could not be assumed to be comparable to a similar number of patients diagnosed in a different setting by a different group of psychiatrists. This probably was an important reason for the conflicting findings reported in the research literature on various types of psychopathology. In the field of clinical psychology, for example, diagnostic psychological test patterns secured in one setting usually failed to be confirmed by investigations in other settings. Although other factors may also have contributed to this sorry state of affairs, the lack of reliability in the diagnosis used as the basis for subject selection was seen as a primary factor—and rightly so. I have written about this and related matters several times in the past and need not go into unnecessary and repetitious detail here (Garfield, 1978, 1983a, 1983b). However, the unreliability of diagnosis was clearly an important matter in all research pertaining to etiology, diagnosis, and treatment in the area of psychopathology.

Some of the more recent diagnostic systems have been developed with full awareness of the past problems of unreliability of diagnosis and, as noted, have been more stringent in defining and specifying their criteria. As also noted, this has apparently led to some improvement in diagnostic reliability, even though problems remain. New problems have been evident also as a result of these new diagnostic systems, and they have been mentioned in the preceding section. One is the lack of agreement between diagnostic systems; the other is the issue of the inclusiveness or exclusiveness of the system. It is worth saying a bit more about these matters.

The fact that there is far from complete agreement among the various diagnostic systems presents a problem in comparing results from different studies which have used different criteria. One can, of course, compare or group studies which have used the same or very similar diagnostic criteria. However, this tends to reduce the number of studies available for any specific comparison, and we are still faced with the issue of interpreting divergent findings where the different systems have been used. This particular problem would be lessened if all future researchers agreed to use DSM-III as their diagnostic system. However, although this might lead to greater agreement among investigators, it would not deal with the problem of inclusion–exclusion.

I have made reference earlier to the problem of excluding a large number of patients from a diagnosis of schizophrenia, but did so mainly in terms of clinical concerns. However, the implications for research are also of some concern. If, for example, research in the area of schizophrenia is based solely on diagnoses secured in a very careful manner from DSM-III and results in studies based only on a selected 30–40% of the cases that might be presumed to be schizophrenic by other diagnostic appraisals, the ability to generalize from the research findings is limited. To the extent that researchers might limit their research only to carefully diagnosed patients on the basis of DSM-III, whereas others in the field at large would be less conservative in this regard, there would tend to be something of a split between research and practice, which is not particularly desirable. Conceivably also, the reduction in diagnoses of schizophrenia would lead to an increase in other diagnoses, which might decrease reliability in these latter diagnoses.

The matter of selecting subjects for research and the accompanying issue of the applicability of research findings to clinical situations is, of course, a matter that is not limited to DSM-III. If the research subjects are not clearly and adequately described, generalization is correspondingly limited. However, if we set up a number of selection criteria, as seems to be the case in research studies these days, generalization is also limited, although in a different manner. Classifying subjects for research purposes appears to be a necessary means for both conducting research and for securing results which potentially can be applied or generalized to other similar samples. Different utility costs, however, are involved when classification systems are either too restrictive or overinclusive. There does not appear to be a simple solution to this problem, but we need to aware of it.

There is one additional aspect that is also worth mentioning. For example, six diagnostic criteria are listed for schizophrenic disorder in DSM-III. The first criterion contains six specific items, at least one of which must be present for a diagnosis. These include the following:

1. bizarre delusions . . .
2. somatic, grandiose, religious, nihilistic or other delusions without persecutory or jealous content,
3. delusions with persecutory or jealous content if accompanied by hallucinations of any type,
4. auditory hallucinations in which either a voice keeps up a running commentary on the individual's behavior or thoughts, or two or more voices converse with each other,
5. auditory hallucinations on several occasions with content of more than one or two words, having no apparent relation to depression or elation,
6. incoherence, marked loosening of associations, markedly illogical thinking, or marked poverty of content of speech if associated with at least one of the following: (a) blunted, flat, or inappropriate affect; (b) delusions or hallucinations; (c) catatonic or other grossly disorganized behavior. (APA, 1980, pp. 188–189)

Although the above category is just one of the categories to be considered in making a diagnosis of schizophrenic disorder, it will serve to illustrate the point to be made here. This pertains to the range of symptomatology that is included within this diagnostic category. Individuals with bizarre delusions, individuals with auditory hallucinations, and individuals who are incoherent with blunted affect or catatonic behavior differ noticeably, yet they all would receive the same diagnosis on Axis I of DSM-III. If some studies utilize patients who primarily manifest bizarre delusions, other studies use patients whose main symptomatology consists of auditory hallucinations, and still other studies include patients who are primarily incoherent, can we expect that the results will be comparable? Is a schizophrenic a schizophrenic a schizophrenic? Is the major classification the really important one for the advancement of knowledge and the most efficacious treatment of such individuals? Or are the different symptomatic features of primary importance?

I have no ready answer for such questions, but I have been impressed with the tremendous variability in personality and behavior among patients bearing the diagnosis of schizophrenia. It is also my belief that categorizing and grouping together such diverse groups of symptomatic behaviors as if they constituted one disease entity or disorder has resulted in the conflicting findings reported many times previously in the literature. Although classification may advance our understanding of phenomena, the classification must have a sound basis which is essentially meaningful. A broad classification may be useful for some purposes, but be of limited value for other purposes. Grouping a wide range of disturbed behaviors into one gross category which actually may include diverse disorders does not appear to be a productive procedure.

Thus, although DSM-III is in many ways an improvement over the preceding classification systems in psychiatry in terms of definition and specificity, it still has some of the basic limitations of such systems. Disorders such as schizophrenia are overly gross and heterogeneous, and in addition such categories as the personality disorders present additional problems of reliability in diagnosis. There is also another feature of DSM-III in particular which I and others have criticized and which deserves special comment (Garfield, 1983a; Garmezy, 1978). This refers to a number of new diagnostic psychiatric classifications appearing in DSM-III.

New and Questionable Diagnostic Categories

Although Spitzer, the chairman of the Task Force that was responsible for the preparation of the DSM-III classification system, stated that the term "disorder" has been chosen as the preferred term for the conditions listed in DSM-III in preference to such terms as "disease" or "illness," "which would seem to be inappropriate for some of the conditions" (Spitzer, Sheehy, & Endicott, 1977, p. 5), psychiatric disorders tend to be viewed and spoken of as illnesses by psychiatrists as well as others. Psychiatrists are physicians and the DSM-III does follow a medical model. The main issue, however, is whether certain categories listed as disorders really belong in a listing of psychiatric disorders. This is particularly true of a number of the developmental disorders listed in DSM-III. The present writer was a participant in a meeting held in 1976 to discuss and critique a preliminary version of DSM-III. Although I submitted a strong criticism of this part of the proposed system, my comments had little impact. Other psychologists have also offered similar criticisms (McReynolds, 1979; Miller, Bergstrom, Cross, & Grube, 1981; Schacht & Nathan, 1977). Since DSM-III is a listing of psychiatric disorders, one has a legitimate right to raise serious questions about the inclusion of problems which are not psychiatric by traditional criteria or any reasonable criteria.

Among the new developmental disorders are "specific reading disorder" and "specific arithmetic disorder." These are most frequently viewed as specific learning problems and would appear to be diagnosed and handled most appropriately by trained persons in the fields of education or educational psychology. Not only are psychiatrists not the professionals best able to deal with such problems, but there is also some potential stigma associated with having a psychiatric disorder and having to see a psychiatrist. There were undoubtedly a number of possible reasons why these and related categories were included in DSM-III, but they would appear to be self-serving interests. As a result of the inclusion of such disorders in DSM-III, psychiatrists and other mental health providers are more likely to be reimbursed by third-party payers for the diagnosis and treatment of specific reading disorder or specific arithmetic disorder. Thus, it seems likely that considerations other than those of a primarily clinical and research nature entered into this determination. The net result is to weaken the classification system and to cast doubt on the overall enterprise.

Besides these specific developmental disorders, there are a few other designated disorders which are also very questionable. Under disorders of impulse control, for example, is listed the category of "pathological gambling." Whether or not such a problem should be considered a form of psychiatric disorder or mental illness would seem to be debatable. Certainly, pathological gambling can have all sorts of negative and distressing consequences, but does it have to be labeled as psychiatric disorder? Many other problems in everyday life may have distressful effects, but they may be viewed as economic and social problems rather than psychiatric ones. Such problems may lead to or be instrumental in causing psychological disturbance, but by themselves they are best left out of the psychiatric classification system. It is of interest to point out that the diagnosis of pathological gambling was used by a defense counsel as an item in behalf of the defendant in a recent trial in a federal court. The attorney had argued that the defendant "suffers from an unusual and newly defined mental disorder—pathological gambling—that prevents him from controlling his behavior" (St. Louis Post-Dispatch, April 13, 1980). However, the jury did not consider this to be an acceptable defense and found the defendant guilty of kidnapping and automobile theft. This appeared to be a case where the label and use of a psychiatric disorder were stretched beyond an acceptable limit.

The issues referred to above go beyond the usual concerns about the uses and reliability of classification systems, but they are of some social significance. A somewhat similar type of problem was evident in the previous psychiatric classifications pertaining to mental deficiency. For example, in DSM-I, a diagnosis of mild mental deficiency was equated with IQs of 70–85. This kind of diagnostic classification appeared to disregard completely the previous history of the use of intelligence tests in this country with respect to mental retardation and had some potentially serious social consequences. According to traditional mental test usage, an IQ of 70 had been viewed as the demarcation point for intellectual subnormality. Using this as a cutoff point, approximately 2.5% of the population would be potentially classifiable as individuals with mental deficiency if other necessary criteria were met. This incidence conforms well to general surveys made in several countries, and statistically an IQ of 70 is about two standard deviations below the mean. However, raising the upper limit for mental deficiency to an IQ of 85, just 5 points below the base of the range for average intelligence, allows 16% of the population to be potential retardates. Such a classification system is obviously faulty and potentially capable of allowing many miscarriages of justice. At least potentially, one-sixth of the population could be diagnosed as mentally deficient if major emphasis was placed on test results. It illustrates that a poor classification system may be worse than no classification system. It can also be mentioned that DSM-II did not utilize the categorization of DSM-I, but followed the classification of the *Manual on Terminology and Classification in Mental Retardation* (Heber, 1959), which differed noticeably from DSM-I. In this classification of mental retardation, "borderline mental retardation" corresponded to an IQ range of 68–83, whereas "mild mental retardation" corresponded to an IQ range of 52–67 (on the revised Stanford–Binet Scale). Individuals previously classified as displaying "moderate" mental deficiency were to be classified as cases with "mild" mental deficiency in the newer system. Mild mental deficiency thus had very different intellectual levels in the two different classification systems.

The above material illustrates that the use of diagnostic classification systems has real consequences. To the extent that there are sometimes wide differences from one edition of the diagnostic system to the next, one can even refer to the lack of reliability of diagnostic categories from one edition to the next. One may also wonder if the diagnoses of patients are changed accordingly when a new system is introduced.

For reasons such as those that have been mentioned as well as possible others, it is important that justified criticisms of diagnostic classification schemes be made and that they be viewed constructively. They may not be able to force a change in the classification system in current usage, but they may have a positive impact on future classifications. For example, the writer wrote a critique of the classification system for mental retardation published by the American Association of Mental Deficiency (AAMD) upon which the comparable system in DSM-II was based (Garfield & Wittson, 1960). Whether due to my efforts or to other factors, I was pleased to note that the classification categories criticized have been replaced with categories that have been used traditionally in psychology and which are in keeping with the studies of the incidence of mental retardation that have been made. This occurred for the AAMD Manual in 1973 (Grossman, 1973) and more recently for DSM-III, which has tended to follow the AAMD Manual in this regard. Allowing for errors of measurement, IQ test scores in the neighborhood of 70 will again be considered as the usual upper limit or cutoff score for considering possible diagnoses of mental deficiency.

Concluding Comments

I have discussed some of the issues and problems associated with diagnostic classification schemes in psychiatry. As indicated, although classification schemes have potential merit and utility, their use in clinical practice and research also reveals their inadequacies and limitations. Unlike classification schemes developed for purely scientific purposes, the more clinically oriented psychiatric systems are a result of a mixture of considerations, some of which have little to do with science. Although DSM-III has been influenced by research considerations much more than the two systems which preceded it, the concerns of different groups of clinicians also had to be considered in the final diagnostic system which was finally accepted. The final system is thus a compromise between different groups with different value systems. The concerns of classification per se had to be tempered by other considerations to which reference was made earlier. Although the real world seemingly demands such compromises, the net result is a classification system which continues some of the deficiencies of the past and introduces a few new ones. As stated by Zubin (1977–1978), "Scientific values were bent to suit the needs of psychiatry, third party payments, certification and economic exigencies of one sort or another including territoriality rights" (p. 5).

An important concern pertains to research which will now be influenced by the new diagnostic system. Research is essential for furthering our knowledge of psychopathology and its attendant implications for diagnosis, treatment, and prevention. To the extent that the present system is different from the previous official system as well as others, how comparable will research data secured previously be to that obtained using the new system? Can the old and new data be meaningfully combined? Research sophistication has increased in recent years, and we can expect that the selection of subjects for research purposes will include other measures in addition to a psychiatric diagnosis based on DSM-III. Although this is clearly a procedure for improving the objectivity of subject description and selection which many of us have recommended, nevertheless, as indicated previously, this does lead to a selectivity of research samples. I do not have a ready answer to this problem. However, I believe we could benefit by further study of those patients that meet certain diagnostic criteria and of those that are excluded. In the long run, this may provide information which could lead to a better diagnostic system. Particularly important are those studies that have focused on prognostic signs and specific subgroups appearing to have some uniqueness. Classification systems should take such important features into account.

REFERENCES

American Psychiatric Association (APA). (1968). *Diagnostic and statistical manual of mental disorders* (2nd ed.). Washington, DC: Author.

American Psychiatric Association (APA). (1980). *Diagnostic and statistical manual of mental disorders* (3rd ed.). Washington, DC: Author.

Astrachan, B. M. *et al.* (1972). A checklist for the diagnosis of schizophrenia. *British Journal of Psychiatry, 121,* 529–539.

Beck, A. T., Ward, C. H., Mendelson, M., Mock, J. E., & Erbaugh, J. K. (1962). Reliability of psychiatric diagnoses. 2. A study of consistency of clinical judgments and ratings. *American Journal of Psychiatry, 119,* 351–357.

Cantwell, D. P., Russell, A. T., Mattison, R., & Will, L. (1979). A comparison of DSM-II and DSM-III in the diagnosis of childhood psychiatric disorders. Agreement with expected diagnosis. *Archives of General Psychiatry, 36,* 1208–1213.

Carpenter, W. T., & Strauss, J. S. (1973). Are there pathognomonic symptoms in schizophrenia? An empirical investigation of Schneider's first rank symptoms. *Archives of General Psychiatry, 28,* 847–852.

Carpenter, W. T., Strauss, J. S., & Bartko, J. J. (1973). Flexible system for diagnosis of schizophrenia: Report from the WHO International Pilot Study of Schizophrenia. *Science, 182,* 1275–1278.

Endicott, J., Nee, J., Fleiss, J., Cohen, J., Williams, J. B. W., & Simon, R. (1982). Diagnostic criteria for schizophrenia. Reliabilities and agreement between systems. *Archives of General Psychiatry, 39,* 884–889.

Feighner, J. P., Robins, E., Guze, S. B., Woodruff, R. A., Winokur, G., & Muñoz, R. (1972). Diagnostic criteria for use in psychiatric research. *Archives of General Psychiatry, 26,* 57–63.

Feinstein, A. R. (1977). A critical overview of diagnosis in psychiatry. In V. M. Rakoff, H. C. Stancer, & H. B. Kedward (Eds.), *Psychiatric diagnosis.* New York: Brunner/Mazel.

Fenton, W. S., Mosher, L. R., & Matthews, S. M. (1981). Diagnosis of schizophrenia: A critical review of current diagnostic systems. *Schizophrenia Bulletin, 7,* 452–476.

Garfield, S. L. (1978). Research problems in clinical diagnosis. *Journal of Consulting and Clinical Psychology, 46,* 596–607.

Garfield, S. L. (1983a). *Clinical psychology. The study of personality and behavior* (2nd ed.). Hawthorne, NY: Aldine.

Garfield, S. L. (1983b). Methodological problems in clinical diagnosis. In H. E. Adams & P. B. Sutker (Eds.), *Comprehensive handbook of psychopathology.* New York: Plenum Press.

Garfield, S. L., & Wittson, C. (1960). Some reactions to the revised "Manual on Terminology and Classification in Mental Retardation." *American Journal of Mental Deficiency, 64,* 951–953.

Garmezy, N. (1978). DSM-III. Never mind the psychologists; is it good for the children? *Clinical Psychologist, 31*(3 and 4), 1–6.

Gift, T., Strauss, J., Ritzler, B., Kokes, R., & Harder, D. (1980). How diagnostic concepts of schizophrenia differ. *Journal of Nervous and Mental Disease, 168,* 3–8.

Grossman, J. (Ed.). (1973). *Manual on terminology and classification in mental retardation.* Baltimore, MD: Garamond/Pridemark Press.

Heber, R. (1959). A manual on terminology and classification in mental retardation. *American Journal of Mental Deficiency, Monograph Supplement, 64,*(2).

Hunt, W. A. (1980). History and classification. In A. E. Kazdin, A. S. Bellack, & M. Hersen (Eds.), *New perspective in abnormal psychology.* New York: Oxford University Press.

Hunt, W. A., Wittson, C. L., & Hunt, E. B. (1953). A theoretical and practical analysis of the diagnostic process. In P. H. Hoch & J. Zubin (Eds.), *Current problems in psychiatric diagnosis.* New York: Grune & Stratton.

Klein, D. N. (1982). Relation between current diagnostic criteria for schizophrenia and the dimensions of premorbid adjustment, paranoid symptomatology, and chronicity. *Journal of Abnormal Psychology, 91,* 319–325.

Klorman, R., Strauss, J. S., & Kokes, R. F. (1977). Premorbid adjustment in schizophrenia, Part III. The relationship of demographic and diagnostic factors to measures of premorbid adjustment in schizophrenia. *Schizophrenia Bulletin, 3,* 214–225.

Kramer, M. (1965). Classification of mental disorders for epidemiologic and medical care purposes: Current status, problems, and needs. In M. M. Katz, J. O. Cole, & W. E. Barton

(Eds.), *The role and methodology of classification in psychiatry and psychopathology* (Public Health Serv. Publ. No. 1584) Washington, DC: U.S. Government Printing Office.

Kreitman, N. (1961). The reliability of psychiatric diagnosis. *Journal of Mental Science, 107,* 876–886.

Mattison, R., Cantwell, D. P., Russell, A. T., & Will, L. (1979). A comparison of DSM-II and DSM-III in the diagnosis of child psychiatric disorders. II. Interrater agreement. *Archives of General Psychiatry, 36,* 1217–1222.

McReynolds, W. T. (1979). DSM-III and the future of applied social science. *Professional Psychology, 10,* 123–132.

Miller, L. S., Bergstrom, D. A., Cross, H. J., & Grube, J. W. (1981). Opinions and use of the DSM system by practicing psychologists. *Professional Psychologist, 12,* 385–390.

Overall, J. E., & Hollister, L. E. (1979). Comparative evaluation of research diagnostic criteria for schizophrenia. *Archives of General Psychiatry, 36,* 1198–1205.

Pasamanick, B., Dinitz, S., & Lefton, H. (1959). Psychiatric orientation and its relation to diagnosis and treatment in a mental hospital. *American Journal of Psychiatry, 116,* 127–132.

Schacht, T., & Nathan, P. E. (1977). But is it good for the psychologists? Appraisal and status of DSM-III. *American Psychologist, 32,* 1017–1025.

Schmidt, H. O., & Fonda, C. P. (1956). The reliability of psychiatric diagnosis: A new look. *Journal of Abnormal and Social Psychology, 52,* 262–267.

Singerman, B., Stoltzman, R. K., Robins, L. N., Helzer, J. E., & Croughan, J. L. (1981). Diagnostic concordance between DSM-III, Feighner, and RDC. *Journal of Clinical Psychiatry, 42,* 422–426.

Spitzer, R. L., & Endicott, J. (1978). *Schedule for the affective disorders and schizophrenia* (3rd ed.). New York: Biometrics Research, New York State Psychiatric Institute.

Spitzer, R. L., Endicott, J., & Robins, E. (1975). Research diagnostic criteria (RDC). *Psychopharmacology Bulletin, 11,* 22–24.

Spitzer, R. L., Endicott, J., & Robins, E. (1978). *Research diagnostic criteria for a selected group of functional disorders* (3rd ed.). New York: Biometrics Research, New York State Psychiatric Institute.

Spitzer, R. L., & Fleiss, J. L. (1974). A reanalysis of the reliability of psychiatric diagnosis. *British Journal of Psychiatry, 125,* 341–347.

Spitzer, R. L., Sheehy, M., & Endicott, J. (1977). DSM-III: Guiding principles. In V. M. Rakoff, H. D. Stancer, & H. B. Kedward (Eds.), *Psychiatric diagnosis.* New York: Brunner/Mazel.

Strauss, J. S., Kokes, R. F., Klorman, R., & Sacksteder, J. L. (1977). Premorbid adjustment in schizophrenia: Concepts, measures, and implications. I. The concept of premorbid adjustment. *Schizophrenia Bulletin, 3,* 182–185.

Taylor, M. A., Greenspan, B., & Abrams, R. (1979). Lateralized neuropsychological dysfunction in affective disorder and schizophrenia. *American Journal of Psychiatry, 136,* 1031–1034.

Tsuang, M. T., & Dempsey, M. (1979). Long-term outcome of major psychoses. II. Schizoaffective disorder compared with schizophrenia, affective disorders, and a surgical control group. *Archives of General Psychiatry, 36,* 1302–1304.

Zubin, J. (1977–1978). But is it good for science? *clinical psychologist, Winter, 31*(2), 3–7.

CHAPTER 5

Diagnosis: Distinguishing among Behaviors

Kurt Salzinger

The burden of this chapter is to argue that what we need in distinguishing among behaviors is the knowledge given us by the appropriate underlying science. In order to eliminate any possible anticipatory apprehension, I will say at the outset that the appropriate science is psychology, particularly behavior theory.

In the first part of the chapter, I will present some of the failures of the new American Psychiatric Association (APA) system of classification (DSM-III). Then I will outline the kinds of behavioral information that we must have at hand before we begin to characterize behavior as "abnormal." This will be followed by a discussion of alternative ways of classifying behavior. In the next section, I will describe radical behavior theory. Finally, in the last part I will present the concept of the behavioral mechanism (Salzinger, 1980) and show how such a concept provides us with a useful method of classifying behavior.

Before fulfilling any of the promises above, however, I wish to make a few remarks on that much maligned word, "behavior." Everybody studies behavior, or as W. N. Schoenfeld used to say in his Learning Seminars at Columbia, "We are all behaviorists." The point is not to make some imperialistic pronouncement here; rather, it is to reason with the reader and to impress on him or her that whether we talk about action, emotion, or thought, our referent is always behavior. Now sometimes we stay close to it when describing what "ails" the patient and sometimes we stray so far away that it is hard indeed to find the referent behavior that gave rise to the

Kurt Salzinger. Department of Social Sciences, Polytechnic Institute of New York, Brooklyn, New York, and New York State Psychiatric Institute, New York, New York.

interviewer statement about the patient, but always, I maintain, we assert that our statements about the patient are inspired by his or her behavior.

What is often referred to as interpretation—psychoanalytic or any other kind—is what has given rise to much of the debate raging in this field. The interpreters among us say with pride that they are not content to deal with mere behavior, whereas the behaviorists maintain that they want to measure what is there, not what the observer believes must underlie the behavior. This discussion requires that we shed our prejudices and simply try to determine exactly what it is that the two camps are trying to do. First, those who interpret insist that interpret is what all of us do, and they are right. Before everybody jumps on me and calls me an enlightened behaviorist, however, implying that others of us are not, let me explain that behaviorists also interpret, if we mean by "interpret" that we define behaviors functionally rather than topographically. I should add here that I am not trying to represent all kinds of behaviorists—partial, unconfirmed, cognitive, or reformed behavioristic. I speak here only from the point of view of a radical behaviorist (Skinner, 1974).

Now why do I say that it is right to describe a behaviorist's observation as interpretation? Because we do not describe an action by restricting ourselves to surveying the responding limb's anatomy or its force. We describe behavior in terms of its consequences. Those responses that have the same consequence are considered to be members of the same response class. For example, all the responses that are followed by a mother feeding her baby are members of the same response class and therefore can be considered to be the same in terms of that criterion. This is where we interpret, or put another way, where we go beyond the single observation of a particular behavior. Having clarified a frequent and serious misinterpretation of the behavioral approach, we are ready to speak of the failings of DSM-III.

Some of What DSM-III Has Failed to Do

1. Although much has been made of a changing orientation in the new diagnostic system, from being theory infested to being truly Baconian, that is, empirical, it is simply not so. The fact that the official book states it is theory-free means that it is dutifully repeated and means that people might be taken unawares. At least earlier on, everybody knew that theory directed the kind of classification system being set up here. The present system is a little like selling cigarettes without stating the warning about the health hazards incurred when smoking.

What are the theoretical underpinnings of DSM-III? They are the basic medical assumptions about abnormal behavior: that it represents a sign or a symptom, that it is part of a "mental" disorder, that the signs are objective (presumably observed by the examiner) indicators, and that the symptoms are the subjective complaints by the patient. This is not simply a classification empirically arrived at. It is based on a theory that signs and symptoms are not important in and of themselves, but that we must look for some underlying cause, which in the current scene means a biochemical one or (still) a concept such as "anxiety." The point here is that in classifying behavior, we must listen to the oft repeated argument by anthropologists that we will better understand our own culture by learning about the different assumptions made by cultures alien to our own. It is then that we learn that things need not be done as we "always" have done them because they are so "natural" and "obvious." So as still another introductory but critical remark here, it is important for the reader to become aware of the many different ways in which one can classify behavior and that no matter what method we ultimately use, each has a theory underlying it. Thus, I repeat, DSM-III is not empirical. To the degree that the authors of this classification system were interested in producing an empirical system, they have failed.

2. Another argument given for DSM-III is its usefulness in communicating with other mental health personnel. Yet this justification for the new DSM is hard to reconcile with the fact that the APA had representation on the committee responsible for the creation of an international system when it started its work, and still the APA went its own way. In addition, it needs to be underlined that communication does not take place merely for the sake of trading war stories, but presumably for conveying information about the usefulness of a particular treatment with a particular kind of patient. The critical question then is, does this system of classification allow mental health experts to communicate with one another? The answer right now is not yet in. I do not believe that we know, except perhaps in some very obvious cases where any layperson could recognize the symptoms and signs we are responding to. As far as the complex system of "any one from A and any two from B with none from C," and so forth, we simply do not as yet know whether the substitutability is functional. Such substitutability is an empirical problem, one that behaviorists have long been wrestling with in such complex areas as language behavior (Salzinger, 1967). It is not obvious that the patterns of behavior that constitute the many combinations of selections from the various categories are reproducible.

Let us look at an example of a pattern that may seem somewhat frivolous, but that still makes the point. Supose we were interested in drawing the conclusion that someone's appearance was deteriorating. Assume we were making use of the following "facts." A patient comes into the examination room wearing very old brown shoes, a wrinkled suit, eyeglasses not quite clean, and dirty fingernails. It is clear that such signs might be substitutable for one another only under certain circumstances. Their meaning would clearly be different if the person involved were a blue-collar or a white-collar worker, rich or poor, from one social class or another, from one ethnic group or another, if he had slept all night on the train, or had just come to work, and so forth. Similar arguments can be made concerning symptoms. Analogously, is it reasonable to give equal weight to neologisms, loose associations, poverty of speech, and so on, in arriving at the conclusion of thought disorder? Should we not react differently if the person is foreign born, lower class, or without sleep before the interview? Add to this that whereas we agree on what constitutes old shoes, a wrinkled suit, and dirty fingernails, we find such concepts as "loose associations" more elusive.

The list of criteria which now forms a part of the diagnostic procedure is no doubt an improvement, but it is not a solution to the problem of reliable, never mind valid, diagnosis. The criteria are hypotheses to be tested (assuming one accepts the basic assumptions of this model in the first place). An improvement in communication is to be expected only if the definitions involved are functional, that is, if they are related to the conditions under which the patient's behavior is emitted. Without knowledge of those conditions, one is not communicating all of the relevant information. Again, notice that interpreters (dynamic, psychoanalytic, or what have you) would say that description of behavior alone does not say anything about the meaning of the behavior in question. Behaviorists behave similarly. They speak of the functional definitions of behavior. What looks like hallucinations may after all consist of someone talking on the telephone or practicing for a part in a play or even role playing for an important encounter. Later on, we will specify how one arrives at functional definitions of behavior.

3. In medical school, prospective physicians get a grounding in the basic sciences, we are told. And so they do—in biochemistry and anatomy, but very little happens when they talk of behavior. Here what they get is that same old nineteenth-century psychology that talked of "will" and other long rejected concepts of warmed over psychology which the teaching psychiatrists got when they were in medical school. But psychology, like other fields, has made some important discoveries in this century, not to speak of more recent discoveries in this decade or year. The description of thought disorder in schizophrenic patients is perhaps a good example of the appeal to outdated concepts. The description of schizophrenia includes the concept of "loosening" of associations, forgetting entirely a whole range of new concepts available in the area of psycholinguistics which have produced new theories of language and thought and new methods of studying them. The same holds for other areas of psychology. Some relevant research has been done with animals and with normal human beings, but some has been performed with exactly the kinds of patients that the DSM purports to describe. Let us look at one more outstanding example of omission of fields of knowledge in constructing the new DSM. Two new axes of DSM-III are the severity of psychosocial stressors and the highest level of adaptive functioning. These new ways of describing patients were at least in part stimulated by research in this area, and yet DSM-III makes no mention of such obvious tools of measurement as the lists of stressful life events (Dohrenwend & Dohrenwend, 1982), which provide ways of characterizing the social environment. Instead, keeping to the tradition of using yesteryear's concepts, it employs an

8-point rating scale to characterize the severity of psychosocial stressors. DSM-III follows that up by using the same kind of scale to speak of the highest level of adaptive functioning despite the fact that for years we have had available empirically established socioeconomic levels and occupational levels in handbooks listing occupations in an encyclopedic manner. In sum, this failing can be described as the deliberate ignoring of entire fields of knowledge that could have provided precision of measurement and eventually validity. Certainly this cannot be achieved using the primitive tools now employed.

4. DSM-III fails to pay attention to the methodological problems raised by any complicated system of classification, never mind by a system that has distinguished itself by its low level of reliability in the past. The judgments that are required from those who are to render the diagnoses are stated in so matter-of-fact a tone that one might think that anybody even half motivated to obtain the information could do so with ease. In fact, the magnitude of the problem of making diagnoses is at least as great with respect to obtaining the information on which to base the required judgment as is the system of classification itself. There are two primary problems: The first is how to obtain the necessary information on which to base one's judgment (Salzinger, 1959, 1978), and the second is how to assess and combine the information once it has been obtained to render that diagnostic judgment. In that regard, Millon (1981) has pointed out that the system has not made up its mind as to whether to label categorically (which it does for the most part) or along a dimension.

The first problem, that of deciding how to obtain the information, is troubled by the fact that the diagnostician must trust the information provided by the very person who in some obvious contexts is not to be trusted. The patient may, for example, be suffering from hallucinations and delusions that would make him or her less than a trustworthy informant. This is more than a bootstrap operation and considerably less than reliable information.

Another problem is produced by the fact that the interviewer can be influenced by any number of outside factors, such as his or her theory of functioning or the prejudice held against or for the ethnic, sexual, or socioeconomic group to which the patient belongs, to actually modify the very thing which is supposed to be only observed (Salzinger & Pisoni, 1958, 1960, 1961). What is more, the complications involved are many. First is the degree to which the patient changes his or her behavior as a function of the kinds of responses that the interviewer reinforces. Second, however, is the degree of conditionability of the patient which varies as a function of his or her history and possibly as a function of the particular constellation of behaviors that we characterize as the patient's disorder. In a study on the relationship of rate of conditioning to outcome of schizophrenia, we found that the higher the rate of conditionability, the shorter the number of days that patients spent in a hospital (Salzinger, Portnoy, & Feldman, 1966). This study makes it clear that the effect of interviewer influence on the very process he or she would like to observe is even more complicated than the fact of mere influence because that influence interacts with the patient's influenceability. These, then, are the factors that would affect the diagnosis made by the mental health expert. Ignoring them in the makeup of any diagnostic system is foolhardy, since such factors can indeed make even a good system of classification fail.

One method recently employed to get around the problem of the influence of the interviewer has been the structured interview. Although these interviews make some attempt to control the questions asked and sometimes even the wording, they have nothing to say about the reinforcement contingencies and thus are clearly inadequate in controlling any interviewer influence. We must add to this the fact that most interviewers are quite unaware of reinforcer effects, and because of that, this influence is even more pernicious than the more obvious one of how questions are asked. By well-placed reinforcements, even though not intentionally placed there, the interviewer can make the verbal content and the nonverbal responses increase or decrease and thus the very behavior on the basis of which one is supposed to decide somebody's diagnosis.

Assuming that somehow we have solved the problems of obtaining the information from the patient in an objective way, we are left with the problem of how that information is used by the interviewer. The interviewer obviously is reacting to the appearance and general behavior of the patient as well as to his or her background characteristics, all of which will color the intake of information. In addition, the interviewer does not generally take notes, never mind tape-recording the interview. A fallible memory in combination with an inadequate set of instructions on exactly how to obtain and weigh different kinds of information cannot lend much reliability to the resulting diagnosis. DSM-III, although having the advantage of a list of criteria, nevertheless describes the patient in such a vague way as to invite differing responses from different diagnosticians. The description of thought disorder in schizophrenia alluded to above provides a good example: "loosening of associations, in which ideas shift from one subject to another completely unrelated or only obliquely related subject, without the speaker showing any awareness that the topics are unconnected" (DSM-III, p. 182). A whole series of critical terms are left undefined: "ideas," "ideas shifting," "subjects completely unrelated" and "obliquely related," "awareness," "showing awareness," "topic" (the latter term apparently being used as a synonym for idea). And this is but one sentence in a long book with many vague or at least undefined terms being repeatedly used. It is an improved manual compared to the preceding ones, but it is not improved enough.

5. Another important gap in DSM-III, and a surprising one at that, is ethics in diagnosis. No mention is made of any consideration of possible abuse of diagnostic procedures, and this in the face of such actual abuses, not only in other countries but even in this country. The APA has certainly been

aware of this problem vis-à-vis Russian psychiatry. In addition, we clearly need to worry about the biasing effects of the patient's social standing, gender, ethnic group membership, and so on, in interfering with an objective kind of diagnostic process. How do we make judgments of Axis V of occupational productivity without taking into account the patient's ethnic group membership? The answer does not come easily. However, not saying anything at all about this is not an answer either.

This then constitutes a brief summary of some of the difficulties in DSM-III. Further development of some of these criticisms and others is to be found in many places (e.g., Eysenck, Wakefield, & Friedman, 1983; Salzinger, 1978). The point of this chapter will be not to scoff at DSM-III, but rather to suggest the foundations of other systems of classifications that are more likely to be helpful in eventually applying appropriate treatment to patients.

Another System of Classification

The object of this chapter will be to explain how radical behavior theory can be the basis of a better system for classifying human behavior than the currently accepted system. However, to make this point more generally, I will provide another example of how one can classify behavior based on a different theoretical orientation in order to show the reader that more than one adequate system exists for classifying behavior. In general, one can say that a lack of theory to back up a system of classification is not a virtue; in fact, it is hard to see how such a system could ever exist. What we need is a system that has some basis in fact *and* in theory—meaning that the theory serves to explain at least some set of facts adequately.

Ethologists provide an excellent example of classification, one that has been long revered as a way of categorizing animals and plants. Ethologists have been interested in classifying the behavior of organisms along similar lines. Using Darwin's principle of adaptation, Scott (1956) proposed a classification for the analysis of the behavior involved in the social organization of different animals. The categories of this system are as follows:

1. Contactual Behavior. Clearly this is one of the most basic ways of describing the behavior of various animals, and clearly it can be used to describe the behavior of human beings also. Such behavior ranges from actual physical contact through communication by gesture and speech and culminates through such other forms of communication at a distance as letters and messages brought through others.

2. Ingestive Behavior. The importance of the intake of food is obvious for human infants; equally clear is the importance of that process in the establishment of early social relations. It continues to be critical as a class of

behavior in the way in which people overeat and undereat, sometimes to the extent of endangering their health.

3. Eliminative Behavior. This particular function sometimes goes awry in various psychiatric disorders. It has also been prominent in theories of psychopathology, particularly with respect to the formation of personality, to take but one example.

4. Sexual Behavior. In the study of animals, this function includes courtship as well as copulation; the significance of sexual behavior in human beings need not be elaborated for an audience of mental health workers because of the use of that behavior as a cornerstone in some theories of psychopathology, and because it is a form of behavior which in its own right sometimes becomes disordered.

5. Epimeletic Behavior. This form of behavior is often referred to as maternal behavior; it consists essentially of giving care and attention. Grooming behavior is a good example of this class of behavior in animals. Among human beings such behavior, that is, the caretaking behavior, has recently been given more attention in the discussions of social support networks. Their role is obviously important with respect to prevention and amelioration of abnormal behavior.

6. Et-epimeletic Behavior. This is the counterpart of the above class of behavior. It is the kind of behavior that evokes care from others. Such behavior is very obvious in human beings when they are infants. In adults, it is perhaps best displayed as one form of coping behavior.

7. Agonistic Behavior. This form of behavior has in recent years been given a great deal of attention in our society. It refers to behavior in which animals are in conflict with one another. This includes fighting, escape, and passive behavior. This is particularly interesting given the concept of passive aggression in the abnormal literature.

8. Allelomimetic Behavior. This label describes behavior in concert, as is displayed in schools of fishes or flocks of birds. Group-coordinated behavior is also to be found among human beings when they are in crowds or in smaller groups in which they stimulate one another to produce behavior quite different from that displayed when they are alone.

9. Investigative Behavior. When an animal is placed in a new environment, it engages in exploratory behavior. Such a class of behavior is never mentioned with respect to psychopathology. Is asocial behavior perhaps an example of behavior emitted in the absence of exploring what is appropriate in different environments?

10. Territoriality. Animals manifest this kind of behavior by staking out the boundaries of their territory. To some degree students of human behavior have been using this concept as a kind of metaphor. On the other hand, one can see a rather close resemblance between the animal concept of territoriality and the concept that seems to explain the boundaries people set about their environment to prevent its invasion by other people.

The above is an example of a system that classifies behavior. It is useful to ethologists. I am not suggesting that it should necessarily be embraced for the classification of abnormal behavior. On the other hand, I do wish to point to other systems of classifying behavior that have been useful in classifying the behavior of other living organisms and that, because they are founded in a basic science, have a good deal to be said for them. In this case, Darwin's concept of adaptation gives this system a generality that the present psychiatric system does not have. The present psychiatric system is based on common-sense empirical notions much overlayed with a theory of disease that has not been informed as to the variables that control behavior. What is interesting about this situation is that DSM-III is not based on one of the relevant basic sciences. Those sciences that deal with behavior—ethology, psychology, sociology, and anthropology—are very much ignored in DSM-III. The point here is not so much to convince the reader of the advantage of selecting the above system as a way of classifying abnormal behavior; rather, it is to show that sciences do exist that could at least form a beginning for a better way of classifying abnormal behavior than now exists. The remainder of this chapter will be dedicated to persuading the reader of the wisdom of embracing behavioral analysis as a way of determining what is wrong with patients and how to help them.

What Is a Behavioral Analysis?

A full answer to this question rightfully requires a book rather than a few paragraphs. Here I will only sketch out an answer.

To begin with, let me say that this kind of analysis has been successfully applied to discovering what happens in the course of the diagnostic interview itself (Salzinger, 1978). Behavior analysis is useful not only for learning to understand the behavior of the patient, but also for understanding the behavior of the interviewer/diagnostician. Here the purpose is not to analyze DSM-III or its cognates. The purpose of this chapter is to examine what a behavioral analysis sans medical model diagnosis can do in furthering our understanding of patients and ways of aiding them.

Let us first look at the reinforcement contingency:

$$S^D \ldots R \rightarrow S^R$$

where S^D is the discriminative stimulus, that is, the occasion on which a particular class of responses is reinforced, R is the class of responses, and S^R is the reinforcing stimulus, that is, a consequence of behavior that increases the frequency of occurrence of the behavior it follows.

Each part of the reinforcement contingency is critical to an explanation of behavior. The S^D, for example, makes it clear not only that there are occasions on which behavior is reinforced, but others on which no reinforcement is forthcoming. In addition, the likelihood of reinforcement differs from one occasion to another, and the particular S^D signals the schedule in effect. The schedules may differ, for example, in having a reinforcement contingency dependent on the number of responses emitted versus having a contingency dependent on the occurrence of at least one response plus the passage of some minimal period of time. In sum, the S^D is very important because it exerts control over behavior by being presented to the person being studied. The kind of control it exerts is dependent on the reinforcement history of the person, thus often explaining why different people behave differently in the presence of the same stimulus.

This brings us quite close to the notion of appropriateness of behavior, a concept which is useful for talking about "normality." The advantage of the S^D is that it provides us with a concept of greater generality than does "appropriateness." Our behavior varies radically as a function of the discriminative stimuli that act on us. This is quite obvious when we compare our behavior when lecturing to a group of students to our behavior when engaged in play with a 3-year-old. Indeed, when our behavior is the same under these varying circumstances, we know that something is wrong. Also interesting about all of this is the fact that we do not need to say to ourselves, "Look, you are now interacting with a 3-year-old; don't lecture to him." Many other kinds of behavior are generated by different S^Ds, such as how we behave in the water, on the gym floor, sitting at a desk, playing chess, standing in a subway, running after a cat, operating a lathe, making love, meeting a new person, or seeing a friend. This flexibility in behaving differently on different occasions is undoubtedly, as already pointed out, a mark of being normal. On the other hand, it should be equally obvious that the person whose behavior varies completely with such discriminative stimuli would also be considered to be abnormal, perhaps psychopathic. Even in the layperson's sense, a person whose behavior is governed entirely and solely by current stimuli (i.e., being uninfluenced by other possibly conflicting reinforcement contingencies) could not be trusted to carry out many tasks and could not therefore be trusted to provide one with the reinforcements that govern the observers' (the others') behavior.

Let us look at some examples of such behavior. You strike a bargain with a woman to buy her house in a week at a certain price. Five minutes later, another potential buyer enters offering a higher price and she strikes the same bargain with that person, cutting you out of the deal. You would either accuse her of being a crook or a "sick" person. Another example might be a man telling you, "You are the most beautiful woman in the world," followed by his saying the very same thing, in your presence, to another woman. Still another example, and one we are unfortunately less and less surprised at, might be a politician promising more welfare to a group of the poor and less welfare to a group of corporation executives. The point is that, in general, behavior has lawfulness matching the reinforcement contingencies signaled by the S^D. The form that lawfulness takes depends on our particular reinforcement history. When the discriminative control that we observe in other individuals does not match ours, then we begin to act in a variety of ways that typically cause a change in the person's behavior. When we are unsuccessful in producing that change, then we resort to various more extreme moves such as ostracizing or merely avoiding such people, jailing them, or putting them in mental hospitals.

Of course, there can be other aberrations in the S^D. . . R relationship, for example, that relationship might simply be a very weak one, or the same S^D might control different responses at different times. One must be very careful here not to conclude that the relationship is unreliable when an S^D controlling the behavior in question is simply one that the observer had not noticed before. Nevertheless, unreliable control by S^Ds is quite common when one considers the behavior of children. The extent to which such an unreliable relationship also characterizes what we call abnormal behavior is a matter for investigation.

Let us now look at the response in our equation, R. The first point to be noted about the concept of response is that, contrary to the calumny so often directed at a behavioristic approach, it is not at all atomistic. When we speak of response in the reinforcement contingency relationship, we are actually talking about a response class. The definition of that class is a functional one, that is, it is based on an empirical investigation of which responses follow the same time course as a function of the same stimuli. Sometimes the topography of these response members is the same, but more often than not the members of a response class differ in topography. The interested reader is directed to look at the problem of a response class in the area of verbal behavior (Salzinger, 1967) for a more detailed discussion and good example of the complexity of this problem. One implication of all this is that we cannot always know beforehand which responses are members of which response class. In many cases we must first engage in an empirical investigation.

Response class membership may vary from one S^D to another and also from one S^R contingency to another, even for a given individual. This added complexity cannot be glossed over; it is a critical aspect of a correct behavioral analysis of why a particular individual behaves in particular ways in particular situations. Thus, the critical question of whether a person's agressive verbal behavior portends his or her aggressive nonverbal, especially violent behavior depends on whether or not the verbal responses are members of the same response class as the physical responses. In some cases, possibly correlated to the person's membership in particular ethnic groups, they are members of the same class, whereas in others they are in different classes. We must also remember that all members of a particular class are not equally strong members of that class. Some responses are members of several response classes, with varying probabilities of occurrence depending on the particular response class being controlled at that time. For some people, then, violent physical and verbal behavior might be equally strong members of the class of aggression; for others, verbal responses might be highly probable and the physical considerably less so.

We return here once again to note that the idea of "meaning" of behavior, which is so central to the psychoanalytic approach, has an analogue in the concept of response class and its control. Without having to invoke the concept of overcompensation, we can point out that in some individuals flattering might well constitute a member of the same response class as vilifying, or in some cases, hitting. Indeed, it appears to be the custom in some cultures to first flatter those that are later unmercifully criticized. Here we have a nexus of cultural and idiosyncratic variables possibly producing the same effect. As the reader must have noticed, the concept of response class is indeed very complicated rather than constituting a simple atomistic approach. We need only to reiterate here that it never makes sense to examine any responses without knowing at the same time what controlling stimuli are acting on them.

This brings us directly to the last part of the reinforcement contingency, namely, the S^R. It would be well at the outset to point out that what constitutes a reinforcing stimulus to one person does not necessarily do so for others and that, as with S^Ds, it depends on the individual's particular reinforcement history. Some reinforcers are of course primary ones and thus may well be universal and predictable. It turns out, however, that even primary reinforcers, those that do not require any conditioning to have reinforcing properties, still can and do acquire conditioned reinforcer properties. People's reactions to the reinforcers of sex and food differ quite a bit. In some individuals they are negative rather than positive, in others they appear to have but a minimal reinforcing value altogether.

The examples are quite obvious from the point of view of abnormal behavior. Some people stay away from sexual stimulation that is normally supposed to be positively reinforcing, some people obviously do not find food positively reinforcing, some find only certain kinds of foods positively reinforcing, some find particular foods negatively reinforcing, and so on. Clearly, even though we might well start out with the same universal reinforcers, it does not take long before we are changed by the conditioning history that we undergo.

When it comes to nonprimary reinforcers, it should be obvious that the variation from person to person is truly very large, depending almost wholly on the conditioning history of the individual. When we speak of fetishes, we are then paying tribute to a special conditioning history. It is probably an unusual history we are talking about in that most of us do not have fetishes; on the other hand, one can imagine how such conditioning could have taken place to produce the particular problem. Other kinds of "minority" reinforcers are not labeled abnormal; for example, some people collect special kinds of paintings or plates or stamps; when one begins to talk of collecting insects in ways other than, say, pinning butterflies up on a board, the authorities begin to become suspicious and talk of eccentricities that might well turn into "abnormal" labels. Some negative reinforcers (i.e., negative for most of us) are deemed to be signs of masochism or sadism. In our society, it is probably safe to say that for most of us the delivery as well as the receipt of physical pain constitutes a negative reinforcer, that is, an event from which one escapes or which one avoids. But once more, it does not take much imagination to picture how such events can become positive reinforcers.

With this general introduction to reinforcers, we will now provide some definitions that should make it clear that we are not merely talking about reward and punishment or about feedback. First, it is necessary to realize that we must talk about three basic concepts: punishment, positive reinforcement, and negative reinforcement. Punishment is a stimulus which reduces the frequency of the response it follows by suppressing it. It follows from this statement that what is meant, except in the case of traumatic punishment, is that the behavior that fails to occur after the delivery of punishment will come back in and of itself simply with the passage of time. In other words, the effect of punishment generally does not alter behavior in a lasting fashion.

The concept of reinforcement is quite different. A reinforcer is an event that strengthens behavior in a lasting fashion. A positive reinforcer is usually defined as a stimulus that strengthens the behavior that produces it; a negative reinforcer, on the other hand, is an event that strengthens the behavior that eliminates or prevents it from occurring. Notice that we are defining reinforcement in terms of strengthening responses both in the cases of positive and negative reinforcement. In other words, negative reinforcement and punishment are not the same phenomenon at all. Note also that the term "strengthen" refers to the particular reinforcement contingency in effect. For example, the usual contingency is to make the S^R contingent on the rate of response; usually that means that the S^R produces an increase in response rate, but one can also make the reinforcement contingent on a decrease in response rate or on a particular rate of response, such as speaking in rhythm, dancing, or engaging in other behavior in a certain temporal order. The reinforcement contingency can also concern any other particular aspect of the response such as its strength, its speed, to whom it is to be directed, in the presence of which stimulus it is to be emitted, and its content.

One more general concept must be discussed and that is "intermittency." It turns out that although a certain number of initial reinforcements must occur on a continuous basis, once this period has gone by, then intermittent reinforcement produces behavior that is stronger than behavior that is only continuously reinforced. This is, of course, one of the critical discoveries about behavior. In "real" life, reinforcement usually does not come on a continuous basis, or at least not for long. Given that condition, it becomes crucial to show what effect this intermittency has on behavior. And the answer is that such behavior is stronger than behavior that is continuously reinforced. A good example of intermittently reinforced behavior is shown in the phenomenon of temper tantrums displayed in infants. The inexperienced caretaker often responds to such crying by checking whether everything is all right only *some* of the time (if we assume that coming to a baby that is left alone otherwise is positively reinforcing, then we have a case of intermittent reinforcement), thus defeating his or her own goal of getting the baby to go to sleep. We can cite a benign effect of intermittent reinforcement in its production of perseverance in problem-solving tasks.

One measure of the strength of behavior is its resistance to extinction. Extinction occurs when behavior is no longer reinforced, as would have happened in the case above if the caretaker had stopped checking the baby. Extinction produces the following effects: emotional behavior, an initial increase in frequency and strength of behavior formerly reinforced, and eventually a reduction in the earlier reinforced response with a concomitant increase in variability of behavior. It follows from this description that the occurrence of increased variability in behavior ought to make the observer look for a recent period of extinction. To make such a judgment, it becomes obvious one must know something about the behavior occurring not only at the time of observation, but at the period preceding it.

This becomes a good place to dispense with another stereotype about behavior theory, namely, that behaviorists are interested only in the current situation. This is not true. As we just illustrated with extinction, one finds out about current contingencies acting on behavior by examining the route by which the current behavior came to be here at this time. Sometimes knowing that past is not useful, but one can make that judgment only after examining that past. A slight demurrer is necessary here, namely, that we are not talking about the distant past which cannot usually be accurately ascertained, nor is it likely to have an effect on current behavior.

The Behavioral Mechanism

In a recent paper (Salzinger, 1980), I suggested that what the area of abnormal psychology needs is to work out the behavioral mechanisms for the various aberrations that we observe in abnormal psychology. The behavioral mechanism points out the particular relationships that are responsible for particular aberrations. For example, an outburst of emotion can be a function of an aversive stimulus presentation. That stimulus can be a conditioned aversive stimulus or a primary aversive stimulus (one that requires no conditioning to be aversive), the withdrawal of a positive reinforcement, or extinction, to give but three examples. In a paper (Salzinger, 1975) in which I referred to this phenomenon as models for abnormal behavior, there are other conditioning paradigms showing how various abnormal behaviors could be engendered. Here I will only talk about the behavioral mechanism that I have posited to explain the behavior we refer to as schizophrenic (Salzinger, 1984).

The behavioral mechanism in question is called the immediacy hypothesis. It states that schizophrenic behavior is in large part determined by stimuli that are immediate in the environment of the patient. Clearly anyone responding to stimuli which are immediate must do so at the expense of the more remote ones and is bound to run into trouble in our society. In the cited paper, I showed how the various symptoms of schizophrenia could be produced by a condition such as the preponderant control by immediate stimuli in the person's environment.

Let us look at some examples of the kinds of behaviors usually associated with schizophrenia and let us determine whether the immediacy hypothesis, as a behavioral mechanism, would be capable of producing such behavior. Bizarre delusions in which the basic idea is obviously absurd, such as believing that one's thoughts are being broadcast widely, constitute one example. Such a belief rests on taking things out of context. The immediate stimulus in this case might be somebody anticipating what one is about to say (on the basis of what had been said before or what somebody else indicated he or she would say); responding to the context, that is, to nonimmediate stimuli, would soon have clarified what really happened. In addition, responding preponderantly to immediate stimuli might lead that person to confront others with that idea, thus getting them to respond with incredulity and in less than a friendly manner. Responding to one's thoughts as if they were broadcast may also reflect an inability to discriminate what one says from what one thinks. Clearly, those two have in common self-generation of verbal behavior; in thought it presumably is subvocal behavior, whereas in talk (broadcast) it is vocal behavior. Given the similarity of vocal and subvocal behavior and the tendency to respond to the immediate stimulus, one can see how there can be confusion of the two.

Hallucinations appear to be subject to a similar interpretation. Gould (1948, 1949, 1950) showed that patients complaining of hearing voices were in fact engaging in subvocal behavior, sometimes measurable only by means of an instrument, but sometimes audible to the naked ear, since in some cases it consisted of whispering. In other words, hallucinations also appear to be a function of an inability to discriminate the difference between either thinking or talking to oneself as opposed to someone else talking. Again, the response to the immediate stimulus makes it more likely that the person would confuse the two, since the immediate aspect of speech is the same, at least to the ear, whether it comes from one's own mouth or that of another source.

Incoherence is another characteristic ascribed to schizophrenic behavior. Here too we can talk about responding to immediate stimuli in a preponderant way as providing the mechanism for a class of abnormal behavior. Normally, verbal behavior requires the speaker (and the hearer) to respond to long strings of responses and to have those long strings act as S^Ds for further verbal behavior. However, when the speaker responds primarily to immediate stimuli, that is, to the last word or words only, that would lead to the kind of incoherence so often remarked about. This is so because having words relate only to the last word or even two or three words within a sentence would lead one to the kinds of statistical approximations to English that Miller and Selfridge (1950) generated. One does have the feeling that it should make sense because, for the most part, it is grammatically correct; the short strings over which these relationships pertain, however, make this meaning limited indeed.

What are the implications of the above? We are able to posit a route by means of which particular behavioral aberrations might arrive, that is, the behavioral mechanism by which they are created. When we know how they are created, we can investigate how they will interact with other variables, ranging from the biochemical to the anthropological. Thus, for example, if we accept the immediacy hypothesis as representing the behavioral mechanism for schizophrenic behavior, we can then speculate how such a person would respond to reinforcement which was much delayed. Clearly, if there are other consequences, those that intervene between the response and the delayed reinforcement would control the behavior. Such a tendency is also there for normal individuals, but it would be exaggerated for those with the immediacy tendency.

People who respond to immediate stimuli would have difficulty making themselves understood, as we already noted. They would respond to stimuli out of context, since in some important sense responding to immediate stimuli almost constitutes an operational definition of responding out of context. They would have difficulty responding to jokes and other abstract material. They would tend to respond to stimuli that were current at the expense of those that were past and, thus, one would expect faster extinction (Salzinger & Pisoni, 1960). At the same time, one might expect them to be better at puns and to be better able to concentrate on tasks requiring behavior that is controlled by immediate stimuli only. If they had jobs that did not oblige them to respond in obvious ways to remote stimuli, then one would forecast that in that subculture, they would survive quite well. One can also see that such inclinations would tend to be overlooked in children in whom one does not expect as much responding to remote stimuli as in adults.

It is also instructive to consider how responding in this manner would interact with therapeutic techniques. Indeed, it becomes clear why token economies based on immediate reinforcement work so well in controlling the behavior of the most regressed schizophrenics. It suggests that one should make use of behavioral prosthetic devices which extend the time or bring closer the stimuli that are important to control the behavior of those people. It suggests also that we ought to condition such people, if at all possible, to respond to increasingly more remote stimuli.

A behavioral mechanism allows one to create order in the jumble of symptoms that one otherwise has to consider in making a diagnosis. Perhaps even more important, the approach of discovering the behavioral mechanism to explain the behavior in question allows one to classify behavior as being caused through a particular route of action. It does not imply that the cause is environmental or genetic; indeed, it remains quite neutral with respect to that. The tendency to respond to immediate stimuli could be genetic and biochemically controlled through, say, the increased amount of dopamine present at the synapses. That greater amount could be caused genetically, through drugs, through some conditioning procedure of long standing, or through a sudden appearance of an S^D that has been powerful in other contexts. In fact, the same behavior might be a function of different behavioral mechanisms. Note that this is not like saying that we want to find out what the underlying disease is for a range of symptoms. Rather, this is a way of analyzing for the behavioral mechanisms that intervene between the cause (biological, environmental) and the resulting abnormal behavior.

Given that the same behavior could have been produced through entirely different mechanisms, the implication is that they would point toward different causes and therefore toward different treatments, whether we are talking about biological, verbal, or behavioral. The implication of the concept of behavioral mechanism is also that what we must classify is not behaviors—a point we started with—or people—another point made early on—but rather the behavioral mechanism through which the undesirable behavior came about and/or by which it is now being maintained. This approach would allow us to look for different routes to explain various aberrant behaviors or to find the same routes for them, depending on our findings regarding the behavioral mechanism through which the behavior occurs.

Clearly, one can see that incoherence could be caused through the mechanism of an inadequate vocabulary, as is sometimes found in foreign speakers; some words may be misused and certain sentence structures might be translated literally by a person conversant in one language to another, producing nonidiomatic speech and a lack of understanding in the new language. German sentence structure in English was, in fact, used by Mark Twain to produce a humorous rendition of English. Responding to immediate stimuli only (as posited for schizophrenia) is, of course, still another mechanism by which incoherence could be produced. One could also think of incoherence in depressed individuals. The mechanism of the production of incoherence here might be the paucity of speech. For people in a manic state, the mechanism for incoherence might involve the speed with which they speak. Because of the speed with which they act and speak, they might well be unable to respond to what they had said before, with the consequence that their successive responses would not be related to one another. Indeed, the recent suggestion that manic patients are like schizophrenics in incoherence of language is exactly the kind of interpretation that could be clarified by the use of the concept of the behavioral mechanism. For behavior that has already been shown to be quite different in different cases, the behavioral mechanism would be able to distinguish those cases from one another before having to resort to, say, the delivery of different kinds of somatotherapy to distinguish between the behaviors produced through different behavioral mechanisms.

The final question that one might want to ask about behavioral mechanisms as a way of classifying behavioral aberrations is whether this is a substitute for the currrent system of diagnosis. The answer at the moment must be "not yet," since this approach is simply in the form of a suggested program rather than a system. On the other hand, one would think it would be useful to have it operate at the same time as the current DSM system. By allowing the two different systems to compete with one another, one can then select between them on the basis of data rather than conjecture. The way in which one can now proceed is to use both the deductive and the empirical method to determine what single or small number of possible mechanisms could produce the kind of behavior that is of interest.

It needs to be stressed that the behavioral mechanism responsible for the initial production of the aberrant behavior need not be the same one that is currently maintaining the behavior. Take, for example, the child that cries regularly in the middle of the night. In the beginning, this behavior may have been produced by a medical condition that required a caretaker to come in and minister to the baby. This particular sequence of events can, as all behavior therapists will recognize, produce conditioning of the crying response if the entry of the caretaker is a positive reinforcer. If the caretaker continues to respond to the crying of the baby even when there is no longer any medical need, then we have the behavioral mechanism of the caretaker reinforcing the crying behavior as a very simple and direct explanation of the behavior. What is more, we have a way of eliminating such aberrant behavior by extinction and/or some other methods which we need not go into here.

As mentioned, I have written about this topic before under the heading of models of abnormal behavior (Salzinger, 1975). There I showed how different abnormal behaviors might have been started in various ways. Emotional behavior could result, to take one example, from extinction, from operant reinforcement applied to the emotional behavior, from primary aversive stimulation, from a conditioned aversive stimulus, or from a combination of these behavioral mechanisms. This makes clear that a great deal of both deductive and inductive work needs to be done to determine which particular behavioral mechanism is responsible for which particular aberrant behavior. A good deal of the deductive work has been completed in that behavior theory already has many interesting paradigms.

The next step is to apply those behavioral mechanisms to the problem behaviors. I will make no attempt here to map out how one comes by this information. That would be a paper or a book in itself. However, it is sufficient to say that one would do best if one could observe the behavior in question; if that is impossible, then obviously the interview—structured if at all possible—and checking with people other than the person in trouble, together with some paper and pencil questionnaires would help to obtain the necessary information. Finally, many mechanisms can be studied experimentally.

Summary

The object of this chapter was to describe an alternative way of distinguishing among different abnormal behaviors. In the first part, some of the failures of DSM-III were reviewed. The second part of the chapter demonstrated the existence of at least one viable alternative system of classification. The third part showed that one cannot examine behavior apart from the stimuli in the environment that control it. Finally, the last part of the chapter showed how one could use the concept of the behavioral mechanism to shed light on how the aberrant behavior came to be. It was suggested that a search for behavioral mechanisms is a reasonable alternative to the existing systems of classification in this field.

REFERENCES

Dohrenwend, B. S., & Dohrenwend, B. P. (Eds.) (1982). *Stressful life events and their contexts*. New York: Neale Watson Academic Publications.

Eysenck, H. J., Wakefield, J. A., & Friedman, A. F. (1983) Diagnosis and clinical assessment: The DSM-III. *Annual Review of Psychology, 34*, 167–193.

Gould, L. N. (1948). Verbal hallucinations and activity of vocal musculature: An electromyographic study. *American Journal of Psychiatry, 105*, 367–372.

Goulds, L. N. (1949). Auditory hallucinations and subvocal speech: Objective study in a case of schizophrenia. *Journal of Nervous and Mental Disease, 109*, 418–427.

Gould, L. N. (1950). Verbal hallucinations as automatic speech: The reactivation of dormant speech habit. *American Journal of Psychiatry, 107*, 110–119.

Miller, G. A., & Selfridge, J. A. (1950) Verbal context and the recall of meaningful material. *American Journal of Psychology, 63*, 176–185.

Millon, T. (1981). *Disorders of personality. DSM-III: Axis II*. New York: Wiley.

Salzinger, K. (1959). Experimental manipulation of verbal behavior: A review. *Journal of General Psychology, 61*, 65–94.

Salzinger, K. (1967). The problem of response class in verbal behavior. In K. Salzinger & S. Salzinger (Eds.), *Research in verbal behavior and some neurophysiological implications*. New York: Academic Press.

Salzinger, K. (1975). Behavior theory models of abnormal behavior. In M. L., Kietzman, S. Sutton, & J. Zubin (Eds.), *Experimental approaches to psychopathology*. New York: Academic Press.

Salzinger, K. (1978). A behavioral analysis of diagnosis. In R. L. Spitzer & D. F. Klein (Eds.), *Critical issues in psychiatricc diagnosis*. New York: Raven Press.

Salzinger, K. (1980). The behavioral mechanism to explain abnormal behavior. *Annals of the New York Academy of Sciences, 340*, 66–87.

Salzinger, K. (1984). The immediacy hypothesis in a theory of schizophrenia. In W. D. Spaulding & J. K. Cole (Eds.), *Nebraska symposium on motivation: Theories of schizophrenia and psychosis.* Lincoln: University of Nebraska Press.

Salzinger, K., & Pisoni, S. (1958). Reinforcement of affect responses of schizophrenics during the clinical interview. *Journal of Abnormal and Social Psychology, 57,* 84–90.

Salzinger, K., & Pisoni, S. (1960). Reinforcement of verbal affect responses of normal subjects during the interview. *Journal of Abnormal and Social Psychology, 60,* 127–130.

Salzinger, K., & Pisoni, S. (1961). Some parameters of the conditioning of verbal affect responses in schizophrenic subjects. *Journal of Abnormal and Social Psychology, 63,* 511–516.

Salzinger, K., Portnoy, S., & Feldman, R. S. (1966). Verbal behavior in schizophrenics and some comments toward a theory of schizophrenia. In P. Hoch & J. Zubin (Eds.), *Psychopathology of schizophrenia.* New York: Grune & Stratton.

Scott, J. P. (1956). The analysis of social organization in animals. *Ecology, 37,* 213–221.

Skinner, B. F. (1974). *About behaviorism.* New York: Knopf.

CHAPTER 6

The DSM-III and Clinical Child Psychiatry

Jules R. Bemporad and Mary E. Schwab

After half a decade of dedicated labor, the third edition of the *Diagnostic and Statistical Manual of Mental Disorders* (American Psychiatric Association, 1980) appeared, attracting a good deal of attention and controversy. Reviewers (Cooper & Michels, 1981) have emphasized the DSM-III's nonetiological frame of reference, its use of operational criteria which facilitates research and scientific communication, the multiaxial classification system, as well as the lack of a coherent organizing principle to the overall system of diagnosis. While some have criticized particular aspects of the DSM-III sections on adult disorders (such as the exclusion of neurosis as a diagnostic entity or the listing of homosexuality only if this is at odds with the individual's self-image), the majority of comments have been favorable. Less attention has been paid to the section, "Disorders Usually First Evident in Infancy, Childhood, and Adolescence," especially regarding the appropriateness of applying a diagnostic system designed for adult disorders to the everyday psychiatric problems of children. This chapter will discuss that section of DSM-III and review recent studies which have used DSM-III in various child psychiatric patient populations. For simplicity, this part of the classification system will be referred to as the childhood section.

This childhood section is much larger than the analogous section of the DSM-II, with over four times as many categories which the authors state reflects "a great increase in knowledge in this area." The diagnoses of this

Jules R. Bemporad. Department of Psychiatry, Harvard Medical School, Boston, Massachusetts.

Mary E. Schwab. Children's Outpatient Services and Department of Psychiatry, Harvard Medical School, and McLean Hospital, Boston, Massachusetts.

section can be divided into five major groups: intellectual, behavioral, emotional, physical, and developmental.

The intellectual disturbances comprise the category of mental retardation. The behavioral category includes attention-deficit disorder, with or without hyperactivity, and the various conduct disorders: undersocialized aggressive and nonaggressive, socialized aggressive and nonaggressive, and atypical. The conduct these conduct disorders describe consists of repetitive and persistent patterns of behavior which violate the rights of others or societal rules.

Some of the emotional disorders appear confined to those manifesting anxiety in various situations. Others in this category, such as elective mutism, oppositional disorder, and identity disorder, do not exhibit a common unifying symptom. The physical disorders are divided into three major categories. The first involves various problems around eating; the second involves stereotyped movements; and the last is a mixture of what used to be called habit disorders: stuttering, enuresis, encopresis, sleepwalking, and sleep terrors.

The developmental group consists of disorders that are manifested by impairment or delays in development. These are divided into pervasive developmental disorders which include autism and autistic-like disturbances and specific developmental disorders such as reading or arithmetic disorders. The latter groups are coded on Axis II rather than Axis I to ensure their being reported when they occur with other disorders, as they often do.

Finally, DSM-III includes diagnoses listed as V codes, which represent conditions that are a focus of attention or treatment, but are not attributable to any mental disorder. This group of conditions is in keeping with the ICD-9, which contains a supplementary classification of factors influencing health status and contact with health services. There are various V codes which refer to childhood problems, such as borderline intellectual functioning, childhood or adolescent antisocial behavior, academic problem, phase-of-life problem, parent–child problem, and other specified family circumstances.

These categories present the essence of the childhood section of the DSM-III. Disorders that may be found in children that are not listed in this section are thought to be covered adequately in the various adult parts of the DSM-III. Table 6-1 contains a list of each of the disorders described in this section.

Table 6-1
*DSM-III Diagnoses: Disorders Usually First Evident in
Infancy, Childhood, or Adolescence*

Mental Retardation
    Mild mental retardation
    Moderate mental retardation
    Severe mental retardation
    Profound mental retardation
    Unspecified mental retardation

Table 6-1 (*continued*)

Attention Deficit Disorder
  With hyperactivity
  Without hyperactivity
  Residual type

Conduct Disorder
  Undersocialized, aggressive
  Undersocialized, nonaggressive
  Socialized, aggressive
  Socialized, nonaggressive
  Atypical

Anxiety Disorders of Childhood or Adolescence
  Separation anxiety disorder
  Avoidant disorder of childhood or adolescence
  Overanxious disorder

Other Disorders of Infancy, Childhood, or Adolescence
  Reactive attachment disorder of infancy
  Schizoid disorder of childhood or adolescence
  Elective mutism
  Oppositional disorder
  Identity disorder

Eating Disorders
  Anorexia nervosa
  Bulimia
  Pica
  Rumination disorder of infancy
  Atypical eating disorder

Stereotyped Movement Disorders
  Transient tic disorder
  Chronic motor tic disorder
  Tourette's disorder
  Atypical tic disorder
  Atypical stereotyped movement disorder

Other Disorders with Physical Manifestations
  Stuttering
  Functional enuresis
  Functional encopresis
  Sleepwalking disorder
  Sleep terror disorder

Pervasive Developmental Disorders
  Infantile austism
  Childhood onset pervasive developmental disorder
  Atypical

Specific Developmental Disorders (these are coded on Axis II)
  Developmental reading disorder
  Developmental arithmetic disorder
  Developmental language disorder
  Developmental articulation disorder
  Mixed specific developmental disorder
  Atypical specific developmental disorder

However, this expanded number of diagnoses for children is not the sole new contribution of the DSM-III. In a recent article on the childhood section, Spitzer and Cantwell (1980) enumerated a number of other advances which, in their opinion, support the superiority of the DSM-III over past systems of classification, particularly the DSM-II. Spitzer and Cantwell cite the DSM-III's specific criteria of mental disorder, correctly noting that previous classification systems did not attempt such definition. The specifications for mental disorder given in the DSM-III are a pattern of behavior that is associated with distress or disability, that is due to behavioral, psychological, or biological factors, and that is not resulting only from the relationship of the individual to society. Other advances cited by these authors include the nonetiological, phenomenological approach to diagnosis which avoids espousing any theoretical viewpoint. They also note the comprehensive systematic description of each disorder which lists for each entity information about associated features, age of onset, possible cause, impairment, complications, prevalence, sex ratio, familial pattern, and differential diagnosis. Another innovation is the multiaxial classification which is a worthwhile step toward a fuller description of each child. Also singled out for praise is the attempt to establish the usefulness and reliability of the DSM-III by field testing. Lastly, these authors present as advances the specific appendices which contain decision trees for help in differential diagnosis, an updated glossary, and a comparative listing of DSM-II diagnoses as relating to their new counterparts.

Proponents of this new system cite these and other features that make the childhood section of DSM-III clearly superior to its DSM-II predecessor, but on a number of points, DSM-III appears to fall short as a viable and practical classification scheme for childhood psychopathology. Let us look at some of the criticisms that have been raised.

The first criticism is perhaps unfair, given the strictures within which the DSM-III committee had to work, those of conforming as closely as possible to the ICD-9; yet this criticism is also a very important and basic one. The essence of this criticism is whether any system designed for the diagnosis of adults can ever be applicable to the problems of children. This critique goes beyond the individual diagnosis to the very definition of mental disorders as reported by Spitzer, Williams, and Skodol (1980). Anna Freud (1965) has long labored over what constitutes psychopathology in childhood, that is, when the clinician should consider a child's difficulties as serious enough to propose treatment. She discusses at length the criteria of subjective distress and impairment of functioning, the two factors given as the basis of mental disorders by the DSM-III. While appropriate as indices of disturbance in adults, she discards both as insufficient and unreliable indicators of psychopathology in children. Freud argues that often parents suffer more from a child's disturbance than the child, who may be unperturbed by encopresis, temper tantrums, or food fads. She continues, "The most seriously disturbed children, such as those with mental or moral deficiencies, retardations, autisms, and childhood psychoses, are completely oblivious of their illness, with maximum distress, of course, caused to the parents" (pp. 120–121). As for impairment of functioning, Freud warns practitioners not to base their assessment on this criterion, for the child's level of functioning normally fluctuates unceasingly. For Freud there is but one aspect of the child's activity that can give an accurate picture or pathology: the blockage of the developmental processes. She writes, ". . . there is only one factor in childhood the impairment of which can be considered of sufficient importance . . . the child's capacity to move forward in progressive steps until maturation, development in all areas of the personality, and adaptation to the social community have been completed. Mental upsets can be taken as a matter of course so long as these vital processes are left intact. They have to be taken seriously as soon as development itself is affected, whether slowed up, reversed or brought to a standstill altogether" (p. 123).

Freud is arguing that often symptoms in themselves are relatively unimportant, as are other objective manifestations of disturbance, as long as normal development proceeds at a proper rate and course. However, she is saying more; she is saying that one cannot apply adult criteria of psychopathology to children. Achenbach (1980) makes the same point, stating that since most major adult disorders have no clear counterparts in children, we cannot indiscriminately apply adult-oriented diagnostic constructs to children. Children must be assessed in terms of their need for continued development. Achenbach writes, "The absence of positive adaptive behavior and the failure to progress along one or more dimensions of development are often more salient in childhood abnormalities than are symptoms like those considered pathognomonic of adult disorders" (p. 397).

While a definition of disorder based on distress and disability has these inherent limitations when applied to children, DSM-III's deemphasis on the individual's relationship to society as an aspect of disorder raises further problems. Again, the difficulty is basically that a consideration of development is essential to the assessment of health or disorder in children. A key feature of healthy psychological growth involves learning how to get along in one's social context: making friends, working cooperatively at age-appropriate tasks, and obeying a reasonable number of rules. For children, disturbances in social adjustment are frequent presenting problems and may indicate the need for treatment. While DSM-III recognizes this to some degree through the inclusion of the conduct disorders in the childhood section, downplaying the social dimension in the definition of childhood disorder risks building into our way of thinking a model which ignores the importance for health of learning how to adjust to one's social environment.

Ignoring this developmental orientation and thus using the same criteria for mental disorder for children as for adults may be the result of having to produce one document which encompasses child and adult syndromes. However, it may also be because the authors of the DSM-III aspire to an avoidance of all theory, including the developmental approach, or because they conceptualize disorders as quasi-autonomous entities, divorced from the total individual's age-dependent attempt to cope with a changing environment. Yet to ignore development is not to remain theoretically pure; it is to deny a blatant fact, namely, that the individual undergoes major changes through the life cycle. A static model of disturbance may be more applicable to adults in whom the rate of development is relatively slow and personality patterns appear somewhat fixed. However, children change very rapidly and as such are quite distinct from their adult counterparts in health or disease. The DSM-III appears to ignore the framework of development, and in the childhood section, it really presents a classification for adults who presented symptoms before age 18. This is somewhat analogous to having to practice pediatrics with a classification geared for the internist treating adults. Actually, Spitzer and Cantell (1980) use this medical analogy in describing the rationale for utilizing the same adult classification for children for those disorders *not* listed in the childhood section (e.g., affective disorders and schizophrenia). Because the essential features of certain diseases, such as measles or pneumonia, are the same in children and adults, description of psychiatric disorders can be used for children if the clinical picture is similar. Actually, there are many medical diseases that share the same essential features—in terms of pathological processes or presenting symptoms—in children and adults that differ greatly in their severity, course, and complications in these two age groups. Mumps in the child is usually a mild disease; in the adult it is often serious. In contrast, juvenile diabetes carries a much grimmer prognosis than does adult onset diabetes. The various endocrinopathies or vitamin deficiencies affect a growing child much more severely than a more slowly changing adult. Even identical symptoms should evoke different etiological possibilities in children and adults. Seizures in a child are rarely caused by brain tumors while in adults they often are. On the other hand, a child with hypertension always should be suspected of an underlying malignancy, but adults with the same clinical complaint rarely should. Therefore, there is sufficient evidence from medicine that children are not just little adults, but are qualitatively different beings. Yet these physiological differences between child and adult are miniscule compared to the enormous contrasts seen in the area of cognition, emotion, and volition.

A consequence of this disregard of the developmental approach is that the DSM-III ignores some conditions in childhood that may be the result of development itself. For example, the GAP Report (Group for the Advancement of Psychiatry, 1966), which is specifically and totally devoted to children, lists a category of healthy responses in order to emphasize the positive strengths in the child and avoid the diagnosis of health only by the exclusion of pathology. It often occurs that during development the child will manifest transient symptoms which are indications of normal progress. Such developmental crises might be the 8-month anxiety of the infant, the phobias of the preschooler, the rituals of the latency age child, and the sporadic faddish behavior of the adolescent. These symptoms are manifestations of health when viewed developmentally and should have been so noted had an appropriate category been developed in the DSM-III. The need for such a category, listing the healthy responses and transient reactive symptoms as well as deviations from proper development, is greater for children than adults because these conditions account for a large number of the presenting problems of children seen by mental health specialists.

For example, in a study of 310 symptomatic children attending a psychiatric clinic which tested the use of the GAP Report as a research project (Bemporad, Pfeifer, & Bloom, 1970), almost 9% were given a diagnosis of healthy response. Similarly, about 15% were given a diagnosis of developmental deviation, and almost 20% were diagnosed as transient reactive disorders. Therefore, when a developmentally oriented system of classification was utilized, almost 44% of children seen in a psychiatric clinic showed evidence of disturbances that could not be called "mental disorders" in the DSM-III sense, but were reactions of a developing child who encountered some internal or external obstacle to the growth process.

Having made this plea for a separate classification for children, let us turn to several specific aspects of the DSM-III. First, in reviewing the diagnoses listed, it becomes apparent that there is a great disparity in the validity of the entities described. For adult psychiatric disorders, Woodruff, Goodwin, and Guze (1974) have attempted a thoroughly detailed and validated description of certain syndromes similar to that found in the DSM-III. However, they warn that not every patient can be diagnosed by these categories. For those who cannot, these authors preferred the term "undiagnosed" which in their words is more appropriate than a label incorrectly implying more knowledge than exists. These researchers acknowledge that precise information about prognosis and other factors exists only for a handful of conditions. A comparable situation exists in current child psychiatry. For example, the existence of early infantile autism as a disease entity has been repeatedly referred to in the literature for almost 40 years. Hundreds, if not thousands of articles as well as numerous books have appeared about autistic children. A separate journal has now been launched dedicated to this childhood affliction. Other DSM-III disorders, such as Tourette's Disease, an attention deficit disorder with hyperactivity, anorexia nervosa and, possibly, elective mutism stand out as specific and independent syndromes. These disorders are indeed well described and defined by the authors of the DSM-III. However, these authors give a similar stamp of scientific objectivity to very vague and questionable symptom pictures which do not always fall into predictable and reliable syndrome packages. Syndromes such as avoidant disorder, oppositional disorder, and identity disorder simply do not have the same coherence or validity as does infantile autism. These are "soft" diagnoses that vary from child to child in terms of severity, etiology, course, complications and prognosis. In its zeal to appear scientific, DSM-III may give to these global reactions what Rutter and Shaffer (1980) have called the "spurious impression of objectivity." It may be unreasonable to expect all diagnoses to be proven to the extreme before inclusion in a classification system; however, it is not the inclusion of these "soft" diagnoses that is objectionable as the manner of their presentation in the DSM-III—as if they contained the same validity as time-tested syndromes. For these softer diagnoses, a humbler approach seems warranted, professing doubt as to not only their associated features, but whether they should actually constitute separate entities and can be classified as mental disorders. Some psychiatric problems of childhood do cluster into neat packages of clearly defined syndromes, but many, perhaps the vast majority, do not.

Second, in addition to the disparity in validity of diagnoses, questions have been raised as to the conceptual origin of the diagnostic entities. The lack of empirical derivation has been pointed out by Achenbach (1980), who has been involved in putting together a taxonomy of childhood disorders by factor-analytic studies of large numbers of children for about the past two decades. In the course of these studies, Achenbach has found groups of factors which fall together in repeated studies. He has been able to divide disturbed children into internalizing and externalizing groups. Smaller clusters of symptoms in the internalizing group led to syndromes categorized as depressed, social withdrawal, somatic complaints, and schizoid obsessive. In the externalizing group, symptoms clustered around syndromes described as hyperactive, sexual problems, delinquent, aggressive, and cruel. In comparing these factor-analytic studies to the DSM-III childhood diagnosis, Achenbach finds good agreement on some syndromes and questionable correspondence on others. He finds little empirical support for attention deficit disorder without hyperactivity, undersocialized conduct disorder without aggression, and separation or avoidant disorder (other than a presentation with generalized withdrawal and anxiety). He questions the existence of oppositional disorder other than as an aggressive syndrome, pervasive developmental disorder other than schizoid, and identity disorder entirely as a valid entity. He also finds no DSM-III diagnosis for some syndromes derived from his empirical studies. These are the childhood depressive syndromes, which he believes are different from adult affective disorders, and the cruel syndrome—which is a cluster of characteristics, seen predominately in girls from age 6 to 16, consisting of cruelty, bullying, meanness, attacking others, and destroying others' belongings.

This is not a plea for the adoption of Achenbach's nosology. As Achenbach says (1980), "because I consider DSM-III and the empirical derivation of syndromes to be but different facets of the same quest, I view them as complementary contributions to knowledge and services" (pp. 395–396). In the discrepancies, we should find the most intriguing questions. For example, several diagnoses that correspond least to Achenbach's taxonomy are new to our diagnostic system, originating with the DSM-III. The manner through which the authors come up with the various diagnoses is not specified, but validation through large-scale empirical or epidemiologic sampling of presenting childhood symptoms is a needed next step.

Third, as previously stated, many children present with various problems in development and not with specific fixed disorders, so it is often difficult for the clinician to make a diagnosis of mental disorder. The inadequacy of the older DSM-II may have been responsible for many clinicians disregarding that official nomenclature and simply diagnosing every child, no matter what, as "adjustment reaction." Garmezy (1978) has considered this problem in reference to the DSM-III. He writes, "the entire taxonomy has been made vulnerable by an over-reaching effort of the creators of the children's section to bring under psychiatry's wing deficits and disabilities that are not mental disorders" (p. 4). We must ask whether it is justifiable to call problems in growing up disorders and whether, because of the changeable nature of the child, clinicians in practice will want to label these as disorders when it appears that they are transient.

The authors of DSM-III have accounted for children whose problems are not attributable to a mental disorder by the establishment of the V code diagnosis. Yet, these V codes present certain problems, theoretical and practical, for the clinician. In terms of theory, it is difficult to know when a problem goes beyond a V code severity to a mental disorder. In contrast to the detail lavished on the regular diagnosis, the description of the V code diagnosis is cursory at best. Usually, the diagnostic description for a mental disorder is repeated with the conclusing proviso, "not attributable to a mental disorder." Many V code entities are vague and at times difficult to differentiate from the disorder diagnoses. For example, the demarcation between phase-of-life problem (a V code entity) and adjustment disorder is unclear. Phase-of-life problems include those associated with going to school, parental control, starting a new career, marriage, divorce, and retirement. An adjustment disorder appears to be a reaction to the same life events except that the difficulty is "in excess of a normal and expected reaction to the stressor." What constitutes a "normal and expected reaction" is not supplied, and obviously this estimation may vary from clinician to clinician. In other cases, the criterion is one of chronicity: One antisocial act does not make a mental disorder, but a history of antisocial acts does. Perhaps the most arbitrary division is the case of borderline intellectual functioning representing an IQ in the 71–84 range, which is not a mental disorder. An IQ of 70 or below signifies mental retardation, which is a mental disorder, although the authors allow flexibility of 5 points on either side for individual cases. The ceiling of 70 was chosen because this was considered to be the upper limit of adaptive functioning. Most individuals above this figure may be seen as able to adapt to social needs. Yet, individuals with an IQ above 70 may still suffer distress and show evidence of a disability, all associated with behavioral, psychological, or biological factors, which is their definition of a mental disorder. Here the criterion for disorder is actually the relationship of the individual to society, which earlier was pointed out as inappropriate. Beyond this contradiction, however, is the arbitrary line between disorder and no disorder.

This would be an academic matter if few children fit the V code diagnoses; however, children usually do not present with structured and stable diseases, but with idiosyncratic difficulties in growing up. We inadvertantly tested out the number of children who would receive V code diagnoses in our outpatient clinic at the Massachusetts Mental Health Center. Following a presentation (as well as smaller group meetings) explaining the DSM-III diagnostic system, six child psychiatry fellows were asked to use the DSM-III to diagnose their current patients. It should be stated that our clinic serves a relatively sicker population than would be found in private practice. We are often referred children who cannot be handled by outreach or affiliate clinics, and the families that we serve will often ignore a child's psychopathology until or unless it reaches relatively severe proportions. Yet, even in this clinic population, we found that 19 of 73 outpatients, or 26%, were given V code diagnoses on Axis I. This would indicate that over one-fourth of the children being seen either did not merit the label of a mental disorder or could not be fitted into an existing disorder category. This finding is in keeping with other studies of clinic populations using DSM-II. Jacobson and colleagues (1980) report that of 1063 children seen in four different clinical settings, 43% had diagnoses of transient situational disturbances, social maladjustment, or nonspecific conditions. Only between 3 and 10% were seen as having a mental disorder. Therefore, there is some question as to the suitability of the DSM-III to reflect the problems presented by children to psychiatric clinics. The difficulty appears to be in the emphasis on narrow definitions of disorders rather than broader based categories, such as those included in the GAP Report, which may more accurately reflect the real-life complexity of disturbed children. Again, the question of need for a separate children's classification arises.

A final criticism of the DSM-III childhood section involves the field trials to ensure reliability and usefulness. The specific field trials for this section are described in a series of articles by Cantwell, Russell, Mattison, and Will (1979a, 1979b; Mattison, Cantwell, Russell, & Will, 1979; Russell, Cantwell, Mattison, & Will, 1979). They consisted of mailing 24 case reports describing a variety of conditions to 20 volunteers who were asked to diagnose the children described according to the DSM-II and DSM-III classifications, as well as fill out questionnaires on other issues, such as the ease of using the DSM-III. The volunteers consisted of 8 faculty members and 12 trainees, all with the Department of Child Psychiatry at UCLA, all of whom were told not to discuss the case material with others. After receiving instructional packets of DSM-II and DSM-III materials, each volunteer was sent four cases every 6 weeks from which they completed research questionnaires which formed the data base for the field study.

The research design employed immediately poses methological problems. We are not told how the 24 case examples were chosen, except that the
researchers believed them to provide a broad range of diagnostic possibilities.
Twenty volunteers seems a small number to test the usefulness of a diagnostic system, especially when 60% were still in training. A more telling objection might be that all of the evaluators came from the same department of
the same medical center. The individuals seem to have been taught or to
have taught the same courses and to share a certain view of childhood
psychopathology, as is true at most training centers. They are hardly representative of the broad range of clinical orientations of the various practitioners who would eventually be asked to use the DSM-III. The use of case
reports rather than examination of live patients or videotapes also has its
drawbacks in that case reports tend to predigest clinical material and to
emphasize only selected aspects, but perhaps this modality was necessary for
expediency. However, it should be noted that 3 of the 24 case reports were of
mentally retarded children, and since the case report data included psychometric test results, these reports may have included materials which "gave
away" the diagnosis, thus favoring high reliability.

Although certain biases may have favored agreement with the expected
diagnoses, the results of the field trials do not seem to confirm this. There
was indeed high agreement for "neat package" diagnoses such as autism or
Tourette's disease, or diagnoses made by an objective test, as in the case of
retardation. The other proposed diagnoses, however, did not fair so well.
There was only 15% agreement with the expected diagnosis on separation
anxiety disorder and from 25 to 30% agreement on the various conduct
disorders. The overall level of evaluator agreement with the expected diagnoses for the entire field trial was 49%, indicating that the evaluators picked
the "wrong" diagnosis a little over half the time. In discussing this finding,
the researchers state that "a source of variation in diagnostic reliability may
be the clinical complexity of the individual case rather than defects in the
classification system itself" (Cantwell et al., 1979a, p. 1213). However, one
may also interpret the results as indicating that the classification is adequate
for simple cases or neat package diagnoses, but not for the complicated
presentations of psychopathology. Yet, it is the latter that the bulk of the
patient population presents to clinicians.

A separate study on interevaluator reliability showed that this parameter was slightly worse for the DSM-III than the DSM-II—54 to 57% (Mattison et al., 1979). Here again there was high agreement on organic or established diagnoses and poor agreement on complex cases. Finally, 46% of the
evaluators reported some difficulty in coding Axis I diagnoses with the
DSM-III (Russell et al., 1979).

It would appear that these field trials, limited as they were, might have
indicated to the authors of DSM-III that their categories may have been too
specific and possibly did not represent adequately the complex problems

presented by child psychiatric patients. Rather, the authors were encouraged by the results, concluding that their new system was superior to the DSM-II.

Despite these criticisms, the task of devising an adequate diagnostic system, especially in a field like child psychiatry, is a difficult one indeed. At this stage of the field's development, a working document is needed for use in studies designed to assess the validity of proposed syndromes and to help delineate new ones. DSM-III certainly serves this purpose, and a number of investigators have begun, although work in this area has lagged behind that on adult psychopathology and nosology. This is probably due to the smaller number of investigators in child psychopathology and to the need for DSM-III-based assessment techniques, which have only recently been developed. Let us look at the findings of several investigators who have examined the usefulness of the DSM-III childhood section. Of the diagnostic entities, the application of the DSM-III depression criteria to the childhood population has been most thoroughly studied.

Cytryn, McKnew, and Bunney (1980) made a point-by-point comparison of four sets of diagnostic criteria for depression in childhood: the criteria of Cytryn and McKnew, the Weinberg criteria, Kovacs' Children's Depression Inventory (CDI), and DSM-III. They found a great deal of concordance among the four sets of criteria and concluded that diagnostic criteria for affective disorders are similar for children and adults, and that DSM-III is a valid system for diagnosing depression in the child population. Such convergences argue in part for the validity of childhood depression as defined by DSM-III, but fuller understanding will await field studies designed to clarify issues such as the number of children who are depressed and would be helped by treatment, but who do not have symptoms to qualify them for a DSM-III diagnosis.

Carlson and Cantwell (1982) recently compared the Weinberg and DSM-III criteria for depression. Both sets of criteria trace their lineage to the Feighner adult diagnostic criteria, but Weinberg modified these specifically for use with children. In this study, the sample consisted of 102 children, ages 7 to 17, who were referred to a children's outpatient clinic. Of the 28 diagnosed by DSM-III as having an affective disorder, 22 also met the Weinberg criteria for acute depression. But examining the converse reveals that of the 38 who met Weinberg criteria, only 22 met DSM-III criteria. Thus, the DSM-III criteria appear more restrictive than the Weinberg criteria that had been developed for use with children. While it is difficult to tell which criteria are "right," the real concern is whether the DSM-III net is too narrow, at least for this diagnosis in children, and will lead to diagnostic and treatment decisions which exclude those depressed, but not quite depressed enough, children. Puig-Antich (1982b), in discussing this study, points out that further validation work is needed, but that "we should keep open the possibility that the lower limit of DSM-III major depression may be too high and exclude true depressives from their proper diagnosis" (p. 291).

Puig-Antich (1982a) has reported on the occurrence of DSM-III conduct disorder in one-third of a sample of 43 prepubertal boys with major depressive disorder (diagnosed by RDC criteria, which are very similar to DSM-III criteria). With successful treatment of the depression, which included tricyclic medication, the conduct disorder subsided in 11 of the 13 boys. On follow-up, when antidepressant treatment was discontinued, a relapse of the conduct only occurred if there was a relapse of the depressive syndrome. Puig-Antich hypothesizes that improvement in the conduct disorder may be mediated by improvement in the depression and that the depression may trigger the emergence of conduct disorder. However, it should not surprise us that unhappy children are likely to be angry and misbehave, and to do so repetitively if unhappy for a long time. Other investigators have noted the simultaneous occurrence of behavior disorder and depression. In their article "Unmasking Masked Depression in Children and Adolescents" (1980), Carlson and Cantwell note that while behavior disturbance may appear to overshadow the depression, "To an alert clinician conducting a thorough interview . . . the depression will not be masked" (p. 449). Thus, while it may be useful to conceptualize certain patterns of misbehavior as conduct disorder, by applying incompletely validated diagnostic categories, we may also run the risk of dichotomizing the individual when a single, cohesive formulation is in fact possible.

Cantor, Evans, Pearce, and Pezzot-Pearce (1982) applied the DSM-II criteria for schizophrenia to a sample of 30 psychotic children and adolescents. These patients could be diagnosed according to DSM-III criteria, except for the stipulation of a deterioration from a previous level of functioning, but there were important differences in clinical presentation, depending on the child's age. For example, severe language disturbances (neologisms, echolalia, clanging) were uncommon among the adolescent patients, although for a substantial number of these patients, such symptoms had been documented in childhood. Also, the delusions of the adolescent group revealed the bodily concerns typical of that age, while the delusions of the prepubertal children involved aspects of identification, for example, with "Mr. Control" or various television characters. A full understanding of childhood and adolescent psychopathology requires us to consider symptoms in their developmental context.

Earls (1982) has applied DSM-III to a sample of 14 3-year-old children who were found on initial screen to have behavior problems severe enough to warrant psychiatric evaluation. All 14 could be assigned DSM-III diagnoses. In discussing the application of DSM-III to these young children, Earls notes that difficulties were encountered when parents reported symptoms as troublesome which did not meet DSM-III criteria. For example, while night enuresis is common at age 3 and frequently will not be clinically significant, day enuresis and encopresis are less common, but these were often reported as symptoms of concern in the behaviorally maladjusted group. Yet the DSM-III criteria for age of onset between 4 and 5 years did not allow inclusion of this information in the diagnostic assessment. In considering the use of DSM-III with this age group, Earls suggests that future revisions of DSM-III should modify Axis V (Highest Level of Adaptive Functioning in the Past Year) to indicate the severity of disorder. He notes that the presence of behavior problems at this early age often carries important prognostic implications, as behavioral maladjustment is likely to persist in a substantial number of children. A diagnostic system, to be maximally useful, should contain information relevant of prognosis when it is known. For the child, this involves appreciating that continuity of development (or lack of it) is key to the understanding of psychopathology and health.

In a retrospective study of childhood patients with anorexia nervosa, Irwin (1981) found that 7 of 13 children who were hospitalized for this disorder did not meet DSM-III criteria for the diagnosis. Because a latency age girl will have a smaller percentage of total body fat than an adolescent or adult, he suggests that the DSM-III requirement of 25% total weight loss (even including the projected weight gain for age from pediatric growth charts) is too stringent and that, particularly in the younger population, refusal to maintain adequate hydration should be added to the diagnostic criteria.

This brief review of some recent work with the DSM-III childhood section suggests that its application has been somewhat successful in diagnosing certain children who fit the system as it currently stands and in indicating modifications for future diagnostic systems. The major criticisms boil down to the following points: (a) psychopathology must be considered in a developmental context; (b) criteria for diagnosis must be more flexible and reflect the complexity of the individual patient; (c) newer syndromes need validation; and (d) while there is a need for a uniformly usable system, clinical relevance should not be sacrificed for what is measurable. The previously mentioned GAP system had avoided these pitfalls by basing its classification on developmental theory and the needs of clinicians. Unfortunately, DSM-III did not profit from that work, and we have a document that is sometimes more appropriate to static adult disorders and the requirements of researchers than to the needs of children and clinicians working with children. Many of the criticisms leveled at the childhood section may reflect the need to incorporate this section into a manual for use with adult patients, a state of affairs which may well have been beyond the control of the authors of this section. However, if we are to take diagnosis seriously, and we must, since the diagnoses listed by practitioners may affect the direction of funding by government agencies and the selective creation of treatment programs, then diagnosis should reflect the problems we encounter in everyday clinical experience. If not, then every patient will once again casually be labeled as adjustment reaction.

In the larger view, classifications are not simply the result of scientific inquiry, but are actually social documents. The GAP Report appeared 20 years ago and reflects the psychodynamic and social orientation of the 1960s. Today, there is a greater effort to make psychiatry more scientific and to make it fit the medical model of disease. We live in an age of greater accountability, decreasing funds for social programs, and greater reliance on third-party payments. The DSM-III reflects such pressures.

Things were not much different in the past. In the appendix to his book, *The Vital Balance*, Menninger (1963) gives a history of psychiatric classifications, identifying two major orientations: the Linnean and the Hippocratic. Today, we might loosely call these orientations the splitters and the lumpers. The splitters usually have been in academia or research with a scientific approach to medicine, while the lumpers mainly have been practitioners with a humanistic and pragmatic attitude to diagnosis. An interesting case in point was Philippe Pinel, who spent years compiling a medical taxonomy. He eventually proposed a huge and detailed classification of illness in which an abbreviated psychiatric nosology ran 8 pages. Right after the publication of this work, he left his scholastic pursuits, being called as a physician to the Salpetriere Hospital in Paris. Within 3 years, during which he actually had to treat and refer psychiatric patients, he reduced his complex classification of mental illness to only four basic types.

It is our belief that a similar transformation will occur to the childhood section of the DSM-III—that many of the new specific diagnoses will die from lack of use and that more pragmatic, broad-spectrum diagnoses will be added. What is obviously needed is a large, national field test in which a substantial number of practitioners may report their utilization or the DSM-III diagnoses and the ease of difficulty that is experienced with this new classification. There is no doubt that the childhood section of DSM-III is vastly superior to its predecessor. It does contain many valuable advances, such as multiaxial classification, a good description of most syndromes, and an appreciation of the variety of child psychopathology. In addition, there was an attempt at field testing its utility. Most importantly, it gives the field a system with which to work and establishes a common language for clinicians and researchers, one that we all expect will undergo development and refinement.

REFERENCE

Achenbach, T. M. (1980). DSM-III in light of empirical research on the classification of child psychopathology. *Journal of the American Academy of Child Psychiatry, 19*, 395–412.

American Psychiatric Association. (1980). *Diagnostic and statistical manual of mental disorders.* (3rd Ed.) Washington, DC: Author.

Bemporad, J. R., Pfeifer, C. M., & Bloom, W. (1970). Twelve month's experience with the GAP classification of childhood disorders. *American Journal of Psychiatry, 125*, 658–664.

Cantor, S., Evans, J., Pearce, J., & Pezzot-Pearce, T. (1982). Childhood Schizophrenia: Present but not accounted for. *American Journal of Psychiatry, 139*, 758–762.

Cantwell, D. P., Russell, A. T., Mattison, R., & Will, L. (1979a). A comparison of DSM-III and DSM-III in the diagnosis of childhood disorders. I. Agreement with expected diagnosis. *Archives of General Psychiatry, 36*, 1208–1213.

Cantwell, D. P., Russell, A. T., Mattison, R., & Will, L. (1979b). A comparison of DSM-II and

DSM-III in the diagnosis of childhood psychiatric disorders . IV. Difficulties in use, global comparisons and conclusions. *Archives of General Psychiatry, 36,* 1227–1228.

Carlson, G. A., & Cantwell, D. P. (1980). Unmasking masked depression in children and adolescents. *American Journal of Psychiatry, 137,* 445–449.

Carlson, G. A., & Cantwell, D. P. (1982). Diagnosis of childhood depression: A comparison of the Weinberg and DSM-III criteria. *Journal of the American Academy of Child Psychiatry, 21,* 247–250.

Cooper, A. M., & Michels, R. (1981). DSM-III: An American view. *American Journal of Psychiatry, 138,* 128–129.

Cytryn, L., McKnew, D. H., & Bunney, W. E. (1980). Diagnosis of depression in children: A reassessment. *American Journal of Psychiatry, 137,* 22–25.

Earls, F. (1982). Application of DSM-III in an epidemiological study of preschool children. *American Journal of Psychiatry, 139,* 242–243.

Freud, A. (1965). *Normality and pathology in childhood.* New York: International Universities Press.

Garmezy, N. (1978). DSM-III. Never mind the psychologists: Is it good for the children? *Clinical Psychologist, 31,* (3).

Group for the Advancement of Psychiatry. (1966). *Psychopathological disorders of childhood.* (GAP Rep. No. 62). New York: Author.

Irwin, M. (1981). Diagnosis of anorexia nervosa in children and the validity of DSM-III. *American Journal of Psychiatry, 138,* 1382–1383.

Jacobson, A. M., Goldberg, I. D., Burns, B. J. et. al. (1980). Diagnosed mental disorder in children and use of health services in four organized health care settings. *American Journal of Psychiatry, 137,* 559–565.

Mattison, R., Cantwell, D. P., Russell, A. T., & Will, L. (1979). A comparison of DSM-II and DSM-III in the diagnosis of childhood psychiatric disorders. II. Interrater agreement. *Archives of General Psychiatry, 36,* 1217–1222.

Menninger, K., Hoeper, E. W., Hankin, J. R., & Hewitt, K. (1963). *The vital balance.* New York: Viking Press.

Puig-Antich, J. (1982a). Major depression and conduct disorder in prepuberty. *Journal of the American Academy of Child Psychiatry, 21,* 118–128.

Puig-Antich, J. (1982b). The use of RDC criteria for major depressive disorder in children and adolescents. *Journal of the American Academy of Child Psychiatry, 21,* 291–293.

Russell, A. T., Cantwell, D. P., Mattison, R., & Will, L (1979). A comparison of DSM-II and DSM-III in the diagnosis of childhood psychiatric disorders. III. Multiaxial features. *Archives of General Psychiatry, 36,* 1223–1226.

Rutter, M., & Shaffer, D. (1980). DSM-III: A step forward or back in terms of the classification of child psychiatric disorders? *Journal of the American Academy of Child Psychiatry, 19,* 317–394.

Spitzer, R. L., & Cantwell, D. P. (1980). The DSM-III classification of the psychiatric disorders of infancy, childhood and adolescence. *Journal of the American Academy of Child Psychiatry, 19,* 356–370.

Spitzer, R. L., Williams, J. G. W., & Skodol, A. E. (1980). DSM-III: The major achievements and an overview. *American Journal of Psychiatry, 137,* 151–164.

Woodruff, R. A., Goodwin, D. W., & Guze, S. B. (1974). *Psychiatric diagnosis.* New York: Oxford University Press.

CHAPTER 7

A Critical Analysis of DSM-III as a Taxonomy of Psychopathology in Childhood and Adolescence

Herbert C. Quay

Criticism of the childhood and adolescence section of DSM-III (American Psychiatric Association, 1980) is not new; it was subject to considerable published criticism before the final version appeared in print (e.g., Garmezy, 1978; Schacht & Nathan, 1977; Zubin, 1978). These early critiques dealt with a variety of issues including whether or not the various syndromes constitute mental disorders and/or medical conditions, the issue of medical control of diagnosis and treatment, and the effects of labeling. Most of these concerns were subsequently discussed by Rutter and Shaffer (1980) in the context of a much broader critique of the published version. Millon (1983) has recently responded to many of the criticisms raised. While these issues may be relevant to both the clinical and administrative uses of DSM-III, as may a host of problems associated with Axes II, III, IV, and V (see Garmezy, 1978; Rutter & Shaffer, 1980), the critical scientific questions have to do with the adequacy of DSM-III as a taxonomy of psychopathology in childhood and adolescence.

It is the intent of this chapter to examine the scientific merits of the major categories of Axis I, "Disorders Usually First Evident in Infancy, Childhood, or Adolescence," of DSM-III.[1,2] The major question to be addressed is the extent to which DSM-III meets the generally accepted criteria for a good classification system for behavior, including the empirical founda-

1. Hereinafter when we refer to DSM-III, we are referring to this section only.
2. We have omitted consideration of mental retardation which, as Rutter and Shaffer (1980) have pointed out, is not really appropriate for inclusion in Axis I. We have also omitted consideration of adult disorders which may be used with children and especially adolescents.

Herbert C. Quay. Departments of Psychology and Pediatrics, University of Miami, Coral Gables, Florida.

tions for its categories, the reliability associated with its use, and the differential validity of its groupings of disorder. We will also comment briefly on
the operational criteria associated with the diagnostic categories.

Criteria for the Adequacy of a Behavioral Classification System

A great deal has been written about criteria for judging behavioral taxonomies, and various authors have put forth various guidelines (e.g., Cromwell,
Blashfield, & Strauss, 1975; Quay, 1979; Rutter, 1965). While writers have
differed in the length of their lists of criteria and in their emphases as to
which are most crucial, a short consensus list is not difficult to construct. It is
also the case that many of the criteria form a hierarchy so that if a given
lower level criterion is not met, the system will fail on higher level criteria as
well.

It is generally agreed that the defining characteristics of the taxonomic
categories should be as observable as possible. If general constructs are used,
they should have external referents. Thus, if "provocative behavior" is to be
a characteristic of oppositional disorder, then this term should have an
operational definition.

Without operationality and observability, it is not likely that the second
criterion, discriminability, will be well met. Discriminability refers to the
extent to which observers can, in fact, discriminate one disorder from others.
Discriminability necessitates that different disorders be indexed by different
observable characteristics.

Observability and discriminability clearly influence the reliability of diagnostic categories. Psychometrics recognizes various kinds of reliability, but
the type most directly relevant to the evaluation of DSM-III is interrater
reliability. To what extent do two clinicians arrive at the same diagnosis for a
given series of cases? Stability reliability ("test–retest") is also relevant, but is
more complex since the time interval over which stability is assessed can, and
usually does, influence the degree of stability.

Observed covariation of the elements of a disorder is also of importance.
In the statistical sense, a taxonomic category is composed of elements which
covary (occur together). It is this covariation of its characteristics that actually defines the disorder. The degree of covariation can be determined by
statistical techniques such as internal consistency reliability and factor and
cluster analysis.

Finally, validity is another critical area of concern which we will discuss
at length below.

Validity

Validity most commonly involves comparing the test or measure in question
against some already established criterion whose validity is prima facie or has

already been established. There is, of course, no infallible criteria against which the list of disorders in DSM-III can be compared. One can only test the system against a number of criteria, none of which is perfect. Under ideal circumstances, there would be research relating the various disorders to different etiologies, to differential responses to various interventions, and to outcome. Such research would validate the taxonomy by demonstrating that the different disorders have different etiologies, respond to different types of intervention, and have different outcomes. The system is too new, of course, to have generated such research.

At present, the most reasonable way to inquire about validity is to determine what relation there is between the DSM-III disorders and those which have been derived out of other approaches to the development of a taxonomy of disorders of childhood and adolescence.

Multivariate statistical research aimed at the discovery of the structure of psychopathological disorders among children and adolescents has been going on for some 40 years. Basically, the various multivariate analytic methods first determine the actual, observed covariation (correlation) between more or less specific characteristics reflective of psychopathology and then elucidate the patterns (factors or clusters) among the observed covariations. The results of many such studies have previously been summarized from somewhat different perspectives by Achenbach and Edelbrock (1978), Dreger (1982), and Quay (1979).

While a discussion of the technical aspects of this type of research is beyond the scope of this chapter, the reader should be aware that the results of any given study depend upon the methods by which the data were collected, the nature of the samples studied, and the particular technique of statistical analysis utilized. The reviews cited above contain more information on these influences.

It is also important to recognize that matching the results of the different studies is not by any means perfectly straightforward. To determine whether Jones's conduct disorder factor is the same as Smith's undersocialized aggressive syndrome, especially when the two factors contain few of the same variables in common, requires judgment on the part of the reviewer. Such judgment can, of course, be influenced by preconceptions of what "ought to be."

Despite these problems, the results of the multivariate investigations are the richest source of data available. The more than 55 published studies spanning the years 1946 to the present cover a very wide range of subjects, clinical and normal, and have utilized a variety of methods of data collection and analytic techniques. Thus, the commonalities among them cannot be due to use of a single type of sample, method of data gathering, or statistical analysis.

A review of the multivariate studies leads first to the conclusion that some syndromes are more frequently found than are others. One therefore has to deal with the problem of how often is often enough. Does one swallow make a summer; if not, how many are required? The writer's solution to this problem is to arbitrarily consider syndromes appearing in more than 10 studies as strongly replicated, while those appearing in 10 or fewer studies as weakly replicated. It should be noted that this "box score" is done without reference to the quality or extensiveness of any particular study, since criteria which have been advanced to judge the worth of any individual study are not without arbitrary elements themselves.

A total of 55 studies have been surveyed and are reported on here.[3] Table 7-1 presents those dimensions most often found along with six characteristics most often associated with each of the dimensions.

The conduct disorder syndrome has almost universally been found and is robust across ages, sexes, and types of samples. Socialized aggression has been less frequently found and is most likely to emerge in adolescent samples who are legally delinquent. Involvement with peers in socially disapproved activities is a clearly central feature. While illegal behavior of one sort or another has frequently been associated with socialized aggression, care should be taken not to equate delinquency and socialized aggression. Those who are legally delinquent may manifest any of the syndromes of deviance found in the multivariate literature.

The attentional problem syndrome has also very frequently emerged, some variant of it being discernible in more than 30 studies. It is clear that the current shift of terminology away from hyperactivity toward an emphasis on attentional problems is well taken; motor underactivity appears in this syndrome with greater frequency than does overactivity.

The dimension of anxious-depressed withdrawal has also been very robust, having occurred in about four-fifths of the studies reviewed. This broad-band dimension subsumes features of anxiety, depression, and social withdrawal. There is very, very little evidence from the multivariate literature that supports separate and distinct syndromes of anxiety and depression in children (see also Lefkowitz & Burton, 1978).

There has been much less frequent emergence of a syndrome of schizoid unresponsiveness involving introversion and social withdrawal, but neither thought disorder nor anxiety. It is possible that this dimension simply reflects an extreme of the introverted personality.

In 10 studies there has appeared a syndrome reflecting poor peer relations, but without accompanying anxiety, depression, or general unresponsiveness. This dimension may simply reflect a very limited repertoire of social skills rather than a psychopathological disorder, and we have chosen to label it social ineptness.

A dimension reflecting commonly held conceptions of psychotic disorder has relatively rarely emerged due, at least in part, to the infrequent inclusion of children manifesting psychotic behavior in most samples studied. Furthermore, items related to psychosis have not often appeared in the various

---

3. Thirty-seven of these studies were reviewed earlier (Quay, 1979). An additional list may be obtained from the author.

Table 7-1

Replicated Dimensions Arising in Multivariate Statistical Analysis with
Six Frequently Associated Characteristics of Each

Conduct Disorder
  Fighting, hitting, associative
  Disobedient, defiant
  Temper tantrums
  Destructiveness
  Impertinent, impudent
  Uncooperative, resistant

Attention Problems
  Poor concentration, short attention span
  Day dreaming
  Clumsy, poor coordination
  Preoccupied, stares into space
  Fails to finish, lacks perseverance
  Impulsive

Motor Overactivity
  Restless, overactive
  Excitable, impulsive
  Squirmy, jittery
  Overtalkative
  Hams and makes other odd noises

Social Ineptness
  Poor peer relations
  Likes to be alone
  Is teased, picked on
  Prefers younger children
  Shy, timid, lacks self-confidence
  Stays with adults, ignored by peers

Somatic Complaints
  Headaches
  Vomiting, nausea
  Stomachaches
  Muscle aches and pains
  Elimination problems

Socialized Aggression
  Has "bad" companions
  Truant from home
  Truant from school
  Steals in company with others
  Loyal to delinquent friends
  Belongs to a gang

Anxious–Depressed Withdrawal
  Anxious, fearful, tense
  Shy, timid, bashful
  Withdrawn, seclusive
  Depressed, sad, disturbed
  Hypersensitive, easily hurt
  Feels inferior, worthless

Schizoid Unresponsive
  Won't talk
  Withdrawn
  Sad
  Stares blankly
  Confused

Psychotic Disorder
  Visual hallucinations
  Auditory hallucinations
  Bizarre, odd, peculiar
  Strange ideas and behavior
  Incoherent speech
  Repetitive speech

rating scales and checklists used to obtain the data. One study (Prior, Boulton, Gazjago, & Perry, 1975) aimed specifically at eliciting syndromes of childhood psychosis did find evidence for two syndromes, one of which involved early onset and very severe impairment. More research into dimensions of psychoses in children is clearly warranted.

Fewer than 10 studies have isolated dimensions wherein excess motor activity has appeared in the absence of attentional and/or conduct problems. This syndrome is, however, relevant to a distinction between attention problem with and without hyperactivity. Finally, a dimension composed of somatic complaints was found in 10 studies. There were no other variables, such as tension, anxiety, and withdrawal, which regularly occurred in this syndrome. Table 7-2 provides a "matching" of DSM-III diagnoses to dimensions arising out of the multivariate research. It is immediately apparent that, with the exception of the Attention Deficit Disorder category, there are a considerable number of DSM-III categories for which there is no empirical counterpart.

In the Conduct Disorder category, there is very strong support for the Undersocialized, Aggressive, and Socialized, Aggressive subgroups, but no support for the Undersocialized, Nonaggressive, or Socialized, Nonaggressive subcategories. With regard to Anxiety Disorders, by far the most frequently found multivariate dimension is one which encompasses anxiety, depression, and social withdrawal. The Social Ineptness Dimension, weakly replicated, can only be suggestively equated to Avoidant Disorder.

With respect to the category of "other disorders," there is only weak multivariate support for just one of the five: Schizoid Disorder.

Table 7-2

A Comparison of Major DSM-III Diagnostic Categories and Dimensions of Disorder Arising Out of Multivariate Statistical Analyses

DSM-III Disorder	Statistically derived dimension[a]
Attention Deficit Disorder	
314.01 With hyperactivity	*Attention problems with motor excess*
314.00 Without hyperactivity	*Attention problems without motor excess*
Conduct Disorder	
312.00 Undersocialized, aggressive	*Conduct disorder*
312.10 Undersocialized, nonaggressive	
312.23 Socialized, aggressive	*Socialized aggression*
312.21 Socialized, nonaggressive	
Anxiety Disorders	
309.21 Separation anxiety disorder	
313.21 Avoidant disorder	Social ineptness
313.00 Overanxious disorder	*Anxious-depressed withdrawal*
Other Disorders	
313.89 Reactive Attachment Disorder of infancy	
313.22 Schizoid disorder	Schizoid–unresponsive
313.23 Elective mutism	
313.81 Oppositional disorder	
313.82 Identity disorder	
Pervasive Developmental Disorders	
299.0x Infantile autism	*Psychotic disorder*
299.9x Childhood onset pervasive Developmental Disorder	*Psychotic disorder*

[a]Statistically derived dimensions considered well replicated in italics; less well-replicated dimensions in roman letters. See text.

As we have seen, multivariate studies have usually elicited only a single dimension of psychosis. However, the most comprehensive study did find two dimensions, one strongly suggestive of infantile autism. In any case, there is no empirical support for the diagnostic category of Childhood Onset Pervasive Development Disorder.

Overall and Pfefferbaum (1982) have approached the validity problem in another way. They examined the consistency of psychiatrists' concepts of emotional and behavioral disorders by an application of Q-type marker variable factor analysis to rating-scale descriptions of hypothetical typical patients in each of 18 diagnostic groups. Multivariate profiles provided by their psychiatrist subjects were considered consistently adequate if they projected clearly on the same Q factor. Their analysis aimed at determining diagnoses which were and were not clearly understood by different judges and identifying particular judges whose concepts of diagnostic groups deviated from the majority.

Five experienced child and adolescent psychiatrists were given 18 copies of a 63-item 7-point rating scale for rating symptoms and behaviors of childhood disorders. The judges were asked to use the rating forms to discribe the average level of severity of each item for typical patients in 18 diagnostic categories.

The profiles of each judge were then intercorrelated and factor analyzed by the marker variable method described in detail by Overall and Pfefferbaum (1982). Results indicated that the 90 (5 judges × 18) ratings could be accounted for by only six factors. This finding indicates that 18 unique profiles, based on the 18 diagnostic groups, did not emerge; only six distinct patterns of psychopathology were present.

All five of the Conduct Disorders and Oppositional Disorder were clearly associated with one factor and one factor only. Infantile Autism, Pervasive Developmental Disorder, and Schizophrenia fell on a single factor. Separation Anxiety, Anorexia Nervosa, Overanxious Disorder, and Identity Disorder lacked a single factor, as did Attention Deficit Disorder, with and without Hyperactivity. Elective Mutism, Schizoid Disorder, and Avoidant Disorder occurred together. Major Depression stood alone. There is, of course, a clear parallel of these findings with those based on the analyses of observed behaviors discussed above in that supposedly separate forms of disorder are not differentiated and far fewer diagnostic categories were substantiated than appear in DSM-III. The major categories of Conduct Disorder, Psychotic Disorder, Attention Deficit Disorder, and Anxiety–Withdrawal Disorder were well substantiated.

While reliability of actual diagnoses will be discussed below, this study also provided data on the extent to which profiles for the 18 disorders were similar across judges; that is, did the judges rate typical cases of the 18 disorders similarly on the 63 items of the rating scales?

Quite good consensus was found for all disorders except Conduct Disorder, Socialized, Nonaggressive type, Oppositional Disorder, Overanxious

Disorder, Identity Disorder, Schizoid Disorder, and Avoidant Disorder. Agreement between the judges does not mean, however, that they all differentiated among the disorders, since we have already seen that they did not. For example, all judges described three subtypes of conduct disorder similarly, while at the same time not differentiating among them.

On the basis of what has been elucidated as the result of extensive multivariate investigations, it is clear that DSM-III has far more categories than have been empirically verified. Earlier critics (Achenbach, 1980; Garmezy, 1978; Rutter & Shaffer, 1980) have leveled this charge as well. This is not to say, however, that future research will not or cannot provide empirical verification for additional DSM-III categories. Nevertheless, given the extensive nature of the research reviewed and the results of the reliability studies to be considered below, such verification for many of the narrower categories seem highly unlikely.

Reliability

For a diagnostic system to be useful, users must assign some reasonable proportion of cases to the same diagnostic category. This attribute is generally labeled interrater reliability. It is to the great credit of the developers of DSM-III that they were concerned with reliability and began assessing it prior to release of the final version of the taxonomy. These efforts are referred to as field trials and the data may be found in Appendix F of DSM-III (see also Spitzer & Forman, 1979; Spitzer, Forman, & Nee, 1979).

In these field trials the participating clinicians were volunteers who were asked to jointly evaluate from 1 to 4 patients after having had the experience of evaluating at least 15 patients of their own using a draft version of DSM-III. The reliability interviews were generally initial diagnostic evaluations. There were two phases of field trials; in Phase 1, approximately 60% of the assessments were done in separate evaluations, while in Phase 2, about 66% were done separately. Overall, 84 clinicians participated.

In both phases, degree of agreement was assessed using the kappa statistic (Cohen, 1960) which corrects for chance agreement as calculated from the frequency with which a given diagnosis is used by both judges.

The results of both Phase 1 and Phase 2 are given in Table 7-3 which provides both the kappa value and the percentage of all cases in each category. A problem that is immediately apparent is that relatively few of the categories with which we are concerned were assessed; no reliabilities were obtained for any of the subtypes of Attention Deficit Disorder, Conduct Disorder, or Anxiety Disorder. An additional difficulty in interpreting the results arises from the widely varying number of cases upon which the reliabilities were based. Only for Conduct Disorder and Attention Deficit Disorder would the actual number of cases assessed by likely to lead to a

Interrater Reliabilities of the Major DSM-III Diagnostic Categories

DSM-III disorder	Field trials Phase 1 (κ)	(%)	Phase 2 (κ)	(%)	Reliability study[a] "Expected" agreement (%)	Interrater agreement (%)	(κ)	cases (%)[b]	(κ)	cases (%)[c]	Mean weighted kappa[c]
Attention Deficit Disorder	.58	15.5	.50	14.6					.76	9.2	.68
With hyperactivity					75	75	—	1	.73	8.2	
Without hyperactivity									.05	1.0	
Conduct Disorder	.61	26.8	.61	38.2				22.1	.53	30.1	.60
Undersocialized, aggressive							.75		.59	8.2	.67
Undersocialized, nonaggressive					30	30	.86		.18	9.2	.32
Socialized, aggressive					70	70	.60		-.04	3.1	
Socialized, nonaggressive									.32	6.2	
Anxiety Disorders	.25	8.5	.44	16.4				6.3	.67	21.0	.52
Separation					15	55	.47		.72	14.4	
Avoidant									.05	2.1	
Overanxious									.65	4.6	
Other Disorders	.79	8.5	.73	9.1				2.1	.39	24.6	.64
Reactive Attachment									.37	3.6	
Schizoid											
Mutism											
Oppositional									.39	20.0	
Identity									.28	1.0	
Pervasive Developmental Disorder	.85	5.6	-.01	1.8							
Infantile Autism					100	100	1.00				
Childhood Onset											

[a] From Cantwell, Russell, Mattison, and Will (1979).
[b] From Strober, Green, and Carlson (1981).
[c] From Werry, Methven, Fitzpatrick, and Dixon (1983).

stable estimate. The very dramatic differences (85 vs. −.01) in the reliability of pervasive Developmental Disorder is quite possibly the result of a very few agreements in Phase 1 versus a very few disagreements in Phase 2.[4]

Two subsequent studies (Cantwell, Russell, Mattison, & Will, 1979; Mattison, Cantwell, Russell, & Will, 1979) utilized a different approach to assessing reliability. They prepared 24 actual case histories upon which 20 psychiatrists completed standardized diagnostic questionnaires. Reliability was assessed both by the extent to which the raters agreed with the "expected" diagnosis (the diagnosis considered most appropriate by the researchers) and the extent of agreement among the raters.

Once again, many of the diagnostic categories of concern here were not used (see Table 7-3), but the reliability of some of the subtype diagnoses was assessed. The measure of reliability was percentage of agreement which does not correct for chance agreement and is thus more "liberal" than kappa.

Strober, Green, and Carlson (1981) assessed reliability on a series of 95 adolescents consecutively admitted to a hospital. Diagnoses were based on a joint interview using a structured mental-status examination, nursing observations, and referral materials. The kappa statistic was used to calculate degree of agreement. In this study, somewhat more of the subtype categories were used, but the number of patients falling into many of them were very limited (see Table 7-3).

The largest scale study to date has been that of Werry, Methven, Fitzpatrick, and Dixon (1983). In this study, 195 successive admissions to an impatient unit in Auckland, New Zealand were assigned a diagnosis by one or more of six clinicians. Diagnoses were made on the basis of a presentation of the case at ward rounds in the week of the patient's admission to the unit. The presentation was usually made by a person not actually involved in assigning the diagnosis, and this person was instructed not to use diagnostic terms during the discussion of the case.

This study utilized many more of the diagnostic categories of interest here and, due to their sample size, agreement was usually based on more cases than in the earlier studies (see Table 7-3).

It is of interest that all of the studies have utilized differing methodologies, each of which have facets that would tend either to increase or decrease the degree of agreement among raters.[5] However, except in a very few instances, degree of agreement in categories common to two or more studies does not differ appreciably.

Werry et al. (1983) have calculated a mean weighted kappa for the studies reviewed here plus two others. Their values may be found in Table 7-3.

---

4. Rutter and Shaffer (1980) have criticized the methodology of the field trials, but as we are no longer dependent upon them for reliability estimates, we refer the reader to their paper for their criticism.
5. Hyler, Williams, and Spitzer (1982) compared reliabilities obtained for either joint or single interviews and case summaries in adult cases and found the former generally to be higher.

These obtained reliabilities can be interpreted in a number of ways. For example, Werry *et al.* concluded that overall, the system is of satisfactory reliability and the value of (overall) kappa obtained (.70) approximates that of other studies which have used this statistic. There is very little meaning to this particular kappa, however, as no patient is diagnosed as "overall."

An inspection of Table 7-3 leads us to a number of conclusions. First, despite the efforts of various researchers to date, the reliability of many of the major Axis I diagnostic categories remains insufficiently examined, either because there are no data or because the data came from a single study where sample sizes in many categories were very small. Thus, there is nothing we can say about the reliability of Reactive Attachment Disorder, Elective Mutism, and Childhood Onset Pervasive Developmental Disorder except that these disorders must occur with extremely low frequencies, if they exist at all.

There is relatively little that we can say about Attention Deficit Disorder without Hyperactivity, Socialized Nonaggressive Conduct Disorder, Avoidant Disorder, Schizoid Disorder, Oppositional Disorder, and Identity Disorder except that in the series where they were diagnosed (Werry *et al.*, 1983), the interrater reliability was extremely unsatisfactory.

Turning now to categories of greater frequency, the picture is somewhat brighter. The major category of Attention Deficit Disorder, while showing rather poor reliability in both phases of the early field trials, was found to be quite reliable in later studies. The subtype with Hyperactivity seems equally reliable. The major category of Conduct Disorder fares reasonably well, as do the Undersocialized Aggressive and Socialized Aggressive subtypes. The Undersocialized Nonaggressive subtype is not at all reliable, nor is the Socialized Nonaggressive, as noted previously.

The major category of Anxiety Disorders is below the rather minimal level of .60 for the Conduct Disorders. For the subtypes, there are little data, but what data are available suggests the only Overanxious Disorder is acceptably reliable.

The Other Disorders, as a group, seem diagnosed with reasonable reliability (overall kappa of .64). However, data on the subtypes are either lacking or, as noted above, reflect serious unreliability.

As a group, the Pervasive Developmental Disorders were, as noted above, highly reliable in Phase 1 of the field trials, but totally unreliable in Phase 2. The one case history of Infantile Autism was rated with perfect agreement in both the Cantwell *et al.* (1979) and Mattison *et al.* (1979) studies. More work clearly needs to be done in assessing the reliability of these disorders.

Taking what data are available, it is of interest to compare the reliabilities of those categories for which there was strong confirmation, weaker confirmation, or no confirmation for the multivariate statistical research (see Table 7-2).

The strongly supported categories of Attention Deficit Disorder and Undersocialized Aggressive Conduct Disorder are of satisfactory reliability. The strongly supported Socialized Aggressive Conduct Disorder fares less well, particularly in the Werry *et al.* study, although its prevalence in their series was very low.

Overanxious Disorder, also well supported empirically, was assessed only by Werry *et al.*, where it was found to be reasonably reliable (.65). While there is good evidence in the empirical literature for at least one, if not two, forms of Psychotic Disorder, the reliability data are too limited to draw any conclusions.

The two disorders judged to be confirmed with much less certainty, Avoidant Disorder and Schizoid Disorder, were reported upon only by Werry *et al.*, where they were infrequent and unreliable. For those many disorders for which there is an absence of empirical confirmation, there is generally an accompanying absence of reliability. Notable examples here are Undersocialized Nonaggressive Conduct Disorder, Oppositional Disorder, and Identity Disorder.

All in all, there is, as might be expected, considerable correspondence between empirical confirmation (or lack thereof) of a category and its reliability. Thus, the data from these reliability studies published to date reinforce the conclusions drawn from the review of the multivariate studies that DSM-III has far too many unvalidated and unreliable diagnostic categories. Among those categories considered here, there seems little reason to include Undersocialized Nonaggressive and Socialized Nonaggressive Conduct Disorder, Avoidant Disorder, Schizoid Disorder, Oppositional Disorder, and Identity Disorder in a taxonomy of child and adolescent psychopathology. Other lesser disorders such as Reactive Attachment Disorder, Separation Anxiety Disorder, and Childhood Onset Pervasive Developmental Disorder are also good candidates for exclusion. Some doubt is even cast on Attention Deficit Disorder without Hyperactivity.

The Operational Criteria

DSM-III differs from its predecessors in another significant way. For most of the disorders, operational criteria are provided giving decision rules for the diagnosis of the disorder.

For example, the operational criteria for Conduct Disorder, Undersocialized Aggressive are as follows:

Diagnostic criteria
   A. A repetitive and persistent pattern of aggressive conduct on which the basic rights of others are violated, as manifested by either of the following:

1. physical violence against persons or property (not to defend someone else or oneself), e.g., vandalism, rape, breaking and entering,
   fire-setting, mugging, assault
2. thefts outside the home involving confrontation with the victim
   (e.g., extortion, purse-snatching, armed robbery)

B. Failure to establish a normal degree of affection, empathy, or bond
   with others as evidenced by no more than one of the following
   indications of social attachment:
   1. has one or more peer-group friendships that have lasted over 6
      months
   2. extends himself or herself for others even when no immediate
      advantage is likely
   3. apparently feels guilt or remorse when such a reaction is appro-
      priate (not just when caught or in difficulty)
   4. avoids blaming or informing on companions
   5. shares concern for the welfare of friends or companions

C. Duration of pattern of aggressive conduct of at least 6 months.

D. If 18 or older, does not meet the criteria for Antisocial Personality
   Disorder.

These criteria were developed to increase the reliability of the various
categories. While we know from the foregoing discussion that some categories are diagnosed reliably, but that many others are not, there are further
implications of the use of these diagnostic decision rules. The fundamental
problem is that they were not arrived at empirically. The use of including
and excluding criteria should follow from some form of statistical prediction
analyses wherein it is demonstrated that these rules have a measurable
degree of validity for predicting, when both the base rate of the disorder and
the cost of false positives and false negatives are considered. Since such
research has not been done, the utility of the operational criteria is open to
serious questions.

While the use of the arbitrary operational criteria *may* have enhanced
reliability in some cases (certainly not too many), the operational criteria as
they stand may very well do nothing to enhance validity. That two or more
clinicians agree to a diagnosis does not make that diagnosis correct. While
reliability sets a ceiling on validity, even perfect reliability does not guarantee
validity. Assume that two individuals were give tape measures and told to
find objects whose combined dimensions equaled 36 inches. After the objects
were collected, we would likely find excellent interrater agreement as to
their measurement, but we would have in hand a collection of objects whose
only common characteristic was that the sum of their dimensions was 36
inches.

The operationality notion is seductive and may easily lead the unwary to
infer validity where none exists. Had the criteria been empirically established, the decision rules could have increased validity. Given the nonempiri-

cal basis by which they were established, no such implications in regard to validity accrue. For an extended discussion of these and other issues in fixed diagnostic rules, see Finn (1982).[6]

The Future

As DSM-IV is sure to follow, we offer the following suggestions aimed at making it as reliable, valid, and useful a taxonomic system as possible. We do not claim that these suggestions are exhaustive or entirely original.

1. Diagnostic categories that are empirically unverified and unreliably used should be excluded.

2. Those remaining should be sharpened and their defining characteristics should be brought more in line with results of multivariate statistical studies.

3. The operational criteria, if retained in the form of disorders present versus absent decision rules, should be based on empirical research.

4. Consideration should be given to revising the notion of operational criteria so that their presence of absence contribute to a severity score rather than to a yes–no decision on diagnosis. Such would dimensionalize diagnoses to make them less of an "all-or-none" affair and would make for easier comparison of clinical diagnoses, with data obtained from psychometric assessment techniques.

Such simplification and shaping of the taxonomy would increase its overall reliability and make it a more reliable, valid, and thus useful system for both clinical and research purposes. A simplified, reliable, and valid taxonomy might well be adopted in educational and legal–correctional settings as well as in the mental health arena, thus fostering better communication and increasing cooperation in dealing with behavior problems common to all three social systems.

REFERENCES

Achenbach, T. M. (1980). DSM-III in light of empirical research on the classification of child psychopathology. *Journal of the American Academy of Child Psychiatry, 3,* 395–412.
Achenbach, T. M., & Edelbrock, C. S. (1978). The classification of child psychopathology: A review and analysis of empirical efforts. *Psychological Bulletin, 85,* 1275–1301.

6. Millon (1983) has argued that the DSM-III categories are "conceptual prototypes, and not tangible entities. Hence, it would not only be specious but paralogical to aspire to develop sophisticated discriminations such as criterion 'weights'" (p. 818). Since the DSM-III will be used to diagnose individuals and supposedly to plan treatments based on that diagnosis, not to develop the diagnostic criteria in the most sophisticated way possible would seem to us to be even more paralogical.

American Psychiatric Association. (1980). *Diagnostic and statistical manual of mental disorders* (3rd ed.). Washington, DC: Author.

Cantwell, D. P., Russell, A. T., Mattison, R., & Will, L. (1979). A comparison of DSM-II and DSM-III in the diagnosis of childhood psychiatric disorders. I. Agreement with expected diagnosis. *Archives of General Psychiatry, 36,* 1208–1213.

Cohen, J. (1960). A coefficient of agreement for nominal scales. *Educational and Psychological Measurement, 20,* 37–46.

Cromwell, R. L., Blashfield, R. K., & Strauss, J. S. (1975). Criteria for classification systems. In N. Hobbs (Ed.), *Issues in the classification of children* (Vol. 1). San Francisco, CA: Jossey-Bass.

Dreger, R. M., (1982). The classification of children and their emotional problems: An overview. II. *Clinical Psychology Review, 2,* 349–385.

Finn, S. E. (1982). Base rates, utilities, and DSM-III: Shortcomings of fixed-rule systems of psychodiagnosis. *Journal of Abnormal Psychology, 91,* 294–302.

Garmezy, N. (1978). Never mind the psychologists: Is it good for the children? *Clinical Psychologist, 31,* 1–6.

Hyler, S. E., Williams, J. B. W., & Spitzer, R. L. (1982). Reliability in the DSM-III field trials. Interview v case summary. *Archives of General Psychiatry, 39,* 1275–1278.

Lefkowitz, M. M., & Burton, N. (1978). Childhood depression: A critique of the concept. *Psychological Bulletin, 85,* 716–726.

Mattison, R., Cantwell, D. P., Russell, A. T., & Will, L. (1979). A comparison of DSM-II and DSM-III in the diagnosis of childhood psychiatric disorders. II. Interrater agreement. *Archives of General Psychiatry, 36,* 1217–1222.

Millon, T. (1983). The DSM-III: An insider's perspective. *American Psychologist, 38,* 804–814.

Overall, J. E., & Pfefferbaum, B. (1982). An investigation of the consistency of diagnostic concepts among five child and adolescent psychiatrists. *Multivariate Behavioral Research, 17,* 435–445.

Prior, M., Boulton, D., Gajzago, C., & Perry, D. (1975). A classification of childhood psychoses by numerical taxonomy. *Journal of Child Psychiatry and Psychology, 16,* 321–330.

Quay, H. C. (1979). *Classification.* In H. C. Quay & J. S. Werry (Eds.), *Psychopathological disorders of childhood* (2nd ed.). New York: Wiley.

Rutter, M. (1965). Classification and categorization in child psychiatry. *Journal of Child Psychiatry and Psychology, 6,* 71–83.

Rutter, M., & Shaffer, D. (1980). DSM-III. A step forward of a step backward in terms of the classification of child psychiatric disorders. *Journal of the American Academy of Child Psychiatry, 19,* 371–394.

Schacht, T., & Nathan, P. E. (1977). But is it good for the psychologists? Appraisal and status of DSM-III. *American Psychologist, 32,* 1017–1025.

Spitzer, R. L., & Forman, J. B. W. (1979). DSM-III field trials. II. Initial experiences with the multiaxial system. *American Journal of Psychiatry, 136,* 818–820.

Spitzer, R. L., Forman, J. B. W., & Nee, J. (1979). DSM-III field trials. I. Initial diagnostic reliability. *American Journal of Psychiatry, 136,* 815–817.

Strober, M., Green, J., & Carlson, G. (1981). Reliability of psychiatric diagnoses in hospitalized adolescents. Interrater agreement using DSM-III. *Archives of General Psychiatry, 38,* 141–145.

Werry, J. S., Methven, R. J., Fitzpatrick, J., & Dixon, H. (1983). The inter-rater reliability of DSM-III in children. *Journal of Abnormal Child Psychology, 11,* 341–354.

Zubin, J. (1978). But is it good for science? *Clinical Psychologist, 31,* 1–7.

CHAPTER 8

A Sociopolitical Perspective of DSM-III

Esther D. Rothblum, Laura J. Solomon, and George W. Albee

The development and publication by the American Psychiatric Association (APA) (1980) of the third edition of *The Diagnostic and Statistical Manual of Mental Disorders* (DSM-III) was preceded and followed by a number of critical articles discussing its relevance for target populations, for science, and for mental health professionals. Schacht and Nathan (1977) discussed the advantages and large disadvantages of DSM-III for psychologists. Zubin (1977–1978) critically evaluated the value of DSM-III as a scientific instrument and found it wanting. Garmezy (1978) focused his critique on the unfortunate implications of DSM-III for children; Kaplan (1983) pointed out its harm for women. The present chapter will continue this critical tradition by considering DSM-III largely from a social and political perspective.

We will begin by contrasting individual versus societal models of causation for psychopathology. Next, we will discuss the prevalence and duration of mental disorders and the nature of the populations so afflicted. We will then focus on several unfortunate aspects of diagnosis including (a) the evidence that the current diagnostic system is a reflection of sociocultural developments rather than scientific data, (b) evidence of the harmful and iatrogenic consequences of a pathology-based classification system in the field, and (c) the tendency for research funding to follow the establishment of diagnostic categories. We will examine the removal from DSM-III of the diagnostic category of homosexuality as a mental disorder and the inclusion of the diagnostic category of ego-dystonic homosexuality to illustrate political factors in operation in this classification system.

Esther D. Rothblum, Laura J. Solomon, and George W. Albee. Department of Psychology, University of Vermont, Burlington, Vermont.

We do support the use of a system of classification, and we recognize the value of scientific research to enhance communication and reliability in the description of subject characteristics. Nevertheless, it is our contention that classification in the area of psychopathology consistently has emphasized negative aspects of social functioning, with resulting stigmatization of the affected population and exoneration of the forces responsible for creating psychopathology.

Psychopathology clearly is associated with poverty and powerlessness, but these relationships are not acknowledged by the model that seeks and finds causal defects in individuals rather than in societies.

An alternative social model looks to social pathology as causal and suggests social change as remediation and as prevention. Vance (1977) has done a thorough review of the relationship between mental disabilities and low social status with associated powerlessness. She shows how many of these mental disabilities and disorders are rooted in the ways this culture socializes women as well as blacks and others who are at the lowest levels of poverty. The individual development of members of these high-risk groups involves the socially induced learning of role models appropriate to low status, the failure of many to develop an internalized locus of control, their failure to learn to delay gratification, to control reactivity, and the failure to develop "perceptual–cognitive differentiation in the discrimination of external reality, self, and feelings" (p. 221). Vance chooses the term "passivity" as the best way to reflect the consequences of an overpowering hostile social environment. She regards perceptual–cognitive passivity as "the greatest single source of vulnerability distress" (p. 223) in low-status human beings.

Vance describes the inverse relationship between rates of psychopathology and socioeconomic status, the higher rates of personality disorders and schizophrenia among the poor, and she reports that, proportionally, state hospital admission rates for the black poor are 75 times that for whites! Prevalence rates for other mental disorders are three or four times greater for blacks than for whites. Women have more depression, and other anxiety-related disorders are reportedly higher among women both in rural and in urban areas. Women also tend to accumulate in the state hospitals, either because they are more inclined to become chronic, or because, historically, it has been more difficult to find community placements for them.

These and similar findings, widely known and reported, tend to be neglected or ignored by the current psychiatric explanatory model which continues to diagnose individuals and to search for personal defect as cause.

The Cause of the Causes

Joffe (1982) has suggested an important concept that we should consider in looking at behavioral and emotional disorders. He admonishes us to seek the cause of the causes. Very often when we concern ourselves with a particular form of psychopathology that we try to understand or to prevent, we concentrate our efforts on one or more apparently specific proximate causes. If we are interested in preventing the conditions associated with premature pregnancy resulting in infants and children at high risk for later psychopathology, we may discover that such early pregnancies are common among the teenage unemployed and underemployed, undernourished, inner-city black women who have inadequate sexual knowlege. When we also find that most of these young women do poorly in schoolwork, we conclude that we have identified some conditions that may represent important "causes." The discovery of these causes may lead us to attempt prevention programs that involve sex education, remedial reading, nutritional counseling, and job training. We have failed to take the critical step of identifying the cause of the causes. We must ask what causes poverty, school dropout, unemployment, low self-esteem, boredom, and hopelessness in these inner-city teenagers? If we do not ask what are the social conditions that are responsible for the slums and for the high rate of black unemployment and low self-esteem, then we are not dealing with an important cause of the causes. If we focus only on the proximate causes, we fail to examine the important underlying reasons for the poor life prospects facing these young people that lead them to have low self-esteem and to become high-risk prospects for emotional disturbances.

In a similar way, we may find specific personality disorders that identify men who have been guilty of rape or the sexual abuse of children. But we neglect to look for the larger cause in the sexist nature of our society with its emphasis on male domination of females, with the focus in the mass media on male violence and female passivity, and with a pervasive and subtle sexism that is everywhere present. What is the cause of the cause? What causes sexism and what can we do about sexism as a cause of psychopathology? Our research should begin to examine the distribution of sexism and its relationship to the power structure of the industrial society, a power structure that survives through exploitation, patriarchal religion, and militarism.

Our model to explain psychopathology has profound implications for efforts at prevention. Because primary prevention efforts are rooted in a particular set of hypotheses about the modifiability of human behavior and the ultimate improvability of society through the abolition of social classes, better child-rearing practices, and modification of abolition of those social institutions that have led to discrimination against the poor, the powerless, ethnic and racial minorities, women, and the elderly, we may conclude that a prevention ideology must reject views that regard human nature and human society as fixed and unmodifiable. A prevention ideology therefore will be more allied with social-environmentalist as opposed to nativist viewpoints. And a prevention model is more likely to find a sympathetic receptivity from those with political views shared by persons on the left and to encounter opposition from supporters of the status quo, those with more conservative political views who favor individual treatment and diagnosis of personal defect.

The Delusion of the Liberals

It is probably a delusion to believe that we can improve the next *Diagnostic and Statistical Manual of Mental Disorders* by gentle constructive criticism of the current psychiatric diagnostic system. There is a very common liberal delusion that objective evaluation, sweet rationality, and helpful criticism of injustice and exploitation will lead to a better world. Trying to improve the present system of psychiatric diagnosis is very much like efforts at improving laissez-faire capitalism, or any one of the world's major patriarchal religions, by pointing out inconsistencies, logical fallacies, injustices, and even sheer associated nonsense. While both rapacious capitalists and masculist priests may tolerate learned disputations about certain obscure or confusing doctrinal issues and thereby foster the illusion that free discussion exists, woe to those who challenge the whole structure, who claim that the profit motive is dishonest, and that those who live by it are often self-seeking exploiters of their fellow human beings. And woe to those who question the divinity of this or that religious figure or who ridicule the doctrinal nonsense and sexism that form the core of most major religions. As two nineteenth-century social scientists, Marx and Engels (1848/1936), long ago pointed out: "The ruling ideas of each age have ever been the ideas of its ruling class." Our own society is so thoroughly suffused with beliefs in the right of inheritance, in property rights, in ultimate retribution for sinners and heavenly rewards for good behavior, and, in the present context, in the belief that crazy behavior results from an individualized and personal defect or sickness, that these beliefs are never questioned because they are promulgated and encouraged by those who favor and support the current societal status quo. Like sexist beliefs, like the belief that the poor are responsible for their own poverty, so the belief that there are underlying, internal organic (though as yet undiscovered) causes of mental illnesses is part of the broad organized attitudinal structure that absolves all of us from the need to correct the injustices that lead to emotional distress by blinding us to the power of social injustice.

So in a volume that celebrates the medical model, that examines and reexamines the genetic, the neurological, the biochemical, the psychodynamic—in short, the individualistic and personal bases for psychopathological behavior—we become the token critics placed on display as evidence of "broadly representative views." The strength of the psychiatric model, of course, is strong enough to endure the funky criticism of some token radicals. Or so it is implied.

This is a dangerous risk. Successful revolutions always begin with a flagrant challenge of the ideas of the powerful. What ideas do we want to challenge and what are we willing to substitute in their place? We wish to state that we believe that the evidence does not support the view that "most mental illness is caused by genetic and organic factors," and so we do not believe that it is proper to try to diagnose diseases where none exists; nor do we believe that help for those damaged by social injustice should involve "treatment" relying on the administration of drugs, shock, and other physical forms of intervention and forced incarceration. Second, we argue that the present emphasis on one-to-one individual therapy, using drugs and involuntary incarceration for the poor, and individual psychotherapy for the affluent, is both hopeless and ineffective, benefiting only the powerful and affluent caregivers directly and the established social structure indirectly.

One-to-one intervention is hopeless because the numbers who are emotionally damaged by the system are so large and the medical illness model is so inappropriate. Let us look for a moment at the dimensions of the problem.

The Numbers Involved

According to most informed estimates (Albee, 1982; Klerman, 1980; President's Commission on Mental Health [PCMH], 1978; Ryan, 1969), some 15% of the population of the United States exhibits mental conditions described as "hard-core mental illnesses" by Klerman and as "serious emotional disturbances" by those who disavow the illness model. Whichever model is used, some 32–36 million persons in the United States exhibit conditions such as depression, incapacitating anxiety, addiction to alcohol and drugs, organic mental disorders, including chronic brain syndromes in the elderly, as well as the functional psychoses such as schizophrenia. This "hard-core group" does not include millions of persons with psychosomatic physical conditions such as hypertension resulting from stress, nor the very large number of other persons who experience acute emotional upsets as a consequence of life crises. In recent years in the United States, for example, there have been, annually, approximately one million divorces, shown by Bloom (1978) to be a significant source of stress leading to any of several different damaging emotional reactions; in addition, there is the stress of the loss of loved ones through death which frequently results in severe emotional distress and/or reactive depression. Large numbers of other persons experience emotional crises. Involuntary unemployment, for example, has been shown (Brenner, 1973, 1977) to produce any of several severe consequences, including a rise in admissions to mental health clinics and mental hospitals, an increased incidence of cirrhosis of the liver, alcoholism, fatal accidents, suicide, and an excess of deaths from all causes.

In 1978, the President's Commission on Mental Health (PCMH) reported on the frightening number of underserved and unserved persons in the field of mental health. Who are these underserved and unserved? They are described in several different places in the Commission's report. They include children, adolescents, and the elderly—all of whom are identified repeatedly as underserved by mental health professionals. These three groups together represent "more than half" of the nation's population. Then there are the minority groups that include 22 million black Americans, 12 million Hispanic Americans, 3 million Asian and Pacific Island Americans, and 1 million American Indians and Alaska natives. All of these groups are underserved or, in many instances, inappropriately served by persons insensitive to cultural differences or incompetent in appropriate languages. While clearly the groups overlap somewhat with other groups identified as underserved, we are not yet at the end of the list. Five million seasonal and migrant farm workers are largely excluded from mental health care. The Task Panel on Women (1978) reported that women often do not receive appropriate care in the mental health system; neither do persons who live in rural America, nor in small towns, nor in the poor sections of American cities; neither do 10 million persons with alcohol-related problems, nor an unspecified but growing number of persons who misuse psychoactive drugs, nor the very large number of children and parents involved in child abuse, nor 5 million children with learning disabilities, nor physically handicapped Americans, nor 6 million persons who are mentally retarded. In all, according to the PCMH, only 7 million individuals are actually seen each year by the entire mental health system! And the lion's share of mental health funds (70%) is spent on inpatient care, serving a small fraction of those needing help.

Kramer (1981) has raised some important and alarming questions about what he refers to as "the rising pandemic of mental disorders" throughout the world. He points out that the United States faces, in the decades immediately ahead, a steadily increasing prevalence rate of serious mental disorders as well as an increase in medical diseases involving hypertension and cerebrovascular accidents. The growth in frequency of these conditions will result from the large increase in the number of persons in those age groups who are at higher risk for their development, as well as the steadily increasing duration of such chronic conditions directly resulting from the development of effective techniques for prolonging the lives of affected individuals. In brief, more people throughout the world are living into middle age and old age, and the chronic mental and physical conditions that are more likely to occur with advancing years are not only occurring, but are being treated in ways that prolong their duration.

Societal Values and Diagnosis

Scientific research is often described as a systematic and objective procedure. One pictures the scientist pursuing knowledge by testing hypotheses, then reconceptualizing scientific principles to explain the resulting data. This reconceptualization leads to further research and to further knowledge about the field. A college textbook on abnormal psychology (Davison & Neale, 1982) describes the scientific method as follows:

> A scientific approach requires first that propositions and ideas be stated in a clear and precise way. Only then can scientific claims be exposed to systematic probes and tests, any one of which could negate the scientist's expectations about what will be found. Statements, theories, and assertions, regardless of how plausible they may seem, must be testable in the public arena and be subject to being disproved. The attitude of science is an extremely doubting one. (p. 121)

Contrary to the scientific ideal, we suggest that "the attitude of science is an extremely doubting one" primarily in the case where scientific data contradict established societal beliefs; that is, sociocultural developments heavily determine the direction of science.

Because scientific research evolves from the testing of alternative hypotheses, it is confined and limited by the ability or willingness of researchers to conceptualize those hypotheses that contradict the status quo. We have developed a sophisticated methodology for testing hypotheses, but not for determining which hypotheses we will test. The process of generating hypotheses is not objective, yet it profoundly influences the type of research that is conducted and, therefore, the types of results that are obtained. In short, we search for evidence to confirm our hypotheses, and our system of research is not as objective as we would like to believe, particularly in the area of psychopathology. Let's take an example.

A statement frequently encountered in the psychiatric literature (and in nearly every psychology and psychiatry textbook) holds that the evidence is fairly clear that schizophrenia has a strong genetic component. Lamb and Zusman (1979) say: "Mental illness is probably in large part genetically determined and it is probably therefore not preventable, at most only modifiable" (p. 13). Erlenmeyer-Kimling (1977) says: "The cumulative evidence supports a general hypothesis of hereditary involvement in the predisposition to schizophrenia" (p. 70).

We want to be certain that it is clear that the existing research supporting the genetic basis of schizophrenia must be strongly suspect. Let us explain the reasons for making such a strong statement. Beginning in 1965 there has been in process a major Cross-National Project for the Study of the Diagnosis of Mental Disorders in the United States and the United Kingdom. It is still going on, with teams based in New York and London. One of the study's major findings is that there is a dramatic difference in readiness to diagnose schizophrenia and depression between groups of clinical psychiatrists in the United States and in Britain (Professional Staff of the U.S.-U.K. Cross National Project, 1974). In addition to specially trained project psychiatrists, there has been a frequent exchange of professional staffs between the two countries and careful examination of diagnostic habits and preferences of clinical psychiatrists in each country. It is reported that "the paramount finding of the work reviewed here is that the American psychiatrists, in general, applied the diagnosis of schizophrenia to a much wider variety of clinical conditions than did their British colleagues" (p. 85). There was a "dramatic preponderance" of the diagnosis of schizophrenia in the New York sample as compared to the London sample. Among psychiatrists drawn from the institutes with the strongest orientation for research and teaching (the New York State Psychiatric Institute and the Maudsley Hospital in London), the most striking cross-national differences were obtained. Where London psychiatrists saw manics or character disorders, New York psychiatrists saw schizophrenics. The London psychiatrists tended to diagnose schizophrenia more frequently in males; many people whom Americans called schizophrenic were called manic–depressives, neurotics, and personality disorders by the British. New York psychiatrists clearly had "a bias toward diagnosing schizophrenia in black patients" (p. 88). Over a 40-year period, the percentage of all annual admissions labeled schizophrenic increased dramatically in New York, but remained fairly level in London. When British and American psychiatrists were shown videotapes of "patient" interviews and were asked to make a diagnostic judgment, "in general, the American psychiatrists rated each and every patient in the videotape series as having more, or more severe, psychopathology than did their British colleagues" (p. 93).

Let us quote some of the conclusions of this major cross-cultural study:

> The evidence presented from the series of studies strongly indicates that the diagnoses routinely made in clinical practice should not be relied upon in epidemiological studies. . . .
>
> Given that hospital statistics gathered in one region report a higher rate of schizophrenia than statistics from hospitals in another region, this observation no longer justifies pursuing the hypothesis that the patients in the two regions are different. . . .
>
> The criteria applied to patient populations may vary even between different wards of the same hospital system, and between different time periods in the same wards. . . .
>
> An apparent rise or fall of a population of schizophrenic patients cannot be translated into a projection for the need of facilities in the future, since the trend may reflect no more than a change in the popularity of the diagnosis. Nor can adherence to new treatment policies be gauged from diagnostic statistics. . . .
>
> Corresponding problems are encountered in comparing the treatment and outcome of schizophrenics in different hospitals; such a comparison would not be useful unless the label of schizophrenia was known to refer to similar groups of patients in the various hospitals. (pp. 93–96)

If the diagnosis of schizophrenia is so unreliable between the two countries, between different regions of the same country, and in the same hospital over time, then it follows that genetic research on schizophrenia, based as it must be on diagnoses made by different psychiatrists in different wards, different hospitals, and different parts of the country [and in the case of the research by Kallmann (1938), from records at least 25 to 100 years old], can be no more reliable than the unreliable criterion! If the staff of this cross-national project believes it must warn against trusting studies involving treatment outcome because of the unreliability of the diagnoses of schizophrenia and of the affective psychoses, then a similar warning clearly should be posted for genetic studies. The cross-national study report concludes that there is an enormous amount of overlap between the clinical picture called schizophrenia and that called affective disorder, with the British preferring the latter diagnoses and the Americans the former when applied to the same cases!

According to Zubin (1977–1978), new classification systems of mental disorders allegedly are developed to improve science, yet in reality are based on more mundane practicalities. The development of DSM-III stemmed not so much from research on etiology or treatment of psychopathology, but from "entrenched clinical practice and such considerations as utility, ease of application, acceptability to practitioners, third party payments, professional considerations and other extraneous influences" (Zubin, 1977–1978, pp. 1, 7). While classification systems are believed to evolve out of advances in science, their progress more likely is based instead on sociocultural–political factors.

A major component of scientific methodology is to discover differences—to isolate a chemical element or to apply a toxin specific to a particular type of bacteria. In the mental health professions, the consequence of discovering differences is to focus on the negative, maladaptive components of behavior. It is deviance from the norm in the negative direction that is pinpointed, explained, and treated. There is comparatively less information on resilience with coping. By probing for deviance, often using exclusively clinical populations as our data base, we discover, for example, what factors covary with depression or stress. Such research, however, does not provide us with knowledge about individuals who do not become depressed or who cope effectively with excessive stress.

Kamin (1974, 1983) has examined carefully the "politics" of genetic explanations of behavior. He describes how the percentage of a particular disorder attributed to a genetic influence varies markedly over the years as a function of society's attitudes about genetic versus environmental influences. If one were to look at the research on the genetics of schizophrenia, it would appear that this disorder is less "heritable" for this generation than for the preceding one! Certain data that are out of synchrony with social norms may be ignored. Inconsistent data may be difficult to publish. Kamin (1983) has discussed his attempts to publish his book on the politics of IQ tests. Repeatedly, various publishers expressed an interest in the manuscript and sent a copy to prominent researchers for review. These researchers then strongly advised against publication. Society and its science struggled to maintain the status quo.

A corollary of the tendency to believe that classification systems evolved out of science is the belief that treatment methods have evolved from classification systems. Rather, as Sharma (1970) has stated, "The history of the development of social forces in Western societies shows that 'mental hospitals' and their precursors preceded the emergence of psychiatry, both as a 'scientific' discipline and as a profession" (p. 248). According to Sharma, psychiatric hospitals were created out of the need to create and maintain social order, particularly to deal with deviates among the lower socioeconomic classes. Once these "hospitals" were established, there was a need for diagnostic labeling of deviancy. The norm used in classifying the "illnesses" of hospital "patients" was ". . . a standard that implicitly adopted middle-class, Protestant, agrarian values" (Sharma, 1970, p. 249). It is not surprising that, as a consequence, classification systems of abnormal behavior focus disproportionally on "diagnoses" that are more common among the poor or the institutionalized and pay less attention to problems in living that affect the more affluent, less disruptive middle and upper classes. Subdivisions among diagnostic categories were often established after prolonged observation of psychiatric hospital patients. Even today, most of our knowledge of the behavior of schizophrenic or psychopathic individuals is based on research conducted on public hospital inpatients or prison inmates. Sharma (1970) indicates that this system of basing nosology on existing conditions in institutions is comparable to basing the theory of law and our legal system on the institution of prisons.

Despite the clear influence of cultural and political factors on classification of abnormal behavior, it is the individual, not society, that is "blamed" for deviance by receiving the diagnostic label. Unusual individual behavior is not tolerated; the deviant individual is treated or institutionalized to protect society. Schacht and Nathan (1977) have criticized DSM-III for its lack of emphasis on the interconnectedness of the individual with his or her cultural context. Etiology and treatment continue to be internally rather than externally directed. Yet historically, there are few psychological disorders that meet the requirements of being entirely organic in nature. Schacht and Nathan recommended viewing individual and environment as ". . . roles that permit flexible interchange of observables" (p. 1021). Just as the individual cannot be understood or classified without regard for his or her environmental context, so too must we recognize that our system of classification is inextricably linked to its social context. Failure to acknowledge the social and cultural influences in our system of psychopathology can only further distort our investigations of human functioning.

The Harmful Consequences of Labeling

In science a Type I error is a cardinal sin. In contrast, in the field of medicine it is widely accepted that it is more dangerous to overlook an active "case" of a disease than to mistakenly diagnose disease in a well person. So medicine more often treats a person who is *not* ill than the reverse. Psychiatry has incorporated this medical orientation toward illness in both its nosology and its practice to the detriment of people who are harmed or stigmatized by psychiatric intervention and labeling. This medical perspective leads to a search for pathological characteristics in those who might otherwise be considered healthy individuals. This perspective also promotes errors in the direction of cautious, dependence-oriented treatment. For example, Mendel and Rapport (1969) investigated whether the severity of a person's symptoms was related to the decision to hospitalize and found the severity of symptoms to be unrelated to the decision to hospitalize. Rather, decisions to hospitalize were heavily influenced by (a) indications of prior hospitalizations on the record, (b) the relative clinical inexperience of the decision maker, and (c) a focus on the medical model in the training of the decision maker. In short, professionals erred in the direction of hospitalizing persons who might not need such hospitalization on the basis of prior hospitalization and the professional's training in the medical bases of mental disorders.

The authors of DSM-III cautioned that abnormality is continuous with wellness, that "there is no assumption that each mental disorder is a discrete entity with sharp boundaries (discontinuity) between it and other mental disorders, as well as between it and no mental disorder" (p. 6). Nevertheless, DSM-III provides clear cutoff points for identifying the presence of disorders and gives exclusion criteria from alternative disorders. The duration of a disorder, or a certain number of symptoms, or a particular age of onset differentiates cases from noncases. It is argued that the distinction between the classes of disorders in terms of specific inclusion and exclusion criteria is important as a common basis for research. Yet, from a clinical perspective and from the standpoint of what happens to an individual, the classification is important as well. Individuals labeled schizophrenic, for example, are not seen as being on a continuum of normal behavior once the classification has been made. Regardless of what the authors of DSM-III say, the classification system supports a discontinuity view of psychopathology.

It is not surprising that humans establish ways of classifying people and/or behavior in attempts to create order and meaning in their observations. However, research suggests that the individual engaging in the behaviors interprets them very differently from the person observing these same behaviors. According to attribution theory (Jones & Nisbett, 1972), individuals tend to attribute their own behavior to the particular situation in which they find themselves. However, observers are more likely to attribute the same behavior, when performed by others, to stable personality characteristics of those other people. For example, the student who talks to his or her professor about handing a paper in late may attribute his or her own behavior to such situational factors as excessive work load, a recent argument with his or her lover, a temporary illness, or interfering demands of his or her part-time job. The professor, on the other hand, is more likely to attribute the student's failure to complete the paper to internal, organismic characteristics such as laziness, general ineptitude, or rebelliousness. Mental health providers are not immune from this attributional tendency. Given our tendencies to interpret the behavior of others in terms of characteristics inherent in the individual, a dysfunction-based system of classification that also places the locus of dysfunction within the person virtually ensures our finding pathology in those individuals who enter our clinic's door.

As a consequence of labeling, we focus attention more on the individual and disregard possible environmental contributions. For example, if a child complains about his or her teacher or school day, we are likely to consider environmental factors as having caused this child's distress. If, on the other hand, we know that this child has been diagnosed as having a learning problem or as being hyperactive, we tend to disregard the problematic environment and attribute the source of the problem within the child. In this way, diagnosis, by focusing attention on defects inside the individual, ultimately serves to blame the victim.

DSM-III clearly states that a diagnosis refers to a "behavioral, psychological, or biological dysfunction, and that the disturbance is not only in the relationship between the individual and society" (p. 6). However, there is little evidence in the criteria of the specific diagnostic categories to take these environmental factors into account. The goodness of fit between the individual and the environment is still important in determining diagnosis. Furthermore, cultural factors can influence how appropriate a particular set of behaviors may be. For example, the average white, middle-class American child, if diagnosed in Finland, would probably be considered as having a conduct disorder; the average Finnish child diagnosed by an American mental health professional would be considered as having a shyness disorder. Undoubtedly, the cultural context determines where a particular behavior falls on the continuum of appropriateness or deviancy.

Although individuals attribute their own behavior to situational variables, they readily believe personality descriptions of themselves made by others. Dmitruk, Collins, and Clinger (1978) demonstrated that even negative personality profiles are overwhelmingly believed by the person assessed. They asked subjects to complete Rokeach's Value Survey and Machover's Figure Drawing Test. A week later, subjects were given a "bogus and uncomplimentary" personality profile that they were told was based on their performance. Subjects overwhelmingly accepted the truthfulness of these interpretations about themselves, even though they knew the reports were based on scanty information. The authors concluded that more objective and standard instruments (such as the DSM-III) could yield even greater acceptance by subjects of negative personal information.

The widely quoted Rosenhan (1973) study in which eight "pseudopatients" gained admission to psychiatric hospitals, were diagnosed and treated by staff, and discharged as "in remission," indicates the resilience of a "set" for psychiatric labeling. Initial diagnostic decisions were maintained while the individuals were inpatients despite the fact that they displayed no schizophrenic behaviors. Further, discharge from the hospital was not viewed as synonymous with "wellness," but rather, the diagnostic label remained attached independently of all evidence of positive functioning. Persons who have had genuine illnesses are rarely called "former pneumonia patients" or "former medical patients," but the term "former mental patient" is inescapable.

The process of psychiatric labeling is particularly alarming when applied to children. Whereas childhood disorders are often transitory, a label is more likely to endure, and the cumulative effects of a label on a child's development can be profound. Garmezy (1978) criticized the childhood diagnoses in DSM-III. Developmental disorders of childhood, which include such diagnoses as oppositional disorder, avoidant disorder, and overanxious disorder, are considered qualitatively different from normal adjustment disorders. According to DSM-III, the child with these disorders is not necessarily likely to "catch up" with other children. This is in marked contrast to the most recent version of the International Classification of Diseases (ICD-9), which includes childhood development delays (rather than disorders) that refer to the child's current functioning and not to permanent diagnoses (Garmezy, 1978). Garmezy further points out that some of the specific developmental disorders of childhood, such as Specific Reading Disorder and Specific Arithmetical Disorder, are not only prevalent in very large numbers of children, but are not necessarily best treated with psychotherapy. Thus, by including such disorders in the DSM-III, we may be creating iatrogenic disorders for many children, and our label may be more powerful than our treatment. Such diagnoses have the further effect of shifting responsibility for intervention from educational professionals to medical therapists whose numbers are insignificant and whose competencies are limited.

As the number of diagnostic categories in a DSM becomes progressively larger, a larger percentage of the population becomes "diagnosable." DSM-III contains fewer organic disorders than DSM-II, but more socially based behaviors (e.g., caffeinism, compulsive gambling). By labeling such social behaviors as psychopathological, we are revealing a lessening tolerance for deviation in our society. At best, we are observing a metamorphosis in which medical practitioners are appointing themselves the arbiters of deviant behavior that was once the province of religious or legal institutions. Individuals who centuries ago might have been excommunicated because of their behavior now face stigmatization by the psychiatric profession. This attempt at control of deviant behavior by psychiatry assumes that people who engage in behaviors judged by others as harmful to themselves are "sick." (Categories for motorcycle riders, sky divers, trapeze performers, and pugilists are not far away!) Psychiatric diagnoses have even pervaded the judicial system. The psychiatric consultants now decide if someone is fit to stand trial.

Antisocial Behavior as Psychiatric Illness

Wootton (1959/1978) examined the intellectual structure dealing with current views of mental health and mental illness, particularly as these concepts relate to persons who exhibit antisocial behavior. First, she says, is the postulate that mental health and mental illness are real, objective, and measurable—not just an expression of value judgments of psychiatrists or reflections of the norms of a particular culture. Mental health is alleged to be as real as physical health, and as definable. From this first postulate it follows that it should be possible to diagnose objectively the presence of mental illness (or mental health) using criteria that are independent of antisocial behavior exhibited by the individuals alleged to be suffering from mental illness. It follows that persons who commit antisocial acts can be divided into two classes: those who have a mental disorder and those who do not. Third, if it is established that a mental disorder exists in a person who has committed antisocial acts, then it is also possible to ascertain whether these acts are caused by the disorder. (This causal relation may not always exist.) It is possible that a person with a mental disorder, say, a paranoid belief that he or she is being persecuted by Martians, at the same time may be guilty of the crime of shoplifting, where there is no apparent necessary connection between the mental disorder and the criminal behavior. This means that it is necessary for the expert to establish that the antisocial behavior was specifically caused by the mental disorder. Then it follows that the antisocial behavior is not only explained by the disorder, but is also to some degree excusable by the presence of the disorder. So mental disturbance may diminish or eliminate moral responsibility and give freedom from legal prosecution. Wootton points out that inasmuch as mental disorder is separate from socially unacceptable behavior, not all persons who exhibit antisocial behavior can be considered mental cases. In other words, two persons who commit the same crime may find very different treatment in the courts because the crime of one is explained by the presence of a mental disorder that caused it, and the crime of the other is judged not to be the product of a mental disorder.

Wootton contrasts all of this with society's attitude toward genuine physical illness. If a person is genuinely sick, he or she will be excused from work. But if a person is alcoholic, or neurotic, or is malingering, society is less inclined to excuse these individuals from fulfilling work obligations. If a person with a high fever or with temporal lobe damage says or does irrational things, society is quite inclined to excuse the behavior as the product of sickness. Attempts to achieve the same kind of social acceptance for those with functional mental disorders have been less successful.

Wootton summarizes her position as follows:

> As definitions of mental illness become even vaguer or deeply entangled in the accepted forms of social conduct, so does it become ever more evident that many of those who are labeled "mentally sick" acquire this label merely because in one way or another they have failed to manage their lives comfortably with the demands of the social environment in which they find themselves. The suspicious, the irritable, the bad-tempered, the aggressive are cajoled or driven by their suffering friends and relatives or by "the

authorities" to seek medical advice—especially, perhaps, if they are of tender years, since the young are generally at the mercy of their elders and
must go and do what they are told. In such cases it is the anti-social
behavior which is the precipitating factor that leads to mental treatment.
But at the same time the fact of the illness is itself inferred from this
behavior: indeed, it is almost true to say that the illness *is* the behavior for
which it is also the excuse. But any disease, the morbidity of which is
established *only* by the social failure that it involves, must rank as fundamentally different from those of which the symptoms are independent of social
norms. (p. 225)

Psychiatric Diagnosis as an Instrument of Control

Psychiatric diagnosis often is used as a method of social control. It is not only
in the Soviet Union that political dissidents, antiestablishment rebels, and
opponents of the prevailing social order are labeled as psychiatrically ill. The
Karen Silkwood case in Oklahoma is a beautiful example of attempts by a
powerful industry to use political and police influence to try to discredit a
woman who was a labor organizer and a critic of questionable safety methods. She was called a sexual deviate and a drug addict. The practice of
labeling and even incarcerating persons who oppose injustice is well established. For a long time it was not questioned. Szasz (1977) pointed out: "The
most powerful justification for an act, especially for a socially established
practice, is no justification at all" (p. 5). He notes the absence of any reference
to slavery in the U. S. Constitution and the absence, in most psychiatric
textbooks, of any mention of involuntary patienthood. But neither, for most
of our history, has there been any reference to, or justification for, sexism
and racism. It is important to recognize that when powerful groups have
their practices questioned and challenged and begin to have to explain their
actions, they have begun to lose their power. As the French say, "Qui
s' excuse, s' accuse."

Szasz describes the justifications and excuses that have begun to appear
to explain the necessity of psychiatric labeling and involuntary incarceration.
He identifies three categories of justification. The first identifies "them" as
different in kind from "us." "They" are defective, constitutionally inferior,
genetically damaged, biochemically abnormal. By putting them in a class
outside the pale of normal society, the mentally ill are classified as things
rather than as people. A second justification for labeling is to argue that we
normal members of society are endangered by "them"; they constitute a
threat because of their inability to control their aggression. We must protect
ourselves by locking them up. Third, it is decided that "they" are also
dangerous to themselves, and that we are doing a kind and selfless duty by
locking them up to protect them from themselves; in other words, we are
helping them by depriving them of their liberty.

The facts are reasonably clear. An overwhelming majority of the persons to whom we give psychiatric labels are not different in kind from the rest of us. Freud's most important message, as Bruner (1957) pointed out, was his emphasis on the continuity between the mind of the child and the mind of the adult, the continuity between the world of waking reason and the world of dreams, the continuity between the sane and the insane. This is why it is so important for psychiatry to search unceasingly for evidence of a disease or defect, to try to establish a discontinuity. And the evidence that an overwhelming majority of persons labeled as psychiatrically ill are not dangerous to others or to themselves is a fact to be denied as frequently and decisively as possible.

In summary, DSM-III was constructed to be inclusive of psychopathology rather than exclusive. Despite the stated assumption that abnormality is continuous with health, there are clear cutoff points for each diagnostic category in DSM-III. Given a dysfunction-based system of classification, mental health professionals are likely to attribute behavior to negative internal, organismic variables of the individual. Attribution theory suggests that individuals attribute their own behavior to situational variables; however, research indicates that individuals overwhelmingly accept personality "interpretations" of themselves, even when such personality profiles are negative. Research also suggests that once a diagnostic label is assigned, it is fairly resistant to change. Furthermore, the diagnosis focuses attention on the individual and away from the environmental context. The process of labeling is particularly alarming for use with children, given the stability of labels and the transient nature of many childhood disorders. Finally, the large number of diagnostic categories in DSM-III suggests a possible trend toward progressively lesser tolerance of deviancy in society and/or progressively greater control of social behavior by the psychiatric profession.

Allocation of Funds for Research

There is something both silly and sinister about the growth in numbers, and the broadening of content, of psychiatric diagnoses. From DSM-I in 1952 to DSM-II in 1968 to DSM-III in 1980, the number of separate diagnostic groups has increased from 60 to 145 to 230. If this neat linear rate of growth continues, we can expect DSM-VI to offer something like 400 diagnostic choices to be available by the turn of the millenium. As things now stand, a clear majority of the population has a psychiatric disorder; indeed, many of us have multiple psychiatric disorders, what with tobacco addiction withdrawal symptoms, episodic alcohol abuse, marital problems, worry over children who are seemingly afflicted with developmental arithmetic disorder (apparently genetic), and all. The silliness is compounded by the determination of the psychiatric profession to retain control of third-party health scheme reimbursement of treatment, claiming that all of these varied mental disorders—like stuttering, developmental arithmetic disorder, pathological gambling, histrionic personality disorder, simple phobia, cannabis abuse, transient tic disorder, to identify a few—are medical problems that must be treated by a psychiatrist (or any other physician), but not by other professionals or laypersons without medical referral and/or supervision.

The sinister and frightening part of this story is the fact that psychiatrists and many otherwise normal, educated people in the society take all this diagnostic mumbo jumbo quite seriously. Psychiatry draws on the power and mystique of medicine to enhance its credibility. Weak ideas, expressed by powerful people, acquire a potency in excess of their quality.

As classification systems evolve, funds for research and intervention seem to follow. Ironically, the majority of funding awards by the National Institute of Mental Health (NIMH) are for specific areas of mental disorder, particularly DSM diagnostic categories. As the number of specific disorders in the DSM have grown linearly in size through its first, second, and third editions, new diagnostic categories now constitute fundable research and clinical areas. Over the next few years, we might expect that relatively infrequent DSM-III categories (e.g., gender identity disorder of childhood, kleptomania, factitious disorder) may have funding priority over problems in functioning that are more prevalent (e.g., stress), but that are omitted from DSM-III.

The progression from DSM-I to -II to -III makes apparent the research/funding cycle. Funding for a diagnostic category results in increased research in that area. Increased research results once again in increased subcategories of that diagnostic category and more funding. In general, as funding priorities have changed with the recent trend toward social conservatism, sociocultural determinants of psychopathology have been deemphasized in favor of biological approaches. If this trend continues, then future versions of DSM will increasingly focus on organic/genetic diagnostic categories rather than sociocultural influences. It is difficult to break out of the perceptual funding/research cycle. Funding dictates research and research dictates funding. The classification system in use appears to influence both heavily.

The classification system's influence on the research/funding cycle is especially grave for the area of prevention. Prevention historically has been locked out of research support for several reasons. First, it is claimed that there is no large body of prevention research, and research begets funding which begets research. Second, medical model spokespersons hold that it is necessary to know the specific causal etiology of a disorder before one can prevent it. This view assumes that there must be a single or discrete causal agent for each disorder. A casual look at DSM-III categories reveals that the identification of specific causation is unlikely for most diagnoses. Thus, prevention research, from a medical model perspective and from a DSM-III base, is largely untenable. Finally, even the Prevention Research Center at NIMH, a center presumably oriented toward preventing psychopathology and maintaining wellness, requires focus on specific mental disorders for funding. DSM-III is the basis for funding decisions. DSM-III exclusively categorizes pathology. Thus, ironically, prevention cannot enter a research/funding cycle unless it becomes dysfunction oriented.

Individuals and organizations that benefit from the allocation of funds are heavily dysfunction oriented. The medical profession, as the primary architect of the DSM-III classification system, thus increases in power and influence. It is reasonable to assume that the medically oriented classification system has become the foundation for determination of third-party payments. DSM-III determines who gets reimbursed for what conditions. By expanding DSM, there are potentially ever more reimbursable categories for the medical profession. As the medical profession attains increased control of reimbursement, nonmedical professionals are excluded. Schacht and Nathan (1977) evaluated the significance of DSM-III for psychologists. They concluded that as the quantity of diagnoses included in a DSM increases and as physicians are considered by insurance companies and legislatures to have primary responsibility in diagnosis and treatment, psychologists' interventions will be increasingly excluded. Their comments apply equally well to other nonmedical categories of mental health professionals. Physicians and other adherents of the medical model will receive the majority of financial support. Once again, other professionals supporting other views of classification will be locked out of the system.

In summary, the cycle of funding and of research yields more funding for standard diagnostic categories. Dysfunction-oriented institutions profit from this system; prevention or competency-based ones are left out. Insurance companies are more likely to reimburse DSM-III categories of psychopathology. Thus, funding allocations reinforce medical professionals over those who are not medical model oriented.

An Illustration of the Diagnostic System: The Case of Homosexuality

The manner in which the DSM has changed the diagnosis of homosexuality illustrates the preceding points.

Societal attitudes regarding homosexuality have changed only gradually over time. In the eighteenth century, homosexuality was considered immoral on religious grounds, and the medical establishment abhorred all forms of sexuality not resulting in procreation (Morin, 1977). Paralleling this cultural homophobia, the DSMs listed homosexuality as a personality disorder until the 1970s.

As a consequence of cultural mores and the DSM-II listing of homosexuality as a mental illness, research and treatment focused on homosexuality as a disease. First, assessment studies attempted to determine whether homosexuals could be identified by means of projective tests or other unobtrusive measures. Presumably, individuals would not admit to homosexuality when asked directly, just as the label "schizophrenic" is not self-selected by individuals. Thus, projective tests attempted to identify such "evidence" of homosexuality as unconscious hostility toward the opposite sex, which was then used as part of the diagnostic criteria. This research continued despite Hooker's (1957) early landmark study revealing that mental health professionals could not differentiate between projective test responses of heterosexuals and homosexuals when the raters were blind to the sexual orientation of the subjects.

Second, research focused on isolating the causes of homosexuality. A popular theory of etiology focused on family background (Morin, 1977). Homosexuals (and sometimes, but not always, heterosexual controls) were asked about the nature of their relationships with their parents, their role in the family, and the methods of child-rearing they had experienced. Results of in-depth (and usually post-hoc) interviews were interpreted according to psychodynamic theory, particularly with regard to Oedipal conflicts. Another theory of etiology stressed biochemical differences between homosexuals and heterosexuals, particularly focusing on hormones that affected masculine or feminine behavior. Finally, learning theory considered homosexuality to result from negative experiences with the opposite sex. Morin (1977) reviewed this research and concluded that the results are ". . . inconclusive and frequently contradictory."

A third area of research focus in the era of DSM-II was on the degree of adjustment of homosexuals (Morin, 1977). Homosexuals were compared with heterosexuals on numerous psychological measures. Despite the heterosexual bias usually inherent in such measures, Thompson, McCandless, and Strickland (1971) found no differences in adjustment between homosexuals and heterosexuals.

Finally, research investigated the treatment of homosexuality. Generally, this consisted of attempts at reorienting sexual arousal to more normative heterosexual stimuli. Treatment was considered successful when the individual was no longer involved in homosexual activity and had transferred sexual activity to members of the opposite sex.

Thus, psychiatric research on homosexuality mirrored the cultural setting and attitudes. The nature of research conducted on homosexuality reflected the attitudes of a society that viewed homosexuality as a sickness. Research results, when favorable to homosexuality or when unable to substantiate differences between homosexuals and heterosexuals, did not significantly affect psychiatric views or social policy. Homosexuals continued to be encouraged to beome "reoriented" because heterosexuality was considered to be the only appropriate and acceptable form of sexual expression in our society.

Despite all of the research that consistently failed to demonstrate maladjustment in homosexuals relative to heterosexuals, the diagnostic category remained unchanged. However, in the late 1960s and early 1970s, the gay rights movement began to advocate an end to discrimination against lesbians and gay men. It was only then that the APA responded by agreeing to discuss removing the diagnosis of homosexuality from DSM-II. As a result, in 1973, the Nomenclature Committee of the APA voted in favor of changing the DSM-II diagnosis to "sexual orientation disorder." This was further modified in DSM-III to "ego-dystonic homosexuality."

According to DSM-III, the essential features of ego-dystonic homosexuality are "a desire to acquire or increase heterosexual arousal, so that heterosexual relationships can be initiated or maintained, and a sustained pattern of overt homosexual arousal that the individual explicitly states has been unwanted and a persistent source of distress." If we assume that sexual arousal is by definition pleasurable to the individual, then arousal that is "unwanted and a persistent source of distress" can only be culturally induced. Indeed, DSM-III suggests that predisposing factors for ego-dystonic homosexuality consist of "negative societal attitudes that have been internalized." Thus, DSM-III again reflects the mores of particular subcultures: If a culture is homophobic, the individual who is homosexual is more likely to have "internalized negative societal attitudes" and to receive the label of ego-dystonic homosexuality; more tolerant cultures are less likely to instill such values and attitudes in homosexuals.

Research on homosexuality no longer focuses on the presumed inferior functioning of homosexuals, nor on theories of etiology, nor on attempts at reorientation to heterosexuality. Yet there is little research supported on the well-functioning homosexual and on such topics as homosexuals' life-styles, relationships, and children. Ironically, as the diagnostic category of homosexuality is removed from our psychiatric classification system, there is an accompanying decline in funding for research. Once again, our pathology-based system of research is evident. Individual or group differences appear to be interesting to mental health professionals only when the deviation is interpreted as a problem. The search for socially defined weaknesses and pathologies is a major flaw in our classification system.

We have used homosexuality as an example of the social (and religious) origin of a psychiatric classification and declassification. But the whole range of acceptable and nonacceptable sexual behavior could provide a number of other examples of the role of moral values in determining and defining deviance. Recently some elderly women living on the back wards of British mental hospitals were found to have spent their lives in the institution because they were "moral degenerates." They had been committed by their families when, as young women, early in the century, they had become pregnant out of wedlock! As this transgression of conventional morality was a conclusive sign of moral weakness, their righteous Victorian families preferred to lock them up rather than to face the social shame of "illegitimacy." Also, in the nineteenth century in England and America, and in parts of the world still today, a belief that sexual pleasure is dangerous for women led to the surgical mutilation of the genitalia of millions of women. Psychiatry supported this view and extended its proscription for many forms of sexual behavior, including especially masturbation (once viewed as a major cause and/or symptom of insanity). The psychological and psychiatric textbooks just a generation ago listed many sexual "perversions" as symptoms of serious psychopathology. Today many of these behaviors are tolerated and even encouraged as normal and healthy.

Conclusions

Systems of behavioral classification reflect the attitudes and biases of the times and culture. Scientific research on etiology and treatment of disorders is confined by cultural expectations, whether in "hard" areas such as the degree to which schizophrenia is genetically induced, or in "soft" areas such as whether homosexuals are well adjusted.

Our nosology is individual defect based. Not only are clinical populations most often used in research, but differences from the norm are of interest only when in a negative direction. Despite the recognition that social environment influences behavior, it is the individual who is labeled abnormal and must endure the consequences of that label.

The research funding cycle for psychopathology ensures that this defect-based system maintains itself. Furthermore, the medical profession benefits primarily from such a disease-oriented model. To the degree that we continue to follow a defect model, we perpetuate a system by which the medical profession identifies and controls individuals who behave in nonconformist ways and by which support is provided for maintaining the status quo. Such a system is not good for the recipients, the providers, or the society as an evolving system.

The situation will change only when it becomes clear that the classification system of psychiatry is basically a political and social device for protecting the status quo, for maintaining a social order that supports exploitation and injustice.

REFERENCES

Albee, G. (1982). Preventing psychopathology and promoting human potential. *American Psychologist, 37*(9), 1043–1050.

American Psychiatric Association. (1980). *Diagnostic and statistical manual of mental disorders* (3rd ed.). Washington, DC: Author.

Bloom, B. (1978). Chapter 6. Marital disruption as a stressor. In D. Forgays (Ed.), *Environmental influences and strategies in primary prevention.* Hanover, NH: University Press of New England.

Brenner, M. H. (1973). *Mental illness and the economy.* Cambridge, MA: Harvard University Press.

Brenner, M. H. (1977). Personal stability and economic security. *Social Policy, 8,* 2–4.

Bruner, J. (1957). Freud and the image of man. In B. Nelson (Ed.), *Freud and the twentieth century.* Cleveland & New York: World Meridan.

Davison, G. C., & Neale, J. M. (1982). *Abnormal psychology: An experimental clinical approach.* New York: Wiley.

Dmitruk, V. M., Collins, R. W., & Clinger, D. L. (1978). The "Barnum effect" and acceptance of negative personal evaluation. *Journal of Consulting and Clinical Psychology, 41,* 192–194.

Erlenmeyer-Kimling, L. (1977). Chapter 5. Issues pertaining to prevention and intervention of genetic disorders affecting human behavior. In G. W. Albee & J. M. Joffe (Eds.), *Primary prevention of psychopathology: Vol. 1. The issues.* Hanover, NH: University Press of New England.

Garmezy, N. (1978). DSM III. Never mind the psychologists: Is it good for the children? *Clinical Psychologist, 31,* 1–6.

Hooker, E. (1957). The adjustment of the male overt homosexual. *Journal of Projective Techniques, 21,* 18–31.

Joffe, J. (1982). Approaches to prevention of adverse developmental consequences of genetic and prenatal factors. In L. A. Bond & J. M. Joffe (Eds.), *Facilitating infant and early childhood development.* Hanover, NH: University Press of New England.

Jones, E. E., & Nisbett, R. E. (1972). The actor and the observer: Divergent perceptions of the causes of behavior. In E. E. Jones, D. E. Kanouse, H. H. Kelly, R. E. Nisbett, S. Valins, & B. Weiner (Eds.), *Attribution: Perceiving the causes of behavior.* Morristown, NJ: General Learning Press.

Kallmann, F. (1938). *The genetics of schizophrenia.* New York: J. J. Augustin.

Kamin, L. (1974). *The science and politics of I.Q.* Potomac, MD: Erlbaum.

Kamin, L. (1983, March). *The genetics of schizophrenia.* Colloquium presented at the University of Vermont, Burlington.

Kaplan, M. (1983). A woman's view of DSM-III. *American Psychologist, 38,* 786–792.

Klerman, G. (1980). Speech. In G. W. Albee & D. Whitehorn (Chairs), *Faculty symposium on the social and biological origins of mental illness.* Burlington: University of Vermont.

Kramer, M. (1981, May). *The increasing prevalence of mental disorders: Implications for the future.* Paper presented at the National Conference on the Elderly Deinstitutionalized Patient in the Community.

Lamb, H. R., & Zusman, J. (1979). Primary prevention in perspective. *American Journal of Psychiatry, 136,* 12–17.

Marx, K., & Engels, F. (1936). Manifesto of the communist party. In Karl Marx, *Selected Works* (Vol. 1). New York: International Publishers. (Original work published 1848)

Mendel, W. M., & Rapport, S. (1969). Determinants of the decision for psychiatric hospitalization. *Archives of General Psychiatry, 20,* 321–328.

Morin, S. F. (1977). Heterosexual bias in psychological research on lesbianism and male homosexuality. *American Psychologist, 32,* 629–637.

President's Commission on Mental Health (PCMH). (1978). *Report to the President.* Washington, DC: U. S. Government Printing Office.

Professional Staff of the U.S.—U.K. Cross National Project. (1974). The diagnosis of psychopathology of schizophrenia in New York and London. *Schizophrenia Bulletin, 1,* 80–102.

Rosenhan, D. L. (1973). On being sane in insane places. *Science, 179,* 250–258.

Ryan, W. (1969). *Distress in the city.* Cleveland, OH: The Press of Case Western Reserve University.

Schacht, T., & Nathan, P. E. (1977). But is it good for psychologists? Appraisal and status of DSM III. *American Psychologist, 32,* 1017–1025.

Sharma, S. L. (1970). A historical background of the development of nosology in psychiatry and psychology. *American Psychologist, 25,* 248–253.

Szasz, T. (1977). *Psychiatric slavery.* New York: Free Press.

Task Panel on Women. (1978). *Report to the Presidents' Commission on Mental Health.* (Vol. 3). Washington, DC: U.S. Government Printing Office.

Thompson, N. L., McCandless, B. R., & Strickland, B. R. (1971). Personal adjustment of male and female homosexuals and heterosexuals. *Journal of Abnormal Psychology, 78,* 237–240.

Vance, E. (1977). Chapter 12. A typology of risks and disabilities of low status. In G. W. Albee & J. M. Joffe (Eds.), *The primary prevention of psychopathology: The issues.* Hanover, NH: University Press of New England.

Wootton, B. (1978). *Social science and social pathology.* Westport, CT: Greenwood Press. (Original work published 1959)

Zubin, J. (1977–1978). But is it good for science? *The clinical psychologist, 31,* 1, 7.

PART III

CONCEPTUAL ISSUES

What Are the Clinical Credentials of the Psychoanalytic Compromise Model of Neurotic Symptoms?

Adolf Grünbaum

Introduction[1]

By espousing a compromise model of neurotic symptoms, Freudian theory makes the repression etiology generically fundamental to the concept of a psychoneurosis. Hence, in psychoanalytic theory, the rationale for a nosology of disorders is basically etiologic rather than symptom centered. And the various diagnostic categories or personality types are thus anchored in specified sorts of supposedly pathogenic repressions, in consonance with Freud's theory of psychosexual development.

In keeping with their compromise model of psychopathology, psychoanalysts have inveterately prided themselves that their therapy extirpates the causes or actual pathogens of the psychoneuroses, while accusing rival treatment modalities of producing merely cosmetic or evanescent removals of symptoms.

Since psychoanalytic diagnosis and therapy are thus founded on the repression etiology, the merits of its nosologic rationale depend crucially on the credentials of Freud's theory of pathogenesis. Avowedly, that etiologic theory meets time-honored scientific standards on the strength of being abundantly warranted by clinical findings. Hence, I hope to contribute to the appraisal of the Freudian nosology by examining the credentials of the psychoanalytic clinical theory in this chapter.

---

1. The sections following the Introduction of this chapter are drawn from the author's Presidential Address to the American Philosophical Association, delivered in Baltimore on December 28, 1982 (Grünbaum, 1983c).

Adolf Grünbaum. Departments of Philosophy and Psychiatry, University of Pittsburgh, Pittsburgh, Pennsylvania.

Freud's Notion of Scientific Status

Throughout his long career, Freud insisted that the psychoanalytic enterprise has the status of a natural science. As he told us at the very end of his life, the explanatory gains from positing unconscious mental processes "enabled psychology to take its place as a natural science like any other".[2] Then he went on to declare: "Psycho-analysis is a part of the mental science of psychology. . . . Psychology too, is a natural science" (S.E. 1940, 23, 282). Earlier, Freud had firmly rebuffed the antinaturalism and methodological separatism that was championed by the Geisteswissenschaften movement as a framework for psychology and the social sciences. Its votaries deemed causal explanations to be endemic to the natural sciences in view of the lawlike causal connections featured by these disciplines. And they rejected such nomothetic causal explanations as generically alien to the humanistic sciences. For as they saw it, the aim of the study of man ought to be the "hermeneutic" quest for idiographic understanding by such methods as empathy and intuitive self-evidence (Möller, 1976, Chap. 2; Möller, 1978, Chap. 2). In diametrical opposition to this view of the task of psychology, Freud proclaimed:

> . . . the intellect and the mind are objects for scientific research in exactly the same way as any non-human things. Psychoanalysis has a special right to speak for the scientific *Weltanschauung*. . . . If . . . the investigation of the intellectual and emotional functions of men (and of animals) is included in science, then it will be seen that . . . no new sources of knowledge or methods of research have come into being. (S.E. 1933, 22, 159)

In 1895, the psychoanalytic method of clinical investigation by means of free association was only a fledgling mode of inquiry. Likewise, Freud's clinical theory of psychopathology was still nascent. At that very early juncture, he gave a neurophysiological twist to the notion of a scientific psychology. And he couched his then vision of a neurological underpinning for psychic processes in the reductionistic physical idiom of material particles. This biophysical notion animated his 1895 manuscript "Project for a Scientific Psychology" (S.E. 1950, 1, 295). Yet Freud abandoned his reductionistic program within only 2 years of having enunciated it. As he wrote in retrospect:

> . . . every attempt . . . to discover a [brain] localization of mental processes, every endeavor to think of ideas as stored up in nerve cells and of excitations as travelling along nerve-fibres, has miscarried completely. (S.E. 1915, 14, 174)

2. Hereafter any references given to Freud's writings in English will be to this *Standard Edition* under its acronym "S.E." followed by the year of first appearance, the volume number, and the page(s). Thus, the 1940 quotation just given would be cited within the text in abbreviated fashion as follows: S.E. 1940, 23, 158.

By 1900, the legacy of the abandoned neurological model had become the postulation of a bipartite structure of the mind whose principal component systems were the unconscious and the so-called preconscious (S.E. 1900, 5, Chap. vii). The contents of the preconscious system, if not actually conscious, are deemed readily accessible to consciousness. But only the clinical techniques of psychoanalysis are held able to unlock the gates to the unconscious system. Freud now pointedly eschewed the original neurological connotations of the technical vocabulary he had introduced in the 1895 project. Yet he retained this terminology for use in a purely mentalistic sense. Thus, the erstwhile excitation or "cathexis" of a neuron has now become the cathected state of an idea or memory. Likewise, a train of thought is now held to involve the flow of cathexes from one idea to another, so that psychic energy is invested in the mental representations of objects. And the two component systems of the mind were assumed to differ in regard to permitting the flow of psychic energy toward tension discharge. Later, Freud modified his bipartite structural model of the unconscious and the preconscious when he replaced it by three agencies whose functions need not detain us (S.E. 1923, 19, 12–59; 1933, 22, 57–80).

These successive models of the structure and function of the psychic apparatus are often denominated as the "metapsychology" of the psychoanalytic edifice (Laplanche & Pontalis, 1973, p. 250). The separation of the clinical theory of repression from that metapsychology within the edifice is not always sharp. Yet it is vital to appreciate to what marginal epistemic status Freud relegated its metapsychological part amid steadfastly claiming natural science status for his construction overall. The metapsychological models, he tells us, are "a speculative superstructure of psychoanalysis, any portion of which can be abandoned or changed without loss or regret the moment its inadequacy has been proved" (S.E. 1925, 20, 32–33; see also S.E. 1914, 14, 77). And he added pointedly: "But there is still plenty to be described that lies closer to actual experience." The "plenty . . . that lies closer to actual experience" is, of course, none other than his clinically based theory of personality, psychopathology, and therapy. The centerpiece of that corpus of hypotheses is the theory of repression, which features his compromise model of neurotic symptoms, as well as of manifest dream content and of various sorts of slips. These various phenomena are deemed to be "compromises" in the sense of being substitutive gratifications or outlets, for they are held to be conatively vicarious surrogates. Moreover, the clinical theory of repression is often couched in personalist language.

But in conspicuous contrast to his depiction of the metapsychology as "a speculative superstructure" which can be sloughed off, if need be, "without loss or regret," Freud explicitly deemed his clinical theory to be "the most essential part" of what he had wrought. For, as he told us, "the theory of repression is the cornerstone on which the whole structure of psychoanalysis rests. It is the most essential part of it" (S.E. 1914, 14, 16).

Thus, when Freud unswervingly claimed natural science status for his theoretical constructions throughout his life, he did so first and foremost for his evolving clinical theory of personality and therapy rather than for the metapsychology of psychic energy flow. After all, he had been chastened in his early reductionistic exuberance by the speedy demise of his neurobiological model in 1896. Thereafter, he never made the scientific status of the clinical theory parasitic on its would-be subsumption under a primordially scientific metapsychology! Instead, he then perenially claimed his theory of personality and therapy to be authenticated by direct and cogent evidential support originating on his office couch and in his self-analysis. In brief, during all but the first few years of his career, Freud's criterion of scientificity was methodological and not ontologically reductive.

Appraisal of Freud's Arguments for the Psychoanalytic Theory of Repression

Avowedly, his criteria of validation are essentially those of hypothetico-deductive inductivism (S.E. 1914, *14*, 77; 1915, *14*, 117; 1925, *20*, 32). And he took adherence to them to be the hallmark of the scientific probity that he claimed for his theory. Hence, it behooves me to appraise Freud's arguments for his monumental clinical theory of personality and therapy by his own standards. Thus, the verdict that I shall reach on this basis is hardly predicated on the imposition of some extraneous methodological purism. Nor does my application of his avowed norm of scientific rationality to psychoanalysis imply that I deem this touchstone to be *the* criterion of demarcation between science and nonscience. In short, I shall grant Freud his own canon of scientific status in addressing the following key question: Did his clinical arguments vindicate the knowledge claims he made for his evolving theory by labeling it "scientific"?

My answer will be twofold: The reasoning on which Freud rested the major hypotheses of his edifice was fundamentally flawed, even if the probity of the clinical observations he adduced were not in question. Moreover, far from deserving to be taken at face value, clinical data from the psychoanalytic treatment setting are themselves epistemically quite suspect.

The central causal and explanatory significance enjoyed by unconscious ideation in the entire clinical theory rests, I submit, on two cardinal inductive inferences drawn by Breuer and Freud. As we are told in their joint "Preliminary Communication" of 1893 (S.E. 1893, *2*, 6–7), they began with an observation made after having administered their cathartic treatment to patients suffering from various symptoms of hysteria. In the course of such treatment, it had turned out that for each distinct symptom, *S*, afflicting such a neurotic, the victim had *repressed* the memory of a trauma that had closely preceded the onset of *S* and was thematically cognate to this particular symptom. Besides repressing this traumatic memory, the patient had also strangulated the affect induced by the trauma. In the case of each symptom, our two therapists tried to lift the ongoing repression of the pertinent traumatic experience and to effect a release of the pent-up affect. When their technique succeeded in implementing this twin objective, they reportedly observed the dramatic disappearance of the given symptom. Furthermore, the symptom removal *seemed* to be durable.

Impressed by this treatment outcome, Breuer and Freud drew their first momentous causal inference. Thus, they enunciated the following fundamental therapeutic hypothesis: The dramatic improvements observed after treatment were produced by none other than the cathartic lifting of the pertinent repressions. But before the founders of psychoanalysis credited the undoing of repressions with remedial efficacy, they had been keenly alert to a rival hypothesis which derived at least prima facie credibility from the known achievements of the admittedly suggestive therapies. On that alternative explanation of the positive outcome after cathartic treatment, that benefit was actually wrought by the patient's credulous expectation of symptom relief, not by the particular treatment ritual employed to fortify his or her optimistic anticipation. Breuer and Freud believed that they could rule out such an account of the treatment gains, an account to which I shall refer as "the hypothesis of *placebo effect*" (Grünbaum, 1981). In an attempt to counter this challenge, they pointed out that the distinct symptoms had been removed *separately*, such that any one symptom disappeared only after lifting a *particular* repression (S.E. 1893, 2, 7).

And they saw very clearly that the threat posed by the rival hypothesis of placebo effect could be ominous, for, unless they could meet it convincingly it would totally abort their inference of a bold and, in fact, historic etiologic postulate from their fundamental therapeutic tribute to the undoing of repressions. Indeed, I shall argue that, to this day, the whole of the clinical psychoanalytic enterprise is haunted by the mortal threat from the very live possibility of placebo effect. As will emerge, the continuing failure of psychoanalytic research to discredit this altogether reasonable challenge gravely jeopardizes the very foundations of Freud's entire clinical theory. Mind you, the clinical hypotheses compromise not only the asserted therapeutic efficacy of lifting repressions, but also the repression etiologies of the psychoneuroses as well as the compromise models of manifest dream content and of sundry sorts of "Freudian slips."

In any case, at the time, Breuer and Freud believed that their therapeutic results had ruled out the dangerous rival hypothesis of placebo effect. Having inferred the remedial efficacy of undoing repressions, they thought furthermore that this posited therapeutic potency inductively spelled a paramount etiologic moral as follows: A coexisting ongoing repression is causally necessary for the maintenance of a neurosis, N, and an original act of repression was the causal sine qua non for the origination of N. This second ground-breaking causal inference was animated by their supposition that the repressed traumatic memory "acts [pathogenically] like a foreign body which long after its entry must continue to be regarded as an agent that is still at work" (S.E. 1893, 2, 6). The heuristic value of adopting this analogy becomes patent upon recalling that the inferred etiology yielded a deductive explanation of the supposed remedial efficacy of lifting repressions, for, as I noted, if an ongoing repression, R, is causally necessary for the pathogenesis and persistence of a neurosis, N, then the removal of R must issue in the eradication of N.

Note that the affect attached to a traumatic experience, E, can be suppressed (strangulated), but such that there is still conscious awareness of this pent-up affect. Thus, the affect attached to E can be suppressed without also being repressed. For example, Breuer's pioneering patient, Anna O., felt disgust at the sight of seeing a dog drinking water from a glass, but she "said nothing as she wanted to be polite" toward the dog's owner (S.E. 1895, 2, 34). Furthermore, the affect attached to E can be repressed without cognitive repression of E as a whole. Yet when E as a whole is repressed, this repression includes its accompanying affect qua being attached to E.

By the same token, the cognitive restoration of the forgotten E as a whole does also lift the repression of the affect attached to it. But the cognitive repression of E can be lifted without undoing E's affective suppression. Indeed, as Breuer and Freud report, the implementation of just this latter scenario was almost always therapeutically unavailing: "Recollection without [release of the attached pent-up] affect almost invariably produces no [therapeutic] result" (S.E. 1893, 2, 6). Thus, it would be empirically false to deem the mere lifting of the cognitive repression of E without catharsis causally sufficient for the removal of the symptom S.

Hence, we must endeavor to construe the Breuer–Freud etiology of psychoneurosis such that it does *not* entail this empirical falsehood. Yet it would have this untoward consequence if it were taken to assert that both cognitive repression and affective suppresion of E are causally necessary for neurosogenesis.

On the other hand, just the undesirable false consequence is averted—as Carl Hempel and Morris Eagle have each remarked to me—by articulating the founding etiology of psychoanalysis as follows: Either cognitive repression or affective suppression of E, that is, at least one of the two, is causally necessary for neurosogenesis, rather than both. And this version of the etiology would explain the reported therapeutic finding that the cathartic lifting of the repression—that is, the undoing of the affective suppression as well as of the cognitive repression—is causally sufficient for symptom removal. Yet, this same version would not explain, but only allow the observation, made by Breuer and Freud, that mere recall without release of pent-up affect is "almost invariably" unavailing therapeutically.

Though the discharge of pent-up affect is thus deemed therapeutically essential, to accompany the cognitive retrieval of the repressed memory of E, it would be cumbersome to say so whenever one speaks of the presumed therapeutic role of lifting repressions. Therefore, brevity is served by the expository practice of simply crediting the therapeutic gain to the restoration of repressed memories, but with the understanding that affect release is to be copresent.

It is essential to bear in mind that the posited therapeutic efficacy of retrieving repressed memories had provided the sole epistemic warrant for the cardinal etiologic postulate. Clearly, this cognitive dependence was hardly lessened when Freud replaced Breuer's hypnotic technique by the innovative method of free association as the means for uncovering repressed mentation. In fact, though it is widely overlooked, the attribution of thera-peutic success to the removal of repressions not only was but, to this day, remains the sole epistemic underwriter of the purported ability of the patient's free associations to certify causes. Thus, these associations were deemed to be a reliable investigative avenue leading to the detection of the pathogens of neuroses. Analysts such as Strachey (S.E. 1955, 2, xvi) and Eissler (1969, p. 461) have hailed free association as an instrument compara-ble to the microscope and the telescope. And it is asserted to be a trust-worthy means of etiologic inquiry in the sense of licensing the following causal inference: Let a causal chain of the analysand's free associations be initiated by his neurotic symptoms and issue in the emergence of previously repressed memories; then, we are told, this emergence qualifies as good evidence that the prior ongoing repression of these memories was actually the pathogen of the given neurosis.

Whereas all Freudians champion this causal inference, a number of influential ones have explicitly renounced its legitimation by the presumed therapeutic dynamics of undoing repressions. To them I say: Without this vindication, or some as yet unknown other warrant, not even the tortures of the thumbscrew or of the rack should persuade a rational being that free associations can certify pathogens or other causes! For without the stated therapeutic foundation, this epistemic tribute to free associations rests on nothing to date but a glaring causal fallacy. And even that foundation will turn out to be quite flimsy. Therefore, it is unavailing to extol the method of clinical investigation by free associations as a trustworthy resource of etio-logic inquiry, while issuing a modest disclaimer as to the therapeutic efficacy of psychoanalytic treatment. And one is dumbfounded to find that noted psychoanalysts such as George S. Klein have done just that (1976, pp. 36–38). Also amazingly, the renowned analyst Judd Marmor (1968) conjectured that it was the accidental need to earn his livelihood as a psychiatric practi-tioner which drove Freud "to utilize his investigative tool [of free association] simultaneously as a therapeutic instrument" (p. 6). In brief, those who have made it fashionable nowadays to dissociate the credentials of Freud's theory of personality—the so-called "science"—from the merits of psychoanalytic therapy are stepping on thin ice indeed. How very thin will shortly become clear from our scrutiny of the arguments put forward by the mature Freud in place of those he had championed while he was still Breuer's junior collaborator.

Soon after Freud had begun to practice without Breuer, it became devastatingly plain that they had been all too hasty in rejecting the rival hypothesis of placebo effect. The remissions achieved by additional patients whom Freud himself treated cathartically turned out not to be durable. Indeed, the ensuing pattern of relapses, additional treatment, ephemeral remissions, and further relapses gainsaid the attribution of therapeutic credit to the lifting of those repressions that Freud had uncovered. Ironically, he began to be haunted by the triumph of the hypothesis of placebo effect over the fundamental therapeutic tenet that Breuer and he had originally enunciated, for he recognized that the vicissitudes of his personal relations to the patient were highly correlated with the pattern of symptom relapses and intermittent remissions. And, in his own view, this correlation "proved that the personal emotional relation between doctor and patient was after all stronger than the whole cathartic process" (S.E. 1925, 20, 27). But once the repression etiology was thus bereft of therapeutic support, the very corner-stone of psychoanalysis was completely undermined. Hence, at that point, the new clinical psychoanalytic structure tumbled down and lay in shambles.

Nonetheless, Freud was undaunted. Although the excavation of adult repressions had been a therapeutic failure, he conjectured that the uncovering of much earlier ones dating from childhood and sexual in content might well eradicate the neurosis. And he hypothesized further that the patient's free associations would lead to the certification of the early pathogen required for the existence of the affliction (S.E. 1896, 3, 194–199). As he reports, the very early repressions that then emerged were in fact thematically sexual. But when his patients improved and he gave therapeutic credit to the lifting of these childhood repressions, he was apparently no longer able to adduce the separate symptom removals invoked earlier to hold the rival hypothesis of placebo effect at bay. At this stage (1896), his attribution of remedial efficacy to the disclosure of hidden affect-laden mentation took the form of declaring such insight to be at least causally necessary for a cure. Furthermore, Freud's rehabilitation of the generic repression etiology in a new sexual version was now directly built into this newly avowed therapeutic role of insight as follows: Insight could extirpate a neurosis only if it afforded the victum conscious mastery of the particular repression causally required by the pathogenesis of his disorder.

In fact, as I have documented elsewhere (Grünbaum 1984, Chap. 2, Sec. B), from 1896 onward through at least 1917, Freud thought he could claim clinical support for the following extraordinarily strong conjunction of clinical propositions (S.E. 1909, 10, 104; S.E. 1914, 12, 155–56; 1917, 16, 452): A neurosis can be dependably eradicated only by the conscious mastery of the repressions that are causally required for its pathogenesis, and only the therapeutic techniques of psychoanalysis can generate this requisite insight into the specific pathogen. I shall designate this conjunction of two causally necessary conditions as "Freud's master proposition." And I am concerned to point out that once he had equipped himself with the intellectual arsenal contained in it, he was entitled to make a whole series of claims that are each of the first importance for the validation of his enterprise. I shall now develop the ensuing cardinal theses.

1. If a patient has been cured, then the etiologic interpretations that his doctor gave him, at least in the later stages of the analysis, must have been correct or close to the mark. By the same token, insofar as the substantial remission of symptoms can bespeak a genuine cure, this treatment outcome confirms that the analyst has correctly identified the specific pathogen via the patient's free associations. Hence, collectively the successes achieved by psychoanalytic treatment vouch for the truth of the Freudian theory of personality, including its specific etiologies of the psychoneuroses, and even its general hypotheses about psychosexual development.

As a further corollary, the psychoanalytic probing of the unconscious is vindicated as a method of etiologic investigation by its therapeutic achievements. Thus, this method has the remarkable capacity to validate major causal claims by essentially retrospective inquiries without the burdens of prospective longitudinal studies employing experimental controls. Yet these causal inferences are not vitiated by *post hoc ergo propter hoc*. Magnificent, if true!

2. The clinical data furnished by successfully treated neurotics do not result from self-fulfilling predictions. Thus, these data are exonerated from the charge that they forfeit their probative value. According to this reproach, even a patient who engages in frequent emotional outbursts against his analyst will comply with him doctrinally, like a pupil, despite the doctor's best efforts to forego overt or covert communication of his theoretical expectations. Such epistemic contamination of the patient's sundry responses will occur willy nilly, it is charged, because the psychoanalyst will unconsciously yet persuasively insinuate his anticipations in a myriad of subtle ways. And since the analysand has sought out an avowedly Freudian therapist for help, he will want to please the authority figure on whom he now so greatly depends. The ensuing intellectual deference thus makes for *self-fulfillment* of the analyst's theoretical expectations, and thereby for the *spuriousness* of the vauntedly abundant clinical confirmations.

Freud (1954, pp. 334–337) had been stung when even his long-time confrère, Wilhelm Fliess, dropped this skeptical bombshell, which rankled. Yet to his great credit, Freud eloquently came to grips with its grave challenge, emphasizing that it "is uncommonly interesting and must be answered" (S.E. 1917, *16*, 447). And he then met it head-on by enlisting his master proposition in his 1917 lecture, "Analytic Therapy" (S.E. 1917, *16*, 452), to authenticate clinical data as probatively legitimate. Thus, if the patient's assent to his analyst's interpretations is epistemically reliable after all, credence may be reasonably given to the patient's introspective self-observations, once his repressions no longer hold his motives in distorting and obfuscating thrall.

3. Only psychoanalytic treatment can effect genuine cures of neuroses (S.E. 1917, *16*, 458). But if Freud's therapy does enjoy such preeminence, then it can warrantedly take credit for the recoveries of its patients without statistical comparisons with the results from untreated control groups or from controls treated by rival modalities (cf. S.E. 1917, *16*, 461–462). Moreover, when analytic therapy does score remedial triumphs, these gains are not placebo effects, for if the first conjunct of the master propostion is to be believed, the working through of the patient's unconscious conflicts is the decisive therapeutic factor, although the analyst's role as a parent surrogate to him serves as an icebreaker. Freud did recognize that the analysand's so-called "transference" attachment to his doctor plays such a catalytic role in the earlier stages of treatment (S.E. 1926, *20*, 190). Yet he evidently singled out the patient's correct etiologic insight as the one quintessential ingredient "which distinguishes [the therapeutic dynamics of] analytic treatment from any kind of treatment by suggestion" (S.E. 1914, *12*, 155–156; cf. also 1917, *16*, 450–452).

As long as Freud felt entitled to champion his master proposition, he could have confidence in the three sets of remarkable theses I have just formulated. Thus, with one stroke, he had redeemed his 1917 promise (S.E. 1917, *16*, 446–447) to nullify the twofold indictment that suggestion is at once the decisive agent in his therapy and the cognitive bane of the psychoanalytic method of investigation. And, in this way, etiologic hypotheses— which do not themselves pertain at all to either the dynamics or the outcome of analytic therapy—nonetheless were epistemically parasitic on therapeutic results, if only to legitimate the probity of the clinical data on which they were predicated. Yet new evidence then severed the dazzling link that Freud had forged in the master proposition between the conquest of a neurosis and the patient's discernment of its pathogens.

Indeed, by 1926, he himself repudiated the therapeutic indispensability of his type of treatment. And he demoted the psychoanalytic conquest of the analysand's resistances to the status of a mere expeditor of recoveries that were in the offing anyway. As he put it modestly, "as a rule our therapy must be content with bringing about more quickly, more reliably and with less expenditure of energy than would otherwise be the case the good result which in favorable circumstances would have occurred of itself" (S.E. 1926, *20*, 154). But just such spontaneous remission *belies* the master proposition. And once the latter became defunct, even spectacular therapeutic successes became probatively unavailing for the validation of the generic repression etiology by means of that proposition. To boot, in 1937, Freud reported ruefully that a satisfactory psychoanalysis is not even prophylactic against the recurrence of the affliction for which the analysand was treated, let alone does it immunize him against the outbreak of a different neurosis (S.E. 1937, *23*, 216–253). Thus, far from holding out hope for cures, Freud essentially confined the prospects to palliation. But the import of this therapeutic pessimism is shattering, for, even if the master proposition were true, it would need the existential premise of documented cures in order to vouch for the etiologies inferred by means of free association.

As if this were not enough, in recent decades, comparative studies of treatment outcome from rival therapies have failed to reveal any sort of superiority of psychoanalysis within the class of therapeutic modalities that exceed the spontaneous remission rate, gleaned from the (quasi) untreated controls.[3] This result further impugns the master proposition, which entails that only analytic therapy can effect genuine cures of psychoneuroses.

But if analytic treatment is not superior to its rivals in the pertinent diagnostic categories, it becomes quite reasonable—though not compelling— to interpret its therapeutic achievements as placebo effects. If so, then the therapeutic successes of psychoanalysis are not wrought after all by the patient's acquisition of self-knowledge, much to Socrates's sorrow. In this vein, the psychiatrist Jerome Frank has contended that the analyst, no less than his competitor, heals neurotics by supportively counteracting their demoralization, not by excavating their repressions. Indeed, Frank's hypothesis even allows rival therapies to have differential effects in virtue of their differential abilities to mobilize agencies common to all of them. The shared techniques for such mobilization usually include well-practiced rituals, a special vocabulary, a knowledgeable manner, and the therapist's charisma (Grünbaum 1980, pp. 341–351). To be sure, it is still arguable that psychoanalytic treatment gains are not placebogenic. But, as some noted analysts have conceded, the following damaging fact remains: "All-pervading" psychic improvements or even cures can be effected by such rival modalities as behavior therapy, and also by extra clinical life events (Malan, 1976, pp. 147, 172–173, 269). Hence, Freud's master proposition became untenable.

It emerges that this collapse completely undercuts the pivotal therapeutic argument given by the mature Freud to validate his repression etiology of the psychoneuroses and to authenticate the probative value of the clinical data generated by the psychoanalytic method. Thus, the ominous reproach that epistemic contamination by suggestion makes for bogus confirmations bedevils clinical validation after all. Moreover, no empirically viable surrogate for the discredited master proposition capable of yielding Freud's desired conclusions even seems to be remotely in sight.

But it may well be asked impatiently: Why could Freud not dispense with therapeutic arguments altogether and rely instead on other sorts of clinical evidence to furnish support for his specific etiologies? In reply, I contend that the genuine confirmation of his etiologies by intraclinical observations is

3. For a very brief digest of the summary literature on treatment outcome, see Grünbaum (1977, pp 235–250; 1980, pp. 344–345). Detailed argued accounts are given in Smith, Glass, and Miller (1980), in Rachman and Wilson (1980), and in Strupp, Hadley, and Gomes-Schwartz (1977). See especially Prioleau, Murdock, and Brody (1983).

epistemically quite hopeless. And I am concerned to give the main reasons that, in my view, collectively warrant this dismal conclusion.[4]

1. Freud conjectured that the development of a neurosis, N, by an individual, I, depended not only on I's exposure to pathogenic experiences, P, but also on I's hereditary vulnerability. Thus, his universal etiologic hypotheses typically asserted that exposure to P is causally necessary for the pathogenesis of N, not that it is causally sufficient. Any such hypothesis entails the universal retrodiction that all those afflicted by N had suffered P.

In the context of this entailment, Freud's Rat Man case has been invoked to maintain that the psychoanalytic etiology of obsessional neurosis would have been confirmed by clinical evidence corroborating the occurrence of the pertinent retrodicted experience P during the Rat Man's early childhood (Glymour, 1980, p. 272).

Now suppose, for argument's sake, that in his analysis, the Rat Man had reported having retrieved the distant memory of the traumatic sexual event retrodicted by Freud. Assume further for now that credence can be given to so early a memory under the suggestive conditions of a psychoanalysis. Then it is vital to appreciate that the mere retrospective authentication of the bare occurrence of the early trauma hardly bespeaks the causal relevance of this event to the pathogenesis of the Rat Man's obsessions. Surely the mere traumaticity of an event does not itself attest to its etiologic relevance. The human condition would be much worse than it already is if every psychic blow became the specific pathogen of a neurosis. Yet prominent psychoanalysts have reasoned that the causal relevance of an experience P to a neurosis N is supported by the mere fact that anyone beset by N who suffered P instantiates the retrodiction entailed by Freud's etiology (Waelder, 1962, pp. 625–626). Such an inference is no better than *post hoc ergo propter hoc*.

But what if we could also assume that the clinical setting has the epistemic resources to certify retrospectively that all available victims of neuroses other than N had been spared the experience P? Even under this sanguine assumption, the envisaged retrospective clinical testing design is confined to the class of neurotics. And as Blake Barley has observed, this confinement restricts the probative import of the putative findings as follows: At best, they might bespeak the etiologic relevance of the experience P to N within the class of neurotics, but would not lend credence to the Freudian claim of pathogenic relevance in the wider class of persons.

2. Some analysts have told us that the patient himself is able to determine by introspection whether the repressed P was in fact the pathogen of his disorder, once he no longer represses the memory of this episode (Waelder, 1962, pp. 628–629). But this thesis of privileged epistemic access to the causes of psychopathology does not bear scrutiny.

Substantial evidence recently marshaled by cognitive psychologists has

4. For my much fuller statement of these reasons, see Grünbaum (1983d).

shown that even in the case of consciously motivated behavior, a subject does not enjoy special cognitive access to the discernment of the motivational causes of his various actions (Grünbaum, 1980, Sec. 3, pp. 354–367). Though the subject often does have direct access to the individual conscious contents of his mental states, he has only inferential access—just like outside observers—to such causal linkages as actually connect some of his own mental states. The possession of direct access to the content of momentary states of attention or felt affect is a far cry indeed from being uniquely privy to the actual existence of a hypothesized causal nexus between, say, certain infantile experiences and specified adult personality dispositions. No less than in the case of causal hypotheses pertaining to physical states, the subject's avowal of causal connections between his own mental states is based either on the fallible inferences drawn by himself or on those carried out by members of his subculture to whom he gives credence. Hence these avowed causal linkages may be fancied or actual. In short, when a subject attributes a causal relation to some of his own mental states, he does so—just like outside observers—by invoking theory-based causal schemata endorsed by the prevailing belief system.

More often than not, a patient who sought treatment from a Freudian doctor already brings some psychoanalytic beliefs into the therapy, or is at least receptive to etiologic interpretations of his conduct based on the analyst's theoretical stance. No wonder that analytic patients then find the rationale offered to them credible. But this credulity is hardly tantamount to privileged cognitive access to the validity of the ambitious causal claims central to the etiologic reconstruction of the given dysfunction. And, as we saw earlier, the same gullibility may also be responsible for the analysand's therapeutic gains. For these may be due to his belief in his doctor's etiologic reconstruction rather than to the undoing of his repressions. But just as the patient has no direct introspective access to the pathogenesis of his affliction, so also his introspections do not afford him privileged epistemic access to the cause of his therapeutic progress. Thus, he is surely not in a better position to make such a causal attribution than his analyst. And recently, two Freudian investigators of the dynamics of psychotherapies have issued the following agnostic disclaimer: "Psychoanalysts, like other psychotherapists, literally do not know how they achieve their [remedial] results" (Luborsky & Spence, 1978, p. 360).

3. Freud himself emphasized that the patient's poor mnemic performance often simply fails to authenticate the childhood event retrodicted via his etiology (S.E. 1920, *18*, 18; 1937, *23*, 265–266). And, as I have documented elsewhere (1980, p. 353), his writings also multiply attest to the unreliability of purported adult memories of early childhood episodes that had presumably been retrieved by the analysis after being repressed. More recently, research on memory has furnished telling empirical evidence that the patient's supposed ability to achieve noninferential veridical recall of very early repressed experiences is largely a myth.

Experimental studies acknowledged by analysts themselves (Marmor, 1970) have borne out the therapist's contaminating regimentation of purported memories recovered by free association. It can be granted, of course, that requirements of consistency or at least overall coherence do afford the analyst *some* check on what the patient alleges to be bona fide memories. And it is to be understood that the epistemic discounting of early childhood memories purportedly retrieved by the adult patient is not a wholesale derogation of adult memories in daily life. But the malleability of adult memories from childhood by suggestion is epitomized by a report from Jean Piaget (Loftus, 1980, pp. 119–121), who thought he vividly remembered an attempt to kidnap him from his baby carriage along the Champs Elysées. He recalled the gathered crowd, the scratches on the face of the heroic nurse who saved him, the policeman's white baton, the assailant running away. However vivid, Piaget's recollections were false. Years later his nurse confessed that she had made up the entire story, which he then internalized as a presumed experience under the influence of an authority figure.

That psychoanalytic treatment ought not to be regarded as a bona fide memory-jogging device emerges more generally as a corollary of at least three sets of recent research findings elaborated by Loftus (1980): (a) the remarkable extent to which human memory is malleable, (b) the interpolative reconstruction and bending of memories by theoretical beliefs or expectations, and (c) the penchant, under the influence of leading questions, to fill amnesiac gaps by confabulated material. Earlier we saw that theoretical beliefs rather than direct introspection determine the subject's verdicts on causal relations between his own mental states. Similarly, the interpolative reconstruction and bending of memories by theoretical beliefs combine with the malleability of memory by suggestion to generate pseudomemories of events that never occurred, especially when they are temporally remote. In short, the retrospective testing design of the psychoanalytic setting cannot even reliably authenticate the bare occurrence of the retrodicted childhood experience P, let alone its pathogenic role.

It emerges that the proposed clinical vindication of the repression etiology without reliance on the dynamics of Freud's therapy is no less a fiasco than his attempted therapeutic validation. I gave two main reasons for this additional failure: (a) The testing design of the analytic setting appears incompetent to warrant that the retrodicted childhood experience P was, if actual, also pathogenic, and (b) the retrospective methods of this clinical inquiry cannot even reliably authenticate the bare occurence of P. To my knowledge, besides the sorts of arguments I have canvassed, there are no other clinical defenses of Freud's sexual repression etiology of the neuroses.

Hence I draw the following major conclusions: His sexual version of this generic etiology is now devoid of cogent clinical support, just as Breuer's non-sexual cathartic etiologies, which Freud had disavowed as clinically ill-founded. Furthermore, this collapse of the psychoanalytic etiology, I maintain, basically impugns the investigative cogency of free associations in the conduct of etiologic inquiry, for Freud had enunciated his fundamental rule of free association as a maxim of clinical research because he thought that associations governed by it had reliably certified the unconscious pathogens of the neuroses. Yet, just this epistemic tribute is now seen to be gratuitous. Finally, Freud is left helpless to rebut the charge that clinical data forfeit their probative value by epistemic contamination through suggestion, a complaint for which there is good evidence. But, for the sake of argument, assume nonetheless that there is no such forfeiture of probative value and that the patient's clinical responses can be taken at face value after all. It is of fundamental importance to appreciate that even if the clinical data were thus uncontaminated, they would still utterly fail to sustain the causal hypotheses of the psychoanalytic clinical theory of psychopathology, as I have argued.

I must emphasize that these bleak results are equally devastating to the currently fashionable revisionist versions of psychoanalysis that go under the names of Kohutian "self-psychology" and of "object relations theory." Insofar as these post-Freudian theories are indeed recognizably psychoanalytic, they do of course embrace some version of the repression etiology. Furthermore, they rely epistemically on free association in the clinical investigation of purported pathogens and other unconscious determinants of behavior, while lifting repressions as one means to effect therapy (Eagle, 1984).[5] But, I submit, precisely to the extent that these outgrowths of Freud's ideas are thus recognizably psychoanalytic in content as well as in method of inquiry and therapy, my epistemic critique of Freud's original hypotheses applies with equal force to the etiologic, developmental and therapeutic tenets of these successors (Eagle, 1983; Grünbaum, 1983a).

As a direct corollary, we are now able to appraise the psychoanalytic theory of dreams as well as Freud's account of sundry sorts of slips or "parapraxes." Both of these renowned hypotheses attribute a decisive causal role to repressed ideation. These two causal attributions were and have remained audacious, if not foolhardy extrapolations from the etiologic function that Freud had ascribed to repression in his explanation of psychopathology, for whereas he claimed to have therapeutic evidence for postulating this pathogenic role, he never produced any independent clinical support for these two momentous extrapolations (Grünbaum, 1984, Chaps. 4 & 5). As

---

5. In the context of the therapeutic theories espoused by the post-Freudian neorevisionists, I have advisedly depicted the undoing of repressions as just "one means" of effecting therapy. The need for this qualification has been stressed by Eagle (1983). As he points out, the Kohutian self-psychologists place less therapeutic emphasis on insight into prior repressions than on the therapist's "empathic mirroring," coupled with the patient's feelings of identification and idealization toward the doctor. But precisely insofar as there is such divergence from the orthodox psychotherapeutic tenet, the warrant for labeling the revised doctrine "psychoanalytic" becomes seriously questionable.

In any case, Eagle (1983) has argued tellingly that the etiologic and therapeutic claims of self-psychology and of object relations theory rest epistemically on bases even more dubious than those of Freud's corresponding hypotheses. Hence, it would be unavailing to adduce the post-Freudian neorevisionist credos in an attempt to blunt the force of the doubts I have raised against orthodox psychoanalysis.

we learn in the opening pages on his method of dream interpretation, the first extrapolation consisted of simply enlarging the epistemic role of free association from being only a method of etiologic inquiry aimed at therapy, to serving likewise as an avenue for finding the purported unconscious causes of dreams (S.E. 1900, 4, 100–101).

Thus, having found that his patients reported their dreams while freely associating to their neurotic symptoms, he drew the following inference: ". . . a dream can be inserted into the psychical chain that has to be traced backwards in the memory from a pathological idea. It was then only a short step to treating the dream itself as a symptom and to applying to dreams the method of interpretation that had been worked out for symptoms" (p. 101). Yet, far from being only heuristic in Freud's view, this cavalier extrapolative adoption of the symptom model for manifest dream content was avowedly also probative. As he argued: "We might also point out in our defense that our procedure in interpreting dreams [by means of free association] is identical with the procedure by which we resolve hysterical symptoms; and there the correctness of our method is warranted by the coincident emergence and disappearance of the symptoms" (S.E. 1900, 5, 528). *Mutatis mutandis*, the same remarks apply to the further extrapolation that slips are likewise mini-neurotic symptoms. Therefore, the claim that the method of free association can reliably certify the unconscious motives of dream formation and of parapraxes is cognitively parasitic on the prior thesis that this method can certify repressions to be the pathogens of neuroses.[6]

But in virtue of the extrapolative justification given for the repression models of dreams and of parapraxes, their epistemic fortunes are dependent on those of Freud's theory of psychopathology (S.E. 1925, 20, 45; 1900, 4, 149). As a consequence of just this epistemic dependence, the ravages from the demise of Freudian psychopathology and of free association as a tool of etiologic certification extend, with a vengeance, to the psychoanalytic theory of dreams and of sundry sorts of "slips."

Originally, Freud had claimed that free association, like Breuer's cathartic method, can certify the required cause of a neurosis by virtue of the method's ability to cure the illness. As Freud put it, "Breuer learnt from his first patient that the attempt at discovering the determining cause of a symptom was at the same time a therapeutic manoeuvre" (S.E. 1893, 3, 35). But, as we saw, the arguments for deeming free association capable of certifying pathogens were not viable. In the wake of their collapse, Freud's extrapolation does not furnish even the shadow of a good reason for supposing that associations governed by his "fundamental rule" can reliably certify the unconscious causes of dreams and of parapraxes.

Indeed, as far as I know, Freud's disciples, either orthodox or revisionist,

6. I have argued in Grünbaum (1983b, Sec. 4) that neither Freud's own account of his *Irma* specimen dream (S.E. 1900, 4, Chap. II) nor Erik Erikson's (1954) attempt to give an orthodox psychoanalytic interpretation of it can serve to accredit free association as a reliable means for identifying dream motives.

have yet to produce any sound reason for crediting free association with the ability to pick out the causes of dream formation. Hence, I claim that the emergence of repressed infantile wishes via free associations triggered by the recall of anxiety dreams and nightmares cannot warrant the hypothesis that these dreams are engendered by such wishes. Indeed, whatever evidence there may be from commonsense psychology that certain particular dreams were generated by unfulfilled wishes, it has now turned out that free association does not have the probative power to underwrite this verdict.

The Futility of Hermeneutics without Causation

Faced with the bleak import of such a skeptical indictment, psychoanalysts will be intent on salvaging their legacy in some form. Some of them will then be understandably receptive to a rationale that promises them absolution from their failure to validate the cardinal hypotheses of their clinical theory. Be of stout heart, they are told, and take the hermeneutic turn. Freud, they learn, brought the incubus of validation on himself by his scientistic pretensions. Abjure his program of causal explanation, some hermeneuticians beckon them, and you will no longer be saddled with the harassing demand to justify Freud's causal hypotheses. One such hermeneutic advocate illustrated this repudiation of causation as follows: "The meaning of a dream does not reside in some prior latent dream [content], but in the manifest dream and the analysand's associations to it" (Steele, 1979, p. 400). Thus, the blandishments of this renunciatory stance include the comforting assurance that the practicing analyst is immune to the taunts from critics who dispute the cost-effectiveness of his therapy. Even for the Freudian psychohistorians, the hermeneutician has the glad tidings that henceforth they can hold their heads high as protagonists of a newly legitimated kind of humanistic discipline. In short, the claim is that the challenge to provide validation of the causal propositions has been obviated, and that the continuing demand for it has therefore become an anachronism.

But as against the generic disavowal of causal attributions advocated by some hermeneuticians, I maintain that it is a nihilistic, if not frivolous, trivialization of Freud's entire clinical theory. Far from serving as a new citadel for psychoanalytic apologetics, the embrace of such hermeneuticians is, I submit, the kiss of death for the legacy that was to be saved. On the other hand, insofar as other hermeneuticians, Paul Ricoeur (1981, Chap. 10), for example, do countenance the retention of causal hypotheses in psychoanalytic explanations, they are no less obligated to substantiate these hypotheses by cogent evidence than the orthodox Freudians, whom they pilloried as scientistically addicted.

Let me illustrate my case against the stated acausal hermeneutic construal of psychoanalytic significance by reference to an allegedly Freudian lapse of memory that has figured as a paradigmatic instance in the literature. To say that a slip of the tongue, pen, ear, eye, or memory is genuinely "Freudian" is to say that it was engendered by a repressed motive. Thus, Freud assimilated a seemingly insignificant slip of the tongue to the status of a mini-neurotic symptom by regarding this lapse as a compromise between a repressed motive that crops out in the form of a disturbance, on the one hand, and the conscious intention to make a certain utterance, on the other.

The pertinent paradigmatic instance of a lapse of memory involves the forgetting of the Latin pronoun "aliquis" (someone), which a young man, Y, omitted when reciting a line from Virgil's *Aeneid* (S.E. 1901, 6, Chap. II). Freud supplied the missing word and enjoined Y to use the restored word as the point of departure for free associations. After a tortuous chain of such associations, punctuated by some interjections from Freud, it emerged that Y had been harboring a presumably repressed fear. An Italian girlfriend, he suspected apprehensively, had become pregnant by him. Freud then told him that this repressed anxiety had undeniably produced his "aliquis" lapse. But Y doubted any such causal nexus, although he was fully aware that his worry was genuine.

Now let me contrast Freud's account of this lapse with the hermeneutic claim that Y's slip lends itself to acausal and yet psychoanalytic interpretation.

The orthodox rationale for calling on Y to let the restored word initiate his free associations was clear. Having deemed the lapse to be a min-neurotic symptom, Freud attributed its occurrence causally to the operation of some repression. And when Y asked him to explain how the forgetting of the pronoun had been brought about, Freud promised to identify the causally relevant repression by winnowing the free associations triggered in Y by the restored word "aliquis" (S.E. 1901, 6, 9). Hence, he then used the surfacing of Y's previously repressed pregnancy worry from these particular associations as grounds for concluding that this very fear—while as yet being repressed before the memory lapse—had caused Y to forget that word. Freud held this inference to be licensed by the principle that a repression, R, present before the commission of a parapraxis by a perxon X qualifies as its cause, if R emerges into X's consciousness in the wake of free associations triggered by his awareness of the content of his error (Grünbaum, 1983b, Sec. 3).

I do not profess to know at all what did cause Y's slip. But, as an immediate corollary of my earlier arguments, I claim that if Y's repressed worry did cause him to forget "aliquis," Freud has completely failed to supply cogent evidence for this causal nexus. This failure to justify his causal inference deserves censure, even if one could grant him quite generally that the analyst does not inject epistemically contaminating influences into the sequence of the associations, as he contended (S.E. 1923, 18, 238). Seriously flawed though it is, Freud's account nonetheless does offer an explanation of slips qua slips by purporting to have identified unconscious motives for their occurrence.

But I submit that the alleged interpretive meaning furnished by the acausal hermeneutic rationale is altogether insensitive to the fact that the word "aliquis" figured in a lapse of memory. Whatever that hermeneutic meaning, I claim that it is not the meaning of a slip qua slip at all! To be sure, the aforecited hermeneutician, no less than the orthodox analyst, sifts the free associations elicited from Y by the restoration of the forgotten word to his awareness. Yet the hermeneutic view now at issue demurely disclaims the postulation of causes (Steele, 1979, p. 400) and thus forsakes the causal import of treating a slip as a mini-neurotic symptom. Hence, according to this construal, the interpretive meaning which is to be revealed by the winnowing of Y's associations avowedly has no causal relevance to the fact that "aliquis" did figure in a lapse. How then can the interpretive meaning revealed by the associative content of "aliquis" be held to be the significance of the *forgetting* of "aliquis" rather than simply the associative import of that word per se, regardless of whether it had been forgotten or not? Indeed, on the acausal hermeneutic rationale, why should Y be asked to associate to the word "aliquis" rather than to one of the words in the line from Virgil that he had not forgotten? Since the emerging meaning is not the meaning of a slip qua slip, how can this acausal rationale provide a reason for supposing that the associations to a forgotten word are richer in interpretive meaning—whatever that is—than the associations to nonforgotten words, or to other associatively evocative items in the subject's life? How then can the hermeneutician see himself as having given any reconstruction at all of Freud's theory of slips qua slips?

What of the reply that, though the associations do not bespeak a cause of a slip, they reveal a great deal about the current psychological makeup of the person who has them? I retort by asking: On what basis does the advocate of acausal hermeneutics infer the psychological makeup of a person from the latter's free associations? Does the inference rely tacitly on presumed causal linkages between personality structure and associational output? If so, the acausalist is not entitled to invoke them, if only because the validation of causal connections would require nonhermeneutic methods that he is unwilling to license. But let us suppose that the generalizations used to draw the requisite inferences as to the associating person's makeup are not causal. Even then, it is at best unclear how they can be validated short of adopting the very methods that the hermeneutician rejects as "scientistic."

Similar considerations warrant the conclusion that the acausal hermeneutic rationale so truncates the repression etiology of the psychoneuroses as to trivialize that etiology qua theory of psychopathology. And a like verdict serves to convict the stated acausal version of the received theory of dreams, as Michael Moore has argued in his telling critique of hermeneutic "rationalization without causation" (Moore, 1983, pp. 32–34).

In a recent book, Esther Menaker (1982) has argued that Freud's one-time disciple Otto Rank repudiated his erstwhile search for causes of personality development, thereby abandoning his own thesis of the role of the birth trauma. Instead, Rank claimed an acausal creative role for an individuating will, a notion that is not explanatory.

Conclusions

I set out to appraise Freud's principal arguments for his monumental clinical theory of personality and therapy. This scrutiny was based on his own avowed inductive standards. By design, I made no mention of any experimental findings, either supportive or adverse. For even toward the end of his life, Freud dismissed purported experimental support for his theory of repression as superfluous, because of an alleged superabundance of clinical confirmations (MacKinnon & Dukes, 1963, pp. 702–703). This epistemic tribute to clinical findings vis-à-vis experimental ones has recently been largely reaffirmed by recognized analysts (Luborsky & Spence, 1978, pp. 350, 356–357). And, as Ernest Jones (1959, Vol. 1, p. 3) has reminded everyone, the results from the psychoanalytic treatment setting are "the real basis of Psychoanalysis. All of Professor Freud's other works and theories are essentially founded on the clinical investigations."

Several conclusions issue from my appraisal of the arguments that Freud and his disciples have rested on their observations:

1. Insofar as the evidence for the psychoanalytic corpus is now held to derive from the productions of patients in analysis, this warrant is remarkably weak.

2. Despite the poverty of the clinical credentials, it may still turn out that Freud's brilliant theoretical imagination was actually quite serendipitous for psychopathology or the understanding of some subclass of slips.

Thus, very recently a psychologist claimed to have found genuine experimental support for the psychoanalytic theory of speech errors (Motley, 1980). He did indeed furnish telling laboratory evidence for the causal relevance of cognitive–affective mental sets, and even of personality dispositions to oral misreadings consisting of phoneme switchings. In this way, the experimenter showed that semantic influences produced by the speaker's mental sets, and external to the intended utterance, effected a prearticulatory semantic editing of the words to be pronounced.

Valuable though they were, the results from these ingenious experiments were probatively irrelevant to the Freudian theory of slips of the tongue, for the mental sets that the investigator manipulated as his independent variable were not repressed ideation. By being conscious (or preconscious) states instead, they failed to realize the initial conditions required by Freud's theory. In fact, the observed misreadings can all be explained by a rival psychological theory that allows *only* conscious motivational influences as generators of slips (Grünbaum, 1984, Chap. 4). Hence, it remains to be seen what a properly designed test would show.

3. In view of my account of the epistemic defects inherent in the psycho-analytic method, it would seem that the validation of Freud's cardinal hypotheses has to come, if at all, mainly from well-designed extraclinical studies, either epidemiologic or even experimental. But that appraisal is largely a task for the future, since extant experimental results have done little to substantiate his major causal assumptions (Grünbaum, 1986).

ACKNOWLEDGMENTS

I am grateful for much encouragement, help, and friendship to Thomas Detre, Morris Eagle, Stanley Rachman, Benjamin B. Rubinstein, and Rosemarie Sand ever since I first began to work in the area of this chapter.

REFERENCES

Eagle, M. (1983). The epistemological status of recent developments in psychoanalytic theory. In R. S. Cohen & L. Laudan (Eds.), *Physics, philosophy and psychoanalysis* (pp. 31–55). Boston, MA: Reidel.

Eagle, M. (1984). Psychoanalysis and modern psychodynamic theories. In N. S. Endler & J. McV. Hunt (Eds.), *Personality and the behavior disorders*, (rev. ed.). New York: Wiley.

Eissler, K. R. (1969). Irreverent remarks about the present and the future of psychoanalysis. *International Journal of Psycho-Analysis, 50,* 461–471.

Erikson, E. (1954). The dream specimen of psychoanalysis. *Journal of the American Psychoanalytic Association, 2,* 5–56.

Freud, S. (1955–1974). In J. Strachey (Ed. and Trans.), *The standard edition of the complete psychological works of Sigmund Freud* (24 volumes). London: Hogarth Press.

Freud, S. (1954). *The origins of psychoanalysis.* New York: Basic Books.

Glymour, C. (1980). *Theory and evidence.* Princeton, NJ: Princeton University Press.

Grünbaum, A. (1977). How scientific is psychoanalysis? In R. Stern, L. S. Horowitz, & J. Lynes (Eds.), *Science and psychotherapy*, (pp. 219–254). New York: Haven Publishing.

Grünbaum, A. (1980). Epistemological liabilities of the clinical appraisal of psychoanalytic theory. *Nous, 14,* 307–385.

Grünbaum, A. (1981). The placebo concept. *Behaviour Research and Therapy, 19,* 157–167. [A much fuller treatment is given in Grünbaum (1985).]

Grünbaum, A. (1983a). Is object relations theory better founded than orthodox psychoanalysis? *Journal of Philosophy, 80,* 46–51.

Grünbaum, A. (1983b). Logical foundations of psychoanalytic theory. In W. K. Essler & H. Putnam (Eds.), *Festschrift for Wolfgang Stegmüller* (pp. 109–152). Dordrecht, Netherlands: Reidel.

Grünbaum, A. (1983c). Freud's theory: The perspective of a philosopher of science. *Proceedings and Addresses of the American Philosophical Association, 57,* 5–31.

Grünbaum, A. (1983d). Retrospective versus prospective testing of aetiological hypotheses in psychoanalytic theory. In J. Earman (Ed.), *Minnesota studies in the philosophy of science* (Vol. X, pp. 315–347). Minneapolis: University of Minnesota Press.

Grünbaum, A. (1984). *The foundations of psychoanalysis: A philosophical critique.* Berkeley & Los Angeles: University of California Press.

Grünbaum, A. (1985). Explication and implications of the placebo concept. In L. White, B. Tursky, & G. E. Schwartz (Eds.), *Placebo: Theory, research, and mechanisms.* New York: Guilford Press.

Grünbaum, A. (1986). Author's Response. *The Behavioral and Brain Sciences, 9* (in press).

Jones, E. (1959). *Editorial preface to S. Freud, collected papers* (Vol. 1). New York: Basic Books.

Klein, G. S. (1976). *Psychoanalytic theory.* New York: International Universities Press.

Laplanche, J., & Pontalis, J. B. (1973). *The language of psychoanalysis.* New York: Norton.

Loftus, E. (1980). *Memory.* Reading, MA: Addison-Wesley.

Luborsky, L., & Spence, D. P. (1978). Quantitative research on psychoanalytic therapy. In S. L. Garfield & A. E. Bergin (Eds.), *Handbook of psychotherapy and behavior change* (2nd ed.) (pp. 331–368). New York: Wiley.

MacKinnon, D. W., & Dukes, W. F. (1963). Repression. In L. Postman (Ed.), *Psychology in the making* (pp. 662–744). New York: Knopf.

Malan, D. H. (1976). *Toward the validation of dynamic psychotherapy.* New York: Plenum Press.

Marmor, J. (1968). New directions in psychoanalytic theory and therapy. In J. Marmor (Ed.), *Modern psychoanalysis* (pp. 3–15). New York: Basic Books.

Marmor, J. (1970). Limitations of free association. *Archives of General Psychiatry 22,* 160–165.

Menaker, E. (1982). *Otto Rank: A rediscovered legacy.* New York: Columbia University Press.

Möller, H. J. (1976). *Methodische Grundprobleme der Psychiatrie.* Stuttgart: Verlag W. Kohlammer.

Möller, H. J. (1978). *Psychoanalyse—Erklärende Wissenschaft oder Deutungskunst?* Munich: W. Fink Verlag.

Moore, M. (1983). The nature of psychoanalytic explanation. In L. Laudan (Ed.), *Mind and medicine: Explanation and evaluation in psychiatry and the biomedical sciences* (Vol. 8, pp. 5–78). Berkeley: University of California Press.

Motley, M. T. (1980). Verification of 'Freudian slips' and semantic prearticulatory editing via laboratory-induced spoonerisms. In V. A. Fromkin (Ed.), *Errors in linguistic performance: Slips of the tongue, ear, pen, and hand* (pp. 133–147). New York: Academic Press.

Prioleau, L., Murdock, M., & Brody, N. (1983). An analysis of psychotherapy versus placebo. *The Behavioral and Brain Sciences, 6,* 275–285.

Rachman, S. J., & Wilson, G. T. (1980). *The effects of psychological therapy* (2nd ed.). Oxford: Pergamon Press.

Ricoeur, P. (1981). *Hermeneutics and the human sciences* (J. B. Thompson, Trans.). New York: Cambridge University Press.

Smith, M. L., Glass, G. V., & Miller, T. I. (1980). *The benefits of psychotherapy.* Baltimore, MD: Johns Hopkins University Press.

Steele, R. S. (1979). Psychoanalysis and hermeneutics. *International Review of Psycho-Analysis, 6,* 389–411.

Strupp, H. H., Hadley, S. W., & Gomes-Schwartz, B. (1977). *Psychotherapy for better or worse: The problem of negative effects.* New York: Jason Aronson.

Waelder, R. (1962). Review of *Psychoanalysis, scientific method and philosophy* (S. Hook, ed.). *Journal of the American Psychoanalytic Association, 10,* 617–637.

CHAPTER 10

Diagnostic Taxa as Open Concepts: Metatheoretical and Statistical Questions about Reliability and Construct Validity in the Grand Strategy of Nosological Revision

Paul E. Meehl

Since I find it hard to conceive that a rational mind could think otherwise, I presuppose that, *ceteris paribus*, careful delineation of the signs, symptoms, and course of a disorder (I cannot interest myself much in the semantic hassle over whether to call it "disease") so as to increase the reliability of classifying clients or patients is desirable. While reliability and validity are not the same thing, it is a psychometric truism that the former bounds the latter, although it is worth mentioning that the bound is the square root of the reliability, so validity can theoretically be larger. Usually the operative validity (net attenuated construct validity) runs far below that upper bound set by the square root of the reliability coefficient. Hence, alterations in the format of assessment or in the content sampled, which might under some circumstances reduce reliability, could nevertheless increase the net attenuated construct validity. Similarly, changes in content or format that increase reliability may theoretically decrease validity. For instance, an alteration in the open-ended, unstructured format of Rorschach administration (as was attempted during World War II to make it possible to test large numbers of individuals and score reliably without inquiry) seemed to eliminate whatever slight validity the instrument had as usually administered.

There is no mystery about this, although it is paradoxical at first look. We may be concerned about the reliability of behavior sampling by two different samplers ("interjudge agreement") or with the trustworthiness of a sample as drawn by an individual judge (how many marbles do we draw from the urn, and how do we draw them?). In either case, the point is this: Whether an interview behavior or a psychological test item is viewed primar-

Paul E. Meehl. University of Minnesota Medical School, Minneapolis, Minnesota.

ily as "sample" or as "sign" (Cronbach & Meehl, 1955), there are kinds of
alterations in the examining situation and in the procedure of response
classification that can alter qualitatively the intrinsic construct validity of the
sample in such a way as to reduce its net validity, despite reliability, in either
of the two senses mentioned, having been enhanced.

I am not arguing that such has occurred in the process of improving our
old Mental Status Examination or in the construction of DSM-III, but
merely that this methodological point should be kept in mind when discussing reliability/validity questions.

It requires neither psychometric nor philosophical expertise to see that
the reliability/validity helps and trade-offs can be somewhat complicated, and
especially so when the aimed at diagnostic construct itself (category or
dimension) is an open concept, lacking a definitive "operational" criterion,
specified implicitly ("contextual definition") by presumably fallible indicators.
In that kind of knowledge situation, we subtly alter meanings as we discover
facts, we amend theoretical definitions as we revise indicator weights. The
basic point can be better brought out by considering the decision to include
an unreliable indicator in a standard examination for "any disease." A general
medical examination always includes blood pressure and not anthropometric
determination of wrist width, despite the mediocre reliability of the former
and $r = .98$ for the latter. We do not find this evidentiary preference puzzling, we simply say, "Blood pressure unreliably measured is a stronger
indicator of more different and important conditions than wrist width reliably measured." Similarly, a psychotherapist who employs dream interpretation (with the manifest–latent content model) would not seriously consider
substituting reliably scorable multiple-choice inquiry for free association
under the Fundamental Rule, despite the grave reliability problems posed by
the classical procedure. One might prefer to avoid Freud's technique altogether, and partly because of unreliability considerations (cf. Meehl, 1983);
what one would almost surely *not* do is retain Freud's core idea and its
entailed technique, while substituting a multiple-choice inquiry in the service
of reliability.

The reasons for desiring diagnostic reliability are well known. The most
important reason is generalizability of research findings by other investigators thinking about their research and by practitioners in applying research
findings to clinical decision making. The easiest way to understand the
former is in terms of the number of pairwise relationships of input and
output variables involved in a decision-making process whether of a theoretical or practical clinical nature (Meehl, 1959). If a set of behavior data (history
and current status, interview, ward behavior, neurological, psychometric)
permit us to classify patients in some "rational" (ultimately "causal"?) way, it
is not necessary that each of the possible n output variables (e.g., treatment
of choice, second choice, prognosis, employability, response to group therapy, suicide risk, genetic risk to offspring) has to be correlated singly pairwise
with all the input variables, a process which would require studying mn

relationships, where mn is in the thousands (Meehl & Golden, 1982, pp. 130–131). Instead, we can first relate the m input variables to the diagnostic dimension or rubric and then relate the diagnostic dimension or rubric to the several output variables of interest. Hence only $(m + n)$ correlations need to be studied. But that process cannot be carried out with any confidence if the relation of some of the input variables to dimension X or categorical rubric C as found at the University of Texas has only a little better than chance relationship between (only partially overlapping) relationships as reported by investigators in Milwaukee. The pulling together of research data to give a coherent interpretation of an alleged psychiatric entity, whether taxonomic or dimensional in nature, presupposes the possibility of scanning the research literature with at least some reasonable confidence that patients called schizophrenic by one investigator are like those called schizophrenic by another. Similarly, suppose a clinician reads a research report claiming that a certain drug is efficacious for paranoid schizophrenics, except when they have a history of an episode, when much younger, of acute catatonic excitement. That report is not helpful to the clinician who lacks rational belief that the investigator was looking at the same indicators of paranoid and catatonic schizophrenia that he or she can now look at in his or her clinical decision making.

It is an interesting question whether one can ever lose by improving reliability, except in the (rare? I don't know) sense discussed above. The main respect in which some workers, and I gingerly include myself here, seem to worry about it is that research aimed at improving, correcting, or—in the extreme case—refuting views implicit in the DSM-III conceptual system will somehow be cramped by an overly enthusiastic view of it, which sometimes takes the form of a dogmatic insistence upon its merits throughout. I have heard research-oriented clinicians express concern about this, but it is difficult to track down persuasive examples where, for instance, an otherwise admirable research proposal was rejected by the peer reviewers on the grounds that it did not employ "official categories" approved by DSM-III. While people talk about this, and one sometimes hears it alleged that it has occurred, I do not myself know of any clear cases. Admittedly, it would be hard to ascertain whether a subtle kind of social process, of the kind that the Supreme Court likes to call a "chilling effect," is taking place. Some researchers might be otherwise disposed to advocate a mild Feyerabendian "proliferation of theories" (Feyerabend, 1970) which he advocates even for cases when the going theories are extremely powerful and well corroborated and, a fortiori, for theories in such primitive fields as psychopathology. Some of them might not be getting research grant money because they have timidly avoided challenging the establishment category system.

Here again, I have no affirmative evidence that such things happen. If they do, it would appear quite easy to find a way around it, and whether it failed would hinge upon whether some peer reviewers have become over-identified with the present product. For example: Suppose I am interested in studying people with a cyclothymic personality makeup who have very mild ups and downs on an endogenous (genetic/biochemical) basis, but who at no time become diagnosably psychotic or even semipsychotic. The psychiatric tradition has connected endogenousness with severity, which there is no strong theoretical reason for insisting upon, although there is a correlation empirically. I don't see why a clinical investigator, behavior geneticist, or neurochemist should in any way be hampered by the received rubrics. He or she can be careful in adhering to criteria for diagnosing manic–depressive disorder as given by DSM-III. It may well be that the only available rubric for some of the other people he or she wants to study is "normal," or even perhaps some *other* piece of non-manic–depressive terminology as specified in DSM-III. Nothing prevents the investigator from saying, in writing up a grant proposal, "It is my empirical conjecture that there are persons who don't manage quite to squeak through the conditions for diagnosing a manic–depressive attack (because of extreme damping in their cyclothymic cycle). But all of my classifications are indicated, and all of the correlations of them with all of the other things I studied, whether psychometric or genetic or familial or whatever, are clearly indicated, so that other investigators may rely on the fact that I stuck literally to the received criteria for making that diagnosis. I have also listed, however, the set of special criteria, together with their time sampling and interjudge reliabilities, that I used to demarcate *my* special subgroup of individuals that do not fit the official rubrics."

At no point does this investigator have to depart from the semantics of DSM-III, nor does he or she have to do any inordinate amount of work in order to include the DSM-III criteria as available for investigators who want to examine his or her data critically. It is, I suppose, imaginable that somebody might want to do something where the task of "double diagnosis" (i.e., according to his or her conjectured criteria for entities or dimensions not in the official list along with the received one) will be a considerable amount of excess work, but I am not aware of any clear showing that that has happened. The diagnostic criteria for DSM-III simply do not involve that much additional work, and most of the overload will arise from his or her idiosyncratic system. Despite the fact that my own views on many categories are quite heterodox, when there is an adoption by an empowered body of clinicians and scientists as to a certain terminology, I think one is not unduly burdened or imposed upon by some extra scientific or clinical toil when the investigator chooses to deviate from it in his or her own research.

An interesting statistical question arises in the "context of discovery" (Reichenbach, 1938, pp. 6–7) where a plausible case—I do not urge that it is more than plausible—can be made for concern about increased difficulty of detecting subtle relationships. I mean by "detection" the development of a clinical hunch and, in a more formalized research context, the problem of the statistical power function failing to detect something that is there. Consider the following: By tightening up the diagnostic criteria, we have increased reliability and, hence (almost certainly), the net attenuated construct validity in identifying the whole class of patients called "schizophrenic." In the course of so doing, we have been forced to eliminate some signs and symptoms that some clinicians have been relying on. Perhaps we ourselves had been doing so, but we are willing to pay this price. We are even willing to pay the price of dropping something that was considered fundamental by the master himself, as, for instance, DSM-III does not include Bleuler's *ambivalence* or his *autism*; or, to take an instance closer to my heart, Rado's *anhedonia* (Meehl, 1962, 1964, 1974–1975, 1975). Less counterconventional, one thinks of the pan-anxiety considered extremely important—perhaps the most important single symptom—in the "pseudoneurotic schizophrenia" syndrome described by Hoch and Polatin (1949). The latter two examples are of course controversial; but as to the former, it is hard to believe that we should omit two of Bleuler's cardinal signs unless this choice is dictated by difficulty objectifying them in the interest of reliability.

I repeat that I am not here disputing the claim that the net attenuated construct validity for identifying the whole class of schizophrenics has been increased by the tightening process, and I am not at the moment concerned with the efficacy of clinical handling, but I am attending to the research context. It is surely possible, and to a statistically and philosophically sophisticated person not even paradoxical, that some subset of patients sharing underlying etiology and psychopathology (genetics, biochemistry, CNS fine structure, and psychodynamics or "personality structure") with the core group of schizophrenias but who, because of modifying genes and normal-range individual differences factors (Meehl, 1975) as well as life history experiences, do not develop the signs and symptoms that have remained in the selected list of DSM-III, or—equally possible despite average heightened reliability—do not have them in sufficient quantity to be clear instances. Such a state of affairs is not only consistent with, but is probabilistically inferable from either the medical model, classical psychometrics, genetics, learning theory, or ordinary trait theory. The point is that clinicians trained to classify patients with the reduced high-reliable list of criteria will not be psychologically disposed to consider the subset of peripheral or borderline cases as belonging to the schizophrenic group (as they should not in applying the objectified criteria). In the context of discovery, this could sometimes operate adversely, since the way you categorize your world, as we all know, will in considerable part determine what you are capable of noticing.

But suppose a perceptive clinician does notice something about these borderline cases and undertakes a systematic research study of something middling complicated and not easy to discern, say, for example, a second-order interaction between phenothiazines and a certain mode of psychotherapeutic intervention (e.g., RET). Now if the polygenic modifiers or environmental factors that make the atypical schizophrenias show a different kind of interaction effect from the core group, that will not be detected statistically, even having been noticed clinically by a gifted clinician, because such cases will only rarely (and mostly due to carelessness in applying the new criteria!) be included in the study. If one believes (as I do) that the psychiatric treatment of the future will involve complicated kinds of actuarial grounds for selecting and sequencing the treatment of choice (Meehl, 1972a, pp. 135–137), early research progress along such lines could be hampered in this way.

I want to emphasize that I'm not here invoking some kind of vague clinical intuitions about "patterns." I am making a simple point about research statistics, that is, that you can't detect a trend that makes a subset of subjects different from the other subjects in a certain group if there aren't any of the subset present in the study. Furthermore, as we move into higher order interaction effects, such as Drug $\times$ Psychotherapy $\times$ Subdiagnosis patterns, the degrees of freedom shrink so that errors of Type II begin to preponderate due to marked reduction in statistical power.

It might be argued that while this may impose an irksome hurdle in the context of discovery at the intuitive stage for the clinician trained in the use of DSM-III, and thinking more or less automatically that way, it will not have any long-run bad effect because the cases not included in such studies will be detectable in studies focusing on some other diagnostic rubric. I think that is an optimistic view because it implies that some sort of massive research network of all possible combinations of everything with everything is going to take place in psychiatry and clinical psychology, which it is not, both for economic and professional interest reasons. Furthermore, what kind of thing is detected will depend upon what initial overall rubric is being studied. If these borderline cases were subsumed under "anxiety state" rather than borderline schizophrenia, the interaction effect between an antipsychotic drug and cognitive therapy will not be a likely subject matter of investigation. Finally, what is perhaps the more serious statistical point, such people will not be found in any one rubric if misdiagnosed because of the tight criteria [by misdiagnosed, I of course mean subsumed to the wrong specific etiological group (Meehl, 1972b, 1977) in the eyes of Omniscient Jones], but are likely to be dispersed. When one disperses a group of people who are heterogeneous in some respects, but homogeneous in some core feature of high causal relevance, into a number of heterogeneous diagnostic categories, the best bet is that they will simply get lost in the shuffle. While I do not claim to know that this is a serious problem, it is not a silly consideration that can be dismissed out of hand without thorough mathematical analysis.

Moving away from what one might call the "political–social–economic" impact of DSM-III, it is worthwhile to examine at a more philosophical level the ways in which a practitioner or researcher may view its categories and dimensions. I can see three (although not sharply demarcated), one of which is admirable, one of which is criticizable but fairly harmless, and only the third of which is scientifically malignant. The first is to view the delineation of a syndrome as an empirically observed (clinically or statistically!) cluster, a syndrome plus course, that suggests to us some kind of underlying causal homogeneity in the subjects who show it; although we may, depending on our theoretical predilections, sit quite loosely to this etiological promissory note. Its justification is mainly communicative and pragmatic, together with whatever degree of faith we have from the history of medicine (and genetics, and psychometrics) that future research will give us a more detailed understanding of whatever historical and "latent" (inner) current processes and structures are at work to produce the covariation of the signs, symptoms, aspects of course, prognosis, and response to treatment. Covariation is the essence of descriptive science and the touchstone of scientific thinking, whether we read such diverse writers as Freud, Skinner, Allport, Murray, Eysenck, Thurstone, or Cattell—strange bedfellows indeed, whose unanimity on *this* point should surely tell us something about how to study the mind! *Ceteris paribus* again, the more standardized the examination can be made, the more objectively described the classification of the responses, and as a result, the greater interjudge agreement by different examiners, and the more striking the empirical "tightness" of the cluster, the better we like the syndrome as an entity. As already stated, it is hard to understand why a rational mind would object to any approach that enhances these desirable properties.

Second, one may believe that DSM-III is the best that can be achieved, at least in the foreseeable future, and may be suspicious or even antagonistic to deviations from it, for either clinical or research purposes. This attitude troubles me, but I should think it can be adequately buffered by the practice I suggested above, that is, that investigators have a responsibility to employ it until it is officially revised by some "culturally empowered" group such as those who constructed it in the first place. But we do not pressure researchers or punish them financially or otherwise, once they have met these conditions in their semantics, for delineating some further conjectural entities or dimensions of their own, hoping to persuade the profession on the basis of clinical experience of better evidence, that they are right.

It is the third attitude which I think is malignant, partly because of its potential chilling effect, but mainly because it is philosophically so terribly mistaken. It says not merely that "this is a good thing so far as it goes, and should not be lightly discarded or whimsically amended." This third view claims it is *the* truth, as a matter of some kind of rigorous definition process. The extreme (simplistic, "vulgar operationist") form of this view is that the very *meaning* of the concepts is contained, exhaustively and explicitly, in the "operational definitions" provided by DSM-III. It would be hard to find one single logician or historian of science today (or for that matter, since around 1935!) who would countenance the conception of scientific method enshrined in this view. I find it puzzling that physicians, or for that matter, psychologists, unless they are of the most dogmatic behaviorist kind, should adopt this position when neither the history of organic medicine, nor of genetics (I don't mean here merely behavior genetics), nor of traditional trait theory in academic psychology, nor of classical psychometrics, gives any support to it. It is simply not true that diseases in organic medicine are "defined by" the syndrome or by the syndrome and course together. Organic diseases are defined by a conjunction of their etiology and pathology when these are known; and otherwise—with much less scientific assurance—as syndromes remaining to be researched so as to be medically understood. A disease entity, as delineated in the early stages of clinical experience and scientific study, at the level of mere syndrome discription when there is as yet no (or minimal and conjectural) knowledge of the etiology or pathology underlying it, is an open concept (Meehl, 1972b, 1977; Cronbach & Meehl, 1955; Meehl & Golden, 1982; Pap, 1953, 1958, Chap. 11). It is neither philosophically rigorous nor scientifically sophisticated to make a literal identification of a disease entity with its currently accepted signs and symptoms. Corresponding to organic medicine's pathology (in a more extended sense than that envisaged by Virchow) is personality structure (genotypic traits, psychodynamics). Corresponding to etiology are, except for an environmentalist fanatic, the genetic predispositions not only to specific mental disorders, but to "temperamental genotypic traits" generally, such as anxiety conditionability, rage readiness, hedonic capacity, general intelligence and the like, and the learning history imposed on an organism whose varied behavior acquisition functions are characterized by such-and-such inherited parameters. Our problem in psychopathology of the so-called functional behavior disorders is obvious, to wit, that we do not possess an equivalent to the pathologist's and microbiologist's report telling us the "right answer" at the conclusion of a clinicopathological case conference (Meehl, 1973, pp. 284–289). If I make a psychodynamic inference, it is not possible for me to ask the psychopathologist whether his stained slides showed the patient's psyche had holes in the superego. To a thoughtful clinician with philosophical sophistication, it is perfectly obvious that disease syndromes are inherently open concepts, as mentioned above. Nothing but dogmatism on the one hand, or confusion on the other, is produced by pretending to give operational definitions in which the disease entity is literally identified with the list of signs and symptoms. Such an operational definition is a fake.

If somebody does not like the medical model (and if that's the case, one wouldn't be taking DSM-III—concocted by a group of psychiatrists for medical purposes—seriously to begin with), he should be reminded that in classical psychometrics (such as factor analysis) or in more recent developments (such as multidimensional scaling), we cannot even write the basic equations, let alone the embedding interpretative text required to give empirical meaning to the variables in those equations, unless a clear distinction is already made between the manifest behavior indicators and the inferred (latent, causal) factors. The same is true of biophysical trait theory as classically elaborated by Allport (1937), Murray (1938), Cattell (1946), and others. Obviously, the great breakthrough in genetics with Mendel, and the rediscovery of Mendel's concepts at the turn of the century, hinged upon the distinction between the genotype and the phenotype. This distinction forced theoretical recognition that under many circumstances or available pedigrees, the weakly stochastic relationship between the two made an inference to genotype impossible.

One simple-minded mistake that I am surprised to find physicians making is to think that if, in a given concrete instance (single case, not class), we do not have a touchstone for testing whether a certain inferred construct property such as a latent disease is present or absent, that lack means that it is scientifically meaningless to ask the question, a view that the logician Carnap, a strongly positivist and tough-minded philosopher of science, refuted definitively almost a half century ago!

The same is true of most variants of learning theory, the old-fashioned kind (Tolman, Hull or Guthrie) as well as the souped up developments in mathematical learning theory, information processing, and cognitive processes generally that took place subsequently. The only plausible exception to the genotypic/phenotypic, inner/outer, inferred/observed distinction in learning theory is strict Skinnerian learning theory which is almost entirely dispositional, although not as "pure" in this respect as some of its adherents like to think when they talk metatheory about it.

I am fond of referring clinical psychology students to a little known 2-page article published many years ago by the late T. A. Peppard (1949), a reputedly brilliant diagnostician who practiced internal medicine in Minneapolis for many years. He made a statistical study of the source of his diagnostic mistakes, using very strict criteria against postmortem findings. Errors of omission (well known to be commoner than errors of commission in medical diagnosis) sometimes occurred because he failed to look for something, other times because he looked for it but didn't give it the proper weight, other times because he made an "error" on a judgment call, and so on. But the interesting thing is that 29% of the errors of omission were attributable, even by very tight standards imposed on himself, to the factor he called "symptoms and signs not found." Of course, all physicians know the concept of "silent disease" such as an undiagnosed staghorn kidney or an early Pick's frontal lobe atrophy, not to mention subjects with an epileptic brain wave who never have a fit and would not be discovered except for being the monozygotic twin of somebody who has a clinically recognizable convulsive disorder. I repeat that I find it strange that one must remind physicians about the distinction between the construct "disease" and its presently accessible symptom picture, although it is not so surprising that some psychologists confuse them.

Finally, of course, the most obvious example, which would still be persuasive to some of my generation, is psychodynamics, whose essence consists in the distinction between the easily observed manifest behavior or self-awareness and the "hidden, latent, underlying source" of some aspect of observable covariation.

Since neither psychodynamics, classical psychometrics, taxometrics, organic medicine, genetics, learning theory, or trait theory has proceeded by explicit identification between theoretical entities and their indicators, it would be strange to hold that rational use of DSM-III requires us to consider its syndromes as literally definitive and totally noninferential.

It might be argued that if the builders of DSM-III had achieved consensus on constructing a purely descriptive (atheoretical, noninferential) "phenomenological" taxonomy, they should have proceeded by applying an appropriate formal cluster algorithm to a huge batch of carefully gathered clinical data, "letting the statistics do the whole job for them," which would have saved a lot of conference time as well as generating a more objective scientific product. This sounds plausible to a psychologist, and maybe to some statisticians, but the main trouble with it is that there is no "accepted" cluster algorithm which is known to be sufficiently powerful to be used in this way (cf. Meehl, 1979). Even if there were such an agreed upon cluster analysis algorithm, one doubts that the committee could have proceeded in that way. The fact is that different clinicians do not share an equally "operational" view, partly for the reasons I have given and partly because of certain clinical (perhaps one could even say ideological) identifications, for example, between organicists and psychoanalysts, biotropes and sociotropes, scientists interested in genes and psychotherapists interested in battle-ax mothers.

I am inclined to think that the next round ought to at least settle on some way of deciding when the orientation should be taxonomic versus dimensional. But that would hinge upon having a sufficiently well-trusted algorithm for determining whether the latent order of a syndrome or dimension should be thought of as taxonic or nontaxonically factorial. Another possibility, which again seems simplistic and arbitrary until you ask what are the reasons for doing it another way, would be to collect all of the information or input kinds of variables, including life history data and the like, that go into diagnosis, and all of the output dispositions that are clinical reasons for making a diagnosis, such as differential response to psychotropic drugs, response to individual and group therapy, danger of acting out, suicide risk, and long-term employability. Absent cogent reasons for giving higher weight to some of these output ones than others, it is arguable that the proper statistical model should be canonical correlation in which we simultaneously optimize the predictability of the most predictable composite on the output side by optimal weights on the input variables. If the various output consequences of clinical importance are not prima facie very different in "importance," if they are, so to speak, qualitatively of equal significance to us in decision making, then the difference in the weights they get might best be to weight them so as to make them collectively most predictable. The justification for defining a syndrome (or a nontaxonic factor) by some subset of input and output considered jointly would be that the canonical correlation between the two sets reach a certain minimum size. It would be interesting, by the way, to ascertain whether such a distribution of candidate canonical correlations would show, if not an actual break, at least some tendency to bimodality, suggesting that some syndromes are "real" and others are more or less arbitrary carvings out by the clinician of regions of slightly greater densification in the multivariate descriptor space (but see Murphy, 1964). My own research interests are such that I consider that the initial distinction between whether one should proceed taxometrically or factorially should be given very great priority in the next revision.

The question as to the desirability of adopting a fixed rule approach to diagnostic criteria involves a complicated mix of statistical, philosophical, and clinical issues that are beyond the space limitations of this chapter and about which I myself have formed no definite opinion. This question has been aired recently in papers by Finn (1982, 1983) and Widiger (1983) [see also Meehl and Rosen (1955), comment by Cureton (1957), and Rorer, Hoffman, La-Forge, and Hsieh (1966)]. In thinking about this difficult question, it is necessary first to distinguish between issues regarding base rate fluctuations in different clinical or research populations and the separate but intimately related issues of clinical utility in treatment and prognosis. In saying these are distinct but intimately related, I mean to emphasize that from the standpoint of scientific realism (surely the implicit assumption of organic medicine, whether medical researchers or practitioners use the philosopher's terminology for it or not!), one does not wish to conflate the probability or corroboration of a diagnostic statement as a factual claim with the seriousness of a mistake. As Widiger worried about in his exchange with Finn, we do not want to adopt a decision rule based on a policy of systematically misdiagnosing patients on the grounds that correctly diagnosing a subset of them would, in certain pragmatic contexts, be too costly or risky or have too many side effects or make them more uncomfortable than the disease makes them, or whatever. Crudely put, the first business of a diagnostic assertion is to be right! We cannot make use of differential utilities and disutilities of clinical errors without at least some crude assessments of diagnostic confidence, whereas we can investigate the optimality of a diagnostic procedure with regard to truth value without referring to any utilities other than the "cognitive utility" of being correct in our assertions. It would seem best, if it can be done and is psychologically acceptable to practitioners, to optimize the diagnoses by some suitable adjustment for known or guesstimated base rates in a given clinical population, and subsequently to raise the question of the various utilities involved in adopting a certain treatment plan or making predictions to the patient, court, employer, insurer, family, or whatever. In that mode of reasoning, the best inferable diagnostic statement is made first and the utilities are plugged in afterward.

But this of course doesn't take care of the base rate problem. Theoretically we know that both the cutting score on a variate which is an indicator of the disease entity and any formal or informal weighting of the scores or way of combining them into a pattern, as in Bayes's formula, should not be done independently of the base rates. In ordinary clinical medicine, practitioners who never heard of the Reverend Thomas Bayes or the subsequent controversy about his ideas (this use of the formula itself is, of course, hardly controversial) make implicit use of it. They know that if you diagnose syphilis in Puerto Rico on the grounds of a positive Wassermann you are likely to fall into errors that you would not make in Minnesota because of the geographic epidemiology of lues versus yaws. Every general practitioner at times says to the patient, "Well, I think you've got the winter crud; there's a lot of that going around these days," an informal Bayesian inference. It is an unsettled question how much the explicit and formalized inverse probability machinery of the statistician should become part of the decision making by a busy doctor. Of course, even given a certain diagnosis, perhaps tentatively arrived at with the intention to be flexible about revising it should the predicted results of a therapeutic intervention fail to materialize in the usual fashion, it is common practice, within the category of patients who meet the diagnostic criteria, to pay attention to the pattern of symptoms that is relevant to treatment choice and to include in this those "extraneous" characteristics (e.g., age, family, income, unrelated concurrent illness) that themselves did not enter into the diagnostic decision proper.

There is nothing either wrong or particularly complicated about any of this. The only question is the extent to which formalization improves or impairs certain of these generally accepted clinical practices. Unfortunately, the behavior of a Bayes theorem computed inverse probability depends in somewhat complicated ways upon the distribution of sign validities, the relationship between valid and false-positive rates, the extent to which the independence assumption of the signs pairwise is not satisfied, how robust the inferred diagnostic p value is with respect to departures from those assumptions, differential responsiveness of error rate at different regions of the base rate continuum, and the like. It would seem that some rather large-scale but also intensive research by statisticians and clinicians would be in order.

I do not think it is safe to assume that because such actuarial refinements are not part of the everyday mental habits of practitioners in organic medicine, then, we don't have to worry about it in psychopathology. There are probably important differences in the latter area. Further, we still do not know the extent to which ordinary clinical practice of organic medicine commits more diagnostic errors than need be because of the extent to which the mathematics of clinical reference is not explicitly employed by the practitioner (Blois, 1980; Dawes, 1979; Dawes & Corrigan, 1974; Engelhardt, Spicker, & Towers, 1979; Goldberg, 1970, 1976; Gough, 1962, Holt, 1970, 1978; Kahneman, Slovic, & Tversky, 1982; Kleinmuntz, 1982; Meehl, 1954, 1956a, 1956b, 1956c, 1957, 1960, 1967; Sawyer, 1966; Sines, 1970). Finally, how one thinks about this and what kinds of research are conducted depend on how confident we are that the underlying psychopathology is intrinsically taxonic (categorical, "typal") versus nontaxonically multidemensional where class concepts and qualitative predicates are only handy rubrics for roughly designating regions in an ontologically continuous descriptor hyperspace.

While the very title of this volume orients us toward revision, one hopes that the intellectual fretfulness of primates and the availability of taxpayer dollars will not induce us to attempt substantial revisions until a large mass of evidence, including experimental research, clinical trials, quantitative analysis of clinical file data, and exchange of experience by seasoned practitioners of various persuasions, puts us in a position to do something more than speculate or nitpick. A tremendous amount of work by able people and a lot of taxpayer money went into generating the present product, and it is foolish to tinker with it very much, let alone undertake a complete overhaul, because it isn't perfect, or because the results of an unavoidable compromise are not located precisely where one might prefer it, given his own theory and practice. Sometimes the best advice is that of the Baptist preacher, "Leave it lay where Jesus flang it." I bethink myself of how difficult it is for me, after 40 years on the Minnesota faculty, to interest myself in interminable discussions about how we should revise the written preliminary examination for the Ph.D. so as to get a better assessment, reduce student anxiety, or whatever. A half century of observation (if I include my student days) reveals mostly primate meddlery, irrational optimism, a disinclination to consult the past, and the Hegelian swing of even short-term history!

It goes without saying that the most important developments one can anticipate that would make it rational to revise are substantive advances in our understanding of mental disorder. But there are also, I think, several metaquestions that it would be desirable to have "settled" (if not exactly *solved*) before the next round of major revision. The reader will discern that the "answers" to these metaquestions involve a mix of mathematical development of statistical methods especially suitable for taxonomic problems, the usual impact of substantive developments upon methodology (no contemporary philosopher of science conceives of methodology as entirely prior to theory), and considerations of clinical utility. I repeat that it is a grave mistake to conflate this last class of questions with questions regarding the intrinsic science, that is, factual validity, of any proposed concept. There are four metaquestions that should meanwhile be addressed by high-competence investigators so that we will be in good methodological shape when the time for major revision arrives. Without dogmatism, I might go so far as to say that in my judgment until these four are answered, at least in the sense of a fairly high consensus among qualified individuals (there is no point in absolute democracy in a field like this!), we are probably not in a cognitive position that warrants a major revision being attempted.

First, what role should a conjectural etiology, when moderately to strongly corroborated, play in the taxonomic strategy? Here one must avoid a simplistic division into "known" and "unverified" etiology, assuming a sharp dividing line where none exists even in organic medicine, genetics, or other fields of knowledge. It is obvious on mere inspection of the present list of rubrics that etiological factors partially understood, and in which varying degrees of "strong influence" as causal factors (Meehl, 1972b, 1977) must have been taken into account at least behind the scenes, have been unavoidable. It will be necessary to have a uniform standard of proof rather than a double standard of methodological morals such as prevails in some quarters today. For example, there are clinicians in the medical and psychological professions who resist recognizing the genetic influences in major mental disorders or, while reluctantly recognizing them, would not want to split the nosology of affective disorders into unipolar and bipolar despite the strong evidence available presently as to the reality of that distinction genetically and its correlates with certain aspects of the syndrome, course, and so on. Yet, some of these same clinicians, while justly pointing out that an absolute hammer blow unavoidable demonstration (there is no such thing as this in empirical science, of course) has not been given for the unipolar/bipolar distinction, will in their own diagnostic thinking rely upon highly speculative psychodynamics, or family factors, or other alleged causal influences, whose degree of evidentiary support at the present time is nowhere in the running with that for the biological distinctions made. This parallels some clinical psychologists who, because of hostility to medicine (or simply poor training at a second-rate school?), continue to decry all psychiatric diagnosis as "mere labeling" or "completely unreliable," refusing to read the quantitative evidence of diagnostic reliability developed in recent years, and then by some obscure mental process (which I confess myself quite unable to understand) proceed to substitute for such "unreliable" psychiatric nosology a batch of unproved, politicized social determiners, or flimsy psychodynamics inferred from an instrument with as low reliability and validity as the Rorschach! That is the sort of thing I mean by double standard of epistemological morals.

Second, the strategic distinction between thinking in terms of dimensions and categories (types, species, taxa, disease entities) remains with us. While one can get by with a kind of compromise between these, the basic theoretical claim of a classification system should be methodologically clear, even if a sizable proportion of patients are not clearly sortable into one or the other (a different question). Sooner or later we should get clear about which of our nosological rubrics are intended to be rough designations of persons location in a multidimensional descriptor space (whether phenotypic or genotypic, psychodynamic or genetic, that's not the point) and which rubrics have a genuine typological (taxonomic) theoretical intent. Thus, for instance, the very meaning of some standard terms in epidemiology and psychometrics, such as "false positive" and "base rate," which can be made tolerably clear on a taxonomic model, becomes fuzzy and—if the point is pressed—hardly interpretable on a nontaxonomic model. An adequate understanding of the philosophical and statistical aspects of this in relation to substantive theories of causation might properly lead us to abandon the idea of rubrics entirely for some subsets of conditions. For example: When I used to teach clinical psychology, in order to make this point I sometimes pushed the following (doubtless exaggerated) doctrine: There are several major mental disorders (e.g., schizophrenia, manic–depression, unipolar depression, delirium tremens, Alzheimer's disease) that are truly taxonomic in nature, and for which category rubrics are semantically strictly appropriate, not merely as rough ways of delineating regions in a continuous descriptor space. There is also, in my opinion, a true entity of the solid gold essential psychopath (sociopathic personality, asocial, amoral type). But when we get to the so-called neuroses and psychophysiological disorders of the neurotic kind, there is only one rubric (with the possible exception of the textbook obsessional neurosis), namely, "psychoneurosis, mixed," a term no longer found in the official nomenclature. The distinctions within that mixed category are quantitative only; they are merely differing degrees of anxiety, depression, somatization, and defense mechanisms in the neurotic mixture. In the long run, it may be worth the trouble to teach clinicians to think more dimensionally than categorically and mold their verbal and inferential habits in those directions.

Third, we should get clearer than we presently are about the matter of sliding cuts on various indicators of an entity in relationship to base rates and various clinical populations in geographic, social classes, and the like, and the relevance of Bayes' theorem. In matters where extremely asymmetrical likelihoods exist for the combination of a small number of high-valid signs, the importance of the base rate, except for the most extreme values, is considerably reduced, and it is probably statistical pedantry to push some kind of Bayes' theorem algorithm onto working clinicians under such circumstances. I think that more mathematical analysis in relationship to the diagnostic habits of practitioners is in order here before altering the character of a psychiatrist's or clinical psychologist's education in this regard. Nobody acquainted with my writings would suspect me of being even faintly "antistatistical" in my biases; but I believe we should think like behavioral engineers in considering ourselves and others as clinical practitioners, taking into account what kinds of psychological disruptions in diagnostic cognitive activity could take place that might reduce net efficiency, even though the underlying mathematical model makes it look like an improvement.

Finally, at the risk of projecting my own current research interests, I would say that a desideratum for the next major revision is agreement upon the general taxometric problem as such, which I see as having two elements: (a) Is a taxometric procedure in psychopathology aimed at anything more than identifying phenotypic clusters, and, if it is, (b) which of the available formal taxometric methods (if any!) have shown themselves capable of detecting an underlying causal structure (whatever its biological or social nature), being meanwhile free of any appreciable tendency to detect taxonic structures that aren't there (Meehl, 1979)? I think it not unduly optimistic to opine that we will have a pretty clear answer to the second question before the end of this decade (Grove & Andreasen, Chap. 17 of this volume; Meehl & Golden, 1982; Sneath & Sokal, 1973).

REFERENCES

Allport, G. W. (1937). *Personality: A psychological interpretation.* New York: Henry Holt.
Blois, M. S. (1980). Clinical judgment and computers. *New England Journal of Medicine, 303,* 192–197.
Cattell, R. B. (1946) *Description and measurement of personality.* New York: World Book Company.

Cronbach, L. J., & Meehl, P. E. (1955). Construct validity in psychological tests. *Psychological Bulletin, 52*, 281–302.

Cureton, E. E. (1957). Recipe for a cookbook. *Psychological Bulletin, 54*, 494–497.

Dawes, R. M. (1979). The robust beauty of improper linear models in decision making. *American Psychologist, 34*, 571–582.

Dawes, R. M., & Corrigan, B. (1974). Linear models in decision making. *Psychological Bulletin, 81*, 95–106.

Engelhardt, T. H., Spicker, S. F., & Towers, B. (Eds.). (1979). *Clinical judgment: A critical appraisal.* Boston, MA: Reidel.

Feyerabend, P. K. (1970). Against method: Outline of an anarchistic theory of knowledge. In M. Radner & S. Winokur (Eds.), *Analysis of theories and methods of physics and psychology. Minnesota studies in the Philosophy of Science* (Vol. 4). Minneapolis: University of Minnesota Press.

Finn, S. E. (1982). Base rates, utilities, and DSM-III: Shortcomings of fixed-rule systems of psychodiagnosis. *Journal of Abnormal Psychology, 91*, 294–302.

Finn, S. E. (1983). Utility-balanced and utility-imbalanced rules: Reply to Widiger. *Journal of Abnormal Psychology, 92*, 499–501.

Goldberg, L. R. (1970). Man versus model of man: A rationale plus some evidence for a method of improving on clinical inferences. *Psychological Bulletin, 73*, 422–432.

Goldberg, L. R. (1976). Man versus model of man: Just how conflicting is that evidence? *Organizational Behavior and Human Performance, 16*, 13–22.

Gough, H. G. (1962). Clinical versus statistical prediction in psychology. In L. Postman (Ed.), *Psychology in the making.* New York: Knopf.

Hoch, P., & Polatin, P. (1949). Pseudoneurotic forms of schizophrenia. *Psychiatric Quarterly, 3*, 248–276.

Holt, R. R. (1970). Yet another look at clinical and statistical prediction. *American Psychologist, 25*, 337–339.

Holt, R. R. (1978). *Methods in clinical psychology: Vol. 2. Prediction and research.* New York: Plenum Press.

Kahneman, D., Slovic, P., & Tversky, A. (1982). *Judgment under uncertainty: Heuristics and biases.* London: Cambridge University Press.

Kleinmuntz, B. (1982). Computational and noncomputational clinical information processing by computer. *Behavioral Science, 27*, 164–175.

Meehl, P. E. (1954). *Clinical versus statistical prediction: A theoretical analysis and a review of the evidence.* Minneapolis: University of Minnesota Press.

Meehl, P. E. (1956a). Clinical versus actuarial prediction. In *Proceedings of the 1955 Invitational Conference on Testing Problems* (pp. 136–141). Princeton, NJ: Educational Testing Service.

Meehl, P. E. (1956b). Wanted—a good cookbook. *American Psychologist, 11*, 263–272.

Meehl, P. E. (1956c). The tie that binds. *Journal of Counseling Psychology, 3*, 163–164.

Meehl, P. E. (1957). When shall we use our heads instead of the formula? *Journal of Counseling Psychology, 4*, 268–273.

Meehl, P. E. (1959). Some ruminations on the validation of clinical procedures. *Canadian Journal of Psychology, 13*, 102–128.

Meehl, P. E. (1960). The cognitive activity of the clinician. *American Psychologist, 15*, 19–27.

Meehl, P. E. (1962). Schizotaxia, schizotypy, schizophrenia. *American Psychologist, 17*, 827–838.

Meehl, P. E. (1964). *Manual for use with checklist of schizotypic signs.* Psychiatry Research Unit, University of Minnesota Medical School, Minneapolis, Copyright 1964.

Meehl, P. E. (1967). What can the clinician do well? In D. N. Jackson & S. Messick (Eds.), *Problems in human assessment* (pp. 594–599). New York: McGraw-Hill.

Meehl, P. E. (1972a). Reactions, reflections, projections. In J. N. Butcher (Ed.), *Objective personality assessment: Changing perspectives* (pp. 131–189). New York: Academic Press.

Meehl, P. E. (1972b). Specific genetic etiology, psychodynamics and therapeutic nihilism. *International Journal of Mental Health, 1*, 10–27.

Meehl, P. E. (1973). Why I don't go to case conferences. In *Psychodiagnosis: Selected papers.* Minneapolis: University of Minnesota Press.

Meehl, P. E. (1974–1975). Genes and the unchangeable core. *VOICES: The Art and Science of Psychotherapy, 38,* 25–35.

Meehl, P. E. (1975). Hedonic capacity: Some conjectures. *Bulletin of the Menninger Clinic, 39,* 295–307.

Meehl, P. E. (1977). Specific etiology and other forms of strong influence: Some quantitative meanings. *Journal of Medicine and Philosophy, 2,* 33–53.

Meehl, P. E. (1979). A funny thing happened to us on the way to the latent entities. *Journal of Personality Assessment, 43,* 563–581.

Meehl, P. E. (1983). Subjectivity in psychoanalytic inference: The nagging persistence of Wilhelm Fliess's Achensee question. In J. Earman (Ed.), *Testing scientific theories. Minnesota studies in the philosophy of science* (Vol. 10). Minneapolis: University of Minnesota Press.

Meehl, P. E., & Golden, R. (1982). Taxometric methods. In P. Kendall & J. Butcher (Eds.), *Handbook of research methods in clinical psychology.* New York: Wiley.

Meehl, P. E., McArthur, C. C., & Tiedeman, D. V. (1956). Symposium on clinical and statistical prediction. *Journal of Counseling Psychology, 3,* 163–173.

Meehl, P. E., & Rosen, A. (1955). Antecedent probability and the efficiency of psychometric signs, patterns, or cutting scores. *Psychological Bulletin, 52,* 194–216.

Murphy, E. A. (1964). One cause? Many causes? The argument from a bimodal distribution. *Journal of Chronic Diseases, 17,* 301–324.

Murray, H. A. (1938). *Exploratory in personality.* London: Oxford University Press.

Pap, A. (1953). Reduction sentences and open concepts. *Methodos, 5,* 3–30.

Pap, A. (1958). *Semantics and necessary truth.* New Haven, CT: Yale University Press.

Peppard, T. A. (1949). Mistakes in diagnosis. *Minnesota Medicine, 32,* 510–511.

Reichenbach, H. (1938). *Experience and prediction.* Chicago, IL: University of Chicago Press.

Rorer, L. G., Hoffman, F. J., LaForge, G. E., & Hsieh, K. E. (1966). Optimum cutting scores to discriminate groups of unequal size and variance. *Journal of Applied Psychology, 50,* 153–164.

Sawyer, J. (1966). Measurement and prediction, clinical *and* statistical. *Psychological Bulletin, 66,* 178–200.

Sines, J. O. (1970). Actuarial versus clinical prediction in psychopathology. *British Journal of Psychiatry, 116,* 129–144.

Sneath, P. H. A., & Sokal, R. R. (1973). *Numerical toxonomy.* San Francisco, CA: Freeman.

Widiger, T. A. (1983). Utilities and fixed diagnostic rules: Comments on Finn (1982). *Journal of Abnormal Psychology, 92,* 495–498.

CHAPTER 11

Psychiatric Diagnosis and Natural Categorization: A Close Analogy

Nancy Cantor and Nancy Genero

Introduction

As clinicians and clinical researchers, we are often in the unenviable position of having to make clear-cut psychiatric diagnoses in a domain that is all but clear-cut. Certainly, there is no immediate solution to this dilemma. A growing literature on natural categorization attests to the difficulties of determining category membership (Rosch, 1978). It emphasizes the uncertainties that permeate the process of categorization at various stages across all domains. Previous work on person categorization and diagnosis (Cantor & Mischel, 1979; Cantor, Smith, French, & Mezzich, 1980; Clarkin, Widiger, Frances, Hurt, & Gilmore, 1983; Genero, Greden, & Markus, 1985; L. Horowitz, Post, French, Wallis, & Siegelman, 1981; L. M. Horowitz, Wright, Lowenstein, & Parad, 1981) provides a conceptual and empirical basis from which to propose that psychiatric diagnosis can be examined by analogy to natural categorization. By doing so, we can familiarize ourselves with the hazards of attempting to deal effectively with psychiatric categories that invariably have fuzzy structures and are therefore difficult to use.

In this chapter, we propose that the future development of DSM (American Psychiatric Association [APA], 1980) can benefit from explicit consideration of issues raised in the study of natural categorization. Among the specific issues which we will consider are the following:

- The advantages and disadvantages of natural categorization
- Structural and procedural aspects of natural categorization

Nancy Cantor, Department of Psychology, and Nancy Genero, Department of Psychiatry, University of Michigan, Ann Arbor, Michigan.

- Application of models of natural categorization to psychiatric diagnosis
- Recommendations for revisions in the diagnostic manual.

Natural Categorization: Advantages and Disadvantages

The way in which we perceptually organize the external environment is largely attributable to the process of natural categorization. It is through this process that we establish relationships among external stimuli to achieve a more meaningful and coherent view of the world (Bruner, Goodnow, & Austin, 1956; Quine, 1969; Rosch, 1978). Thus, natural categorization is adaptive in that it facilitates daily functioning by limiting the amount and the complexity of stimuli. Most of us would be overwhelmed by the staggering amounts of information that we might otherwise have to process. For example, a violin is an object that has a scroll, bridge, neck, chin rest, sound post, fingerboard, tailpin, pegs, strings G, D, A, and E, and so forth. The perceptual composite of these parts, however, produces an object commonly known as a violin. Hence, the categorization of this object as a violin simplifies the encoding, storage, and retrieval of information concerning violins; assists the individual in making inferences, judgments, and predictions about the instrument; and allows the development of a language of commonality. Every day, people group objects (both animate and inanimate) according to similarities in their essential features, label these natural categories, and communicate about the similarities within groups and differences between groups through this system of shared category labels (Cantor & Mischel, 1979).

Although natural categorization provides us with the means to create a manageable view of the world, there are distinct disadvantages. In the process of categorization, homogeneity within groups is emphasized and heterogeneity between groups exaggerated. Unfortunately, cognitive economy is frequently achieved at the expense of continued registration or recognition of the inconsistencies and variability in naturally occurring stimuli (Bransford & Franks, 1971; Posner & Keele, 1968; Walker, 1975). Therefore, although most violins share some basic features, all violins are certainly not the same. However, individuals are less likely to remember the variability once having learned or used the category label, violin (Walker, 1975). Natural categorization does allow us to make broad discriminations; violins do appear to be different from cellos. However, finer distinctions come less easily. It is difficult to find a clean dividing line between violins and the violas, and for the novice it is even more difficult to discriminate a fiddle from a Stradivarius. An expert might argue that sound is the ultimate test of accuracy in categorization here; unfortunately, even the country fiddle can sound like a Stradivarius in the fine-tuned hands of a musical genius (Labov, 1973). The costs of categorization—exaggerating within-group similarity and between-group divisions—are, of course, particularly troublesome when the category objects are people.

The literature on stereotyping provides us with ample evidence of the disadvantages of natural categorization. Stereotypes not only sometimes lead the perceiver to create erroneous assumptions about others (i.e., blacks are lazy, women are weak), they also discourage the perceiver from registering and remembering disconfirming evidence (Hamilton, 1979). As Cohen (1981) points out, an "impression-forming goal encourages perceivers to reduce the complexity of stimuli and thus overlook incongruent information" (p. 444). In the process of organizing the social world into categories, people come to "see" the members of social categories as remarkably similar in attributes and, once again, the between-group divisions are enhanced (Quattrone & Jones, 1980). From the perspective of a "liberal," *all* "conservatives" are antiregulations, antichange, free market-oriented individuals. The liberal sees conservatives as a distinctly different species, despite considerable overlap in opinions and actions on particular issues: lowering interest rates, health care, preventing nuclear war, the space program, social security, reducing the crime rate, and so on. This push toward between-group distinctions may be particularly intense because of the motivation to solidify group loyalties and affiliations (Locksley, Ortiz, & Hepburn, 1980).

The categorization of persons encourages the same host of inaccuracies—distortions in perception and memory—as surface in the inanimate object domain (Cantor & Mischel, 1979). When we think about types of people in the abstract, the most accessible image is of the classic, prototypic exemplar, not the slightly imperfect one—the liberal thinks of George Wallace, not of William F. Buckley, as the representative "conservative" (Kahneman & Tversky, 1973). Over time, the stereotype-inconsistent features of a particular instance somehow get lost from memory and the gaps are filled with consistent features—William Buckley seems more and more to fit the ultraconservative mold (Cantor & Mischel, 1977; Cohen, 1981; Duncan, 1976; Higgins, Rholes, & Jones, 1977; Tsujimoto, 1978). As memories of group members are consolidated, smoothed, and normalized, between-group distinctions really do appear clear and clean—George Wallace and Teddy Kennedy have very little in common politically, or so we think.

To summarize, natural categorization occurs continually and affects all domains of perception. It is adaptive in that it enables individuals to function amidst a profusion of external stimuli. It is maladaptive in that there is a tendency, once having categorized, to exaggerate the similarity among nonidentical stimuli by overlooking within-group variability, discounting disconfirming evidence, and focusing on stereotypic examples of the category. By overestimating the goodness of fit of category members to an ideal representation of the category, perceived divisions between categories are also exaggerated.

Fuzzy Natural Categories

These disadvantages would not be problematic if the world were full of stimuli that fit neatly into well-defined categories. But, the fact is that most natural categories are perceptually "fuzzy" (Rosch, 1978; Wittgenstein, 1953). According to Smith and Medin (1982), natural categories do not have obvious necessary and sufficient *criterial* properties, so that boundaries between closely related categories are ill-defined. Linguists, philosophers, and psychologists alike have all had difficulty specifying criterial or defining features for common object categories like musical instruments, furniture, birds, fish, clothing, and so on (Clark & Clark, 1977; Miller & Johnson-Laird, 1976; Rosch & Mervis, 1975). The failure to specify criterial features that define category membership has two implications of special interest: One is that natural categories are described by a set of correlated (not criterial) features such that members may appear quite different from one another. The other is that the correlated features property of natural categories implies a continuum of category membership, ranging from the very clear or "typical" examples of a category to the very unclear, questionable "atypical" cases (McCloskey & Glucksberg, 1978; Smith, Shoben, & Rips, 1974). Some examples of the continuum of typicality in category membership include the following: violins—Stradivarius to home-made fiddle; fruit—apple to tomato; birds—robins to chickens; chairs—kitchen chair to beanbag chair. Because of correlated features, quite "good" examples of a category may appear surprisingly different. Similarly, the more atypical a stimulus is, the more different it becomes to include it within a single category—Is a tomato a fruit or a vegetable? Are Ku Klux Klan members conservatives or terrorists? The other complication in natural categories is that there is a potential for tremendous overlap in the characteristic features descriptive of closely related categories—fruits and vegetables share many characteristic features, so do violins and violas, and even conservatives and liberals. This runs counter to the intuitive notion of well-defined, orthogonal categories with clearly demarcated boundaries.

Psychiatric Diagnosis

Psychiatric diagnostic systems typically have been devised by analogy to the supposedly well-defined taxonomies of traditional biological classification systems (see Chapter 18 of this volume). Recently, however, there appears to be a shift away from the analogy to classical taxonomic systems and a move toward the recognition that diagnostic categories are fuzzy and replete with internal variability. For example, the DSM-III describes diagnostic categories with larger sets of correlated features rather than selected criterial ones and specifies guidelines for diagnosis that recognize the heterogeneity among similarly diagnosed patients. It is our belief that this shift from a classical to a fuzzy classification model is now only implicitly acknowledged in DSM-III; this shift goes unnoticed by practicing clinicians because the fundamental emphasis in the manual is still a descriptive one (see ASA, p. 7). The fuzzy structure of diagnostic categories is presented as a problematic deviation from a clear diagnostic system. Atypical cases are handled in postscripts, encouraging clinicians to become exceedingly focused upon a narrow set of typical examples. Information about the "how to's" of handling fuzzy diagnostic categories is embedded within appendices (e.g., decision trees for differential diagnosis and multiaxial evaluation system). The clinician is not encouraged to view these procedures as integral to working with fuzzy categories. In the remainder of this chapter, we will explore these structural–procedural issues more fully and identify ways in which clinicians might better be alerted to variability within and between diagnostic categories.

Fuzzy Structure and Flexible Procedures in Natural Categorization

For our purposes it is convenient to think of the fuzzy structure of natural categories in two ways: fuzziness within categories that makes it difficult to specify "what a target instance *is*," and fuzziness between neighboring categories that makes it cumbersome to know "what a target instance *isn't*" (L. M. Horowitz *et al.*, 1981). These structural properties make natural categorization difficult and raise procedural questions. In order to ease exposition, we will consider separately the questions about categorization that arise from within-category variability and those procedural concerns arising from the between-category overlap in natural taxonomies. Table 11-1 is presented to help the reader keep track of these various structural–procedural concerns.

Variability within Categories

Natural categories do not have sets of necessary and sufficient criterial features descriptive of the category numbers. Consequently, the members of natural categories define a continuum of goodness of fit in the category; there exists a number of ways to be a "good" example of any particular category; borderline or atypical cases which do not fit well in single categories abound. These structural properties have been illustrated earlier in our discussion. The category of fruit has a continuum of membership from apple to fig; apples and bananas are "good" fruit, but share few common features that specify them as fruit; tomato is an atypical fruit often confused as a

Table 11-1

Fuzzy Natural Categories: Structure, Process, Questions, and Solutions

Question	Structure	Process	Questions	Solutions
What is it?	Within category No criterial features Continuum membership Multiple "good" exemplars Atypical exemplars	Similarity matching to closest target category	Appropriate comparison standard?	Summary prototype Disjunctive exemplar Shifting criterion of match depending upon goals, expertise, context
What isn't it?	Between categories Overlapping categories Imperfect feature nesting	Differentiation from neighboring categories	Appropriate contrast set?	Distinct contrast set Plausible alternative categories Evolving contrast set to match goals, context, expertise.

vegetable. The left panel of Table 11-1 lists the within-category structural properties of interest here.

The within-category structure of natural categories has implications for the process of categorization, that is, for answering the question: What is it? Because natural categories are not well defined, there is no simple procedure such as checking a set of criterial features for categorizing a target instance. Categorization is a similarity-matching process, that is, the more features that a target instance has which are also characteristic of the category, the more likely it is to be categorized with that label (Cantor & Mischel, 1979; Rosch & Mervis, 1975; Tversky, 1977). And the criterion for a good match may shift, depending upon the expertise and goals of the categorizer and the context of other target instances (Murphy & Wright, 1982). Apples are clearly fruit because of the many fruit-like features they possess; figs, on the other hand, share few of these characteristically fruit-like features. The characterization of figs as atypical fruits would not apply in the eyes of a fig-grower intimately knowledgeable about figs. These features of the process of natural categorization are also listed in Table 11-1.

What questions are raised by this characterization of within-category variability and a similarity-matching process? First, in order to carry out the similarity-matching process, there must be a representation of the category's characteristic meaning—a standard of comparison that represents what the category is. Second, given the variability of likely instances, this category representation must be well suited to highlight, rather than to hide, the continuum of goodness of fit of category instances. Third, the category representation and matching rule must incorporate a shifting criterion of fit dependent upon the expertise and goals of the categorizer and the context of categorization. These questions are presented in Table 11-1 and will be considered in more depth in a subsequent section.

Overlap between Neighboring Categories

Natural taxonomies are characterized by a variety of categories at different levels of abstraction (e.g., food, produce, apples, Granny Smiths) and of different degrees of closeness in meaning (e.g., apples–pears vs. apples–figs). Moreover, the fuzziness of structure characteristic of natural categories applies to natural taxonomies as well. Natural taxonomies are characterized by a property known as imperfect feature nesting; that is, the features descriptive of an abstract category such as fruit are not always all characteristic of a subset category such as tomato (Rosch, Mervis, Gray, Johnson, & Boyes-Braem, 1976). Also, categories at one level of abstraction in a taxonomy (e.g., apples and pears) often overlap considerably in terms of their descriptive features; the boundaries between natural categories are ill-defined (Smith & Medin, 1981). Together these structural properties of natural taxonomies, listed in the bottom left panel of Table 11-1, sometimes make it difficult to tell "what a target instance is not."

Categorization, therefore, necessarily involves two processes: similarity matching to decide what an instance is, and differentiation to decide what an instance is not. The former is made difficult by the variability within natural categories, the latter is made cumbersome by the overlap between neighboring categories within a taxonomy. In order to be sure that a target instance is an apple, it would be nice to assure oneself that it is not a pear. However, because neighboring categories such as apples and pears overlap considerably in characteristic features, this differentiation process may not be routine; in fact, the fruit buyer may actually find an apple–pear. The categorizer may need to choose more distinct categories (e.g., apple vs. banana) to differentiate satisfactorily. Choosing a contrast set is a tricky process because neighboring categories overlap in meaning to different degrees. The differentiation process is presented in Table 11-1 as the necessary consequence of fuzzy taxonomic structure.

What questions are raised by the imperfect structure of natural taxonomies and the necessity in categorization to differentiate as well as to similarity match? First, as illustrated above, the choice of a contrast set is crucially important in the categorization process—there should be a procedure to guide in the establishment of an appropriate contrast set. Second, to be effective for differentiation, the contrast set must include relatively distinct, nonoverlapping categories. However, that distinct contrast set may not help when an instance truly falls between overlapping categories. So, the categorizer must be continually open to revision, perhaps changing to a set of overlapping categories in order to describe "borderline," atypical cases. These questions, presented in Table 11-1, will be considered in more depth in the following section.

The foregoing discussion has raised two classes of questions that follow from the fuzzy structure and flexible procedures of natural categorization. In the next section, we will consider these two classes of concerns. First, we will consider issues of choice of representation that grow out of the desire to characterize what something is. Then we will look at issues of choice of contrast sets that emerge from the process of deciding what something is not. In each case, the literature on natural categorization will form the basis for discussion, while data from our studies of psychiatric diagnosis will provide the springboard for applications to that domain. Ultimately, since people simultaneously decide what an instance is and is not, the unified categorization process will be considered in the context of diagnostic goals and purposes.

Representational Models

Prototype Approach

There are several approaches to natural categorization that have been developed in response to these problematic concerns. One successful approach has been the prototype model (Rosch, 1978; Rosch & Mervis, 1975). This approach is based on a similarity-matching procedure whereby category membership is determined by the degree of similarity between a particular instance and a standard of comparison, the prototype. According to L. M. Horowitz et al. (1981), "a prototype is a kind of theoretical ideal, a theoretical standard against which real people can be evaluated. The more closely the person approximates this idea, the more the person typifies the concept" (p. 568).

Consider the prototype for "bird." It is a summary or abstract representation of what we generally know about birds, that is, birds are swift, graceful, warm-blooded, lay eggs, have feathers, wings, beaks, can fly, sing, molt, build nests, have keen sight, keen hearing, little sense of smell, and can be domesticated and kept as pets. The reader will note that some of these bird-like features are more characteristic of birds (e.g., fly) than are others in the list (e.g., kept as pets). According to the prototype approach, a particular bird need not possess the entire set of possible bird features to be included within the category. Moreover, no single feature is necessary or sufficient to determine category membership. For example, typical birds such as robins, bluejays, canaries, and sparrows share a high degree of similarity or featural overlap, and these typical birds possess many of the most characteristic bird-like features. As typical instances of the target representation "bird," these birds can be readily identified as members of the category. In contrast, consider birds such as the ostrich, penguin, and chicken. These are said to be atypical instances in that they share fewer features with the members of that category and possess fewer of the most characteristic bird-like features (e.g., these birds do not fly). It should be emphasized, however, that not even the most typical bird is likely to possess the total number of possible features characteristic of the prototype.

To illustrate further, let us now apply the prototype approach to the DSM-III diagnostic category of Major Depressive Disorder. The manual lists dysphoria and the following features as being commonly associated with the illness:

1. Poor appetite or significant weight loss;
2. Insomnia or hypersomnia;
3. Psychomotor agitation or retardation;
4. Loss of interest or pleasure in usual activities, or decrease in sexual drive not limited to a period when delusional or hallucinating;
5. Loss of energy; fatigue;
6. Feelings of worthlessness, self-reproach, or excessive or inappropriate guilt;
7. Complaints or evidence of diminished ability to think or concentrate, such as slowed thinking, or indecisiveness not associated with marked loosening of associations or incoherence;
8. Recurrent thoughts of death, suicidal ideation, wishes to be dead, or suicide attempt.

As a whole, these features constitute a summary prototype of this diagnostic category. These features are not criterial (necessary and sufficient), but rather represent a continuum from the most to least characteristic depressive-like feature. DSM-III represents a departure from the classical "necessary and sufficient" features approach to categorization. For example, the manual indicates that a diagnosis for depression can be made if dysphoric mood and any four of the eight symptoms are present. In evaluating a patient, the more similar the patient's symptoms are to the set of features that describe the category, the more reliable and confident the diagnosis will be (McCloskey & Glucksberg, 1978). It is also clear, however, that in reality, patients can be quite heterogeneous when it comes to clinical features. Depressives, for example, can differ in symptomatology (e.g., psychomotor retardation vs. agitation; insomnia vs. hypersomnia), and more broadly, differences would be observed in age, sex, education, family income, and social histories. The prototype model allows for deviations from the theoretical ideal by acknowledging that some cases will be less similar to the standard of comparison than others. It is this correlational structure that warns the clinician of variability within diagnostic categories, that is, that no two depressives will be identical and that some depressives will be more similar to the prototype for depression than others. This approach is based on a continuum of goodness of fit, or that there are many ways to be a good example of a category, and that atypical cases are an integral and meaningful part of natural categories. The most significant contribution that the prototype approach can make to the process of psychiatric diagnosis is to provide a representation that highlights this within-category variability, encouraging more flexibility in determining diagnostic categorization.

Exemplar Approach

Another representational model which acknowledges that there are many ways to be a good example of a category is the exemplar or the multiple-examples approach to categorization (Smith & Medin, 1981). Although the prototype model is a significant improvement over the classical "necessary and sufficient" features approach, the possibility of the excessive use of a summary prototype to exaggerate goodness of fit still exists; that is, the categorizer may be tempted to view the atypical case as more typical of the category once the decision for inclusion is made. The exemplar model, however, proposes an explicitly disjunctive view of categories. An exemplar-based prototype stresses the use of multiple concrete examples in determining category membership. Smith and Medin (1981) suggest the two following assumptions for this model: (a) that all exemplars in the concept representation are retrieved and available for comparison, and (b) that an instance is judged to be a concept member only if it provides a sufficient match to at least one exemplar (p. 148). Note that "all exemplars" to be retrieved and available for comparison are the good exemplars stored in memory that represent the category. In considering our previous example, the category bird need not be represented by one summary representation or prototype. Instead, the categorizer would retrieve good examples of birds (e.g., robins, sparrows, bluejays, and canaries). Therefore, the inclusion of an instance in the bird category would be accomplished by matching the instance in question to all other known examples of the category. As long as the instance matches at least one of the examples retrieved, it can be regarded as a member of the category (Brooks, 1978; Holyoak & Glass, 1975; Kossan, 1978; Medin & Schaffer, 1978; Walker, 1975).

In applying the exemplar-based approach to the diagnostic evaluation of a depressed individual, the clinician would retrieve all stored examples of typical depressives. Comparing the similarity between the individual and multiple examples of depressives, the clinician would determine that Mr. X is a depressive because he is just like Mr. Y, Mrs. A, and Ms. C, who are examples of depressives. By using separate "disjunctive" exemplars to determine category inclusion, the clinician becomes acutely aware of those cases that do not match the stored exemplars. This is a direct consequence of the exemplar-matching process itself; that is, as one repeats the matching process from instance to exemplar over and over again, any dissimilarities between an atypical case and retrieved typical exemplars will be magnified. In this way, the exemplar model highlights within-category variability.

Similarity Matching to Summary and Exemplar Prototypes: "What Is It?"

The summary and exemplar prototype models both use a similarity-matching procedure for categorization. The basic prediction, in this regard, is straightforward: The more typical an instance is of a category, the more reliably and confidently will it be categorized as such (McCloskey & Glucksberg, 1978); that is, the greater the featural overlap between X and its prototype, or between X and the retrieved Y exemplars, the greater the reliability and confidence in determining category membership—in deciding what X is. We refer to this effect as the typicality effect in natural categorization. In order to confirm the utility of these models in the psychiatric domain, we need to show the basic typicality effect in diagnosis.

Diagnosis: The Typicality Effect

Cantor *et al.* (1980) examined psychiatric diagnosis as a function of prototype categorization. First, 13 experienced clinicians listed features characteristic of nine diagnostic categories from DSM-II (APA, 1968) (Functional Psychosis, Schizophrenia, Affective Disorder, Paranoid Schizophrenia, Schizoaffective, Chronic Undifferentiated, Manic–Depressive—Manic, Involutional Melancholia, and Manic–Depressive—Depressed). For each category, a consensual prototype, comprising the features listed by three or more clinicians, was generated. These prototypes provided standards of comparison to judge the typicality of real patients and to test the typicality prediction for diagnostic judgments.

In order to ascertain the role of typicality in the diagnostic categorization process, Cantor *et al.* (1980) asked another group of nine experienced clinicians to diagnose 12 patients. The clinicians made diagnoses on the bases of unedited case histories from the files of the Palo Alto Veterans Administration Hospital Psychiatric Unit. Of the 12 patients, 3 had been diagnosed in the hospital as belonging to each of four categories: manic–depressive— manic (MDM), manic–depressive—depressed (MDD), paranoid schizophrenic (PS), and chronic undifferentiated schizophrenic (CUS). For each category, there were three cases at different levels of typicality. The typical patient had a case history containing from 8 to 13 features in the consensual prototype for that category, the medium typical patient presented from 5 to 8 features in the prototype, and the low typical patient's case history included 4 prototype features. The nine clinicians read each case history and assigned a diagnostic label (from the four target categories) and a confidence rating representing the degree to which the patient fit that category label (from 1 to 7).

The main prediction of the prototype model for these data concerned the comparison between typical and atypical patients; that is, it was expected that the accuracy (match to hospital diagnosis) and reliability of clinical diagnoses would increase with typicality. This prediction was substantially confirmed. The distinction between typical (high and medium) versus atypical (low) patients was quite clear for all four categories on accuracy and on confidence. For example, averaged over the four categories, the mean number of correct diagnoses per category (out of 9) of atypical patients was 4.75 and that for high and medium typical patients was 8.00. A similar comparison of mean confidence ratings (1–7) for correct diagnoses resulted in mean confidence of 3.32 for atypical patients and 4.52 for high and medium typical patients. Analysis of variance performed on a combined accuracy–confidence score clearly revealed the predicted typicality effect ($p < .001$).[1] These results were particularly impressive because the diagnoses were based on unedited case histories, and the experimenters' assignment of patients to levels of typicality was based on overlap with consensual prototypes generated by the earlier set of clinicians. Despite this, the typicality predictions held for this new set of clinical diagnoses.

These data suggest that psychiatric categorization mirrors natural categorization in many respects. In diagnostic categories, there appears to be a continuum of goodness to fit, a number of ways to be a good example of the

---

1. A significant category $\times$ typicality effect ($p < .005$) did not modify the basic typical versus atypical distinction in accuracy–confidence, though high typical patients were not always diagnosed more accurately-confidently than medium typical patients.

category, and atypical cases exist. The typicality effect on diagnostic categorization is consistent with the similarity-matching process proposed by the summary and exemplar prototype models.

The next issue of interest is how to facilitate the similarity-matching process without exaggerating goodness of fit between instances and the category representation. It seems quite possible that one of these two models functions better in serving that aim. It is possible that the exemplar model may better serve to highlight within-category variability as it is based on multiple-disjunctive exemplars.

Diagnosis: Summary versus Exemplar Prototypes

Genero and Cantor (in press) performed two studies in order to compare the utility of the summary and exemplar prototypes in alerting clinicians to the variability in typicality. A teaching paradigm was used in which clinicians were presented with summary or exemplar prototypes describing four psychiatric diagnostic categories. In each study, the clinicians were asked to diagnose typical and atypical patients from these four categories, to rate the degree of fit of each patient in the diagnostic category, and to provide a rating of satisfaction with each diagnosis. In the first study, novice clinicians were taught about the four categories with either summary or exemplar prototypes. The second study primed the already formed knowledge of expert clinicians by presenting summary or exemplar prototypes. We predicted an advantage of the exemplar-based over the summary-based representational model in alerting clinicians to the distinction between typical and atypical patients. This prediction was based upon the idea that exemplar priming might be particularly effective in inducing retrieval of a variety of already stored category exemplars to use in the diagnoses. The greater number of exemplar comparisons, the more likely the clinicians would recognize variations in typicality.

The basic typicality prediction was confirmed in both the novice and expert samples. Analyses of variance on a measure of agreement with hospital diagnosis revealed that agreement was greater for typical than atypical patients in all four categories across both models for the experts ($p < .001$), and in all four categories for novices using the summary prototype model, and in three out of four categories for novices using the exemplar prototype model ($p < .001$).[2] Again, the typicality effect in the agreement analyses may be traced to increasing accuracy for typical versus atypical cases.

These results replicate the Cantor et al. (1980) findings and underscore the utility of a similarity-matching perspective on psychiatric diagnosis. However, our primary concern was to test the differential utility of these

---

2. In both analyses there were significant category × typicality effects because the typicality distinction was stronger for some categories than others.

two representational models. In that regard, analyses of the clinicians' ratings of confidence with the diagnoses (defined as a joint measure of degree of diagnostic fit between the patient and the chosen category and degree of satisfaction with the information provided) revealed support for the differential utility of the exemplar prototype model for experts. A significant typicality × model interaction in a MANOVA on the satisfaction–fit measures indicated that the discrepancy in confidence for typical versus atypical cases was especially strong in the exemplar (vs. summary) condition for experts. Experts distinguished more in their satisfaction and fit ratings between typical and atypical cases after being provided with illustrative exemplars rather than summary prototypes. Highlighting discrepancies in confidence for typical and atypical cases is important precisely because clinicians were more reliable in their diagnostic judgments of typical cases.

It is tempting to speculate that for experts who have many stored exemplars to use in the matching process, the discrepancy in satisfaction between typical and atypical cases may be heightened by the process of repeated multiple comparisons. This speculation assumes that the presentation of our exemplar descriptions simply primed the experts to retrieve their own exemplars and to repeatedly match each presented case against the exemplars from the most likely category. In the summary prototype condition, the experts may have settled for single case–prototype comparisons. That comparison process may not have provided the basis for as much variation in feelings of satisfaction as did the multiple-exemplar comparisons. Of course, these remain as speculations, since we do not know the details of the matching process actually used in the summary and exemplar prototype conditions. It should be noted, however, that for experts a manual is really similar to a priming tool. Consequently, exemplar representations in a manual might serve expert clinicians particularly well, encouraging them to reflect upon the typicality distinction.

The data from the novice sample are interesting in two respects: First, the replication of the basic typicality effect across both model conditions is encouraging support for the appropriateness of conceiving of diagnosis as a similarity-matching process. However, unlike the expert sample, novices distinguished between typical and atypical cases in their confidence ratings more clearly in the summary prototype than in the exemplar condition. This apparent advantage of learning from summary prototypes (vs. exemplars) of the typicality distinction is intriguing. It may well be that when first understanding diagnostic categories, summary prototypes best allow the novice to grasp the fuzzy structure of diagnostic categories. The summary representation in coordination with instructions about fuzzy categories may serve novices particularly well, better than would explicitly disjunctive exemplars. Since the novices do not have their own extensive store of exemplars upon which to draw (Mervis, 1984), the disjunctive exemplar model may not function as well for them as would the summary prototype representation.

The foregoing section has been concerned with the process of similarity matching—deciding what something is—in the context of fuzzy natural and diagnostic categories. Although we have not been able to support decisively one representational model over another, the diagnostic data do support the generality of a similarity-matching model and suggest conditions under which one representational model might better serve the clinician over another model. Regardless of the choice of representational model, the clinician needs to remain cognizant of the variability inherent within psychiatric categories. The similarity-matching procedure can assist the clinician to detect the many ways in which different patients can be good and bad exemplars of a diagnostic category. There are two distinct advantages to recognizing variability within psychiatric categories: The awareness of variability prevents the clinician from excessively applying ideal categories and narrow labels with which to characterize cases, and also provides the clinician with substantially more flexibility in setting a criterion of match when dealing with fuzzy categories. We will return to a discussion of these advantages after considering the complementary process to similarity matching, that is, differentiation or evaluating what a target instance is not.

Differentiation: "What Isn't It?"

We indicated previously that similarity matching and differentiation are two procedures involved in determining category membership. The former tells us what an instance is by assessing the featural similarities between X and the target category Y, whereas the latter tells us what an instance is not by indicating the ways in which X is distinct from other neighboring categories. Both the summary and exemplar representational models presented earlier include procedures to capture the featural similarities between a target instance X and its category Y. They also include procedures to determine the absence of such similarity between X and other neighboring categories A, B, C, and so on. In the prototype model, the typicality of an instance increases as a function of both overlap with the target category prototype and dissimilarity from prototypes of neighboring categories (Cantor & Mischel, 1979; Rosch & Mervis, 1975). An apple is a "good" fruit because it shares many fruit-like features and does not possess many vegetable-like features. Quite simply, the apple seems more fruit-like to the extent that it is not very much like a vegetable. Similarly, the exemplar approach assumes that "X can be categorized as an instance or subset of Y if and only if X retrieves a criterial number of Y's exemplars before retrieving a criterial number of exemplars from another contrasting concept" (Smith & Medin, 1981, p. 147). In that case, a typical fruit like an apple will retrieve many fruit exemplars before retrieving many vegetable exemplars.

Since differentiation plays an important role in natural categorization, the choice of a contrast set is a crucial facet of categorization. Earlier in this discussion, we illustrated the ways in which the fuzziness within natural categories complicates the similarity-matching process. Similarly, the fuzzy structure of natural taxonomies makes differentiation cumbersome and the categorizer should be well advised of the procedural issues involved in selecting an appropriate contrast set (see Table 11-1).

The fuzzy structure of natural taxonomies within the psychiatric domain may be quickly illustrated by reference to the Cantor *et al.* (1980) data. Working with a taxonomy of Functional Psychosis drawn from DSM-III, we observed both imperfect feature nesting and overlap between neighboring categories in the clinicians' prototypes. Categories varied considerably in the degree to which their prototype features appeared in the prototypes of their subset categories: Of the 17 prototype features for Schizophrenia, 11 were nested in the prototypes of all 3 subcategories of Schizophrenia. Only 1 of the 16 prototype features of Affective Disorders appeared in the prototypes for all 3 subtype disorders, while 6 of the Affective Disorder features did not appear in any 1 of the 3 subtype prototypes.

Similarly, and more strikingly, the prototypes for neighboring categories in the DSM-II taxonomy overlapped in features to a considerable degree and in unexpected ways. For example, the prototypes for manic–depressive—manic (MDM) and manic–depressive—depressed (MDD) were relatively distinct (only two overlapping features), while the prototypes for manic–depressive—manic and paranoid schizophrenia were unexpectedly similar (six overlapping features); the prototypes for paranoid schizophrenia and chronic undifferentiated schizophrenia were even closer in meaning (eight overlapping features). This fuzziness in taxonomic structure is actually the rule rather than the exception in natural category taxonomies (Cantor, Mischel, & Schwartz, 1982; Rosch *et al.*, 1976). Consequently, it is essential to be quite careful in selecting contrast sets.

Choice of Contrast Sets

The aim of the differentiation process is to help characterize what an instance is not; for that purpose a contrast set should highlight between-category distinctions (e.g., MDM vs. MDD). However, the categorizer needs to be aware of the considerable and often unexpected overlap between categories in different branches of natural taxonomies (e.g., PS and MDM). The contrast set should not be used inflexibly to highlight category distinctiveness at the expense of missing the points of real overlap. Maintaining a sense of the overlap between categories may be very useful in describing borderline, atypical instances. The choice of a contrast set, therefore, is by no means a clear-cut issue in fuzzy taxonomies; the categorizer may need to shift contrast sets repeatedly to capture both useful distinctiveness and real overlap between categories.

The choice of a contrast set, then, should be swayed by two concerns that may conflict: In order to facilitate the differentiation process, the contrast set should include relatively distinct neighboring categories. However, in order to facilitate categorization of borderline, atypical cases, the contrast set must make use of the intercategory overlap. For purposes of exposition, it may be useful to consider these two concerns separately, as if the categorizer first operates to facilitate the differentiation process and then to handle borderline cases.

Distinct Contrast Sets

In order to facilitate the differentiation of an instance from neighboring categories, the contrast set should contain categories with distinctive summary prototypes or collections of exemplars. Frequently, in order to choose a contrast set with reasonably distinct categories, it may be necessary to pay close attention to the level of abstraction of the categories (Cantor & Mischel, 1979). Rosch and her colleagues (1976) have suggested that there may be a "basic" level of taxonomic abstraction. The basic level of abstraction jointly maximizes richness of description and distinctiveness between neighboring category prototypes. This basic level typically represents a medium degree of abstraction; very abstract categories tend not to have rich prototypes (e.g., furniture), while very specific categories tend to have prototypes that are quite rich but not very distinctive from neighboring categories (e.g., rocking chair and kitchen chair). In many natural taxonomies, the middle level may allow for contrast sets with rich and yet distinctive prototypes (e.g., chairs vs. tables). Cantor *et al.* (1980) hinted at a similar phenomenon in the DSM-II taxonomy. The very specific diagnostic categories were quite overlapping in prototypes (e.g., PS, CUS), while the slightly more global comparison of Schizophrenia and Affective Disorders provided for a more distinctive comparison.

However, the choice of contrast set cannot proceed with an inflexible rule about level of abstraction; such a rigid rule would never work with fuzzy natural taxonomies. For example, Blashfield and Sprock (1983) correctly point out that the Schizophrenia/Affective Disorder comparison actually does not maximize richness–distinctiveness; rather, a mixed contrast set of Schizophrenia, MDD, MDM would be more optimal by these criteria. The PS/CUS categories overlap considerably, and many features of Schizophrenia are nested in PS, CUS; thus, Schizophrenia serves as a good representation of their most critical features. By contrast, MDD and MDM are relatively distinct categories and much meaning is lost by moving to the level of abstraction represented by the Affective Disorder category.

Plausible Alternative Categories

Atypical cases frequently reflect the overlap in characteristic features between neighboring categories. Consequently, a contrast set that maximizes intercategory distinctiveness will not be of much help in characterizing atypical cases. In order to acknowledge faithfully the borderline quality of an atypical case, the diagnostician will need to turn to a contrast set containing plausible alternative categories that overlap in meaning. Suppose, for example, that a patient's features provided a borderline match to those of MDM and were quite distinct from MDD, but only somewhat distinct from the Schizophrenia prototype. The clinician could use these differences as conclusive evidence of the appropriateness of the MDM label, but that would really be an exaggeration of fit. Instead, the clinician might rework the contrast set to include some plausible alternative categories with prototypes that overlap with the MDM prototype. In this case, the present data suggest that {PS} might form a plausible alternative category to MDM. The previous distinct contrast set of {S, MDD} can only serve to hint at the direction of the atypical overlap—toward the schizophrenia categories—and now the new contrast set can better specify the *exact* nature of the atypicality of the patient.

Actually, our diagnostic data are suggestive of a preference for close alternative categories in choice of diagnosis for atypical patients. When our novice and expert clinicians misdiagnosed atypical patients, they tended to choose the category whose prototype provided the next best match to the features in the atypical case history. Of the expert misdiagnoses of atypical patients, 74% went to the category with the prototype providing the second best match to the case history, while 59% of the novice misdiagnoses followed this pattern. Another way of looking at the misdiagnoses of atypical patients is as follows: Since the PS and CUS categories overlap considerably, we would expect that misdiagnoses of an atypical Schizophrenic patient would remain within the "S" branch. By contrast, since the MDD and MDM categories are quite distinct, misdiagnoses of atypical patients from one of these Affective Disorder categories may switch to PS or CUS, categories which actually overlap more with MDM or MDD. The data supported that prediction. Of misdiagnoses by novices of schizophrenic atypicals, 68% remained within that branch as compared to 20% of affective disorder misdiagnoses. The percentages for experts were almost identical to those for novices (62% vs. 14%). In other words, when these clinicians had trouble diagnosing atypical patients, they turned to a plausible alternative category among the four alternatives provided in the study.

In Genero and Cantor (in press), clinicians were restricted from using a mixed diagnostic level, even for atypical patients. Certainly, in most settings the way in which a final diagnosis reflects the atypicality of a patient would depend on the diagnostic goals and purposes. For example, the overlap in mood and thought disorder features in an atypical MDM case could be captured for insurance purposes by a Schizoaffective diagnosis. For purposes of communication among colleagues, a mixed MDM–PS diagnosis might better capture the exact slice of overlap in mood–thought disorder. There are times when a diagnostic label need not convey all of the specifics of the atypicality of a case and other times when communication about atypicality will be enhanced by a more specific mixed diagnosis.

In sum, contrast sets are constructed to help the clinician see what a patient is not; in this regard, the distinctions between categories are emphasized. However, the process of differentiation should not be used to force a fit between an atypical patient and a target category. Differentiating between an instance and neighboring distinctive categories may sometimes need to evolve into similarity matching between the instance and a number of overlapping categories. The switch from a distinct contrast set to plausible alternative categories may help a clinician arrive at a mixed diagnosis that best captures the borderline quality of many cases. It is helpful to begin with distinct sets, for even with atypical cases the differentiation process may narrow the number of plausible alternatives. However, the process must then evolve to reflect better the atypicality of the target instance.

Similarity Matching and Differentiation

Until this point, we have discussed similarity matching and differentiation as if these are two quite separate procedures in natural categorization. In reality, the individual simultaneously works toward a characterization of what the target instance *is* and what it *is not*. Similarity matching and differentiation function in tandem to help the individual select a category that best fits the target instance, given the set of likely categories. Since there are no explicit criteria of fit/not fit in natural categorization, the assessment of a good similarity match and a good contrast set will always be a relative judgment, quite tied to the context of observation and the individual's goals and purposes.

In an effort to illustrate how these two processes function together within a domain like diagnostic categorization, we propose the following step-by-step simulation of a diagnostic assessment. Our intention is to show the ways in which the similarity matching and differentiation procedures can be used in consort with summary and exemplar representations and distinct contrast sets and plausible alternative categories. Summary prototypes provide quick and easy guides to overlap between categories and, thus, should be of help in the construction of contrast sets. Exemplars help to underscore the variability within categories and, hence, serve the similarity-matching process quite well. The integration of these models should prevent the exaggeration of within-category fit and between-category divisions. It is our hope that the judicious mixing of these varied representations and contrast sets can enable the diagnostician to identify clear matches and yet communicate about atypical cases as well.

Simulation of Diagnostic Assessment

Step 1. The clinician typically enters the diagnostic process with a hunch about the most likely target category (or categories) based on past experience with the relevant patient population. This hunch can be seen as derived from a quick similarity match of the patient's case to a diagnostic prototype (e.g., similar to MDM) and, perhaps, from an informal differentiation from prototypes of neighboring categories (e.g., different from MDD). On the basis of the initial matches and differences, the clinician can construct a distinct contrast set so as to attempt to minimize prototype overlap between the likely target category (MDM) and the neighboring categories {MDD, S}.

Step 2. Having used the diagnostic prototypes to facilitate a quick match (MDM) and having constructed the first contrast set {S, MDD}, the clinician would turn to similarity matching between the target case and the exemplars for each category in the contrast set. The repeated exemplar-matching process will be useful in highlighting any atypicality as well as underscoring a clear fit. At this point, a clearly "good" case will be seen via good exemplar matches and distinct exemplar contrasts. Of course, the criteria for good matches and good contrasts are inherently unstable (tied to goals, context, expertise). Unlike the DSM-III approach which specifies a threshold number of features for a similarity match, the prototype exemplar models leave that threshold purposely vague, to be specified in the context of each categorization.

Step 3. Suppose instead that upon closer examination, the case only partially fits into the initial target category (MDM), is quite distinct from one category (MDD), but isn't terribly distinct from the other contrast category (S). This should signal some atypicality and initiate the construction of a new contrast set—the set of plausible alternative categories. In order to derive the new contrast set, the clinician will look for categories with prototypes that overlap with the initial target category (MDM). Actually, the prior differentiation process will help in this process as well. For example, the moderate match to both MDM and S in this case may signal some schizoaffective overlap and prompt the clinician to check the fit to specific S categories (CUS, PS). A match to the exemplars of the new contrast categories may suffice to isolate a better fit for the atypical case (e.g., PS).

Step 4. The isolation of a reasonable match may not occur if the case is truly borderline or atypical. In that instance, the clinician would try to find a mixed diagnosis that preserves information about the nature of the atypicality (i.e., which categories together provide a good description). This mixed diagnosis can be represented at different levels of abstraction (e.g., Schizoaffective or MDM/PS), depending upon the goals of the clinician. The more concrete representation may be especially useful in communicating with colleagues about the details of a case. However, a more abstract description of the atypicality in the case (e.g., Schizoaffective) may be perfectly suitable for third-party payment purposes.

Summary Comments

The primary thesis of this chapter is that psychiatric diagnosis can be viewed as an instance of natural categorization; as such, the diagnostic enterprise is subject to the procedural difficulties associated with the fuzzy structure of natural categories (see Table 11-1). In order to be an effective teaching device, a diagnostic manual should ideally give as much attention to the structure of diagnostic categories and the process of operating with fuzzy categories as it gives to the descriptive content of those categories. Without these procedural guidelines, clinicians will be likely to consider variability among the cases they encounter as "error" and run the risk of exaggerating the fit of a case to a category for the sake of "precision." By contrast, a manual that explicitly emphasizes material on structure and process is more likely to convey the message that variability in case-category fit may be more the rule than the exception. The task of a diagnostic manual should be to teach clinicians to be self-consciously flexible in operating with fuzzy categories and taxonomies; rigid standards of match and finer category descriptions will not rid the domain either of atypical, bothersome cases or the imprecision of overlapping categories.

Our preliminary review has emphasized the following points of interest that may deserve attention in the manual:

• Category membership is really a matter of degree. Each category properly contains a set of members arrayed along a continuum of fit; there are many ways to be a good example of a category and just as many ways to barely belong in a category.

• Category representations can be achieved in many ways; summary and exemplar prototypes are each useful representations.

• Exaggeration of goodness of fit of an instance to a target category is a frequent problem in the similarity-matching process. Matching to exemplar-based representations, which are explicitly disjunctive in distinguishing instances, can help to minimize this problem.

• Categorization properly involves both similarity-matching and differentiation processes.

• Contrast sets can also be based upon different principles; distinct and plausible alternative sets are two useful examples.

• Exaggeration of divisions between categories is a frequent problem in the differentiation process. Use of both distinct contrast sets and then plausible alternative categories can help to minimize this problem.

• Criteria for match and differentiation must be flexibly responsive to the particular diagnostic goals and the context of diagnosis.

These points may be incorporated into the revised manual quite simply by building upon, highlighting, and expanding features that are already a part of DSM-III. The present category descriptions are already in the form of prototypes, though the exact criteria of number of features required for similarity matches should be replaced by flexible, shifting criteria. Similarly, exemplar descriptions are occasionally included in the manual. Again, this material could be expanded to provide exemplar representations within each category description. Certainly, novice clinicians stand to gain much from exposure to exemplars and exemplar matching as a tool to increase recognition of within-category variability. The suggestion of inclusion of exemplar representations in a manual raises many questions: How many exemplars per category? Should atypical as well as typical exemplars be included? What procedures should be used for generating representative exemplar descriptions? These promise to be thorny issues, causing much debate if exemplar-based representations are considered.

DSM-III could also be revised in a manner that gives more weight to differentiation in the diagnostic process. At present, Axis II in the multiaxial system and the decision trees provide plausible alternative categories if and when an initial tentative diagnosis fails to provide a good fit to the case. Building upon these aspects of DSM-III, a revised manual could stress the differentiation process more by suggesting the use of contrast sets for *all* diagnoses. For example, a list that states degree of prototype overlap between all pairs of diagnostic categories would facilitate the construction of distinct and plausible alternative contrast sets. Such a list may alert clinicians to the areas of unexpected overlap that frequently occur in natural taxonomies. In this way, the manual could explicitly encourage the construction of new contrast sets as initial diagnostic hunches become progressively defined or revised.

We believe that revisions in the diagnostic manual should explicitly recognize the variability within diagnostic categories and the overlap between categories by emphasizing the utilization of similarity-matching and differentiation procedures. However, even with these additions, the central unresolved problem would remain—the patient population will never fit clearly into well-defined diagnostic categories. The similarity between psychiatric diagnosis and fuzzy models of natural categorization appears to be real; the contrast to classical models of categorization is impressive. Therefore, the answer is not to ignore the real variability in cases or treat poor case-category fits as error to be steadily reduced by procedural and descriptive improvements in the manual. Rather, attempts to recognize the link between diagnosis and natural categorization and to provide methods for working *with* fuzzy categories should constitute the major thrust of future developments in psychiatric diagnostic manuals.

ACKNOWLEDGMENTS

We are indebted to Sara Freeland for her help in preparation of this chapter, to Howard Wolowitz for his invaluable conceptual and practical assistance in the running of our studies, and Howard Wolowitz, Paula Nurius, Camille Wortman, and Joseph Veroff for their comments on earlier drafts. This research was supported by grant BNS-8022253 from the National Science Foundation.

REFERENCES

American Psychiatric Association (APA). (1968). *Diagnostic and statistical manual of mental disorders* (2nd ed.). Washington, DC: Author.

American Psychiatric Association (APA). (1980). *Diagnostic and statistical manual of mental disorders* (3rd ed.). Washington, DC: Author.

Blashfield, R., & Sprock, J. (1983). *A replication study on the use of prototypes for understanding psychiatric classification.* Unpublished manuscript, University of Florida, Gainesville.

Bransford, J. D., & Franks, J. J. (1971). The abstraction of linguistic ideas. *Cognitive Psychology, 2,* 331–350.

Brooks, L. (1978). Nonanalytic concept formation and memory for instances. In E. Rosch & B. B. Lloyd (Eds.), *Cognition and categorization.* Hillsdale, NJ: Erlbaum.

Bruner, J. S., Goodnow, J., & Austin, G. (1956). *A study of thinking.* New York: Wiley.

Cantor, N., & Mischel, W. (1977). Traits as prototypes: Effects on recognition memory. *Journal of Personality and Social Psychology, 35,* 38–48.

Cantor, N., & Mischel, W. (1979). Prototypes in person perception. In L. Berkowitz (Ed.), *Advances in experimental social psychology* (Vol. 12). New York: Academic Press.

Cantor, N., Mischel, W., & Schwartz, J. (1982). A prototype analysis of psychological situations. *Cognitive Psychology, 14,* 45–77.

Cantor, N., Smith, E., French, R. de S., & Mezzich, J. (1980). Psychiatric diagnosis as prototype categorization. *Journal of Abnormal Psychology, 89,* 181–193.

Clark, H. H., & Clark, E. V. (1977). *Psychology and language.* New York: Harcourt Brace Jovanovich.

Clarkin, J. F., Widiger, T. A., Frances, A., Hurt, S. W., & Gilmore, M. (1983). Prototypic typology and the borderline personality. *Journal of Abnormal Psychology, 90,* 575–585.

Cohen, C. E. (1981). Person categories and social perception: Testing some boundaries of the processing effects of prior knowledge. *Journal of Personality and Social Psychology, 40,* 441–452.

Duncan, B. L. (1976). Differential social perception and attribution of intergroup violence: Testing the lower limits of stereotyping blacks. *Journal of Personality and Social Psychology, 34,* 590–598.

Genero, N., & Cantor, N. E. (in press). Exemplar prototypes and clinical diagnosis: Towards a cognitive economy. *Journal of Social and Clinical Psychology.*

Genero, N., Greden, J., & Markus, H. (1985). *Cognitive differences between unipolar and bipolar depression.* Unpublished manuscript, Clinical Studies Unit, University of Michigan, Ann Arbor.

Hamilton, D. L. (1979). A cognitive-attributional analysis of stereotyping. In L. Berkowitz (Ed.), *Advances in experimental social psychology* (Vol. 12). New York: Academic Press.

Higgins, E. T., Rholes, C. R., & Jones, C. R. (1977). Category assessibility and impression formation. *Journal of Experimental Social Psychology, 13,* 141–154.

Holyoak, K. J., & Glass, A. L. (1975). The role of contradictions and counterexamples in the rejection of fake sentences. *Journal of Verbal Learning and Verbal Behavior, 14,* 215–239.

Horowitz, L., Post, D., French, R., Wallis, K., & Siegelman, E. (1981). The prototype as a construct in abnormal psychology: A clarifying disagreement in psychiatric judgments. *Journal of Abnormal Psychology, 90,* 575–585.

Horowitz, L. M., Wright, J. C., Lowenstein, E., & Parad, H. W. (1981). The prototype as a construct in abnormal psychology. I. A method for deriving prototypes. *Journal of Abnormal Psychology, 90*, 568–574.

Kahneman, D., & Tversky, A. (1973). On the psychology of prediction. *Psychological Review, 80*, 237–251.

Kossan, N. E. (1978). *Structure and strategy in concept acquisition.* Doctoral dissertation, Stanford University, Stanford, CA.

Labov, W. (1973). The boundaries of words and their meanings. In C. J. Baily & R. Shuy (Eds.), *New ways of analyzing variations in English.* Washington, DC: Georgetown University Press.

Locksley, A., Ortiz, V., & Hepburn, C. (1980). Social categorization and discriminatory behavior: Extinguishing the minima intergroup discrimination effect. *Journal of Personality and Social Psychology, 39*(5), 773–783.

McCloskey, M., & Glucksberg, S. (1978). Natural categories: Well defined or fuzzy sets? *Memory and Cognition, 6*, 462–472.

Medin, D. L., & Schaffer, M. M. (1978). A context theory of classification learning. *Psychological Review, 85*, 207–238.

Mervis, C. B. (1984). *The role of cognition and language in early lexical development.* Paper presented at a symposium at Michigan State University, East Lansing.

Miller, G. A., & Johnson-Laird, P. N. (1976). *Language and perception.* Cambridge, MA: Harvard University Press.

Murphy, G. L., & Wright, J. C. (1982). *Changes in conceptual structure with expertise: Differences between real-world experts and novices.* Unpublished manuscript, Stanford University, Stanford, CA.

Posner, M. I., & Keele, S. W. (1968). On the genesis of abstract ideas. *Journal of Experimental Psychology, 77*, 353–363.

Quattrone, G. A., & Jones, E. E. (1980). The perception of variability within in-groups and out-groups: Implications for the law of small numbers. *Journal of Personality and Social Psychology, 38*(1), 141–152.

Quine, W. V. (1969). *Ontological relativity and other essays.* New York: Columbia University Press.

Rosch, E. (1978). Principles of categorization. In E. Rosch & B. B. Lloyd (Eds.), *Cognition and categorization.* Hillsdale, NJ: Erlbaum.

Rosch, E., & Mervis, C. (1975). Family resemblances: Studies in the internal structure of categories. *Cognitive Psychology, 7*, 573–605.

Rosch, E., Mervis, C., Gray, W., Johnson, D., & Boyes-Braem, P. (1976). Basic objects in natural categories. *Cognitive Psychology, 8*, 382–439.

Smith, E. E., & Medin, D. L. (1981). *Categories and concepts.* Cambridge, MA: Harvard University Press.

Smith, E. E., Shoben, E. J., & Rips, L. J. (1974). Structure and process in semantic memory: A featural model for semantic decisions. *Psychological Review, 81*, 214–241.

Tsujimoto, R. N. (1978). Memory bias toward normative and novel trait prototypes. *Journal of Personality and Social Psychology, 36*, 1391–1401.

Tversky, A. (1977). Features of similarity. *Psychological Review, 84*, 327–352.

Walker, J. H. (1975). Real-world variability, reasonableness judgments, and memory representations for concepts. *Journal of Verbal Learning and Verbal Behavior, 14*, 241–252.

Wittgenstein, L. (1953). *Philosophical investigations.* New York: Macmillan.

CHAPTER 12

Psychiatric Diagnosis: A Reconsideration Based on Longitudinal Processes

John S. Strauss

DSM-III has provided the basis for much progress in psychiatric diagnosis by emphasizing the issues of reliability and clarity for diagnostic categories. In general, as behooves a still young field, primary emphasis on diagnostic criteria has been on the most obvious manifestations of pathology, symptoms and syndrome patterns. These tend to be assessable in reliable ways, form the basis for identifying many aspects of psychopathology, and are accepted as central in many schools of thought and across many cultures.

In spite of the progress represented by DSM-III, the criticisms raised by this document suggest that beyond the problems always generated by something new, there are more fundamental concerns involved. Although DSM-III attempts to be "atheoretical," like any diagnostic system, it involves certain basic assumptions and ways of looking at its subject matter. The range of potentially important variables and vantage points for any system of classification is simply too great to allow the construction of a system without making assumptions and key choices. In selecting symptoms and syndromes as a basis for classification, DSM-III involves the assumption that these are more valid for defining diagnostic groups than, for example, underlying biological variables or psychological processes. And, to be sure, in the past, theoretical notions of processes underlying the nature of psychopathology, while interesting and important, have often involved a considerable amount of speculation based on a very limited foundation of systematically collected data.

It is still too early to provide a comprehensive scheme for establishing a diagnostic system based on clearly demonstrated underlying processes. Fur-

John S. Strauss. Department of Psychiatry, Yale University Medical School, New Haven, Connecticut.

thermore, it is increasingly apparent that the nature of psychiatric disorders, their etiology, course, and the factors that influence them are simply too complex to permit accepting a comprehensive scheme of diagnosis founded on the limited information that is currently available. Nevertheless, it is possible to begin using the principles of Kraepelin, who himself borrowed extensively from Sydenham, who borrowed from Hippocrates, who may have borrowed from still earlier physicians, to apply one concept that has had consistent importance for establishing diagnostic categories in the field of medicine. This principle is, as rephrased by one group, "diagnosis is prognosis." Stated otherwise and in slightly more detail, the course of a disorder and the factors that affect it help to identify disease processes, which in turn must form the basis for diagnostic categories and criteria.

The basic concept is relatively straightforward and important. A disease is a manifestation of some kind of pathologic process. The nature of the process may be identified and understood by attending to its course and to the variables that influence it. In essence, the principle is that when exploring and trying to understand a mysterious object, one valid approach is to see the way the object responds to a variety of situations and events. If the object changes over time, studying its evolution provides further crucial information about its nature.

Pursuing the Kraepelinian contribution to psychiatry, we have found that recent findings suggest factors that need more attention in reconsidering diagnostic concepts. In this chapter, some of these findings will be described briefly along with the implications they have for diagnostic categories and criteria. As part of this explication, there will be an attempt to include a broad range of data in order to reduce perhaps erroneous assumptions about what aspects of the course of disorder are valid and invalid and to limit preconceptions that might be based on one or another theoretical framework that could exclude crucial factors. The findings on course of disorder can be considered under the headings of prognostic factors, individual–environment interactions, and longitudinal principles.

Prognosis in Psychiatric Disorder

Recent results from studies on the course of a variety of psychiatric diagnostic categories have demonstrated the heterogeneity of their outcomes (Ciompi, 1980; Marks, 1971; Strauss & Carpenter, 1974; Weissman, Prusoff, & Klerman, 1978). Currently, therefore, diagnosis is not prognosis beyond an extremely rough level of approximation. More recent data suggest, furthermore, that prognosis is not a unidimensional phenomenon related to any single characteristic. Rather, there are several aspects of outcome in psychiatric disorder, each of which is somewhat independent of the rest. Symptom type is somewhat independent from symptom severity as these evolve over time (World Health Organization [WHO], 1979). Other measures of pathology involving functional incapacity in social relations, work, and the need for hospitalization are somewhat independent of each other as well as of symptom type and severity. Thus, attention to outcome, taken broadly, suggests that there are several different ongoing processes involved in psychiatric disorder, each influencing the others and being influenced by them, but each also having some independence from the others as well (Strauss, Kokes, Carpenter, & Ritzler, 1978).

If diagnosis, syndrome-based diagnosis, is not a sufficient basis for prognosis in these various aspects of outcome, then what is? To some extent, each aspect of outcome is predictable by knowing previous levels or type of functioning in its respective domain. Thus, previous symptom type is a partial predictor of future type of symptoms (WHO, 1979). (Major changes in symptom type over time are not rare, however [Cheadle, Freeman, & Korer, 1978; Strauss, 1983b].) Symptom severity helps to predict future symptom severity (Strauss & Carpenter, 1977). Specific predictive relationships also tend to exist for work functioning, social relations functioning, and need for hospitalization. Based on such findings, we have suggested that the course of disorder might best be viewed as involving several open-linked systems of functioning. Each of these systems has some of its own determinants, and each is influenced by and has some influence on the others.

Individual–Environment Interaction

Beyond this basic prognostic structure, however, other aspects of the course of disorder can be identified, especially by attending to treatment and environmental factors that influence it. Research has shown that course is influenced by psychotropic medications (Weissman et al., 1979), certain family environment factors, such as "expressed emotion" (Vaughn & Leff, 1976), and by other variables, such as stressful life events (Cooke & Hole, 1983) and social supports (Aneshensel & Stone, 1982).

Besides these impacts of the environment on the person, research, especially the studies of life events and the mechanisms of depression, has suggested that the patient's subjective experience and interpretation of the meaning of situations and events are important in determining course of disorder (Coyne & Gotlib, 1983; Folkman, Schaefer, & Lazarus, 1979). We have even argued that the so-called "expressed emotion"—certain types of communication by family members of a psychiatric patient—may relate less to a postulated concept of stimulus level in a physiological sense than it does to the specific meaning characteristics of expressed emotion as an attack on the patient's self-esteem and identity boundaries (Strauss, 1983a).

Finally, the patient as an active person also appears to be of major importance in the course of disorder. Narrow versions of the medical model are inclined to see the patient as a passive recipient of the disease process. But clinical experiences and recent research suggest several ways in which the person can take an active role influencing the course of pathology and recovery. These ways include not only the customary considerations of treatment collaboration (interestingly termed "compliance"), but the ways in which the patient selects and deals with environmental contexts and situations, and in many instances even takes measures to control his own symptoms (Breier & Strauss, 1983).

But how can environmental impact, subjective experience and interpretation, and the active role of the patient be considered together in understanding prognosis? In a series of reports (Strauss, Loevsky, Glazer, & Leaf, 1981), an empirically based model has been developed for defining individual–environment interactions as they affect the course of disorder. It appears that certain characteristics ("components") of the individual–environment interaction—structure, self-esteem, involvement, and social contact—can be identified that help to determine the impact of individual–environment interactions. It may even be possible to identify, for purposes of understanding and ultimately for diagnosis, what the person needs from the environment (self-esteem, involvement, structure, social contact) and the "contexts" (e.g., work, family, friends, treatment) in which such needs can be met or frustrated. The subjective experience and interpretations of meaning by the patient and role of the patient as an active agent as these influence individual–environment interactions can also be incorporated into this conceptual structure.

Longitudinal Principles

Besides attending to prognostic variables and individual–environmental interactions, a third source for clarifying processes in the course of disorder becomes apparent by focusing on the evolution of disorder rather than merely on its "outcome." Current diagnostic concepts in DSM-III that deal with course, such as "chronic" and "subchronic," are essentially static in nature. However, preliminary findings (Strauss, Hafez, Lieberman, & Harding, 1985) suggest that the course of disorder rarely, if ever, follows a straight line. Systematically collected data are beginning to show that course is irregular and that these irregularities may reflect phases, phases suggesting the existence of definable sequential processes. For example, in the course of disorder for some persons there appears to be one or more "moratorium" periods in which no major alteration in severity of disorder or in functioning takes place. These periods are often followed by a "change point" in which rather rapid shifts occur. Such patterns and their variations as they exist over extended periods of time may also suggest the evolution of certain developmental processes involving vulnerabilities, coping mechanisms, and structures of meaning that may be important to the disorders themselves. Basic biological processes, such as changes in dopamine systems with aging, may also constitute important aspects of the evolution of disorder. The longitudinal patterns generated in these ways and the principles that govern them may have major implications for understanding prognosis and the nature of pathological and recovery processes.

Thus, following the precepts of Kraepelin, Sydenham, Hippocrates, and others brings us to a fascinating, but complex view of the nature of psychopathology and the reconsideration of diagnostic validity from the longitudinal perspective.

Is all this complexity necessary? Studies of psychopharmacologic agents, abnormal brain physiology, and other aspects of psychopathology and treatment have uncovered increasingly the complexities of nervous system function. But isn't it still possible to keep a simple model of psychopathologic processes and diagnostic types? For example, even though the healing of a fracture will be influenced by the amount of rest it is given, the tightness of the cast, the metabolic state of the individual, and perhaps even by the patient's psychological well being, it may be adequate to diagnose the fracture itself without involving these other factors. Isn't it possible to assume that these various considerations are all more or less variations on an "average expectable environment"?

This depends more on expediency than absolute knowledge. If an illness generally runs a specific course leading to recovery with only rare exceptions, then perhaps the other factors are of minimal importance. But if that course is highly variable and often not benign, and if a variety of characteristics are known to affect it in significant ways, then consideration of these variables and the processes by which they act may be crucial.

The justification for a more complex perspective is the increased accuracy it may provide to deal with clinical and research observations; it involves the sacrifice of simplicity for validity. For now at least, it may be necessary to emphasize openness to a number and range of factors rather than the simplicity and kind of closure that may ultimately be desirable. Remaining open to complexity and diversity may be essential in spite of desire for closure using psychoanalytic, biological, descriptive, or other explanations. These, if accepted prematurely, may lead to ignoring or discounting factors suspected or even known to be crucial.

Recognizing that providing definitive answers to identifying the underlying processes in psychiatric disorder is still not possible, but noting that course of disorder is crucial to recognizing such processes, perhaps what is known about course can be used to influence DSM-IV just as more basic prognostic characteristics influenced DSM-III (Strauss, 1975). What specifically can be suggested? The following principles are important.

1. Diagnosis based on symptom type alone is inadequate to reflect prognosis and hence to represent adequately the processes of disease and recovery.

2. Whatever the pathologic processes are, they are not totally independent of environmental factors, but are influenced by them. The way in which environmental factors influence these processes seems likely to provide clues to the nature of the processes. Concepts of diathesis and stress have been useful efforts in this direction. However, far more specificity, perhaps using the model of components and contexts mentioned earlier, is desirable for improving on and clarifying these very general and very rough approximations.

3. The subjective experience of the patient cannot be ignored in attempting to understand the course of disorder and processes of disease and recovery. Descriptive characteristics, such as symptoms and environmental features, are important in defining diagnostic categories and are relatively easy to assess reliably. But the person's other subjective experiences, the way the environment is interpreted, issues of meaning, feelings such as confidence or fear, also affect improvement and recurrence. To some extent, the field has been discouraged by previous claims and promises regarding the understanding of subjective experiences such as these. Although the claims were often overstated and the assessment of these processes is complex, neither reason is adequate for avoiding a major attempt to develop creative ways for looking at the role of such subjective experiences in the course of psychopathology and their relevance to diagnosis.

4. The active role of the patient in collaborating with treatment, choosing contexts and activities, and in controlling his or her own symptoms also appears to be an important part of the course of disorder and needs to be included in diagnostic systems. In this area too, excessive claims and negations from certain belief systems have made dealing with the issue very difficult. Nevertheless, exploration of ways to insert the patient's active role into the diagnostic system may be important for more valid diagnostic concepts.

5. Longitudinal principles may provide key information on types of disturbance. To the extent that a longitudinal conceptual system—for example, describing phases and their evolution—can be validated, it provides for a dynamic psychiatry in which the principles of state change and state maintenance can be identified. Principles and models analogous to those employed in physics (P. Lavori, personal communication, March 24, 1983) can become the goal, permitting a useful progression beyond the more static emphasis of current approaches to descriptive diagnosis in psychiatry.

New diagnostic systems must continue to reflect symptoms and syndromes, but also to attend more closely to the other factors in the course of disorder. Whether this attention is paid through classifying disorders according to their longitudinal characteristics defined in a phase/component scheme, through the definitions of new axes, or by including these considerations within axes defined in broader terms, some movement in this direction is essential.

REFERENCES

Aneshensel, C. S., & Stone, J. D. (1982). Stress and depression: A test of the buffering model of social support. *Archives of General Psychiatry, 39,* 1392–1396.

Breier, A., & Strauss, J. S. (1983). Self-control in psychiatric disorders. *Archives of General Psychiatry, 40,* (10), 1141–1145.

Cheadle, A. J., Freeman, H. L., & Korer, J. (1978). Chronic schizophrenic patients in the community. *British Journal of Psychiatry, 132,* 221–227.

Ciompi, L. (1980). The natural history of schizophrenia in the long term. *British Journal of Psychiatry 136,* 413–420.

Cooke, D. J., & Hole, D. J. (1983). The aetiological importance of stressful life events. *British Journal of Psychiatry, 143,* 397–400.

Coyne, J. C., & Gotlib, I. H. (1983). The role of cognition in depression: A critical appraisal. *Psychological Bulletin, 94,* 472–505.

Folkman, S., Schaefer, C., & Lazarus, R. S. (1979). Cognitive processes as mediators of stress and coping. In V. Hamilton & D. M. Warburton (Eds.), *Human stress and cognition: An information-processing approach* (pp. 265–298). London: Wiley.

Marks, I. (1971). Phobic disorders four years after treatment: A prospective follow-up. *British Journal of Psychiatry, 118,* 683–688.

Strauss, J. S. (1975). A comprehensive approach to psychiatric diagnosis. *American Journal of Psychiatry, 132*(11), 1193–1197.

Strauss, J. S. (1983a). The evolution of psychotherapeutic approaches for affective and schizophrenic disorders. In M. Zales (Ed.), *Affective and schizophrenic disorders.* New York: Brunner/Mazel.

Strauss, J. S. (1983b). Schizoaffective disorders: Just another illness or key to understanding the psychoses? *Psychiatrica Clinica, 16,* 286–296.

Strauss, J. S., & Carpenter, W. T., Jr. (1974). Characteristic symptoms and outcome in schizophrenia. *Archives of General Psychiatry, 30,* 429–434.

Strauss, J. S., & Carpenter, W. T., Jr. (1977). Prediction of outcome in shizophrenia. III. Five-year outcome and its predictors. A report from the International Pilot Study of Schizophrenia. *Archives of General Psychiatry, 34,* 159–163.

Strauss, J. S., Hafez, H., Lieberman, P., & Harding, C. M. (1985). The course of psychiatric disorder. III. Longitudinal principles. *American Journal of Psychiatry, 142,* 289–296.

Strauss, J. S., Kokes, R. F., Carpenter, W. T., Jr., & Ritzler, B. A. (1978). The course of schizophrenia as a developmental process. In L. C. Wynne, R. L. Cromwell, & S. Matthysse (Eds.), *Nature of schizophrenia: New findings and future strategies* (pp. 617–630). New York: Wiley.

Strauss, J. S., Loevsky, L., Glazer, W., & Leaf, P. (1981). Organizing the complexities of schizophrenia. *Journal of Nervous and Mental Disease, 169*(2), 120–126.

Vaughn, C. E., & Leff, J. P. (1976). The influence of family and social factors on the course of psychiatric illness: A comparison of schizophrenia and depressed neurotic patients. *British Journal of Psychiatry, 129,* 125–137.

Weissman, M. M., Prusoff, B. A., DiMascio, A., Neu, C., Goklaney, M., & Klerman, G. L. (1979). The efficacy of drugs and psychotherapy in the treatment of acute depressive episodes. *American Journal of Psychiatry, 136,* 555–558.

Weissman, M. M., Prusoff, B. A., & Klerman, G. L. (1978). Personality and the prediction of long-term outcome of depression. *American Journal of Psychiatry, 135*(7), 797–800.

World Heath Organization (WHO). (1979). *Schizophrenia: An international follow-up study.* New York: Wiley.

CHAPTER 13

Accountability in Psychiatric Diagnosis: A Proposal

Thomas J. Scheff

The purpose of this essay is to attempt to place the problem of the diagnosis of mental illness in a somewhat broader framework than that envisaged by the authors of the *Diagnostic and Statistical Manual* of the APA. Since a diagnosis is the basic datum in psychiatry, I will compare the psychiatric model of diagnosis with the model of the basic datum in science, the reliable number, and the humanistic model, which I will refer to as "valid testimony." I will argue that diagnosis of mental illness fits neither model. For this reason, I propose a measure that might ameliorate some of the deficiencies of psychiatric diagnosis: a videotape record of a brief psychiatric interview. This record would meet the criteria of the humanistic and legal models of the basic datum and be available for use with the scientific model. If this procedure were followed, psychiatric diagnosis might become accountable from both the legal and scientific points of view.

The model of the basic datum in science is what might be called "the reliable number." This model is used in natural science, demography, survey research, and experimental psychology.[1] In these ventures, procedures of measurement are used which ostensibly allow repeatability of findings. The measurements themselves are explicit and objective in the sense that they use instruments that are based on precise interval scales. The procedures used in a census, a sample survey, or a psychological experiment are described in a general way in methodology texts, and purportedly, in an extremely detailed and precise way in the publication of results. Findings

1. For a powerful critique of social science claims to reliability, see Cicourel (1964).

Thomas J. Scheff. Department of Sociology, University of California, Santa Barbara, Santa Barbara, California.

based on this model are accountable in the sense that they are reliable. If one wished to challenge the findings, one could repeat the study in a way virtually identical to the way it was done originally. If one studies exactly the same situation with exactly the same measurement procedures, presumably the results will be the same.

The warrant for the factual nature of scientific findings is based almost entirely on their reliability. The term "reliability" is not used in its vernacular sense to mean truthfulness, but in a technical sense in that it means exactly one thing, and one thing only, repeatability. Since repeatablility is so centrally important in science, it is customary, in natural science at least, to make repeated measurements within a single study, generating a measure of reliability that can be published along with the findings. Even in the most precise and accurate of the sciences, there is always some variation in the actual measurements. These variations may be due either to changes over time in the phenomena being measured or to human error. These variations are always present, even though they are often vanishingly small, at least by the standards that we use in everyday life.

The repeatability of numerical findings in natural science is of such premier importance that a custom is followed which requires that the repeatability of each and every numerical fact published be contained within the fact itself. This is the convention of the "significant digit." According to this convention, the amount of variation in a measurement is signaled by the number of digits reported. A simple example will suffice to illustrate what is meant. Suppose the same phenomena were measured three times with the result 9.11, 9.15, and 9.04. In reporting this result, the number published would be 9.1 rather than 9.10. This presentation warrants that the result was somewhere between 9.05 and 9.15. There was so much variation in the third digit that it is not deemed "significant." This convention is followed so automatically in natural science that it virtually goes without saying. One makes repeated measurements so that one cannot only present a finding, but also signal its reliability. The warrant for the truth of classification in the natural science model, the reliability of measurement, is signaled in every datum presented.

There is another model of the basic datum, the humanistic model, which potentially, at least, may be more appropriate for psychiatric diagnosis than the natural science model. This model, which is based on valid testimony, has an advantage over the natural science model which concerns the issue of validity. The validity of a measurement concerns its generalizability. Are we measuring what we think we are measuring? In the Prisoner's Dilemma game used in experimental social psychology, is the competitiveness of players betting on pennies generalizable to their competitiveness in the real world? The problem of validity of measurement is a much more ambiguous problem than that of reliability. The humanistic model of the basic datum is oriented toward the problem of validity, not reliability.

The humanistic model is based on testimony which has four fundamental characteristics. The testimony comes from an identified person, it is located in time and space, and it involves a multiplicity of extremely detailed information in more than one sensory channel. As can easily be shown, the humanistic model is almost identical to the legal model of admissible testimony. As is much less obvious, it is also closely related to the model of the basic datum found in works of art. First, let us consider each of the four characteristics of valid testimony.

Unlike the basic datum of the reliable number found in demography, survey research, and experimental psychology, the humanistic model requires testimony from an identified person, someone with a name, precisely located in time and space. The criterion of hearsay in law is relevant to these characteristics. Survey data are usually not admissible in court because they are deemed hearsay in that they are not directly from identified persons located in space and time.

The characteristic of a multiplicity of information and channels is related to the legal criterion of the eyewitness account. In principle at least, only a person present at an event is eligible to testify about the event because only then will all the sensory channels of perception come into play. There is actually some flexibility in this requirement in that filmed records of an event may be admissible at times (e.g., a will). Since a filmed record contains more than one channel of perception, both the visual and the audible, the principle seems to be reaffirmed even in this exception.

The criterion of testimony by an identified person located in space and time is, in part, a humanistic version of the repeatability requirement of the natural science model. Any challenge to the truthfulness of testimony from an identified person could be met, presumably, by finding the person again for further testimony. The precise location in space and time locates the event being testified about, allowing for cross-validation by other potential witnesses, somewhat like repeated measurement in the natural science model.

The criterion of voluminous information in many channels is quite different from any criterion of the natural science model, however, and perhaps in some ways, antagonistic to it. The goal in the natural science model is the absolute minimum of information which will allow the testing of a hypothesis, with all extraneous information removed. In the humanistic model, however, redundancy of information seems to be required. The goal seems to be to acquire a great surplus of ambient detail. What purpose does redundancy serve in this model? The answer to this question is not at all obvious. To help frame an answer, it will be useful to consider another ambiguous question, the model of the basic datum in art.

It has been skillfully argued that art and science have the same goal, to show "unity in variety," to use Coleridge's phrase (Bronowski, 1965, p. 16). As already indicated above, however, even if we allow that they have the same goal, it is quite clear that they approach the goal in quite different ways. Science seems to want a single unadorned fact, art a virtual cloud of interrelated facts. Since art itself is so various, I won't attempt to examine this issue in all types of art, but for illustrative purposes, I will refer to the basic datum in the work of one artist, the writer, Marcel Proust.

Many critics have agreed that one of the facets of Proust's art that make it irresistible is its seeming verisimilitude. Apparently the scenes that Proust describes have an enormous weight, a palpableness, of facticity. Even a relatively minor character like the servant Francois springs to life from the printed page. Agreeing that Proust's work has this character is one thing; however, explaining why it does is another. One critic draws a visual analogy:

> In the Fitzwilliam Museum at Cambridge, there is a painting by Ruysdael, a view of Amsterdam from the river Amstel. It expresses not a single afternoon hundreds of years ago, but a particular, selected moment in that afternoon. It has been raining—the fields glisten with rain in the pallid light—and it will rain again. The tender and sallow sun, streaming through a sky patched with black cloud and cineraria blue, touches a few sails on the river; soon they will be shadowed again. It is an interim between storms. (Johnson, 1971, p. 195).

The crucial point that Johnson is making is that this painting is not a generalization, but what William Blake called a "minute particular," in this case, a single moment between storms. Let me carry this furthur than Johnson does, to emphasize her point. Suppose that in looking carefully at this painting, we inspected an individual leaf on one of the trees by the river and saw that on the tip of the leaf, about to fall, was a single drop of rain. This shockingly minute detail would testify that this scene was located in time in some unique, single moment. It may be that it is the singularity of the moment, as testified repeatedly by the minute but numberless ambient details, which gives Proust's work its appearance of facticity.

Proust (1922-1927) appears to be aware of the importance of locating the single moment, not only in practice in his writing, but in theory as well. His first point is that all of the characters in his writing are constructed by adding together particular moments: "It was not Albertine alone that was simply a series of moments, it was also myself" (Vol. xi, p. 101). He recognized the enduring force that this method of construction has: "A great weakness, no doubt, for a person to consist merely in a collection of moments; a great strength also: it is dependent upon memory . . . this moment which it has registered endures still, lives still, and with it the person whose form is outlined in it" (Vol. xi, p. 85). The point that Proust implies about the nature of art is stated explicitly by Salaman in her extraordinary *A Collection of Moments* (1970): Writing becomes art only when it evokes singular moments.

What is it about the singular moment such that once registered in human consciousness, it "endures still, lives still," in Proust's phrase? A well-described moment appears to trigger a process of fundamental empathy which allows one to enter that moment, to be incumbent within it. This process of incumbency may occur to the person who originally lived the moment; it is then a process of reliving it. Incumbency may also occur for another person other than the one who originally lived the moment. Perhaps the description of the other's singular moment triggers the recollection of one of one's own. One recognizes one's own humanness through the experience of another's.

Proust's emphasis on the part played by memory is somewhat too narrow for the purpose of this chapter, which is to relate the model of the basic datum in art to a more general humanistic model. Proust's thesis can be generalized by referring not to memory alone, but to human consciousness, whether of the past, present, or future. The humanistic model of the basic datum, of valid testimony, concerns what might be called the phenomenology of particular moments. If these moments are connected to an identified person, are precisely and singularly located in space and time, and contain a multiplicity of ambient detail in many channels, then they will have virtually universal currency and will strike a note of authenticity to human beings in all times, as great art does.

Perhaps the redundancy of information is the characteristic which is most crucial for giving testimony universal currency. A wealth of detail in many channels could do two things: First, it could establish subtly, indirectly, but indisputably the identity of the persons involved, the passage of time, and location in space in a way that makes that particular moment unique. (I intend the word "unique" to be taken literally: If the cloud of ambient detail is large enough, it establishes the moment as unique, as the many whorls in a fingerprint make each one unique.) These details give the testimony psychological immediacy by allowing for the kind of cross-authentication that is a continuous feature of the common human experience of the phenomenal world. Second, redundancy allows for variations in modes of perception because of cultural or individual differences. In reacting to testimony, each person selects those details most relevant to their own experience. To the extent that there is a multiplicity of detail, to that extent persons with very different backgrounds may each find elements that are relevant to them. The natural science model speaks only to scientists, the humanistic model to all humankind.

The humanistic model of the basic datum is implied in Max Weber's concept of "verstehende soziologie," a social science based on empathic or interpretive understanding rather than merely an objective description of outer appearance. A more recent discussion which seems to imply the reliving of a particular moment can be found in Clifford Geertz's method of "thick description": the ethnographer must give such a detailed description of a scene that the reader can relive it, not just understand it intellectually.

Emerson (1841) had already clearly stated his belief in the necessity of a rigorously empathic approach to history:

> We are always coming up with the emphatic facts of history in our private experience, and verifying them here. All history becomes subjective; in other words, there is properly no history; only biography. Every mind must know the whole lesson for itself—must go over the whole ground. What it does not see, what it does not live, it will not know . . .
>
> We as we read must become Greeks, Romans, Turks, priest and king, martyr and executioner, must fasten these images to some reality in our secret experience, or we shall learn nothing rightly. (pp. 238, 240)

As a final example, here is a description of a trial lawyer's application of the idea of a particular moment in his approach to the jury (Edel, 1982):

> [He attacked the jury] with a mixture of learning, logic, dramatic imagination and eloquence which he knew would prove irresistible. He would cause them to live through the events of the crime or the supposed crime, he would take them through the steps of the transaction, whatever this was, and he would lodge in their heads a picture that it was difficult for the opposing attorney to expel. (p. 245)

The Universality of Emotions

Given the seemingly infinite variation in cultures, codes, and personal experiences, is it possible that all human beings in all places and times have qualities in common? The leading contender for these qualities are the basic emotions, or what William James called the "coarse emotions," fear, grief, anger, shame, and so on; affects which seem to have a strong biological base. Darwin speculated that these emotions were shared by all human beings, and indeed, to some extent with other nonhuman mammals. Recent cross-cultural research by Ekman, Friesen, and Ellsworth (1972), and independently by Izard (1971) seems to support this idea. Peoples from all cultures, even, as in Ekman, Friesen, and Ellsworth's study, an aboriginal tribe which had had no prior contact with Western culture, seem able to identify and consensually label the facial expression of these basic emotions. The ability of the art of antiquity to evoke appropriate emotional responses from modern audiences is another indication of the common human quality of emotion. The universality of the appeal of Greek tragedies and comedies, for example, suggests that emotional reactions of weeping in a tragic context and laughing in a comic context reach to all humankind.

The predominance of the role of emotions in the causation of mental illness has been forcefully suggested by the recent work of Helen B. Lewis. Her pioneering study of the role of shame and guilt in the formation of symptoms (1971) has not yet received the attention it deserves. She uses a large number (59) of lengthy verbatim transcripts from therapy sessions, which she interprets word for word. In an extraordinary tour de force, she demonstrates that if shame and/or guilt are evoked in therapy sessions, but not acknowledged, the patient's symptoms will be exacerbated or new symptoms will be produced. Although this study does not present scientific proof of the causation of symptoms by unacknowledged shame and guilt, it makes an extremely plausible case.

In a more recent theoretical work, Lewis (1981) goes on to propose a sweeping modification of psychoanalytic theory, which would simplify it and bring it into much closer accord with the facts that are known. She proposes that psychoanalytic theory and practice actually center on emotions rather than instincts, as originally envisioned by Freud. The most critical translation from instincts to emotions is the substitution of attachment for the sexual instinct and anger for the instinct of aggression. These substitutions lead to a restatement of Oedipal conflict into a much simpler and empirically testable series of hypotheses than Freud's formulations. Lewis indicates how other emotions, especially combinations of shame, guilt, and anger, figure prominently in all mental illness, and how particular emotions, such as fear in paranoia and grief in depression, are central in certain syndromes.

Using Freud's case histories, Lewis is able to account for the decreasing effectiveness of Freud as a therapist by examining his management of the patient's emotional responses. Freud's earliest psychotherapeutic technique (Freud & Breuer, 1895/1966) was based entirely on the patient's emotional responses (abreaction). These treatments were often very brief and virtually always effective (Scheff, 1979). Lewis suggests that as Freud became more and more convinced of the central role of sexual repression in symptom formation, he increasingly ignored the patient's affects, leading to longer and longer treatment and less successful outcomes. For example, she compares two obsessional cases, the "Rat-man," treated successfully in 11 months in 1907, and the "Wolf-man" in 1918, whose treatment lasted 4 years and was terminated unilaterally by Freud in what he later acknowledged was a technical mistake.

The most dramatic illustration of the fruitfulness of Lewis's analysis when applied to Freud's cases is Dora. She was an 18-year-old when she entered treatment with Freud for what her father characterized as depression. She told Freud that she had been subjected since she was 14 to what today might be called sexual harassment, by her father's best friend, Herr K. She went on to explain the unsavory situation in which she had become unwillingly involved. When she complained to her father of Herr K.'s advances, he denied their reality. She then learned that her father was involved in an affair with Frau K., and she reasoned that he was rejecting the reality of her complaints to avoid a confrontation with Herr K. When she complained to her mother and to Frau K. (who had been her best friend), she received no support from them either. Given a situation in which the four adults who were most important to her had rejected her, she felt humiliated and enraged.

Apparently Freud took steps to check her story and found it entirely accurate. Rather than respond to her feelings of outrage, however, he began conducting treatment by analyzing Dora's dreams, particularly their unacknowledged sexual content. Lewis argues that even if Freud's analysis of Dora's dreams were completely accurate, they were quite beside the point. Freud joined the other four adults in rejecting her perception of the reality in which she was involved and the justice of her emotional reactions to that reality. In a move that puzzled Freud to his dying days, Dora unilaterally left treatment. Lewis argues that Freud's theory of sexual repression led him astray. Instead of focusing on Dora's sexuality, he should have helped her acknowledge and work through the immediate interpersonal situation in which she found herself and the affects of shame, guilt, and anger to which it gave rise. By converting psychoanalytic theory into a description of the dynamics of emotion, Lewis seems able to account for Freud's therapeutic successes and failures much more successfully than Freud himself could.

Lewis's very detailed analysis of emotional dynamics may also point in the direction of answering an otherwise very puzzling question about the contours of the "particular moments," which were referred to earlier in this chapter. Neither Proust nor any other commentator gives us much help in describing the dimensions of particular moments. For example, what is likely to be the duration of one of these moments? (Aaron Cicourel raised this question in response to an earlier draft of this chapter.) One very crude guess as to the outline of particular moments would be that they require only two ingredients: a dramatic scene that involves an understandable context (usually provided by a verbal narrative and/or visual images) and at least one stimulus within this scene that arouses an emotional response in the viewer similar to that aroused in one of the characters in the scene. If we accept this simple conceptualization, then the duration of particular moments might be very brief. P. Ekman (personal communication) has suggested that most authentic emotional arousal (as contrasted with voluntarily enacted emotional displays) is of short duration, approximately 1 or 2 seconds. By this reasoning, a recognizable particular moment could involve a single dramatic scene which caused the viewer to have an emotional response and to relate that response to the context of the dramatic scene. This whole process might be as brief as 1 or 2 seconds.

It appears to me, however, that this model of a particular moment might be too simple to perform the functions I have assigned to it. The difficulty is the requirement that the viewer must connect a context with his felt emotion, which would seem to militate against the universality that we are requiring. The narrative/visual context of a dramatic scene is usually couched in symbols, and these symbols are almost always culture-bound. How could particular moments be universal if they are presented through culturally bound contexts?

Lewis's descriptions of the evocation of affect suggest a way out of this dilemma. She notes that affects are seldom evoked singly, but in sequences which involve two or more affects. For example, one may feel ashamed that one is ashamed (because the first shame response seems unjustified, for example) or ashamed that one is angry. One may feel guilty when one feels joy. Some of the sequences that Lewis describes involve more than two emotional responses. In pathological grief, for example, one may first experience grief in a context of loss, then anger at the lost one, then shame or guilt that one is angry. This chain involves three different emotions: grief, anger, and shame or guilt.

Many of the sequences described by Lewis are interpersonal. Person A shows scorn toward Person B, Person B displays shame, Person B then shows anger toward Person A, and finally Person A is ashamed because he is angry. This sequence contains four discrete affective states distributed among two persons. Sequences containing only two affects are more common: Person A is angry at Person B, who becomes ashamed or guilty.

The affect sequences described in detail by Lewis may be relevant to the problem posed above: How can particular moments be universally recognizable if they are dependent on a culture-bound context? The affect sequences with two or more links may provide a partial answer to this question. Although never completely free of the verbal/visual context for its interpretative meaning, an affect chain provides its own context: If each authentic emotional display is universally recognizable, the first affect would provide a context for the second, or the first and second for the third, and so on. Seeing another person becoming increasingly ashamed of feeling ashamed might be universally recognizable, even if the context in which the first emotion arose in the sequence is not understandable. If this model of the particular moment proves useful, the duration would be longer than the first model I proposed, since 1 or 2 seconds would be required for each affect. The duration for these sequences would be at least 2 or 3 seconds for a two-affect chain, and as much as 8 or 10 for a chain with four affects.

These comments on the contours of particular moments are only speculative, of course, and need considerable empirical verification before they can be relied on. They are presented only to suggest the plausibility of the idea of a particular moment as a model of the basic fact in valid testimony and the centrality of emotions in this model.

Conclusions and Recommendations

Does psychiatric diagnosis fit either model of the basic datum? It is quite clear that it does not fit the natural science model of the reliable number. First of all, there are few if any numbers involved in diagnosis. The judgments on which diagnoses are based are not measured with instruments that are systematic and objective, but rest on intuitive, common human classifications. These classifications are usually nominal (either-or) rather than the quantitative ordinal or interval scales upon which the natural science model depends. Numbers are useful when extremely precise and reliable measurements are made, since they allow the presentation of a great deal of information concisely. In the absence of precision and reliability, one should probably use descriptive terms to make classifications.

The more important question about the appropriateness of the natural science model to diagnosis is its reliability. Even if the classification are only nominal, if they are highly reliable, the natural science model might still be appropriate. How reliable are psychiatric diagnoses? I won't pretend to give a complete review of this intricate issue, since it would require a survey of a sizable literature. Instead, I will attempt a brief and therefore somewhat oversimplified answer. Stated bluntly, in terms of requirements of the natural science model, psychiatric diagnosis is usually quite unreliable. Earlier research on reliability reveals a bewildering array of estimates, most of them quite low. To further support this asssessment, I will briefly discuss the evidence on reliability presented in the DSM-III itself, the "Field Trials of Interrater Reliability" (Appendix F).

For the most important dimension of diagnosis in DSM-III, the clinical syndromes (Axis I), the mean coefficient of agreement for two diagnosticians classifying the same patient is .72. There are 17 main categories of diagnosis along this axis, with the largest proportion of patients in the sample ($N = 331$) falling into the categories of Schizophrenic Disorders and Affective Disorders (combined proportion is 53%). The highest coefficient of agreement is for Substance Use Disorders (.80) and the lowest for Factitious Disorders ($-.005$). The negative number means that there was more disagreement than agreement for this particular diagnosis, and for one other (Dissociative Disorders).

By what standards are we to judge these results? The authors themselves say that .70 constitutes "good" agreement. The coefficients for seven (which contain 24% of the patients in the sample) of the 17 classifications fail to meet the author's standards. Even in those 10 classifications in which the coefficients of agreement meet the author's standard, the reliability still may be unacceptably low by the standards of the natural science model. To draw on an analogy from a field of natural science, say geology, suppose that 25 or 30% of the experts disagreed with the classification of a specimen as granite, but said that it was feldspar or some other rock. For science, this finding would represent an intolerable state of ambiguity about the basic classifications in the field.

Another difficulty with the reliability reported in DSM-III is that it does not represent the "true reliability" of psychiatric diagnosis using DSM-III, but something else, which might be called an "ideal reliability." The conditions under which the data for these field trials were drawn are not at all like the conditions under which the usual psychiatric diagnosis is made. The raters knew that they were involved in a reliability study and in most cases even knew with whom their own diagnosis was going to be compared. It seems likely that they would have taken extra time and care with their diagnoses for this reason. A true reliability would involve conditions of diagnosis when the raters did not know that their diagnoses were to be evaluated. For the reasons indicated above, it would seem that psychiatric diagnosis comes nowhere near fitting the natural science model of the basic datum.

Since the humanistic model of the basic datum does not require reliability, it is conceivable that psychiatric diagnosis might meet the humanistic model's requirements, which concern valid testimony. In a minimum way, it seems to meet the first three criteria: Diagnosis is made by, and concerns, an identified person and is located in time and space. In its present form, however, it does not meet the fourth criterion of containing a multiplicity of detailed information in more than one sensory channel. Even the lengthy written descriptions of the results of a psychiatric examination (which are sometimes required in legal testimony) usually do not contain enough detail to establish a particular unique moment in the life of the patient. Most of the descriptive terms that are used are psychiatric concepts which gloss the circumstances of the patient's appearance and actions. As they are presented today, psychiatric diagnoses are more like stereotypes, divested of ambient detail. They are not reliable enough to fit the requirements of the natural science model and contain too little information to meet the requirements of the humanistic model.

Given the present state of the art of diagnosis, I propose that it would become more accountable both legally and scientifically if the humanistic model were stressed more and the natural science model stressed less. The movement away from the natural science model might be symbolized by changing the five-digit classification scheme in the next revision of the DSM. These five digits, complete with a decimal between the third and fourth digit, intimate a precision and reliability which diagnosis does not have. If my reading of the reliability evidence is correct, there is some doubt whether diagnosis is reliable enough to use one significant digit, let alone five. In the place of this pseudonumerical scheme, I would suggest a more modest nominal system. The designation BFN-QR would serve the same classificatory purpose as 553.46, but be less likely to invoke an image of science which is not appropriate.

My second suggestion would move psychiatric diagnosis toward the humanistic model of the basic datum: A videotape record should be made of at least some portion of each diagnostic interview. This record would make available to interested parties the multiplicity of ambient detail in more than one sensory channel that the humanistic model of valid testimony requires and that is missing from present-day psychiatric diagnosis. The videotape record need not cover the entire interview; even 5 minutes of tape contains a vast amount of information, far more than enough to establish a particular moment in the patient's life. It has been shown that facial expressions of emotion may change very rapidly: Expressions that last a quarter of a second or less are referred to as "microexpressions" and are particularly frequent in clinical interviews when stressful topics are under discussion (Haggard & Isaacs, 1966). There are 30 frames/second in video. Five minutes would contain 9000 frames. The use of the Facial Action Coding System (Ekman & Friesen, 1978) makes each tape available for scientific use in relating facial expression to verbal statements, responsiveness of the patient verbally and emotionally to the interviewer's questions, and so on.

In addition to recording a portion of the psychiatric interview, it would probably be useful to have the patient give a brief account of his or her own experience of the situation. Finally, it would be important for the examining psychiatrist to personally introduce the interview excerpt, providing his or her and the patient's name, the date, location, and also the type and amount of psychoactive drugs the patient has been given, if any, since these appear to have important effects on the patient's expressiveness.

Relinquishing attempts to force psychiatric diagnosis into the natural science model and videotaping some portion of the psychiatric interview might be a long step toward making diagnosis legally accountable by moving toward the humanistic model of the basic datum in the classification of mental illness. This same move might also have the paradoxical effect of making diagnosis scientifically accountable, since it would generate a record of particular moments that could provide a foundation for precise and reliable observations.

How would these suggestions affect a future addition of the DSM if they were to be carried out? Two suggestions have already been made: first, that the scheme of numeric classification be changed to an alphabetic one to signal the move away from the natural science model toward a model of valid testimony. The second suggestion was to have the diagnostician record at least a portion of the diagnostic interview on videotape so that a verbal/visual record would be available. My third and final suggestion would be to ask each diagnostician to review the tape in order to find some episode to comment on and relate to his or her diagnosis. This last step would introduce the possibility that another diagnostician might make an independent assessment of the segment of the tape that was mentioned in the diagnosis. This step would conceivably make it possible to falsify the documented portion of the original diagnosis.

I don't foresee that these changes would have large immediate effects on the diagnostic system or the process of diagnosis which it assumes. (One exception comes to mind: It is possible that the existence of videotape records of the diagnostic interview might introduce immediate changes in the legal status of diagnosis.) In the long run, however, it might produce substantial changes. If diagnosticians are asked to document some portion of their judgments with the videotaped record, they might begin to try to articulate the perceptual processes and intuitive judgments they make and to demand systematic training in this process, particularly with respect to the recognition of the verbal and nonverbal expression of emotion. Such demands might lead ultimately to some sharing of the burden of the problems of diagnosis with related disciplines. The description of pathological and normal emotional processes and their relationship to verbal expression is a problem of basic research for psychology, sociology, and anthropology, as well as for psychiatry. The problem of documenting diagnoses with a videotaped record could conceivably lead to a fruitful alliance among these disciplines.

ACKNOWLEDGMENT

This chapter has benefited from the detailed comments on an earlier draft by Aaron Cicourel.

REFERENCES

Cicourel, A. V. (1964). *Method and measurement in sociology.* New York: Free Press.

Bronowski, J. (1965). *Science and human values.* New York: Harper & Row.

Edel, L. (1982). *Stuff of sleep and dreams.* New York: Harper & Row.

Ekman, P., & Friesen, W. (1978). *Facial action coding system.* Palo Alto, CA: Consulting Psychologists Press.

Ekman, P., Friesen, W., & Ellsworth, P. (1972). *Emotion in the human face.* Oxford: Pergamon Press.

Emerson, R. W. (1841). *Lectures and essays.* New York: Library of America.

Freud, S., & Breuer, J. (1966). *Studies of Hysteria.* New York: Avon. (Original work published 1895)

Haggard, E. A., & Isaacs, K. S. (1966). Micromomentary facial expressions as indicators of ego mechanisms in psychotherapy. In L. A. Gottschalk & A. H. Auerbach (Eds.), *Methods of research in psychotherapy.* New York: Appleton-Century-Crofts.

Izard, C. (1971). *The face of emotion.* New York: Appleton-Century-Crofts.

Johnson, P. H. (1971). Triumph over time. In P. Quennell (Ed.), *Marcel Proust: 1871-1922.* New York: Simon & Schuster.

Lewis, H. B. (1971). *Shame and guilt in neurosis.* New York: International Universities Press.

Lewis, H. B. (1981). *Freud and modern psychology.* New York: Plenum Press.

Proust, M. (1922-1927). *Remembrance of things past.* (C. K. S. Moncrieff, Trans.) (12 vols.). London: S. Hudson, Chatto.

Salaman, E. (1970). *A collection of moments: A study of involuntary memories.* London: Longman.

Scheff, T. J. (1979). *Catharsis in healing, ritual, and drama.* Berkeley: University of California.

CHAPTER 14

Bootstrapping toward a Classification System

W. C. Corning

For the past several years, I have been increasingly interested in and concerned about the processes by which the fields of psychology and psychiatry generate languages, systems of conceptualizations and constructs, and theoretical formulations. It has always seemed reasonable to expect that when human beings are engaged in the acts of perceiving, categorizing, classifying, and interpreting human behavior, that we first and foremost become aware of epistemological issues, that we, second, remain eclectic with respect to the available methodological avenues in discovering "reality," and lastly, that our fabrications of reality are accepted as tentative and incomplete guesses subject to modification or outright burial as new and verifiable data emerge. On the surface, it would seem that there should be little disagreement among mental health professionals with respect to these expectations. However, as an outsider whose involvement in this area is relatively recent and admittedly ingenuous, my impression is that the above three expectations are rarely observed among the clinical and research activities of mental health professionals.

In this chapter, a brief discussion of epistemological and methodological topics will be presented, the problems of a behaviorally based approach will be reviewed, some alternative and I hope more objective "taximetric" and "bootstrap" approaches will be outlined, and examples of findings that support suggested strategies will be presented. I cannot offer ultimate panaceas for the problems in the mental health area, but perhaps some of the ideas and methodologies that are reviewed will stimulate more critical self-examination and effect changes in traditional practices.

W. C. Corning. Department of Psychology, University of Waterloo, Waterloo, Ontario, Canada.

The Relativity of Labels and Concepts

The basic terminology and conceptual structures developed by the mental health sciences reflect biases. These biases are imposed by the nature of the human sensory, perceptual, and brain structures as well as by the nature of the particular human subculture in which the professions operate. At a more general level, Ludwig von Bertalanffy (1962) has rendered a most considered discussion of this subject in an essay entitled, "The Relativity of Categories." Von Bertanlanffy rejects any Kantian notion of absolute universals governing the course of human cognitive discovery, arguing that there is (a) biological relativism where human psysiological states and psychophysical organizations influence the development of perception and thought, and (b) cultural relativism where social and cultural factors affect the course and nature of science. As examples of the former, he points out that our perception of time is influenced by bodily temperature and that the history of physics would probably have been quite different if the human being had X-ray vision. With respect to cultural relativism, there are numerous demonstrations of how the course and interpretations of scientific activities are influenced by current economic, social, or political circumstances (Gergen, 1973; Halleck, 1971; Reich, 1983).

However, science is not entirely controlled by these biases, according to von Bertalanffy. Our perceptions and cognitive constructs, whatever their limitations and distortions, are not "wrong." They represent a utilitarian and adaptive transaction with the world. They are correct only in the sense that, for the circumstances in which they evolved, they "work": ". . . perception and experience categories need not mirror the real world; they must, however, be isomorphic to it to such degree as to allow orientation and survival" (p. 241).

Von Bertalanffy goes on to argue that both of these relativistic influences could be minimized by the process of deanthropomorphism: "It is an essential characteristic of science that it progressively de-anthropomorphizes, that is, progressively eliminates those traits which are due to specifically human experience" (p. 242).

Lest this be misinterpreted, it should be strongly emphasized that the argument is not to depreciate the role of the human being (mental health professional and/or client) in the diagnostic–therapeutic process, but to explore methods by which we increase our awareness of these biases and develop procedures which transcend them and permit the mental health profession to achieve a higher order understanding of its defined areas of human dysfunction. As will be argued later, a deanthropomorphized professional would consider that a client's pathology could reside in (a) the individual (a metabolic/organic abnormality), (b) the professional (theoretical orientation, technical skills, social status), (c) social circumstances such as family patterns or subcultural stresses, or (d) any combination of these factors. At the practical level, it is important to note that there is a problem which requires attention and resolution, but if we are to circumvent the limitations and biases that are inherent when humans perceive and interpret human behavior, then we must follow the route of other sciences. Procedures must be found which permit us to remain cognizant and reactive to human problems, but which allow us to research and interpret these areas in ways that supersede the limitations and biases of the human observer. Our science cannot be dictated by the immediate experience and should be capable of arriving at more universal approximations of "reality."

Von Bertalanffy offers a "perspectivistic" compromise, a view that recognizes the importance of the immediate and pragmatic aspects of human experience and cognition, and yet offers an approach that can expand these views, an approach that reduces the egocentrism. A quantitative, objective evolution of knowledge would be possible via symbolic systems whereby we move from the immediate, practical transactions to those levels which transcend the limitations of our psychophysical and cultural structures.

> In a way, progressive de-anthropomorphism is like Muenchausen pulling himself out of the quagmire on his own pigtail. It is, however, possible because of a unique property of symbolism. A symbolic system, an algorithm, such as that of mathematical physics, wins a life of its own as it were. (p. 244)

Von Bertalanffy's perspectivistic approach is not reductionistic or, in other words, does not attempt to reduce all science to physics. It is an attempt to develop procedures that ensure that each level of scientific evolution can be accepted as valid with respect to the problems that are relevant for that level, but also recognizes that the scientific concepts and technologies at each of these levels have limitations and that it is possible and natural for knowledge to move beyond these limitations. Relying upon von Bertalanffy's arguments as a basic orientation, the question of whether the language, concepts, and diagnostic procedures of psychiatry and psychology can be criticized on the same grounds will be examined.

Behavior as a Basis for the Behavioral Sciences?

It is clear that it is human behavior and the behavioral expressions of cognitive processes which compel us to organize conceptual frameworks and scientific disciplines in order to better understand and cope with what human beings and human social structures do. There is nothing unreal about the transactions that we perceive. If I am informed by a nurse that a certain person is physically aggressive on the day that he or she is scheduled for my EEG assessment, I readily accept that information and use it in adaptive ways. Such terminology is certainly useful and communicates relevant information about perceived, overt transactions.

The behavioral sciences have been constructed upon such perceptions, and our textbooks reflect our fascination and belief in these basic perceptions. It is common to find standard textbooks with chapter headings on "mental retardation," "gifted children," "learning disabilities," "autism," "conduct disorders," "psychoses," and so on. Academic treatises, journals, research areas, and grant awards are also organized around these behavioral organizations.

My involvement in the origin and evolution of psychological concepts and categories stems from comparative neuropsychological and neurophysiological research. Using behavior as the organizing basis, considerable effort was expended investigating and documenting common biophysical mechanisms in various species (Corning, Dyal, & Lahue, 1976; Lahue & Corning, 1975). The rationalization for these efforts derived from the enviable success enjoyed by molecular biologists in their discovery and subsequent elaboration of those cellular events which accounted for the transmission and establishment of information from generation to generation. Our assumption was that a carefully defined behavioral function should have corresponding physiological substrates, and that sufficient comparative documentation of this correspondence would enable generalizations to be made about human brain function. We selected "habituation," or the process of learning not to respond, as the best comparative end point because it is generally considered to be the simplest form of learning. There also exist well-defined and operationally established behavioral criteria for this adaptation (Thompson & Spencer, 1966). When species were compared with respect to the biochemical and physiological mechanisms which subserved habituation, we found that cats, flatworms, and single-celled animals could fulfill the same behavioral criteria, but that there was a wide disparity in the biological processes which permitted the same behavioral goal, even among animals of closely related species (Lahue & Corning, 1975).

Ontogenetic Convergence

In phylogeny, it is common to find that animals of widely differing ancestry and physiological makeup evolve similar features. This process is usually referred to as convergence. An analogous operation occurs within the lifetime of different individuals where common behavioral and cognitive functions are achieved in spite of physiological and anatomical dissimilarities. This has been termed "ontogenetic convergence." The significance of this for the behavioral sciences is that, on the basis of behavioral and cognitive similarities alone, we may not assume homologous mechanisms or processes.

A good illustration of scientists who often ignore process heterogeneity may be found in the research and writings of the ethologist, where traditionally, behavior is used to classify and to systematize relations between species in the same way that bone structure is used by morphologists to describe similarities and dissimilarites among various animals. Konrad

Lorenz, Niko Tinbergen, and others have maintained that behavior can be used to discern evolutionary position and lineage. An early attack upon this position was launched by Daniel Lehrman (1953, 1955), who used mother love in ring doves as an example. There is certainly "maternal" behavior, nest "protection," motherly "attention" to the newly hatched squab, even to the point of regurgitating food "in order to" feed the squab. However, mothering in the pigeon is not what is seems to be. Lehrman's research demonstrated that the ring dove sits on the egg because of a hormonally induced patch that develops on her underside. When the area is anesthetized, incubation behavior ceases. Cool stones as well as eggs would elicit incubation. The regurgitation of food seems to be an example of motherly "self-sacrifice," but was seen in a different context when research showed that the crop sac, which becomes engorged with food, was also a source of irritation. When it was anesthetized, "mother" failed to feed the squab. The relationship between the two can be defined as one of reciprocation: The wildly pecking squab hits the crop sac, causing regurgitation and the appearance of food. The mother, in turn, experiences temporary relief of the peripheral irritation, and the two acquire a learned series of responses to each other. The behavioral sequence of mothering, while seemingly familiar with respect to our perception and experiences, takes on a totally different meaning if one deanthropomorphizes.

It is recognized that these examples from comparative research will not impress the clinician whose day-to-day interaction with human cognitive dysfunction and emotional disturbance is obviously more pressing. However, the following two clinical cases should help to support the argument that behavior, by itself, may not be the strongest organizing point in attempts to understand its development and modification.

Ruth Kirk's (1972) theoretical speculation about the causes of schizophrenia is most relevant to the present discussion. One case used in support of her argument involved a young girl who had, until her enrollment in school, a normal developmental history. An undetected perceptual handicap (letter reversal) led to the formation of emotional withdrawal, a "retarded" profile, and subsequent social difficulties. The child's behavioral symptomology was a product of her own disability and the reaction of others to her learning and social characteristics. In other words, the learning disability led to a social interaction handicap which increased and compounded the child's problem. The behavioral end point, a potential "schizophrenic" syndrome, was not the best way to understand (and subsequently treat) the child. Upon discovery of the perceptual handicap, communication between relevant persons and the girl improved, and therapeutic regimes were more appropriately organized.

The second case is drawn from a brain–behavior assessment program which I conduct at the University of Waterloo in collaboration with Richard Steffy. Children involved in this program are given a computerized EEG analysis (John *et al.*, 1977) as well as neuropsychological and psychometric assessments. The 12-year-old boy, D. T., had been doing below acceptable work in core subjects for several months and was, as his principal euphemistically put it, scheduled to be "retained." The key problems were a progressive deterioration of skills in core subjects, an inability to maintain attention, and low motivation. All teachers noted a frequent "drifting" and "spaced out" demeanor. Results from the WISC-R indicated considerable scatter on performance items, with verbal scores normal. The EEG data showed excess slow frequency in the right occipital and left frontal regions and abnormally low correlations between left and right occipital leads. An opthamological examination confirmed the EEG findings and demonstrated visual deficits in the lower nasal quadrant as well as eye–motor control dysfunctions. His behavioral characteristics and the psychometric and EEG test results began to make sense. Subsequent interviews with D. T. yielded information that further clarified matters. Two years earlier, he had fallen and hit his head while playing in an area that was off limits. To avoid being caught, he did not tell his parents about the incident and for weeks tolerated severe headaches and dizziness. The symptoms eventually subsided, but he would still become moderately dizzy, particularly in bright light, and the family doctor began to treat him for a sun allergy.

The behavior, in both these cases, was misleading and could have led to incorrect classifications of the children as well as to inappropriate and perhaps harmful therapeutic attempts. In D. T.'s case, one suggestion was that behavior modification techniques be invoked in order to increase his attention span. However, it was sustained attention that led to headaches and dizziness and, in fact, the opposite strategy was called for—classroom tasks involving visual attention were shortened and changed often. Since the left half of his visual field was impaired, his classroom seating position was also changed so that blackboard viewing was easier. His educational performance improved rapidly following the implementation of these strategies.

There are other examples of ontogenetic convergence in the clinical and experimental literature. Children who are born without a corpus callosum manage to achieve normal behavior and cognitive end points and, on the surface, are indistinguishable from their peers (Cuénod, 1972). Rosner (1970) has noted the remarkable capacity of the immature brain to establish normal functions after extensive damage, a property that accounts for the frequent observation by pediatric neurologists that children with nervous system injuries do not show the same symptomology as adults with identical injuries. The experimental literature has also provided many examples where normal and identical behavioral and cognitive capacities are achieved by dramatically altered brains [see Thatcher and John (1977) for a review of this literature]. By way of summary, it is generally found that in animals the effects of a disrupted physiology on behavior depend upon pre- and postlesion treatment, upon whether the lesion(s) was single or in multiple stages, and upon the age of the animal. Given the correct combination of circumstances, what was once considered a devastating surgical insult could result in little change in an animal's capacities.

Too much reliance upon perceived behavioral categories can also interfere with research progress (Corning & Steffy, 1979). If a researcher wishes to explore, for example, the causes of process schizophrenia, the traditional approach is to organize experimental and control groups around specific behavioral criteria, such as a group of process patients identified by more than one independent diagnosis, a group of hospitalized but nonschizophrenic patients, and a group of normals. The hypothesis might be that some biochemical factor x is the key predisposing cause for the syndrome. Statistical analyses may turn out to be negative, resulting in the unwarranted conclusion that factor x is not a primary cause. Using the heterogeneity argument reviewed earlier, it may be that in an experimental group of 20, 5 actually had factor x, and their contribution to the group mean is mitigated. Another researcher may by chance capture a much larger number of factor x's in the experimental group and achieve statistically significant differences, leading to the conclusion that factor x is involved in the development of schizophrenia. This possibility may explain the slow progress and often controversial nature of mental health research.

Disciplinary Egocentrism: The Necessity for Multilevel Data

One way of discerning whether process heterogeneity exists in a behavioral or cognitive function is to incorporate relevant multilevel data and concepts. "Multilevel" simply refers to other disciplines. Reliance upon external transactions alone is ". . . an indication of the immaturity of the science, an age when the external and obvious engross the attention" (Herrick, 1924, p. 12). As an example, the concept of the gene received verification and gained power from the data generated in microbiology (the transformation and conjugation experiments with *Escherichia coli*), histochemistry (the documentation of chromosomal characteristics), biochemistry (the research of cellular readout and control mechanisms), and behavioral genetics (drosophila and mouse mutation studies). The original focus upon overt, phenotypic features has been expanded so that we now have a much more integrative conceptualization. Each level of information, although quite different from the data of other levels, corresponds with the total concept of the gene and its operations. Transformation from one level to the other is possible.

Some may be quick to point out that many areas in the behavioral and psychiatric sciences are involved in multidisciplinary efforts (e.g., see Millon, 1969). I would agree, but reply that it is common practice for us to attempt to organize other levels on the basis of a behavioral or cognitive category before the relationships or transformations between the levels have been established. Investigators have looked for molecules that specifically subserve learning and memory, even to the point of claiming to have found a "light avoidance" polypeptide in mice (Ungar, 1970). Others have attempted to find "memory" in limbic areas, "consciousness" in the reticular formation, "aggressiveness" in the amygdala, and a "percept" in a single cell. Such disciplinary egocentrism is reminiscent of the attempts by the phrenologists to establish correspondences between psychological categories and skull conformations. The assumption is that the category remains intact in the anatomy, the physiology, and the chemistry. However, there is a growing body of research that questions these facile transformations between the behavior and the physiology.

There are also signs of a reduction in disciplinary egocentrisms as exemplified in the research of E. R. John (John, 1967, 1972, 1977; Thatcher & John, 1977). John has challenged the position that memory can be "a thing in a place," at least in mammalian brains. In general, his research has demonstrated that there are correspondences between the average statistical properties of neural masses and certain behavioral, perceptual, and cognitive phenomena. When examining the relationships between single cells and the neural masses, the correspondences decrease. A transformation rule is needed, and John's research and theory has proposed various transformations between molecules and cells, cells and neural masses, and neural masses and the anatomy. Approaches such as this will help to advance knowledge rather than protect paradigms. In addition, this multilevel approach may help to uncover mechanisms that may lead to disordered thought. The categorization of disordered thought by itself is unlikely to be of much help in locating and understanding relevant transformation points.

The foregoing discussion concerning unilevel and multilevel approaches is not meant to argue for the "universal professional" who knows all disciplines. It is intended to increase caution in our assumptions about our constructs (such as mental retardation) and in our interpretations of research data. Unilevel constructs and categories can have value. For example, a behavioral ecologist who is studying the effects of a high-power radar installation may want to classify the surrounding animal population into "flying" and "nonflying." Similarly, the classification of river inhabitants into "sessile" and "nonsessile" would be useful when assessing the potential effects of a proposed dam. With respect to the daily administration of the mental health ward, the implementation of therapy, behavioral management techniques, medication, and so on would be impossible unless we had a system of describing and organizing behavior. Terms such as "passive-aggressive," "catatonic," "hyperkinesis," or "zoophilia" are useful, but they are as arbitrary and as limited as the ecological classification examples that were provided.

Zing Yang Kuo (1969), in his final publication, offered what I consider to be most cogent discussions of conceptualized behavior within its environmental and organic contexts.

Kuo objected to the standard compartmentalizations of behavior and their concomitant labels because they implied goals on the part of the behaving organism and because they reflected the purposes of the observer or experimenter. He objected to the reliance upon overt bodily movements and so on, as perceived by the human observer. Kuo viewed the study of behavior as necessarily multidisciplinary because

The extrinsic changes are merely a portion of the total pattern. The activities or changes taking place inside the body are not just physiological bases or physiological counterparts of behavior; they are inseparable portions of the total pattern of behavioral gradients.

Just as philosophers have tried to separate mind from the body, modern students of behavior are apt to separate physiology from behavior. But, under the concept of behavioral gradients, the physiological level and the behavioral (overt movement) level form an integrated inseparable total pattern in which the activity of different parts and organs varies from time to time in intensity and extensity. (p. 94)

DSM-III as an Organizing Device

Considering my previously published discussions on current psychiatric diagnostic and labeling practices (Corning, 1975b, 1977; Corning & Steffy, 1979), the invitation to submit a contribution to a compendium focusing upon the DSM seemed analogous to asking an astrophysicist to comment on the utility of horoscopes in sending a space probe to Jupiter. My past views of traditional diagnostic and classification procedures have been negative, but I shall attempt to deanthropomorphize and arrive at some propitiatory statements about the utility of this manual.

The Necessities for Diagnosis and Classification

It should be understood that I have little quarrel with the need to identify symptoms or signs in an individual (the process of diagnosis), to develop procedures whereby individuals are grouped on the basis of their shared characteristics (the process of classification), and with the need to assign some identifying marker to the category (the process of labeling). These processes organize symptom clusters for clinical/research purposes, they permit the gathering of statistical data about the incidence and characteristics of the syndrome, and they facilitate the organization of funds, institutions, and personnel. As Gerald Senf (personal communication) once put it, it would be unsettling to walk into a doctor's office with an ailment, recieve an examination, and then have the doctor say to you, "I've never seen anything like this before."

The Problems with Diagnosis and Classification

There have been many publications criticizing the diagnostic and classification procedures in the mental health professions (for reviews, see Braginsky & Braginsky, 1974; Goffman, 1961; Sarbin, 1967; Szasz, 1970). With respect to my own involvement in these processes, I find the following problems to be most important.

First, as mentioned in the initial segment of this chapter, the symptoms that attract our attention mirror our personal and cultural biases. What is deemed abnormal may be more of a lack of tolerance within a society than a problem within the indivdual. For instance, until a few years ago, the medical profession considered homosexuality an illness. This "disease" lost its medical status by vote at a psychiatric convention obviously because the attitudes and tolerance of a society had shifted, not because any disease was cured. The danger of manuals that define symptom arrays and pronounce them as normal or abnormal is that they reify the category and locate the deviance within the persons with the symptoms. The "medical model" approach has not traditionally presented our conceptualizations of abnormality within social and cultural contexts, although with some categories such as schizophrenia, there has been a growing interest in familial patterns (e.g., see Bowen, 1961). The process entrenches the category, isolates it from relevant social, economic, and cultural factors, and gives it an inertia which is difficult to overcome. This model has also been moderately intransigent with respect to research findings that should modify or delete the criteria upon which the diagnosis has been made.

In order to bring the preceding points into a more practical framework, the category "mental retardation" will be used to amplify my arguments. To begin with, in our culture educational progression is age based, and we have developed "intelligence" tests that are used to assess and predict future educational success because of their predictive validity in this one area of Western culture.[1] It is clear that in any reasonable sampling of children, a normal distribution curve will result when they are given an "IQ" test. Our educational system, bent on servicing the norm and streamlining its efficiency in this endeavor, engages in what the Braginskys (1974) refer to as "social sanitizing," that is, they want children who are not coping with their curricula to be removed from the mainstream classroom. They are considered to be retarded and given alternate social and educational programs. The question is, if I were to create a pill that raised all IQ scores by 50 points, would we see the end of mental retardation in our culture? It has been suggested by others (Raines, Kituse, Duster, & Freidson, 1975) that our societal criteria often produce the deviance, for example, there would not be any criminals without laws.

With respect to social and cultural contexts, an excellent discussion of this problem has been presented by Mercer and Richardson (1975) who have researched the incidence of mental retardation labeling in minority groups and have found a significant degree of over labeling. Using a multifactor model which includes IQ scores as well as family expectations and other relevant variables, they construct a more realistic and quantitative estimate of retardation. In addition, the dimensional aspects and the modification

---

1. I've often wondered why there is no "AQ test" that assesses children for altruistic retardation in our culture.

potentials of individuals included in the category are rarely emphasized. Studies such as those of Tizard (1962) and Skeels (1966) suggest that the category (and the label) is an incomplete analysis of the individual's ultimate potential.

To summarize the first point, what I am arguing is that the format of diagnostic manuals, the professional source (the medical community), the theoretical orientation (the medical model or belief that the abnormality is mainly within the individual), and the presentation of categories as stable entities, are misleading, invalid, and could be detrimental with respect to the evolution of knowledge.

My second objection to diagnostic and classification processes stems from my involvement with the strategies of numerical taxonomy (which will be discussed more thoroughly later). A basic aspect of this approach is to let information lead to categories and groupings. Current diagnostic systems and the categories which result organize information before an adequate evidential substrate has been established. Based mainly on a few symptoms which are unilevel (behavioral and cognitive), these systems not only offer categories covering perceived abnormal behavior, but become the critical organizing devices for clinical statements, research designs, and most important, for the organization and implementation of treatments.

In schizophrenia research and treatment, there is increasing evidence that this category represents a collection of separate entities (Cancro, 1972; Douglass & Hays, 1980; Hays, 1973, 1978; Kendler & Hays, 1981, 1982a, 1982b). One may show similar behavioral and cognitive symptoms because of a recent immigration or because of an abnormal brain. However, the category remains unified, and a diagnostic decision of schizophrenia could result in two etiologically different individuals being placed in the same ward and receiving identical treatments.

The opposite situation may also occur. Diagnostic systems may distinguish between mental retardation and learning disabilities. This is a critical dichotomy because in today's society, there are significantly different social and educational consequences, depending upon which category is chosen. As Ross (1980) has argued, an attentional deficit alone (which is a learning disability) could lead to poor performance on IQ tests and to a classification of "retardation." My point is that the dichotomization occurred before scientific research has adequately established the similarities and differences between the two groupings. Separate budgets, institutions, professional personnel, curricula, journals, parental associations, and expectations result before any empirical basis has been established to justify the dichotomy.

A Look at the DSM-III

There is little in the latest DSM that lessens the concerns expressed above. Categories are constructed by committees and approved by vote. Behavioral and cognitive symptoms are the predominant organizers, categorization is

mainly qualitative, and the diagnostic criteria are often limited and/or chal-
lengeable on the basis of present-day research findings, ". . . avoiding the
introduction of new terminology and concepts that break with tradition,
except when clearly needed" (American Psychiatric Association, 1980, p. 2).
Since my own assessment program focuses on children with behavioral and
cognitive difficulties, I shall discuss two categories, Attention Deficit Disorder and Mental Retardation.

There are, as the manual notes, several labels that are used to describe
what they have voted to be labeled Attention Deficit Disorder, such as
Hyperkinesis, Hyperactivity, and Minimal Brain Dysfunction. The various
labels and their research data and theoretical backgrounds are swept aside
because in the view of whatever committee constructed the category, attention is the most prominent and persistent characteristic. Impulsivity and
excess motoric activity are also included in the category which is divided into
Attention Deficit Disorder with Hyperactivity, Without Hyperactivity, and
Residual Type. I would be curious about what operational criteria were used
to define attention and various attentional processes, and, in addition, what
literature demonstrates that there is a clear attentional deficit in all the
categories that were thrown out. Oculomotor abnormalities, short-term
memory deficits, lack of teacher tolerance, and inappropriate classroom
reinforcement procedures may all produce unacceptable performance, but
they are not all "attentional." There is simply not enough research data to
justify this committee-based creation. I have seen hyperactive children who
enter a room, move effectively and rapidly around and over the furniture,
quickly navigate toward and examine several unusual and interesting items
lying around, and do all of this with tremendous skill and at high speed. They
certainly do not have an attentional deficit with respect to monitoring their
position in space and focusing upon items in the environment. A "deficit" of
some sort exists, but I strongly object to a committee's pronouncement that
it is attentional or that it is necessarily within the child.

The diagnostic criteria for this category are probably representative of
the major problems for most categories contained in the DSM-III—they are
limited, nondimensional, and fail to include situational variables. For example, category C, Hyperactivity, has as its diagnostic criteria the following
(DSM-III, p. 44):

(1) runs about or climbs on things excessively
(2) has difficulty sitting still or fidgets excessively
(3) has difficulty staying seated
(4) moves about excessively during sleep
(5) is always on the go or acts as if driven by a motor

These are qualitative statements that are highly correlated and, accordingly,
do not represent an adequate and objective sampling of behavior. Now if a
child is running around (criterion 1), he is obviously not sitting still (2) and
consequently has difficulty staying seated (3), and therefore can be described

as always on the go (5). "Movement during sleep" (4) has to be researched more thoroughly in various samples before it becomes a valid criterion. Frankly, I find such attempts to organize knowledge and establish criteria to be professionally sophomoric, especially when, as in the case of hyperactivity, the committee decides that "at least two of the following" are necessary for a diagnostic statement. Category C has essentially one criterion—movement.

The section also fails to note that hyperactivity is situational [see Ross (1980) for an excellent discussion of this point]; it may be more normal than people realize (Werry & Quay, 1971), and it may reflect different tolerances and expectations among school and parents (Langhorne, Loney, Paternite, & Bechtoldt, 1976).

The section on mental retardation is most disappointing because it remains ensconced in the highly debatable notion of "intelligence" and in the IQ test as an instrument to assess cognitive capabilities. The IQ score is the major diagnostic feature and remains the basis upon which an individual is considered to be "mildly," "moderately," "severely," or "profoundly" retarded. These labels by themselves are highly questionable because of their pejorative consequences, but more importantly, the different levels of categorization can have markedly different effects upon how the child is educated and treated socially. At a more general level, I question the use of the term "retardation" to describe all people with IQ test and educational subnormality. Although the DSM-III claims to be atheoretical, the assumption behind this term is that there is delayed development and that future cognitive potential will be limited. Borrowing somewhat from Ross (1980), I find that the term "performance deficit" might be more neutral, since IQ tests measure responses to questions and demands.

The manual also includes "adaptive behavior" as a criterion, but is not very specific about what facets of daily existence should be examined. Adaptive behavior scales are judged to be insufficiently valid and reliable to be the only basis for evaluation and, according to the manual, clinical judgment must be involved. This criterion remains weak and permits the clinician considerable variability in what is selected and how it is evaluated. The IQ score remains, unfortunately, the major classification device in spite of increasing evidence that altered environments and alternate educational strategies can dramatically improve IQ scores. The rigidity of the DSM-III with respect to the reliance upon IQ scores does not reflect the changes, both in conceptual orientation and in terms of research results, that are occurring in this field. It continues to perpetuate limited and questionable diagnostic procedures.

Overall, I view the DSM-III as a lexicon that standardizes our terminology. It is important, as it is in law, for example, that the language represent and describe essentially the same phenomena for those who use it. This process is never perfect, but it does enhance communication. Like all linguistic systems, it will organize and limit our perceptions of behavioral and cognitive processes. As a "statistical" manual, it is certainly not very dimensional. Qualitative classifications prevail and numerical exercises are mainly assigning numbers to categories, much like assigning numbers to football players according to their position.

The Taximetric Approach

Taxonomic structures traditionally used in biology can be criticized along the same lines. However, out of these criticisms a variety of techniques have emerged that attempt to circumvent the relativistic biases, expand the domain of relevant measure sets, and construct classification schemes which are based upon more objective and repeatable procedures. In general, these approaches comprise the field of "numerical taxonomy," and they developed because of increasing dissatisfaction with the logic, the methods, and the taxonomic schemes used by biologists to classify various species of animals and plants.

For a biological taxonomist, the initial bias occurs when the compelling "symptoms," such as an array of jaw bones, are assembled. From such arrays, similarities and dissimilarities are noted and classifications emerge. Other arrays (such as skulls and fossils) are also found, and eventually a taxonomic scheme emerges which defines the criteria by which a species may or may not be a member of a certain class. Subsequent evidence (carbon dating, for example) that may suggest an alteration in the scheme tends to be disregarded because the classification system has had longevity and has gained acceptance, and because it fits the overall conceptual orientation and bias of the field (in biology, this would be the belief in evolution). The problems in this process are quite similar to those discussed with respect to classification in the mental health professions: (a) there is a limited sampling of data; (b) the selection and weighting of the data depend upon the biases and theoretical orientation of the classifier; (c) a taxonomic scheme eventuates and is accepted because of its paradigm compatibility (see Kuhn, 1962); and (d) subsequent information that does not support the scheme is simply not used for classification purposes; that is, a "classification tautology" arises where the initial data not only set up the categories, but are then used to include or exclude later information.

The numerical taxonomic position has at its core the ideas of Michael Adanson, an eighteenth-century botanist. His arguments were as follows (reviewed by Sneath & Sokal, 1973):

1. Classifications are best when information content is high; therefore, if as many measurements as possible are obtained, the categorization process is more robust.

2. A priori, all measures have equal weight. Thus, the jaw bones discov-

ered by the anthropologist and the compelling paranoid hallucination observed by the clinician are reduced to a status equal to all other measures, such as carbon dating for the former and oculomotor data for the latter.

3. Groups are formed because the members of any group are more like each other across the multidimensional set than any of the others; separate groups arise because of the lack of shared features.

4. Classification is objective and atheoretical.

Present-day numerical taxonomists have introduced some additional concepts that are compatible with the Adansonian position. They have challenged the propensity among scientists to organize data according to its predominant and compelling features, that is, its essence. As discussed by Sneath and Sokal (1973), the use of a single or few measures to make a classification is a monothetic approach, an Aristotelian strategy that defines the inevitable and universal properties of a category. Thus, there are liquids and nonliquids, unicellular and multicellular organisms, animals with and without hemoglobin, and so on. In contrast to this, they have introduced the concept of polytheticism (Beckner, 1959; Sokal & Sneath, 1963) in which a category or group has the following characteristics:

1. Each member of the group has a significant number of the properties characterizing the group.

2. Each property or measure is, in turn, possessed by a significant proportion of the group.

3. No feature has to be found in every member of the category.

With this approach, the goal is to find natural groupings and affinities independently of a priori assumptions and interests.

> Thus there are birds that lack wings, vertebrates that lack red blood and mammals that do not bear their young. In such cases a given . . . class is established because it contains a substantial portion of the characters employed in the classification. Assignment to the taxon is not on the basis of any single property but on the aggregate of properties, and any pair of members of the class will not necessarily share every character. (Sokal, 1966, p. 197)

The application of polythetic classification schemes in science has been slow to develop because it is easier and perhaps psychologically more comfortable to be Aristotelian and seek out a unifying feature that appears to describe a complicated set of apparently related events. Cognitive consonance is obtained, but accuracy suffers. Sokal proposes that with the advent of present-day computer technology, polytheticism, and the procedures by which polythetic classifications are developed can be documented, and that given the same information, different scientists will arrive at the same classification result.

What has evolved from this strategy is a set of techniques which are possible only because of advances in computer technology and which permit the use of multidimensional data sets and large numbers of subjects in order to ascertain whether there is any "structure." These techniques, usually referred to as clustering methods, generally attempt to organize units (or individuals) according to their similarities across many measures; that is, they disclose and summarize the coefficients of relationship and the structure of the matrix. What is important is that the methodology used to organize groupings is objective, repeatable, and deanthropomorphizing. It is essentially a computer algorithm. It need not be acceptable because any grouping only obtains "reality" as a consequence of replication and validation through corresponding research findings and clinical utility.

The numerical taxonomic approach is essentially a "bootstrapping" procedure where groups and relevant measure sets are continually refined. Thus, the approach with a problematical population such as a school of learning disabled would be to select a set of measurement domains such as medical data, neuropsychological data, psychometric assessment, school performance, and neurophysiological measures. The population is then given the various tests. Each individual's data set is subjected to a clustering algorithm which would agglomerate profiles with the greatest affinities across the multidimensional array of measures. Measures that best discriminate between the groups are retained, while those that have poor discriminative power would be deleted. The whole procedure is repeated on another population whose data are added to the first. A reclustering can be carried out, and with larger numbers and a more refined measure set, group structure should be further clarified. Each child's position in the group or distance from the group mean can be stated quantitatively and forced categorization can be avoided; that is, there will be some children who fall between two or more groups or are simply unclassifiable. This entire bootstrapping process provides a quantitative and operational means classification, it evolves objectively as new subjects are added and the measure set is gleaned, and it remains sensitive to the dimensionality of each individual. Once clusters have been validated and shown to be reliable, various remediation strategies can be administered to particular groups and compared with respect to their effectiveness in changing the salient abnormal characteristics of the clusters. This was essentially the program that I helped implement at New York Medical College (see John et al., 1977).

The above sequence of procedures would seem to be quite similar to the bootstrap approach outlined by Von Bertalanffy. However, the numerical taxonomic ideology is easier to outline than it is to effect. Richard Steffy and I have discussed some of the associated problems in a previous publication (Corning & Steffy, 1979), so I shall provide only a brief review here.

First, it is impossible to deanthropomorphize in the selection of subjects. We cannot remove ourselves from our cultural surround and our perceptions of normality and abnormalilty. It is undoubtedly true that there are many people whose behavior and actions are harmful to themselves and to others, but are not targeted for assessment and classification because of our cultural biases. At best, we can hope for a sufficiently broad-based measure set that includes environmental as well as individual data in the hope of being accurate with respect to the source(s) of abnormality. It is also important, particularly with respect to numerical taxonomy, to maintain some degree of population heterogeneity by adding normals as well as other problematical samples to the subject pool. This not only ensures that the norms represent true estimates, but aids interpretation and understanding of the perceived abnormality. As will be discussed in the following section, a child with an abnormal brain feature may be found in a normal, learning disabled, or delinquent population, depending upon family circumstances. Only by using multidisciplinary measures and heterogeneous populations can we evolve a more accurate and objective understanding of targeted populations.

A second problem involves the selection of measures. Given the necessity of multidisciplinary assessment, there must be literally thousands of potentially relevant tests. Again bias is introduced. Our particular technical expertise will certainly dictate which measurement domains are emphasized. As argued by Steffy and myself, two critical requirements for a test are that it diagnose (identify and predict) and/or that it provide information about process. The latter demand is critical if we are to circumvent the ontogenetic convergence problem discussed earler and if appropriate remediation regimes are to be selected. The selection of any test battery depends upon money, availability of trained personnel, reliability and validity, the availability of normative standards, and their sensitivity to the dysfunctions that are apparent in the targeted population.

A final problem concerns the acceptance and interpretation of the classification system generated by the computer. Computers and clustering algorithms are not "intelligent." They are stupid machines rigidly following a sequence of instructions which have to be created and analyzed by a human scientist. There are several different classes of clustering algorithms, and each is likely to provide a different structuring of "reality" for the same set of data (Blashfield, 1976). The type of similarity index, the nature of the measure set's distribution, and the algorithm's mathematics can affect the outcome of a clustering. There are procedures that can help guide the investigator's choices, such as that of Bartko, Strauss, and Carpenter (1971) where artificial "patient" data with known groupings were subjected to different similarity measures and clustering algorithms in order to ascertain which methods best reconstructed the groups. Again, this procedure is not independent of bias because it relies upon our a priori conceptualizations of what groups exist and what the characteristics of a measure set will be for the groups. Assuming that we do locate a trustworthy clustering procedure, we are finally left with its results—the clustering of individuals in multidimensional space or "hyperspace." It is likely that in many cases, if the groupings don't make any sense, the results will be ignored. To be entirely fair to the computer and its algorithm, the results of a clustering program need to be subjected to the same criteria as other medical and psychological classification schemes: Does the structure improve diagnosis, understanding, and treatment?

Bootstrapping Bargain Basement Style[2]

The preceding overview of numerical taxonomy may have suggested to the reader that in its ideal form, large amounts of funds are necessary to support all the required personnel, obtain sufficient computer capacity, and implement proper computer programming. Given the advantages of multiple measures and multilevel data sets, large numbers of subjects are required, since at least a 10:1 subject to measure ratio is needed for the clustering algorithms. The New York Medical College program was permitted a modest excursion with respect to applying the ideology of numerical taxonomy, through a population of over 900 learning-disabled children, at a cost of over $2 million. After a sabbatical year involved in developing this project, I returned to Canada and an annual research budget of $6000–14,000. I had discovered a bit of reality.

The first stage was purely physical. Through theft, coercion, vague promises of future coauthorship, and threats of temper tantrums, I managed to obtain a 22-channel EEG amplifier system, a graduate student who knew how to program, free access to the department's PDP 11/40, and the unqualified support of departmental chairpersons. A promise of future payment to clinical trainees assured me of psychometric data. I was bent upon unraveling the heterogeneity of learning and cognitive disorders, but was aware that I was a neurophysiologist with some knowledge of psychometric skills without much money. Fortunately, my colleague, Richard Steffy, agreed (for the most part) with my strategies, and with his expertise in clinical psychology and neuropsychology we implemented an assessment program which focused upon problematical children in general, but was necessarily limited to electroencephalographic and psychometric domains.

As a first step toward bootstrapping, we decided to focus upon two areas which seemed to have sufficient validation: EEG slow frequency and the Wechsler Intelligence Scale for Children—Revised, or WISC-R. We chose these two sets for the following reasons:

1. EEG slow frequency (1.0–7.0 Hz) has been shown to covary with maturation (decreasing with age), neuropathology (such as tumors), and certain functional disorders such as learning disabilities.

2. The WISC-R has demonstrated predictability with respect to educational success and moderate discriminative power between normal and dysfunctional groups.

2. The research findings discussed in this section have been recently published (Corning, Steffy, & Chaprin, 1982).

The second step was to obtain a heterogeneous population of children. Through assessment contracts with social service and educational agencies, we began a program of brain–behavior assessments. Once the program was operative, private referrals increased and to date, we have assessed well over 500 children. In order to ensure that our population was truly heterogeneous, we actively solicited children who were not known to have any behavioral, cognitive, or emotional disorders. In all, our population contained juvenile delinquents, hyperactives, slow learners, learning disabled, emotionally disturbed, and the perceived normals. Although children in the program received other assessments, depending upon the case, almost all participants were given WISC-Rs and the EEG.

Our major interest was in establishing whether there were any relationships between two measurement domains, the electrophysiological and the psychometric, independently of the symptom categories that constituted the basis for an assessment referral. Our belief in ontogenetic heterogeneity led us to ignore, at least with respect to our research design and statistical analyses, the behavioral/cognitive classifications. We also decided to organize groups on the basis of EEG slow wave measures and then look for WISC-R characteristics that were unique for any of the groups. The major reason for this procedure is that the EEG data have been shown to be independent of socioeconomic factors (John *et al.*, 1977). Thus, the groups that were formed were free from both behavioral labels and cultural bias.

The EEG and WISC-R data were analyzed for the first 92 children (ages 9–14) in the program. The EEG data were obtained from bilateral electrodes placed over frontal, central, parietal, occipital, and temporal areas. These data were digitized on the PDP 11/40 and subjected to fast Fourier transforms yielding relative and absolute power calculations in all standard EEG bandwidths, as well as interhemispheric correlations for bilateral pairs of electrodes. All records were then ranked from highest to lowest with respect to slow-frequency indices (.5–7.0 Hz) and a developmental index, the $\theta:\alpha$ ratio. Ranking procedures were designed so that two groups emerged: children with high amounts of slow frequency in most areas of the brain (group DSF indicating "diffuse slow frequency") and children with consistently low rankings in all leads (group NF).

The results were as follows:

1. The DSF group showed significantly lower WISC-R scores on all verbal items and on the Block Design and Object Assembly subtests. Verbal and performance IQs were 92.6 and 101.3, respectively, for group DSF and 112.1 and 113.8 for group NF.

2. Correlations were then carried out among all the WISC-R subtest scores in both groups. For group DSF 61 of 66 correlations exceeded a p value of .05, while only 17 of 66 were significant for group NF.

3. Using a stepwise discriminant function, we ascertained whether the WISC-R subtest and IQ scores could be used to classify the EEG groups. We

found an 88% correct classification, with the Information subtest being the most powerful discriminator.

4. WISC-R scores were then used in a cluster analysis. Two groups emerged: a group with low intelligence scores and high subtest scatter, and children with high IQs. Of interest were the WISC-R characteristics of DSF children who appeared in the high IQ group as compared to the low IQ DSF group. Analyses showed that while there were general differences in average IQ scores, the profiles were the same across WISC-R subtests.

5. Interhemispheric correlations derived from the EEG waves were significantly higher for the DSF group.

6. Of the 19 perceived normal children in the study, 14 appeared in the group NF. Group DSF clearly contained a mixture of the dysfunctional categories.

With respect to the arguments and purposes of the present chapter, the study demonstrates that there are valid relationships between two different levels of measurement and that these relationships exist independently of the perceived disorders. The EEG groupings, free of bias, were quite different in terms of corresponding WISC-R data, and the WISC-R data in turn could predict the EEG categories. This finding should increase confidence in using these two measurement domains in developing a classification system. There is both process information and predictive power in the two sets.

From the electrophysiological data, there is evidence of a developmental difference. EEG slow frequency decreases with age and group DSF was significantly high. Interhemispheric correlations were also greater in the DSF children. Since current dogma states that with development there is increasing right–left differentiation, the higher subtest correlations in the DSF group, combined with the other data, suggest a tentative category of "brain organization difference." Calling it a "lag" is premature and unnecessary, since the issue can be resolved by retesting DSF children 2 or more years later (this study has recently been completed and data are currently being analyzed). It is possible that the DSF profile represents a developmental event that is different and will not change.

Based upon the data obtained in our initial study, we can hypothesize that DSF children have a brain that is less functionally differentiated with respect to the verbal and spatial skills assessed in the WISC-R. Reading, for example, may rely more upon the configurational features of words, and educational curricula might require less reliance upon linguistic devices. The latter suggestion is based upon the finding that their scores for most Performance items on the WISC-R were normal. However, whether this tentative category represents a maturational lag or a "stuck" syndrome will be resolved empirically, not by vote or label, and its future evolution or demise will be dependent upon other relevant data (such as determining whether there is a true physiological delay in terms of brain maturation indices). Additional measurement domains need to be explored in order to validate the initial findings. Additional DSF syndromes are also required because it is likely that within this group, there will be subgroups with variations along several dimensions, and a larger population will be needed in order to determine objectively how much heterogeneity exists within the category.

Assuming that the brain organization difference category does exist, the final question is, why does the category contain such diverse behavioral and cognitive dysfunctions, including a few perceived normals? We return to the opening discussions concerning the utility of perceived disorders in the mental health professions. These humanly based perceptions are real and represent the observed transactions between persons and their environments. The person brings to the environment a differently organized brain, one that interacts with mainstream demands in alternate ways. Within a secure and supportive environment, this person can learn not to steal hubcaps, but cannot learn to read, at least not at the same speed or with the same strategies as a mainstreamer. He or she is "caught" and labeled as learning disabled at ages 9 to 10 because the cumulative evidence indicates that maintaining the current educational course is not working. A child with the same syndrome who exists in an unstable environment or in a family where school performance is not considered important finds school to be a negative experience, gains social status and rewards elsewhere, and is caught with the hubcap and the label of juvenile delinquent before someone detects a reading disability. As part of any classification system that would strive for increased predictability, and etiological understanding, such situational and environmental data are critical. For example, the DSF "normals" in our initial analyses were mostly from economically and socially stable environments. Diagnostic systems, such as the DSM-III, should consider these factors as being just as important as the diffuse slow-frequency substrate because, in a sense, they guide the organic being toward certain end points. Ideally, it may be possible, given a diffuse slow-frequency profile combined with adequate sociometric and psychometric data, to classify a child as potentially normal, as potentially delinquent, as potentially learning disabled, and so on. The use of such verbiage reflects to some degree the interactive nature of organism and environmental circumstances, but more importantly, it reflects our technical capacity to effect changes in behavioral and cognitive modes. It is an evolving and unstable diagnostic and classification approach because as new information and syndromes are acquired, the structure of reality changes. Structuring classification systems mainly on the basis of the end point (juvenile delinquent, schizophrenic, learning disabled, etc.) does not seem to be as informative or as helpful to the child.

Conclusions: Overcoming Stasis

It seems that I've come full circle, beginning with the argument that our humanly based perceptions of behavior are unreliable and concluding with the argument that the organism–environment transaction, the perceived behavior, is as important as any other measurable domain. However, there are different ways of approaching the study and organization of behavior, and to be moderately paraphrastic, my purpose is not to bury behavioral and cognitive symptomology, but to praise its value within certain contexts and logical constraints. The opening arguments of the chapter focus upon the biases inherent in our construction of behaviorally based categories and concepts, and yet emphasize the immediate utility of such constructs. The use of behaviorally based perceptions to organize other levels of analysis is criticized and the characteristics of the DSM-III are examined in light of these various problems and limitations.

What is offered is a deanthropomorphizing and bootstrapping approach whereby valid multidimensional and multilevel sets provide the basis for organizing symptom clusters which are comparatively free from bias and, in fact, may organize reality in different but utilitarian ways. The field of numerical taxonomy as well as a less elegant but conceptually compatible strategy are discussed as potential bootstrap strategies.

There is little doubt that the bootstrap approach, if pursued in the mental health sciences, would seriously challenge traditional models and procedures as reflected in diagnostic systems such as the DSM-III. The plan initially requires rather unsettling requirements from the mental health practitioner—an initial admission of ignorance, an avoidance of diagnostic labels that connote cause and knowledge without supportive facts, an eclectic view with respect to diagnostic data, a tolerance for flexible and changing classification systems, and the recognition that the compelling symptomology (which is most likely the reason for the referral) is only a fragment of the realm of pertinent data and may not be the most important fragment. Egocentrism and stability suffer, but classification evolution and accuracy are gained with these requirements.

Immobility can be appealing. Printed statements and criteria are psychologically comforting, especially when ordained by committees of professionals. But the mental health sciences are still too immature with respect to their research findings and technical expertise to accept as valid these early attempts to organize "knowledge." Such attempts probably impede progress.

To close, I would like to relate an incident which happened to me several years ago. Circumstances required that I bring my younger son, then age 6, to my office for the day. Normally, I try to avoid all 6-year-olds as they are too active, too inquisitive, and seem to have no adaptive purpose in life. Since it was necessary that I chair a thesis defense, I collected chalk, paper, crayons, candy bars, and a machine-dispensed cup of alleged chicken broth with the hope that even a 6-year-old might be kept entertained for an hour or so. The thesis defense lasted longer than expected and when I returned to my office, I was met with an unusual sight. Situated neatly, in a semicircle, were stacks of papers and file folders. There was a pile of long yellow note sheets, short yellow note sheets, long white sheets, short white sheets, long medium brown file folders (emptied of course), short medium brown folders, manilla folders, and a very tall pile of typed sheets, standard size. A picture of my oldest son was stuffed inside an envelope with his name on it, a categorization decision with Freudian significance. All my filing cabinets were empty. "Hi dad, your office was a mess and I got it all straight."

I trust that our categorization procedures in the mental health sciences can proceed beyond this Aristotelian level of organization. If you are wondering about my reaction to my son's "categorization" exercise, I managed what can best be described as a horizontal smile, a "thank you," and silently prayed for the day when he would achieve cognitive Nirvana and could orgainze my files on the basis of the information they contained.

ACKNOWLEDGMENTS

The preparation of this chapter and a significant portion of the author's research has been supported by a grant from The National Science and Research Council of Canada.

The author would like to thank Dr. Pat Wainwright for her willingness to review the first draft. I am also deeply indebted to my friend and colleague, Richard Steffy, Dr. Alan Goebel of the Waterloo Board of Education, David Greenstein, Director of Educational and Family Services, Robert Ewart of the department shop, Alice Bast and the department staff, and the 550 children who have tolerated us.

REFERENCES

American Psychiatric Association. (1980). *Diagnostic and statistical manual of mental disorders* (3rd ed.). Washington, DC: Author.

Bartko, J. J., Strauss, J. S., & Carpenter, W. T. (1971). An evaluation of taxometric techniques for psychiatric data. *Classification Society Bulletin, 2,* 2–28.

Beckner, M. (1959). *The biological way of thought.* New York: Columbia University Press.

Blashfield, R. (1976). Mixture model tests of cluster analysis: Accuracy of four agglomerative hierarchical methods. *Psychological Bulletin, 83,* 377–388.

Bowen, M. (1961). A family concept of schizophrenia. In D. D. Jackson (Ed.), *The etiology of schizophrenia* (pp. 346–371). New York: Basic Books.

Braginsky, B., & Braginsky, D. (1974). *Mainstream psychology: A critique.* New York: Holt, Rinehart & Winston.

Cancro, R. (1972). The causes of schizophrenia. *Annals of Internal Medicine, 77,* 647–648.

Corning, W. C. (1975a). The problem with Porky Pig. In J. A. Dyal, W. C. Corning, & D. M. Willows (Eds.), *Readings in psychology: The search for alternatives* (pp. 206–210). New York: McGraw-Hill.

Corning, W. C. (1975b). Introduction to madness, or, what's in a name? In J. A. Dyal, W. C. Corning & D. M. Willows (Eds.), *Readings in psychology: The search for alternatives* (pp. 247–248). New York: McGraw-Hill.

Corning, W. C. (1977). Seeing is not believing. In I. Taylor (Ed.), *The Lakehead review* (Vol. 9, pp. 70–80).

Corning, W. C., Dyal, J. A., & Lahue, R. (1976). Intelligence: An invertebrate perspective. In R. Masterton, W. Hodos, & H. Jerison (Eds.), *Evolution, brain and behavior* (pp. 215–263). Hillsdale, NJ: Erlbaum.

Corning, W. C., & Steffy, R. A. (1979). Taximetric strategies applied to psychiatric classification. *Schizophrenic Bulletin, 5,* 294–305.

Corning, W. C., Steffy, R. A., & Chaprin, I. C. (1982). EEG slow frequency and WISC-R correlates. *Journal of Abnormal Child Psychology, 10,* 511–530.

Cuénod, M. M. (1972). Split-brain studies. Functional interaction between bilateral central nervous structures. In G. H. Bourne (Ed.), *The structure and function of nervous tissue* (Vol. 5). New York: Academic Press.

Douglass, A. B., & Hays, P. (1980). An objective study of relationships and discontinuities between paranoid schizophrenia and Kretschmer's syndrome or sensitive delusions of reference. *Acta Psychiatrica Scandinavica, 61,* 387–394.

Gergen, K. (1973). Social psychology as history. *Journal of Personality and Social Psychology, 26,* 309–320.

Goffman, E. (1961). *Asylums.* New York: Doubleday.

Halleck, S. (1971). *The politics of therapy.* New York: Science House Inc.

Hays, P. (1973). Aeiological theories in relation to research on clinical classification. *Canadian Psychiatric Association Journal, 18,* 254–256.

Hays, P. (1978). Taxonomic map of the schizophrenias, with special reference to puerperal psychosis. *British Medical Journal, 2,* 715–780.

Herrick, J. (1924). *The neurological foundations of animal behavior.* New York: Henry Holt.

John, E. R. (1967). *Mechanisms of memory.* New York: Academic Press.

John, E. R. (1972). Switchboard versus statistical theories of learning and memory. *Science,* 850–864.

John, E. R., Karmel, B. Z., Corning, W. C., Easton, P., Brown, D., Ahn, H., John, M., Harmony, T., Prichep, L., Toro, A., Gerson, I., Bartlett, F., Thatcher, R., Kaye, H., Valdes, P., & Schwartz, V. E. (1977). Neurometrics: Numerical taxonomy identifies different profiles of brain functions within groups of behaviorally similar people. *Science, 196,* 1393–1410.

Kendler, K. S., & Hays, P. (1981). Paranoid psychosis (delusional disorder) and schizophrenia. *Archives of General Psychiatry, 38,* 547–551.

Kendler, K. S., & Hays, P. (1982a). Familial and sporadic schizophrenia: A symptomatic, prognostic and EEG comparison. *American Journal of Psychiatry, 139,* 1557–1562.

Kendler, K. S., & Hays, P. (1982b). Schizophrenia with premorbid inferiority feelings. *Archives of General Psychiatry, 39,* 643–647.

Kirk, R. (1972). Perceptual defect and role handicap: A theory of the etiology of schizophrenia. In D. Hawkins & L. Pauling (Eds.), *Orthomolecular psychiatry.* (pp. 71–92). San Francisco, CA: Freeman.

Kuhn, T. S. (1962). *The structure of scientific revolutions.* Chicago, IL: University of Chicago Press.

Kuo, Z. Y. (1969). *The dynamics of behavior development: An epigenetic view.* New York: Random House.

Lahue, R. & Corning, W. C. (1975). Synthesis: A comparative look at vertebrates. In W. C. Corning, J. A. Dyal, & A. O. D. Willows (Eds.), *Invertebrate learning* (Vol. 3, pp. 147–177). New York: Plenum Press.

Langhorne, J. E., Loney, J. Paternite, C. E., & Bechtoldt, H. P. (1976). Childhood hyperkinesis: A return to the source. *Journal of Abnormal Psychology, 85,* 201–209.

Lehrman, D. S. (1953). A critique of Konrad Lorenz's theory of instinctive behavior. *Quarterly Review of Biology, 28,* 337–363.

Lehrman, D. S. (1955). The physiological basis of parental feeding behavior in the ring dove. *Behavior, 7,* 242–286.

Mercer, J., & Richardson, J. G. (1975). "Mental retardation" as a social problem. In N. Hobbs (Ed.), *Issues in the classification of children.* (pp. 463–486). San Francisco, CA: Jossey-Bass.

Millon, T. (1969). *Modern psychopathology.* Philadelphia, PA: Saunders.

Raines, P.M., Kituse, J. I., Duster, T., & Freidson, E. (1975). The labelling approach to deviance. In N. Hobbs (Ed.), *Issues in the classification of children.* (pp. 88–100). San Francisco, CA: Jossey-Bass.

Reich, W. (1983, January, 30). The world of soviet psychiatry. *New York Times Magazine.*

Rosner, B. S. (1970). Brain functions. *Annual Review of Psychology, 21,* 555–594.

Ross, A. O. (1980). *Psychological disorders of children.* New York: McGraw-Hill.

Sarbin, T. (1967). On the futility of the proposition that some people is labelled "mentally ill." *Journal of Consulting Psychology, 31,* 447–453.

Skeels, H. M. (1966). Adult status of children with contrasting early life experience, *Monographs of the Society for Research in Child Development, 31* (Serial No. 105).

Sneath, P., & Sokal, R. R. (1973). *Numerical taxonomy.* San Francisco, CA: Freeman.

Sokal, R. R. (1966). Numerical taxonomy. *Scientific American, 205,* 106–116.

Sokal, R. R., & Sneath, P. (1963). *Principles of numerical taxonomy.* San Francisco, CA: Freeman.

Szasz, T. (1970). *Ideology and insanity.* New York: Doubleday.

Thatcher, R., & John, E. R. (1977). *Functional neuroscience: Vol. 1. Foundations of cognitive processes.* Hillsdale, NJ: Brlbaum.

Thompson, R. F., & Spencer, W. A. (196). Habituation: A model phenomenon for the study of neuronal substrates of behavior. *Psychological Review, 73,* 16–43.

Tizard, J. (1962). The residential care of mentally handicapped children. In *Proceeding of the London conference on the scientific study of mental deficiency* (pp. 659–666).

Ungar, G. (1970). *Molcular mechanisms in memory and learning.* New York: Plenum Press.

Werry, J. S., & Quay, H. C. (1971). The prevalence of behavior symptoms in younger elementary school children. *American Journal of Orthopsychiatry, 41,* 136–143.

PART IV
METHODOLOGICAL SCHEMES

CHAPTER 15

Construct Validation Approach to Psychiatric Classification

Harvey A. Skinner

Introduction

Classification is a basic process man uses for ordering the universe, for simplifying a large amount of information through the placement of objects or events into definable subsets. Riese (1945) has argued that this economizing principle of the human intellect is essential for learning. In science, classifications generally evolve from the initial description of events to the formulation of underlying causal mechanisms or scientific theories (Hempel, 1965). Thus, scientific knowledge falls into different strata. The discovery of nonrandom patterns among observations, such as a clinical syndrome, stimulates attempts at explaining the causal mechanisms which are generally unobservable (e.g., a virus). This process continues in each era until an impasse is reached beyond which we lack either the imagination or technical resources to penetrate (Harré, 1972).

Perhaps the best example of this stratification process is the periodic system of elements which began with preliminary groupings such as potassium and sodium due to observations about their common characteristics, was then systematized by Mendeleev in his formulation of the periodic table, and was subsequently refined through understanding of atomic structure and chemical valency. Today, we appear on the verge of unveiling yet another stratum by finding evidence of the subatomic particle that would lend credence to a unified theory of the four fundamental forces of nature: electromagnetism, gravity, a "strong" force that holds atoms together, and a "weak" force that controls radioactive decay.

Harvey A. Skinner. Addiction Research Foundation, and Department of Preventive Medicine and Biostatistics, University of Toronto, Toronto, Ontario, Canada.

In contrast to these impressive developments, progress has been much slower in the classification and understanding of psychiatric disorders. This rate of progress may seem odd given the extensive history of psychiatric classification (Menninger, 1963) and the equally rich storehouse of psychiatric theories and research (Freedman, Kaplan, & Sadock, 1975). Moreover, during the past 20 years there has been an explosive growth in the use of statistical techniques such as cluster analysis to identify psychiatric disorders (Blashfield & Aldenderfer, 1978). Given the diverse attempts to improve psychiatric nosology, why have we failed to penetrate lower strata in our understanding of most psychiatric disorders?

Although various factors may be adduced as possible explanations, three issues should be emphasized. First, much of the theorizing in psychiatry, such as psychoanalytic theory, is not couched in a form that is readily open to empirical evaluation and falsification. In his doctrine of falsifiability, Popper (1972) argued that the essential aspect of a "scientific" theory is that it suggests refutation rather than proof. Empirical evidence is valuable for its power to falsify hypotheses. Theoretical conjectures and auxiliaries are *corroborated* to the extent that they have survived increasingly risky tests (Meehl, 1978). The need for more scientific theorization has been underscored by Birley (1975) who concluded that psychiatry is presently "littered with a mixture of irrefutable theories which explain a great deal, and refutable theories which explain only a very little" (p. 399).

A second reason involves problems with the measurement or recognition of a disorder. In recent years, considerable efforts have been directed toward upgrading the reliability of psychiatric diagnoses through the use of explicit operational definitions. An example of this evolution is the diagnostic criteria proposed by Feighner *et al.* (1972) that were extended in the Research Diagnostic Criteria (Spitzer, Endicott, & Robins, 1975) and further refined before incorporation in DSM-III (American Psychiatric Association, 1980). However, there is still considerable room for improvement in the standardization of criteria (Taylor, 1983; Zwick, 1983) and in the development of optimal diagnostic rules that are sensitive to shifts in base rates across clinical settings (Finn, 1982). Another troublesome issue concerns the construct validity of diagnostic techniques (Cronbach & Meehl, 1955). In brief, what confidence do we have that the diagnostic process (operational criteria) actually taps the putative disorder (hypothetical construct)? Ideally, each construct should possess *fundamental* measurement, that is, an explicit operational and theoretical meaning (Torgerson, 1958).

A third reason has to do with the conservative nature of official classifications. Traditional diagnostic systems such as DSM-III are based to a great extent on consensual agreement among expert clinicians that the diagnostic categories "make sense." The foremost reason for a broad-band classification is to allow health care professionals to communicate about clinically recognizable conditions (Spitzer, Sheehy, & Endicott, 1977). However, from his investigation of why a common classification of the mental disorders (ICD-6) had failed to gain acceptance, Stengel (1959) concluded that the root of the problem was different assumptions about etiology by various schools of psychiatry. Stengel (1959) recommended deleting all etiological implications and advocated a focus on unambiguous operational definitions of diagnostic categories. Similarly, etiological concepts were downplayed in DSM-III in order to facilitate its acceptance by clinicians from different schools of thought (e.g., psychodynamic vs. behavioral vs. biological). In justifying this tack, Spitzer (1980) argued that "clinicians can agree on the identification of mental disorders on the basis of their clinical manifestations without agreeing on how the disturbances come about" (p. 7).

Clearly, there are opposing forces in the development of psychiatric classifications, especially an official system such as the DSM. If truly significant advances are to be made in the upcoming DSM-IV, then they will likely come from developments in theory and etiology. However, the history of psychiatric classification strongly reinforces the downplaying of theoretical/ etiological elements in order to facilitate clinical acceptance. These forces may interact to cause a trade-off between scientific quality and clinical acceptance of the diagnostic system (Skinner & Blashfield, 1982). Thus, a key challenge for DSM-IV is to achieve a synergism between theory formulation and empirical classification methods, while at the same time fostering clinical acceptance of the diagnostic system. This chapter discusses issues that are vital for achieving these aims.

Theoretician's Dilemma

Most of the current diagnostic concepts in psychiatry have resulted from careful observations by clinicians of a small number of "classic" cases (e.g., Kraepelin, 1899). Schizophrenia, manic-depression illness, paranoid psychosis, obsessional states, anxiety neurosis, hysteria, and senile dementia were all derived by clinical observations and inferential reasoning without the assistance of statistical methods or predetermined theoretical models (Garside & Roth, 1978; Meehl, 1979). After the recognition of a clinical syndrome, attention generally focuses upon prognosis and therapy; that is, does knowledge of the syndrome help one decide what form of treatment will reduce disability as well as predict the future course and outcome? Following careful research, increased confidence may be placed upon the diagnosis of a disorder and its treatment and management (e.g., pharmacotherapy of endogenous depression with tricyclic antidepressants). Ultimately, the emphasis shifts toward the construction of an explanatory theory for understanding the etiology and pathogenesis of the disorder. However, as Feinstein (1977) points out, etiological proof for most psychiatric disorders presents formidable problems. This statement applies to many other areas of medicine as well. For instance, insulin provides a powerful therapy for the management of diabetes despite limits in our knowledge about the etiology of this disorder.

Thus, the traditional sequence in the development of a diagnostic concept begins with a provisional description of the clinical syndrome, shifts to an emphasis on examining prognosis and therapy, and finally progresses to developing a theoretical understanding of its etiology and pathogenesis. This sequence raises questions about how important theory is to the initial development of a psychiatric classification. A fundamental issue is the extent to which hypothesized constructs are invoked instead of a direct description of behavior itself. Whereas the behavioral approach involves a direct sampling of criterion behavior (Taylor, 1983), theory-based models first assess hypothetical constructs and then use them to predict criterion behaviors such as treatment outcome. Goldfried and Kent (1972) have argued that the behavioral approach is more useful, since it requires fewer inferences and is directly amenable to empirical analyses. This contrast between approaches exemplifies the theoretician's dilemma. According to Hempel (1965), "Why should science resort to the assumption of hypothesized entities when it is interested in establishing predictive and explanatory connections among observables? Would it not be sufficient . . . to search for a system of general laws mentioning only observables?" (p. 179). In brief, can this theoretical detour be avoided?

Certainly with the mature sciences there are compelling examples of how theoretical constructs enable the establishment of predictive order among complex observations. In medicine, this development can be seen in the shift from descriptive (symptomatic) to more theoretical (etiological) terms and in the treatment of the "cause" of a disease rather than its overt symptoms. Classic examples include tertiary syphilis, chronic tuberculosis, and pernicious anemia, which can have diverse manifestations among major organ systems. Nevertheless, a single causative mechanism has been identified for each disease, specifically: the spirochete, tubercle bacillus, and vitamin B_{12} deficiency, respectively.

In contrast, with most psychiatric disorders the etiology is unknown. Zigler and Phillips (1961) warned against the dangers of premature inference and advocated an accelerated program of descriptive research. They argued that etiological considerations should represent an end point as opposed to the beginning of a psychiatric classification. Cluster analytic studies of psychopathology provide an excellent example of this empirical tradition. However, the naive empiricism inherent in much of this research has been criticized (Blashfield, 1980; Skinner, 1981). Cluster analytic studies have tended to be largely descriptive in orientation and are analogous in many respects to the empirical approach to test construction exemplified by the Minnesota Multiphasic Personality Inventory (MMPI) (Wiggins, 1973). Too often, a clustering algorithm has been applied to a convenient date set as an end in itself. Few attempts have been made to determine whether the derived types have prognostic value with respect to treatment outcome or to integrate the types with previous research.

Just as Loevinger (1957) has argued the need for developing a theoretical model to underlie an assessment instrument, similar arguments can be made for integrating an empirically based classification within a scientific theory. The major issues are how and at what rate we should progress from a descriptive orientation to an emphasis on theoretical entities in psychiatric classifications. The principles of construct validation as discussed by various writers provide a powerful methodology for the development and evaluation of theory-based classifications (Campbell & Fiske, 1959; Cronbach & Meehl, 1955; Embretson, 1983; Jackson, 1971; Loevinger, 1957; Messick, 1981).

Construct Validation Framework

Although various criteria have been proposed for the evaluation of psychiatric classifications (Blashfield & Draguns, 1976a, 1976b), there is a need for an integrated paradigm. Figure 15-1 presents such a framework based on the principles of construct validation (Skinner, 1981), where emphasis is placed on the continual interplay between the theory development and empirical analyses. A key tenet is that a psychiatric classification should be viewed as a scientific theory that is open to empirical falsification (Meehl, 1979; Popper, 1972).

In brief, the theory formulation component of Figure 15-1 involves a precise definition of the typal constructs, their functional linkages or nomological network, and hypothetical relationships to external variables such as treatment outcome. Central to theory development are the use of "ideal type" constructs and structural models. Second, the internal validation component entails the choice of relevant statistical techniques for deriving the

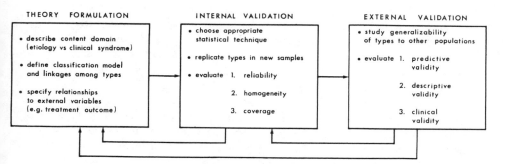

Figure 15-1. *Synopsis of the construct validation approach to classification research.*

empirical taxonomy and an evaluation of the diagnostic system's reliability, homogeneity, and coverage. Third, the external validation component involves a series of studies that address the prognostic value of the diagnostic types as well as their clinical meaningfulness, descriptive validity, and generalizability to other populations and settings. All three components interact to form a program of research in which successive refinements are made to both the empirical typology and the underlying theoretical model. This framework is meant to serve as a metatheory of classification, which should have heuristic value for the development and evaluation of particular diagnostic systems.

Ideal Type Constructs

The use of ideal type constructs in theory construction has a considerable history (Hempel, 1965; Jung, 1921/1971; Wood, 1969). Each ideal type may be defined as a hypothetical pattern of attributes (e.g., clinical signs and symptoms, personality characteristics, history, family background) that is characteristic of a subset of individuals in the population. Ideal types are mental constructs that may be used to summarize observed characteristics among relatively homogenous groups of individuals. For example, the schizoid taxon (Meehl, 1962) represents a class of individuals who are postulated to have a particular genetic constitution that predisposes them to cognitive slippage, social aversiveness, anhedonia, and ambivalence. Certain ideal types are hypothesized in a population with each member being more or less related to each type (Skinner, 1979a). In an interesting metaphor, Kretschmer (1925) has termed this mixture the "constitutional alloy."

The ideal type construct is analogous to the prototype view of psychiatric diagnosis advanced by Cantor, Smith, French, and Mezzick (1980). It is assumed that membership in a prototype is defined by correlated features, not the necessary presence of all defining features. This issue has been widely discussed in biological classification through the distinction between monothetic and polythetic groups (Sneath & Sokal, 1973). With monothetic groups, a unique set of features is both sufficient and necessary for membership in the diagnostic category. For example, a manic-affective disorder should include distinct periods with a predominantly elevated mood as well as symptoms of increased activity, talkativeness, flight of ideas, inflated self-esteem, distractibility, and decreased need for sleep. According to the classical view of categorization, a patient must have *all* defining features in order to receive the diagnosis (Cantor *et al.*, 1980).

In contrast, with polythetic groups, individuals are placed together that have a large number of shared characteristics, but no single feature is essential to group membership or is sufficient to make an individual a member of the diagnostic category. The polythetic or prototype view resolves certain problems concerning the existence of borderline cases, heterogeneity among members of a diagnostic category, and variation among category members with respect to their typicality (Cantor *et al.*, 1980). For instance, Jung (1921/1971) theorized that individuals classified according to the broad types of introversion or extraversion will also vary within each type according to the psychological functions of thinking, feeling, sensation, and intuition. Each function will be present, more or less, in a given individual. Jung (1921/1971) argued that "there can never be a pure type in the sense that it possesses only one mechanism with the complete atrophy of the other" (p. 6). Thus, the ideal type concept is better able to accommodate real patients who do not fit neatly into rigidly defined categories (Strauss *et al.*, 1979).

The metaphysical status of ideal type constructs can vary according to contrasting paradigms (Harré, 1972). First, a construct may serve only the pragmatic role of connecting facts into systematic knowledge, without having an independent meaning. For instance, in the science of mechanics it is possible to remove the construct of force and still explain the phenomena of motion using a different construction such as energy. Similarly, clinical observations would be summarized in terms of ideal type constructs that have only systemic existence by being grounded in a nomological network. Messick (1981) has termed this perspective the constructivist view. Alternatively, the theoretical construct may be seen as an essential part of understanding the phenomena and as having real existence. An example from pathology is the concept of virus, which is a microorganism that is hypothesized to cause transmission of certain diseases. One cannot eliminate the concept of virus without introducing a radically different conception of the disease. This perspective is called the realist view by Messick (1981), who gives as an example, Cattell's (1957) theory of source traits as causes of observed consistencies in behavior. Finally, Messick (1981) discusses the constructive-realist view which assumes that causal entities exist outside the mind, but also purports that they can only be understood in terms of constructs that summarize overt behavior.

Structural Models

Various models have been used for describing relationships among psychiatric disorders. These structures represent quite different notions about what constitutes a "type," and may serve as a basis for specifying linkages among ideal type constructs (nomological network). This section will briefly review four basic structures and then discuss several hybrid models that hold considerable promise.

Hierarchical structures classify individuals into subsets which are themselves successively classified into groups at higher levels in the hierarchy. This approach is popular in psychiatry because it permits differentiation among clinical syndromes according to nested categories, and yet the hierarchies are relatively easy to learn and use. With respect to differential diagnosis, hierarchical structures resemble decision trees. Once a particular branch has been selected, one need only consider the limited number of categories at that node. Hence, a hierarchical structure can summarize a substantial amount of information in a readily usable form. For example, a four-tiered hierarchy of depression (Figure 15-2) has evolved from research by psychiatrists at Washington University, St. Louis (Feighner *et al.*, 1972; Winokur, Codaret, Baker, & Dorzab, 1975). The general category of affective disorder is differentiated into a primary disorder (depressive or manic illness that is not preceded by other psychiatric disorders) and a secondary disorder (illness preceded by another psychiatric disorder or accompanied by a life-threatening physical illness). Then, primary affective disorders are subdivided into unipolar (depression only) and bipolar (depression and mania) types. Based on family history and age at illness onset, the unipolar disorder is further divided into either a depression spectrum or a pure depression illness.

In contrast to the nesting of syndromes within a hierarchy, dimensional systems display relationships among individuals in a multidimensional space. This approach emphasizes quantitative variation rather than all-or-none alterations. In other words, a particular disorder, such as the alcohol dependence syndrome (Edwards & Gross, 1976), is held to exist in degrees, and the severity of the disorder is measured by an individual's location on that dimension (Skinner & Allen, 1982). In the classification of depression, dimensional systems have been described by both Kendell (1968) and Eysenck (1970). For instance, Kendell (1968) proposed a single dimension that contrasts psychotic from neurotic depression. This psychotic/neurotic continuum evolved from Kendell's unsuccessful attempts to demonstrate a valid boundary between the two illnesses (Kendell, 1976). On the other hand, Eysenck (1970) argued that the two independent dimensions of psychoticism and neuroticism are necessary to explain variation in symptomatology exhibited by depressed patients.

Categorical approaches are characterized by internally cohesive, nonoverlapping classes; that is, an individual either does or does not have a particular disorder. In contrast to the quantitative nature of dimensional systems, categorical structures assume qualitative differences among disorders. Within a dimensional framework, discrete types should be identifi-

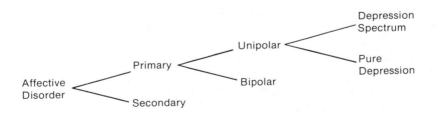

Figure 15-2. *Four-tiered hierarchy of depression.*

able by marked areas of discontinuity between the different types. This structure is best illustrated by the classic medical model where a specific disease agent is proposed as a causative mechanism for a disease. In the classification of depression, the number of categories has ranged from a single depressive illness to five distinct types (Kendell, 1976). Of particular note are two systems that were derived empirically using cluster analysis. Overall, Hollister, Johnson, and Pennington (1966) identified three subtypes: anxious-tense, hostile, and retarded depression, whereas Paykel (1971, 1972) found four categories: psychotic, anxious, hostile, and young depressives with personality disorder. Both studies found that certain subtypes responded better to a different form of drug therapy.

Circumplex structures have been popular, especially in the literature on interpersonal behavior. Here, variation among individuals appears to be continuous in the form of a closed circle or circumplex (Guttman, 1954). Figure 15-3 illustrates a perfect circumplex of interpersonal variables described by Wiggins (1979). In this schema, variables adjacent to each other share features in common (e.g., cold and aloof), whereas logically opposed concepts are located opposite each other (e.g., warm vs. cold). The two-dimensional circular ordering of interpersonal variables has a history that

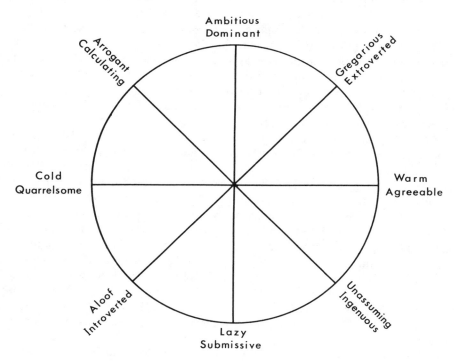

Figure 15-3. *A circumplex model of interpersonal behavior.*

may be traced as far back as Galen's four temperatures (sanguine, choleric, melancholic, and phlegmatic) described in the second century A.D. Moreover, similar models of interpersonal behavior have been proposed for the study of parents and children (Benjamin, 1974), adults (Leary, 1957), psychotic patients (Lorr, Klett, & McNair, 1963), college students (Stern, 1970), and marital and family systems (Olson, Sprenkle, & Russell, 1979). Thus, the circumplex structure has proved to be quite popular because of its descriptive power and apparent ubiquity in diverse areas of normal and abnormal functioning.

In review, it is important to recognize that the four basic structures represent quite different conceptual approaches to psychiatric disorders, and a substantial body of literature surrounds the controversy over which structure is most valid (Kendell, 1975; Maxwell, 1972; Strauss, 1973). A perplexing problem is that alternative models are often applied in the same area with plausible evidence offered in support of each. One road out of the controversy is to consider hybrid models that integrate key elements of the basic structures. The merits of this strategy are well illustrated in physics where the theory of quantum mechanics resulted from an integration of the seemingly disparate wave theory and particle theory of light. Degerman (1972) has provided an excellent description of structural models that result from either the composition or nesting of structures. Two of the more promising combinations include the class-quantitative and radex models.

In the class-quantitative approach, quantitative dimensions are superimposed on discrete categories; that is, individuals are classified into discrete groups, but there is quantitative variation within each group. This model is evident in the development of multiaxial systems for psychiatric diagnoses (Mezzich, 1979). By including separate axes for phenomenology, etiology, course, and social functioning, these systems allow one to differentiate the presenting clinical syndrome from etiology and precipitating factors. Certainly, the best current example of a multiaxial system is DSM-III. Earlier versions of the DSM had been criticized because a patient was "forced" into a single diagnostic category. In contrast, the multiaxial system of DSM-III allows primary and secondary diagnoses as well as the potential for multiple determinants by including physical (medical) disorders, psychosocial stressors, and level of adaptive functioning. The clinical syndromes on Axes I and II have an implicit hierarchical structure. For example, the major class of Schizophrenic disorders is divided into five subtypes: disorganized, catatonic, paranoid, undifferentiated, and residual. Along with medical disorders on Axis III, the first three axes represent qualitative classes. On the other hand, the remaining axes involve quantitative ratings of the severity of psychosocial stressors (Axis IV) and level of adaptive functioning in the past year (Axis V). Thus, DSM-III is a hybrid of hierarchical (categorical) and dimensional structures.

The radex structure results from the nesting of quantitative variation within a generalized circumplex (Degerman, 1972). The qualitative aspect is reflected in the angular variation among vectors that are grouped in a hyperspheroid. The quantitative aspect is depicted by the length of the nested radius vectors. An example of the radex structure is the vector model of disease states in clinical medicine proposed by Sneath (1975). The course of a disorder is represented by the movement of a vector or point within a multidimensional space of clinical variables. Sneath (1975) draws a distinction between the type of disorder and the severity of its clinical symptoms. Imagine a three-dimensional cube where the center of the space (origin) defines the normal population (Figure 15-4). Normal individuals constitute a swarm of points that are proximal to the origin. As an individual becomes ill, his point moves away from the origin. One can envisage this process as an

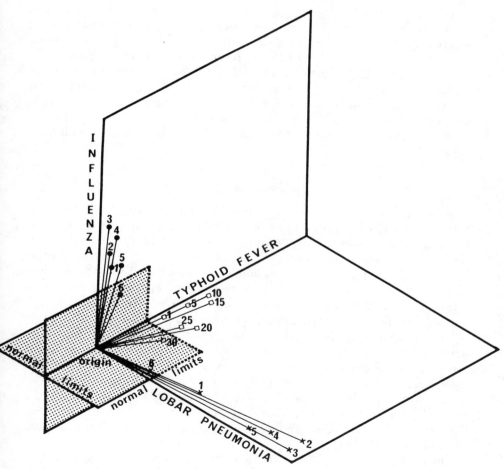

Figure 15-4. *Vector model of diseases in clinical medicine. The vectors depict a patient's status at different days (numbered) in the course of the disease.*

arrow (vector) traveling away from the center of the cube. The length of the vector (distance from the origin) yields a quantitative measure of symptom severity, whereas the direction of the vector (angular location from the origin) denotes the type of clinical disorder.

For instance, each dimension in Figure 15-4 could represent one of the three classical fevers: influenza, lobar pneumonia, and typhoid. The clinical variables which define the disorders could be the vital signs of pulse rate, temperature, and respiration rate. Since influenza is typically a brief fever of rapid onset and fairly quick resolution, one could expect an individual's vector to move up fairly quickly near the influenza axis and subsequently return to the origin in a short time course. However, with acute lobar pneumonia the vector would move out rapidly near the pneumonia axis and measure a considerable distance from the origin to display the critical severity of clinical signs. Finally, typhoid fever is characterized by slow onset and resolution of the clinical signs, with generally only a moderate level of severity. Hence, the vector would gradually move out near the typhoid axis to a moderate length and then slowly return to the origin. For illustrative purposes, Figure 15-4 depicts the three-dimensional model with vectors that represent hypothetical patients at different days. Thus, the radex model provides an important heuristic for representing relationships among syndromes at one point in time (cross-sectional data) as well as for depicting quantitative changes in signs and symptoms during the course of a disorder (longitudinal data).

Construct Modeling

In a recent article on construct validation, Embretson (1983) differentiated between two approaches to construct modeling research: construct representation and nomothetic span. Although Embretson (1983) focused on test theory, her discussion is relevant to classification research. Construct representation stems from an information processing paradigm and involves identifying processes that underlie item responses. The goal is to decompose a task into fundamental processes or strategies. For example, Cliff (1977) derived a model for decomposing the response to a personality item into two processes: (a) an internalized schema that the individual uses to interpret the item, and (b) a self-image that the individual wants to present. Whereas construct representation research focuses on task variability, nomothetic span is assessed by individual differences data. Nomothetic span pertains to the network of relationships of a test to other variables. A nomological network would have a wide span to the extent that individual differences on the test correlate strongly with theoretically related measures under a range of conditions.

In the classification of psychiatric disorders, nomothetic span involves the richness of theoretical relationships among ideal type constructs, their operational definitions, and linkages with external variables. Nomothetic span research would focus on issues such as comparing alternative structural models as a basis for understanding relationships among disorders (e.g., Kendell, 1968, 1976), estimating the reliability of diagnostic procedures (e.g., Grove, Andreasen, McDonald-Scott, Keller, & Shapiro, 1981, Spitzer, Forman, & Nee, 1979), elucidating factors that influence the process of making a diagnosis (e.g., Morey, 1980; Robins, Helzer, Croughan, & Ratcliff, 1981), and evaluating the prognostic implications of different conceptions of a disorder with respect to treatment outcome (e.g., Kendell, Brockington, & Leff, 1979). Thus, emphasis is placed on individual differences regarding the ideal type constructs and the degree to which these individual differences are manifested in theoretically relevant criterion variables.

Construct representation, on the other hand, concerns the system processes (J. G. Miller, 1978) involved in the development, maintenance, and resolution of disorders. Attention is focused on the continuum between healthy and abnormal states as well as the biological, psychological, and social factors involved in system changes (e.g., Engel, 1977, 1980). For instance, a large body of literature has addressed pathways between an individual's exposure to recent life change and the future onset of illness (Barrett, 1979). In the domain of schizophrenia, Zubin and Spring (1977) have proposed a higher order construct of "vulnerability" which interacts with challenging events to produce (or prevent) an episode of the disorder. Indeed, Buchsbaum and Haier (1983) have speculated that psychiatric diagnosis and treatment may be metamorphosized in the future by a shift from systems based on clinical symptoms to alternative concepts such as vulnerability that may be assessed using biological markers.

Internal Validation

The second component of the construct validation framework (Figure 15-1) involves testing the goodness of fit of the theoretical model to data, and then evaluating internal validity properties of the diagnostic procedure, including its reliability, coverage, homogeneity, and robustness (Skinner, 1981). Multivariate statistical methods, such as cluster analysis, have become increasingly popular for internal validation research. Cluster analysis techniques were originally derived to identify "naturally" occurring subgroups in the population of interest (Everitt, 1974; Sneath & Sokal, 1973). However, applications of these methods have had limited impact on psychiatric classification, in part due to the naive empiricism of much of this research (Blashfield, 1980; Skinner & Blashfield, 1982). Recently, there has been a growing emphasis on confirmatory techniques that would allow the comparison of a priori defined structural models (e.g., Hubert & Baker, 1977; Hubert & Subkoviak, 1979), the statistical testing of a conjectured ideal type (e.g., Golden, 1982), and the fitting of hybrid structural models (e.g., Carroll, 1976; Skinner, 1979a). These advancements are consistent with a major revolution that has taken place in the past 15 years with the development of confirmatory techniques for causal modeling (Bentler, 1980). Indeed, multi-variate statistical techniques for confirmatory research provide a powerful technology for addressing the pivotal links between theory and data.

Paul Meehl's work is one of the best illustrations of a synergism between theory formulation and statistical testing of hypotheses. In 1962, Meehl proposed a theory of schizophrenia in which he postulated an ideal type termed the schizoid taxon. According to Meehl (1962), these individuals have a particular genetic constitution that predisposes them to cognitive slippage, social aversiveness, anhedonia, and ambivalence. The genetic aberration is hypothesized to alter single cell functioning and produce an integrative neural defect. Using the MMPI item pool, Golden and Meehl (1979) evaluated three statistical methods for detecting the schizoid taxon, which produced comparable base-rate estimates in a hospitalized psychiatric sample. Although Golden and Meehl (1979) derived an "optimal" 7-item scale for detecting the schizoid taxon, other investigators have raised questions about the diagnostic accuracy and interpretation of this scale (H. R. Miller, Streiner, & Kahgee, 1982). Since MMPI responses are far removed causally from any genetic source, further research may find more powerful indicators of the schizoid taxon among physiological and neurological variables. An important outgrowth of this research is the development of a statistical model for testing the substantive conjecture regarding the existence of an ideal type or taxon. The methodology also includes consistency tests for assessing auxiliary conjectures about assumptions of the model (Golden, 1982; Meehl, 1973).

Another approach is to begin with an explicit structural model of psychopathology, such as the radex structure discussed above in relation to Sneath's (1975) vector model of disease. For example, Skinner has proposed a generalized principal components model which draws a distinction between the severity of maladjustment and the particular clinical syndrome or ideal type (Skinner, 1978, 1979a, 1979b; Skinner & Sheu, 1982). In an application of this model to MMPI data, Skinner and Jackson (1978) identified three superordinate types: Neurotic characterized by somatic complaints, depression, and an immature or egocentric orientation; Psychotic evidenced by unusual thought content, inappropriate affect, emotional agitation, and suspiciousness; and Sociopathic marked by a character disorder and tendency toward social extraversion. Each syndrome defines an orthogonal axis in Figure 15-5. The three types are hypothesized to reflect fundamental ways in which individuals differ, with each type having certain biological and environmental determinants. These dimensional-based types have a historical lineage that may be traced through Eysenck (1970) to Jung (1921/1971) and Wundt (1903). For instance, Eysenck (1970) has argued that neuroticism is associated with the inherited degree of lability in the autonomic nervous system, whereas extraversion is related to the extent of excitation or inhibition in the central nervous system.

The location of an individual's vector in Figure 15-5 is determined by MMPI profile shape, that is, the pattern of ups and downs across the 13

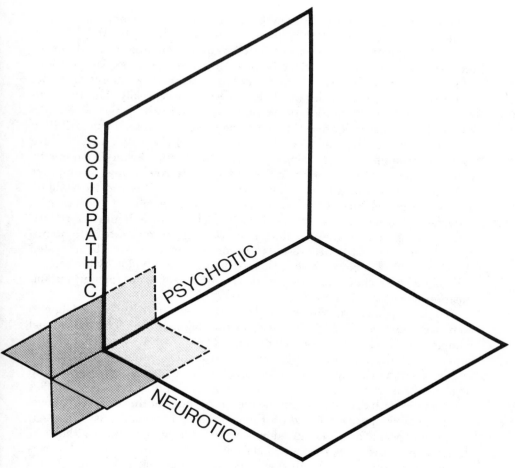

Figure 15-5. *Three-dimensional model of psychopathology.*

clinical scales. Three shape parameters are generated that denote the quantitative resemblance of an individual to each syndrome and also give the coordinates for plotting a vector in Figure 15-5. Another important parameter of the model is profile elevation, which is the mean score across all 13 MMPI clinical scales. This parameter is used to form a fourth axis that describes the degree of symptom severity. It is postulated that elevation provides a more situationally determined index of general maladjustment. Thus, by distinguishing profile shape from elevation, the model integrates aspects of the trait (clinical syndrome) and situational (symptom severity) approaches to the study of psychopathology (Bowers, 1972; Mischel, 1973). Skinner (1984) presents evidence based on longitudinal data that supports this differentiation between parameters. Also, the model has proved to be a powerful framework for comparing MMPI profiles from diverse clinical and normal groups (Skinner, 1979b, 1984; Skinner & Jackson, 1978).

A third illustration of theory-based research is the use of causal modeling (Bentler, 1980). This multivariate procedure attempts to explain relationships (covariances) among observed variables in terms of a theoretical model comprised of latent variables (e.g., ideal types). Conceptually, causal modeling represents an integration of factor analysis and path analysis methods; that is, latent variables are estimated using the common factor model, then structural relationships or "causal" paths among these latent variables are evaluated using linear regression equations. Maximum likelihood parameter estimates and goodness-of-fit indices may be derived using a computer program such as LISREL (Jöreskog & Sorbom, 1978). In a nested fashion, alternative models may be tested statistically to determine which model(s) provides a plausible representation of the causal structure (Bentler & Bonett, 1980). Causal modeling is appealing, since one may incorporate both nomothetic span and construct representation concepts in the models being tested (Embretson, 1983). Nevertheless, this sophisticated methodology is of recent origin and researchers must be cautious about potential misapplications and misinterpretations (Cliff, 1983).

For example, Huba, Wingard, and Bentler (1981) used causal modeling to compare two models of adolescent drug use (Figure 15-6). The first model (simplex) is based on the research of Kandel (1975) who argues that adolescents initiate drug use in a fairly invariant sequence beginning with nonuse and progressing through stages of alcohol use, cannabis use, and on to hard drug use (e.g., barbiturates, heroin). The use of one type of drug implies involvement with drugs lower on the hierarchy, but not those at steps above. An alternative approach based on the common factor model assumes that the use of specific drugs is caused by several underlying latent variables. As depicted in Figure 15-6, the two models differ only in that the simplex uses one less path (parameter). Huba *et al.* (1981) found that either model provided a plausible representation of the observed data, although the simplex model might be preferred because it is more parsimonious. In subsequent analyses, Huba and Bentler (1982) tested various models of psychosocial factors (e.g., rebelliousness, deviance in intimate support systems, peer pressure) as "causes" or antecedents to the use of certain drugs.

Building on theories of interpersonal behavior, Benjamin (1974) proposed a structural analysis of social behavior model (SASB). The two major axes of the model, labeled affiliation and interdependence, are used to describe interpersonal behaviors in three planes: (*a*) focus on the other person, (*b*) focus on the self, and (*c*) focus on introjected behaviors. Since psychiatric diagnoses tend to emphasize interpersonal behavior, McLemore and Benjamin (1979) proposed this model as an alternative to DSM-III. Various studies have examined the internal validity of the SASB model. Support for its construct validity was evidenced by an item factor analysis in which the empirical item loadings were highly congruent with their hypothesized loca-

Stepwise (simplex) model of drug use

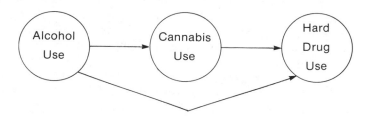

Recursive (common factor) model of drug use

Figure 15-6. *Alternative models of adolescent drug use.*

tion on the two major axes. The utility of the SASB model for family therapy has been illustrated by Benjamin (1977), and the SASB model has been combined with Markov procedures to describe social processes in a dyadic interaction (Benjamin, 1979). Although further research is needed on the external validation component, Benjamin's work is an excellent illustration of a classification system that is based on an explicit structural model.

A final illustration of a theory-based classification is the typology of personality disorders proposed by Millon (1969) and elaborated upon by Millon (1981). Eight personality patterns are hypothesized to emerge from an individual's social learning history: schizoid–asocial, avoidant, dependent–submissive, histrionic–gregarious, narcissistic, antisocial–aggressive, compulsive–conforming, and aggressive–negativistic. In addition, three syndromes are described which represent a more chronic or periodically severe pathology: schizotypal–schizoid, borderline–cycloid, and paranoid. Millon's (1981) typology of personality coping patterns corresponds closely to the personality disorders contained in DSM-III. Several diagnostic instruments have been developed based on this classification model. The most recent instrument, Millon Clinical Multiaxial Inventory, or MCMI (Millon, 1982), followed the construct validation paradigm described by Loevinger (1957) and Jackson (1971). The MCMI manual provides a detailed account of the theory specification, internal validity analyses, and external validation studies. The comprehensive work by Millon provides an excellent demonstration of a classification system that has been developed according to a construct validation framework.

Clinical Acceptance

The third stage of the construct validation framework (Figure 15-1) involves an ongoing series of studies aimed at establishing the prognostic usefulness of the diagnostic concepts, as well as their descriptive validity, clinical relevance, and generalizability to different populations and settings (Skinner, 1981). This research would be motivated by testable hypotheses from the theory formulation stage and would extend the nomothetic span of theoretical concepts to include external criterion variables. For instance, one could conduct randomized trials to determine whether certain subtypes of schizophrenia respond better to individualized treatment approaches postulated at various phases of the disorder (Carpenter & Heinrichs, 1981). Predictive validity is of immediate concern to clinicians. Kendell (1975) argued that "in the last resort all diagnostic concepts stand or fall by the strength of the prognostic and therapeutic implications they embody" (p. 40). At the same time, it is unlikely that a classification of psychiatric disorders will be widely used if clinicians do not feel conversant with the diagnostic concepts. Unfortunately, issues related to clinical acceptance have often been neglected in classification research (Skinner & Blashfield, 1982).

Davis and Salasin (1975) discuss various models for research utilization. Traditional classification systems such as DSM-III have tended to follow a social interaction model. Through an emphasis on face-to-face contacts, this approach is sensitive to human relationships and communication networks that are vital for the dissemination phase of a new classification system. The extensive field trials of DSM-III were aimed at providing data about the way in which the diagnostic concepts would be used. These field trials had the powerful effect of allowing clinicians to make input on the final version of the DSM-III.

In contrast, alternative approaches to psychiatric classification such as cluster analysis research have tended to follow the research, development, and diffusion model, which assumes that a target audience of clinicians will accept an innovation when they see it as an improvement over competitors. From this perspective, clinicians are viewed as a relatively passive group of consumers. Although there has been considerable activity in generating statistically based classifications, the clinical consumers have been less than ecstatic about the product (Skinner & Blashfield, 1982). Too little attention has been given to the dissemination of research findings in a format that is readily seen to be of value to clinicians in their practice. One message is clear. Regardless of the scientific quality of a new diagnostic system, this work will have limited impact unless concerted efforts are directed at fostering clinical acceptance through successive field trials.

In addition, attention should be given to evaluating and improving the clinical validity of a proposed classification. Clinical validity refers to the perceived meaningfulness and relevance of diagnostic concepts to clinicians. According to Overall and Woodward (1975), clinical validity "involves the extent to which the empirically derived types 'ring true' in clinical experience" (p. 215). One approach to evaluating clinical validity is through experiments on clinical judgment. Reed and Jackson (1975) used a model of inferential accuracy to study processes involved in judgments about behavior of prototypes that were drawn from empirically derived patient types. Cantor *et al.* (1980) studied the degree of consensus in clinical features that characterize diagnostic categories. They found that diagnostic prototypes at lower levels in the hierarchy (e.g., paranoid vs. schizo-affective) shared more features in common than prototypes at a higher level (e.g., schizophrenia vs. affective disorder). Also, clinicians diagnosed atypical patients with less accuracy and confidence than more typical patients. Clinical judgment experiments provide valuable information not only about the descriptive power and meaning of diagnostic concepts (ideal types), but also about inferential processes involved in making diagnostic decisions.

Another strategy for evaluating clinical validity is to explore how clinicians organize diagnostic prototypes, and then compare these "conceptual maps" with empirical relationships among real patients. Overall and Woodward (1975) found moderate agreement in a cross-classification of 2,000 real patients with eight prototypes (e.g., florid thinking disorder) based on psychiatrists' conceptions. A key factor underlying discrepancies was that conceptual prototypes tended to magnify distinguishing features and minimize overlapping characteristics with other diagnostic groups. In brief, the conceptual prototypes tended to be more differentiated than real patients. This tendency was clearly demonstrated by Strauss *et al.* (1979) who found that real patients did not fit neatly into the conceptual categories. They concluded that the lack of congruence between real patients and diagnostic categories (conceptual maps) is a major source of dissatisfaction that clinicians have with current psychiatric nomenclature.

Conclusion

From early beginnings, psychiatric classifications have generated much disenchantment and controversy (Menninger, 1963). The recent publication of DSM-III has stimulated yet another round of criticisms and proposed solutions (e.g., Eysenck, Wakefield, & Friedman, 1983; Taylor, 1983). DSM-III, with its emphasis on operational definitions and multiaxial framework, has proved to be more researchable than previous editions. Hopefully, the growing body of research will provide a stepping-stone leading to major improvements in the upcoming DSM-IV. The construct validation paradigm described in this chapter can play a vital role in upgrading the scientific quality of classification research (a) by facilitating an evaluation of the strengths and weaknesses of a given classification, (b) by pointing out areas that require further development, and (c) by encouraging the comparison of alternative systems. However, it would be naive to expect that this research by itself could generate a new classification that would have widespread clinical acceptance. Equal effort must be directed toward fostering the clinical utilization of classification research.

How best can we progress beyond our present stratum of knowledge in the classification of psychiatric disorders? I would speculate that significant breakthroughs will be fueled more by an insightful imagination than by empirical research. However, this imagination must be disciplined through the formulation of theoretical models that are falsifiable in principle and subjected to systematic research aimed at the internal and external validation of diagnostic concepts. All shortcuts are problematic.

ACKNOWLEDGMENT

Many of the ideas expressed in this chapter were refined through fruitful discussions with my colleague Roger Blashfield.

REFERENCES

American Psychiatric Association. (1980). *Diagnostic and statistical manual of mental disorders* (3rd ed.). Washington, DC: Author.

Barrett, J. E. (Ed.). (1979). *Stress and mental disorder.* New York: Raven Press.

Benjamin, L. S. (1974). Structural analysis of social behavior. *Psychological Review, 81,* 292–425.

Benjamin, L. S. (1977). Structural analysis of a family in therapy. *Journal of Consulting and Clinical Psychology, 45,* 392–406.

Benjamin, L. S. (1979). Use of structural analysis of social behaviour (SASB)) and Markov chains to study dyadic interactions. *Journal of Abnormal Psychology, 88,* 303–319.

Bentler, P. M. (1980). Multivariate analysis with latent variables: Causal modeling. *Annual Review of Psychology, 31,* 419–456.

Bentler, P. M., & Bonett, D. G. (1980). Significance tests and goodness of fit in the analysis of covariance structures. *Psychological Bulletin, 88,* 588–606.

Birley, J. L. T. (1975). The history of psychiatry as the history of an art. *British Journal of Psychiatry, 127,* 393–400.

Blashfield, R. K. (1980). Propositions regarding the use of cluster analysis in clinical research. *Journal of Consulting and Clinical Psychology, 48,* 456–459.

Blashfield, R. K., & Aldenderfer, M. S. (1978). The literature on cluster analysis. *Multivariate Behavioral Research, 13,* 271–295.

Blashfield, R. K., & Draguns, J. G. (1976a). Evaluative criteria for psychiatric classification. *Journal of Abnormal Psychology, 85,* 140–150.

Blashfield, R. K., & Draguns, J. G. (1976b). Toward a taxonomy of psychopathology: The purpose of psychiatric classification. *British Journal of Psychiatry, 129,* 574–583.

Bowers, K. S. (1973). Situationism in psychology: An analysis and a critique. *Psychological Review, 80,* 307–336.

Buchsbaum, M. S., & Haier, R. J. (1983). Psychopathology: Biological approaches. *Annual Review of Psychology, 34,* 401–430.

Campbell, D. T., & Fiske, D. W. (1959). Convergent and discriminant validation by the multitrait–multimethod matrix. *Psychological Bulletin, 56,* 81–105.

Cantor, N., Smith, E. E., French, R., & Mezzich, J. (1980). Psychiatric diagnosis as prototype categorization. *Journal of Abnormal Psychology, 89,* 181–193.

Carpenter, W. T., & Heinrichs, D. W. (1981). Treatment-relevant subtypes of schizophrenia. *Journal of Nervous and Mental Disease, 169*, 113–119.

Carroll, J. D. (1976). Spacial, non-spacial and hybrid models for scaling. *Psychometrika, 41*, 439–463.

Cattell, R. B. (1957). *Personality and motivation structure and measurement.* New York: World Book.

Cliff, N. (1977). Further study of cognitive processing models for inventory response. *Applied Psychological Measurement, 1*, 41–49.

Cliff, N. (1983). Some cautions concerning the application of causal modeling. *Multivariate Behavioral Research, 18*, 115–126.

Cronbach, L. J., & Meehl, P. E. (1955). Construct validity in psychological tests. *Psychological Bulletin, 52*, 281–302.

Davis, H. R., & Salasin, S. E. (1975). The utilization of evaluation. In E. L. Struening & M. Guttentag (Eds.), *Handbook of evaluation research* (Vol. 1). Beverly Hills, CA: Sage Publications.

Degerman, R. L. (1972). The geometric representation of some simple structures. In R. N. Shepard, A. K. Romney, & S. B. Nerlove (Eds.), *Multidimensional scaling* (Vol. 1). New York: Seminar Press.

Edwards, G., & Gross, M. M. (1976). Alcohol dependence: Provisional description of a clinical syndrome. *British Medical Journal, 1*, 1058–1061.

Embretson, S. (1983). Construct validity: Construct representation versus nomothetic span. *Psychological Bulletin, 93*, 179–197.

Engel, G. L. (1977). The need for a new medical model: A challenge for biomedicine. *Science, 196*, 129–196.

Engel, G. L. (1980). The clinical application of the biopsychosocial model. *American Journal of Psychiatry, 137*, 535–544.

Everitt, B. S. (1974). *Cluster analysis.* London: Heinemann.

Eysenck, H. J. (1970). A dimensional system of psychodiagnostics. In A. R. Mahrer (Ed.), *New approaches to personality classification.* New York: Columbia University Press.

Eysenck, H. J., Wakefield, J. A., & Friedman, A. F. (1983). Diagnosis and clinical assessment: The DSM-III. *Annual Review of Psychology, 34*, 167–193.

Feighner, J. P., Robins, E., Guze, S. B., Woodruff, R. A., Winokur, G., & Muñoz, R. (1972). Diagnostic criteria for use in psychiatric research. *Archives of General Psychiatry, 26*, 57–63.

Feinstein, A. R. (1977). A critical overview of diagnosis in psychiatry. In V. M. Rakoff, H. C. Stancer, & H. B. Kedward (Eds.), *Psychiatric diagnosis.* New York: Brunner/Mazel.

Finn, S. E. (1982). Base rates, utilities, and DSM-III: Shortcomings of fixed-rule systems of psychodiagnosis. *Journal of Abnormal Psychology, 91*, 294–302.

Freedman, A. M., Kaplan, H. I., & Sadok, B. J. (1975). *Comprehensive text book of psychiatry* (2nd ed.). Baltimore, MD: Williams & Wilkins.

Garside, R. F., & Roth, M. (1978). Multivariate statistical methods and problems of classification in psychiatry. *British Journal of Psychiatry, 133*, 53–67.

Golden, R. R. (1982). A taxometric model for the detection of a conjectured latent taxon. *Multivariate Behavioral Research, 17*, 389–416.

Golden, R. R., & Meehl, P. E. (1979). Detection of the schizoid taxon with MMPI indicators. *Journal of Abnormal Psychology, 88*, 217–233.

Goldfried, M. R., & Kent, R. N. (1972). Traditional versus behavioral personality assessment: A comparison of methodological and theoretical assumptions. *Psychological Bulletin, 77*, 409–420.

Grove, W. M., Andreasen, N. C., McDonald-Scott, P., Keller, M. B., & Shapiro, R. W. (1981). Reliability studies of psychiatric diagnosis. *Archives of General Psychiatry, 38*, 408–413.

Guttman, L. (1954). A new approach to factor analysis: The radex. In P. F. Lazarsfeld (Ed.), *Mathematical thinking in the social sciences.* Glencoe, IL: Free Press.

Harré, R. (1972). *The philosophies of science.* London: Oxford University Press.

Hempel, C. G. (1965). *Aspects of scientific explanation.* New York: Free Press.

Huba, G. J., & Bentler, P. M. (1982). A developmental theory of drug use: Derivation and assessment of a causal modeling approach. *Life-Span Development and Behavior, 4,* 147–203.

Huba, G. J., Wingard, J. A., & Bentler, P. M. (1981). A comparison of two latent variable causal models for adolescent drug use. *Journal of Personality and Social Psychology, 40,* 180–193.

Hubert, L. J., & Baker, F. B. (1977).The comparison and fitting of given classification schemes. *Journal of Mathematical Psychology, 16,* 233–253.

Hubert, L. J., & Subkoviak, M. J. (1979). Confirmatory inference and geometric models. *Psychological Bulletin, 86,* 361–370.

Jackson, D. N. (1971). The dynamics of structured personality tests: 1971. *Psychological Review, 78,* 229–248.

Jöreskog, K. G., & Sorbom, D. (1978). *LISREL IV: Analysis of linear structural relationships by the method of maximum likelihood.* Chicago, IL: National Educational Resources.

Jung, C. G. (1971). *Psychological types.* Princeton, NJ: Princeton University Press. (Original work published 1921)

Kandel, D. B. (1975). Stages in adolescent involvement in drug use. *Science, 190,* 912–914.

Kendell, R. E. (1968). *The classification of depressive illness* (Maudsley Monograph No. 18). London: Oxford University Press.

Kendell, R. E. (1975). *The role of diagnosis in psychiatry.* Oxford: Blackwell Scientific Publications.

Kendell, R. E. (1976). The classification of depressions: A review of contemporary confusion. *British Journal of Psychiatry, 129,* 15–28.

Kendell, R. E., Brockington, I. F., & Leff, J. P. (1979). Prognostic implications of six alternative definitions of schizophrenia. *Archives of General Psychiatry, 36,* 25–31.

Kraepelin, E. (1899). *Psychiatric: Ein lehrbuch fur studierende und artze* (6th ed.). Leipzig: Barth.

Kretschmer, E. (1925). *Physique and character.* (W. J. H. Spratt, Trans.) (2nd Ger. ed.). New York: Harcourt, Brace.

Leary, T. (1957). *Interpersonal diagnosis of personality.* New York: Ronald Press.

Loevinger, J. (1957). Objective tests as instruments of psychological theory. *Psychological Reports, 3,* 635–694.

Lorr, M., Klett, C. J., & McNair, D. M. (1963). *Syndromes of psychosis.* New York: Macmillan.

Maxwell, A. E. (1972). Difficulties in a dimensional description of symptomatology. *British Journal of Psychiatry, 121,* 19–26.

McLemore, C. W., & Benjamin, L. S. (1979). Whatever happened to interpersonal diagnosis? A psychosocial alternative to DSM-III. *American Psychologists, 34,* 17–34.

Meehl, P. E. (1962). Schizotaxia, schizotypy, schizophrenia. *American Psychologist, 17,* 827–838.

Meehl, P. E. (1973). MAXCOV-HITMAX: A taxonomic search method for loose genetic syndromes. In *Psychodiagnosis: Selected papers.* Minneapolis: University of Minnesota Press.

Meehl, P. E. (1978). Theoretical risks and tabular asteriks: Sir Karl, Sir Ronald and the slow progress of soft psychology. *Journal of Consulting and Clinical Psychology, 46,* 806–834.

Meehl, P. E. (1979). A funny thing happened to us on the way to latent entities. *Journal of Personality Assessment, 43,* 563–581.

Menninger, K. (1963). *The vital balance.* New York: Viking Press.

Messick, S. (1981). Constructs and their vicissitudes in educational and psychological measurement. *Psychological Bulletin, 89,* 575–588.

Mezzich, J. E. (1979). Patterns and issues in multiaxial psychiatric diagnosis. *Psychological Medicine, 9,* 125–137.

Miller, H. R., Streiner, D. L., & Kahgee, S. L. (1982). Use of the Golden-Meehl indicators in the detection of schizoid-taxon membership. *Journal of Abnormal Psychology, 91,* 55–60.

Miller, J. G. (1978). *Living systems.* New York: McGraw-Hill.

Millon, T. (1969). *Modern psychopathology.* Philadelphia, PA: Saunders.

Millon, T. (1981). *Disorders of personality: DSM-III: Axis II.* New York: Wiley.

Millon, T. (1982). *Millon clinical multiaxial inventory manual* (2nd ed.). Minneapolis: National Computer Systems Interpretive Scoring Systems.

Mischel, W. (1973). Toward a cognitive social learning reconceptualization of personality. *Psychological Review, 80,* 252–283.

Morey, L. C. (1980). Differences between psychologists and psychiatrists in the use of the DSM-III. *American Journal of Psychiatry, 137*, 1123–1124.

Olsen, D. H., Sprenkle, D. H., & Russell, C. S. (1979). Circumplex model of marital and family systems. *Family Process, 18*, 3–28.

Overall, J. E., Hollister, L. E., Johnson, M., & Pennington, V. (1966). Nosology of depression and differential response to drugs. *JAMA, Journal of the American Medical Association, 195*, 946–950.

Overall, J. E., & Woodward, J. A. (1975). Conceptual validity of a phenomenological classification of psychiatric patients. *Journal of Psychiatric Research, 12*, 215–230.

Paykel, E. S. (1971). Classification of depressed patients: A cluster analysis-derived grouping. *British Journal of Psychiatry, 118*, 225–288.

Paykel, E. S. (1972). Depressive typologies and response to amitriptyline. *British Journal of Psychiatry, 120*, 147–156.

Popper, K. R. (1972). *The logic of scientific discovery*. London: Hutchison.

Reed, P. L., & Jackson, D. N. (1975). Clinical judgment of pathology: A model for inferential accuracy. *Journal of Abnormal Psychology, 84*, 475–482.

Riese, W. (1945). History and principles of classification of nervous diseases. *Bulletin of History of Medicine, 18*, 465–512.

Robins, L. N., Helzer, J. E., Croughan, J., & Ratcliff, K. S. (1981). National Institute of Mental Health diagnostic interview schedule: Its history, characteristics and validity. *Archives of General Psychiatry, 38*, 381–389.

Skinner, H. A. (1978). Differentiating the contribution of elevation, scatter and shape in profile similarity. *Educational and Psychological Measurement, 38*, 297–308.

Skinner, H. A. (1979a). Dimensions and clusters: A hybrid approach to classification. *Applied Psychological Measurement, 3*, 327–341.

Skinner, H. A. (1979b). A model of psychopathology based on the MMPI. In C. S. Newmark (Ed.), *MMPI: Clinical and research trends*. New York: Praeger.

Skinner, H. A. (1981). Toward the integration of classification theory and methods. *Journal of Abnormal Psychology, 90*, 68–87.

Skinner, H. A. (1984). Models for the description of abnormal behavior. In H. E. Adams & P. B. Sutker (Eds.), *Comprehensive handbook of psychopathology*. New York: Plenum Press.

Skinner, H. A., & Allen, B. A. (1982). Alcohol dependence syndrome: Measurement and validation. *Journal of Abnormal Psychology, 91*, 199–209.

Skinner, H. A., & Blashfield, R. K. (1982). Increasing the impact of cluster analysis research: The case of psychiatric classification. *Journal of Consulting and Clinical Psychology, 50*, 727–735.

Skinner, H. A., & Jackson, D. N. (1978). A model of psychopathology based on an integration of MMPI actuarial systems. *Journal of Consulting and Clinical Psychology, 46*, 231–238.

Skinner, H. A., & Sheu, W. J. (1982). Dimensional analysis of rank-order and categorical data. *Applied Psychological Measurement, 6*, 41–45.

Sneath, P. H. A. (1975). A vector model of disease for teaching and diagnosis. *Medical Hypotheses, 1*, 12–22.

Sneath, P. H. A., & Sokal, R. R. (1973). *Numerical taxonomy*. San Francisco, CA: Freeman.

Spitzer, R. L. (1980). Introduction. *Diagnostic and statistical manual of mental disorders* (3rd. ed.). New York: American Psychiatric Association.

Spitzer, R. L., Endicott, J., & Robins, E. (1975). *Research diagnostic criteria (RDC) for a selected group of functional disorders*. New York: Biometric Research Branch, New York State Psychiatric Institute.

Spitzer, R. L., Forman, J. B. W., & Nee, J. (1979). DSM-III field trials: Initial interrater diagnostic reliability. *American Journal of Psychiatry, 136*, 815–817.

Spitzer, R. L., Sheehy, M., & Endicott, J. (1977). DSM-III: Guiding principles. In V. M. Rakoff, H. C. Stancer, & H. B. Kedward (Eds.), *Psychiatric diagnosis*. New York: Brunner/Mazel.

Spitzer, R. L., & Williams, J. B. W. (1980). Classification of mental disorders and DSM-III. In H. I. Kaplan, A. M. Friedman, & B. J. Sadock (Eds.), *Comprehensive textbook of psychiatry* (3rd ed.). Baltimore, MD: Williams & Wilkins.

Stengel, E. (1959). Classification of mental disorders. *Bulletin of the World Health Organization, 21,* 601–663.

Stern, G. G. (1970). *People in context: Measuring person–environment congruence in education and industry.* New York: Wiley.

Strauss, J. S. (1973). Diagnostic models and the nature of psychiatric disorder. *Archives of General Psychiatry, 29,* 445–449.

Strauss, J. S., Gabriel, R., Kokes, R. F., Ritzler, B. A., Van Ord, A., & Tarana, E. (1979). Do psychiatric patients fit their diagnoses? Patterns of symptomatology as described with the biplot. *Journal of Nervous and Mental Disease, 167,* 104–113.

Taylor, C. B. (1983). DSM-III and behavioral assessment. *Behavioral Assessment, 5,* 5–14.

Torgerson, W. (1958). *Theory and methods of scaling.* New York: Wiley.

Wiggins, J. S. (1973). *Personality and prediction: Principles of personality assessment.* Reading, MA: Addison-Wesley.

Wiggins, J. S. (1979). A psychological taxonomy of trait-descriptive terms: The interpersonal domain. *Journal of Personality and Social Psychology, 37,* 395–412.

Winokur, G., Codaret, R., Baker, M., & Dorzab, J. (1975). Depression spectrum disease versus pure depressive disease. *British Journal of Psychiatry, 127,* 75–77.

Wood, A. L. (1969). Ideal and empirical typologies for research in deviance and control. *Sociology and Social Research, 53,* 227–241.

Wundt, W. (1903). *Grundzuge der physiologischen psychologie* (5th ed., Vol. 3). Leipzig: Barth.

Zigler, E., & Phillips, L. (1961). Psychiatric diagnosis: A critique. *Journal of Abnormal and Social Psychology, 63,* 607–618.

Zubin, J., & Spring, B. (1977). Vulnerability: A new view of schizophrenia. *Journal of Abnormal Psychology, 86,* 103–126.

Zwick, R. (1983). Assessing the psychometric properties of psychodiagnostic systems: How do the Research Diagnostic Criteria measure up? *Journal of Consulting and Clinical Psychology, 51,* 117–131.

CHAPTER 16

Classifying Psychotics: Dimensional and Categorical Approaches

M. Lorr

In this chapter we will seek to compare the pros and cons of categorical and dimensional approaches to psychiatric classification. The nature of categories will be examined in light of some recent advances in the psychological literature and from the cluster analytic perspective. Next, the more recent cluster analytic studies of the traditional psychotic categories will be evaluated. The status of psychotic syndromes identified by factor analysis will be reviewed. Following this an effort will be made to contrast dimensions and categorical models of the disorders. The advantages and disadvantages of each mode of classification will be compared. Finally, it will be argued that a mixed model is needed to represent psychopathology. Any planned revision of DSM-III should consider the addition of dimensional measures to the criteria presently available.

The Nature of Categories and Categorization

In the traditional Aristotelian view, a category is defined by a small set of essential characteristics. Membership is determined by the possession of this set of necessary and jointly sufficient attributes. All members of the category must possess all critical characteristics. For example, fever, cough, and a rash must be present for a diagnosis of measles. An additional requirement is needed if two categories have a subset or inclusion relation, as when para-

M. Lorr. Center for the Study of Youth Development, Catholic University of America, Washington, D.C.

noids are regarded as a subset of schizophrenics. Then the defining attributes of the more general category should be included or nested in those of the subset. For instance, the defining characteristics of schizophrenia should be included with those required for the paranoid or the catatonic. Some of the limitations of this traditional viewpoint are (a) the difficulty of specifying a set of defining characteristics, (b) the lack of homogeneity of category members, (c) the less than complete nesting of a category's attributes among its subsets, (d) much variation in member characteristics, and (e) the existence of numerous borderline cases.

Recently, a "fuzzy set" viewpoint has emerged in the psychological literature (Rosch, 1975). Research in natural categorization systems indicates that there are serious problems for the traditional view of categories. The assumptions of specific defining attributes for each category cannot be supported. Membership in a category is determined by possession of different attributes for different members. Mervis and Rosch (1981) found that there are no common defining features for common objects such as birds, fish, furniture, and trees. Borderline cases are common, interjudge agreement is low, and category members are not homogeneous. Some instances are more typical than others and they share certain characteristics. Indeed, cognitive categories are found to be organized around prototypical stimuli and exemplars. Once a category is established new instances are compared to a set of attributes called a prototype. Cantor et al. (1980) found that psychiatric categorization suffers from the same problems as object categorization. To demonstrate the usefulness of the prototype view in psychiatric diagnosis, a group of experienced clinicians were asked to list the clinical features that characterize the prototypical patient for each of nine diagnostic categories. Included were three schizophrenic subtypes and three affective disorders. They found that the assumption of correlated features and imperfect attribute nesting of the prototypes provided a better description of these categories than the assumptions of the classical view. They argued that the prototype view appears to mirror the natural categorization process in many scientific and nonscientific domains. Categorization is probabilistic rather than all or none.

Numerical toxonomists (Sneath & Sokal, 1973) and cluster analysts have long held to a view of classes that has much in common with the prototypic view. Groups of taxa are viewed as based on multiple-correlated characteristics of objects compared; they are said to be polythetic. Generally the term cluster or type is used instead of category. Then a cluster is a set of entities, each member of which is more like all other members of the cluster than it is like entities not in the cluster. The process of clustering is the grouping of entities into homogeneous subsets on the basis of their measured similarity across attributes. Similarity is assessed by comparing entities across a representative set of attributes. Thus no fixed definition of necessary characteristics is assumed. Clusters are generated empirically by means of statistical procedures applied to similarity measures. All in all, the prototype view fits in well with the cluster analytic, although proponents of the former appear not to recognize this condition.

Cluster Analytic Studies

There have been a number of attempts at validation of traditional psychiatric syndromes by cluster analysis. One of the earliest was by Everitt, Gourlay, and Kendell (1971). They hypothesized that clusters emerging would consist entirely of patients with a single diagnosis. The patient samples consisted of 250 consecutive admissions to a New York State hospital and 250 to a hospital in Great Britain. These were examined as part of a cross-national study of diagnosis. Each case was rated on the Present State Examination (PSE) (Wing, Cooper, & Sartorius, 1974) and on a short history form. For the cluster analysis 70 items were selected and reduced to 10 scores by means of a principal component analysis. Two clustering procedures were applied to each of the two dates set, one by Wolfe called NORMAP and another, a partitioning procedure called MacQueens K-means (Everitt, 1980). Included in the sample were groups diagnosed paranoid schizophrenia, residual schizophrenia, schizo-affective schizophrenia, mania, psychotic depression, neurotic depression, alcoholic, and drug addicted.

A 7-group solution was obtained for the English data and a 5-group solution for the United States data. The cluster, most homogeneous diagnostically in both samples, consisted of manics. The psychotic depression group also emerged clearly in both samples. The patients diagnosed as paranoid schizophrenia also separated out rather well. The residual schizophrenic appeared in all analyses, but were less homogeneous in diagnostic composition. In none of the four solutions do neurotics or alcoholics share any clear tendency to form discrete clusters. Failure to cluster may have been due to the lack of a sufficient number of cases with that diagnosis in the data. Another cause may have been incorrect diagnosis. In summary, all four analyses disclosed separate clusters identifiable with the manic, the depressive phases of the manic–depressive disorders, acute paranoid schizophrenia, and chronic or residual schizophrenia. The results are thus supportive of traditional psychotic categories.

A study of schizophrenic subtypes was conducted by Carpenter, Bartko, Carpenter, and Strauss (1976). The study was based on data collected on 1,202 patients in nine countries for the International Pilot Study of Schizophrenia (IPSS). Out of the total sample, 680 representing the major schizophrenic subtypes (simple, hebephrenic, catatonic, paranoid, acute schizophrenic episode, and schizophrenic) provided the data. The PSE (Wing et al., 1974) was used to define 27 dimensions considered basic to descriptions of these disorders. A profile analysis of variance was conducted to test whether the six subtypes were distinctive. The analysis suggested considerable similarity rather than difference in pattern and level of the disorders of the various subtypes. Therefore, cluster analysis was applied to determine whether distinguishable classes could be defined. For the analysis, a sample of 600 was subdivided into 4 subsamples, each of 150 cases, but proportionate in representation of the 5 subtypes.

Two clustering techniques were applied to the four samples, one hierarchical and the other an iterative K-means technique. Since four clusters emerged in each hierarchical analysis there were 16 subgroups. The mean profiles were used as nuclei for the K-means analysis. A six-cluster solution proved best, but because two clusters accounted for only 4% of the patients, these were dropped. The iterative program found essentially the same solution as the hierarchical procedures. The largest, cluster 1, called "typical schizophrenia," was characterized by poor insight, presenting delusions, auditory hallucination, restricted affect, and social withdrawal. Cluster 2, called "flagrant schizophrenic," was distinguished by aberrant agitated or bizarre behavior, incongruent affect, and absence of anxiety. The third cluster, "insightful schizophrenia," shared mainly the cluster 1 symptoms, but had good insight and showed neurotic symptoms. Cluster 4, "hypochondrical schizophrenia," manifested somatic concerns, visual hallucinations, and neurotic symptoms. The authors concluded that the schizophrenic subtypes as currently diagnosed are not differentiated by traditional criteria. However, by use of structured interview techniques and cluster analysis, four groups can be distinguished.

Andreasen, Grove, and Maurer (1980) have reported on a cluster analysis of depressive disorders. Their aim was to ascertain whether depressive disorders vary only in degree of severity or represent a group of two or more discrete disorders. Earlier Paykel (1971) had analyzed a group of 165 depressed patients and found an optimal solution at the level of four groups. These were labeled psychotic, anxious, hostile, and young. The 86 cases studied by Andreasen et al. were evaluated by a structured interview Schedule for Affective Disorders and Schizophrenia (SADS). Patients were diagnosed independently on the Research Diagnostic Criteria (RDC) developed by Spitzer, Endicott, and Robins (1978). The analyses were based on 71 items of SADS that reflected cross-sectional symptoms; longitudinal items were not included. Two methods of cluster analyses were applied: Ward's agglomerative hierarchical program and an iterative reallocation program that seeks an optimal solution using the hierarchical clusters. Following three iterative reallocations, a three-cluster solution was accepted. Next, the clusters were compared on the individual items, the overall severity score, diagnosis, and treatment received. The three clusters differed significantly with respect to severity on which cluster 1 averaged higher. The data indicated that cluster 1 consisted primarily of endogenous depression. Cluster 2 was highest on emotional lability, including anger and alcohol abuse probably corresponding to a reactive neurotic depression. Cluster 3 appeared to represent the minor depressions. In this study, then, there was a fair correspondence between diagnosis and cluster identified.

Strauss *et al.* (1979) raise an interesting question: Do psychiatric patients fit their diagnoses? These authors point out that systems of psychiatric diagnosis have been regularly criticized for their low reliability and their inability to fit accurately the patient coming for treatment. To cover the reasons for low reliability and poor coverage, their study utilized a new method, called the "biplot," for defining groups of similar patients and their relationships to key symptom clusters. By this procedure two-dimensional graphs (biplots) are generated that display patient symptoms as arrows form a common origin, and patients are points on the same plane with the arrows. Sheaves of arrows that point in the same direction represent highly correlated symptoms or syndromes. Clusters of points represent groups of patients with similar symptoms. The first data studied consisted of symptom ratings on 100 "archetypal" patients. These were fictitious subjects on whom ratings had been made on 25 dimensions of symptomatology to fit stereotyped concepts of five diagnostic categories. These categories were neurotic depression, psychotic depression, paranoid schizophrenia, simple schizophrenia, and mania. The second set of data were symptom ratings for a sample of 217 first admissions for functional disorders from two catchment areas. The same 25 symptoms that derived from the PSE were also used with the archetypal patients.

The results for the archetypal data indicated that the symptoms formed the expected syndromes. The patients clustered neatly in each of five locations. In the real patients the biplot showed that the symptoms arranged themselves into syndromes, as with the archetypal patients. On the other hand, most real patients fell in the left-hand portion of the plot. The great majority did not fit neatly into archetypal categories, but clustered randomly together in an area representing low symptom scores. These results were replicated in data from a second catchment area and in a sample of readmissions. The authors close by raising a question of the appropriateness of the current diagnostic system for representing real patients accurately.

The biplot is obviously not a clustering procedure. However, analogous methods called "ordination" are widely applied in numerical taxonomy to confirm or to discover the presence of cluster structure in a set of data. Generally the techniques used are principal components analysis or multidimensional scaling. These are applied to provide a low-dimensional representation of the points in the data. The researcher can then visually inspect the two-dimensional plots of points (representing the patients) to see whether there are separate clusters of points, or the investigator can use the coordinates in a cluster analysis. The method called Q-analysis also determines the number of dimensions that can represent a set of objects and then locate clusters of objects in this space. Thus, biplots and ordination procedures provide confirmatory information for cluster analytic techniques.

The cluster analytic studies reviewed do not offer a consistent view of present-day psychiatric categories. The Everitt *et al.* analyses are supportive of conventional diagnosis. The reason may be that the diagnosis was made with exceptional care for a cross-national study. The Carpenter *et al.* analytic was also carefully collected, but nine different countries were involved with psychiatrists who possibly differed in their psychiatric stereotype of patient classes. The Andreasen analysis is mixed with respect to the validity of diagnosis. These authors did not seek to establish that the cluster found confirmed known diagnoses. They tried to determine whether there were indeed discrete depressive clusters and how these related to severity of depression. The Strauss–Gabriel findings provide little support of conventional diagnostic categories, but good support for dimensional syndromes. In another report, Strauss (1973) asserts that "there is increasing evidence that the dimensional model best fits the nature of psychiatric data . . ." (p. 447).

Dimensional Studies of Psychosis

DSM-III defines a syndrome as a grouping of symptoms that occur together and that constitute a recognizable condition. The use of factor analysis to define such dimensions begun by Moore in 1933 continued into the 1960s. Findings from such analyses were reviewed and summarized by Lorr, Klett, and McNair (1963). Relatively few factor analytic studies of observable symptoms and behavior manifested in a mental status interview have appeared since. Interest shifted to the analysis of self-report forms such as the Minnesota Multiphasic Personality Inventory (MMPI). The present review will be confined to reports of interview-observed behavior and symptoms. Those will be compared to the 12 syndromes established in the Inpatient Multidimensional Psychiatric Scale (IMPS) Lorr et al. (1966). These same syndromes were confirmed in cross-national studies conducted in England, France, Germany, Italy, Japan, and Sweden (Lorr & Klett, 1969). These 12 syndromes are listed in Table 16-1.

The first analysis to be summarized was reported by Spitzer, Fleiss, Endicott, and Cohen (1967). A scoring procedure was needed for the Mental Status Schedule (MSS). The MSS consists of an interview schedule and a matching inventory of 248 dichotomous items. The items were grouped by the investigators into 145 clusters, each consisting of from 1 to 4 items scored by summation. Two principal component analyses followed by a Varimax rotation were applied to the correlations among the clusters based on 1,000 MMS protocols. Thirteen scales were constructed on the basis of these analyses. Eight of these scales match closely with those assessed in IMPS. The 13 scales were as follows: (1) Inappropriate or Bizarre Appearance, (2) Belligerence–Negativeness, (3) Agitation–Excitement, (4) Retardation–Emotional Withdrawal, (5) Speech Disorganization, (6) Suspicion–Persecution–Hallucinations, (7) Grandiosity, (8) Depression–Anxiety, (9) Suicide–Self-Mutilation, (10) Somatic Concerns, (11) Social Isolation, (12) Disorientation–Memory, and (13) Denial of Illness. A comparison of MSS with IMPS indicated a close correspondence or match for eight MSS scales. These are shown in Table 16-1 (Scales 1, 3–8, 10, 12)

Table 16-1

Corresponding Psychotic Syndromes Isolated in Four Studies

Syndrome	Fleiss, Gurland, and Cooper (1971)	Everitt, Gourlay, and Kendall (1971)	Spitzer, Fleiss, Endicott, and Cohen (1967)	Mortorano and Nathan (1972)
Excitement	+	+	+	+
Hostile Belligerence	+			
Paranoid Projection	+	+	+	
Grandiosity	+		+	
Perceptual Distortion	+			+
Anxious Depression		+	+	+
Obsessive–Compulsive	+			
Retardation	+	+	+	
Disorientation	+		+	
Motor Disturbances			+	+
Conceptual Disorganization	+		+	+
Somatic Concern			+	
Depression	+	+		+
Phobic Anxiety	+	+		

Another dimensional analysis may be found in a study by Everitt *et al.* (1971). B. S. Everitt *et al.* selected 70 items, 45 from an early form of the PSE (Wing*et al.* 1974), and 25 from a social history form. The samples consisted of 250 British and 250 United States patients collected in a cross-national study of diagnosis of the mental disorders. Principal component analyses of the two samples disclosed 10 very similar factors. These were interpreted as Depression, Paranoid Schizophrenia, Mania, Drug Abuse, Depressive Delusions, Retardation/Apathy, Schizoid Personality, Manic–Depressive Depression, Hysteria, and Auditory Hallucinations. Of these factors five are quite similar to the IMPS syndromes. The new syndromes are Depression, Hysteria, and Drug Abuse. The remaining factors appear to emerge primarily out of social history variables. These are Hysteria and Drug Abuse. Thus, only the broad Depression factor seems to be novel.

A broader analysis of the PSE was reported by Fleiss, Gurland, and Cooper (1971). They utilized the same 500 cases observed in the British–United States study. Two forms, the PSE with 700 items, and the Psychiatric Status Schedule (PSS) constructed by Spitzer, Endicott, Fleiss, and Cohen (1970), were used. The items were grouped into 185 clusters by consensus of two investigators. Each of the two samples were analyzed by the method of principal components followed by a Varimax rotation. From the analysis 25 factors emerged. Each variable was assigned to the factor with which it correlated highest. The most striking result, according to Fleiss *et al.*, was the separation of Depression and Phobic Anxiety. In most factor analytic studies, Depression and Anxiety define a single factor called Anxious Depression. However, the presence of specific situational conditions that give rise to phobic anxiety and the inclusion of physiological indicators (pounding heart, dry mouth) help to define a phobic anxiety dimension. A Flat Affect factor also seems to merit recognition, but further confirmation is needed. The authors also believe that a Restlessness factor warrants separation from a Mania factor. A fair number of the factors extracted were narrow and may reflect verbal equivalents of the same behaviors. In all, perhaps six of the factors are also found in IMPS, while Depression and Phobic Anxiety are new.

Hautaluoma (1971) sought to test out the syndromes identified in IMPS. He utilized a sample of 1,099 admissions to a Colorado hospital. Data were available in the Menninger Mental Status form, a social history form, and a ward behavior scale. The total sample was subdivided into three subsamples and factor analyzed using the BC-TRY computer program. Nine factors were isolated, but only five corresponded to the 12 IMPS dimensions. These were Hostile, Belligerence, Anxious Depression, Paranoid Projection, Retardation, and Disorientation.

Mortorano and Nathan (1972) sought to isolate the syndromes of psychosis and nonpsychosis measured in the Boston City Hospital Behavior Checklist (BCH-BCL). Symptoms of 924 psychiatric patients were rated on teh BCH-BCL. Correlations among 70 of the 100 items were factored to yield 13 dimensions. Four IMPS factors appear in their findings: Excitement, Paranoid Projection, Motor Disturbance, and Perceptual Distortion. Their depressive factor corresponds more to a psychotic depression than anxious depression. A narrow Anxiety factor appears primarily because of social history data. Their Reactive Depression and Endogenous Depression are likewise based principally on social history. All the IMPS dimensions reflect present-day reports and observations and not history.

The review indicates that between 14 and 16 syndromes are observable in psychotic patients. These have been found in a wide variety of rating schedules structured and semistructured. Included here are the PSE, the MSS, and the IMPS. In addition, there are ward behavior rating forms and checklists that can tap many of the same factors. The relations of behavioral-based syndromes to self-report measures remain relatively unknown. There have been many studies of the MMPI, but the relations of behavioral and self-report dimensions have been seldom studied.

Purposes of a Classification Scheme

It is germaine here to list the more general purposes or uses of a classification scheme for the behavior disorders. On the theoretical side, the conceptual arrangement should fit and advance existing theory and methodology. It should facilitate ongoing thinking and research in the area. On the practical side, the classification should enhance communication among researchers and clinicians. The terminology should provide a nomenclature or language for discussion of ideas as well as patients. An even more valuable use is to provide predictions for a wide variety of outcomes such as choice of treatment, length of hospitalization, and duration of illness. Another critical purpose is to provide a basis for assessing change over time or the effects of treatment. Criteria are also needed for decision making such as treatment choice, hospitalization, acceptance for military service, and compensation for disability. The kind and severity of the disorder are appraised on the classification scheme. Record keeping is another use that is sometimes forgotten. The epidemiologist may want counts of the prevalence or frequency of occurrence of various disorders. Institutional managers require an accounting of services delivered by whom and for whom. The administrator needs information regarding diagnostic classes in order to request funds for housing, for treatment of patients, and for hiring diagnosticians and therapists.

Evaluative Criteria

In summary, the principal uses of a classification scheme for the behavior disorders are (1) advancement of theory, (2) a language for communication, (3) a basis for prediction of outcome, (4) a method for measuring change, (5) criteria for decision making, and (6) a foundation for record keeping. Next, evaluative criteria are needed to assess how well the scheme functions and how adequate it is for the above purposes. Blashfield and Draguns (1976) suggest reliability, coverage, and descriptive and predictive validity. A modified version will be employed here.

Certainly to be useful a classification scheme must be reliable in the sense that there must be agreement among independent observers. Some of the determinants of reliability are training of the clinicians and specificity and objectivity of the diagnostic rules. The second criterion concerns coverage or the proportion of cases classifiable. The relatively high proportion of unclassified cases is one of the limitations of the categorical conception and a principal advantage of a dimensional scheme. Third, a classification scheme should be judged by the extent to which it can explain the natural variance of the phenomena. It should account for differences between individuals on the characteristics involved and should be able to allocate each individual to one of the available categories. From this viewpoint the allocation of people to discrete categories, as in traditional diagnosis, is greatly wasteful of information. Here a quantitative approach is superior. However, even a factor analytic model discards much information as when a structured interview with 250 items is reduced to, say, 12 syndromes.

By descriptive validity Blashfield and Draguns (1976) refer to homogeneity of categories within a classification. However, if the scheme is dimensional in nature a preferable term would be construct validity. At the conceptual level a category or type is a cognitive construct such as a syndrome or trait. A type thus represents a range of discriminably different entities treated as if equivalent. A factor or syndrome is a dimension of individual differences or constructs intended to explain what is common to a set of attributes. In the language of cluster analysis a category or type is a subset of persons characterized by the properties of isolation (separateness) and coherence (homogeneity). These characteristics can be appraised by application of suitable cluster algorithms. The dimensional structure of a set of syndromes is determined by appropriate factor analytic procedures. The predictive validity of a classification can be evaluated only piecemeal. If categories are involved, then treatment response and diagnosis interactions must be demonstrated. Should the scheme be multidimensional, then multiple regression techniques are applied and replicated to show which dimensions predict the desired effect.

Pros and Cons for Categories

Categories or types clearly facilitate communication, since a wide range of information is conveyed in reporting a person to be a schizophrenic, a paranoid, or a sociopath. They are easy to remember, to report, and to differentiate from persons in general. Like all class concepts, they provide direction for practical behavior. We know what to expect, how to relate, and how to treat socially, and often professionally. Biologists call such classes "natural" because they convey a high content of information and can be used for many purposes. The established categories are especially useful for understanding and treating individual patients.

Classification schemes are especially important in the formulation of research designs. Controlled experiments concern classifications relating treatment conditions to measured dependent variables. In conducting research or treatment effectiveness on the genetic basis of behavior disorders, it is particularly useful to partition a larger sample into smaller homogeous subsets. For instance, depressives have been subdivided into the anxious, the hostile, and the retarded in order to evaluate various drugs.

As indicated earlier, categorical classes are essential for record keeping and institutional management. Clinic and hospital administrators are required to keep records on such matters as services rendered for particular classes of patients. In requesting funds from legislative bodies it is usually necessary to specify the type of patients to be treated and the kinds of drugs or supplies needed. Thus, regardless of their limitations, psychiatric categories satisfy a practical need.

The limitations of the typal approach will now be sketched. A critical one is the loss of information. It is often forgotten that in classification as well as in measurement the method of grouping of persons or attributes loses information. Any encoding of behavioral phenomena discards some information. If the presence or absence of 10 symptoms is noted, there are potentially 2^{10} or 1,024 different symptom patterns available. Adding up the number of symptoms into one scale also combines many bits of information into one index. Grouping together individuals with similar score patterns on the MMPI into a class represents a substantial loss of information. In any typology the measurement domain is partitioned, often arbitrarily, into coarser groupings with a consequent loss of variance. Similarly, there is a loss of degrees of freedom when a larger sample of, say, 1,000 is partitioned into, say, 7 subgroups, each with a smaller number of cases. The loss may come from the coarseness of grouping and from the index used to assess similarity. Gleser (1968) contends that typologies are unnecessary where more refined measures are available for decision making. In a recent review, Eysenck, Wakefield, and Friedman (1983) state the belief that "diagnostic categories are a scientific anachronism" (p. 185). They should be replaced by dimensional measurement.

In addition to loss of information, there is the question whether categories are arbitrary and imposed by the diagnostician or the cluster analyst. As was seen in the Strauss data (1979), patients may not fall into traditional diagnostic classes. Everitt (1980) likewise demonstrated that the cluster analytic algorithms often impose structure on data when none exists. An elliptical cluster of points is often partitioned into two clusters. There are others, however, who point out that clusters may represent facts of nature. There are certainly many who believe that in the psychoses there is enough evidence that the schizophrenic and the manic-depressive disorders have a sound genetic basis for their separation. Meehl (1979) is a strong proponent of this viewpoint. For him, a taxon, as a class entity, must have a nonarbitrary basis; it is a class of persons who belong together.

Arguments favoring the categorical model for psychosis are fairly strong. The affective and schizophrenic groups have had a long tradition of acceptance, although the Kraepelinian subtypes remain uncertain. In interviews the symptom rating nearly always appears as a reversed J-shaped distribution. There is also support from recent cluster analytic studies, as was seen in the reviews reported.

The Dimensional Approach

The alternative to the categorical is the dimensional approach. An increasing number of investigators have come to agree that most of the behavior disorders are better represented by continuous quantitative variables: Most recognized syndromes in the behavior disorders are quantitative variables about which individuals differ in degree. Each person may be represented by a profile of p scores, or a point in p-dimensional attribute space. Since no arbitrary cutoffs are imposed on patient loci in p space, there are no mixed, undiagnosed, or atypical cases. The end result is maximum flexibility for later categorization and complete rather than partial coverage. Cutoffs can be set or altered depending upon the need, and not upon category boundaries.

Another major advantage of the dimensional model is its superiority for evaluating change. Almost no investigators evaluate a drug treatment by examining the diagnosis. Quantitative measures such as observer ratings and self-reports are applied to appraise treatment effects. Greater efficiency in predicting outcomes represents another advantage over categorical data. Empirical studies have repeatedly demonstrated that multiple linear regression is substantially superior to the use of subgroups in accounting for criterion variance. At best, subgroup (categorical) information can be added in the form of "dummy" variables to regression equations. Then it is possible to determine whether the new information adds significantly to the variance accounted for by the quantitative variables.

The categorical and dimensional views of psychiatric abnormality were compared by Lang (1978) in a study of neurotics, schizophrenics, and alcoholics. Lang's argument was that many forms of psychopathology simply reflect gross deviations of continuous dimensions of personality and not discontinuities with qualitative change points. His three aims were (1) to compare the extent of agreement between psychiatrically assigned diagnoses and computer-generated diagnoses, (2) to contrast the categorical-dimensional approaches by using Eysenck's Neuroticism score as an index of severity of maladjustment, and (3) to check the degree of "collinearity" between Neuroticism and Extraversion dimensions and the Tryon–Stein–Chu symptom clusters from the MMPI. The sample consisted of 157 diagnosed cases. A discriminant function analysis carried out on the basis of three types of scores correctly assigned 70% of the patients to their diagnostic categories. However, the "hit rate" rose to 90% when patients were aligned on a continuity of severity. The results also showed that Eysenck's Extraversion and Neuroticism variable has much in common with the MMPI clusters. To carry out the second aim, patients were subdivided into low, moderate, and high Neuroticism clusters irrespective of diagnosis. The 26 univariate F tests showed that neurotics, schizophrenics, and alcoholics differed on 12 of the 26 measures used, but 18 significant F's emerged when the patients were subdivided by Neuroticism score. The implication is that it may be easier to depict patients in terms of degree of pathology on a continuous variable than to fit them into predetermined classes. Lang concludes that the categorical model does not provide a good fit for the actual empirical characteristics of the population.

Kendell (1975) has also considered the problems relating to choice between categories and dimensions. In the process he critically evaluated Eysenck's arguments. Eysenck sees the disease concept as inappropriate for mental disorders. Psychiatric diagnoses are unreliable because the boundaries of the categories are imposed rather than found. Factor analysis, he asserts, fails to reveal evidence of clustering; factor scores are continuous, not discontinuous. He claims that by means of criterion analysis it is possible to determine whether the psychoses and neuroses are separate or continuous and graded. He proposes a three-dimensional system of Neuroticism, Psychoticism, and Extraversion-Introversion. Kendell's counterarguments are that Eysenck is justified in claiming continuity between psychotics and normals only with respect to the region his arbitrary test battery measured. None of the devices used resembles the methods ordinarily applied by clinicians. In sum, Kendell argues that Eysenck has never proved his case for use of criterion analysis.

A Mixed Model

The material presented here contrasted the categorical and dimensional bases for classifying patients. It is worthwhile to note that the use of quantitative criteria has increased substantially in DSM-III. The diagnostic criteria for the various disorders are quantitative in nature, although cutoffs or bounds are set for each condition. To this can be added a more or less explicit recognition that nearly all criteria (symptoms) can be regarded as dimensional in nature, including delusions and hallucinations. Strauss (1969) has argued that conceptualizing hallucinations and delusions as points on continua rather than discontinuous entities allows for more accurate evaluation of those symptoms. Some criteria that Strauss suggests for defining such continua are (a) degree of the patient's conviction of the objective reality of the experience, (b) the extent to which the patient was influenced by cultural determinants, (c) the amount of time spent preoccupied with the experiences (pervasiveness), and (d) the implausibility of the experience. In many cases a simple judgment of presence or absence makes these symptoms seem more distinct than they actually are.

What we would like to propose is use of a mixed model in future modifications of DSM-III. A quantitative set of measures that represent the major syndromes is needed most. These could be added to the present criteria. A plausible source could be a stripped down version of the PSE (Wing et al., 1974) or the SADS (Spitzer et al., 1970). A factor analysis of a broad set of protocols would yield a reduced set of scales for use with the DSM. Thus, each patient would be described in turn by a diagnostic group and by a standardized syndrome profile. In this way schizophrenia and the affective disorders could each be represented by a distinctive quantitative profile.

The syndrome measures could be used to evaluate the patient's present status and changes due to treatment. These same scales could then be employed as independent variables for predicting various outcomes of interest. A third important use would be in cluster analytic studies. The scale scores could be fed into programs designed to establish hierarchical arrangements, say, for schizophrenics or to confirm or extend currently accepted categorical classes.

REFERENCES

American Psychiatric Association. (1980). *Diagnostic and statistical manual of mental disorders.* (3rd ed.) Washington, DC: Author.

Andreasen, N. C., Grove, W. M., & Maurer, R. (1980). Cluster analysis and the classification of depression. *British Journal of Psychiatry, 137,* 256–265.

Blashfield, R. K., & Draguns, J. G. (1976a). Evaluation criteria for psychiatric classification. *Journal of Abnormal Psychology, 85,* 140–150.

Blashfield, R. K., & Draguns, J. G. (1976b). Toward a taxonomy of psychopathology: The purpose of psychiatric classification. *British Journal of Psychiatry, 129,* 574–583.

Cantor, N., Smith, E. E., French, R., & Mezzich, J. (1980). Psychiatric diagnosis as a prototype categorization. *Journal of Abnormal Psychology, 89,* 181–195.

Carpenter, W. T., Bartko, J. J., Carpenter, C. L., & Strauss, J. S. (1976). Another view of schizophrenia subtypes. *Archives of General Psychiatry, 33,* 508–516.

Everitt, B. (1980). *Cluster analysis* (2nd ed.). New York: Halsted Press.

Everitt, B. S., Gourlay, A. J., & Kendell, R. E. (1971). An attempted validation of traditional psychiatric syndromes of cluster analysis. *British Journal of Psychiatry, 119,* 379–412.

Eysenck, H. J., Wakefield, J. A., Jr., & Friedman, A. F. (1983). Diagnosis and clinical assessment: The DSM-III. *Annual Review of Psychology, 34,* 167–194.

Fleiss, J. L., Gurland, B. J., & Cooper, J. E. (1971). Some contributions to the measurement of psychopathology. *British Journal of Psychiatry, 119,* 647.

Gleser, G. C. (1968). Quantifying similarity between people. In M. M. Katz, J. O. Cole, & W. E. Barton (Eds.), *The role and methodology of classification in psychiatry and psychopathology.* Washington: Government Printing Office.

Hautaluoma, J. (1971). Syndromes, antecedents and outcomes of psychosis: A cluster-analytic study. *Journal of Consulting and Clinical Psychology, 37,* 332–344.

Kendell, R. E. (1975). *The role of diagnosis in psychiatry.* Oxford: Blackwell Scientific Publications.

Lang, R. J. (1978). Multivariate classification of day-care patients: Personality and as a dimensional continuum. *Journal of Consulting and Clinical Psychology, 46,* 1212–1226.

Lorr, M., & Klett, C. J. (1969). Cross-cultural comparison of psychotic syndromes. *Journal of Abnormal Psychology, 74,* 531–543.

Lorr, M., Klett, C. J., & McNair, D. M. (1963). *Syndromes of psychosis.* New York: Macmillan.

Lorr, M., McNair, D. M., & Klett, C. J. (1966). *Impatient multidimensional psychiatric scale.* Palo Alto, CA: Consulting Psychologist Press.

Meehl, P. E. (1979). A funny thing happened to us on the way to the latent entities. *Journal of Personality Assessment, 43,* 564–581.

Mervis, C. B., & Rosch, E. (1981). Categorization of natural objects. *Annual Review of Psychology, 32,* 89–115.

Mortorano, R. D., & Nathan, P. E. (1972). Syndromes of psychosis and nonpsychosis: A factor analysis of a systems analysis. *Journal of Abnormal Psychology, 80,* 1–10.

Paykel, E. S. (1971). Classification of depressed patients: A cluster analysis derived grouping. *British Journal of Psychiatry, 118,* 275–288.

Rosch, E. (1975). Cognitive representation of semantic categories. *Journal of Experimental Psychology, General, 104,* 192–233.

Sneath, P. H. A., & Sokal, R. R. (1973). *Numerical taxonomy.* San Francisco, CA: Freeman.

Spitzer, R. L., Endicott, J., Fleiss, J. L., & Cohen, J. (1970). Psychiatric status o schedule: A technique for evaluating psychopathology and impairment in role functioning. *Archives General Psychiatry, 23,* 41–55.

Spitzer, R. L., Endicott, J. E., & Robins, E. (1978). *Research diagnostic criteria for a selected group of functional disorders* (3rd ed.). New York: Biometric Research Branch, New York State Psychiatric Institute.

Spitzer, R. L., Fleiss, J. L., Endicott, J., & Cohen, J. (1967). Mental status schedule: Properties of factor analytically derived scales. *Archives of General Psychiatry, 16,* 476–493.

Strauss, J. S. (1969). Hallucinations and delusions as points on continua function. *Archives of General Psychiatry, 21,* 581–586.

Strauss, J. S. (1973). Diagnostic models and the nature of psychiatric disorder. *Archives of General Psychiatry, 29,* 445–449.

Strauss, J. S., Gabriel, R., Kokes, R. F., Ritzler, B. A., Autumn, V. O., & Tarana, E. (1979). Do psychiatric patients fit their diagnosis? *Journal of Nervous and Mental Disease, 167,* 105–113.

Wing, J. K., Cooper, J. E., & Sartorius, N. (1974). *The measurement and classification of psychiatric symptoms.* London & New York: Cambridge University Press.

CHAPTER 17

Multivariate Statistical Analysis in Psychopathology

William M. Grove and Nancy C. Andreasen

Clinicians and researchers interested in studying psychopathology are often intimidated by the field of multivariate statistical analysis, which has burgeoned in the past three decades. Nevertheless, a familiarity with these techniques is necessary for the investigator interested in doing serious research on phenomenology, psychopathology, and nosology. While they offer no panaceas (nothing does), these techniques have considerable utility and power for discovering new approaches to classification, validating traditional schemes, and determining which symptoms of a particular diagnosis have the strongest predictive power. The purpose of this chapter is to describe these statistical methods in a relatively simple and clear fashion and to illustrate how they can be used in the study of psychopathology.

The practicing clinician usually has a clear scheme for classifying patients which has grown out of clinical observations gathered over many years, as did Kraepelin's demarcation of various psychotic illnesses. Alternatively, it may have been achieved by dividing the population of patients on a variable of some practical or theoretical interest, such as response to lithium carbonate or failure to suppress cortisol secretion in response to dexamethasone. Whatever the source, a nosology must survive tests of its validity if it is to prove useful. Many multivariate techniques are of value in determining the construct validity of psychopathological classification systems.

On the other hand, clinicians and researchers may wish to attempt to develop an entirely new system for classifying patients. This may arise

William M. Grove. Department of Psychology, University of Minnesota, Minneapolis, Minnesota.

Nancy C. Andreasen. Department of Psychiatry, University of Iowa, Iowa City, Iowa.

because little is known about a group of disorders (a situation quite common in child psychopathology) or because existing classifications are of uncertain validity and new ones appear to be needed. In the past decade, methods for isolating new homogeneous syndromes from mixed populations of individuals have proliferated under the general rubric of numerical taxonomy. As the name implies, data gathered systematically on individuals are used in statistical procedures to detect taxa, to isolate their characteristics, and to assign individuals to groups.

Numerical taxonomic methods can be used either in exploratory or confirmatory analyses. In exploratory analyses, the investigator uses the results of numerical taxonomy to suggest divisions of patients into groups. This may yield new systems of classification. In confirmatory analyses, numerical taxonomy can also be used to study clinically derived classifications by examining the syndromal homogeneity of existing diagnostic groups. If the system developed by numerical taxonomy matches the existing groups well, then the existing classification system has been in some sense mathematically validated. It is convenient to explain methods for generating homogeneous groups of patients first. Then we will examine statistical procedures that help to validate existing classes.

Methods of Numerical Taxonomy

To catalog the available procedures in this field would make a list longer than this chapter. Several excellent summaries of these methods are available (Anderberg, 1973; Everitt, 1980; Hartigan, 1975). In particular, Everitt's book is a quite readable introduction to the field, as is his highly condensed article summarizing the problems confronting the user of some of these analyses (Everitt, 1972).

Numerical taxonomic procedures may be divided into three basic kinds: inverse factor analysis, cluster analyses, and mixture models. Inverse factor analysis involves factor analyzing a matrix of intercorrelations among people. This used to be a common technique of numerical taxonomy in psychiatry (e.g., Raskin, Schulterbrandt, Boothe, Reatig, & McKeon, 1972), but the results are very difficult to interpret and are subject to various artifacts (Fleiss, Lawlor, Platman, & Fieve, 1971). Inverse factor analysis has been largely supplanted by cluster analysis. The essential feature of cluster analysis is that patients are grouped according to some defined measure of similarity so that clumps of patients, alike on a profile of measurements, are formed. Mixture models, on the other hand, proceed by assuming that the patients come from a mathematically describable mixture of probability distributions. For example, it might be assumed that patients come from one of two normal distributions on a dimension of "endogenomorphic" features. The endogenomorphic patients (Klein, 1974) would come from the upper distribution on this dimension, while the nonendogenomorphic would come from a distribution centered further down on the dimension. Both methods capture some of the flavor of what the clinician does when he or she creates a taxonomy. Cluster analysis is the mathematical equivalent of Kraepelin's summer vacation pastime of sorting patients' charts into like-featured groups. In mixture analysis, the supposition that patients form true groups is given mathematical form: Either the patient comes from one distribution or from another. There are no truly intermediate cases.

The user of each of these techniques faces similar problems. First, a patient population appropriate for study must be chosen. Second, a set of patient descriptors must be selected that will maximize chances of detecting order in a welter of patient characteristics. Third, a mathematical method for isolating the groups must be chosen. Finally, criteria must be found for determining whether a merely arbitrary division of patients or a truly valid typology has been found. We will examine each of these questions in turn.

The choice of patient populations can be critical. The chief danger is that an unrepresentative choice of clinical populations can mislead the investigator, making a vagary of sampling appear to be of taxonomic significance. For example, an ongoing controversy in British psychiatry has been whether endogenous depression is a distinct form of illness from "neurotic" or "reactive" depressions, or whether they form a continuum. If a continuum, patients simply range from a "neurotic-like" extreme to an endogenous-looking extreme, in which case it is arbitrary to classify cases categorically into endogenous and nonendogenous types. The Newcastle group, led by Sir Martin Roth, has long championed the binary view (Carney, Roth, & Garside, 1965), while Kendell (1969), following the lead of Sir Aubrey Lewis, has argued that depressive illnesses fall on a continuum. Suppose a study were conducted that gathered data on depressed patients, rejecting from inclusion any patient showing atypical or mixed features of both endogenous and reactive depression. Further suppose that the two groups studied then appeared quite distinct. Obviously, the resulting data set would be worse than useless, since it depended on rejecting the very cases which would prove a dichotomous typological model false. From this example, one can see the importance of representative sampling in nosologic research. One must study all patients who have features of the illness one wishes to type. The easiest way to ensure fair sampling is to examine consecutive admissions to a clinic or hospital, rejecting cases only when their illnesses are clearly unrelated to the ones under study.

Given a representative sample of patients, they must also be assessed with suitable measuring instruments. It has been customary in cluster analytic studies to use many measures, but this is not an essential requirement of these methods. The rationale for using dozens to hundreds of signs and symptoms in cluster studies is this: It is supposed to be the best way not to beg the question of classification (by assuming the important discriminating variables to be known at the outset). However, if one is trying to determine the homogeneity of *existing* clinical groups (in contrast to trying to develop a new nosology), most signs and symptoms may not be relevant to distinguishing the groups. For example, manic symptoms might be of rather limited use in subtyping anxiety disorders. In general, confirmatory numerical taxonomic studies will use fewer signs and symptoms than exploratory studies; this properly reflects the greater a priori knowledge of the disorders in a confirmatory study.

Whether 10 symptoms or 100 are used to characterize patients, all measurements must be reasonably reliable and repeatable. It is best if previous research has established high interrater and interlaboratory agreement on measures, as well as proving that the measures to be used have important correlates. This caveat is often ignored in studies using cluster analysis.

It is often possible to make modestly reliable measurements more useful for taxonomic work by grouping like measures into scales. This can be done by intuitive or statistical data reduction methods. Items can be grouped into clumps with similar content, or factor analysis (discussed later) can be used to reduce numerous measures to a more parsimonious handful. If content similarity is used to group items into scales, it is wise to correlate items within scales to ensure that the grouping is empirically supported.

Cluster Analysis

One of the most complex decisions facing the investigator is the choice of a particular method of cluster or mixture analysis. In particular, the number of competing cluster algorithms outstrips the ability of all but aficionados to keep up.

Cluster algorithms are either hierarchical or nonhierarchical. Hierarchical methods produce a "tree," in appearance like a phylogenetic tree, typically printed upside down so that the branches open downward. Individuals sit at the tips of branches at the base of the tree; as one moves up the tree, they are joined into successively larger groups. The two most similar individuals are joined nearest the bottom of the tree: the two least similar individuals or groups are joined nearest the top, producing just one group at the root.

Such trees define a hierarchy, and they can be produced by either agglomerative or divisive methods. Agglomerative methods form the tree from the bottom up by successively fusing individuals or groups together. Divisive methods form trees by taking the whole sample at the outset and dividing it on some measure of dissimilarity. One of the two groups thus formed is then redivided, and so on until N individuals are left at the bottom of the tree. Divisive methods have not found much favor among numerical taxonomists, as they tend to make an initial erroneous division from which they are unable to recover. Even within the group of agglomerative hierarchical methods there are many different algorithms.

There also exist nonhierarchical methods of cluster analysis. In perhaps the most useful of these methods, called the K-means algorithm, the user specifies the number of groups to be formed from the data. The method then uses some procedure for forming initial groups (perhaps using the output of other cluster methods) and reallocates cases from cluster to cluster to optimize some measure of similarity. Reallocation of cases continues until moving each case again will not improve cluster homogeneity. As with other cluster methods, homogeneity can be measured in various ways. For example, the sum of all within-cluster similarity coefficients could be maximized, or within-cluster variances could be minimized.

How is the investigator to choose a method when each claims some advantage over the others? Happily, a number of studies in the past few years have compared cluster techniques in terms of their chief desirable property: their ability to recover the true groups present in an artificially constructed mixture. These studies were reviewed by Milligan (1981), and a few conclusions stand out. First, all available methods perform much better when groups are clearly distinct, homogeneous clumps than when groups are poorly separated on available measures. Second, the liability to error of even the best performing cluster algorithms is great, especially when groups are not clearly distinct. Third, no one method uniformly dominates the others in comparative trials: There is usually an interaction of method with data structure, so that with some data, one method does best, while rank order changes for other sorts of data. However, we are happy to report that the interaction of method used with type of data is not so strong that no overall winners emerge from these "Kentucky Derby" trials of cluster analysis procedures.

In fact, across a broad range of data structures, two methods stand out as preferable. Neither one routinely dominates the other, but they are usually two of the top three methods in comparative studies. These two methods are average linkage and Ward's method. Average linkage assigns cases to groups so that the average similarity of pairs of cases within a group is maximized. Ward's method assigns cases to groups so that the sum of squared deviations of cases from cluster means is minimized (a measure closely related to minimizing within-cluster variances).

In studies comparing the nonhierarchical K-means algorithm to average linkage and Ward's method, K-means also performed well. Particular advantage may be gained when a good agglomerative hierarchical cluster method (such as Ward's method) is used to get starting clusters, followed by use of the K-means algorithm (Andreasen & Grove, 1982).

The reader should note that the comparative studies referred to here and in Milligan (1981) are purely empirical. They depend for results on the particular mixture of groups used in each study. No guarantee can be made that these cluster algorithms would work well on data unlike those examined in these studies. For example, if the investigator has signs that show very great intercorrelation within clusters, average linkage and Ward's method tend to perform much worse than another method known as single linkage. This method joins individuals to existing groups if they are highly similar to any single member of an existing group. This leads to elongated clusters that are just chains of individuals in a string. However, with very highly inter-correlated measures, this can be the true shape of the underlying groups, and single-linkage clustering can recover it best.

Quite a few studies in psychiatry have used cluster analysis to type patients. The methods have a natural appeal because, as noted above, their categorization of patients bears a close resemblance to the process of syndrome isolation in clinical medicine. These methods have been especially popular in the study of depression; the literature has been recently reviewed by Blashfield and Morey (1979). In particular, Ward's method has been regularly employed, as by Paykel and Rassaby (1978), by Andreasen and Grove (1982), and by Mattusek, Luks, and Nagel (1982).

Mixture Models

The appropriate uses of mixture models are at present less well understood than clustering algorithms. Few studies have examined the usefulness of mixture models, either from a statistical standpoint or by using them to type psychiatric patients. The principal choice to be made in mixture analysis, after having decided what population to study and what measures to make, is what kind of statistical model to posit. For example, the most common model in mixture analysis is that of a mixture of two or more normal distributions. Fleiss (1972) gave an example of this for the problem of subtyping depression, and recently it has been employed to study the construct of anhedonia in depression (Fawcett, Clark, Scheftner & Gibbon, 1983).

However, even supposing that one postulates a mixture of normal distributions, choices still remain. When there are (as usual) multiple signs which may distinguish between groups, one has to specify a form for the mixture of multivariate normal distributions. This general mixture model supposes that each individual is described by several measurements, each of which is normally distributed within groups. However, measures may be uncorrelated within groups or correlated within groups. The model that specifies correlations within groups must further specify whether the correlations are the same within all groups or differ from group to group. The most flexible model, postulating different correlations within each group, is the most difficult mathematically and can prove numerically insoluble (Hartigan, 1975, p. 114). Procedures for estimating the parameters of such models were given by Day (1969). Everritt (1981b) has performed Monte Carlo studies of the power of a test for the number of types in a mixed population, based on multivariate normal mixture models. He found that unless groups were quite widely separated and all were large (N per group $\geq$ 100), the test for the presence of types was not very powerful.

Another mixture model coming into use in psychiatry is the latent class model. The usual latent class model supposes that the observed data are from a mixture of distributions. Unlike the multivariate normal mixture model, however, the latent class model assumes that the signs are not normally distributed, but are categorical (usually dichotomous). It is further assumed that within classes, the signs are independent; that is, for a group of subjects, all of whom fall in a given group, knowing their status on one sign is of no use in predicting their status on another sign. In this model, any observed covariation among signs is due to the mixture of two or more groups. This assumption can be made more plausible by considering that if there is one cause of large effect (e.g., a single major gene locus segregating in families) which leads to the development of one type of illness, then the other (randomly operating) causes will not lead to symptom covariation. This model was introduced in psychopathology by Meehl (1973), and elaborate procedures for estimating the quantities in the model were used by Golden and Meehl (1979). More statistically optimal estimation procedures were given by Goodman (1974).

Recently, this model has been used in two instances. Golden and Meehl (1979) considered whether a schizotypal class could be detected using just answers to the Minnesota Multiphasic Personality Inventory (MMPI) items. Young, Tanner, and Meltzer (1982) examined whether a core class of schizophrenics was isolated in common by various operational criteria for diagnosing schizophrenia.

An exciting aspect of both these uses is that one set of parameters estimated by these latent class models is the sensitivities and specificities of the indicators. The sensitivity of a sign is the proportion of true "cases" who possess that sign. The specificity is the proportion of true "noncases" who do not possess the sign. These quantities are ordinarily only estimable when a "gold standard" diagnosis is available, against which diagnostic signs can be validated. Latent class methods offer promise as a way to "lift oneself by one's bootstraps" from a state of partial ignorance about the groups present to a judgment about the validity of diagnostic signs.

However, the reader ought not to feel that this mathematical wizardry will obviate the need for clinical validation of groups. The problem shared by almost all numerical taxonomic methods is that they invariably produce groups. The groups may be totally spurious, but groups are produced nonetheless. There are two approaches which may help distinguish between real and misleading groupings. These may be called the internal and the external validation approaches, respectively.

The internal approach to validation relies on working out tests for the existence of types, from the fit of the data used in producing a typology to an assumed typological model. It is often possible to produce tests which will, with reasonable fidelity, say "Yes" when true groups are present and "No" when they are not. For example, in cluster analysis, Mojena (1977) has worked out a test that uses information printed out by agglomerative hierarchical cluster programs in order to tell what is the true number of groups in the sample. This test relies on the fact that if two natural groups are joined to form a mixed group, then the within-group similarity for the new, mixed group should be much lower than the within-group similarity in each of the old groups. Lee (1979) has developed another test that is based on the fact that cluster programs capitalize on chance; that is, in making within-group similarity as great as possible, they will seize even on noise in the data to increase similarity. Lee has taken the approach of estimating how much disparity between clusters can be accounted for by capitalization on chance. If groups differ by more than this amount, then there are presumably true types in the data. Other tests for spuriousness have been worked out by Golden and Meehl (1979) for the latent class model. The simplest of these is to graph the distribution of probabilities of having a syndrome. If there are two types, each subject has some probability of belonging to one of the groups. These probabilities can be graphed as a frequency distribution. Golden and Meehl have found that this distribution should be U-shaped, implying that few subjects are assigned intermediate probabilities of having the syndrome. If the graph is not U-shaped, the two types may well be spurious.

It has been asserted repeatedly that the presence or absence of a bimodal distribution of scores on some continuous variable is a criterion for the presence or absence of true types. For example, Kendell (1968) computed a discriminant analysis between clinically classified endogenous and nonendogenous depressed patients (for a discussion of discriminant analysis, see below). According to Kendell, scores on the canonical variate separating the two groups ought to be bimodal if true subtypes of depressed existed. He found no bimodality, in contrast to Carney et al. (1965), who found clear-cut bimodality. However, population bimodality is a sufficient but not necessary condition for the existence of types. Everitt (1981a) and Fleiss (1972), among others, have pointed out that this is a very stringent criterion, only met when the groups are very widely separated and neither type of patient is too infrequent. Therefore, the similar failure of Paykel, Prusoff, and Klerman (1971) to find bimodal distributions of factor scores is also not telling evidence against a typology of depression.

Valuable as these statistical indications of cluster validity may be, they are unlikely to replace external evidence of cluster validity. By these we mean the use of cluster membership to predict important clinical validators, patient symptoms (other than those used to form clusters), course of illness, response to treatment, patterns of familial transmission, and so on. The acid test of a nosology is its predictive validity, for two reasons. First, a good nosology should have some practical clinical value, since (as in the rest of clinical medicine) diagnosis should bear a strong relationship to prognosis and treatment response, and for genetically transmitted diseases, to familial factors as well. Second, and just as important, the presence of reliable clinical correlates of group membership argues for the reality of a postulated diagnostic entity. The first criterion is pragmatic, the second Platonic.

Validation of Classification Schemes

A number of multivariate statistical techniques are especially valuable for validating existing classifications, whether these classifications are clinical or mathematical in origin. These include factor analysis, multivariate analysis of variance, discriminant analysis, and log-linear models. Space will not permit coverage of other methods, such as multiple regression analysis, which are of use from time to time, but are not of special relevance to the nosologist in psychopathology.

Factor Analysis

Factor analysis can be used to reduce the number of variables on hand severalfold before undertaking numerical taxonomic studies. It also has a general usefulness in aiding the investigator to see how various measures intercorrelate. Factor analysis assumes that the pattern of intercorrelations of a number of variables can be accounted for by a linear statistical model. A linear model is one in which one variable is, except for errors of prediction, equal to a weighted sum of other variables in the model. In factor analysis subjects' scores on observed variables are assumed to be weighted sums of their scores on the unobserved factors. Often the table of weights for predicting variable scores from factor scores, called the matrix of factor "loadings," can be interpreted so that one reduces the number of variables one has to work with, with no loss of information.

However, some cautions are in order. Factor analysis was developed on the assumption that all subjects come from the same population. When subjects come from two or more groups that are mixed together, then factors based on item intercorrelations in the mixed group will be partly a function of within-group correlations and partly a function of the difference between groups on the items. In the extreme case of two very widely separated groups of about equal size, bimodal factor score distributions can emerge. One clue that a mixed group has been factor analyzed is when a large factor with some big positive loadings and some big negative loadings emerges. However, other situations can lead to similar findings, and these so-called "bipolar" factors must be interpreted with caution. A second caution is that there are very many varieties of factor analyses and even more methods of "rotating" factor loadings after they have been computed. The purpose of rotating factor loadings is to increase their interpretability by making the variable break into groups which load highly on one factor and as little as possible on other factors. These factor analyses and rotating methods get very technically complicated. The classic reference on the subject is Harman (1976).

Factor analysis has long been used in psychiatry. It was applied frequently to the detection of depressive syndromes. An excellent review of the results of major factor analyses of depressive syndromes is that of Mendels and Cochrane (1968).

Multivariate Analysis of Variance

Multivariate analysis of variance (MANOVA) offers a method of comparing groups on profiles of measures simultaneously. The usual analysis of variance compares groups on one variable at a time. MANOVA tests several measures at once. It does this by finding the weighted sum of dependent measures that shows a maximal univariate F statistic. If there are more than two groups, it then finds the weighted sum of dependent measures, uncorrelated with the first combination, which maximizes a second univariate F test. In all, the number of such combinations is equal to the number of groups less one, or the number of dependent variables (whichever is less). Since the maximization of the F tests by combining dependent variables capitalizes on chance, the significance tests for MANOVA are complex. The overall test establishes whether the groups contrasted are equal on all dependent measures. But there is more. Not only does MANOVA test all groups for equality on all variables, but it can also afford a method for analyzing profiles of scores.

For example, a widely used psychopathology interview, the Schedule for Affective Disorders and Schizophrenia (SADS) (Endicott & Spitzer, 1978), yields eight scales organized by type of symptom: depressed mood and ideation, depression-associated features, endogenous features, anxiety symptoms, suicidal ideation and behavior, manic features, psychotic features, and formal thought disorder. It makes a useful picture of a group's symptoms to graph the average standardized scale scores as a profile. Using MANOVA, the investigator can decide whether two or more predefined groups (e.g., psychotic vs. endogenous vs. reactive depression) have the same overall profile elevation (roughly corresponding to overall severity of illness), and independently of profile elevation, whether they have the same profile shape. Profile shape is crucial to the psychiatric taxonomist, since one ordinarily wants to find groups that differ not merely in severity of illness, but also in type of predominant symptoms. A test of identical profile shape between groups establishes presence or absence of differences in predominant symptom type between groups. This strategy was used to validate clusters in a cluster analytic study done by the authors (Andreasen, Grove, & Maurer, 1980). It was demonstrated that profile shape differences (type of symptoms) accounted for one-third of between-cluster variance, while profile elevation (severity of illness) accounted for two-thirds of the variance.

Investigators using MANOVA must confront a number of problems. Several times as many subjects per groups as there are variables are required (recommendations range from 3 to 10 subjects per variable per group). Variables are supposed to be normally distributed, although this is apparently not critical as long as measures are at least quasi-continuous, not highly skewed, and not bimodally distributed within groups. The measures are supposed to have the same variances and covariances within groups. If this assumption is grossly violated, the significance levels associated with tests of multivariate equality between groups may be compromised. The equality of covariance matrices should be checked when MANOVA is done; tests are described by Harris (1975), who also gives a good introductory discussion of MANOVA. Harris, however, fails to inform the reader that the test of equal within-group covariance matrices is rather sensitive to nonnormally distributed variables.

Discriminant Analysis

Discriminant analysis is in some respects closely related to MANOVA, and it is a very important technique with considerable promise in developing diagnostic systems both for research and for clinical practice. Unlike techniques discussed to this point, discriminant analysis must always begin with groups of patients who have already been classified into diagnostic groups. It finds a combination of scores that maximally discriminates between these groups, as does MANOVA. However, instead of trying to maximize the significance of between-group differences, as MANOVA does, discriminant analysis attempts to find the variables (or symptoms) that produce the most accurate classification of patients into known groups. When the data are normally distributed within groups and when the within-groups variances and covariances are the same, these objectives of MANOVA and discriminant analysis are identical. This produces the usual linear discriminant function. This function is *not* the same as the linear combination of scores with a maximum F statistic, which is called the first canonical variate in discriminant analysis literature. Beware: Some computer manuals confuse the two. If there are more than two groups to be classified, there will be one less discriminant function than there are groups or as many functions as there are variables, whichever is less.

A useful piece of output from discriminant analysis is the hit-rate table, showing the performance of the discriminant functions in classifying subjects into groups. However, discriminant functions capitalize on chance. If the performance of discriminant functions is evaluated on the same sample in which they were developed, the investigator may get an overly optimistic idea about how good the discrimination is. There are two solutions to this problem: cross-validation (trying them out on a new sample) or correcting for the capitalization on chance. A correction can be made by the following procedure, called jackknifing: Calculate the discriminant functions with the first case left out, and use them to classify the first case. Repeat this, leaving out each case in turn, and record all the results together in a new hit-rate table. This table gives a fair estimate of the expected performance of the discriminant functions obtained in the population from which the subjects were drawn. Discriminant functions usually misclassify more subjects with a rare condition than with common ones. If the analysis is redone in a new sample with different rates of the various illnesses, different results will be obtained; the effectiveness of discriminant analysis varies with the base rates.

What can the investigator do if the variables show a different pattern of covariation in one group than in another? Quadratic discriminant analysis can help here. It finds a combination of measures to discriminate that is not a weighted sum of measures, but instead is a weighted sum of squares and cross-products of measures. However, this method requires many observations per group and per variable in order to get reliable results. Both linear and quadratic discriminant analysis and the "leaving-one-out" method are described by Lachenbruch (1975) in detail.

When dichotomous or categorically classified symptoms are used as diagnostic indicators, linear and quadratic discriminant analysis may not be useful. Instead, a classification rule such as the following may be tried: Find all patients in a standardization sample who show the same pattern of symptoms as the patient to be classified, and classify the test patient into whichever diagnosis most of the patients with the same symptoms had. This is the optimal rule for categorical discriminators. However, if the table of symptoms has many items in it, the available cases (unless vast samples are available) will be spread too thinly for reliable results. Various schemes to get around this problem by combining similar symptom patterns to increase group size are described by Goldstein and Dillon (1978).

Discriminant analysis has been very widely used in psychiatry, often to demonstrate that certain signs and symptoms are particularly important in making a differential diagnosis. These demonstrations depend on the size of coefficients of various signs and symptoms in the canonical variates. All other things being equal, the symptoms with largest weights are most useful in making differential diagnoses. However, usually all other things are not equal, and judgment is called for in interpreting statistics purporting to measure the importance of discriminators.

An example of discriminant analysis was given by Fowler, Liskow, Tanna, Lytle, and Mezzich (1980). They used nine variables to distinguish between primary affective disorder and schizophrenia. These nine variables were chosen from a plethora of measures that significantly discriminated between the two groups. This of course capitalizes on chance, since some variables will be significant by mere accident. The authors evidently thought they were protecting against chance-based variable selection by using the leaving-one-out procedure for estimating cross-validated hit rates. This is a common misunderstanding. If the variables chosen for use in a discriminant analysis are selected by stepwise equation fitting or by previously showing significant group differences in the calibration sample, the leaving-one-out method will not compensate for such capitalization on chance. The leaving-one-out method compensates for capitalization on chance in the choice of weights for the variables in the discriminant function, given that the correct variables are in the equation. Lachenbruch (1975) suggests that no more than four or five variables be selected by stepwise addition of variables to a discriminant function. The previously mentioned strictures on sample size for MANOVA also apply to discriminant analysis. Quadratic discrimination needs especially large samples.

A valuable aspect of the Fowler *et al.* study was that the criterion diagnoses were made using rigorous diagnostic criteria. This is especially important in discriminant analysis, since errors in classifying the patients used to develop a discriminant function can result in considerable error.

Log-Linear Models

The last technique we will discuss is just becoming well known in psychopathology research and is the most recently developed of all the techniques we have mentioned. Log-linear models are uniquely suited to the type of data often available to the psychopathology researcher. These models are an advanced way of analyzing contingency table data in which data are categorized and in which at most relations of ordering obtain between categories. The fundamental log-linear model assumption is that the logarithms of frequencies in table cells are a linear function of effects in the model. Such models often provide parsimonious accounts of the cooccurrence of signs, symptoms, diagnoses, and correlates thereof, for which multiple regression and other linear models often provide poor fits.

An example will illustrate this point. Cadoret, Cain, and Grove (1980) fit linear and log-linear models to adoption study data on the prevalence of alcoholism in the adoptees with and without biological relatives with alcohol abuse. Various environmental and family history predictors were examined to see if they could predict adoptee alcoholism. The best fitting multiple regression model accounted for less than 10% of the variance in adoptee diagnosis. A simple log-linear model using just one predictor (biological background for alcoholism) accounted for over 75% of the variance in frequency of alcoholism among adoptees. Cloninger and his colleagues at Washington University have also made extensive use of log-linear models and discriminant analysis in predicting adoptee alcohol abuse (Bohman, Sigvardsson, & Cloninger, 1981; Cloninger, Bohman, & Sigvardsson, 1981).

A standard reference in this field is Bishop, Fienberg, and Holland (1975), who gave many examples of the use of these models in biomedical studies. In using these techniques one needs a lot of data, especially if many factors are being examined simultaneously. For example, studying eight dichotomous factors as predictors of another dichotomous variable gives 512 cells in the contingency table. Even with 50-50 splits on every variable, with 1,000 cases there will be on average just two cases per cell. Usually in practice many cells have very few data points. Suggestions for overcoming this problem are discussed at length by Bishop *et al.* (1975). We expect that more and more researchers will be using these procedures now that major statistical packages offer good programs for performing the required computations (which can be extensive).

Summary

The literature on multivariate statistical techniques is too vast to survey comprehensively in a brief chapter. We have attempted to describe how multivariate statistics can be harnessed to serve many different purposes. Techniques such as cluster analysis can be used to develop new empirically based systems of classification. Investigators using cluster analysis and related techniques hope that they may permit us to see new typologies or relationships to which ossified traditional classification schemes have blinded us. Other techniques, such as discriminant analysis, approach the problem of nosology from the opposite direction. They begin with groups of patients who have already been classified using some recognized nosological system and proceed to identify the symptoms that have the greatest utility for classifying patients within this system. Imaginative investigators can move back and forth between these two extremes. The nosological classes produced by a cluster analysis can be compared with those produced by traditional clinical systems, thereby providing a test of validity for each. Discriminant function scores can be graphed and examined for bimodality, thereby providing a kind of test for the existence of independent typologies. As these examples indicate, the uses of multivariate analysis are numerous. As new methods such as mixture models and log-linear models are developed and used in clinical research, we can hope to steadily improve our understanding of phenomenology and nosology.

REFERENCES

Anderberg, M. R. (1973). *Cluster analysis for applications*. New York: Academic Press.

Andreasen, N. C., & Grove, W. M. (1982). The classification of depression: A comparison of traditional and mathematically derived approaches. *American Journal of Psychiatry, 139,* 45–52.

Andreasen, N. C., Grove, W. M., & Maurer, R. (1980). Cluster analysis and the classification of depression. *British Journal of Psychiatry, 137,* 256–265.

Bishop, Y. M. M., Fienberg, S. E., & Holland, P. W. (1975). *Discrete multivariate analysis: Theory and practice.* Cambridge, MA: MIT Press.

Blashfield, R. K., & Morey, L. C. (1979). The classification of depression through cluster analysis. *Comprehensive Psychiatry, 20,* 516–527.

Bohman, M., Sigvardsson, S., & Cloninger, C. R. (1981). Maternal inheritance of alcohol abuse: Cross-fostering analysis of adopted women. *Archives of General Psychiatry, 38,* 965–969.

Cadoret, R. C., Cain, C., & Grove, W. M. (1980). Development of alcoholism in adoptees raised apart from alcoholic biological relatives. *Archives of General Psychiatry, 37,* 561–563.

Carney, M. W. P., Roth, M., & Garside, R. F. (1965). The diagnosis of depressive syndromes and the prediction of E.C.T. response. *British Journal of Psychiatry, 111,* 659–674.

Cloninger, C. R., Bohman, M., & Sigvardsson, S. (1981). Inheritance of alcohol abuse: Cross-fostering analysis of adopted men. *Archives of General Psychiatry, 38,* 861–868.

Day, N. E. (1969). Estimating the components of a mixture of normal distributions. *Biometrika, 56,* 463–474.

Endicott, J., & Spitzer, R. L. (1978). A diagnostic interview: The schedule for affective disorders and schizophrenia. *Archives of General Psychiatry, 35,* 837–844.

Everitt, B. S. (1972). Cluster analysis: A brief discussion of some of the problems. *British Journal of Psychiatry, 120,* 143–145.

Everitt, B. S. (1980). *Cluster analysis* (2nd ed.). New York: Halsted Press.

Everitt, B. S. (1981a). Bimodality and the nature of depression. *British Journal of Psychiatry, 138,* 336–339.

Everitt, B. S. (1981b). A Monte Carolo investigation of the likelihood ratio test for the number of components in a mixture of normal distributions. *Multivariate Behavioral Research, 16,* 171–180.

Fawcett, J., Clark, D. L., Scheftner, W. A., & Gibbon, R. D. (1983). Assessing anhedonia in psychiatric patients: The pleasure scale. *Archives of General Psychiatry, 40,* 79–84.

Fleiss, J. L. (1972). Classification of the depressive disorders by numerical typology. *Journal of Psychiatric Research, 9,* 141–153.

Fleiss, J. L., Lawlor, W., Platman, S. R., & Fieve, R. R. (1971). On the use of inverted factor analysis for generating typologies. *Journal of Abnormal Psychology, 77,* 127–132.

Fowler, R. C., Liskow, B. I., Tanna, V. L., Lytle, L., & Mezzich, J. (1980). Schizophrenia–primary affective disorder discrimination. I. Development of a data-based diagnostic index. *Archives of General Psychiatry, 37,* 811–814.

Golden, R. R., & Meehl, P. E. (1979). Detection of the schizoid taxon with MMPI indicators. *Journal of Abnormal Psychology, 88,* 217–233.

Goldstein, M., & Dillon, W. R. (1978). *Discrete discriminant analysis.* New York: Wiley.

Goodman, L. A. (1974). The analysis of systems of qualitative variables when some of the variables are unobservable. Part I. A modified latent structure approach. *American Journal of Sociology, 79,* 1179–1259.

Harman, H. H. (1976). *Modern factor analysis* (3rd rev.). Chicago, IL: University of Chicago Press.

Harris, R. J. (1975). *A primer of multivariate statistics.* New York: Academic Press.

Hartigan, J. A. (1975). *Clustering algorithms.* New York: Wiley.

Kendell, R. E. (1968). *The classification of depressive illnesses.* London: Oxford University Press.

Kendell, R. E. (1969). The continuum model of depressive illness. *Proceedings of the Royal Society of Medicine, 62,* 335–339.

Klein, D. F. (1974). Endogenomorphic depression: A conceptual and terminological revision. *Archives of General Psychiatry, 31,* 447–454.

Lachenbruch, P. A. (1975). *Discriminant analysis.* New York: Hafner.

Lee, K. L. (1979). Multivariate tests for clusters. *Journal of the American Statistical Association, 74,* 708–714.

Matussek, P., Luks, O., & Nagel, D. (1982). Depressive symptom patterns. *Psychological Medicine, 12,* 756–773.

Meehl, P. E. (1973). MAXCOV-HITMAX: A taxonomic search method for loose genetic syndromes. In *Psychodiagnosis: Selected Papers.* Minneapolis: University of Minnesota Press.

Mendels, J., & Cochrane, C. (1968). The nosology of depression: The endogenous-reactive concept. *American Journal of Psychiatry, 11,* Supplement.

Milligan, G. C. (1981). A review of Monte Carlo tests of cluster analysis. *Multivariate Behavioral Research, 6,* 379–407.

Mojena, R. (1977). Hierarchical grouping methods and stopping rules: An evaluation. *Computer Journal, 20,* 359–363.

Paykel, E. S., Prusoff, B., & Klerman, G. L. (1971). The endogenous–neurotic continuum in depression: Rater independence and factor distributions. *Journal of Psychiatric Research, 8,* 73–90.

Paykel, E. S., & Rassaby, E. (1978). Classification of suicide attempters by cluster analysis. *British Journal of Psychiatry, 133*, 45–52.

Raskin, A., Schulterbrandt, J. G., Boothe, H., Reatig, M., & McKeon, J. J. (1972). Some suggestions for selecting appropriate depression subgroups for biochemical studies. In T. A. Williams, M. M. Katz, & J. A. Shields, Jr. (Eds.), *Recent Advances in the psychobiology of depressive illness.* Washington, DC: U.S. Government Printing Office.

Young, M. A., Tanner, M. A., & Meltzer, H. Y. (1982). Operational definitions of schizophrenia: What do they identify? *Journal of Nervous and Mental Disease, 170*, 443–447.

CHAPTER 18

Structural Approaches to Classification

Roger K. Blashfield

In the field of biology, classification has been a central topic for the past 300 years. Biologists have subdivided the general topic of classification into three areas: *classification, identification,* and *taxonomy* (Simpson, 1961). Classification, in the precise sense of the word, refers to the activity of forming categories or classes of entities; identification is used to describe the assignment of new entities to an already existing set of categories. The presentation of a metaphor may help make this distinction clear. Imagine a boy with his collection of marbles. He decides to sort his marbles into piles. He puts the pretty marbles into one pile, his "shooters" into another, the marbles he will trade in another, and finally the chipped marbles into a fourth pile. The activity of forming the piles is what biologists mean by *classification*. If a friend comes along and gives the boy a new marble, *identification* is the process he utilizes to decide into which pile he should place the new marble. In medicine and psychiatry, the activity biologists describe as identification is usually denoted by the term *diagnosis*.

Neither classification nor identification/diagnosis will be the focus of this chapter. Instead, this chapter will address the third area, *taxonomy*. Taxonomy is the term that biologists use to refer to the theoretical study of classification. Part of the reason for the importance of taxonomy is that biological classification is very much intertwined with evolutionary theory. Currently, there are three competing theoretical perspectives about biological classification: evolutionary systematics, numerical taxonomy, and cladistics. These three theoretical perspectives will be discussed later in the chapter.

Roger K. Blashfield. Department of Psychiatry, College of Medicine, University of Florida, Gainesville, Florida.

There has been relatively little literature in the field of psychopathology that addresses taxonomy. Most writers who have discussed psychiatric classification (e.g., Cantor, Smith, French, & Mezzich, 1980; Panzetta, 1974) seem to assume that the theoretical principles which govern the formation of classification systems are or should be self-evident. The present chapter will attempt to partially alter this state of affairs by focusing on theoretical concepts regarding classificatory systems. To start, taxonomic concepts from biological classification will be introduced. The reason for the initial emphasis on biological classification is the extensive history of this area of classification. Moreover, initial developments in medical classification were often patterned after biological classification (Faber, 1930). The second section of the chapter will use the concepts from biological taxonomy to analyze contemporary psychiatric classification. Generally this section will show that there are substantial structural differences between these two systems. Finally, concepts from the research of cultural anthropologists on folk classifications of living organisms will be presented. It will be argued that psychiatric classification has a structure more similar to these folk classifications than it is similar to biological classification as recognized by modern science.

Taxonomic Approaches to Biological Classification

To begin the discussion of taxonomy, the initial focus will be on a monograph called *The Language of Taxonomy* (1954) by the logician, John Gregg. In his monograph, Gregg attempted to explicate the structure of biological classification using principles from logic and from set theory. Modern taxonomists consider Gregg's treatise to be overly formal (Simpson, 1961). Nonetheless, Gregg's analysis provided a useful structural perspective on biological classification, especially for readers who are not familiar with the details of biological classification.

To begin the discussion of the structural features of biological classification, let us look at Figure 18-1. This figure shows the classification of the cat family. Listed on the figure are the common English names for the various categories of cats. In parentheses are shown the scientific names of the categories in Latin. Since spoken languages often do not make the precise distinctions among categories of animals which are necessary for a scientific classification of biological organisms, it has become a standard practice since the work of Linnaeus to use Latin names for categories.

Gregg introduced a system of names to describe the structural features in biological classification (see also Buck & Hull, 1966). For example, the term *categories* is used to refer to all of the names shown in Figure 18-1 (most biologists prefer the term *taxa* instead of "categories"); that is, all names shown in Figure 18-1 are names of specific categories in the cat family. Gregg also pointed out that categories (taxa) refer to sets of objects. The

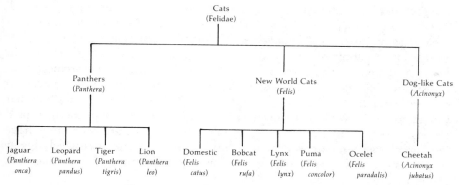

Figure 18-1. *Classification of the cat family.*

category name, *Felis catus* (domestic cat), refers to the class of housecats such as the three cats in my household whose names are Mittens, PS, and Mehitable. For the purpose of this chapter, the names of my three pet cats will be described as the names of *entities*. Entities are the members of the various categories in the classification. A third level of name which is important to understanding biological classification is the name of *ranks*. For instance, *Felis catus*, *Panthera tigris*, and *Panthera leo* are all names of different species. The term *species* is the name of a specific rank. The great classifier, Linnaeus, was also the innovator who proposed a set of names to be used for the ranks of biological classification. These names included "kingdom," "phylum," "order," "family," "genus," and "species." In Figure 18-1, all categories that belong to the same rank occur along the same row of the figure, a conventional practice when displaying the hierarchical arrangement among categories in a biological classification. To summarize, there are three types of names in biological classification:

Type I   names—the names of entities (e.g., Mehitable)
Type II names—the names of categories (e.g., *Panthera leo*)
Type III names—the names of ranks (e.g., species)

Gregg also proposed three relationships which can exist among the types of names. The first relationship is *membership*. This relationship can occur between any two names which are one type apart. For instance, my pet cat Mehitable is a member of the category *Felis catus*. "Jai," a tiger cub at Marine World/Africa USA, is a member of the category *Panthera tigris*. The category *Panthera tigris* is a member of the rank named "species," just as the category Felidae is a member of the rank named "family."

Another relationship that can exist is the relation of inclusion. Inclusion is a relation that can only occur within a given type of name. The category Felidae includes the categories *Felis*, *Felis catus*, *Felis concolor*, *Panthera tigris*, and so on. The relationship of inclusion will occur between two names of the same type when all members of the first name are also members of the second. Thus, the category *Felis catus* is included under Felidae because all entities which are members of *Felis catus* are also members of Felidae.

A third relationship that can exist among names is that of hierarchy. In his monograph, Gregg proposed an exact definition of a hierarchical relationship using set theory. Subsequent analyses have shown deficiencies in the precise definition given by Gregg (Buck & Hull, 1966). Basically, what Gregg proposed was that a hierarchy is a complex relationship among Type II names. A hierarchical relationship requires that names at lower ranks have less members than names at higher ranks, that there are successively fewer names as the hierarchy moves upward, and that all names of the same rank are mutually exclusive.

The hierarchical relationship among Type II names in biological classification is extremely important. As will be shown later, most of the current controversies about theoretical approaches to biological classification concern the details of the hierarchical relationship among categories. Taxonomists in biology are very concerned about the hierarchical nature of classification.

One concept was introduced above almost parenthetically when attempting to explain what a hierarchical relationship is. This concept was *mutually exclusive*. Most biologists would agree that a classification of cats should be both *mutually exclusive* and *exhaustive*. The property of being mutually exclusive means that if a particular animal is a member of one category, then it cannot also be a member of another category. For instance, my cat Mehitable is a member of the category *Felis catus*. The property of being mutually exclusive would be defied if this domestic cat were also a member of the category *Felis pardalis* (ocelot). The property of being exhaustive means that categories should exist to contain all possible entities in the classification. If an animal is a cat, there should exist a species name to which that cat is a member.

One structural feature not discussed by Gregg is the definition of names. Buck and Hull (1966) suggested that there are two major types of definitions of names. One definition is an *extensional* definition. In this type of definition, a name is defined by listing its members. An extensional definition of *Felis catus* would contain the names of all domestic cats. In the same way, an extensional definition of the name "genus" would list the names of all categories (e.g., *Felis, Panthera, Homo*) which are members of that rank. In general, extensional definitions for the names of ranks and categories are not practical. For instance, there are millions of domestic cats in the world. Listing the names of all domestic cats would be an impractical task.

The other definition is called an *intensional* definition. Using this type of definition, a name is defined by listing the characteristics which are necessary for an object to be a member of the name. Thus, the intensional definition of *Felis catus* would list the characteristics of the domestic cat which could be used to decide whether a particular cat belonged to this particular category or not. Notice that categories are defined intensionally by using the characteristics of entities; in the same way, an intensional definition of a rank would require the listing of characteristics of categories which are necessary for assigning a given category to that rank.

Intensional definitions can be subdivided further into *monothetic* and *polythetic* (Bailey, 1973; Sokal & Sneath, 1963). In the monothetic definition of a category, the characteristics, all of which are necessary, are listed. The other form of an intensional definition is called a polythetic definition. Using this definitional form, all characteristics listed in the definition are not necessary, but some subsets of the characteristics are jointly sufficient.

To clarify the distinction between monothetic and polythetic definitions, consider a category named X. Category X is defined intensionally by five characteristics: a, b, c, d, and e. A monothetic definition would be symbolized as follows:

$$(a \ \& \ b \ \& \ c \ \& \ d \ \& \ e)$$

where the symbol "&" means "and." In this definition, all five characteristics must be present in order for an entity to belong to the category. If an entity has four of the five characteristics, it would not belong to the category.

A polythetic definition of category X, by contrast, might be symbolized as follows:

$$(a \ \& \ b \ \& \ c \ \& \ d) \ \vee \ (a \ \& \ c \ \& \ e) \ \vee \ (b \ \& \ d \ \& \ e)$$

where the symbol "∨" means "or." In this polythetic definition of category X, if characteristic e is present, an entity needs to have only two of the remaining four characteristics to be identified as a member of the category (either characteristics a and c or characteristics b and d). If characteristic e is not present, all four of the other characteristics must be present.

Biologists have found that intensional definitions, which are pragmatically useful and permit the identification of new cases, will be polythetic. Specifying characteristics, all of which are necessary for membership to a category (i.e., monothetic definitions), is rarely feasible for natural categories (Beckner, 1959). The members of natural categories are often highly similar in terms of the defining characteristics, but rarely are they identical in terms of these characteristics.

Animals have large numbers of characteristics. In a very general way, these characteristics can be grouped into divisions such as morphology, behavior, physiology, and biochemistry. Thousands and perhaps millions of characteristics could be used in the classification of biological organisms. To propose an intensional definition in terms of all characteristics would be as impractical as an extensional definition.

Frake (1972) used the concept of *contrast set* to denote what characteristics should be the foci in any intensional definition. A contrast set refers to the collection of names from which a given name must be distinguished when it is defined. In biological classification, a contrast set would consist of all categories occurring immediately below a common node in the hierarchy. Thus, the contrast set for the category *Felis catus* would consist of all categories which are included under the genus named *Felis*. The characteristics that are necessary in an intensional definition of *Felis catus* are those characteristics which are necessary for distinguishing among the different species of this genus. Thus, in defining *Felis catus*, one does not have to list the general characteristics of all cats. Those characteristics would be used in defining the category Felidae [whose contrast set consists of other family names such as Candidae (dog family), Mustelidae (weasels and skunk), and Ursidae (bears)].

As noted earlier, the hierarchical arrangement among categories has become a central aspect to biological classification. Part of the reason for the importance of the hierarchical arrangement of categories is that the hierarchical pattern among categories can suggest the evolutionary process by which different species came into being. Three schools of thought have developed in biological classification about the nature of hierarchical relationship among categories.

One school of thought is called *numerical taxonomy* (Sneath & Sokal, 1973; Sokal & Sneath, 1963). This school argues that biological classification should be organized by the similarity of entities. All entities that have highly similar characteristics should belong to the same category. The ranks reflect the homogeneity of the categories. Categories at the lowest rank (species level) should be highly homogeneous across all possible characteristics, while categories at higher levels (e.g., phylum level) would be relatively heterogeneous.

The numerical taxonomy school is best known for the explicit classification process it has proposed. Numerical taxonomists have suggested that a classifier should collect as much information as possible across as many characteristics as possible on the entities being classified. Once information has been gathered across a wide range of characteristics, a statistical procedure called *cluster analysis* should be used to empirically organize similar entities into categories (Clifford & Stephensen, 1975; Everitt, 1980). Then the categories at the lowest (most specific) rank can be arranged hierarchically according to their similarity using cluster analysis. Numerical taxonomists have favored cluster analysis procedures to create classifications because these methods can handle vast amounts of data that can overwhelm human classifiers and also because cluster analysis procedures are statistical techniques which are not affected by human biases. However, the numerical taxonomy school has fallen into disfavor because there are serious statistical issues associated with the known cluster analysis methods and because the classifications created through cluster analysis have often been unsatisfactory (Cormack, 1971; Nelson & Platnick, 1981).

A second school of thought about biological classification is called *cladistics* (Wiley, 1981). Cladists are strongly opposed to the notion of organizing biological classification purely on the basis of similarity of characteristics. Cladists argue that the most important property of any biological classification is the evolutionary information contained in its hierarchical structure. Cladists believe that each node in the hierarchy of biological classification should represent a point of change in evolutionary history. Evolution, not similarity, is the organizing principle of biological classification, according to the cladists.

To persons who are not familiar with the details of biological classification, the position advocated by the cladists of using evolution as the organizing principle seems plausible. However, to biologists, the classifications that can result from cladistics may be strange. For instance, crocodiles and birds have a more recent evolutionary ancestor than do crocodiles and alligators. Cladists favor a hierarchical arrangement in which crocodiles and birds are subsets of a common category—a decidedly nontraditional arrangement (Mayr, 1981).

The third school of thought about biological classification is called *evolutionary systematics* (Mayr, 1969; Simpson, 1961). This is the traditional school of thought. Its main organizing principle is information retrieval. Evolutionary systematists agree that both similarity and evolution are important bases for forming classifications. However, either similarity or evolution if taken alone can lead to strange classification systems. Hence, systematists attempt to compromise and to form classifications which optimize both similarity and evolutionary history. Thereby, evolutionary systematists hope to create classifications that are useful to other biologists when storing, organizing, and retrieving information about organisms. However, because evolutionary systematics is essentially advocating a compromise position, the decisions made by classifiers from this school of thought necessarily contain subjective elements. Both numerical taxonomists and cladists reject evolutionary systematics as being less rigorous and less scientific than their perspectives.

To conclude, the preceding discussion of biological classification has introduced and briefly described a number of concepts which taxonomists have utilized when discussing the problems of classification. This presentation about biological classification has not exhausted the topic. Biological taxonomists use a number of other concepts such as *phenogram*, *synapomorph*, *phenetic*, and *polarity*. Interested readers should examine books such as Nelson and Platnick (1981), Simpson (1961), Sneath and Sokal (1973), and Wiley (1981) for a discussion of these and many other concepts.

Taxonomic Concepts from Biology Applied to Psychiatric Classification

In this section, the application of the previously developed taxonomic concepts to the classification of psychopathology will be explored. The particular classification which will be the focus in this section will be the DSM-III.

Proposition 1: *There are parallels between biological and psychiatric classifications.*

A number of ostensible parallels exist between biological classification and the classification of psychopathology. First, both classifications use a hierarchical organization of categories. Figure 18-2 shows some of the categories from the DSM-III arranged in a hierarchical pattern which parallels the hierarchical structure of biological classification shown in Figure 18-1. Second, the historical roots of both systems have many communalities. Linnaeus, the Swedish botanist, was one of the most significant persons in the history of biologist classification. Linnaeus was also concerned with medical classification and proposed a major classification of diseases (King, 1958). His ideas were influenced by the classificatory activities of the important seventeenth-century physician, Syndenham. This historical relationship is important, since psychiatric classification is usually considered a subset of the classification of medical diseases. Third, one of the three theoretical schools of thought described above, the numerical taxonomists, has stimulated a large amount of research about the classification of mental disorders (Lorr, 1966, 1983). Currently, there are over 200 published articles and books which have used some form of cluster analysis to create alternative classifications of the various mental disorders (Blashfield, 1984). The dramatic rise of interest in cluster analysis within the psychopathology literature can be attributed to the influence of the numerical taxonomists (Blashfield & Aldenderfer, 1978).

These facts do suggest that parallels between biological classification and psychopathological classification are indeed plausible. However, when a rigorous application of the concepts of biological taxonomy is attempted, the parallels between the two systems become less clear.

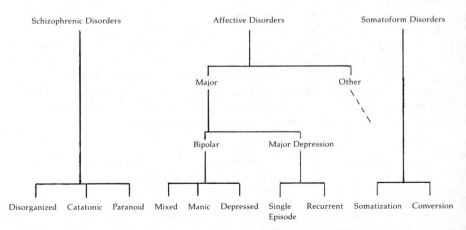

Figure 18-2. *Hierarchical pattern of some categories from DSM-III, paralleling the structure of the biological classification of Figure 18-1.*

Proposition 2: *It is not clear whether the entities in the DSM-III are patients or disorders.*

A good place to begin the analysis of the parallels between biological and psychopathological classification is with the three types of names which Gregg proposed when discussing structural properties. The names shown earlier in Figure 18-1, the classification of the cat family, are all names of categories. Categories also·exist in the DSM-III. The names of categories in the latter system are shown in Figure 18-2. In effect, the categories of the DSM-III are the various mental disorders which this system recognized. About 250 separate categories are presented in the DSM-III system. More specifically, names like "schizophrenic disorders," "major depressive disorder," "schizotypal personality disorder," and "anorexia nervosa" are all names of categories.

What then are the entities (Type I names) in the DSM-III? The most obvious answer to this question is patients. Patients are the objects that are diagnosed (identified). It is the characteristics (symptoms, behaviors, etc.) of patients which are used in the intensional definitions of the categories. When the homogeneity of categories is studied, it is analyzed by computing the variance across patients along various clinical assessments on these patients.

In short, it would seem that the entities in the DSM-III are patients. However, the authors of the DSM-III are quite explicit in rejecting this interpretation (American Psychiatric Association, 1980). They assert that disorders, not patients, are the objects being classified in the DSM-III (cf. Ghiselin, 1974; Hull, 1976). Why do they make this assertion?

Proposition 3: *If patients are the entities, then either the property of mutually exclusive categories is defied or a logical structure for overlapping categories is needed.*

A major reason for rejecting the notion that the entities in the DSM-III are patients is that the DSM-III classification system permits the use of multiple diagnoses; that is, it seems quite plausible that a patient who is diagnosed as having anorexia nervosa could also have a severe snake phobia which needs treatment. However, if the same patient is a member of two different categories, then the property of mutually exclusive categories would be defied.

Another reason for rejecting the notion that patients are the entities in the DSM-III is because psychiatric diagnoses generally have strong negative connotations and because there is a tendency by both patients and clinicians to reify the diagnoses assigned to patients. In other words, if psychiatric diagnoses are to be assigned to people, then these diagnoses can be seen as "bad labels" which tend to "stick" to people. Representative of this position is Szasz's caustic suggestion that "classifiers should be classified, not people." By asserting that patients are not the objects of the DSM-III classification, the authors of the DSM-III are attempting to circumvent the labeling issue.

Regarding the issue of overlapping categories, some work has been done on the logical structure of classification systems which would allow overlap. In particular, two British taxonomists, Jardine and Sibson (1971), have suggested mathematical models for classification systems which would permit and support the existence of significant overlap among categories (see also Zadeh, 1965).

Moreover, the issue of overlapping categories is probably not as serious an issue as it might seem in the DSM-III. First, the authors of the DSM-III defined a number of categories in such a way that overlap was not permitted between commonly used categories (e.g., the definition of the category "schizophrenic disorders" requires that the category "affective disorders" is ruled out). Second, even among categories that are permitted to overlap, multiple diagnoses are rare (Rutter, Shaffer, & Shepherd, 1975). Clinicians usually assign only one diagnosis to a patient.

Finally, to state that the DSM-III is a classification of disorders is tautological. Of course, it is a classification of disorders, just as biological classification is a classification of taxa. Taxa and disorders are general names for the categories in these two classifications. To claim that the DSM-III is a classification of disorders is simply to avoid defining the entities (i.e., Type I names) in this system.

Proposition 4: *No names exist for the ranks in the DSM-III.*

The third type of name which Gregg discussed in his structural approach to classification was ranks. Ranks are the higher level concepts to which all categories at the same level in the hierarchical system belong.

Names for ranks do not exist in the DSM-III; that is, there are no terms in the DSM-III which are analogous to the concepts of species, genus, order, family, and so on in biological classification. Although categories such as "schizophrenic disorders," "affective disorders," and "somatoform disorders" all exist at the same level in the hierarchical outline of the DSM-III, no explanation is given why they occur at the same level, nor is any definition provided for the rank to which they might belong.

It is interesting to speculate what might be a reasonable name for a rank in the DSM-III. One possible name for the lowest level rank in the DSM-III system would be "disease." Categories such as "paranoid schizophrenia," "anorexia nervosa," "recurrent major depression," and "substance abuse disorder (cocaine)" would all be diseases (i.e., members of the rank named disease). Thus, the definition of disease would need to be expressed in terms of the characteristics of categories which are necessary for membership in this rank.

If the name disease was used as the name of a rank (i.e., if "disease" is analogous to the biological term "species"), then it would be necessary to distinguish between the terms "mental disorder" and "disease." Mental disorder is the most inclusive name for categories in the DSM-III. If a patient is diagnosed as belonging to the category "schizophrenia," the patient also must belong to the superordinate category called "mental disorder." Thus, the intensional definition of mental disorder would distinguish between persons who have some form of psychopathology and those persons who are psychiatrically normal.

Disease, in contrast, would *not* be defined by referring to characteristics of patients, nor would its definition resolve the demarcation problem of deciding who is normal and who is abnormal. Instead, the definition of disease would be used to specify what categories belong to the class of diseases and therefore what categories should be recognized in a scientifically viable classification of psychopathology.

The possible analogy between the terms "species" and "disease" is quite important for the development of an adequate classification of psychopathology. The term "species" has an extended and controversial history over the past two centuries of writing about biological classification (Blackwelder, 1967). Different taxonomists have proposed different explicit definitions of this concept. Classifiers in biology recognize that to adopt a specific resolution to the definition of species is to take a strong stand which will dramatically affect the details of the biological classifications. Controversies over the meaning of species continue in the present literature. The different theoretical schools described earlier all have different positions about the concept of species.

The concept of disease also has an extensive and controversial history. Providing an adequate definition of this concept has proved to be a very difficult theoretical task. Notice that to claim that the term "disease" is analogous to the term "species" is in itself controversial. The making of this analogy is tantamount to accepting the medical model—a perspective to psychopathology which has been criticized for a number of theoretical and political reasons (Caplan, Englehardt, & McCartney, 1981).

Regardless of what term is used to designate the lowest rank in the hierarchical organization of mental disorders, it should be clear that the choice and definition of this term will have a major effect on the organization of psychopathological classification.

Proposition 5: *The diagnostic criteria in the DSM-III are polythetic, intensional definitions.*

One of the three major changes from the DSM-II to the DSM-III was the use of diagnostic criteria when defining categories (the other two changes were the major reorganization of the categories and the adoption of a multiaxial system). When viewed from the perspective of biological taxonomy, diagnostic criteria are polythetic, intensional definitions. Diagnostic criteria a la the DSM-III are intensional definitions because they involve the listing of the characteristics of patients. Diagnostic criteria are polythetic because a patient does not need to have all characteristics in order to be identified as belonging to a category. However, it should be noted that there are a number of disorders in the DSM-III which are given monothetic, not polythetic, definitions; that is, the diagnostic criteria for some categories require that the patients have all of the characteristics listed in the definition of that category. Generally the categories that are given monothetic definitions are those that have poorly formulated diagnostic criteria (e.g., "depersonalization disorder") and/or those categories that are rarely used in applied clinical practice (e.g., "pyromania").

Proposition 6: *There is no analogy in traditional biological classification to the multiaxial system of the DSM-III.*

Another important innovation in the DSM-III was the adoption of a multiaxial system which invited clinicians to assign five diagnoses to a patient (clinical syndrome, personality disorder, medical disorder, psychological stressor, and level of adaptive functioning). Traditional biological classifications are not multiaxial. Some authors have talked of forming different biological classifications using the different types of information which might be available on organisms. Thus, one might create a classification of animals based solely on the behaviors these animals can exhibit; another classification could be created from the study of the morphological characteristics of these animals; and yet a third classification might be created by analyzing the biochemical characteristics of the animals (what amino acids are present, what types of protein synthesis occur, etc.). However, most biologists tend to agree with the evolutionary systematists that it is more desirable to attempt to create a "natural" classification rather than different specific classifications of the same organisms (Gilmour, 1937); that is, a classification of animals should be sufficiently general so that it takes into account biochemical, morphological, and behavioral information. Animals that belong to the same categories should be relatively homogeneous across all of the types of information relevant to the comparative study of animals. In short, the evolutionary systematists implicitly have adopted the metaphysical position that natural categories of animals do exist, and it is the job of classifiers to isolate and correctly label these naturally occurring classes of organisms.

In the area of psychopathological classification, a number of authors have suggested that a "linguistic conventionalism" view of classification is more appropriate (cf. Corning & Steffy, 1979). These authors suggest that a number of different classifications of psychopathology exist, each of which might be quite adequate for the specific purpose for which it was intended; that is, one classification might serve quite well in describing the behavioral characteristics of patients, while another classification might contain the relevant etiological information, and yet a third classification might be most relevant to the choice of the best therapeutic approach to the patient. None of these classifications would be more natural than one other. All would be important within the context of the purpose for which it was designed. In other words, diagnostic labels are linguistic conventions which are not necessarily superior or inferior to another possible set of diagnostic labels. From this perspective, no particular classification of psychopathology will be "natural." Hence, creating and using different classifications (e.g., the different axes in the DSM-III) for different purposes could markedly increase the usefulness of a system.

Principles of Folk Classifications

The preceding analysis should have made it clear that the concepts of biological classification cannot easily be applied to the classification of psychopathology. The next section of this chapter will discuss another approach to classification which may help clarify some of the structural aspects of psychiatric classification. This section will introduce a few principles of classification discovered by cultural anthropologists when they studied how non-Western cultures have classified living organisms. These non-Western classifications of living organisms are called "folk classifications." In the following analysis, a few of the principles which have been abstracted from folk classifications will be presented and then followed by an attempt to apply these principles to the classification of psychopathology.

Principle 1: *Folk classifications are hierarchically organized.*

One consistent finding in all studies of non-Western biological classifications is that they have a hierarchical structure. For example, Figure 18-3 displays some of the categories of mammals recognized by the Rofaifo, a group of people who live in the New Guinea highlands (Dwyer, 1977). All categories shown in Figure 18-3 are listed in the native language of the Rofaifo. English language terms for some of the categories found in this classification are 'pig' (*Yabo*), 'dog' (*Hula*), 'cassowary' (*Orona*), 'dasyure' (*Rano*), 'giant rats' (*Himi-Fuema*), and 'water rats' (*Homo*). Notice that this partial classification of mammals by the Rofaifo contains five ranks. Most ethnobiological classifications have from three to six ranks in their hierarchical structures (Berlin, 1978). However, users of folk classifications rarely recognize the concept of ranks, and speakers usually cannot offer any coherent explanation of why various categories occur at certain levels in the hierarchical structure.

The consistent finding of a hierarchical arrangement among categories in folk classifications suggests that the use of a hierarchical organization is a common conceptual device which all humans invoke in their classification systems. Hierarchical organizations have a number of pragmatic conceptual features including (*a*) providing memory aids, (*b*) allowing a system with a large number of categories to be subdivided into manageable chunks, and (*c*) postulating an implied decision tree which can be used in the assignment of a new entity to a category within the system.

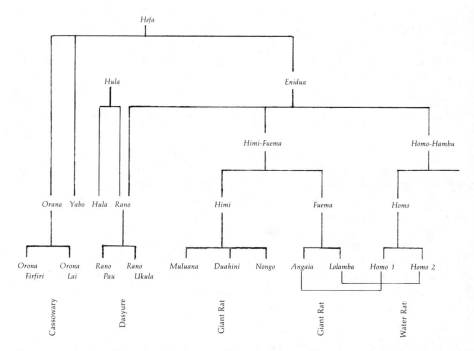

Figure 18-3. *Partial classification of mammals by the Rofaifo, illustrating a hierarchical arrangement in folk classifications.*

Like folk classifications, the DSM-III has a hierarchical organization among its categories. Like folk classifications, the DSM-III does not contain names for ranks, nor is any explanation given why certain categories occur at a common level in the hierarchical system. Also like folk classifications, a major implicit reason for the use of a hierarchical organization of categories in the DSM-III is the conceptual simplicity this structure permits in a classification with over 250 categories.

Principle 2: *At least three types of categories exist in folk classifications: generic, variety, and kingdom.*

Berlin (1978) suggested that at least three types of categories exist in ethnobiological classifications: generic, varieties, and kingdom. (Actually, Berlin postulated five to six types of categories, but the other types will not be addressed for the sake of simplicity.) Generic categories are categories such as *Rano* ('dasyure'), *Yabo* ('pig') and *Hula* ('dog') in the Rofaifo system. These categories have a number of characteristics including the following: (*a*) they occur in the middle ranks of the hierarchical organization of categories; (*b*) they are represented by linguistically simple names (e.g., names with one word or even one syllable); (c) these categories are recognized and reliably identified by all speakers of the language; and (d) these categories can be translated as corresponding to categories existing in scientific classification systems. In short, generic categories are the "natural taxa" of folk classifications.

Varieties are categories that usually occur at the lowest ranks of ethnobiological classifications. Linguistically, a variety is often given a binomial form of name. Examples of varietal categories in our folk classification of cats are "Persian cat," "Siamese cat," and "Angora cat." One of the two words in the name of a variety denotes the generic category which includes it ("cat"). In terms of characteristics, varieties are usually separated on the basis of one or, at most, very few sets of characteristics. For example, the variety names listed above are primarily separated on the color, texture, and length of the fur of these cats. In addition, the characteristics that separate various subordinate categories are characteristics that have significance for a given culture. For instance, in our culture, the domestic cat is a common pet, and the variety names refer to different breeds which have been separated to emphasize the beauty of these pets. Finally, the subordinate categories are often specific to a given culture. Thus, a culture to which bananas are an important source of food may have a complicated set of subcategories of banana trees, while another culture which emphasizes hunting may have complicated varietal categorization of deer.

The highest category in a folk classification is a kingdom. A category at this rank is often called a "unique beginner" because there is only one category and because it includes all other categories in the classification. An example of kingdom in our folk classification is the term "plant." Linguistically a kingdom-level category is interesting because most folk classifications do not have a term or even a simple phrase for such a category. Instead, when anthropologists have attempted to inquire about the most inclusive category in a botanical classification, they will be greeted with comments such as "those things that do not walk, do not move, possess roots, and are all planted in the earth." In effect, users of a folk classification have difficulty defining or naming a kingdom-level category. The descriptions they do give for a kingdom often appear to be idiosyncratic and to vary markedly across speakers. For instance, other folk descriptions for the kingdom of plants are "all leaves" and "green things that try to reach the sun."

These three types of category names can be applied to psychiatric classification. The unique beginner for the DSM-III is probably the term "mental disorder," though the DSM-III does not specifically use or define this category. Like kingdom-level categories in folk classifications, the category mental disorder is not easily defined, and a consensus definition which could be used to separate "psychiatrically normal" from "psychiatrically abnormal" would be difficult to obtain.

The generic categories in the DSM-III are probably diagnostic categories such as "schizophrenia," "paranoia," "hysteria," "alcoholism," and "mania"

(Cantor *et al.*, 1980; Feighner *et al.*, 1972). These categories all have one-word names; they are categories that have international recognition; and they are probably the concepts that have sufficient utility to be retained in some form within future classificatory systems, even as these future systems are improved.

The varietal categories are subcategories in the DSM-III such as the subtypes of schizophrenia: "paranoid schizophrenia," "catatonic schizophrenia," "disorganized schizophrenia," and "undifferentiated schizophrenia." All four categories are names with binomials. They are defined by a small number of characteristics; the first three subtypes of schizophrenia are defined by the occurrence of an outstanding symptom complex ("paranoia," "catatonia") while the fourth subcategory (i.e., "undifferentiated schizophrenia") is the variety which contains all patients not having any of the prominent symptoms of the first three subtypes.

To conclude, Berlin's typology of categories in folk classifications does seem plausible when applied to the classification of psychopathology.

Principle 3: In the hierarchical organization of folk classifications, categories occasionally overlap, and frequently category names do not exist at all ranks.

Although folk classifications are similar to traditional scientific classifications in that both are hierarchical, differences in the details of the hierarchical structures do exist. Compare the hierarchical outlines shown in Figures 18-1 and 18-3. In Figure 18-3, some categories overlap. For instance, *Angaia* (a variety of giant rat) and *Homo 1* (a variety of water rat) both contain relatively large rats, and the membership of these categories is not mutually exclusive. In general, most non-Western cultures do not insist on mutually exclusive categories. In contrast, the standard scientific classification of living organisms contains categories at every rank which are then subdivided at the next lowest rank. This pattern does not occur in Figure 18-3. Category names are absent along a number of ranks.

Both category overlap and absent category names at some ranks are characteristics of the DSM-III hierarchy. The issue of category overlap was mentioned earlier, since the DSM-III permits multiple diagnoses. The existence of absent category names at some ranks is shown in Figure 18-2. Specifically, there are no category names between the general category of "schizophrenic disorders" and the specific subtypes (e.g., "paranoid schizophrenia").

Concluding Comments

This chapter started its discussion of the structural features of classification by presenting a series of concepts from taxonomic analyses of scientific, biological classifications. Some of the concepts focused on the hierarchical organization of biological classification (entities, categories, ranks) while others concerned forms of definitions (monothetic, intensional, extensional). When an attempt was made to apply these concepts to psychiatric classification, specific analogies were difficult to complete. For instance, when applying Gregg's three types of names to psychiatric classification, clear instances of only one could be found. Patients are probably the entities of the DSM-III, but the authors of this classification specifically argue against this interpretation. Also, the DSM-III does not specify what might be the ranks of this system. The most likely candidate as an analogy to "species" is the concept of "disease." However, the definition of disease, particularly as applied to psychopathology, is still quite problematic.

The final section of the chapter then introduced some structural concepts and principles abstracted from studies of folk classifications by anthropologists. It was argued (*a*) that humans generally use hierarchical structures in their classification systems, (*b*) that there are three broad types of categories in folk classifications, and (*c*) that folk classifications contain overlapping categories. All three features have obvious parallels in the DSM-III.

The main reason for writing this chapter was to demonstrate how little is understood about the structure of psychiatric classification. Discussions of taxonomy abound in biology. Theoretical analyses of classification systems are also important topics in cultural anthropology, developmental psychology, and cognitive psychology. In psychiatry, theoretical analyses of classification are infrequent.

This chapter attempted to overcome some of the deficiences concerning the structural understanding of psychiatric classification by focusing on ideas from scientific and folk classifications of living organisms. Interestingly, it would seem that the structure of the DSM-III is more like a folk classification than a scientific classification—a comparison which comments on the primitive state of knowledge about the classification of psychopathology.

Besides suggesting how little is known about psychiatric classification, this chapter also suggested topics which could be fruitful for future study. These topics would include the logical structure of hierarchical systems, ethnobiological analyses of folk classifications, and taxonomic studies of other areas of classification such as medical classifications.

Classification is a fundamental process in all sciences. A classification system contains the concepts which are the building blocks for a theory within that science. In order to improve our knowledge of psychopathology, we must advance our knowledge about psychiatric classification.

REFERENCES

American Psychiatric Association. (1980). *Diagnostic and statistical manual of mental disorders* (3rd ed.). Washington, DC: Author.

Bailey, K. D. (1973). Monothetic and polythetic typologies and their relation to conceptualization, measurement and scaling. *American Sociological Review, 38,* 18–33.

Beckner, M. (1959). *The biological way of thought.* New York: Columbia University Press.

Berlin, B. (1978). Ethnobiological classification. In E. Rosch & B. B. Lloyd (Eds.), *Cognition and categorization.* Hillsdale, NJ: Erlbaum.

Blackwelder, R. E. (1967). *Taxonomy: A text and reference book.* New York: Wiley.

Blashfield, R. K. (1984). *The classification of psychopathology: Neo-Kraepelinian and quantitative approaches.* New York: Plenum Press.

Blashfield, R. K., & Aldenderfer, M. S. (1978). The literature on cluster analysis. *Multivariate Behavioral Research, 13,* 271–295.

Buck, R. C., & Hull, D. L. (1966). The logical structure of the Linnean hierarchy. *Systematic Zoology, 15,* 97–111.

Cantor, N., Smith, E. E., French, R. D., & Mezzich, J. (1980). Psychiatric diagnosis as prototype categorization. *Journal of Abnormal Psychology, 89,* 181–193.

Caplan, A. L., Englehardt, H. T., & McCartney, J. J. (Eds.). (1981). *Concepts of health and disease: Interdisciplinary perspectives.* Reading, MA: Addison-Wesley.

Clifford, H. T., & Stephenson, W. (1975). *An introduction to numerical classification.* New York: Academic Press.

Cormack, R. M. (1971). A review of classification. *Journal of the Royal Statistical Society, Series A, 134,* 321–367.

Corning, W. C., & Steffy, R. A. (1979). Taximetric strategies applied to psychiatric classification. *Schizophrenia Bulletin, 5,* 294–305.

Dwyer, P. D. (1977). An analysis of Rofaifo mammal taxonomy. *American Ethnologist, 4,* 425–445.

Everitt, B. (1980). *Cluster analysis* (2nd ed.). New York: Halstead Press.

Faber, K. (1930). *Nosography: The evolution of clinical medicine in modern times.* New York: Harper (Hoeber).

Feighner, J. P., Robins, E., Guze, S. B., Woodruff, R. A., Winokur, G., & Muñoz, R. (1972). Diagnostic criteria for use in psychiatric research. *Archives of General Psychiatry, 26,* 57–63.

Frake, C. O. (1972). The ethnographic study of cognitive systems. In J. A. Fishman (Ed.), *Readings in the sociology of language.* The Hague: Mouton.

Ghiselin, M. T. (1974). A radical solution to the species problem. *Systematic Zoology, 23,* 536–544.

Gilmour, J. S. L. (1937). A taxonomic problem. *Nature (London), 139,* 1040–1042.

Gregg, J. R. (1954). *The language of taxonomy.* New York: Columbia University Press.

Hull, D. L. (1976). Are species really individuals? *Systematic Zoology, 25,* 174–191.

Jardine, N., & Sibson, R. (1971). *Mathematical Taxonomy.* London: Wiley.

King, L. S. (1958). *The medical world of the eighteenth century.* Chicago, IL: University of Chicago Press.

Lorr, M. (Ed.). (1966). *Exploration in typing psychotics.* Oxford: Pergamon Press.

Lorr, M. (1983). *Cluster analysis for social scientists.* San Francisco: Jossey-Bass.

Mayr, E. (1969). *Principles of systematic zoology.* New York: McGraw-Hill.

Mayr, E. (1981). Biological classification: Toward a synthesis of opposing methodologies. *Science, 214,* 510–516.

Nelson, G., & Platnick, N. (1981). *Systematics and biogeography: Cladistics and vicariance.* New York: Columbia University Press.

Panzetta, A. F. (1974). Towards a scientific psychiatric nosology: Conceptual and pragmatic issues. *Archives of General Psychiatry, 30,* 154–161.

Rutter, M., Shaffer, D., & Shepherd, M. (1975). *A multi-axial classification of child psychiatric disorders.* Geneva: World Health Organization.

Simpson, G. G. (1961). *Principles of animal taxonomy.* New York: Columbia University Press.

Sneath, P. H. A., & Sokal, R. R. (1973). *Numerical taxonomy.* San Francisco, CA: Freeman.

Sokal, R. R., & Sneath, P. H. A. (1963). *Principles of numerical taxonomy.* San Francisco, CA: Freeman.

Wiley, E. O. (1981). *Phylogenetics: The theory and practice of phylogenetic systematics.* New York: Wiley.

Zadeh, L. A. (1965). Fuzzy sets. *Information and control, 8,* 338–353.

CHAPTER 19

Methodological Issues in Personality Disorder Diagnosis

Allen Frances and Thomas A. Widiger

The provision within DSM-III of a separate axis devoted to the personality disorders reflects formal recognition of the importance of personality classification to psychiatric diagnosis and treatment planning. The separation of Axes I and II increases diagnostic reliability by encouraging clinicians to distinguish between and consider both the immediate clinical syndrome and a personality disorder rather than forcing an arbitrary choice between them. More importantly, however, there is accumulating empirical data indicating that personality characteristics help predict the course and treatment response of various Axis I conditions, such as unipolar affective disorder (Bielski & Friedel, 1976; Weissman, Prusoff, & Klerman, 1978), bipolar affective disorder (Donnelly, Murphy, & Goodwin, 1976; M. Taylor & Abrams, 1975), clyclothymic disorder (Akiskal, Djenderedjian, Rosenthal, & Kkani, 1977), dysthymic disorder (Akiskal, 1983; Kelly & King, 1979), schizophrenic disorders (Garmezy, 1975), substance abuse (Treece & Nicholson, 1980), and psychophysiological disorders (Haynes, Feinleib, & Kannel, 1980). Personality variables may also be important predictors of psychotherapeutic outcome (Strupp, 1980).

The above research suggests that personality diagnosis is clinically meaningful and useful, but this research has typically involved paper and pencil inventories of a variety of personality dimensions and has not been based upon traditional psychiatric diagnoses, such as those found in Axis II of

Allen Frances. Department of Psychiatry, Cornell University Medical College, and Outpatient Department, Payne Whitney Clinic, New York, New York.

Thomas A. Widiger. Department of Psychology, University of Kentucky, Lexington, Kentucky.

DSM-III. There is in fact very little available data to support the validity of most of the Axis II diagnoses and virtually no data to support the theoretical speculations regarding specific etiology and treatment. The lack of research is in part due to the inherent complications in the diagnosis of personality disorders (Frances, 1980). With the adoption of the method of diagnosing by fixed and explicit rules (Spitzer, Williams, & Skodol, 1980), there should be some improvement in the reliability of classification and thereby in the ability to validate hypothesized covariates of the diagnoses. Fixed and explicit rules, however, have their own inherent complications (Finn, 1982; Widiger, in press), and although Axis II is far superior to its predecessors, it still achieves relatively low reliability for a personality diagnosis in general, and even lower reliability for each particular personality diagnosis (Spitzer, Forman, & Nee, 1979).

Various criteria have been proposed for the evaluation of psychiatric classifications (e.g., Blashfield & Draguns, 1976; Kendell, 1975; Spitzer, Endicott, & Robins, 1975; Spitzer & Williams, 1980; Zigler & Phillips, 1961; Zubin, 1978). Guze (1975), for example, suggests that the validity of a diagnostic construct involves predictions concerning clinical description, laboratory data, discriminant validation, follow-up data concerning theoretically relevant variables, and familial data. Blashfield and Draguns (1976) emphasize adequate reliability (across time and diagnostician), coverage, descriptive validity (homogeneity of category membership with respect to definitional and associate features), and predictive validity (e.g., prognostic and treatment implications). Skinner (1981), however, emphasizes that the evaluation of diagnostic constructs should be integrated with a particular theoretical formulation. And Loevinger (1957) has also argued the need for developing a theoretical model to guide the construction (internal validity) of an assessment instrument, "psychiatric classification should be viewed as a scientific theory that is open to empirical falsification" (Skinner, 1981, p. 69).

DSM-III was intended to be atheoretical because the "inclusion of etiological theories would be an obstacle to use of the manual by clinicians of varying theoretical orientations" (American Psychiatric Association [APA], p. 7). This may, however, be an inherently untenable position. It was thought that because the "definitions of the disorder . . . are described at the lowest order of inference necessary" (APA, 1980, p. 7), they would then be somehow less theoretically biased. Observations inherently have one or another theoretical bias (Weimer, 1979). The DSM-III method of diagnosis simply favors theories that are symptom or behavior oriented (e.g., biological modes) over theories that are more inferential (Frances & Cooper, 1981; Taylor, 1983). The denial of theoretical bias may result in unexpected, discordant, and inconsistent influences. One can identify a potpourri of diverse theoretical biases that influenced the formulation of Axis II (e.g., the influence of Robins on the formulation of the antisocial disorder, of Millon on the avoidant personality, of Frances's use of psychoanalytic constructs in the formulation of the narcissistic personality, and a general bow to popular preferences in the retention of term "borderline"). There was an attempt to organize the Axis II diagnoses into three clusters (odd or eccentric; dramatic, emotional, or erratic; and anxious or fearful; APA 1980), but as Millon (1981) has indicated, this organization lacks any clear utility, in part due to a lack of any theoretical formulation.

The purpose of this chapter is to highlight some of the methodological issues that make personality diagnosis both interesting and difficult. We will begin with a comparison of dimensional and categorical methods that will highlight the advantages and disadvantages of each approach. Next we will discuss four promising dimensional systems (those of Cattell, Eysenck, Leary, and Millon). The second half of the chapter compares the characteristics of classical and prototypal models of categorical assignment. The theoretical and empirical implications of prototypal classification are discussed in some detail. Throughout the chapter, we will emphasize areas that warrant special research attention and will consider ways in which future systems of personality diagnosis may evolve from those now available to us.

Categorical versus Dimensional Methods

Axis II follows the traditional psychiatric (and medical) format of diagnosing personality disorders in terms of discrete, separate syndromes. To the extent that one conceives of personality disorders as specific and unique constellations of personality traits (i.e., a syndrome with characteristic etiology, course, family history, biological markers, and treatment responsivity), a categorical model is most useful (Frances, 1982). For example, the Schizotypal Personality Disorders can be conceived as the phenotypic expression of the latent, discrete taxon of schizotaxia (Meehl & Golden 1982). On the other hand, to the extent that one conceives of personality disorders as extreme variants of normally occurring or common personality traits that are distributed continuously (e.g., the Compulsive Personality Disorder; Pollack, 1979), then a dimensional model is more consistent and useful. DSM-III state that "there is no assumption that each mental disorder is a discrete entity with sharp boundaries (discontinuity) between it and other mental disorders, as well as between it and No Mental Disorder" (APA, 1980, p. 6). Likewise, "it is only when personality traits are inflexible and maladaptive and cause either significant impairment in social or occupational functioning or subjective distress that they constitute personality disorders" (APA, 1980, p. 305). DSM-III, however, also clearly states that this acknowledgment of a continuity between normality and disorder "does not imply a resolution of the controversy as to whether or not these conditions are in fact quantitatively or qualitatively different" (APA, 1980, p. 6).

There has been and will continue to be heated debate over whether psychiatric disorders are best represented as points on a continuum or as discrete categories (Eysenck, Wakefield, & Friedman, 1983; Hine & Williams, 1975; Kelly, 1965; Kendell, 1975; Mezzich, 1979; Strauss, 1973). Dimensional systems of classification have the advantage of providing more flexible, specific, and comprehensive information, while categorical systems tend to be Procrustean, lose information, and result in many classificatory dilemmas when patients fall at the boundaries between categories (Eysenck *et al.*, 1983; Kendell, 1975; Lang, 1978; Strauss, 1975). A categorical taxonomy is typically faced with the dilemma of developing restrictive diagnostic criteria in order to increase the homogeneity of membership (e.g., the DSM-III narrowing of the schizophrenic diagnosis), but is then required to add a number of wastebasket categories to cover the large number of patients who are unable to meet the restrictive criteria (e.g., atypical psychosis, schizophreniform, and schizoaffective disorders).

Proponents of a categorical system argue that it is consistent with past, current, and popular nomenclatures, provides greater ease in communication and conceptualization, and that dimensional systems impede the efforts to discover and validate actual discrete syndromes and specific etiologies (Kendell, 1975; Strauss, 1973, 1975). In regard to the last argument, however, a dimensional system would in fact facilitate research by providing a scale of measurement (i.e., ordinal or interval) that has more power in detecting empirical relationships than the nomimal scale inherent to categorical systems. Furthermore, it is not difficult to translate a dimensional system into a categorical system when the latter is desired (e.g., all persons above a certain score on a dimension receive one categorical diagnosis while those below do not), while a translation from a category membership to a dimensional score may require more information than is available. However, while a dimensional system would provide more precise measurement of the many borderline cases, a surface continuum can conceal underlying discontinuities (e.g., different viruses produce similar, overlapping symptoms, but can be distinguished on immunological grounds).

It is also acknowledged that a categorical system is simpler and more consistent with traditional psychiatric nomenclatures. Although a dimensional measurement of color (e.g., wavelength and intensity) is precise, it can also be less immediately evocative than a categorical statement that a dress is "bright red." These advantages, however, may not be as significant as having the more complete and accurate information that is obtained through dimensional systems. Indeed, the simplicity of categorical systems may be inappropriate to the complexity of the domain of psychopathology, especially in regard to personality disorders. Furthermore, although dimensional systems are more complex, they need not be incomprehensible or cumbersome (Hine & Williams, 1975). To argue that one should continue using categories because they are the past or current method may be to appeal only to tradition and is not really befitting an effort to improve and advance scientific understanding (Hempel, 1961; Kelly, 1965).

For everyday clinical use, it seems likely that the traditional categorical model of personality diagnosis will hold sway for some time, in part due to the additional training and computer resources necessary for an adequate understanding and application of a dimensional model. Thus, an Axis II diagnosis in DSM-IV will probably be quite similar in its form to the current system. Perhaps by DSM-V or VI, personality diagnosis will take on the dimensional method, although Axis I will still be more or less categorical. For research purposes, however, one or several dimensional systems are clearly necessary for most studies or personality disorders and their interaction with other conditions.

If one accepts the advantages of a dimensional system, one is still left with the difficult question of which dimensions optimally map or define the domain of personality disorders for various research and clinical applications. The answer is not obvious, for there are many models to choose from (e.g., Cattell, Eysenck, Fromm, Guilford, Kernberg, Leary, Millon, Royce, Schneider, H. Skinner, and Wolman) and none is without significant problems.

For starters, one could simply convert Axis II to a dimensional structure by instructing clinicians to rate patients (e.g., on a 10-point scale) on each of the 11 personality disorders. The ratings could be generated in various ways: global impression, percentage of satisfied diagnostic criteria, descriptive anchor points, or self-administered standardized inventories. It is unlikely, however, that the current 11 disorders constitute the optimal set of dimensions. Some of the disorders may be so correlated (e.g., Avoidant, Schizoid, and Schizotypal) as to require collapsing, and there are likely to be important dimensions that are not directly represented by any single disorder.

We will describe four popular dimensional structures that were originally formulated by Cattell, Eysenck, Millon, and Leary. They were chosen from among the many possible options because they illustrate different approaches, demonstrate particularly important theoretical and empirical issues, and/or have received empirical attention.

Dimensional Structure of Cattell

Cattell's (1946, 1966, 1970) system of dimensionalizing personality was heavily researched after its initial development, but it has not received sufficient attention during the past 10 years. It is an ambitious attempt to comprehensively study all important personality factors, the relationships among them, and their ability to predict behavior. The ambitious goal may itself have been a source for some of its problems (Guilford, 1975). Cattell began with Allport's list of over 4,000 personality adjectives compiled from Webster's dictionary (Allport & Odbert, 1936). Based on judgments of similarity, these were then condensed into 171 synonym groups. Cattell empirically tested the correlations among these groups and further reduced them to 42 clusters, which he labeled surface traits. These were still correlated with one another and could be factor analyzed further to obtain 16 factors known as source traits (see Table 19-1).

Cattell's efforts were extraordinarily comprehensive, employing a variety of methods of measurement of ability, temperament, and motivation, all of which were constructed in accord with the assumptions of his theoretical model. However, his theory of personality structure was derived essentially from his empirical, factor-analytic research and "the substantive implications of the theory may be said to stand or fall on the appropriateness of the factor-analytic procedures that have been employed in the indentification of the principal constructs" (Wiggins, 1973, p. 497). There is no single right, incontrovertible way to perform factor analysis, and Cattell's particular and at times idiosyncratic approach has been criticized (e.g., the principal component method of factor extraction, the large number of factors extracted, and the complex method of rotating to oblique factors; Eysenck, 1977; Guilford, 1975; Wiggins, 1973). His principal assessment instrument, the 16 PF, has also been criticized for relying too heavily on the idiosyncratic internal, structural validity (i.e., the particular factor analysis) and sacrificing external validity and clinical utility (Rorer, 1972). Goldberg (1981, 1982) has picked up the ball to develop a comprehensive taxonomic structure for personality trait terms, and his efforts are likely to be more fruitful.

The questionable clinical utility of factor-analytically derived structures of personality is also relevant to another mathematical technique, cluster

Table 19-1
Cattell's Source Traits—Popular Label

A.	Outgoing versus reserved
B.	More intelligent versus less intelligent
C.	Emotionally stable
(L.1)	Excitable versus undemonstrative
E.	Assertive versus humble, obedient
F.	Happy-go-lucky versus sober
G.	Conscientious versus expedient
H.	Venturesome versus shy
I.	Tender-minded versus tough-minded
(L.2)	Doubting versus vigorous
(L.3)	Analytical versus unreflective
L.	Suspicious versus trusting
M.	Imaginative versus practical
N.	Shrewd versus forthright
O.	Apprehensive versus placid
(Q.1)	Experimenting versus conservative
(Q.2)	Self-sufficient versus group-dependent
(Q.3)	Controlled versus undisciplined
(Q.4)	Tense versus relaxed

analysis, that is growing in popularity and has been applied to a broad area of psychopathology. Although it would be interesting to derive empirical personality types through the cluster analysis of the distribution of features used to diagnose the 11 Axis II personality disorders, it must be noted that the results of cluster analyses have not received much attention or application by clinicians. An effort to derive a taxonomy of personality disorders through cluster analysis faces the limitations described well in reviews by Blashfield (1980), Corning and Steffy (1979), and Skinner and Blashfield (1982). Many of the criticisms and suggestions are similar to those concerning factor-analytically derived dimensions of personality (Comrey, 1978; Guilford, 1975). Cluster-analytically derived personality disorders are prone to (a) being specific to idiosyncratic mathematical models that derive different solutions than alternative models (e.g., just as different personality structures are derived from orthogonal oblique rotations in factor analysis, different personality disorders would be derived from single complete linkage procedures in cluster analysis), (b) being dependent on and specific to the particular input variables and subject groups used, (c) imposing structure rather than discovering it, and (d) ignoring or at least slighting the external validation of the derived clusters (e.g., covariation of the typology with etiological, demographic, prognostic, and treatment variables). It would, for example, be of more use to develop confirmatory cluster analyses that are related to a theoretical formulation of personality disorders rather than an exploratory search for any and all homogeneous clusters (Skinner, 1981).

Dimensional Structure of Eysenck

Eysenck (1952, 1970, 1981) offers another factor-analytically derived dimensional model of personality. He proposes that the three dimensions of Neuroticism (instability and/or emotionality), Psychoticism, and Introversion–Extraversion (impulsivity and sociability) define the domain of psychopathology (Wilson, 1978). Although Eysenck (1981) describes it as a model of personality, it appears to define the entire domain of psychopathology, including neurotic and psychotic disorders. This at times can be confusing, but it can also provide theoretically derived predictions of the relationship between Axis I and Axis II disorders, assuming an ability to translate Eysenck's terminology into the DSM-III diagnoses. It must be remembered that although Eysenck may use the same terms as other clinicians, his usage often carries a somewhat different meaning. His Introversion–Extraversion dimension, for example, is similar but certainly not equal to other common conceptualizations (e.g., Jung's; Wilson, 1978).

Like Cattell's model, Eysenck's structure is also dependent upon the creator's particular factor analytic preferences, in this case for only a few factors that are orthogonally rotated (Gray, 1981; Guilford, 1975, 1977). However, unlike Cattell, Eysenck offers considerable external (clinical) correlates to corroborate the structure (Eysenck, 1981; Eysenck et al., 1983). He also presents a rather unique learning–physiological theory for the development of the personality structure (e.g., the position on the Introversion-Extraversion dimension is determined in part by arousal level that originates in the ascending reticular activating system and is associated with the ease with which conditioned reflexes are formed). This emphasis on molecular learning–physiological mechanisms, however, may also represent a shortcoming in that clinicians have an understandable difficulty identifying the face validity of these mechanisms (e.g., critical flicker fusion thresholds, number of pauses during a tapping task, ease of eye-blink conditioning, and the amount of saliva generated when a standard amount of lemon juice is placed on the tongue) for the etiology, phenomenology, and treatment of their patients' disorders. There are, however, more traditional self-report inventories with which to measure the dimensional structure (e.g., the Eysenck Personality Inventory; Eysenck & Eysenck, 1971).

Dimensional Structure of Leary

A third alternative dimensional structure for Axis II is the interpersonal circumplex originally formulated by Leary (1957) and subsequently expanded and refined by Kiesler (1982), McLemore and Benjamin (1979), and Wiggins (1982). This dimensional structure was based on both an a priori theoretical formulation and empirical data. Two dimensions define the circumplex. The most commonly considered are affiliation and dominance. Change (1966), however, has indicated how the two basic dimensions can be changed by rotating the axes. Wiggins (1982) has reviewed and integrated the various interpersonal nosologies. Figure 19-1 presents his interpersonal circumplex. The least restrictive assumption concerning the arrangement is that it reflects a circular order, an order without beginning or end. This nonmetric model is referred to as a circumplex (Guttman, 1954). One could also add metric, Euclidean assumptions: (a) Types located opposite to each other reflect opposite poles of a biopolar dimension and have maximal negative correlations; (b) types perpendicular to each other are on poles of orthogonal dimensions and are uncorrelated; (c) positive correlations are maximal between those types close in proximity and decrease as they reach a perpendicular spatial relationship; and (d) the distance from the original reflects the intensity, severity, or rigidity of the subject's manifestations of the dimensions (Wiggins, 1982). The patient may then be described by a dimensional profile of eight scores (each score presenting the magnitude on an octant of the circumplex). There are a variety of other inventories with which to measure the magnitude and location on the circumplex, including the Interpersonal Behavior Inventory (Lorr & McNair, 1965), Benjamin's (1974) Structural Analysis of Social Behavior, and Wiggins's (1979) interpersonal trait terms.

    To the extent that an interpersonal nosology subsumes or accounts for personality traits (Wiggins, 1982), the interpersonal circumplex should also account for the personality disorders. A comprehensive list of personality

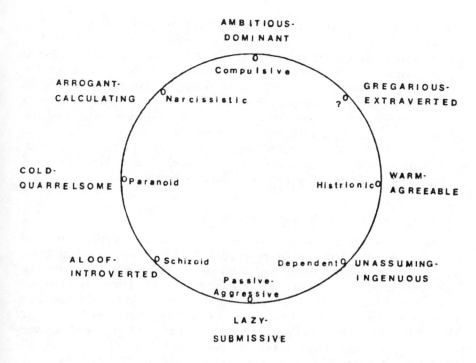

Figure 19-1. *Wiggins's interpersonal circumplex and corresponding Axis II diagnoses.*

disorders should represent and be present within the octants, and preferably should not overload any particular octant (Kiesler, 1982). The circumplex also provides a rich theoretical model for Axis II by generating hypotheses regarding relationships between the disorders and therapeutic prescriptions (Kiesler, 1982). McLemore and Benjamin (1979), for example, propose "antidotal" relationships whereby one elicits the opposite of a currently maladaptive behavior by exhibiting the complement of the opposite. The complementary and opposing relationships are determined by the relative positions on the circumplex(es).

Wiggins (1982) suggested that at least seven of the Axis II disorders "emphasize interpersonal behavior rather than symptoms or social evaluations, and these categories bear a close resemblance to the octants of the interpersonal circumplex" (p. 211). Figure 19-1 also presents his placement of these seven disorders on the circumplex. One might disagree with his placements and his decision to leave off four disorders. The Avoidant and Antisocial disorders, for example, are certainly as interpersonal as the others.

The interpersonal circumplex, however, may not be able to adequately represent all of the features of personality disorders. Conte and Plutchik (1981), for example, verified that the circumplex accounts for the relationship between interpersonal trait terms, but "if other types of descriptors had been included, such as abilities, interests, or intelligence, analysis of the data would most likely not have produced a circumplex due to the increased dimensionality of such data" (p. 707). To the extent that personality disorders involve more than interpersonal disorders, the circumplex will be an inadequate model. The Compulsive personality, for example, involves such cognitive features as indecisiveness (Leary, 1957; Wiggins, 1982) and the Schizoid and Schizotypal disorders are differentiated largely by the cognitive impairments in the latter disorder (Spitzer *et al.*, 1980). One might also argue for the inclusion of a severity dimension (Kiesler, 1982; Millon, 1981) and perhaps an activity–passivity dimension (Millon, 1981).

Dimensional Structure of Millon

The above three dimensional structures are not readily translated into the particular categorical nomenclature of Axis II. This is not a problem, however, for the theoretical model of Millon (1969, 1981), whose dimensional framework is easily translated into the current psychiatric categorical nomenclature. Millon (1969, 1981) proposed that the underlying dimensions are activity–passivity, self–other orientation, and pleasure–pain motivation. "Using this threefold framework as a foundation, Millon (1969) derived personality 'coping patterns' that correspond in close detail to each of the 'official' personality disorders in the DSM-III" (Millon, 1981, p. 55). One might expect that this framework would result in eight categories that result from crossing the two poles of the three dimensions. However, this is not really the case. What he in fact appears to do is to cross four "levels" or types on a self–other dimension (dependent, ambivalent, detached, and independent) with the two poles on the active–passive dimension, to form eight "mild" personality disorders (Millon, 1981, p. 61). He then adds three more categories (Paranoid, Borderline, and Schizotypal) that involves the same dimensions as before, but are considered to be more severe than the other eight. The Schizotypal, for example, is a more dysfunctional variant of the detached pattern and entails the same underlying dimensions as the Avoidant and Schizoid. No disorders are at the poles of the pleasure–pain dimension. The latter dimension is employed only insofar as the Schizoid disorder involves a deficit in the capacity to experience either positive or negative reinforcement, and the Avoidant involves a deficit in pleasure.

Millon (1969, 1981) provides a theoretically derived dimensional structure that can be empirically applied to the categories of Axis II. It would be of interest to assess whether the Axis II disorders are correlated to independent measures of activity–passivity, self–other orientation, and pleasure–pain motivation in the manner hypothesized by Millon (1969, 1981). His theoretical framework has not received the direct empirical attention that it warrants. Given its close correspondence to Axis II, this research should now be forthcoming.

Millon (1982) also offers a self-report inventory, the Millon Clinical Multiaxial Inventory (MCMI), with which to measure Axis II in both a dimensional and a categorical manner. The MCMI first appeared in 1977 (as the MMCI) and was heralded by Butcher and Owen (1978) as the top contender to the MMPI. Its construction was explicitly guided by the substantive, structural, and external considerations of construct validity formulated by Loevinger (1957) and by a consideration of the weaknesses identified in the MMPI (Butcher, 1972). However, as Wiggins (1982) indicated in his brief review, it is strong on substantive grounds, but may have some structural weaknesses. Millon (1982) wished to keep the inventory short enough for practical purposes, but may thereby have compromised its structural validity. "When 20 scales averaging 37 items per scale are scored from a common pool of only 171 items, the psychometric consequences of such a high degree of scale redundancy will almost certainly be unfavorable" (Wiggins, 1981, p. 211). For example, because of the item overlap, one cannot use the scales to independently measure the relationship between the diagnoses or between the diagnoses and external variables (unless one is willing to accept the forced covariations that result from the item overlap). Millon (1982), however, has argued that precisely for the sake of internal structural validity the overlap is necessary to ensure that the scales relate in the manner suggested by the underlying theory. Although it does appear that the inventory's potential may outweigh its limitations, it is unfortunate that research concerning the MCMI is only now beginning to be major journals. Millon (1982) does present external validation data in the inventory's manual, but there is a need for additional convergent and discriminant validation by other investigators. For example, Millon's (1982) criterion judges utilized early variants of the final group of Axis II diagnostic criteria for this reason, Millon's personality labels do differ somewhat in their content from what was included within the Axis II diagnoses.

Prototypal and Classical Categories

A categorical system can be more or less compatible with a dimensional structure, depending upon its assumptions. For example, a distinction has been made between a "classical" and a "prototypal" model of categorization (Cantor & Mischel, 1979; Rosch, 1978; Wittgenstein, 1953). For reasons we will now specify, the prototypal model is considerably more useful.

The classical model of categorization conceives of disorders as qualitative, discrete entities and assumes that the defining features are singly necessary and jointly sufficient, that the boundaries between categories are distinct, and that members are homogeneous with respect to the defining features (Cantor, Smith, French, & Mezzich, 1980). With the help of the philosopher Wittgenstein (1953), cognitive psychologists have demonstrated many problems with the classical model (Rosch, 1978). Although the classical model works well for abstract categories (e.g., "square"), it fails to do justice to the complexity of naturally occurring taxonomic problems. All squares share the features of having four equal sides joined at right angles, and any figure without these features is most definitely not a square (i.e., squares always satisfy the requirements of homogeneity of membership and distinct boundaries). Actual objects, plants, animals, and persons, however, often fail to share a set of singly necessary and jointly sufficient features (Cantor & Mischel, 1979). In most situations borderline cases abound. It is unclear, for example, whether a bookend is a piece of furniture (Rosch & Mervis, 1975) and whether a tomato is a fruit or a vegetable (Smith, Shoben, & Rips, 1974). Even plant species, the specification of which was a stimulant to exact psychiatric classification (Kendell, 1975), are no longer thought to be easily distinguishable (Levin, 1979). If a classical typology is an inappropriate model for classification of objects, birds, and plants, it is clearly inappropriate for psychiatric diagnosis (Cantor et al., 1980).

The fact that a category fails to be classically homogeneous or to have distinct boundaries does not imply invalidity or lack of usefulness. The category "furniture" fails to meet the criteria for a classical category (Rosch, 1978), but it is certainly a very useful concept nonetheless. A more appropriate model for psychiatric diagnosis, and one more consistent with a dimensional system, is the prototypal typology (Cantor & Mischel, 1979; Rosch, 1978) in which definitional features are not considered to be necessary or jointly sufficient. In a prototypal system, membership is heterogeneous, there are overlapping boundaries, and definitional features have varying degrees of validity. Widiger (1982) demonstrated the implications of these characteristics for the controversy concerning the validity of the various Borderline diagnoses, and Clarkin, Widiger, Frances, Hurt, and Gilmore (1983) presented empirical data on this question.

DSM-III is an improvement over DSM-III because it incorporates features of a prototypal system rather than attempting rigidly to adhere to a classical typology (Frances, 1982). Axis II of DSM-III allows for multiple diagnoses and at times (but not always) provides polythetic rather than monothetic diagnostic criteria. However, Axis II is inconsistent and falls far short of realizing the full implications of a prototypal typology. This is one direction in which DSM-IV would be improved. The implications of a prototypal system for heterogeneity of membership, the determination of the diagnostic efficiency of the definitional features, and the validation of hypothesized covariates of each diagnosis will be discussed in turn.

Axis II and Heterogeneity of Membership

In a classical system of categorization, members of the category are presumed to be homogeneous with respect to the defining features. The DSM-III diagnostic criteria for the personality disorders are inconsistent in the extent to which homogeneity is assumed. The criteria for the Avoidant, Dependent, and Shizoid disorders require all of the defining features to be present in order for the diagnosis to be made. This would then assume (or require) homogeneity with respect to the defining features. In contrast, the Paranoid, Histrionic, Passive–Aggressive, and Narcissistic disorders require all of the defining features to be present, but provide multiple cirteria for the assignment of each feature. For example, the Paranoid diagnosis requires pervasive and unwarranted mistrust (homogeneity), but three of eight indicators of mistrust will suffice for the attribution. There are 219 distinct combinations of three or more of eight indicators, irrespective of order (heterogeneity). In further contrast, the criteria for the Schizotypal, Antisocial, Compulsive, and Borderline disorders present a multiple choice in regard to the defining features. For example, only five or eight features need to be present for a diagnosis of a Borderline Personality Disorder, and there are 93 different combinations of five or more of eight features, irrespective of order. In summary, Axis II is inconsistent in the extent to which the members of each category are assumed to be homogeneous with respect to the definitional features.

Which particular disorders are more or less heterogeneous is an empirical question. Heterogeneity that is possible in principle might not be present in actuality. For example, patients who meet the minimal criteria of five features for the Borderline diagnosis might also tend to possess the remaining three, and even if most patients fail to possess all eight, it is still possible that most patients share the same five subset criteria. Clarkin et al. (1983) found in their sample of 26 DSM-III Borderline patients that the prevalence of the definitional features ranged from a high of 88% for the features of impulsivity and affective instability to a low of 35% for intolerance of being alone. There was also considerable variation in the occurrence of the various combinations of features. In other words, not only do the definitions of the disorder vary in terms of their tolerance for heterogeneity of membership, but the heterogeneity that does in fact occur appears to vary according to the defining features.

The extent and focus of heterogeneity is not a trivial issue. It has a direct influence on the relative diagnostic efficiency of each definitional feature and the validation of hypothesized covariates of the syndrome (see below). Certainly the base rate of the syndrome and the true positive rate of the feature will be affected by the extent to which membership is heterogeneous. A fruitful area of research, therefore, would be to determine which of the personality disorders tends to possess a heterogeneous membership and for which features this heterogeneity occurs.

Diagnostic Efficiency of the Definitional Features

In a classical model, all of the definitional features have the same true positive hit rate (i.e., 100%). There can be different degrees of diagnostic

efficiency (i.e., the conditional probability of the diagnosis given the definitional feature; Meehl & Rosen, 1955) only if the features differ in their false-
positive hit rates (percentage of patients without the disorder that do have
the feature) or if changes in the base rate of syndrome have a differential
effect on the false-positive rate.

In contrast, in a prototypal model the definitional features of the disorder can also differ considerably in their true positive hit rates. As a result,
the features of a prototypal system are much more likely to differ significantly in terms of their diagnostic efficiency (Rosch, 1978). This characteristic of a prototypal typology is not explicitly acknowledged by DSM-III. DSM-
III makes a distinction between the "associated features" and "diagnostic
criteria," but there is no indication whether one criterion is more important
to diagnosis than another. The absence of differential efficiency weights in
the diagnosis of Axis II disorders is due to the lack of any relevant empirical
data to support them and the fact that different criteria may have more or
less efficiency, depending on the comparison groups that need to be distinguished. This is another area of fruitful research, with results that would be
of obvious relevance to efficient diagnosis and to DSM-IV.

When determining the diagnostic efficiency of an Axis II definitional
feature, it is also important to consider its efficiency when in various combinations with the other definitional features. A feature with low efficiency
when present alone might become quite important in combination with
certain other features. A localized headache is not especially diagnostic by
itself, but in combination with certain other symptoms (e.g., contralateral
sensory impairments) it can become highly suggestive. Personality disorders
are typically conceptualized as being a constellation of features, and it would
be misleading to dismiss a feature based on its diagnostic efficiency when it is
considered by itself, ignoring its efficiency when it is combined with other
features. This is perhaps obvious, but it is rarely given serious consideration
in psychodiagnostic research. Clarkin et al. (1983), for example, found that
identity disturbance by itself was a relatively inefficient indicator in the
differential diagnosis of Borderline from other personality disorders, but in
combination with unstable-intense relations (a feature with only moderate
diagnostic efficiency when considered alone), the two features diagnosed
with certainty.

The conditional probability of various combinations of features is not
irrelevant to classical categories (again due to the possible variation in false-
positive rates and a differential effect of base rates), but it is certainly far
more important in a prototypal model. In a classical model all of the members
have the same combination of features (i.e., a true positive hit rate of 100%
for one possible combination), while in a prototypal model the true positive
hit rate for various combinations of features can vary considerably. For
example, it is likely that the 93 different possible combinations of features
for a Borderline Personality Disorder (i.e., five or more of eight features) will
differ considerably in terms of their true positive hit rates. As a result, the

conditional probabilities for the various combinations of four or fewer features will also vary considerably.

As a final note, when considering the diagnostic efficiency of any particular feature (or combination of features), it is also important to recognize that the efficiency will vary not only according to the local base rate of the syndrome (Finn, 1982), but also according to the local and/or particular false-positive rate of the feature(s). For example, unstable–intense relations may be an efficient diagnostic indicator of a Borderline diganosis in the setting of a university counseling center, but not at a marriage-family clinic where its false-positive rate will be higher. In addition, it may be an efficient indicator in the differential diagnosis of Borderline versus Schizoid and in Borderline versus Schizophrenia, but not when the differential is Borderline versus Histrionic or Borderline versus Bipolar Affective Disorder, where the false-positive rate may again be higher. The establishment of the diagnostic efficiency of an indicator is obviously not a simple matter.

Validation of Hypothesized Covariates

A classical typology assumes that important covariates of category membership will be observed in each member. What is true for the category is likely to be true for every member (see, e.g., Blashfield & Draguns, 1976; Kendell, 1982). Failure to verify a hypothesis for a sample of patients with a particular diagnosis can then be taken as a falsification of the hypothesis for the diagnosis, assuming no additional auxiliary hypotheses.

However, an assumption of homogeneity with respect to the hypotheses concerning the diagnostic construct is a false assumption for a prototypal typology. If members are heterogeneous with respect to the defining features and meet the criteria for other personality disorders, they may possess characteristics considered to be associated with other diagnoses, and they may not be homogeneous with respect to the hypothesized covariates of their own diagnosis. How can one isolate a specific etiology and therapy for a certain personality disorder if many patients simultaneously also meet the criteria for a variety of other personality disorders?

Research that attempts to test hypotheses regarding a diagnostic construct by comparing groups of patients that meet the minimal criteria for membership (e.g., five of eight features for Borderline, or four of eight for Schizotypal, will likely include enough heterogeneity, overlap, and borderline cases to render group comparisons relatively uninformative (Horowitz, Post, French, Wallis, & Siegelman, 1981). It is possible that increased prototypicality of a member (e.g., possessing eight of eight features rather than five of eight) will result in an increased probability of a verification of hypotheses, just as increased prototypicality results in increased reliability of classification (Cantor et al., 1980). This is the reason for developing more restrictive criteria for schizophrenia and homogeneous subtypes of affective disorders (Andreasen, 1982; Kendell, 1982). It might be best for research concerning personality disorders to follow suit and foucs on the infrequent prototypic members and not rely on those who meet only the minimal DSM-III criteria.

Heterogeneity of membership, however, may be not only common, but pervasive. Prototypic examples of the hypothetical construct may then be too rare to be of much use. Meehl and Golden (1982) described a series of taxometric methods for identifying and validating hypothetical constructs (latent taxons) that are sophisticated alternatives to the simplistic Fisherian group differences research. Their methods, however, may be somewhat difficult to use by the average researcher. Once one abandons the assumptions of classical categories, however, questions arise about the appropriateness of traditional methods for diagnostic validations.

Summary

We have reviewed the DSM-III Axis II format for the classification of personality disorders and have outlined some of the issues that may influence the choice of future methods of diagnosis. We have emphasized two areas of active and important controversies: (a) the value of dimensional versus categorical methods, and (b) the use of prototypal versus classical models of categorization.

A dimensional system of classification presents more flexible, specific, and comprehensive information, while categorical systems tend to be Procrustean, lose information, and result in many classificatory dilemmas. Categorical systems, however, remain the prevalent mode for psychiatric diagnosis, are simpler to apply, and may be more appropriate for the discovery and validation of discrete syndromes and specific etiologies. It seems likely that dimensional approaches will gradually supplant the categorical in the classification of personality disorders (Frances, 1982), especially in research applications. A difficult decision is which of many possible dimensions to use. Four alternative methods were discussed (i.e., those of Cattel, Eysenck, Leary, and Millon).

It was also demonstrated that Axis II is inconsistent in the extent to which it is based on a prototypal or a classical model of categorization. Overlapping boundaries are acknowledged and at times polythetic diagnostic criteria provided, but some disorders still imply a homogeneity with respect to the definitional features, and the diagnostic criteria do not acknowledge that the definitional features are likely to have varying degrees of diagnostic efficiency. It was suggested that research determining the relative diagnostic efficiency of the defining features of a disorder consider the true-positive, local false-positive, and base rates, the particular differential diagnosis from which the specificity values are obtained, and the conditional probability of combinations of features as well as of single features. The implications of heterogeneity of membership and overlapping boundaries for testing hypotheses concerning specific etiology and treatment were also discussed.

REFERENCES

Akiskal, H. (1983). Dysthymic disorder: Psychopathology of proposed chronic depressive subtypes. *American Journal of Psychiatry, 140,* 11–20.

Akiskal, H., Djenderedjian, A., Rosenthal, A., & Khani, M. (1977). Cyclothymic disorder: Validating criteria for inclusion in the bipolar affective group. *American Journal of Psychiatry, 134,* 1227–1233.

Allport, G., & Odbert, H. (1936). Trait-names: A psychological study. *Psychological Monographs, 47,* 1–171.

American Psychiatric Association (APA). (1980). *Diagnostic and statistical manual of mental disorders* (3rd ed.). Washington, DC: Author.

Andreasen, N. (1982). Concepts, diagnosis and classification. In E. S. Paykel (Ed.), *Handbook of affective disorders.* New York: Guilford Press.

Benjamin, L. (1974). Structural analysis of social behavior. *Psychological Review, 81,* 392–425.

Bielski, R., & Friedel, R. (1976). Prediction of tricyclic antidepressant response. *Archives of General Psychiatry, 33,* 1479–1489.

Blashfield, R. K. (1980). Propositions regarding the use of cluster analysis in clinical research. *Journal of Consulting and Clinical Psychology, 48,* 456–459.

Blashfield, R. K., & Draguns, J. (1976). Evaluative criteria for psychiatric classification. *Journal of Abnormal Psychology, 85,* 140–150.

Butcher, J. N. (Ed.). (1972). *Objective personality assessment.* New York: Academic Press.

Butcher, J. N., & Owen, P. (1978). Objective personality inventories: Recent research and some contemporary issues. In B. Wolman (Ed.), *Clinical diagnosis of mental disorders.* New York: Plenum Press.

Cantor, N., & Mischel, W. (1979). Prototypes in person perception. In L. Berkowitz (Ed.), *Advances in experimental social psychology* (Vol. 12). New York: Academic Press.

Cantor, N., Smith, E. E., French, R. D., & Mezzich, J. (1980). Psychiatric diagnosis as prototype categorization. *Journal of Abnormal Psychology, 89,* 181–193.

Cattell, R. (1946). *Description and measurement of personality.* New York: World Book.

Cattell, R. (1966). *The scientific analysis of personality.* Chicago, IL: Aldine.

Cattell, R. (1970). The integration of functional and psychometric requirements in a quantitative and computerized diagnostic system. In A. Mahrer (Ed.), *New approaches to personality classification.* New York: Columbia University Press.

Chance, E. (1966). Content analysis of verbalizations about interpersonal experience. In L. Gottschalk & H. Auerbach (Eds.), *Methods of research in psychotherapy.* New York: Appleton-Century-Crofts.

Clarkin, J., Widiger, T., Frances, A., Hurt, S., & Gilmore, M. (1983). Prototypic typology and the borderline personality disorder. *Journal of Abnormal Psychology, 92,* 263–275.

Comrey, A. (1978). Common methodological problems in factor analytic studies. *Journal of Consulting and Clinical Psychology, 46,* 648–659.

Conte, H., & Plutchik, R. (1981). A circumplex model for interpersonal personality traits. *Journal of Personality and Social Psychology, 40,* 701–711.

Corning, W., & Steffy, R. (1979). Taximetric strategies applied to psychiatric classification. *Schizophrenia Bulletin, 5,* 294–305.

Donnelly, E., Murphy, D., & Goodwin, D. (1976). Cross-sectional and longitudinal comparisons of bipolar and unipolar depressed groups on the MMPI. *Journal of Consulting and Clinical Psychology, 44,* 233–237.

Eysenck, H. (1952). *The scientific study of personality.* London: Routledge & Kegan Paul.

Eysenck, H. (1970). A dimensional system of psychodiagnostics. In A. Mahrer (Ed.), *New approaches to personality classification.* New York: Columbia University Press.

Eysenck, H. (1977). Personality and factor analysis: A reply to Guilford. *Psychological Bulletin, 84,* 405–411.

Eysenck, H. (1981). *A model for personality.* Berlin: Springer-Verlag.

Eysenck, H., & Eysenck, S. (1971). *Manual of the Eysenck personality inventory* (4th ed.). London: University of London Press.

Eysenck, H., Wakefield, J., & Friedman, A. (1983). Diagnosis and clinical assessment: The DSM-III. *Annual Review of Psychology, 34,* 167–193.

Finn, S. (1982). Base rates, utilities, and DSM-III. Shortcomings of fixed-rule systems of psychodiagnosis. *Journal of Abnormal Psychology, 91,* 294–302.

Frances, A. (1980). The DSM-III personality disorders section: A commentary. *American Journal of Psychiatry, 137,* 1050–1054.

Frances, A., & Cooper, A. (1981). Descriptive and dynamic psychiatry: A perspective on DSM-III. *American Journal of Psychiatry, 138,* 1198–1202.

Frances, A. (1982). Categorical and dimensional systems of personality disorder. *Comprehensive Psychiatry, 23,* 516–527.

Garmezy, N. (1975). Process and reactive schizophrenia, some conceptions and issues. In M. Katz, J. Cole, & W. Barton (Eds.), *Classification in psychiatry psychopathology.* Chevy Chase, MD: U.S. Department of Health, Education and Welfare.

Goldberg, L. (1981). Developing a taxonomy of trait-descriptive terms. In D. Fiske (Ed.), *Problems with language imprecision.* San Francisco, CA: Jossey-Bass.

Goldberg, L. (1982). From ace to zombie. Some explorations in the language of personality. In C. Spielberger & J. N. Butcher (Eds.), *Advances in personality assessment* (Vol. 1). Hillsdale, NJ: Erlbaum.

Gray, J. (1981). A critique of Eysenck's theory of personality. In H. Eysenck (Ed.), *A model for personality.* Berlin: Springer-Verlag.

Guilford, J. (1975). Factors and factors of personality. *Psychological Bulletin, 83,* 802–814.

Guilford, J. (1977). Will the real factor of extraversion-introversion please stand up? A reply to Eysenck. *Psychological Bulletin, 84,* 412–416.

Guttman, L. (1954). A new approach to factor analysis: The radex. In P. Lazarsfeld (Ed.), *Mathematical thinking in the social sciences.* Glencoe, IL: Free Press.

Guze, S. (1975). Differential diagnosis of the borderline personality disorder. In J. Mack (Ed.), *Borderline states in psychiatry.* New York: Grune & Stratton.

Haynes, S., Feinleib, M., & Kannel, W. (1980). The relationship of psychosocial factors to coronary heart disease in the Framingham study. *American Journal of Epidemiology, 111,* 37–51.

Hempel, C. (1961). Introduction to problems of taxonomy. In J. Zubin (Ed.), *Field studies in the mental disorders.* New York: Grune & Stratton.

Hine, F., & Williams, R. (1975). Dimensional diagnosis and the medical student's grasp of psychiatry. *Archives of General Psychiatry, 32,* 525–528.

Horowitz, L., Post, D., French, R., Wallis, K., & Siegelman, E. (1981). The prototype as a construct in abnormal psychology. 2. Clarifying disagreement in psychiatric judgments. *Journal of Abnormal Psychiatry, 90,* 575–585.

Kelly, C., & King, G. (1979). Behavioral correlates of the 2-7-8 MMPI profile type in students at a university mental health center. *Journal of Consulting and Clinical Psychology, 47,* 679–685.

Kelly, G. (1965). The role of classification in personality theory. In M. Katz, J. Cole, & W. Barton (Eds.), *The role and methodology of classification in psychiatry and psychopathology* (Public Health Publ. No. 1584). Washington, DC: U. S. Government Printing Office.

Kendell, R. (1975). *The role of diagnosis in psychiatry.* Oxford: Blackwell Scientific Publications.

Kendell, R. (1982). The choice of diagnostic criteria for biological research. *Archives of General Psychiatry, 39,* 1334–1339.

Kiesler, D. (1982). *The 1982 interpersonal circle: A taxonomy for complementarity in human transactions.* Richmond: Virginia Commonwealth University Press.

Lang, R. (1978). Multivariate classification of day-care patients: Personality as a dimensional continuum. *Journal of Consulting and Clinical Psychology, 46,* 1212–1226.

Leary, T. (1957). *Interpersonal diagnosis of personality.* New York: Ronald Press.

Levin, D. (1979). The nature of plant species. *Science, 204,* 381–384.

Loevinger, J. (1957). Objective tests as instruments of psychological theory. *Psychological Reports, 3,* 635–694 (Monograph No. 9).

Lorr, M., & McNair, D. (1965). Expansion of the interpersonal behavior circle. *Journal of Personality and Social Psychology, 2*, 823–830.

McLemore, C., & Benjamin, L. (1979). Whatever happened to interpersonal diagnosis? A psychosocial alternative to DSM-III. *American Psychologist, 34*, 17–34.

Meehl, P., & Golden, R. (1982). Taxometric methods. In P. Kendall & J. N. Butcher (Eds.), *Handbook of research methods in clinical psychology.* New York: Wiley.

Meehl, P., & Rosen, A. (1955). Antecedent probability and the efficiency of psychometric signs, patterns, or cutting scores. *Psychological Bulletin, 52*, 194–216.

Mezzich, J. (1979). Patterns and issues in multiaxial psychiatric diagnosis. *Psychological Medicine, 9*, 125–137.

Millon, T. (1969). *Modern psychopathology: A biosocial approach to maladaptive learning and functioning.* Philadelphia, PA: Saunders.

Millon, T. (1981). *Disorders of personality: DSM-III: Axis II.* New York: Wiley.

Millon, T. (1982). *Millon clinical multiaxial inventory manual* (2nd ed.). Minneapolis, MN: National Computer Systems.

Pollak, J. (1979). Obsessive–compulsive personality: A review: *Psychological Bulletin, 86*, 225–241.

Rorer, L. (1972). Sixteen personality factor questionnaire. In O. Buros (Ed.), *Seventh mental measurements yearbook* (Vol. 1). Highland Park, NJ: Gryphon Press.

Rosch, E. (1978). Principles of categorization. In E. Rosch & B. Lloyd (Eds.), *Cognition and categorization.* Hillsdale, NJ: Erlbaum.

Rosch, E., & Mervis, C. (1975). Family resemblances: Studies in the internal structure of categories. *Cognitive Psychology, 7*, 573–605.

Skinner, H. (1981). Toward the integration of classification theory and methods. *Journal of Abnormal Psychology, 90*, 68–87.

Skinner, H., & Blashfield, R. (1982). Increasing the impact of cluster analysis research: The case of psychiatric classification. *Journal of Consulting and Clinical Psychology, 50*, 727–735.

Smith, E., Snoben, E., & Rips, L. (1974). Structure and process in semantic memory: A featural model for semantic decisions. *Psychological Review, 81*, 214–241.

Spitzer, R., Endicott, J., & Robins, E. (1975). Clinical criteria for psychiatric diagnosis and DSM-III. *American Journal of Psychiatry, 132*, 1187–1192.

Spitzer, R., Forman, J., & Nee, J. (1979). DSM-III field trials: Initial interrater diagnostic reliability. *American Journal of Psychiatry, 136*, 815–817.

Spitzer, R., & Williams, J. (1980). Classification of mental disorders and DSM-III. In H. Kaplan, A. Freedman, & B. Sadock (Eds.), *Comprehensive textbook of psychiatry/III* (3rd ed., Vol. 1). Baltimore, MD: Williams & Wilkins.

Spitzer, R., Williams, J., & Skodol, A. (1980). DSM-III: The major achievements and an overview. *American Journal of Psychiatry, 137*, 151–164.

Strauss, J. (1973). Diagnostic models and the nature of psychiatric disorder. *Archives of General Psychiatry, 29*, 445–449.

Strauss, J. (1975). A comprehensive approach to psychiatric diagnosis. *American Journal of Psychiatry, 132*, 1193–1197.

Strupp, H. (1980). Success and failure in time limited psychotherapy. *Archives of General Psychiatry, 37*, 947–958.

Taylor, C. (1983). DSM-III and behavioral assessment. *Behavioral Assessment, 5*, 5–14.

Taylor, M., & Abrams, R. (1975). Acute mania: Clinical and genetic study of responders and nonresponders to treatment. *Archives of General Psychiatry, 32*, 863–865.

Treece, C., & Nicholson, D. (1980). DSM-III personality type and dose levels in methadone maintenance. *Journal of Nervous and Mental Disease, 168*, 621–628.

Weimer, W. (1979). *Notes on the methodology of scientific research.* Hillsdale, NJ: Erlbaum.

Weissman, M., Prusoff, B., & Klerman, G. (1978). Personality and prediction of long term outcome of depression. *American Journal of Psychiatry, 135*, 797–800.

Widiger, T. (1982). Prototypic typology and borderline diagnoses. *Clinical Psychology Review, 2*, 115–135.

Widiger, T. (in press). Utilities and fixed diagnostic rules: Comments on Finn (1982). *Journal of Abnormal Psychology.*

Wiggins, J. (1973). *Personality and prediction: Principles of personality assessment.* Menlo Park, CA: Addison-Wesley.

Wiggins, J. (1979). A psychological taxonomy of trait-descriptive terms: The interpersonal domain. *Journal of Personality and Social Psychology, 37,* 395–412.

Wiggins, J. (1982). Circumplex models of interpersonal behavior in clinical psychology. In P. Kendall & J. N. Butcher (Eds.), *Handbook of research methods in clinical psychology.* New York: Wiley.

Wilson, G. (1978). Introversion/extroversion. In H. London & J. Exner (Eds.), *Dimensions of personality.* New York: Wiley.

Wittgenstein, L. (1953). *Philosophical investigations* (G. E. M. Anscombe, Trans.). Oxford: Blackwell Scientific Publications.

Zigler, E., & Phillips, L. (1961). Psychiatric diagnosis: A critique. *Journal of Abnormal and Social Psychology, 63,* 607–618.

Zubin, J. (1978). Research in clinical diagnosis. In B. Wolman (Ed.), *Clinical diagnosis of mental disorders.* New York: Plenum Press.

PART V

PROPOSALS FOR DSM-IV SYNDROMES

CHAPTER 20

Attention Deficit and Associated Childhood Disorders

Dennis P. Cantwell

Introduction

Attention deficit disorder is one of the more common psychiatric diagnoses in childhood. This chapter will discuss the following aspects of this disorder: (*a*) the DSM-III definition and diagnostic criteria for attention deficit disorder as well as the DSM-III proposed subtypes; (*b*) other criteria proposed for the diagnosis of this syndrome; (*c*) other terms that have been used to describe the syndrome; (*d*) the relationship of attention deficit disorder with hyperactivity (ADDH) to other disorders in childhood: conduct disorders, learning disorders, depression, mental retardation, pervasive developmental disorders, brain damage syndromes, and Tourette's syndrome; (*e*) the relationship of the ADDH syndrome in childhood to other psychiatric disorders in adolescence and adult life; (*f*) various etiological hypotheses; (*g*) the treatment of the syndrome in childhood; and (*h*) treatment of the syndrome in adolescence and later life.

Attention Deficit Disorder: DSM-III Definition, Diagnostic Criteria, and Subtypes

For the first time in an "official" diagnostic nomenclature, DSM-III provided detailed descriptions of various disorders. In addition, specific diag-

Dennis P. Cantwell. Neuropsychiatric Institute, University of California, Los Angeles, Los Angeles, California.

nostic criteria were provided for the diagnosis of each of the disorders described in DSM-III.

According to DSM-III, the essential features of ADDH in childhood include a developmentally inappropriate short attention span, impulsivity, and hyperactivity. At home, attentional problems are described as being demonstrated by failure to follow through on requests made by parents and instructions given by the parents and by inability to stick to play activities for periods of time that are appropriate for the child's age. In school inattention is probably more easily recognized. In school, the child's attentiveness and impulsivity are shown by an inability to stay with tasks that other children in the classroom can stay with for significant lengths of time (i.e., not completing work, difficulty organizing work). Teachers often describe the children as children who "do not listen" or who are "easily distractible." Any group situation probably intensifies the child's attentional difficulties, and the classroom setting is probably the worst because of the task demands of the academic setting.

Motoric abnormalities vary somewhat as a function of age. Whereas older children and adolescents may demonstrate only extreme restlessness and fidgetiness, younger children are more likely to manifest gross motor activity and are often described by the parents as "constantly on the go" or "his motor is always running." The quality of the motor activity of the child with ADDH syndrome is every bit as important as the quantitative aspects. The motor activity appears to be non-goal directed and poorly organized. However, it is important to note that in settings where high levels of motor activity are appropriate, such as when playing active sports, the children may not be as easily distinguished on the basis of their activity level from normal children as they are in sedentary settings such as the classroom where high levels of motor activity are inappropriate.

DSM-III also points out that the symptoms of the child's condition may vary from day to day, from setting to setting, and within the same setting from hour to hour. Thus, the diagnosis cannot be ruled out because "he can sit and watch television for hours."

Thus, the core features of the DSM-III-defined ADDH syndrome are inattention, impulsivity, and hyperactivity. Specific, explicit criteria are pinpointed in each of these areas for the diagnosis to be made. At least three of the following must be present for inattentiveness to be diagnosed: (a) often fails to finish things he or she starts; (b) often does not seem to listen; (c) easily distracted; (d) has difficulty concentrating on schoolwork or other tasks requiring sustained attention; and (e) has difficulty sticking to a play activity.

For impulsivity to be present, at least three of the following must be characteristic of the child's behavior: (a) often acts before thinking; (b) shifts excessively from one activity to another; (c) has difficulty organizing work not due to cognitive impairment; (d) needs a lot of supervision; (e) frequently calls out in class; and (f) difficulty in waiting turn in games or group situations.

For hyperactivity to be considered present, at least two of the following symptoms must be characteristic of the child's behavior: (a) runs about or climbs about excessively; (b) has difficulty sitting still or fidgets excessively; (c) has difficulty staying seated; (d) moves about excessively during sleep; and (e) is always "on the go" or acts as if "driven by a motor."

However, these core symptoms are relatively common in many other child psychiatric disorders: conduct disorders, children with mental retardation, pervasive developmental disorders, and other conditions. Thus, DSM-III adds two other inclusion criteria for the diagnosis to be made. In addition to the cross-sectional picture noted above, the onset must be before the age of 7, and the condition must have a duration of at least 6 months. These two criteria are to ensure that one is not dealing with an episodic condition that may present cross-sectionally, like the ADDH syndrome. They emphasize the fact that this is a condition that has very early onset, usually by the age of 3, although the children may not be presented for professional evaluation until they enter a school setting where their behavior may be exacerbated and first brought to attention.

The use of a duration criteria also underscores the fact that this is a relatively chronic problem. This is not a condition that is present for one long period of time such as a year or so and then disappears for long periods of time, although it is true that the children's individual symptoms may vary in intensity from setting to setting and from day to day. This does not mean that the symptoms disappear for long periods of time. Thus, the DSM-III criteria outline specific and explicit behavioral symptoms that must be present in the three core areas and emphasize the fact that this is a condition that has an early age of onset and tends to be chronic.

DSM-III also adds exclusion criteria in that the diagnosis should not be made when the condition is due to schizophrenia, an affective disorder, or severe or profound mental retardation.

Three subtypes of the attention deficit disorder syndrome are proposed in DSM-III: the more commonly recognized ADDH syndrome in which all three core symptoms are present; attention deficit disorder without hyperactivity in which all of the features except hyperactivity are present; and attention deficit disorder residual state.

While it has been clinically recognized for a long time that there are children who present with inattentiveness and impulsivity, but who do not present with motor activity symptoms, the disorder was named for the first time in DSM-III. Thus, there are really no studies of consequence yet to tell us how ADD without hyperactivity compares to ADD with hyperactivity with regard to such things as outcome, response to treatment, family pattern of illness, and relationship to other psychiatric disorders.

Attention deficit disorder residual state in DSM-III is described as a condition in which the individual once met the criteria for ADDH and in which the signs of hyperactivity are no longer present. However, the individual must have had continued presence of the other signs, namely, attentional deficits and impulsivity. Moreover, these symptoms must result in some impairment in social or occupational functioning. Again, the exclusion criteria for ADD residual state include schizophrenia, affective disorder, severe or profound mental retardation, and schizotypal and borderline personality disorders.

The DSM-III criteria for ADDH are specific and explicit. However, they are not "operational," even though the word is often used. Loney (1983) has pointed out that true operational criteria are criteria that spell out the operations that take place in making the diagnosis. Thus, the methods of measuring the various symptoms must be sufficiently detailed so that it can be duplicated by other individuals wanting to replicate any particular procedure. The general process of clinical diagnosis, however, generally includes assimilating information about the child from parents, from teachers, and from other significant individuals in the child's life; observations and interviews of the child himself; and synthesizing this date from several sources to decide whether the child meets the criteria for the categorical diagnosis of ADDH.

Loney (1983) has outlined 10 operational steps in the definition of child psychiatric conditions such as the ADDH syndrome: (a) the selection of symptom dimensions; (b) the definition of the dimensions; (c) the enumeration of symptom descriptors; (d) operationalization of the symptoms and the descriptors so that there are definite measures of symptom dimensions that are sufficiently detailed and can be duplicated exactly; (e) a statistical approach to demarcation between normal and abnormal behavior; (f) combination of symptom information; (g) addition of important nonsymptom factors (i.e., age of onset and chronicity); (h) exclusion of other conditions; (i) demonstration of reliability and utility; and (j) validation of the disorder. Loney has applied this process to the diagnosis of ADDH, and indeed it results in a much more operational and replicable diagnosis.

Barkley (1982) likewise has gone somewhat further than the DSM-III criteria in specifying guidelines for defining the ADDH syndrome. Barkley does specify the symptom pattern of DSM-III, namely, attentional difficulties, impulsivity, and restlessness. He also adds an inability to restrict behavior as an adult demands or as a situation demands and rules out mental retardation, autism, and evidence of significant neurologic and central nervous system disorder. However, he adds more operational dimensional criteria in that the child must place two standard deviations above the mean for his age group relative to the other children on standardized behavior scales for parents and teachers, such as those devised by Conners. He also operationally requires that the child must be rated as a problem in at least 50% of the settings described on a home situation questionnaire for parents and the school situation questionnaire for teachers.

Thus, Loney and Barkley both have outlined the combination of categorical and dimensional criteria that are likely to lead to more reliable diagnoses between investigators or clinicians if they follow the Loney process or the Barkley process. It is beyond the scope of this chapter to discuss in detail the contrast between the DSM-III approach, the Barkley approach, and the Loney approach. What is important is that the process of diagnosis of ADDH is being considered in a much more scientific way than has been previously done. Barkley's review (1982) of a cross section of scientific papers on the ADDH syndrome over a 20-year period found that almost two-thirds used nothing more than the opinion of the investigators that the ADDH syndrome was present without specifying any criteria used in making their decisions.

A final note on this topic worth mentioning is the other terms that have been used almost synonymously to describe this syndrome over the years. These include terms such as the hyperkinetic reaction of childhood (which was the official term in DSM-II) and the hyperactive child syndrome. Both of these terms are behaviorally oriented, that is, they do not imply any etiology in their title, but do imply that one symptom pattern (the motor activity symptoms) is more important than the others. They are thus given primacy of importance in the diagnostic term.

The term was changed in DSM-III to attention deficit disorder syndrome with the various subtypes described above because it was felt that compared to the activity symptoms, the inattentiveness and impulsivity were probably "more important" because they are always present in younger children, including those who do not have hyperactivity and also seem to persist more over time. It should be recognized, however, that the impulsivity is probably as equally important in the syndrome as the attentional symptoms are, and possibly a better name would have included both symptom clusters in the title so that attentional symptoms are not given overall importance.

However, there are other terms that have been "unofficially" used synonymously with this syndrome as well. These include terms such as the minimal brain damage syndrome and the minimal brain dysfunction syndrome. These terms are not behaviorally oriented; they are not simply descriptive; but they imply an etiology in that they suggest some type of brain damage or brain dysfunction being present. Unfortunately, in many cases, if not most cases, that are described in the literature, the presence of the symptom pattern was in and of itself enough to indicate that the child had brain damage or brain dysfunction.

We know now that the great majority of children who present with the clearly defined ADDH syndrome described in DSM-III do not have true evidence of brain damage, if by brain damage one means some actual deficit in the structure of the brain. Brain dysfunction is a somewhat softer term, and brain dysfunction may occur with or without actual damage to the brain. However, the measurement of brain dysfunction in children is tenuous at best and certainly cannot be quantified, as a term such as minimal brain dysfunction suggests. (If there is a minimal brain dysfunction, there is a maximal brain dysfunction.) At present, the techniques do not exist for quantifying brain dysfunction and all that that implies in children. Terms such as minimal brain dysfunction and minimal brain damage should be abandoned.

ADDH Syndrome: Relationship to Other Disorders in Childhood

There are some conditions that may be confused with, may coexist with, or may have other relationships with the ADDH syndrome that are important in childhood. These include conduct disorders, learning disorders, depressive disorders, mental retardation, the pervasive developmental disorders, true brain damage syndromes, and Tourette's syndrome. These will be taken up in turn.

Conduct Disorders

Conduct disorders are characterized by a repetitive and persistent pattern of conduct in which the individual either violates the basic rights of others or violates major age-appropriate societal norms. Like the ADDH syndrome, conduct disorders are overt behavior disorders. They tend to begin early in life, are more common in males, and are relatively chronic. The subclassification of conduct disorders is a somewhat muddled area. DSM-III specifies four subtypes: undersocialized aggressive and nonaggressive, and socialized aggressive and nonaggressive. On the other hand, other authors, such as Robins (1966), suggest that the most important subclassification of conduct disorders are mild, moderate, and severe. It is beyond the scope of this chapter to discuss this controversy. However, it is important to discuss the relationship of the ADDH syndrome in childhood to conduct disorders in childhood.

The DSM-III approach to the relationship between ADDH and conduct disorders is that these are separate disorders diagnosed by specific and explicit criteria. It is recognized that they often occur together, and indeed when both are present, both diagnoses should be made. However, there are other authors, particularly British authors, such as Shaffer and Greenhill (1979) and Sanberg, Rutter, and Taylor (1978), who feel that ADDH and conduct disorder may just be different names for variants of the same condition. They point out that both are similar with regard to their clinical symptomatology, that is, they are overt behavior disorders. They are more common in males and have similar etiologic factors, family genetic factors, and natural history. Sanberg et al. (1978) are some of the leading British espousers of the view that the ADDH syndrome as diagnosed in the United States overlaps considerably with conduct disorder as diagnosed in Britain. In Britain, the diagnosis of ADDH is reserved for a much smaller number of children, generally with demonstrable neurological abnormalities and lower IQ, who present with a transsituational symptom pattern of inattentiveness, impulsivity, and motor activity.

On the other hand, American investigators, particularly exemplified by Loney (1980) and Barkley (1982), suggest that there are important differences between ADDH and conduct disorders. It is true that ADDH children may in fact also be diagnosed as having conduct disorders, and children with diagnosable conduct disorders may be found to have an underlying ADDH syndrome as well. A study conducted at Iowa by Stewart, Cummings, Singer, and deBlois (1981) on an inpatient service found that about three-quarters of children with a conduct disorder had hyperactivity, and two-thirds of children with hyperactivity had a conduct disorder.

However, Loney (1980), also at Iowa, has produced data that are very important concerning the differentiation between ADDH and conduct disorders. Loney and her colleagues have produced data suggesting that there are two independent dimensions of behavior, one of aggressive behavior (or conduct symptomatology) and one of hyperactivity–inattentiveness, and these independent dimensions have concurrent validity and different contemporary and long-term correlates. A fourfold subgrouping using these two independent dimensions of hyperactivity and conduct disorder produced four groups of children who differed at follow-up. Loney and her colleagues have also produced data (Langhorne & Loney, 1979) to suggest that childhood conduct symptomatology, particularly aggression, is much better than the hyperactivity–inattentiveness dimension as a predictor of certain aspects of adolescent outcome—most particularly, antisocial behavior.

Barkley (1982) points out that there are independent investigators who have used factor analytic methods and have found separate independent factors for inattentiveness, motor activity, and conduct disorder using various parent and teacher rating scales. The inattentive factors do not show the same patterns of intercorrelation as the conduct disorder factors do with measures of teacher and peer interaction, attitudes in classroom, and achievement.

In summary, some children with the ADDH syndrome do in early childhood demonstrate significant conduct symptomatology. When this occurs, both diagnoses of the ADDH syndrome and conduct disorders should be diagnosed. It is likely from the available data that the conduct symptomatology is probably a better predictor of certain aspects of adolescent outcome—including antisocial behavior, self-esteem problems, and others. It is also probably true that certain children with the ADDH syndrome, even in the absence of significant conduct symptomatology in childhood, may develop conduct disorder in later life or antisocial personality in early adulthood. This will be discussed below when considering the relationship of the ADDH syndrome in childhood to other psychiatric conditions of adolescence and early adulthood.

What is needed are comparative studies of children with "pure ADDH," "pure conduct disorder," and with both ADDH and conduct disorder. These groups should be compared at baseline and over time on a wide variety of parameters, including measures of attention, activity, impulsivity, laboratory learning, academic performance, other cognitive areas, association with other problems, neurophysiology, biochemistry, family history of psychopathology, and short- and long-term response to stimulant drug treatment. Only in this fashion can the question of overlap of ADDH and conduct disorder be definitively answered.

Learning Disorders

The definition of learning disorders is almost as muddled a field as the definition of attention deficit disorder. Loose terminology is one problem that makes definitions difficult. "Ability" is a term best used to connote an underlying, often inferred capacity. "Performance" is a term best used to describe observed behavior. "Deficit" is a term best used to describe something less than expected, and "disorder," to describe a recurring pattern causing some degree of distress or disadvantage. Therefore, a performance deficit is observed lower than normal performance in learning, while a disability is not observed but is inferred in the performance.

A proper definition of a learning disorder must give a specified level of performance deficit and must take into account the regression effect of chronological age and performance IQ. For example, 2 years behind expected performance is not the same performance deficit for children of different chronological ages and differing IQs. When learning disorder is defined as performing significantly below a level in an academic subject predicted on the basis of chronological age and IQ, it is quite clear that children with ADDH also have learning disorders. In our own work (Cantwell & Satterfield, 1978), about three-quarters of our ADDH boys were underachieving to some degree in all three academic subjects—reading, spelling, and mathematics. More than one-third were a full grade below their expected level in at least two academic subjects. When compared to a normal control group of children, the ADDH children were more severely academically retarded in that they were academically retarded in more academic subjects and to a greater degree in each of these subjects. However, it is also quite clear that not all ADDH children have learning disorders when defined this way. Moreover, although there is a good degree of overlap, there are certainly a large number of children with learning disorders who do not have the ADDH syndrome.

Most modern clinicians feel that learning disorders have a multifactorial etiology. Four leading views are that (*a*) linguistic problems are the most important etiologically in learning disorders; (*b*) visual perceptual disorders are important in some; and (*c*) some combination of both of these is important along with memory and attention factors; (*d*) ecologic or environmental factors are considered to be a major issue (i.e., poor teaching or inadequate opportunity for instruction). When one looks at the core disabilities of ADDH children, it is not surprising that a significant number would be expected to have learning disorders. It is probable that some ADDH children have their learning disorders on the basis of the fact that they have attentional difficulties and/or impulsivity.

However, Cantwell and Baker (1980) have shown that there is an intimate relationship between early speech and language delay, attention deficit disorder, and learning disorder. First, children with early speech and language disorders are at risk for a variety of psychiatric problems, the most prominent being attention deficit disorder with hyperactivity. Moreover, a significant number of these children when they first present for speech and language disorders are already demonstrating significant academic problems, and as they grow older, the percentage with academic problems increases even though their speech and language disorders tend to improve with time. Finally, when one takes those children with speech and language disorders who are already demonstrating significant academic problems, one also selectively picks out a group that is highly likely to have psychiatric disorder. In one study, Cantwell and Baker (1980) showed that 83% of those children with early speech and language delay who also had a significant learning disorder also had a DSM-III diagnosable psychiatric disorder. This was compared to 30% of the same population of speech and language disordered children who did not have any significant learning disorders. The most prominent psychiatric disorder among those already demonstrating significant learning disorders was ADDH. Douglas (1980) suggests that children with ADDH and children with learning disorders have different underlying disabilities. However, she suggests that the outcome of both of these disabilities—ADD and LD—is quite similar in many respects because they both lead to comparable secondary difficulties and over time tend to look more and more alike.

Douglas also suggests that ADDH children may have difficulties in acquiring the strategic problem-solving skills required for the process of learning to take place. She has demonstrated that ADDH children differ from normal children when given learning tasks that require them to devise their own strategies for remembering associations in a paired associate learning task. However, they do not differ as much from normal children when the pairs are already associated in a known and consistent way. The fact that ADDH children tend to do less well on memory tasks in a free recall situation, but not in a cued recall situation, suggests the same thing (i.e., that when the strategy is already there, as in cued recall situations, the ADDH children do as well as normals; but in a free recall situation that requires children to make up their own strategies to remember things, they do not do as well).

In summary, a significantly large number of ADDH children will also demonstrate learning disorders. However, clinical studies and factor analytic studies suggest that there are ADDH children who do not have learning disorders, and that there are a significantly larger number of learning-disordered children who do not meet the criteria for the ADDH syndrome. Ongoing work suggests that the core disabilities in the two groups may be different. Comparative long-term studies of ADDH children without learning disorders, pure learning-disordered children without ADDH, and ADDH children with learning disorders would help to unravel this puzzle.

Depressive Disorders

As we shall see later in this chapter, a number of authors, including Mendelson, Johnson, and Stewart (1971) and Weiss, Minde, Werry, Douglas, and Nemeth (1971), have commented on the frequency of depressive symptomatology in ADDH children once they have reached the age of adolescence. Not as frequent comment has been made about the relationship of ADDH and depressive disorders in childhood. At least part of this is due to the fact that the field of childhood depression is a relatively new one. The prevailing view for a long time was that children in the prepubertal age range either did not become depressed or, if they manifested depression, the clinical picture was not analogous to that seen in adults. However, more recent studies suggest that indeed a substantial number of psychiatrically referred children may have a depressive syndrome which presents clinically the way it presents in adults, that is, with dysphoric mood, anhedonia, guilt, hopelessness, suicidal ideation, and melancholic vegetative symptoms such as insomnia, anorexia, and weight loss.

Weinberg was one of the first to point out in his early studies of affectively disordered children (Weinberg, Rutman, Sullivan, Pencik, & Dietz, 1973) that there were some who had preexisting ADDH whose ADDH symptomatology was made worse when their depressive disorder developed, and returned to the baseline level when their depressive disorder was treated and/or remitted.

Carlson and Cantwell (1979), in a study of 102 systematically interviewed parents and children referred to the UCLA Neuropsychiatric Institute, found that 28 (or 27%) of the total had a diagnosis of ADDH, according to DSM-III criteria. However, 28 also had a DSM-III diagnosable affective disorder (or 27%) of the total. Eight of these children had a history of ADDH that was longstanding, and when they presented for evaluation, they had a superimposed affective disorder. Thus, 30% of the ADDH population had a superimposed affective disorder, and 30% of the depressed children had a preexisting history of ADDH. This may be due to the independent association of two relatively common syndromes in psychiatrically referred children. One could make a case that the ADDH child who "does not make it in our society," who does not succeed in school, who is rather "klutsy" and not good in sports, and who has poor peer relationships, may develop a depressive disorder as a reaction to his core symptoms of the ADDH syndrome. It is also reported that a depressive disorder may develop in an ADDH child as a reaction to treatment with stimulant medication.

Mental Retardation

The essential features in mental retardation are significantly subaverage intellectual functioning resulting in or associated with deficits or impairments in adaptive behavior, with both of these occurring before the age of 18. The diagnosis of mental retardation is made whether or not there is a coexisting mental or physical disorder. Significantly subaverage intellectual functioning is defined as an IQ of 70 or below on an individually administered IQ test. The prevalence of other mental disorders is three or four times greater among children with mental retardation than in the general population. The more common mental disorders present in the mentally retarded include stereotyped movement disorders, infantile autism, and the ADDH syndrome. However, it is generally accepted that in a significant number of cases of the ADDH syndrome associated with mental retardation the attention deficit may be qualitatively different than the attention deficit in nonretarded ADDH children.

Aman (1983) has pointed out that the percentage of mentally retarded children with the ADDH syndrome who improve behaviorally with stimulant drugs is less than the percentage of nonretarded children with the ADDH syndrome who improve. Moreover, even in those who "improve" behaviorally with stimulant drugs, there may be a negative effect on the attentional process and subsequent deterioration of cognitive function. The reason for this, Aman postulates, is that the nature of the attention deficit disorder in the retarded with the ADDH syndrome is fundamentally different from the nature of the attention deficit in nonretarded children with the ADDH syndrome. He suggests that the retarded have a fixed narrow attention span which is worsened by stimulant medication, while the nonretarded have an overflow attention span which is narrowed, leading to improvement with stimulant medication.

Thus, the ADDH syndrome may occur in conjunction with mental retardation. However, the therapeutic implications and prognostic implications are probably not the same as they are for nonretarded children with the ADDH syndrome.

Pervasive Developmental Disorders

The pervasive developmental disorders are characterized by the distortions in the development of multiple basic psychological functions that are involved in the development of social skills and language such as attention, perception, reality testing, and motor movement. DSM-III describes two major types—infantile autism and pervasive developmental disorder, childhood onset. In the past, many names have been ascribed to these disorders, including atypical children, childhood schizophrenia, and childhood psychosis. However, the term pervasive developmental disorder describes most accurately the core clinical disturbance: many basic areas of psychological development that are affected at the same time and to a severe degree. The use of a term such as childhood schizophrenia suggests a link with adult schizophrenia, as does the use of a term such as childhood psychosis. Such links are tenuous at best for infantile autism and are unknown for the heterogeneous group of children who would fall under the rubric of pervasive developmental disorder, childhood onset. As with the mentally retarded, children with these syndromes may indeed have an attention deficit disorder syndrome as well. Some do respond to stimulant medication for their core ADDH symptoms, although not for their core symptoms of the pervasive developmental disorder. Thus, in some cases it is important to make a diagnosis of ADDH in children with pervasive developmental disorders. On the other hand, a significant number of pervasive developmental disordered children, especially those with infantile autism, are also mentally retarded, and the same cautions about the nature of the attention deficit in these children probably applies as it does to other retarded children.

Brain Damage Syndromes

Brain damage in its literal sense should be used to describe a condition in which there is a definite structural change in the brain. Brain dysfunction should be used when there is an abnormal functioning in the brain, such as an abnormal electrical discharge. In the Isle of Wight study, Rutter, Graham, and Yule (1970) found that less than 5% of children, ages 10 and 11, who had clinically significant psychiatric disorders also had detectable pathological disorders of the brain. This compares with a prevalence rate of 6.4 per 1,000 for pathological disorders of the brain in the total child population of the island. The figures from this large-scale, carefully conducted and controlled epidemiologic study indicate that only a minority of children with clinically significant psychiatric disorder has demonstrable evidence of damage to the brain. They also indicate, however, that compared to the general population of children, those with psychiatric disorder do have an increased prevalence rate of abnormality of the brain.

Looking at the situation the other way around, Rutte found that about 7% of the 10- and 11-year-olds were found to have clinically significant psychiatric disorder. Those with chronic physical disorders not involving the brain, such as asthma and diabetes, had a rate of psychiatric disorder of about 12% (almost twice as high as that of the general population). The most striking finding was that 35% of the children with definite brain disorders had psychiatric disorders. That is five times higher than the rate for the general population and three times higher than that for children with chronic disorders that did not involve anatomical abnormality in brain structure.

Children with uncomplicated epilepsy (brain dysfunction without brain damage) have a psychiatric disorder rate of about 28%. Children with epilepsy who also had definite abnormalities above the brain stem had a rate of about 58%, while children who had lesions above the brain stem without epilepsy had a rate of about 37.5%.

This carefully designed study indicates very definitely an increased prevalence rate of psychiatric disorder in children with demonstrable brain damage, and likewise a comparable prevalence rate in children with at least one form of abnormal brain functions, but with no demonstrable physical abnormality of the brain as uncomplicated epilepsy. Those who had both an abnormality in brain structure and in brain function had an even higher rate in psychiatric disorder. However, it was also worth noting that there was no type of psychiatric disorder that was uniquely associated with the presence of brain damage or brain dysfunction. In particular, the ADDH syndrome was not a unique outcome of children with known brain damage or brain dysfunction. Thus, the use of terms such as the brain damage behavior syndrome, minimal brain damage, or minimal brain dysfunction to describe the great majority of children with the ADDH syndrome is scientifically and pragmatically incorrect.

It is true that some children with demonstrable brain damage and brain dysfunction will have an ADDH syndrome. However, only a small minority (probably less than 5%) of children with the ADDH syndrome has demonstrable brain damage. As with the association of ADDH with mental retardation and pervasive developmental disorders, there is serious question as to whether the nature of attention deficit and the therapeutic implications and prognostic implications of the ADDH syndrome are the same as they are in children without known brain damage.

Tourette's Syndrome

A condition that has recently gained attention for its association with the ADDH syndrome is Tourette's syndrome. Tourette's is characterized by the recurrent involuntary repetitive rapid movements called tics. These include multiple vocal tics. The movements can be voluntarily suppressed for minutes to hours, and the intensity frequency and the location of the symptoms may vary over weeks or months. The prevalence of this condition is probably greater than previously thought, with Leckman, Detlor, and Cohen (1983) giving a figure of 1 per 1,500 of the population. Peak onset is around age 7, but can be anywhere from age 3 to age 16. It is not always severe; it tends to be a broad spectrum of dysfunctions. It does tend to run in families, and there probably is a genetic factor operating as one etiologic agent. It is not always a lifelong problem and, in fact, may wane over time.

Cohen suggests that from 30% to 40% of Tourette's patients give a history of ADDH in their early years of life. Many of them developed multiple motor tics after they had been first treated with stimulants, and a few developed a full blown Tourette's syndrome after the use of stimulants. There is usually a positive family history in this subgroup for multiple tics and/or Tourette's syndrome. Whether those ADDH children who later develop Tourette's syndrome would have developed Tourette's without treatment with stimulant medication is obviously an unknown factor. The presence of tics in an individual with ADDH and/or a strong family history of

Tourette's syndrome or tics should raise caution with the use of stimulant medication to treat the ADDH syndrome.

Relationship of Childhood ADDH to Other Disorders in Adolescence and Adult Life

Loney, Kramer, and Milich (1981) point out that there are three theories of outcome of the ADDH syndrome in childhood, adolescence, and adult life. One is a developmental delay theory; one is a continual display theory; and the third is the eventual decay theory.

In the developmental delay theory, ADDH is postulated as some type of maturational or developmental lag. It is postulated that the children are on the "right" developmental track, but just moving at a slower pace, and then over time will eventually normalize by adolescence or early adult life. Until very recently, this was the prevailing view about the outcome of childhood ADDH.

In the continual display theory, the postulate is that the core symptoms of inattentiveness, impulsivity, motor activity, and so on will remain and lead to what in DSM-III terms is an ADD residual state in adolescence and adult life. Moreover, some secondary and psychological symptoms may develop, such as low self-esteem, which complicate the picture in adult life.

The eventual decay theory postulates a much more serious outcome. In this theory the childhood ADDH is considered to be a precursor to the development of severe psychopathology in adult life, including such conditions as antisocial personality disorder, alcoholism, affective disorders, serious academic retardation, other types of personality disorders, and even schizophrenia.

The problem in assessing this literature is that the relationship between childhood ADDH, that is, the picture at time one, and outcome in adolescence (time two) or in adult life (time three) is complicated by the design of the particular study. There are three types of studies that are used to relate childhood conditions to adolescent and adult outcomes: the real time prospective study, the follow-back study, and the catchup prospective study as named by Robins (1966).

In the real time prospective study, the childhood ADDH subjects are selected at time one in childhood by the investigator and studied by the investigator. They are then prospectively followed for a period of time and reevaluated at time two at adolescence and at time three in adult life. This is the only type of the three studies in which one investigator can select and study the index subjects and the control subjects and is the only one acceptable to test true treatment effects because random assignment is possible to treatment, to no treatment, or to one type of treatment versus another type of treatment. However, there are some serious problems in dealing with a real time prospective study. One of the difficult ones is subject attrition. Data from follow-up studies of psychiatric subjects suggest that those patients who are most difficult to find and follow-up are the ones who are demonstrating the most significant psychopathology. Moreover, with patients that are being prospectively followed for a long period of time (such as 10 and 20 years), the investigators age as the children do. Not only do the investigators age, but science ages and matures, so that early measures which may have been "state-of-the-art measures" at time one in childhood may look very crude at time two and time three in adolescence and adult life.

In the second type of study, the follow-back study, the subjects are selected at time two at adolescence or time three in adulthood. They are selected on the basis of some particular outcome(s) (such as delinquency or alcoholism). Then an attempt is made to locate early records to see how many of these adolescents or adults with a particular type of outcome had childhood histories of ADDH. The problems here are that one must rely on existing records for time one data, and one must select a particular outcome group and thus may miss other types of outcome. Moreover, if one relies only on early records for a childhood diagnosis of ADDH, one will miss those in the adolescent or adult population who may in fact have had ADDH in childhood, but were not seen anywhere and have no records at time one.

A modification of the follow-back study has been performed by Wender, Reimher, and Wood (1981), who attempted to find adults who were still manifesting symptoms suggestive of ADDH and who indeed had other types of psychopathology in adult life. Rather than relying on existing records, they attempted to make a retrospective diagnosis of ADDH based on both the subjects' and parents' histories of childhood behavior and the use of standardized rating scales.

The third type of study, the catchup prospective study, combines elements of the first two types. The sample is identified as an ADDH childhood sample at time one in childhood. However, they are identified from existing childhood records. One then studies them at time two in adolescence or time three in adult life after the population has "aged." The classic example of this type is Lee Robins's follow-up study of a childhood guidance population, published in the book *Deviant Children Grown Up* (1966).

There are other issues as well in looking at the relationship of childhood ADDH to certain types of adolescent and adult outcomes aside from the design of the study. One is the selection of index sample and selection of controls. Obviously, the diagnostic criteria used to select the index sample, whether it is broad criteria or narrow criteria, may affect the outcome results simply because different populations are being selected by different criteria.

Other important issues, in addition to core diagnostic criteria, are what additional conditions such as learning disorders, conduct disorders, and depressive disorders are present in childhood in addition to the ADDH. If some of these are present, the adult outcome or the adolescent outcome may be as much due to the additional conditions as they are to the ADDH syndrome. Where one obtains a sample may be important. For example, one could plausibly make a case that populations of ADDH children obtained from schools would have a less pathological outcome than those that are obtained from psychiatric clinics. It is likely that a substantial number of those selected from the school population will not have been referred to a psychiatric clinic, and it is plausible to assume that those who already have a psychiatric referral in childhood may have a more severe outcome. One could make a similar case comparing ADDH children from a private pediatric practice to that seen in a psychiatric clinic. To this author's knowledge, this has never been substantially demonstrated, but it certainly is plausible.

When the control should be selected (either initially at time one, time two, or at time three) is also an important issue. It may be that ADDH children grow into certain types of problems which would be missed if the controls in the ADDH population were not selected at the same time.

Where one obtains controls and how to match the control subjects to the index ADDH subjects are important questions. If they are matched for race, sex, social class, IQ, presence of learning disorders, presence of conduct disorders, and so on, then none of these can figure in as predictive factors in outcome.

Last, interval factors between time one and time two and between time one and time three are very important, and yet they may be hard to measure. Two common interval factors are various types of treatment intervention whose efficacy may be very hard to determine by retrospective information and life events. It is clear that certain types of stressful life events are associated with the development of certain types of psychopathology in adolescence and adult life. These may be difficult to determine retrospectively as well, and yet may be what explains the outcome rather than the presence of childhood ADDH.

Given these caveats then, we will attempt to selectively review some relevant studies of the outcome of childhood ADDH in adolescence and adult life. Overall, the large number of published studies of the outcome of childhood ADDH in adolescence and adult life have postulated widely varying outcomes. Aside from complete normality, other postulated outcomes in adolescence and adult life include attention deficit disorder residual state, antisocial personality disorder, other personality disorders, very significant academic retardation, affective disorders, alcoholism, and schizophrenia. Several recent reviews of the evidence for these various outcomes are available (Cantwell, 1975). For the purposes of this chapter, we will review some of the relevant studies suggesting these various types of outcomes.

The study by Minkes, Rowe, and Minkes (1967) probably deserves most recognition and is one of the first, if not the first, to point out that the outcome was not essentially one of developmental delay. She identified 18 children seen at Johns Hopkins Child Psychiatry Outpatient Department between 1937 and 1946. All of the children were retrospectively diagnosed as

ADDH from clinical records on the basis of the presence of a defined behavioral syndrome. Moreover, none of the patients had seizure disorders, were mentally retarded, or had a diagnosis of psychosis. The mean age at first clinic visit was 7 years, with a range from 2 years, 7 months, to 15 years, 6 months. Of the original 18, 14 were followed up, with a follow-up period ranging from 14 to 27 years and a mean age of 24 years. The age at follow-up ranged from 22 to 40.

The clinical status at follow-up indicated that the outcome was anything but rosy. Only eight were self-supporting. Two were definitely retarded and entirely supported by their families, and four were institutionalized for psychosis. Moreover, four of the eight who were self-supporting at follow-up had spent some time in institutions such as jails, juvenile halls, and hospitals for the retarded. Three still demonstrated evidence of restlessness and concentration difficulties (one at the age of 24). Follow-up IQ was more than 10 points lower than initial IQ in five cases.

Weiss and her colleagues (1971) in Montreal are conducting a prospective study of 155 ADDH children who were referred to the psychiatric outpatient clinic of the Montreal Children's Hospital. There have been a series of reports over the years of various subgroups of this population, with the latest reports being into late adulthood. Four to six years after initial evaluation, 64 ADDH children were reevaluated. The follow-up results indicated that as a group the children had improved in the target symptoms of hyperactivity, distractibility, aggressive behavior, and excitability. However, they were not normal in these areas. They were still rated as more disturbed in all of these areas than a normal control group matched for age, sex, and IQ. Interestingly, distractibility, rather than hyperactivity was now the major complaint of the mothers.

Psychiatric evaluation of the grown-up ADDH children in adolescence revealed no cases of psychosis, although three did show marked schizoid personality traits. One-quarter had a history of significant antisocial behavior, with 15% having been already referred to the courts. Nearly one-third had no steady friends. Emotional immaturity, lack of ambition, and a severe inability to maintain goals were the main pathological traits reported by the mothers. The examining child psychiatrist was also impressed by this lack of ambition and by the marked depression and low self-esteem demonstrated by the children at interview.

Rather marked educational retardation was present in a significant number of these children, with 70% having already repeated at least one grade and more than a third having repeated two grades. A total of 10% were in special classes, and 5% had already been expelled from school. Teachers reported that these children were still more restless, more antisocial, and less able to concentrate than their classmates. The poor academic functioning was emphasized in a later report by Minde *et al.* (1971), who compared the academic performance of a subsample of 37 of these children with a performance of 37 same-sexed, non-ADDH classmates. By the age of 11, 21 of the

ADDH group (as opposed to 6 of the control group) had repeated one or more grades in school. The ADDH children scored significantly lower than the controls, and 10 out of 12 school subjects with the ADDH group equaled the performance of their peers only in nonacademic subjects such as physical activity. A detailed look at the battery of psychometric test results indicated that the ADDH group had uneven cognitive patterns and a preponderance of verbal difficulties that made academic progress in a normal class setting unlikely, particularly combined with their restlessness and inattention.

In a similar prospective study, Stewart and his colleagues (1981) interviewed both mothers and subjects who had presented to the St. Louis Children's Hospital 2 to 5 years earlier. There were 80 adolescents who had received a previous diagnosis of ADDH. The history from the mothers revealed that about half of the children were significantly improved. However, this improvement tended to be in hyperactivity per se. The increase in antisocial behavior was quite striking. Two-thirds were said to be incorrigible by their parents. More than 20% had long histories of antisocial behavior and were considered likely to have antisocial personalities as adults. Nearly 60% had some contact with police, 17% on three or more occasions. More than one-quarter had been referred to the juvenile court. More than one-third had threatened to kill their parents. Seven percent carried concealed weapons. Fifteen percent had set fires.

Poor school performance was also a characteristic finding similar to what the Montreal group found. One-quarter were attending some type of special school or class. Nearly 60% had failed two or more grades. Nearly three-quarters of the group still had concentration and attention problems in the classroom. Some 60% were considered by the teachers to be a discipline problem, while 17% had already begun truanting. Nearly half of the children were experiencing depressive symptoms at follow-up, with frequent periods of low mood and poor self-image. Fifteen percent had either talked of or attempted suicide. Of the adolescents, 62% told the investigators that they were disgusted with themselves.

Rapoport and her colleagues (Riddle & Rapoport, 1976) also found that about 15% of their adolescent subjects at follow-up were experiencing some depressive reactions.

J. H. Satterfield (personal communication, 1983) and his colleagues are following up 150 ADDH and 88 normal control subjects who had been studied by them 8 years previously. At the time of one part of the follow-up, arrest records from childhood through adolescence, as recorded in the Los Angeles County Probation Department's automated juvenile index, were compared between the ADDH group and controls. The offenses were classified into two broad types—serious and nonserious. Nonserious offenses included status crimes, alcohol intoxication, possession of less than an ounce of marijuana, vandalism, and petty theft. Serious crimes included robbery, burglary, grand theft, grand theft auto, and assault with a deadly weapon.

The mean ages at follow-up were 17.3 and 16.9 years for the ADDH and control group, respectively.

The first comparison was the percentage of subjects in each group arrested at least once for a serious offense in three broad social class distributions—lower, middle, and upper. For the ADDH population, this figure was 58%, 38%, and 52%, as compared with 11%, 9%, and 2% in the normal control group. The figures for multiple arrests for serious offenses in the two groups (ADDH vs. controls) in the same three social class groups were as follows: for the ADDH group, 45%, 25%, and 28%; for the normal control group, 6%, 0%, and 0%.

The final comparison was the rate of institutionalization for delinquent behavior by the time of follow-up. Of the ADDH group, 25% had been institutionalized for delinquent behavior compared to one subject (less than 1%) of the control group. Thus, the ADDH group had rates of serious offenses in lower, middle, and upper class—5, 4, and 26 times higher than the control group. For multiple serious offenses, their rates were 7, 25, and 29 times higher than the controls. The rate of institutionalization for ADDH subjects was about 20 times higher than the control group.

In a subsample of this population, 35 ADDH youths were compared to their brothers who were between 1 year younger or 1 year older. The mean age of the ADDH group was 17.6 years compared to 18.4 years for their brothers. Similar comparisons were made as above. The percentage of ADDH youths arrested at least once for a serious offense was 46% compared to 14% in their non-ADDH brothers. The multiple arrest record for a serious offense was 27% versus 5%. The institutionalization rate was 27% versus 0%. Thus, this study suggests a very strong correlation between a history of childhood ADDH and very serious antisocial delinquent behavior in late adolescence. Since official arrest records were used, these results are not biased either high or low by either overreporting or underreporting of serious antisocial behavior by either parents or subjects themselves.

In a similar comparison of 65 ADDH boys and their brothers at the University of Iowa, Loney, Whaley-Klahn, Kosier, and Conboy (1981) reported the following results when the subjects were between ages 21 and 22. Using strict diagnostic criteria and standardized measures of evaluation, 45% of the ADDH group currently qualified for a diagnosis of antisocial personality as opposed to 18% of their brothers, and 14% of the ADDH currently qualified for a diagnosis of alcoholism as opposed to none of the brothers. Other drug abuse was equally present in both groups, 9% for the ADDH group and their brothers. There was an overlap between antisocial personality and alcoholism in that 23% had both, and 43% had either antisocial personality or alcoholism.

In two recent studies, Wender *et al.* (1981) have attempted to use a modified version of the follow-back design. Working with the Salt Lake Community Mental Health Center and private practitioners, the Wender group asked for referrals of white patients between the ages of 21 and 45 years whose major complaints in adult life were impulsivity, irritability, restlessness, and emotionality. They excluded patients with diagnoses of schizophrenia, primary affective disorder, organic brain syndrome, or mental retardation. Then using previously designed rating scales rather than childhood records, they attempted to make a retrospective diagnosis of ADDH in these subjects. In one study they were able to do this in 26 subjects.

Several findings are worth emphasizing. First, there was an excess of females in the sample, which also occurred in a previous attempt to do a similar study. This suggests either that females have a more persistent form of the disorder or that the common outcomes of childhood ADDH in males in adult life are conditions that are not seen by the mental health sector, but by other sectors—possibly the legal one.

Even with the exclusion criteria noted above of certain definite psychiatric disorders, the prevalence of diagnosable psychopathology was quite high. Many of the 26 patients had multiple diagnoses. Six were alcoholic, 6 had drug abuse, 2 were hysterics, 7 had antisocial personality disorder, 15 had generalized anxiety disorder, and 21 had various types of dysphoric disorders.

The Wender group made some pertinent observations about the affective disorders seen in these adult ADDH patients. They noted that the patients had complained of labile mood that began in childhood, and it was characterized by both up periods and down periods lasting from hours in length to days in length. While many of the mood changes were precipitated by life events, it was also noteworthy that these individuals had a propensity to construct life situations for themselves that created stressful life events. As time went by, the ups began to disappear, to be replaced by down periods.

Wender felt that this syndrome was similar to what had previously been described by others as emotionally unstable character disorder. The latter is described as beginning in adolescence and being responsive to lithium compounds. This mood disorder in the ADDH adults tended to begin in childhood, and almost universally the subjects had a dysphoric response to lithium—not a positive response. Some of the subjects had a dramatic response to stimulant medication in that their mood lability decreased, depression improved, and the high periods became fewer. They responded unpredictably, however, to tricyclic medications, which is not surprising since they generally do not have pervasive anhedonia that characterizes good responders to tricyclic medication.

Wender predicted that these mood disorders in the ADDH adults would probably respond best to monoamine oxidase inhibitors, since they affect the metabolism of dopamine as well as serotonin and norepinephrine. However, this was not systematically studied.

The data presented thus far suggest that the strongest correlations of childhood ADDH and adolescent and adult psychopathology tend to be in the antisocial spectrum of disorders, with some recent data suggesting that there may be atypical affective disorders as outcomes as well. However, there are also isolated reports of other psychopathological entities as outcomes of childhood ADDH. Explosive personality or episodic dyscontrol has been suggested by Morrison and Minkoff (1975) as an outcome, and they suggest that these individuals have a rather dramatic response to tricyclic medication. And some investigators have suggested that a substantial number of those adolescents and adults given a borderline personality diagnosis may have a history of childhood ADDH.

The last suggestion of some investigators is that there is a particular subtype of schizophrenics who have a childhood history of ADDH and who do not respond well to neuroleptics, but have a good response to stimulant medication without a worsening of the schizophrenic symptomatology. These are generally in the realm of case reports such as that by Huey et al. (1978), Huessy (1954), and Bellak (1979). Huessy and Bellak suggest that this subgroup responds to low doses of tricyclics.

Etiological Theories, Subgroups, and Mechanism of Relationship of the Childhood ADDH to Other Psychiatric Disorders

Several recent comprehensive reviews of proposed etiological factors in the ADDH syndrome are available (Ross & Ross, 1982; Whalen, 1983). Among the postulated etiological factors, the following are included: family-genetic factors, biochemical factors, neurophysiological factors, true brain damage or minimal or minor brain damage, environmental precipitants (such as lead level), certain aspects of diet (such as sugar and food additives and food colorings), a response to academic failure, and possible environmental psychological mechanisms. Obviously when so many postulated etiological agents exist for one particular condition, it is safe to say that we do not really know the etiology and that the etiology in some cases is probably multifactorial. In other cases, there may be one primary, necessary, and sufficient etiological cause which would lead to the further hypothesis that there may be etiologically distinct subgroups of childhood ADDH. Thus, phenotypically one would diagnose ADDH by DSM-III criteria, but etiologically one would have a heterogeneous group of patients.

Thus, one might further postulate that the different results of outcome of childhood ADDH in adolescence and adult life are not simply due to the factors described above (i.e., study design, initial subject selection, interval factors, etc.). Rather, one could postulate that different outcomes are due to the fact that one is dealing with etiologically distinct subgroups in the beginning. Thus, one could say that the relationship between childhood ADDH and antisocial personality as an example is due to the perpetuation of some original psychobiological deficit which presents as childhood ADDH and manifests itself in adult life as antisocial personality. However, one could also state that there may be a remission of the initial psychobiological deficit, but there may be a persistence of secondary symptoms of an antisocial nature due to induced dynamic factors.

The Satterfield group (J. H. Satterfield, personal communication, 1983) does have very preliminary data on a small number of their subjects at around age 18 to suggest that there are electrophysiological differences between those individuals who do not demonstrate serious antisocial behavior and those who have multiple arrest records for serious offenses. Garfinkel (1982) and his group have been following up Bradley's original patients in Providence, Rhode Island. Even in adult life many continue to have shorter attention spans than normal controls. Moreover, they tend to be normalized by stimulant medication, and there is a suggestion of different hormonal responses to psychostimulant medication between the "grown up ADDH" individual and normal controls. Much more research in this area is needed.

Treatment

The literature in this area of ADDH in childhood is dominated by short-term studies of response to psychostimulant drug treatment. More recently, there have been comparative studies of stimulant treatment in combination with behavior modification compared to stimulant medication alone and behavior modification alone. There is increasing evidence that the outcome of this condition untreated or briefly treated with stimulants alone may not be as rosy as one had originally predicted.

There is increasing attention to several treatment issues: First, since these children tend to have multiple handicaps, and since this is an etiologically heterogeneous group of children, may not a multimodality treatment approach be more effective in childhood? Second, if effective treatment is instituted in childhood, how long does it have to last? Third, if effective treatment is instituted in childhood, does it have any effect on adolescent or adult outcome? And last, do stimulant medications tend to have the same type effect on adolescents and adults with ADDH residual state possibly complicated by other psychiatric disorders as they do in children with the ADDH syndrome?

The first question tends to be answered in the affirmative by Satterfield, Satterfield, and Cantwell (1981) in their multimodality study of children treated over a 3-year period. Based on an individual multidimensional approach to evaluation and an individual multimodality treatment plan commensurate with each child's disabilities, treatment plans were implemented by members of the research staff working together as a coordinated therapeutic team. Treatment included individual education therapy, individual psychotherapy and group therapy for the children, individual psychotherapy and group therapy for the parents, family therapy, behavior modification, special educational programs, and carefully titrated dosages of stimulant medication for those in whom it was effective. Measures of the child's behavior at home and at school, academic performance, delinquent behavior, and emotional adjustment were obtained initially and after 1, 2, and 3 years of treatment.

What was quite striking is that measures for all of these factors improved rather dramatically at 1, 2, and 3 years. This included demonstrated changes in academic performance by standardized testing—one of the few long-term studies to report this type of outcome. Moreover, since approximately 50% of the patients dropped out of treatment after 1 year or 2 years, groups receiving less and more treatment could be compared on various outcome measures. At 3-year follow-up, the group receiving more treatment was found to be further ahead educationally, to be demonstrating less antisocial behavior, to be more attentive, to have better adjustment at school and at home, and to be rated more globally improved by the treating psychiatrist and by parents than children in the group receiving less treatment.

A substantial number of the children dropped out of treatment after 1 or 2 years precisely because they were doing so well, and the parents no longer wished to continue in a multimodality treatment program, but rather opted to get stimulant medication from their private doctor. The stimulant medication alone, in the absence of the other aspects of the treatment program, tended to lead to an outcome of 3 years that was significantly poorer in most areas than that obtained by those who stayed in the multimodality treatment program for the full 3 years.

Thus, the available evidence does suggest that a properly instituted and consistently administered treatment program can make a substantial impact on the child's behavior at home and at school, academic performance, self-esteem, antisocial behavior, and other symptomatology. However, the question of whether such a therapeutic program administered properly and effectively in childhood has any lasting effect on adolescent and adult outcome is essentially unanswered. There is some suggestion from the Loney follow-up study mentioned above that those whose symptoms responded best to stimulants in childhood may have had somewhat less in the way of substance abuse in adolescence and early adult life.

It seems clear that childhood ADDH in adolescence and adult life will be in a substantial number of cases complicated by other types of psychopathology, as described in the studies reviewed above. Thus, multimodality treatment approach is probably even more necessary with adolescents and adults than it is with children. On the other hand, there is a growing body of evidence—some from case reports, some from systematic studies (such as that of Wender)—to suggest that adolescents and adults may in fact have dramatic responses to stimulant medication, such as methylphenidate and Dexedrine, as well as to other medications, such as the tricyclic antidepressants.

Summary and Conclusions

This chapter has attempted to address several salient issues about the syndrome of childhood ADDH. It is quite clear that this common behavioral syndrome, when diagnosed phenotypically even by very strict diagnostic criteria, is etiologically heterogeneous. It is also becoming increasingly evident that there is a relationship between ADDH in childhood and other types of childhood psychopathology. Moreover, the idea that most childhood ADDH eventually disappears with time and is some type of developmental delay is dying a slow death. It does look at a substantial number of children with the ADDH syndrome who continue to demonstrate in adolescence and early adult life some of the same core symptoms that they did in childhood. Moreover, other psychopathological entities seem to develop in adolescence and adult life, particularly those in the antisocial spectrum of disorders.

What limited evidence there is suggests that intensive, effective treatment in childhood can significantly alter various types of psychopathology over at least a 3-year period. However, whether treatment of any type significantly alters adolescent or adult outcome is simply unstudied at the present time. What little evidence there is with regard to drug treatment of adolescents and adults suggests that whatever causes the rather dramatic and unique response that children with ADDH have to psychostimulants is still present in a substantial number of adolescents and adults. Future research needs to address the question of subgroups, etiologically different subgroups, their relationship to various types of adolescent and adult outcomes, and their responses to various forms of therapeutic intervention.

REFERENCES

Aman, M. G. (1983). Psychoactive drugs in mental retardation. In J. L. Matson & F. Andrasik (Eds.), *Treatment issues and innovations in mental retardation*. New York: Plenum Press.
Barkley, R. (1982). Guidelines for defining hyperactivity in children: Attention deficit disorder with hyperactivity. In B. E. Lahey & A. B. Kazdin (Eds.), *Advances in clinical psychology* (Vol. 5). New York: Plenum Press.
Bellak, L. (1979). Psychiatric aspects of minimal brain dysfunction in adults: Their ego function assessment. In L. Bellak (Ed.), *Psychiatric aspects of minimal brain dysfunction in adults*. New York: Grune & Stratton.
Cantwell, D. P. (Ed.). (1975). *The hyperactive child: Diagnosis, management, and current research*. New York: Spectrum.
Cantwell, D. P., & Baker, L. (1980). Academic failures in children with communication disorders. *Journal of the American Academy of Child Psychiatry, 19*, 579–591.
Cantwell, D. P., & Satterfield, J. H. (1978). Prevalence of academic underachievement in hyperactive children. *Journal of Pediatric Psychology, 3*, 168–171.
Carlson, G. A., & Cantwell, D. P. (1979). Unmasking masked depression in children and adolescence. *American Journal of Psychiatry, 137*, 445–449.
Douglas, V. I. (1980). Self-control techniques. Higher mental process in hyperactive children: Implications for training. In R. M. Knights & D. J. Bakker (Eds.), *Treatment of hyperactive and learning disordered children—current research*. Baltimore, MD: University Park Press.
Garfinkel, B. D. (1982). *The neuroendocrine response to d-amphetamine in individuals with residual attention*

deficit disorder. Paper presented at the annual meeting of the American Academy of Child Psychiatry, Chicago, IL.

Huessy, H. R. (1954). The adult hyperkinetic. *American Journal of Psychiatry, 131,* 724–725.

Huey, L. Y., Zetin, M., Janowsky, D. S., & Judd, L. L. (1978). Adult minimal brain dysfunction and schizophrenia: A case report. *American Journal of Psychiatry, 135,* 1563–1565.

Langhorne, J. E., Jr., & Loney, J. (1979). A four-fold model for subgrouping the hyperkinetic MBD syndrome. *Child Psychiatry and Human Development, 9,* 153–159.

Leckman, J. F., Detlor, J., & Cohen, D. J. (1983). Gilles de la Tourette syndrome: Emerging areas of clinical research. In S. B. Guze, F. J. Earls, & J. E. Barrett (Eds.), *Childhood psychopathology and development.* New York: Raven Press.

Loney, J. (1980). Hyperkinesis comes of age: What do we know and where should we go? *American Journal of Orthopsychiatry, 50,* 28–42.

Loney, J. (1983). Research diagnostic criteria for childhood hyperactivity. In S. B. Guze, F. J. Earls, & J. E. Barrett (Eds.), *Childhood psychopathology and development.* New York: Raven Press.

Loney, J., Kramer, J., & Milich, R. (1981). The hyperkinetic child grows up: Predictors of symptoms, delinquency, and achievement at follow-up. In K. D. Gadow & J. Loney (Eds.), *Psychosocial aspects of drug treatment for hyperactivity.* Boulder, CO: Westview Press.

Loney, J., Whaley-Klahn, M. A., Kosier, T., & Conboy, J. (1981). *Hyperactive boys and their brothers at 21: Predictors of aggressive and antisocial outcome.* Paper presented at the meeting of the Society for Life History Research and Psychopathology, Monterey, CA.

Mendelson, W., Johnson, N., & Stewart, M. A. (1971). Hyperactive children as teenagers: A follow-up study. *Journal of Nervous and Mental Disease, 153,* 273–279.

Minde, K., Lewin, D., Weiss, G., Laviguer, H., Douglas, V., & Sykes, E. (1971). Hyperactive child in elementary school: A five-year controlled follow-up. *Exceptional Children, 38,* 215–231.

Minkes, M. J., Rowe, J. S., & Minkes, J. H. (1967). Twenty-five year follow-up study on the hyperkinetic child with minimal brain dysfunction. *Pediatrics, 39,* 393–399.

Morrison, J. R., & Minkoff, K. (1975). Explosive personality as a sequel to the hyperactive child syndrome. *Comprehensive Psychiatry, 16,* 343–348.

Riddle, K. D., & Rapoport, J. L. (1976). A 2-year follow-up of 72 hyperactive boys. *Journal of Nervous and Mental Diseases, 162,* 126–134.

Robins, L. (1966). *Deviant children grown up.* Baltimore, MD: Williams & Wilkins.

Ross, D. M., & Ross, S. A. (1982). *Hyperactivity: Current issues, research, and theory.* New York: Wiley.

Rutter, M., Graham, P., & Yule, W. (Eds.). (1970). *A neuropsychiatric study in childhood.* Philadelphia, PA: Lippincott.

Sanberg, S. T., Rutter, M., & Taylor, E. (1978). Hyperkinetic disorder in psychiatric clinic attenders. *Developmental Medicine in Child Neurology, 20,* 279–299.

Satterfield, J. H., Satterfield, B. T., & Cantwell, D. P. (1981). Three-year multimodality treatment study of 100 hyperactive boys. *Journal of Pediatrics, 98,* 650–655.

Shaffer, D., & Greenhill, L. (1979). A critical note on the predictive validity of the hyperkinetic syndrome. *Journal of Child Psychology and Psychiatry, 20,* 61–72.

Stewart, M. A., Cummings, C., Singer, S., & deBlois, C. S. (1981). The overlap between hyperactive and unsocialized aggressive children. *Journal of Child Psychology and Psychiatry, 22,* 23–45.

Weinberg, W. A., Rutman, J., Sullivan, L., Pencik, E. C., & Dietz, S. G. (1973). Depression in children referred to an educational diagnostic center. *Journal of Pediatrics, 83,* 1065–1072.

Weiss, G., Minde, K., Werry, J. S., Douglas, V. I., & Nemeth, E. (1971). Studies on the hyperactive child. VIII. Five-year follow-up. *Archives of General Psychiatry, 24,* 209–214.

Wender, P. H., Reimher, F. W., & Wood, D. R. (1981). Attention deficit disorder, minimal brain dysfunction in adults: A replication study of diagnosis in drug treatment. *Archives of General Psychiatry, 38,* 449–456.

Whalen, C. K. (1983). Hyperactivity, learning problems, and the attention deficit disorders. In T. H. Ollendick & M. Hersen (Eds.), *Handbook of child psychopathology.* New York: Plenum Press.

CHAPTER 21

The Interpersonal Approach to Understanding Depression

Gerald L. Klerman and Myrna M. Weissman

Introduction

As discussed in Chapter 1 of this volume, the interpersonal school is one of the contemporary United States schools of psychopathology. Early in the development of this school, its leaders in the Baltimore/Washington area reported on their clinical experience with depression. Sullivan (1953a) discusses depression at numerous points in his writings, particularly in *Conceptions of Modern Psychiatry*.

In 1954, Mable Blake Cohen and associates published their observation of 12 cases of manic–depressive insanity being treated in intensive individual psychotherapy (Cohen, Blake, Cohen, Fromm-Reichmann, & Weigert, 1954). Although the major therapeutic efforts of the interpersonal school have been devoted to schizophrenia, a number of significant theoretical and clinical reports have appeared about depression. At the same time, important empirical studies have contributed to a research base for the interpersonal approach.

Disrupted interpersonal relations often result in mood changes. And although disruptions of interpersonal relationships are not in themselves "necessary and sufficient" to produce clinical depressions, interpersonal difficulties are usually associated with clinical depression.

Gerald L. Klerman. Department of Psychiatry, Cornell University Medical College, and Department of Psychiatry, New York Hospital, New York, New York.

Myrna M. Weissman. Depression Research Unit, Department of Psychiatry, Yale University Medical School, New Haven, Connecticut.

While past and ongoing interpersonal relationships are related to depression, we cannot always establish the direction of causation. Henderson (1980) notes that persons with clinical depression may exaggerate and distort problems in their interpersonal relations because of their current affective state and cognitive dysfunction. The symptoms of the depression may be adversely affecting the patient's close interpersonal relations, and/or the patient's personality may make that person less competent to establish mutually satisfying interpersonal relationships and maintain attachments.

This chapter examines the relationship between changes in interpersonal relations and normal depressed mood, then explores the effect of disrupted interpersonal relationships on clinical depression as correlates and as consequences. Research on personality, interpersonal relations, and depression will be discussed. Finally, the therapeutic application of the interpersonal approach will be discussed and the interpersonal therapy for depression (IPT) will be described.

Theoretical and Empirical Sources

The theoretical basis for understanding depression in an interpersonal context is a distinctly American contribution to psychopathology and mental health. The earliest theoretical writing from the interpersonal school was by Adolf Meyer, whose psychobiological approach to understanding mental disorders placed great emphasis on the patient's experiences (Meyer, 1957). In contrast to Kraepelin's concept of disease entities derived from Continental European psychiatry, Meyer applied Darwin's concept of adaptation to understanding psychiatric illness. Meyer saw psychiatric illnesses as part of the patient's attempt to adapt to the environment, usually the psychosocial environment, and considered that a patient's particular response to environmental changes reflected early developmental experiences, especially interpersonal experiences in the family and social groups.

Among Meyer's associates, Harry Stack Sullivan stands out for his articulation of the theory of interpersonal relations. His writings linked clinical psychopathology to anthropology, sociology, and social psychology (Sullivan, 1953a, 1953b). Sullivan asserted that psychiatry is the scientific study of people and interpersonal processes, as distinct from the exclusive study of mind, society, or brain. Emphasis on interpersonal and social factors in the understanding and treatment of the depressive disorders is evident in the work of many other clinicians, especially the work of Fromm-Reichmann (1960) and Cohen et al. (1954), and more recently that of Arieti and Bemporad (1978). Becker (1974) and Chodoff (1970) are also among those who have emphasized the social roots of depression and the need to attend to the interpersonal aspects of the disorder, and Frank (1973) has stressed the general importance in psychotherapy of focusing on current interpersonal situations.

Interpersonal Relations and Normal Depressive Mood

As a result of mammalian evolution, human beings are born with the capacity to experience and express a range of emotional stages, including fear and anxiety, sadness and depression, anger, hostility, and rage, and pleasure and elation. While there is considerable controversy as to the number of fundamental emotions and the role of biological and experiential factors in their development in individuals, there is almost universal agreement that sadness is the normal equivalent of depression, and that the capacity to experience sadness is a fundamental human emotion evident in the infant during early development.

Sadness and an occasional depressed mood are a normal part of the human condition, and feelings of sadness are a nearly universal response to disruptions of interpersonal relations. The most useful discussions of the relationship between disrupted interpersonal relations and normal sadness are found in studies of attachment bonding and of bereavement.

Attachments and Bonds

Attachment theory, as developed by Bowlby (1969), proposes that humans have an innate tendency to seek attachments and that these attachments contribute to the survival of the species and to individual satisfaction. Attachments lead to reciprocal, personal, social bonds with significant others and to experiences of increased warmth, nurturance, and protection and a decrease in levels of psychomotor activity such as attention, vigilance, and increased muscle tone.

Intense human emotions (love, hate, envy, rivalry, desire for nurturance) are associated with the formation, maintenance, disruption, and renewal of attachment bonds. Investigations by ethologists applied to mother–child relationships have demonstrated the importance of attachment and social bonds to human functioning. Humans of all ages are vulnerable to impaired interpersonal relations if strong attachment bonds do not develop early. Individuals are vulnerable to depression when attachment bonds are disrupted.

Bowlby (1969) provides a link between developmental theories, particularly those derived from psychodynamic principles, and animal research based on ethological concepts. In this view, depression is the emotional response to the disruption of attachment bonds. This response is evident in mammals and primates. In humans, in addition to the behavioral response, there are the cognitive and mental representations. Mental representations and the capacity for language endow human beings with the possibility of anticipating their own death and the death of loved ones. Thus, the anticipation of the disruption of attachment bonds comes into mental life relatively early in childhood and serves as an important regulator of behavior. The threat of disruption of attachment bonding is often used as punishment and to control child behavior. The fear of disruption of attachment bonds is a frequent theme in novels and in human relationships, particularly with those that have sexual and erotic components, both heterosexual and homosexual.

Bowlby argues that attachment bonds serve a survival function. The attachment of the helpless child to the mother aids the offspring's biological survival, especially by providing protection from predators. The continued presence of a secure attachment figure helps the child explore its physical environment, make peer contacts, and achieve group membership.

The way affectional bonds are made is determined and learned largely within the family, especially but not exclusively during childhood. The threat of loss of an important attachment figure creates anxiety and sadness, and frequent threats of such loss may predispose to later depression. Many mental disorders may be the result of an inability to make and keep affectional bonds. Bowlby concludes that human beings of all ages are happiest—most effective and competent—when they are confident that one or more trusted persons are available for help in times of trouble. For most adults in Western societies the main attachments are with a few persons, of whom the spouse is usually but not always the most prominent, followed by close relatives, offspring, and friends (Henderson, 1977). Bowlby's work has been extended by Rutter (1972) to show that the child's relationship with others besides the mother can also create attachment bonds and that disruption and deprivation of these bonds can contribute to the onset of depression.

On the basis of such observations, Bowlby (1977) proposed a general approach to psychotherapy: Psychotherapy should help the patient examine current interpersonal relationships and understand how they have developed from experiences with attachment figures in childhood, adolescence, and adulthood. Parker (1978), among others, describes effective psychotherapy as similar to optimal parenting. Ideal psychotherapy should combine caring with nonpossessive warmth and should provide, as part of the interpersonal therapeutic relationship, a cognitive explanation of distortions of past relationships.

The concept of attachment bonds provides a theoretical basis for understanding the interpersonal context of depression and for developing psychotherapeutic strategies to correct the distortions produced by faulty attachments in childhood. Moreover, attachment theory has stimulated a body of empirical research in the association between interpersonal relationships and depression.

Bereavement, Grief, and Mourning

The death of a loved one is an irreversible disruption of an attachment and almost universally produces sadness, grief, and mourning. The universality of this response has led many theorists to regard it as a normal variant of the clinically depressed state. Attention to the similarities and differences between grief and depression was first given by Freud and Abraham, who emphasized that mourning following the death of a loved one is not a pathological condition. Both saw mourning as similar to "melancholia" in the pattern of symptoms, with the exception that loss of self-esteem is absent in mourning but prominent in clinical depressions. As Freud (1917/1957) stated, "In mourning it is the world which has become poor and empty; in melancholia it is the ego itself."

These observations have been partly confirmed by empirical studies of the bereaved (Lindemann, 1944; Osterweis, Solomon, & Green, 1984). Both men and women respond to the death of a loved one with unhappiness and depressive symptoms (Weissman *et al.*, 1979), but not all depressed patients have low self-esteem and feelings of worthlessness and guilt, and only a minority of mourners express guilt and fall in self-regard. Most grieving persons recover and only a few require treatment (Clayton, Desmarais, & Winokur, 1968). Grieving persons who are at risk for developing a depression are those who perceive themselves as having few emotional, physical, or financial supports available to them (Maddison, 1968; Maddison & Walker, 1967; Walker, MacBride, & Vachon, 1977). Grief is a normal reaction to the disruption of a bond by death, but the presence of other attachments protects against a pathological outcome to grief (Parker, 1978).

Life Events, Stress, and Depressive Mood and Symptoms

As will be described later, the developments of a specific technique for scoring the intensity of life events has provided a research tool for investigators in many areas of psychopathology. Life events, particularly the disruption of attachment bonds, represents a particular stressor and one of the important stimuli to the stress response in contemporary human life. Whether or not there is increased stress in modern life remains a matter of some conjecture. Nevertheless, in a modern urban industrial society, the necessity to move from one community to another for education, military service, promotion, and advancement results in the frequent making and breaking and remaking of attachment bonds and calls upon personality characteristics of individuals which are often experienced adversely.

A number of large-scale studies have indicated that depressive mood and symptoms do occur in response to these changes (Ilfeld, 1977; Klerman, 1982; Paykel, 1982; Pearlin & Lieberman, 1977).

While there is almost universal agreement that life events serve as a stressor in normal life, controversy remains as to whether the depressive response to those situations is a sufficient explanation of clinical depression. Among the various stressors that have been studied, disruption of attachment bonds is one of the most common experienced in modern life. In the extreme form, this is experienced in states of bereavement, where the grief and mourning responses are universal. Less extreme than bereavement are the disruptions that come with geographic movement, refugee status, marital discord, separation and divorce, and normal developmental transitions, such as the end of child rearing ("the empty nest") and retirement (Klerman, Weissman, Rounsaville, & Chevron, 1984).

Interpersonal Relations as Antecedent to Clinical Depression: The Role of Childhood Experience

While disruption of attachment bonds produces feelings of sadness, they do not necessarily produce clinical depression. The relationship between life events, including those that involve disruptions of attachment bonds, and clinical states of depression remains a matter of controversy. It is not likely that a single factor theory based on separation and loss can explain clinical depression. Only a small percentage of individuals who experience disruption of attachment bonds react with feelings of loss and with symptoms similar to those of depression. The majority of individuals adapt to such environmental stressors. Therefore, some additional factor related to individual vulnerability must be taken into account. Some theories attribute this vulnerability to genetic and constitutional factors. Other theories attribute this vulnerability to the result of adverse childhood experiences and intrafamilial relations.

The Childhood of Adult Depressives

Although adults' retrospective reports of their childhood are particularly prone to bias, they have been useful for generating hypotheses. A number of studies have investigated adult depressive patients' descriptions of their early years. The published studies bear out findings that depression in parents is associated with similar emotional problems in their offspring. Adult depressives are more likely to have suffered in childhood from family discord, parental neglect, rejection, and abuse (see Orvaschel, Weissman, & Kidd, 1980, for a review).

Certain early childhood experiences are generally considered to predispose to development of psychopathology in adulthood. In particular, loss of a parent in childhood has been implicated in the development of adult depression. The parental bond can be disrupted through death, geographic separation, or divorce. Emotional separation of parent from child—lack of caring, emotional distance, overprotection, or child abuse—may also impair parent–child bonding.

Parental Loss and Separation during Childhood

The relationship between loss of a parent in childhood and subsequent adult depressive disorders has been studied extensively. When all research problems are taken into account, there is little evidence that it is the death of the parent itself that increases the child's vulnerability to later depression in adulthood (Tennant, Bebbington, & Hurry, 1980). The adverse effects are probably explained by the quality of the parenting which replaces that of the dead parent or the qualities of the parenting before the loss. But the fact remains that death of a parent in childhood can increase the likelihood of depression in the face of life stress in adulthood.

On the basis of these observations, recent research has been directed toward understanding the quality of parent–child relationships preceding loss by death or separation. It has become clear that the parenting role need not be provided by the biological parent (Birtchnell, 1980). Rutter found that children temporarily separated from parents because of family discord became better adjusted emotionally if they were later placed in a harmonious family setting. Parker (1979) found a close relationship between adult depression and poor parental care in childhood irrespective of whether the care was provided by the biological parent.

A disrupted, unloving relationship between a child and his or her parent or parent substitute can increase the child's vulnerability to depression as an adult. Parker found that adult depressed patients, compared with normal controls, more frequently reported low maternal care and/or greater maternal overprotection. These associations were not influenced by the levels of symptoms and were confirmed by the mothers' independent reports of their interactions with their offspring. These patterns were not found in bipolar depressives.

Depression in Children and Adolescents

The existence of childhood depression has been a controversial issue in child psychopathology (Bemporad, 1982). Recently, however, there has been a major shift in thinking about the diagnosis of depression in childhood. Current studies are beginning to overcome many of the difficulties surrounding the evaluation of childhood depression, such as the problem of distinguishing between symptom and syndrome and the need to separate symptom clusters according to developmental age. Depression is now recognized as a frequent symptom in adolescent patients (Evans, 1975). In the Isle of Wight (Rutter, Graham, Chadwick, & Yule, 1976), depression or suicide was not found to be frequent among the general preadolescent population, and only a small number of children overall were actually suffering from clinically significant depression. However, many of the adolescents in this British study reported feelings of inner distress, self-depreciation, and suicidal ideation (Rutter et al., 1976).

Connell (1972) proposed that depressed children be divided into two groups—those who had a precipitating event and those who manifested a long history of depression with no obvious precipitant. The latter group had a higher incidence of depressive illness in the family. In fact, among depressed children, a family history of psychiatric illness is commonly observed. Brumbach, Dietz-Schmidt, and Weinberg (1977) found a history of affective disorders in 89% of the depressed children's families and in over 60% of the mothers of the depressed children. Poznanski and Zrull (1970) reported high rates of marital discord and parental depression in the families of depressed children and described many of the parents as rejecting and hostile, often suffering from personality problems. Puig-Antich et al. (1979) found serious family discord or mistreatment of children in 11 out of 132 cases and a family history of psychiatric disorder (depression, mania, alcoholism, or schizophrenia) in 61% of the relatives of the children.

It is now agreed that depressive illness occurs in preadolescent and adolescent children and that it can be reliably diagnosed on the basis of symptom criteria (Kovacs, Feinberg, Crouse-Novak, Paulauskas, & Finkelstein, 1984). The presence of a depressed parent and/or a positive family history of affective disorder strongly contributes to depression in childhood, particularly when the depression is chronic and does not appear to have a clear-cut psychosocial precipitant (Kovacs *et al.*, 1984).

The families of depressed children are similar to those described by adult depressed patients recalling their childhood experiences. The depressed children's homes are characterized by family discord, parental rejection, and an increased frequency of parental psychopathology, although the psychopathology is not always depression. A disruptive, hostile, and generally negative environment, or depression in the parent has adverse effects on the child and is frequently reported in depressed children and adult depressed patients about their childhood.

Children in Families with Depressed Parents

A number of researchers have investigated the effects of depressed parents on their children. Children in families with one or two depressed parents are more likely to show psychopathology than the children of normal parents. Rolf and Garmezy (1974) found more withdrawn, shy, and socially isolated behavior among the children of depressive mothers than for control children. Weintraub, Neale, and Liebert (1975) noted higher levels of classroom disturbance, impatience, disrespectful or defiant behavior, inattentiveness, and withdrawal, and lower levels of comprehension, creativity, and relatedness to the teacher for both the children of schizophrenic mothers and the children of depressed mothers than for their control counterparts. Gamer, Gallant, Grunebaum, and Cohler (1977) found the children of psychiatrically ill parents to have disturbances in attention, particularly when confronting complex tasks. Welner, Welner, McCrary, and Leonard (1977) found that depressed mood, death wishes, fighting, psychosomatic concerns, and anhedonia were significantly more common in the children with a depressed parent than in the controls. They also noted that 11% of the children of depressives had five or more depressive symptoms, with 7% meeting the criteria for probable or definite depression, as compared with none in the control group.

Weissman, Paykel, and Klerman (1972) investigated the parental role performance of a group of 35 depressed women and a matched group of 27 normal women. During the acute depressed episode, they found the depressed women less involved with their children, impaired communication, increased friction, lack of affection, and greater guilt and resentment. The depressed mothers were more overprotective, irritable, preoccupied, withdrawn, emotionally distant, and/or rejecting. Disturbed functioning in the children of these depressed mothers was noted in approximately 59% of the 109 children. This proportion was even larger (64%) when only those children at early adolescence or younger were considered. The children manifested hyperactivity, enuresis, depression, school problems, truancy, drug abuse, and delinquency.

It is now clear that children in families in which one or both parents are depressed are at greater risk for psychopathology in general and for depression in particular. It is not clear how many of these effects are genetic and how many are due to social and environmental transmission; most likely there is usually a combination of both influences. Other factors, too, such as marital discord, low socioeconomic status, and peer relations, undoubtedly play a role.

This literature has recently been reviewed by Beardslee, Bemporad, Keller, and Klerman (1983). The evidence is now growing that being raised in a family where one or both parents have depression or other clinical conditions places the child at risk. This risk increases after the onset of puberty, and by the end of adolescence, the often noted predominance of females over males becomes clearly manifest.

Recent research indicates an increase in the prevalence of depression over past decades and earlier age of onset. This evidence for a cohort effect (Klerman et al., in press) has stimulated considerable interest in identifying those historical and cultural forces which may account for these changes in epidemiology. This earlier age of onset, noted in epidemiologic studies, probably accounts for the growing clinical awareness of childhood depression.

Interpersonal Difficulties and the Onset of Clinical Depression in Adulthood

As childhood interpersonal experiences can predispose to adult depression, so some aspects of interpersonal relations in adulthood can also be associated with onset and perpetuation of clinical depression.

Social Stress and Life Events

Since Holmes, Goodell, and Wolf (1950) observed that the rate of medical illness increased with the number of stressful life events, research has frequently demonstrated the relationship between stress, especially over recent events, and the onset of many medical and psychiatric illnesses, particularly depression (Paykel, 1979; Paykel et al., 1969; Rabkin & Struening, 1976; Schless & Mendels, 1977; Uhlenhuth & Paykel, 1973).

The New Haven group's work is most relevant to depression (Paykel *et al.*, 1969). In the 6 months following a stressful life event, they found a sixfold increase in the risk of developing a clinical depression. Marital discord was the most common event before the onset of depression. This research group also found that "exits" of persons from the individual's life during the preceding 6 months had occurred more frequently with depressed patients than with the control group.

In another study, Myers, Lindenthal, and Pepper (1975) interviewed a community sample in 1967 and again in 1976 and found a relationship between stressful life events and psychiatric symptomatology, often depression.

Bloom, Asher, and White (1978), in a critical analysis of several studies related to the consequences of marital disputes and divorce, linked these marital disruptions with a variety of emotional conditions, including depression.

Similar observations by Ilfeld (1977) were based on a survey of over 3,000 adults in Chicago. Depressive symptoms were closely related to the degree of stress, especially stresses in marriage and in parenting. In a further look at these Chicago adults, Pearlin and Lieberman (1977) found that persisting problems within an intact marriage were as likely to produce depressive symptoms and distress as the disruption of the marriage by divorce or separation.

Social Supports

As research indicated the adverse effects of life events as stressors for many forms of medical and psychiatric illness, the concept soon emerged that the presence of social supports serves to buffer the adverse effects of life events, and that in the presence of adequate social supports, life events would not have the deleterious effects that had previously been documented.

Using Bowlby's concept of attachment, Henderson and associates in Australia conducted a series of studies that examined the importance of social supports in the production of psychopathology. Henderson's work began with a careful analysis of the concept of care-eliciting behavior, an essential part of attachment bonding. "Care-eliciting behavior" is described as "a pattern of activity on the part of one individual which evokes from another, responses which give comfort" (Henderson, 1974). Comfort includes close body contact and verbal expressions of concern, esteem, or affection. These findings are based on animal observation by the ethologists Harlow and Suomi (1974) and Goodall and Hamburg (1971) on studies of human infant–parent interactions. Henderson notes that ethological studies of care-eliciting behavior have been limited to the young, and in agreement with Bowlby and Ainsworth, he proposes that attachment behavior, including care-eliciting behavior, remains part of the behavioral repertoire of humans throughout life. During childhood and adolescence, as the repertoire changes and enlarges, new relationships develop; these are usually quite strong with one or two people and less intense with a larger group. Adults, like infants and children, are distressed when separated from loved ones. When distressed, they seek the closeness of a few persons known or expected to be comforting. Such care-eliciting behavior has probably conferred considerable reproductive and evolutionary advantages; since it is one mechanism for male–female attraction and bonding, it provides a means of maintaining strong social bonds among members of the group.

Weiss (1975) and Henderson (1977) note that close personal relations— that is, social bonds—provide intimacy, social integration through shared concern, opportunity to receive nurturance, reassurance of worth, a sense of a reliable alliance, and guidance. Deficient social bonds in the adult environment are associated with neurotic symptoms, often depression. Patients with neurotic disorders, primarily depression, spend the same amount of time with their primary group as matched normal controls, but proportionately more of the interactions were affectively unpleasant. Neurotic depressives had fewer good friends and fewer contacts outside the household; they had fewer attachment figures and felt that these attachment figures gave them insufficient support (Henderson et al., 1978).

The clinical association between weak social bonds and neurosis, mostly depression, was confirmed in an epidemiologic study of a random sample of the general population in Canberra, Australia (Henderson, Duncan-Jones, Byrne, Scott, & Adcock, 1979). The value of strong social bonds in protection against the development of neurotic symptoms was even greater when the individual was faced with adversity (Henderson, 1980; Henderson et al., 1978; Henderson, Byrne, Duncan-Jones, Scott, & Adcock, 1980). Recognizing the considerable difficulty of teasing apart cause and effect, Henderson (1980, 1981) also conducted a longitudinal study in an attempt to determine the direction of causation. He noted that the association between weak social bonds and neurosis could be due to "persons with a disturbance of mood reporting unfavorably on adequate relations or being uncongenial company, driving away the support they need and seek. A third factor—personality— may lead to both the development of symptoms and to the inability to form mutually satisfying interpersonal relations" (Henderson et al., 1978). Lack of social bonds is a risk factor for the onset of neuroses, and adequate social relationships, both closely affectional and more diffuse, can protect against neurosis. The crucial aspect of social bonds seems to be, not their availability, but how adequate they are perceived to be when one is under stress.

Intimacy

Among the aspects of social support, Brown and his colleagues, among others, have paid special attention to the importance of an intimate relationship with ease of verbal communication and expression of positive emotional regard.

Intimacy has been proposed as an important component of care-eliciting and supportive interpersonal relations. Research on this aspect of attachment bonding in relationship to the development of depression was reported by Brown, Harris, and Copeland (1977). In their survey of women living in the Camberwell section of London, they found that the presence of an intimate and confiding relationship with a man, usually the spouse, was a strong protection against the development of a depression in the face of life stress. Roy (1978) has replicated this finding in a study of 84 depressed women compared to a matched group without history of depression.

In similar research with medically ill patients, Miller and Ingham (1976) found that both men and women who reported the lack of an intimate confidant to general physicians had more severe psychological symptoms, usually depression.

Marital Discord

Recent epidemiologic data, particularly from the New Haven site of the Epidemiologic Catchment Area Project, confirm a host of earlier clinical and epidemiologic studies by other investigators that marital discord is a significant correlate of major depression (Leaf, Weissman, Myers, Tischler, & Holzer, 1985).

Marriage serves as society's response to the individual adult's need for human attachment (Hinchliffe, Hooper, & Roberts, 1978) and society's need to reproduce the species and nurture children. Ideally, the social and legal contract provides a secure economic and social base for rearing children and creates an opportunity for each partner's needs for mutual care, concern, and affection to be expressed within the stability and security of a committed relationship. Therefore, the actual or threatened disruption of the marital attachment through disputes, separation, or divorce is one of the most common and serious disruptions of attachment in adulthood and is often related to the occurrence of depression.

Although there is controversy about the sequence of marital problems and depression, some relationship between the two has long been recognized and has become increasingly well documented. Marital difficulties, especially arguments, are the most frequently reported events in the lives of depressed women during the 6 months before they sought treatment (Paykel, 1979). Weissman and Paykel (1974) found that marital relationships were the most impaired areas of functioning of acutely depressed women compared to their normal neighbors. The marriages of depressed women were characterized by disengagement, poor communication, friction, and sexual problems. These impairments were slow to resolve and persisted long after the women had symptomatically recovered from their depressions. These studies, as well as Brown's study of intimacy, highlight the importance of the marital relationship in the development and course of depression in women.

Following the evidence that persistent marital disputes are a common circumstance in the development of depressive symptoms for many women,

Rounsaville, Weissman, Prusoff, and Herceg-Baron (1979) studied the relationship between marital disputes and the clinical course of moderate to severe depression in women. Among a group of depressed women who received psychotherapy and/or antidepressant drugs for acute depression, they found that the majority of women coming for treatment had marital disputes. Depressed women with marital disputes differed from those without disputes in the process and outcome of psychotherapy in that women with marital disputes showed less improvement in their symptoms and social functioning and had a greater tendency to relapse. However, within the marital dispute group, women who were able to effect an improvement in their marital relationships during treatment showed an improvement in depression and social adjustment equal to that of the patients who had no marital disputes at the onset of treatment, which demonstrates a correlation between improvement of marital disputes and improvement of depression.

Sustaining marital disputes or repeatedly attaching to a partner who is unsuitable may reflect persistent personality difficulties. The majority of women who left their original partner and subsequently became involved with the same or a new man became further involved in marital strife. These women may be inadvertently seeking self-destructive attachments, suppressing their awareness of the partner's negative traits until it is too late, or their involvement in repeated disputes may be due to lack of an appropriate repertoire of social skills for close interpersonal relations.

Interpersonal Difficulties as a Consequence of Clinical Depression

In addition to the important role that difficulties in interpersonal relations play in the predisposition to depression derived from childhood experiences and in the onset and perpetuation of clinical depression in adolescence and adulthood, we must consider the impact of depression on the individual's interpersonal relations and the consequences of the depression for the patient's marriage, family, work, and community activities.

Impact on Interpersonal Communication and Interactions

Several studies that examine the impact on a nondepressed person with someone who is depressed can help us understand the processes by which interpersonal relationships become disrupted as a consequence of depression.

The usual response of significant others to normal sadness, disappointment, and depression, and to grief and mourning is sympathy, support, encouragement, and offers of assistance. However, as time goes on, this positive response often gives way to frustration, friction, and withdrawal.

Coyne (1976), studying the interaction between depressed patients and those around them, found that depressed people elicited unhelpful responses. When college women were asked to interact with both depressed and nondepressed women patients and with nonpatients, they evaluated depressed patients more negatively than nondepressed patients. Furthermore, there was an increase in depression, anxiety, and hostility among the college women who talked with acutely depressed patients.

In similar work, Hammen and Peters (1978) had male and female college students rate other male and female students who played standardized depressed or nondepressed roles in telephone conversations. Depressed persons of the opposite sex were strongly rejected. Female raters made relatively little distinction between depressed males and females in role impairment. Male raters, however, considered the depressed females more impaired. And as in Coyne's study, the "normal" students were depressed after their interaction with the depressed ones.

The findings of these short-term studies have implications for clinical practice and theory. Depressed individuals are "depressing" to have around; they are evaluated negatively and often avoided. The effects of long-term interaction with depressed people can be even more adverse. Kreitman, Collins, Nelson, and Troop (1971) and Collins, Kreitman, Nelson, and Troop (1971) have investigated the effects on marital relationships of women living with a neurotic (mainly depressed) husband. Sixty male outpatients and their wives were interviewed and compared with 60 control couples (Kreitman et al., 1971). Wives of patients were five times as likely to be impaired as control wives in household roles, social activities, health, and child-rearing activities. Wives of patients were also twice as likely as control wives to have a psychiatric history. The longer the marriage, the more incapacitated the patients' wives became as compared to wives of controls.

The observation that spouses of depressed patients have higher than expected rates of mental illness and emotional problems could be due to assortative mating—the tendency of predisposed depressives to seek out and marry other future depressives even before the onset of clinical symptoms—or to pathogenic influence—that is, the adverse effects upon a clinically normal person of continued interaction with a depressed spouse (Merikangas, 1982).

Similar findings about the detrimental impact of depressed patients' social communication patterns have been reported by Merikangas, Ranelli, and Kupfer (1979), who found in addition that a change in marital communication patterns predicted good treatment response. Patients who had responded to antidepressant drug treatment demonstrated improved communication with their spouses, including better dyadic conversation and more interaction.

Hooper, Roberts, Hinchliffe, and Vaughan (1977) also observed the communication interactions of depressed patients and their spouses. In a detailed study, 20 depressed patients interacting with their spouses and with a stranger during the acute episode and at recovery were matched with a comparison group of surgical patient controls and their spouses. Using tape recordings, the researchers observed that discussions around everyday interpersonal and family situations and general philosophical issues which pose a problem may be dealt with in maladaptive ways (Hinchliffe, Hooper, Roberts, & Vaughan, 1975; Hinchliffe, Vaughan, Hooper, & Roberts, 1977, 1978; Hooper et al., 1977). The communication interactions of depressives were more negative, less responsive to the partners, more responsive to strangers, and more self-preoccupied. The high level of tension and hostility, a prominent feature in the marriages of depressed patients, arises from the patients' diminished social responsiveness. The diminished social responsiveness in turn produces uncertainty and insecurity in the marital relationship and increases the patient's fear of possible loss of the loved person. This is followed by guilt and remorse, which in turn generates further anxiety and tension. Hostility leads to the spouse's withholding and remoteness and resultant angry demands by the patient for reassurance from the spouse.

Marital Separation and Divorce

Although marital disputes are most often viewed as a factor precipitating depression, Briscoe and Smith (1973) have examined the hypothesis that divorce is a consequence of depression. They interviewed 139 divorced individuals and assessed the presence of affective disorders before, during, and after the divorce. Of the sample, 32% met the criteria for unipolar depression. In general, individuals who had been depressed before divorce were significantly more likely to be depressed afterward.

Briscoe and Smith also found that the divorced women had often been depressed during the marriage, whereas the men became depressed after the separation. The depressive symptoms of 17 of the 45 were judged as having contributed to the marital disruption rather than being the result of the divorce.

Men and women react differently to marital discord. Women seem more likely to become depressed during a marriage dispute, often as the result of specific stresses contributing to the friction.

Work, Family, and Community Adjustments

Weissman and Paykel (1974) studied 40 depressed women and 40 normal neighbors in an Italian working-class neighborhood and described that the depression influences social, family, and community adjustment. The maladjustments associated with an acute episode persisted during treatment and after recovery.

The impairments of the acutely depressed woman reach into all her roles—wife, mother, worker, and community member. Role impairments were marked in work and in the intimate relationships of marriage and parenthood. They were less marked in relationships with friends, acquaintances, and the extended family. Consistent with the guilt and self-negation of depression, the patient's subjective distress about her performance was more marked than her objective signs of impairment.

Dissatisfaction and distress reported at work were greater than the loss of attendance at work or decreased functioning there. Despite their discomfort, a considerable proportion of depressed women remained at work. Interestingly, women who worked outside the home showed less impairment in their work than the housewives who were at home. Occupations outside the home seem to have a protective effect on depression. Women in the labor force report greater financial security, but also are enhanced by the sense of participating in the larger world, even if these jobs are not professional or lead to career advancement.

Depressed women express increased hostility in the family, and it is directed much more toward husband and children than work associates and friends. In good marriages, the women withdraw from the spouse in an effort to protect him from the effects of depression, and the husbands in turn are more protective toward them. On the other hand, depressed patients with poor marriages blame the spouse for their depression, and the marital conflict is intimately involved with the patient's symptoms.

Relationships with children are also markedly impaired and the manifestations vary with the stage of the family life cycle. Depressed mothers with infant children tend to be overconcerned, helpless, guilty, and sometimes overly hostile. With young school-age children, the mothers' attitudes vary from irritability to lack of emotional involvement. There is often intense conflict with adolescent children. The adolescent learns to exploit the mother's helplessness rather than give her sympathy. Finally, the children's departure from the home precipitates more feelings of loss and depression for the mother.

Interpersonal Relations and Recovery from Depression

As symptomatic recovery of the depression occurs, there is a tendency for social adjustment to improve, but the improvement is slower than of symptoms. Thereafter, the adjustment remains more or less static, or it may even worsen over the next year. Although the depressed person's improvement is considerable, it is not complete.

Work performance improves rapidly as the patient's depression improves. However, impairments in family relations are slower to improve, suggesting that enduring personality factors are operating independently of the depressive symptoms.

Symptomatic relapse is accompanied by a rapid worsening of social functioning. In particular, the patient's work performance worsens and dependency and family attachment increases. Even after recovery, communication with close family and friends may be inhibited by friction, and resentment and argumentative behavior often persists.

Many of the interpersonal disturbances of depression are a consequence of the illness; most impairments subside with recovery, but many return with symptomatic relapse. However, intrafamilial tension and problems in child rearing may persist.

Personality, Interpersonal Relations, and Depression

The classic Greek medical writings of Hippocrates describe the role of temperament predisposing to melancholia. Through the centuries many clinicians have observed attributes of character and individual disposition that make some people vulnerable to depression. Twentieth-century views of the depression-prone personality derive mainly from the observations of clinicians working with clinically depressed patients. The psychoanalytic approach postulates that those who tend to be depressed are dependent on direct or indirect narcissistic inputs from others for their self-esteem. The cognitive approach holds that they have an enduring cognitive set of negative attitudes about themselves and are highly sensitive to situations that reinforce these negative attitudes. The learned helplessness theory proposes that people who can't alter or prevent negative situations become apathetic and reduce their goal-directed behavior. The behavioral approach would emphasize the deficient instrumental behaviors of depressives, such as social skills (the ability to behave in ways that elicit positive reinforcement from others); in this approach, low self-esteem is regarded as a consequence of the lack of positive social reinforcement.

The interpersonal approach has emphasized undue interpersonal dependency as a major vulnerability for depression. Following the paper by Cohen et al. (1954), most interpersonal theorists emphasized the relationship of the depressive's self-esteem to ongoing relationships, characterized by dependency.

The ideal design for testing these approaches would be to first study a group of people when they are without depressive disorders to assess their personality, then follow them to see which ones become depressed later on. The approach would come closer to disentangling personality traits from the symptoms of the disorder. Unfortunately, this research design is too expensive and time consuming to be practical. The alternative approach is to study depressed persons after they have recovered. This method is not without its limitations, because personality assessments during and after the recovery period may still be contaminated by the consequences of having been ill or the presence of mild residual symptoms.

Zuckerman, Prusoff, Weissman, and Padian (1980) studied depressed outpatients who received psychotherapy, pharmacotherapy, or a combination of the two. Patients with premorbid low neuroticism and high extraversion, as measured by the Maudsley Personality Inventory (MPI-N) (Eysenck, 1962), improved significantly in social and interpersonal adjustment compared to patients with premorbid high neuroticism and low extraversion. These findings, which were consistent regardless of which treatment was used, suggest that there is a subgroup of depressives with neurotic personality traits that predispose them to continued interpersonal difficulties. Similar results were found when these patients were followed up 1 year later (Weissman, Kasl, & Klerman, 1976) and 4 years later (Weissman & Bothwell, 1977).

This approach to assessing the personality characteristics of depressed patients has been used systematically by Hirschfeld and Klerman (1979). A total of 73 depressed and 24 manic inpatients at four major university hospital centers were compared after their symptoms had abated. The depressed patients were significantly abnormal, with greater likelihood to break down under stress, have less energy, more insecurity, interpersonal sensitivity, greater tendency to worry, less social adroitness, more neediness, and more obsessionality. Manic patients were much more nearly normal according to the measures of personality included in the assessment battery.

The findings for the nonbipolar depressed patients were consistent with the excessive dependency described in psychoanalytic theory, the negative attitudes and learned helplessness emphasized by the cognitive theorists, and the deficient instrument behaviors of behavior theory. The depressed patient who emerges in this profile is introverted, lacking in self-confidence, unassertive, dependent, pessimistic, and self-perceived as inadequate.

Hostility increases during the acute episode, but there is only a small decrease after recovery, so that the recovered depressed women still displayed more hostility than her neighbors. Clearly, formulations that relate depression to an internalization of hostility and an inability to externalize must be revised. Of course, the classical psychoanalytic formulations suggest something more complex than simply, "depression equals anger turned inward": They do not posit a direct inhibition of external hostility, but an increase of hostility directed inward on an introjected object (Klerman, 1982).

English writers have proposed a tendency to neuroticism in depressives (Foulds, 1965). Two areas of neurotic maladjustment most characteristic of the recovered depressive are interpersonal friction and inhibited communication.

The concepts of interpersonal dependence as a crucial personality trait predisposing to depression have been the subject of recent research by Hirschfeld et al. (1983). The confirmation of this hypothesis has been made difficult by the important impact that emotional states, particularly sadness, depression, and anxiety, have on self-reported assessments of personality. In this respect, there is convergence between the interpersonal research and the evidence for cognitive distortions proposed by Beck, Rush, Shaw, and Emery (1979). Nevertheless, follow-up studies by Hirschfeld *et al.* (1983) indicate that interpersonal dependency persists to the extent that assessments of personality made during the recovery phase are not an accurate mode of assessing preexisting personality. These findings lend support to the hypothesis that interpersonal dependency may be a predisposing factor in adult depression.

Therapeutic Application

The development of an interpersonal conceptualization of depression arose in the context of treatment. In fact, many of the early hypotheses about the relationship of interpersonal relations to depression were derived from therapeutic settings and from clinicians involved in treating adult depressives with psychotherapy.

Gradually there has emerged psychotherapeutic efforts based on interpersonal theory. Most of these efforts involved long-term treatment, particularly that described by Cohen *et al.* (1954) and by Arieti and Bemporad (1978). More recently, short-term treatment [interpersonal psychotherapy for depression (IPT)] has been developed (Klerman *et al.*, 1984).

Goals of Short-Term IPT with Depression

The conceptual framework for IPT develops directly from an interpersonal conceptualization of depression. However, IPT *does not* assume that interpersonal problems "cause" depression. Whatever the cause, depression occurs in an interpersonal context. The therapeutic strategies of IPT is to understand that context and resolve the dispute. IPT views depression in three levels: (*a*) symptom formation, the development of depressive affect and other symptoms; (*b*) social and interpersonal relations, which are disrupted in association with symptoms; and (*c*) personality—the predisposition to symptoms, particularly enduring traits such as inhibited expression of anger, guilt, poor psychological communication with significant others, and/ or difficulty with self-esteem.

IPT intervenes in the first two of these three processes, symptom formation and social and interpersonal relations. Because of IPT's relatively brief duration, IPT is not expected to have a marked impact upon enduring aspects of personality structure, although personality functioning is assessed. While some longer term psychotherapies have been designed to achieve personality change using the interpersonal approach (Arieti & Bemporad, 1978), these treatments have not been assessed in controlled trials.

IPT facilitates recovery from acute depression by relieving depressive symptoms and by helping the patient become more effective in dealing with those current interpersonal problems that are associated with the onset of symptoms. Symptom relief begins with helping the patient understand that the vague and uncomfortable symptoms are part of a known syndrome, which is well described, understood, and relatively common, and which responds to a variety of treatments and has a good prognosis. Psychopharmacologic approaches may be used in conjunction with IPT to alleviate symptoms more rapidly. Improvement in interpersonal relations begins with exploring which of four problem areas commonly associated with the onset of depression—grief, role disputes, role transition, or interpersonal deficit—is related to this particular patient's depression. IPT then focuses on the particular interpersonal problem as it relates to the onset of depression. See Table 21-1 for an outline (Klerman *et al.*, 1984).

IPT Compared with Other Psychotherapies

The authors of IPT agree with Frank (1973) that the procedures and techniques in many of the different psychotherapies have much in common. Many of the therapies emphasize helping the patient to develop a sense of

Table 21-1
Stages and Tasks in the Conduct of IPT

Stages	Tasks
Early	Treatment of depressive symptoms
	Review of symptoms
	Confirmation of diagnosis
	Communication of diagnosis to patient
	Evaluation of medication need
	Education of patient about depression (epidemiology, symptoms, clinical causes, treatments, prognosis)
	Legitimation of patient's "sick role"
	Assessment of interpersonal relations
	Inventory of current relationships
	Choice of interpersonal problem area
	Therapeutic contract
	Statement of goals, diagnosis, problem area
	Medication plan
	Agreement
Middle	Treatment focusing on problem area
	Grief reaction
	Interpersonal disputes
	Role transition
	Interpersonal deficits
Termination	

mastery, combating social isolation, restoring the patient's feeling of group belonging, and helping the patient to rediscover meaning in life. The psychotherapies differ, however, on whether the patient's problems lie in the far past, the immediate past, or the present.

IPT focuses primarily on the patient's present, and it differs from other psychotherapies in its limited duration and its attention to current depressive symptoms and the current depression-related interpersonal context. Given this frame of reference, IPT includes a systematic review of the patient's current relations with significant others. IPT also differs in that it was developed for the treatment of a single group of disorders—the depressive disorder.

IPT is time-limited and not long term. Considerable research has demonstrated the value for most patients' current problems and for most symptom states of short-term, time-limited psychotherapies (usually once a week for less than 9–12 months). While long-term treatment may still be required for changing personality dysfunctions, particularly maladaptive interpersonal and cognitive patterns, and for ameliorating or replacing dysfunctional social skills, evidence for the efficacy of long-term psychotherapy is limited. Long-term treatment also has the inherent potential disadvantage of promoting dependency and reinforcing avoidance behavior. Psychotherapies that are short term or time-limited aim to minimize these adverse effects.

IPT is focused and not open-ended. In common with other brief psychotherapies, IPT focuses on one or two problem areas in the patient's current interpersonal functioning, and these are agreed upon by the patient and the psychotherapist after several evaluation sessions. The content of sessions is therefore focused and not open-ended.

IPT deals with current and not past interpersonal relationships. The IPT therapist focuses the sessions on the patient's immediate social context, as it was just before and as it has been since the onset of the current depressive episode. Past depressive episodes, early family relationships, and previous significant relationships and friendship patterns are, however, assessed in order to understand overall patterns in the patient's interpersonal relationships.

IPT is concerned with interpersonal, not intrapsychic phenomena. In exploring current interpersonal problems with the patient, the psychotherapist may observe the operation of intrapsychic defense mechanisms such as projection, denial, isolation, undoing, or repression. In IPT, however, the psychotherapist does not work on helping the patient see the current situation as a manifestation of internal conflict. Rather, the therapist explores the patient's behavior in terms of interpersonal relations. The example of how dreams are handled is analogous. Although the therapist does not usually ask the patient to recall dreams, patients may spontaneously report them. When this occurs, the psychotherapist may work on the dream by relating its manifest content and associated affects to relevant current interpersonal problems.

IPT is concerned with interpersonal relationships, not cognitive-behavioral phenomena per se. IPT attempts to change how the patient thinks, feels, and acts in problematic interpersonal relationships. Specific negative cognitions or behaviors such as lack of assertiveness and lack of social skills are not in themselves a treatment focus in IPT. They are considered only in relationship to significant persons in the patient's life and for the ways that they impinge upon these interpersonal relationships.

In common with cognitive-behavioral therapy, IPT is concerned with the patient's distorted thinking about him or herself and others and with the relevant options for change. The IPT therapist may work with the patient about his or her distorted thinking by calling attention to discrepancies between what the patient is saying and doing or between the patient's standards and those of society in general. Unlike cognitive-behavioral therapies, however, IPT does not attempt systematically to uncover such distorted thoughts, give homework, or prescribe methods of developing alternative thought patterns. Rather, the IPT psychotherapist calls the patient's attention to distorted thinking in relation to significant others as the evidence arises during the psychotherapy. The IPT psychotherapist will often visit with the patient to explore the effect of his or her maladaptive thinking on interpersonal relationships.

The patient's personality is very frequently the major focus in psychotherapy. IPT does not expect to make an impact on personality. It recognizes, but does not focus on, the patient's personality characteristics. Moreover, IPT does not make the assumption that persons who become depressed have unique personality traits. This assumption is still questionable and requires further testing; so far, research on this question has not yielded any conclusive answers.

Interpersonal Approaches and Psychoanalytic Theory and Therapy

The authors' goal in developing IPT was not to create a new psychotherapy, but to make explicit and operational a systematic approach to depression and to base that approach on accepted theory and empirical evidence. Much of IPT incorporates what many, perhaps most, psychoanalytic and dynamic psychotherapists do. This reflects the extent to which the interpersonal approach has permeated American psychotherapeutic practice, a trend whose historical roots are probably twofold. In the first place, most of the founding psychotherapists and practitioners and theorists of the interpersonal approach, including Sullivan, Fromm-Reichmann, Cohen, and Stanton, were initially trained in Freudian psychoanalysis. While they disagreed with many aspects of classic psychoanalytic theory and practice, the role of early childhood experience and the existence of unconscious mental processes were not the sources of this disagreement. Their disagreement arose over the existence of libido, the dual instinct theory (eros and death instincts), and the relative importance of biological, instinctive forces compared with social and cultural influences on personal development and current functioning. A second historical force was the expansion of psychotherapy following World War II, which coincided with widespread national concerns about social change, racial and sexual equality, personal well-being, and the enhancement of personal potential and individual happiness. Such cultural values are highly compatible with scientific and professional pursuits that focus on interpersonal relations and personal development throughout the life cycle.

For purposes of theoretical clarity and research design, the authors have nonetheless often found it useful to highlight the differences between the interpersonal and the psychodynamic approaches to human behavior and mental illness. The essential focus of a pure psychodynamic approach is on unconscious mental processes and the role of intrapsychic memories, wishes, fantasies, and conflicts in determining behavior and psychopathology. The essential focus of a pure interpersonal approach is on social roles and interpersonal interactions in the individual's past and current life experiences. Both the interpersonal and the psychodynamic approaches are concerned with the person's life span and the important role of early experiences and persistent personality patterns at all developmental stages and in all areas of personal functioning. However, in understanding personal functioning, the psychodynamic psychotherapist is concerned with object relations, while the interpersonal psychotherapist is concerned with interpersonal relations. Put another way, the psychodynamic psychotherapist listens for the patient's intrapsychic wishes and conflicts, while the interpersonal psychotherapist listens for the patient's role expectations and disputes.

A comprehensive theory would ideally incorporate both these approaches, along with biological, behavioral, and other views. Given the current state of knowledge, however, the authors believe it timely and valuable to focus clearly on one approach, to explore its validity, and to examine its utility through systematic research, especially through controlled trials of efficacy and other outcomes.

Evidence for Efficacy

One of the significant features of IPT is the extent to which it has been tested for efficacy. The results of two controlled studies have been reported (Klerman, DiMascio, Weissman, Prusoff, & Paykel, 1974; Weissman et al., 1979). These studies indicate the value of IPT in reducing symptoms in the acute episode and in facilitating clinical remission and promoting interpersonal relations as part of maintenance therapy. IPT has been chosen as one of the two forms of psychotherapy for the National Institute of Mental Health Collaborative Study of the Psychotherapy of Depressed Patients. This study is now under way in three centers and will compare IPT with cognitive behavior therapy, imipramine, and a control group receiving placebo and psychological management. The results of this study should be forthcoming within the next year or so.

Long-Term Interpersonal Psychotherapy of Depression

Although this chapter has described the form of short-term therapy called IPT, it is important to note that there are long-term forms of psychotherapy based on interpersonal principles. This has been described in detail by Arieti and Bemporard. In this form of therapy, the focus is not so much on the reduction of symptoms and improvement in social functioning during the acute episode as it is on working on the long-term personality difficulties which are implicated in the predisposition to depression. At the present time, no systematic empirical data from controlled studies exist as to the efficacy of long-term treatment.

Conclusions

This chapter has reviewed the theoretical basis for an interpersonal approach to depression, emphasizing the broad conceptual framework developed by Adolf Meyer and Harry Stack Sullivan.

The specific application to depression rests heavily on empirical research on childhood, particularly that influenced by Bowlby and also by ongoing studies of life events and interpersonal functioning of depressives. Epidemiologic findings from community surveys now provide empirical support for the role of interpersonal disruptions as a significant correlate of major depression, and a variety of interpersonal psychotherapies for depression, both brief and long term, have been developed. One brief interpersonal psychotherapy (IPT) specifically designed for symptom reduction and the improvement of interpersonal relations during acute symptomatic depressive episodes is currently being tested in a National Institute of Mental Health-sponsored multicentered clinical trial.

Looking to the future, it is expected that the findings from epidemiologic, clinical, and therapeutic studies will result in modifications of the interpersonal concept of depression and then integration with genetic and biological concepts of depression. The interesting question is not whether interpersonal problems "cause" depression, but rather what aspects of the patient's social interpersonal environment interact with what type of predisposition and for what type of depression.

Acknowledgments

Portions of this chapter have appeared in previous publications. Appreciation is expressed to the *American Journal of Psychiatry* and the American Psychiatric Press for permission to reproduce sections of previous work.

REFERENCES

Arieti, S., & Bemporad, J. (1978). *Severe and mild depression. The psychotherapeutic approach.* New York: Basic Books.

Beardslee, W. R., Bemporad, J., Keller, M. B., & Klerman, G. L. (1983). Children of parents with major affective disorder: A review. *American Journal of Psychiatry, 140,* 825–832.

Beck, A. T., Rush, A. J., Shaw, B. F., & Emery, G. (1979). *Cognitive therapy of depression.* New York: Guilford Press.

Becker, J. (1974). *Depression: Theory and research.* New York: Wiley.

Bemporad, J. R. (1982). Childhood depression from a developmental perspective. In L. Grinspoon (Ed.), *Psychiatry 1982 annual review.* Washington, DC: American Psychiatric Press.

Birtchnell, J. (1980). Women whose mothers died in childhood: An outcome study. *Psychological Medicine, 10,* 699–713.

Bloom, B. L., Asher, S. J., & White, S. W. (1978). Marital disruption as a stressor: A review and analysis. *Psychological Bulletin, 85,* 867–894.

Bowlby, J. (1969). *Attachment and Loss: Vol. I. Attachment.* London: Hogarth Press.

Bowlby, J. (1977). The making and breaking of affectional bonds. II. Some principles of psychotherapy. *British Journal of Psychiatry, 130,* 421–431.

Briscoe, C. W., & Smith, J. B. (1973). Depression and marital turmoil. *Archives of General Psychiatry, 28,* 811–817.

Brown, G. W., Harris, T., & Copeland, J. R. (1977). Depression and loss. *British Journal of Psychiatry, 130,* 1–18.

Brumbach, R. A., Dietz-Schmidt, S., & Weinberg, W. A. (1977). Depression in children referred to an educational diagnostic center—diagnosis and treatment and analysis of criteria and literature review. *Diseases of the Nervous System, 38,* 529–535.

Chodoff, P. (1970). The core problem in depression. In J. Masserman (Ed.), *Science and psychoanalysis.* New York: Brune & Stratton.

Clayton, P., Desmarais, L., & Winokur, G. (1968). A study of normal bereavement. *American Journal of Psychiatry, 125,* 168–178.

Cohen, M. B., Blake, G., Cohen, R., Fromm-Reichmann, F., & Weigert, E. (1954). An intensive study of twelve cases of manic-depressive psychosis. *Psychiatry, 17,* 103–137.

Collins, J., Kreitman, N., Nelson, B., & Troop, J. (1971). Neurosis and marital interactions. III. Family roles and functions. *British Journal of Psychiatry, 119,* 233–242.

Connell, H. M. (1972). Depression in childhood. *Child Psychiatry in Human Development, 4,* 71–85.

Coyne, J. C. (1976). Depression and the response of others. *Journal of Abnormal Psychology, 85,* 186–193.

Evans, J. (1975). Depression in adolescents. *Proceedings of the Royal Society of Medicine, 68,* 565–566.

Eysenck, H. (1962). *Manual of the Maudsley personality inventory.* San Diego, CA: Educational and Industrial Testing Service.

Fieve, R. R. (1975). *Moodswing.* New York: Bantam Books.

Foulds, G. A. (1965). *Personality and personal illness.* London: Tavistock Publications.

Frank, J. D. (1973). *Persuasion and healing: A comparative study of psychotherapy.* Baltimore, MD: Johns Hopkins University Press.

Freud, S. (1957). Mourning and melancholia. In J. Strachey (Ed. and Trans.), *The standard edition of the complete psychological works of Sigmund Freud* (Vol. 14). London: Hogarth Press. (Original work published 1917)

Fromm-Reichmann, F. (1960). *Principles of intensive psychotherapy.* Chicago, IL: Phoenix Books.

Gamer, E., Gallant, D., Grunebaum, H. U., & Cohler, B. J. (1977). Children of psychotic mothers. *Archives of General Psychiatry, 34,* 592–597.

Goodall, J., & Hamburg, D. (1971). *In the shadow of man.* Boston, MA: Houghton Mifflin.

Hammen, C. L., & Peters, S. D. (1978). Interpersonal consequences of depression: Response to men and women enacting a depressed role. *Journal of Abnormal Psychology, 87,* 322–332.

Harlow, H. H., & Suomi, S. J. (1974). Induced depression in monkeys. *Behavioral Biology, 12,* 273–279.

Henderson, S. (1974). Care-eliciting behavior in man. *Journal of Nervous and Mental Disease, 159,* 172–181.

Henderson, S. (1977). The social network, support and neurosis: The function of attachment in adult life. *British Journal of Psychiatry, 131,* 185–191.

Henderson, S. (1980). A development in social psychiatry. The systematic study of social bonds. *Journal of Nervous and Mental Disease, 168,* 63–69.

Henderson, S., Byrne, D. G., & Duncan-Jones, P. (1982). *Neurosis and the social environment.* Sydney: Academic Press.

Henderson, S., Byrne, D. G., Duncan-Jones, P., Adcock, S., Scott, R., & Steele, G. P. (1978). Social bonds in the epidemiology of neurosis. *British Journal of Psychiatry, 132,* 463–466.

Henderson, S., Byrne, D. G., Duncan-Jones, P., Scott, R., & Adcock, S. (1980). Social relationships, adversity and neurosis: A study of association in a general population sample. *British Journal of Psychiatry, 136,* 574–583.

Henderson, S., Duncan-Jones, P., Byrne, D. G., Scott, R., & Adcock, S. (1979). Psychiatric disorder in Canberra: A standardized study of prevalence. *Acta Psychiatrica Scandinavica, 60,* 355–374.

Henderson, S., Duncan-Jones, P., McAuley, H., & Ritchie, K. (1978). The patient's primary group. *British Journal of Psychiatry, 132,* 74–86.

Hinchliffe, M. K., Hooper, D., & Roberts, F. J. (1978). *The melancholy marriage.* New York: Wiley.

Hinchliffe, M. K., Hooper, D., Roberts, F. J., & Vaughan, P. W. (1975). A study of the interactions between depressed patients and their spouses. *British Journal of Psychiatry, 126,* 164–172.

Hinchliffe, M., Vaughan, P. W., Hooper, D., & Roberts, F. J. (1977). The melancholy marriage: An inquiry into the interaction of depression. *British Journal of Medicine and Psychology, 50,* 125–142.

Hinchliffe, M. K., Vaughan, P. W., Hooper, D., & Roberts, F. J. (1978). The melancholy marriage: An inquiry into the interaction of depression. III. Responsiveness. *British Journal of Medicine and Psychology, 51,* 1–13.

Hirschfeld, R. M. A., & Klerman, G. L. (1979). Personality attributes and affective disorders. *American Journal of Psychiatry, 136,* 67–70.

Hirschfeld, R. M. A., Klerman, G. L., Clayton, P. J., Keller, M. B., McDonald-Scott, P., Larkin, B. H. (1983). Assessing personality: Effects of the depressive state on trait measurement. *American Journal of Psychiatry, 140,* 695–699.

Holmes, T. H., Goodell, H., & Wolf, S. (1950). *The nose: An experimental study of reactions within the nose of human subjects during varying life experiences.* Springfield, IL: Charles C Thomas.

Hooper, D., Roberts, F. J., Hinchliffe, M. K., & Vaughan, P. W. (1977). The melancholy marriage: An inquiry into the interaction of depression. I. Introduction. *British Journal of Medicine and Psychology, 50,* 113–124.

Ilfeld, F. W. (1977). Current social stressors and symptoms of depression. *American Journal of Psychiatry, 134,* 161–166.

Klerman, G. L. (1982). Testing analytic hypotheses: Do personality attributes predispose to depression. In A. Jacobson & D. Parmelee (Eds.), *Psychoanalysis: A contemporary appraisal.* New York: Brunner/Mazel.

Klerman, G. L. (1983). Evaluating the efficacy of psychotherapy. In P. J. Clayton & J. E. Barrett (Eds.), *Treatment of depression: Old controversies and new approaches.* New York: Raven Press.

Klerman, G. L., DiMascio, A., Weissman, M. M., Prusoff, B. A., & Paykel, E. S. (1974). Treatment of depression by drugs and psychotherapy. *American Journal of Psychiatry, 131,* 186–191.

Klerman, G. L., Lavori, P. W., Rice, J., Reich, T., Endicott, J., Andreasen, N. C., Keller, M. B., & Hirschfeld, R. M. A. (in press). Birth cohort trends in rates of major depressive disorder among relatives of patients with affective disorder. *Archives of General Psychiatry.*

Klerman, G. L., Rounsaville, B. J., Chevron, E. S., Neu, C., & Weissman, M. M. (1979, June). *Manual for short-term interpersonal psychotherapy (IPT) of depression.* Unpublished manuscript, fourth draft.

Klerman, G. L., Weissman, M. M., Rounsaville, B. J., & Chevron, E. S. (1984). *Interpersonal psychotherapy of depression.* New York: Basic Books.

Kovacs, M., Feinberg, T. L., Crouse-Novak, M. A., Paulauskas, S. L., & Finkelstein, R. (1984). Depressive disorders in childhood. *Archives of General Psychiatry, 41,* 229–237.

Kreitman, N., Collins, J., Nelson, B., & Troop, J. (1971). Neurosis and marital interactions. IV. Manifest psychological interaction. *British Journal of Psychiatry, 119,* 243–252.

Leaf, P., Weissman, M. M., Myers, J., Tischler, G., & Holzer, C. (1985). *Risks and correlates of major depression in one urban community.* Unpublished paper presented at the American Psychopathologic Association.

Lindemann, E. (1944). Symptomatology and management of acute grief. *American Journal of Psychiatry, 101,* 141–148.

Maddison, D. (1968). The relevance of conjugal bereavement for preventive psychiatry. *British Journal of Medicine and Psychology, 41,* 223–233.

Maddison, D., & Walker, W. (1967). Factors affecting the outcome of conjugal bereavement. *British Journal of Psychiatry, 113,* 1057–1067.

Merikangas, K. (1982). Assortative mating for psychiatric disorders and psychological traits. *Archives of General Psychiatry, 39,* 1173–1180.

Merikangas, K., Ranelli, C., & Kupfer, D. (1979). Marital interaction in hospitalized depressed patients. *Journal of Nervous and Mental Disease, 167,* 689–695.

Meyer, A. (1957). *Psychobiology: A science of man.* Springfield, IL: Charles C Thomas.

Miller, P., & Ingham, J. G. (1976). Friends, confidants and symptoms. *Social Psychiatry, 11,* 51–58.

Myers, J. K., Lindenthal, J. J., & Pepper, M. P. (1975). Life events, social integration and psychiatric symptomatology. *Journal of Health and Social Behavior, 16,* 421–427.

Orvaschel, H., Weissman, M. M., & Kidd, K. K. (1980). Children and depression: The children of depressed parents; the childhood of depressed patients; depression in children. *Journal of Affective Disorders, 2,* 1–16.

Osterweis, M., Solomon, F., & Green, M. (Eds.). (1984). *Bereavement: Reactions, consequences, and care.* Washington, DC: National Academy Press.

Parker, G. (1978). *The bonds of depression.* Sydney: Angus & Robertson.

Parker, G. (1979). Parental characteristics in relation to depressive disorders. *British Journal of Psychiatry, 134,* 138–147.

Paykel, E. (1979). Recent life events in the development of depressive disorders. In R. A. Depue (Ed.), *The psychobiology of depressive disorders: Implications for the effects of stress.* New York: Academic Press.

Paykel, E. S. (1982). Life events and early environment. In E. S. Paykel (Ed.), *Handbook of affective disorders.* New York: Guilford Press.

Paykel, E. S., Myers, J. K., Dienelt, M. N., Klerman, G. L., Lindenthal, J. J., & Pepper, M. P. (1969). Life events and depression: A controlled study. *Archives of General Psychiatry, 21,* 753–760.

Pearlin, L. I., & Lieberman, M. A. (1977). Social sources of emotional distress. In R. Simmons (Ed.), *Research in community and mental health.* Greenwich, CT: JAI Press.

Poznanski, E., & Zrull, J. P. (1970). Childhood depression. *Archives of General Psychiatry, 23,* 8–15.

Puig-Antich, J., Perel, J. M., Lupatkin, W., Chambers, W. J., Shea, C., Tabrizi, M. A., & Stiller, R. L. (1979). Plasma levels of imipramine (IMI) and desmethylimipramine (DMI) and clinical response in prepubertal major depressive disorder: A preliminary report. *Journal of American Academic Child Psychiatry, 18,* 616–627.

Rabkin, J. G., & Struening, E. L. (1976). Life events and illness. *Science, 194,* 1013–1020.

Rolf, J. E., & Garmezy, N. (1974). The school performance of children vulnerable to behavior pathology. In D. F. Ricks, T. Alexander, & M. Roff (Eds.), *Life history research in psychopathology* (Vol. III). Minneapolis: University of Minnesota Press.

Rounsaville, B. J., Weissman, M. M., Prusoff, B. A., & Herceg-Baron, R. L. (1979a). Marital disputes and treatment outcome in depressed women. *Comprehensive Psychiatry, 20,* 483–490.

Rounsaville, B. J., Weissman, M. M., Prusoff, B. A., & Herceg-Baron, R. L. (1979b). Process of psychotherapy among depressed women with marital disputes. *American Journal of Orthopsychiatry, 49,* 505–510.

Roy, A. (1978). Vulnerability factors and depression in women. *British Journal of Psychiatry, 133,* 106–110.

Rutter, M. (1972). *Maternal deprivation reassessed.* London: Penguin Books.

Rutter, M., Graham, P., Chadwick, O. F. D., & Yule, W. (1976). Adolescent turmoil—fact or fiction? *Journal of Child Psychology, 17,* 35–56.

Scarf, M. (1980). *Unfinished business: Pressure points in the lives of women.* New York: Doubleday.

Schless, A. P., & Mendels, J. (1977). Life events and psychopathology. *Psychiatry Digest, 28,* 25–35.

Scott, J. P., Stewart, J. M., & DeGhett, V. S. (1977). Separation in infant days: Emotional response and motivational consequences. In J. P. Scott & E. C. Senay (Eds.), *Separation and depression, clinical and research aspects.* Washington, DC: American Association for the Advancement of Science.

Spiegel, J. P. (1957). The resolution of role conflict within families. *Psychiatry, 20,* 1–16.

Sullivan, H. S. (1953a). *Conceptions of modern psychiatry.* New York: Norton.

Sullivan, H. S. (1953b). *The interpersonal theory of psychiatry.* New York: Norton.

Tennant, C., Bebbington, P., & Hurry, J. (1980). Parental death in childhood and risk of adult depressive disorders: A review. *Psychological Medicine, 10,* 289–299.

Uhlenhuth, E. H., & Paykel, E. S. (1973). Symptom intensity and life events. *Archives of General Psychiatry, 28,* 473–477.

Walker, K., MacBride, A., & Vachon, M. (1977). Social support networks and the crisis of bereavement. *Social Science, 11,* 35–41.

Weintraub, S., Neale, J. M., & Liebert, D. E. (1975). Teacher ratings of children vulnerable to psychopathology. *American Journal of Orthopsychiatry, 45,* 839–845.

Weiss, R. S. (1975). *Marital separation.* New York: Basic Books.

Weissman, M. M., & Bothwell, S. (1977). The assessment of social adjustment by patient self-report. *Archives of General Psychiatry, 33,* 1111–1115.

Weissman, M. M., Kasl, S. V., & Klerman, G. L. (1976). Follow-up of depressed women after maintenance treatment. *American Journal of Psychiatry, 133,* 757–760.

Weissman, M. M., & Paykel, E. S. (1974). *The depressed women: A study of social relationships.* Chicago, IL: University of Chicago Press.

Weissman, M. M., Paykel, E. S., & Klerman, G. L. (1972). The depressed women as mother. *Social Psychiatry, 7,* 98–108.

Weissman, M. M., Prusoff, B. A., DiMascio, A., Neu, C., Goklaney, M., & Klerman, G. L. (1979). The efficacy of drugs and psychotherapy in the treatment of acute depressive episodes. *American Journal of Psychiatry, 136,* 555–558.

Welner, Z., Welner, A., McCrary, M. D., & Leonard, M. A. (1977). Psychopathology in children of inpatients with depression—a controlled study. *Journal of Nervous and Mental Disease, 164,* 408–413.

Zuckerman, D. M., Prusoff, B. A., Weissman, M. M., & Padian, N. (1980). Personality as a predictor of short-term treatment outcome in depressed outpatients. *Journal of Consulting and Clinical Psychology, 48,* 730–735.

CHAPTER 22

The Bipolar Spectrum Reconsidered

Philippe J. Khouri and Hagop S. Akiskal

Manic–depressive insanity . . . includes on the one hand the whole domain of so-called periodic and circular insanity, on the other hand simple mania, the greater part of the morbid states termed Melancholia. . . . Lastly, we include here certain slight and slightest colorings of mood, some of them periodic, some of them continuously morbid, which on the one hand are to be regarded as the rudiment of more severe disorders, on the other hand pass without sharp boundary into the domain of personal predisposition. In the course of the years I have become more and more convinced that all the above-mentioned states only represent manifestations of a single morbid process.
—EMIL KRAEPELIN (1921)

The nosological boundaries of manic–depressive illness have been considerably broadened in the past few years, in part due to the availability of a relatively specific pharmacologic agent for its treatment (Akiskal & Cassano, 1983). Recent research has shown that some conditions, previously subsumed under schizophrenic, neurotic, and personality disorder rubrics, represent variants of manic–depressive illness. For instance, it is now recognized that (a) mania and (to a lesser extent) depression may manifest mood-incongruent psychotic features (Akiskal & Puzantian, 1979); (b) some forms of mild "neurotic" depression may develop hypomanic episodes during prospective follow-up (Akiskal, Bitar, Puzantian, Rosenthal, & Walker, 1978); (c) other recurrent depressives exhibit brief hypomanic switches on antidepressant medication (Akiskal et al., 1983); and (d) subtle forms of bipolar oscillation at the level of temperament are seen among outpatients (Akiskal, Djenderedjian, Rosenthal, & Khani, 1977). Such findings have led to a formulation in which bipolar illness is viewed as a spectrum of disorders, from the temperamental to the psychotic (Akiskal, 1983a).

Recent work has also shown that bipolar conditions are more common than previously thought, and the unipolar–bipolar ratio may approach unity in some populations (Egeland, 1983). Such findings have evolved from more precise phenomenological assessments of affective disorders, as well as the delineation of "subtle" variants within the bipolar spectrum (Akiskal & Webb, 1983). One must also acknowledge the possibility—particularly relevant to rapid cycling forms of bipolar disorder—that the prevalent use of

Philippe J. Khouri and Hagop S. Akiskal. Department of Psychiatry, University of Tennessee College of Medicine, Memphis, Tennessee.

tricyclic antidepressants may have contributed to the increase in bipolar switches (Kukopulos *et al.*, 1983).

This chapter will review the evidence that supports a partial return to Kraepelin's (1921) broad concept of manic–depressive illness. As psychopathologic evidence for the proposed bipolar spectrum has been documented elsewhere (Akiskal, 1983a), the present discussion will focus on genetic and neurobiological considerations.

Unipolar–Bipolar: Dichotomy or Continuum?

The Perspectives of Kraepelin and Leonhard

Although the relationship of mania to depression has been recognized since antiquity, it was Kraepelin's (1921) systematic work which legitimized the concept of manic–depressive illness as a distinct nosological entity. His unitary system brought together the entire domain of endogenous affective psychoses and affective temperaments.

This work was challenged by Leonhard (1957), another German psychiatrist, whose classificatory schema of affective psychoses was supported by work conducted in Sweden (Perris, 1966), Switzerland (Angst, 1966), and the United States (Winokur, Clayton, & Reich, 1969). The Leonhardian view proposed a sharp distinction between unipolar and bipolar forms of affective disorders, the former involving only depression and the latter including periods of elevated mood. This distinction was originally based largely on differences of familial affective history; other lines of evidence that emerged in later research have been summarized by Fieve and Dunner (1975) and Depue and Monroe (1978). Bipolar forms are characterized by an equal sex ratio, earlier age of onset, more retardation and hypersomnia during depressed periods, high genetic "loading" for affective disorder (both unipolar and bipolar) in consecutive generations, shorter but more frequent episodes, "augmentor" status with the average evoked potential technique, low platelet monoamine oxidase (MAO) activity, tendency toward lower excretion of urinary 3-methoxy-4-hydroxyphenylethyleneglycol (MHPG) when depressed, lowered threshold for developing hypomania during antidepressant treatment, and response to lithium carbonate during elevated and depressed phases. However, in a critical review, Gershon (1978) concluded that none of these differences was sufficiently compelling to argue for a neurobiological separation of unipolar and bipolar disorders. This conclusion has remained essentially unchallenged by findings from research on more recently developed biological markers (Akiskal, 1983b).

Current Perspectives

The unipolar–bipolar distinction clearly had heuristic merit in psychobiological research into affective disorders. However, recent evidence indicates that the family histories of unipolar and bipolar probands may be more similar than dissimilar (Gershon et al., 1982). Furthermore, a spectrum of milder bipolar disorders, forming a phenomenological bridge between unipolar and bipolar disorders, has been delineated (Akiskal, 1983a; Dunner, 1983). Gershon, Baron, and Leckman (1975) have hypothesized that bipolar illness may be the more severe or penetrant of the two disorders, having earlier age of onset, high episode frequency, and lowered threshold for hypomanic and manic decompensation. Some of the previously reported unipolar–bipolar differences may have been due to the considerable dilution of unipolar research samples with dysphoric anxiety states, situational unhappiness, and social misery. This position is supported by the finding that unipolar–bipolar differences become less marked when endogenous depressions are studied (Taylor & Abrams, 1980). In this sense, then, the bipolar–unipolar dichotomy is, in part, a distinction between affective and nonaffective disorder or affective illness and nonspecific dysphoria common to a variety of nonaffective disorders.

Other recent evidence that has eroded the boundary between unipolar and bipolar affective states includes systematic clinical observation that many patients with recurrent primary depressive disorders develop transient hypomanic episodes either spontaneously or upon pharmacologic challenge with tricyclic antidepressants (Akiskal et al., 1978; T. L. Rosenthal, Akiskal, Scott-Strauss, Rosenthal, & David, 1981). Such patients may be cross-sectionally misclassified as unipolar because their hypomanic periods tend to be pleasant or even "productive," and, therefore, seldom reported. Skillful phenomenological questioning or personal follow-up is necessary to document their hypomania. Some of these patients may be classified as "atypical" bipolar (American Psychiatric Association, 1980) or as having bipolar II disorder, bipolar I being reserved for those with full-blown mania (Fieve & Dunner, 1975).

Although the existence of these intermediary affective subtypes argues for a unipolar–bipolar continuum, there is no reason to include all depressions, especially those with late onset and low episode frequency, in such a continuum. Twin studies of affective disorders have a bearing on this issue. The Danish twin study (Bertlesen, Harvald, & Hauge, 1977) reported that bipolar probands had wider monozygotic–dizygotic differences when compared with unipolars. However, this was due to dilution of unipolar cases by nonrecurrent depressions; unipolars with recurrent ($\geq$3 episodes) illness were similar to bipolars. Therefore, genetic factors appear to be most clearly established for bipolar and recurrent depressions; their importance is less established, if not equivocal, for other forms of depression. In all probability, sporadic unipolar depressions arise from the interaction of multiple environmental causes rather than a specific genetic factor (Akiskal & McKinney, 1975). Thus, unipolar illness may exist in two phenotypes (Akiskal, 1983a; Kupfer, Pickar, Himmelhoch, & Detre, 1975): (a) a pure depressive form without bipolar family history and with relatively low episode frequency (unipolar I), and (b) high episode frequency depressions with bipolar family history, that is, a pseudounipolar phenotypical expression of the bipolar genotype (unipolar II disorder). When unipolar II disorders are treated with tricyclic antidepressants, one can expect short-lived hypomanic responses or transformation of the depressive state into a dysphoric–irritable mixed state. For all these reasons, bipolar III would be a better designation than unipolar II. As formulated here, the nosological territory of these pseudounipolar conditions overlaps considerably with that of bipolar II. Thus, lithium may be preferable for these conditions. It is obviously clinically important to identify these potential bipolar depressives. Table 22-1 summarizes findings from recent prospective research to delineate predictors of bipolar outcome in patients presenting with a depressive episode (Akiskal *et al.*, 1983; Strober & Carlson, 1982).

The developments summarized above herald a partial return to Kraepelin's (1921) viewpoint. It would appear that many recurrent depressions belong to a bipolar spectrum, with bipolar II disorder forming an intermediary phenotype between unipolar II and bipolar I disorders. In the remainder of this chapter we shall review the research evidence, especially from a genetic–neurobiological perspective, in support of this modified concept of the bipolar spectrum.

The Emergence of the Bipolar Spectrum

Conceptual Issues

The boundaries of nosological entities in psychiatry are due in part to the assumption of its developers. Clinician-scientists like Kraepelin, who focused on the forest rather than the trees, could visualize a continuum between the psychotic disorganized phase of a manic episode and milder

Table 22-1
Predictors of Bipolar Outcome in Depressive Illness[a]

Onset before 25 years
Acute onset of episode
Primary depression
Hypersomnic–retarded features; stupor
Psychotic depression
Postpartal precipitation
Pharmacologic hypomania
Bipolar family history
Loaded pedigrees
Consecutive-generation affective family history

[a]Adapted from Strober and Carlson (1982) and Akiskal *et al.* (1983).

temperamental mood fluctuations in close relatives of people with these episodes. Thus, family and natural history permitted Kraepelin to postulate the existence of a spectrum of endogenous affective conditions, which he termed manic–depressive illness. Until the early 1970s, Kraepelin's contributions had had relatively little impact on American psychiatry. There were many reasons for this, not the least of which was the lack of evident advantage of such classification when specific treatments did not exist. Further, many psychiatric clinicians and educators were uncomfortable with the notion that genomes could modulate disturbances in overt behavior, thinking, and feelings (D. Rosenthal, 1970).

The paradigm we adopt from Robins and Guze (1970) to examine the hypothesis of a bipolar spectrum is Kraepelinian in several regards, and includes the following steps: (*a*) Emphasis is placed on the phenomenology of the disorders rather than implied mechanisms of causation; (*b*) the diagnostic process is broadened to include family history of psychiatric illness; (*c*) induced alterations in phenomenology by pharmacologic challenge provide additional criteria for reordering the clinical data; (*d*) neurobiological abnormalities that may extend to the entire spectrum of bipolar affective disorders are described.

Phenomenological and Familial Aspects

Phenomenological approaches to psychopathology were accorded relatively little importance in North America until recent years when the work of the St. Louis group (Feighner *et al.*, 1972) made descriptive psychiatry respectable once again, thereby shaping the new zeitgeist of American psychiatry. We summarize below a large number of investigations—bearing on the bipolar spectrum—that have utilized the rigorous observational tools of the neo-Kraepelinian approach as introduced by the St. Louis group.

The concept of bipolar spectrum presented here is modified from Kupfer *et al.* (1975), Fieve and Dunner (1975), Klerman (1981), Gershon *et al.* (1982), and Akiskal (1983a). This spectrum includes the following conditions:

Bipolar I: Patients with single or recurrent manic episodes with or without previous history of depressive episodes
Bipolar II: Those with recurrent early-onset depressive episodes who develop spontaneous periods of hypomania
Bipolar III (unipolar II): Similar to bipolar II, with the exception that hypomania occurs upon pharmacologic challenge only
Cyclothymia: Persons with lifelong traits of emotional instability manifested by cyclical, biphasic, and abrupt mood shifts with concomitant psychomotor, circadian, and cognitive manifestations occurring on a lower plane of severity—and of shorter duration—compared with major forms of bipolar illness

The concept of a bipolar spectrum evolved, in part, as a reformulation in three areas insofar as they relate to affective disorders: psychosis, neurotic depression, and precipitating factors.

Psychosis: The equation of psychosis with schizophrenia is one of the main reasons for the well-known findings of overdiagnosis of schizophrenia vis-à-vis mania in North America (Cooper *et al.*, 1972). If psychosis is identified by the presence of delusions and hallucinations, then many manics not only develop psychosis, but also a paranoid psychosis (Akiskal & Puzantian, 1979). Misdiagnosis of mania as schizophrenia is most commonly due to overemphasis of cross-sectional phenomenology. A study of the natural progression of mania (Carlson & Goodwin, 1973), however, reveals that paranoid mania belongs to the severe end of the bipolar spectrum.

Neurotic Depression: This is presently a more or less defunct nosological term. A University of Tennessee study (Akiskal *et al.*, 1978) showed that many patients initially classified as neurotic depressives (because of mild symptoms that seemed "reactive" to psychosocial events) developed hypomanic or even manic episodes during prospective follow-up. Change in polarity occurred in 18% of such patients during a follow-up period of 3–4 years. Even chronic neurotic depressives—currently subsumed under the dysthymic rubric in North America—were found to develop hypomania during prospective observation (Akiskal, 1983c); however, antidepressant challenge was required for eliciting latent bipolar tendencies in these patients. Such findings emphasize the common existence of very mild endogenous depressive states under the guise of "neurosis," which when viewed in longitudinal perspective, belong to a bipolar spectrum, albeit an attenuated spectrum where hypomanic manifestations are brief and sporadic.

Precipitating Factors: A large volume of literature (reviewed by Lloyd, 1980) implicates psychosocial factors in affective disorders, whether manic or depressed. However, one may question whether such factors are etiologic, as the overwhelming majority of people exposed to aversive life circumstances do not develop such episodes (Akiskal, 1979). Thus, it seems necessary to postulate an interaction between predisposing and precipitating causes (Akiskal & McKinney, 1975). The outcome of such interaction depends on genetic–temperamental factors, character traits (or habitual modes of maintaining psychological homeostasis through defense mechanisms), as well as the number and severity of psychosocial stressors. Geneticists use the concept of liability to explain the way in which a combination of multiple factors, both genetic and nongenetic, increases the risk of a given disorder (Falconer, 1967; Reich, Cloninger, & Guze, 1975). Heritability is the genetic component of the liability. The threshold for manifestations of a disorder will be reached by various permutations of genetic and nongenetic factors for each disorder, and even for individuals with the same disorder. For example, in some forms of bipolar I illness with adolescent onset, heritability may be so high that nonheritable factors play a minimal role in the clinical expression of the vulnerability. By contrast, in those who develop bipolar illness after age 50, following exposure to a tricyclic or steroidal medication, the heritable component may be less important.

Family history data suggest that bipolar disorders have a higher threshold of liability than unipolar disorders (Perris, 1982), perhaps reflecting greater heritability. Another interpretation, favored by Gershon *et al.* (1975), is that bipolar and unipolar affective disorders share a common genetic diathesis, bipolar disorders having higher threshold of expression. The positive response of early onset unipolar cases to lithium salts (Bowden, 1981) is consistent with this hypothesis.

Kraepelin (1921) was alerted by his experience with patients' families to the presence of attenuated forms of the disorders among close kin. He noted that the temperamental characteristics of cyclical moodiness in some relatives represent the same morbid process as manic–depressive psychosis, albeit in an attenuated form. However, his approach was methodologically flawed by the fact that temperamental peculiarities were described in the family members of known manic–depressives. The more critical question is whether cyclothymic probands, chosen without regard to family history, will exhibit bipolar family history in excess of that expected by chance. This aim has been accomplished in research conducted in Jerusalem (Gershon & Liebowitz, 1975), Memphis (Akiskal *et al.*, 1977), and Buffalo, New York (Depue *et al.*, 1981). The strongest evidence that cyclothymic and related depressive temperamental disorders represent *formes frustes* of manic–depressive illness is provided by their prevalence in monozygotic pairs, where one of the co-twins has a classical bipolar diagnosis (Bertlesen *et al.*, 1977). That these cyclothymic conditions predispose to major affective episodes is seen in prospective observations demonstrating the occurrence of such episodes in nearly a third (Akiskal *et al.*, 1977).

Within the bipolar spectrum, different clinical forms of the disorder appear to be on a quantitative continuum with different thresholds of expression. The distinction between bipolar II and bipolar III (unipolar II), for instance, is based on whether hypomania is spontaneous or pharmacologically induced.

Family history merely suggests a relationship between particular phenotypes and genotypes. In such studies the behavioral phenotype is used as the best approximation for inferring the presence of a genotype. Another approach—the high-risk biochemical paradigm (see, e.g., Buchsbaum, Coursey, & Murphy, 1976)—uses a biochemical measure such as platelet MAO to predict phenotypic and family history characteristics. The high-risk behavioral strategy—based on detailed examination of behavioral phenotypes— remains the more orthodox strategy at this writing. Using this strategy, a University of Tennessee study (Akiskal, Downs, Jordan, Watson, Daugherty, & Pruitt, in press) demonstrated the presence of spectrum disorders in the juvenile offspring and sibs of known bipolar probands. As shown in Table 22-2, nearly 90% of this large group of referred symptomatic subjects met the criteria for milder phenotypical forms of bipolar disorder, including cyclothymia, dysthymia, and polysubstance abuse. We tentatively consider polysubstance abuse in the families of bipolars as a phenotypic variant of bipolar illness because, during a mean follow-up of 3 years, all 11 subjects

Table 22-2
Types of Onset in the Referred Children and Younger Siblings of Bipolar Patients[a]

Types of onset	N (total = 68)	Percentage
Affective onset (N = 57)		
Acute		
Major depressive episode	24	35.3
Manic episode	8	11.8
Mixed state	3	4.4
Intermittent		
Dysthymic disorder	12	17.7
Cyclothymic disorder	10	14.7
Undiagnosed at onset (N = 11)		
Polysubstance abuse	11	16.2

[a]Summarized from Akiskal, Downs et al. (1985).

with such abuse history evidenced clear-cut evidence for cyclothymic and dysthymic disorders.

Pharmacologic Considerations

Current evidence indicates that cyclothymic (Akiskal, Khani, & Scott-Strauss, 1979), bipolar II (Dunner, 1983), and unipolar II (Kupfer et al., 1975) disorders, just like classical bipolar I disorder, respond to lithium carbonate. Although one must be cautious in using pharmacologic response as a validating principle, the fact that the range of proved effectiveness of lithium in psychiatry (Jefferson, Greist, & Ackerman, 1983) is largely limited to bipolar disorder can be considered as partial support for the concept of a bipolar spectrum. Finally, pharmacologic mobilization of hypomania is shared by cyclothymic conditions (Akiskal et al., 1977), dysthymic and major depressive disorders with bipolar family history (Akiskal et al., 1983; T. L. Rosenthal et al., 1981), and classical bipolar I forms of manic–depressive illness (Bunney, 1978).

Neurobiological Considerations

We may have exhausted the limits of phenomenological, family, and twin studies, and course variables as far as further delineation and dissection of the bipolar spectrum, and it would seem that newer thrusts in this area must come from neurobiology. Neuroendocrine strategies, polysomnography, and assaying receptor sensitivity with agonists or antagonist substances are the most promising research tools at this time.

Although failure of serum cortisol to suppress following administration of dexamethasone probably represents a state abnormality (Carroll, 1982), other neuroendocrine abnormalities such as blunted thyrotropin response to thyrotropin-releasing hormone stimulation may represent trait factors (Loosen & Prange, 1982). Shortened REM latency (Kupfer, Foster, & Coble, 1978) and its cholinergic induction (Sitaram, Nurnberger, Gershon, & Gillin, 1982) could also represent trait abnormalities. The absence of normalization of REM abnormalities following clinical recovery, and the correlation of such REM abnormalities in dysthymia with bipolar family history (Akiskal, 1983c, 1984) is in line with this suggestion. Interestingly, a University of Tennessee study (Akiskal, 1984) has demonstrated that hyperthymic subjects who have never been manic—like dysthymic subjects not in the midst of a major depressive episode—exhibit shortening of the REM latency. Many patients with dysthymic, cyclothymic, and hyperthymic disorders meet DSM-III criteria for borderline personality. The adjacent figure shows that the REM latencies of these borderline patients are indistinguishable from those of affective controls, but very different from those of nonaffective (histrionic and sociopathic personality) and nonpsychiatric controls (Akiskal, Yerevanian, Davis, King, & Lemmi, 1985). This means that many so-called borderline personalities represent borderline manic–depressive psychosis.

Another promising area in the neurobiological dissection of affective

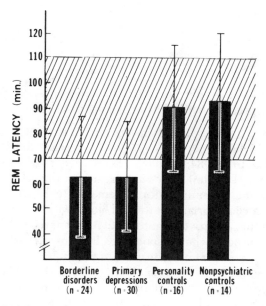

Figure 22-1. *REM latency in DSM-III borderline, depressive, and control groups (Scheffé; p < .05). Hatched area represents the range for published norms. Reprinted with permission from Akiskal (1984).*

disorders is the field of brain neuroreceptor sensitivity. Earlier attempts at correlating manic and depressive subtypes with alterations of various bio- genic amines and their metabolites such as MHPG and 5-hydroxyindole- acetic acid (5-HIAA) have not led to definitive findings. The simplicity of those models was deceptive because it excluded the influence of other neurotransmitter systems such as acetylcholine modulation of emotion and behavior (Janowsky, El-Youssef, Davis, & Sekerke, 1972) and omitted recep- tor supersensitivity or subsensitivity as important factors. Variations in receptor sensitivity often cannot be detected by measurement of neuro- transmitters or their metabolites in the periphery (cerebrospinal fluid, blood, urine). Challenging receptor function with agonists or antagonists provides a more sensitive indicator of pathogenesis and vulnerability. Recent work using clonidine—a noradrenergic receptor agonist—suggests down-regula- tion or "numbing" state in affective disorders (Siever & Uhde, 1981); the numbing persists after treatment of the episode and suggests a trait abnor- mality. The more provocative development in receptor physiology is the recent finding (Nadi, Nurnberger, & Gershon, 1984) of increased density of muscarinic acetylcholine receptors from skin fibroblasts in individuals with major affective disorders and their ill relatives with a spectrum of major *and* minor affective disorders. This finding, which is in line with abnormalities in REM latency and cholinergic REM induction, supports the notion of choli- nergic supersensitivity in depression.

Comparison of the Concepts of Bipolar and Schizophrenia Spectrum Disorders

Before we conclude, it would be instructive to contrast what we know about the bipolar spectrum with that of the schizophrenia spectrum.

1. The notion of a schizophrenia spectrum (Meehl, 1962) is contested by some (Abrams & Taylor, 1983; Stevens, 1981) whereas others emphasize its heuristic value (Khouri, 1984; Khouri, Haier, Rieder & Rosenthal, 1980). The phenomenological dissimilarities are greater in the schizophrenia spec- trum, and the common denominator(s) remains to be delineated. In the bipolar spectrum, cyclical variation of mood along with other vital functions such as sleep, appetite, and psychomotor activity is shared by all forms and is the target morbid process that responds to lithium. Kraepelin (1921) and Bleuler (1950) observed that autism or "retrenchment" is a common out- come to all forms of schizophrenia. Nonetheless, the phenomenological disparities between the paranoid and nonparanoid forms suggest more than one common denominator. Emotional flatness (expressed or nonexpressed) and psychosis are two other candidates. Emotional disintegration manifested as breakup in previous affective links and emotional distancing and disrup-

tion in the processes that modulate the physical expression of emotions are shared by some relatives of schizophrenics; however, available studies do not discriminate between relatives of paranoids and nonparanoids. Psychosis defined as proneness to experience perceptual deceptions such as hallucinations, delusion of self-reference, and persecution is also shared by some relatives of schizophrenics, but whether retrenchment from reality, emotional disintegration, and psychosis are trait or state disturbances remains an unresolved question. All of these dilemmas may explain why schizotypal disorder remains less well defined than cyclothymic disorder and its variants.

2. The pharmacological bridge does not exist in the schizophrenia spectrum due to the lack of well-defined phenomenological targets and the relative nonspecificity of the antipsychotic agents compared with lithium salts.

3. Neurobiological abnormalities such as reduced MAO activity and ventricular enlargement have been found only in small subgroups of schizophrenic patients (Buchsbaum & Haier, 1983) and do not seem to be shared by the entire spectrum. By contrast, abnormalities in REM latency (Akiskal, 1983a), arecoline REM induction (Dube et al., 1985), and increased density of muscarinic receptors in skin fibroblasts (Nadi et al., 1984) seem to be shared by most forms of primary affective disorders, but generally not by anxiety disorders.

It is likely that bipolar illness represents a more discrete and less heterogeneous psychopathologic entity than schizophrenia. This means that affective disorder research might be at an advantage in terms of delineating neurobiological mechanisms common to the entire bipolar spectrum.

Summary

Four criteria are required to demonstrate relatedness between specific behavioral disorders.

1. Shared core phenomenological disturbances: In the bipolar spectrum, cyclical fluctuations in mood and circadian functions of sleep, libido, appetite, and psychomotor activity span a spectrum from the paranoid, disorganized manic to the episodically and intermittently depressed individual with pharmacologically mobilized hypomania.

2. Overlapping family histories with increased risks of other spectral disorders for each discrete entity within the spectrum: Several studies have met this criterion.

3. Shared response to the same pharmacologic agents: We are not suggesting that a genetic relationship exist between two disorders if they respond to the same agent; however, the pharmacologic mobilization of hypomania by antidepressants and the prophylactic response to lithium in

cyclothymia and bipolar II, unipolar II disorders suggests shared neuropharmacologic substrates with more classical bipolar disorders.

4. Neurobiological abnormalities such as shortened REM latency and cholinergic supersensitivity: These appear shared by almost all the phenotypes within the bipolar spectrum.

Such developments hold the promise of identifying milder phenotypes of bipolar disorder during an early phase of its inception—using trait markers to distinguish them from phenocopies—with the ultimate purpose of halting their progression to more seriously disruptive mood swings. This is of great public health interest, given the fact that milder affective temperamental disorders seem to be associated with achievement and creative thrust, while the extreme expressions of the bipolar spectrum cause major disruption in family life and serious morbidity and mortality.

REFERENCES

Abrams, R., & Taylor, M. A. (1983). The genetics of schizophrenia: A reassessment using modern criteria. *American Journal of Psychiatry, 140,* 171–175.

Akiskal, H. S. (1979). A biobehavioral approach to depression. In R. A. Depue (Ed.), *The psychobiology of depressive disorders: Implications for the effects of stress.* New York: Academic Press.

Akiskal, H. S. (1983a). The bipolar spectrum: New concepts in classification and diagnosis. In L. Grinspoon (Ed.), *Psychiatry update: The American Psychiatric Association Annual Review.* Washington, DC: American Psychiatric Press.

Akiskal, H. S. (1983b). Diagnosis and classification of affective disorders: New insights from clinical and laboratory approaches. *Psychiatric Developments, 1,* 123–160.

Akiskal, H. S. (1983c). Dysthymic disorder: Psychopathology of proposed chronic depressive subtypes. *American Journal of Psychiatry, 140,* 11–20.

Akiskal, H. S. (1984). Characterologic manifestations of affective disorders: Toward a new conceptualization. *Integrative Psychiatry, 2,* 83–88.

Akiskal, H. S., Bitar, A. H., Puzantian, V. R., Rosenthal, T. L., & Walker, P. W. (1978). The nosological status of neurotic depression: A prospective three-to-four year examination in light of the primary–secondary and unipolar–bipolar dichotomies. *Archives of General Psychiatry, 35,* 756–766.

Akiskal, H. S., & Cassano, G. B. (1983). The impact of therapeutic advances in widening the nosologic boundaries of affective disorders: Clinical and research implications. *Pharmacopsychiatry, 16,* 111–118.

Akiskal, H. S., Djenderedjian, A. H., Rosenthal, R. H., & Khani, M. K. (1977). Cyclothymic disorders: Validating criteria for inclusion in the bipolar affective group. *American Journal of Psychiatry, 134,* 1227–1233.

Akiskal, H. S., Downs, J., Jordan, P., Watson, S., Daugherty, D., & Pruitt, D. B. (1985). Prospective course of affective disturbances in the referred children and younger sibs of manic–depressives. *Archives of General Psychiatry, 42,* 996–1003.

Akiskal, H. S., Khani, M. K., & Scott-Strauss, A. (1979). Cyclothymic temperamental disorders. *Psychiatric Clinics of North America, 2,* 527–554.

Akiskal, H. S., & McKinney, W. T., Jr. (1975). Overview of recent research in depression: Integration of ten conceptual models into a comprehensive clinical frame. *Archives of General Psychiatry, 32,* 285–305.

Akiskal, H. S., & Puzantian, V. R. (1979). Psychotic forms of depression and mania. *Psychiatric Clinics of North America, 2,* 595–617.

Akiskal, H. S., Walker, P. W., Puzantian, V. R., King, D., Rosenthal, T. L., & Dranon, M. (1983). Bipolar outcome in the course of depressive illness: Phenomenologic, familial and pharmacologic predictors. *Journal of Affective Disorders, 5,* 115–128.

Akiskal, H. S., & Webb, W. L. (1983). Affective disorders. Part I. Recent advances in clinical conceptualization. *Hospital and Community Psychiatry, 34,* 695–702.

Akiskal, H. S., Yerevanian, B. I., Davis, G. C., King, D., & Lemmi, H. (1985). The nosologic status of borderline personality: Clinical and polysomnographic study. *American Journal of Psychiatry, 142,* 192–198.

American Psychiatric Association. (1980). *Diagnostic and statistical manual of mental disorders* (3rd ed.). Washington, DC: Author.

Angst, J. (1966). *Zur atiologie und nosologie endogener depressiver psychosen.* Berlin: Springer-Verlag.

Bertlesen, A., Harvald, B., & Hauge, M. (1977). A Danish study of manic-depressive disorders. *British Journal of Psychiatry, 130,* 338–351.

Bleuler, E. (1950). *Dementia praecox or the group of schizophrenias* (J. Zinkin, Trans.). New York: International Universities Press.

Bowden, C. (1981). Lithium-responsive depression. *Comprehensive Psychiatry, 19,* 227–231.

Buchsbaum, M. S., Coursey, R., & Murphy, D. I. (1976). The biochemical high-risk paradigm: Behavioral and familial correlates of low platelet monoamine oxidase activity. *Science, 194,* 339–341.

Buchsbaum, M. S., & Haier, R. J. (1983). Psychopathology: Biological approaches. *Annual Review of Psychology, 34,* 401–430.

Bunney, W. E. (1978). Psychopharmacology of the switch process in affective illness. In M. A. Lipton, A. DiMascio, & K. F. Killam (Eds.), *Psychopharmacology: A generation of progress.* New York: Raven Press.

Carlson, G., & Goodwin, F. (1973). The stages of mania. *Archives of General Psychiatry, 28,* 221–228.

Carroll, B. J. (1982). Clinical applications of the dexamethasone suppression test for endogenous depression. *Pharmacopsychiatria, 15,* 12–24.

Cooper, J. E., Kendell, R. E., Gurland, B. J., Sharpe, L., Copeland, J., & Simon, R. (1972). *Psychiatric diagnosis in New York and London.* London: Oxford University Press.

Depue, R. A., & Monroe, S. M. (1978). The unipolar–bipolar distinction in the depressive disorders. *Psychological Bulletin, 85,* 1001–1029.

Depue, R. A., Slater, J. R., Wolfsetter-Kaush, M., Klein, D., Coplerud, E., & Farr, D. (1981). A behavioral paradigm for identifying persons at risk for bipolar depressive disorders: A conceptual framework and five validation studies (Monograph). *Journal of Abnormal Psychology, 90,* 381–437.

Dube, S., Kumar, N., Ettedgui, E., Pohl, R., Johns, D., & Sitaram, N. (1985). Cholinergic REM-induction response: Separation of anxiety and depression. *Biological Psychiatry, 20,* 408–418.

Dunner, D. L. (1983). Subtypes of bipolar affective disorder with particular regard to bipolar II. *Psychiatric Developments, 1,* 75–85.

Egeland, J. A. (1983). Bipolarity: The iceberg of affective disorders. *Comprehensive Psychiatry, 24,* 337–344.

Falconer, D. S. (1967). The inheritance of liability to diseases with variable age of onset, with particular reference to diabetes mellitus. *Annals of Human Genetics, 31,* 1–20.

Feighner, J. P., Robins, E., Guze, S. B., Woodruff, R. A., Winokur, G., & Muñoz, R. (1972). Diagnostic criteria for use in psychiatric research. *Archives of General Psychiatry, 26,* 57–63.

Fieve, R. R., & Dunner, D. L. (1975). Unipolar and bipolar affective states. In F. Flach & S. Draghi (Eds.), *The nature and treatment of depression.* New York: Wiley.

Gershon, E. S. (1978). The search for genetic markers in affective disorders. In M. A. Lipton, A. DiMascio, & K. F. Killam (Eds.), *Psychopharmacology: A generation of progress.* New York: Raven Press.

Gershon, E. S., Baron, M., & Leckman, J. F. (1975). Genetic models of the transmission of affective disorders. *Journal of Psychiatric Research, 12,* 301–317.

Gershon, E. S., Hamovit, J. R., Guroff, J. J., Dibble, E., Leckman, J. F., Sceery, W., Targum, S. D., Nurnberger, J. J., Golden, L. R., & Bunney, W. L. (1982). A family study of schizoaffective, bipolar I, bipolar II, unipolar and normal control probands. *Archives of General Psychiatry, 39,* 1157–1167.

Gershon, E. S., & Liebowitz, J. H. (1975). Sociocultural and demographic correlates of affective disorders in Jerusalem. *Journal of Psychiatric Research, 12,* 37–50.

Janowsky, D. S., El-Youssef, M. R., Davis, J. M., & Sekerke, H. (1972). A cholinergic–adrenergic hypothesis of mania and depression. *Lancet, 2,* 6320.

Jefferson, J. W., Greist, J. H., & Ackerman, D. L. (1983). *Lithium encyclopedia for clinical practice.* Washington, DC: American Psychiatric Press.

Khouri, P. J. (1984). Toward a validation of the concept of borderline schizophrenia. *Comprehensive Psychiatry, 25,* 367–371.

Khouri, P. J., Haier, R. J., Rieder, R. O., & Rosenthal, D. (1980). A symptom schedule for the diagnosis of borderline schizophrenia: A first report. *British Journal of Psychiatry, 137,* 140–147.

Klerman, G. L. (1981). The spectrum of mania. *Comprehensive Psychiatry, 22,* 11–20.

Kraepelin, E. (1921). *Manic–depressive insanity and paranoia.* Edinburgh: E. & S. Livingstone.

Kukopulos, A., Caliani, B., Tundo, A., Minnai, G., Floris, G., Reginaldi, D., & Tondo, L. (1983). Rapid cyclers, temperament and antidepressants. *Comprehensive Psychiatry, 24,* 249–258.

Kupfer, D. J., Foster, F. G., & Coble, P. (1978). The application of EEG sleep for the differential diagnosis of affective disorders. *American Journal of Psychiatry, 135,* 69–74.

Kupfer, D. J., Pickar, D., Himmelhoch, J. M., & Detre, T. (1975). Are there two types of unipolar depression? *Archives of General Psychiatry, 32,* 866–871.

Leonhard, K. (1957, trans. 1979). *The classification of endogenous psychoses* (5th ed.). New York: Irvington Publishers.

Lloyd, C. (1980). Life events and depressive disorder reviewed. II. Events as precipitating factors. *Archives of General Psychiatry, 37,* 541, 548.

Loosen, P. T., & Prange, A. J. (1982). Serum thyrotropin response to thyrotropin-releasing hormone in psychiatric patients: A review. *American Journal of Psychiatry, 139,* 405–416.

Meehl, P. E. (1962). Schizotaxia, schizotypal, schizophrenia. *American Psychologist, 17,* 827–838.

Nadi, N. S., Nurnberger, J. J., & Gershon, E. S. (1984). Muscarinic cholinergic receptors on skin fibroblasts in familial affective disorder. *New England Journal of Medicine, 311,* 225–230.

Perris, C. (1966). A study of bipolar (manic–depressive) and unipolar recurrent depressive psychoses. *Acta Psychiatrica Scandinavica, Supplementum, 253.*

Perris, C. (1982). Depression: Pointers to a hereditary factor in its etiology. In J. Korf & L. Pepplinkhuizen (Eds.), *Depression: Molecular and psychologically based therapies—an integrative view.* Drachten: TGO Foundation.

Reich, T., Cloninger, C., & Guze, S. B. (1975). The multifactorial model of disease transmission. I. Description of the model and its use in psychiatry. *British Journal of Psychiatry, 127,* 1–10.

Robins, E., & Guze, S. B. (1970). Establishment of diagnostic validity in psychiatric illness: Its application in schizophrenia. *American Journal of Psychiatry, 126,* 983–987.

Rosenthal, D. (1970). *Genetic theory and abnormal behavior.* New York: McGraw-Hill.

Rosenthal, T. L., Akiskal, H. S., Scott-Strauss, A., Rosenthal, R. H., & David, M. (1981). Familial and developmental factors in characterological depressions. *Journal of Affective Disorders, 3,* 183–192.

Siever, L. J., & Uhde, T. W. (1981). New studies and perspectives on the noradrenergic receptor system in depression: Effects of the α_2-adrenergic agonist clonidine. *Biological Psychiatry, 19,* 23–26.

Sitaram, N., Nurnberger, J. I., Gershon, E. S., & Gillin, J. C. (1982). Cholinergic regulation of mood and REM sleep: Potential model and marker of vulnerability to affective disorder. *American Journal of Psychiatry, 139,* 571–576.

Stevens, J. (1982). Neuropathology of schizophrenia. *Archives of General Psychiatry, 39,* 1131–1139.

Strober, M., & Carlson, G. (1982). Bipolar illness in adolescents with major depression: Clinical, genetic and psychopharmacologic predictors in a three- to four-year prospective follow-up investigation. *Archives of General Psychiatry, 39,* 549–555.

Taylor, M. A., & Abrams, R. (1980). Reassessing the bipolar–unipolar dichotomy. *Journal of Affective Disorders, 2,* 195–217.

Winokur, G., Clayton, P., & Reich, T. (1969). *Manic–depressive illness.* St. Louis, MO: C. V. Mosby.

CHAPTER 23

Implications of the Vulnerability Model for DSM-IV with Special Reference to Schizophrenia

Joseph Zubin

Introduction

It is generally agreed that DSM-III is atheoretical, steering a midcourse between the Scylla of theory and the Charybdis of practice. Despite this precarious balance, it is hoped that DSM-III will improve clinical practice by tightening the definitions of the categories of disorder, and will also improve research by specifying the characteristics of patients included in research designs so that replication becomes possible. However, if further progress is to be made, we must eventually incorporate the diagnostic schema into a theoretical structure. The purpose of this chapter is to review some of the more fruitful theoretical models that are now operative and try to integrate them into a superordinate vulnerability model that will incorporate the findings of each of the disciplines contributing to psychopathological knowledge. Methods for identifying the presence of the various specific disorder categories, based on the parameters of the vulnerability model, will be suggested as a new axis for DSM-IV. Before presenting this new axis, we shall briefly review the status of DSM-III from this new perspective.

Reliability

The first step in any classification schema is observation of the phenomena in the area of interest. Such observations have accumulated in psychopathology over the past 34 centuries; the specific phenomena of psychopathology observed by our predecessors form the matrix from which are drawn the specific symptoms, signs, syndromes, and individual items of

Joseph Zubin. Veterans Administration Medical Center and University of Pittsburgh School of Medicine, Pittsburgh, Pennsylvania.

psychopathology that constitute our various classification instruments (DSM-III, RDC, PSE, SADS, etc.). The standardization of these instruments has increased the reliability of our diagnoses, but has left validity relatively untouched. Thus, we are in the position of having developed a new, reliable thermometer, but do not yet know what it indicates.

Even the reliability of the new instruments has been called into question, since the individual items and symptoms of psychopathology have not yet been defined sufficiently to ensure that different interviewers have the same criteria in mind when deciding whether a given symptom or sign is actually present. We need research criteria for the individual items similar to the research criteria for diagnosis. Wing, Cooper, and Sartorius (1974) have gone a long way in providing such definition for many items in the glossary of their manual for the Present State Examination (PSE), but much still remains to be done.

To achieve this, we need to lay aside our rating scales and interviews once in a while and observe the patient the way our predecessors did which, in the process, provided us with phenomenological observations that we have codified into our interviews.

Are Rigorous Definitions Required?

One of the hopes of the authors of DSM-III was to introduce more rigor in the definition of the categories in the nomenclature. But is it necessary that a category be defined rigidly in a close-ended way, like a mathematical concept? If this were necessary, such a widely useful concept as "species," for example, would go by the board, as Julian Huxley (1940) has pointed out.

If biologists cannot define species rigorously, we need not be shamefaced that we cannot rigorously define schizophrenia, or for that matter, mental disorder itself. The test of a good definition is not ironclad rigor, but usefulness.

For the scientists who are interested in the disorder and its causes, approximate open-ended definitions are sufficient, since they are continuously testing and probing the borders of the definitions and extending them or contracting them as the facts warrant. For the clinician interested in the individual patient about whom decisions need to be made, a specific diagnosis is necessary, and that is why the Research Diagnostic Criteria (RDC) are so necessary, even though they are still in the research stage.

Validity

We cannot be satisfied with reliability alone—we must also ask whether our judgments are valid. Of the four types of validity—predictive, construct, concurrent, and content (Cronbach & Meehl, 1955; MacCorquodale & Meehl, 1948)—we will deal only with the first two—predictive and construct validity, since concurrent validity is really a type of reliability and content validity refers to whether the measure covers adequately the entire area under investigation.

Predictive Validity

Outcome and course of the disorder provide criteria for the predictive validity of the diagnosis. Thus, if the diagnosis of affective disorder leads to a more rapid release than the diagnosis of schizophrenia, this can be taken as a vindication of the diagnosis, since this is the outcome we would expect. The narrower definition of schizophrenia, according to DSM-III, for example, may indeed lead to a greater homogeneity in outcome in the category of schizophrenia as well as in the complementary category of schizophreniform psychosis. It would be expected that many patients with the strict definition of schizophrenia required by DSM-III would tend to have a poor outcome, since chronicity is built into the definition of strict schizophrenia and, similarly, many of the schizophreniform patients would tend to have a good outcome, since they comprise individuals who have not yet or are not likely to become chronic. But the results are not uniform for all the patients. There must be additional forces at work in the production of good and poor outcomes over and above the diagnostic label.

Construct Validity: Scientific Models of Etiology

What else do we expect patients in a given category to have in common besides similarity in outcome? These expectations constitute the constructs whose validity is sought. They have been embodied in a set of scientific models for etiology that have been classified in two domains: field theory domain, consisting of the ecological, developmental, and learning theory models, and the molecular or biological domain, consisting of genetic, internal environment, and neurophysiological models (Zubin, 1972). Each of these models leads to certain expectancies or hypotheses, and these have been postulated elsewhere (Zubin, 1972). Here we will give only brief examples of these expectancies.

Accepting the genetic model, we would, for example, expect the most valid diagnostic system to be the one that showed the highest transmission rate of schizophrenia in relation to consanguinity or the highest concordance rate in identical twins. A comparison of several diagnosticians (American, British, and Swedish) was made in the Gottesman and Shields twin study, and the highest concordance rate was found in Essen-Möller's diagnoses (Gottesman & Shields, 1972).

Accepting the ecological model, we would, for example, expect to find the highest rates of schizophrenia in individuals occupying the deprived, isolated, and oppressed ecological niches in our cities—and this indeed turns out to be the case.

Accepting the developmental model, we would, for example, expect the highest rates among those who, according to Sullivan and later verified by Kreisman (1970), never had a close or intimate friend, that is, had deviant friendship patterns in their adolescence.

Accepting the learning theory model, we would expect that families with deviant rearing patterns and individuals with negative reinforcement histories would give rise to more psychopathology.

Accepting the internal environment model, we would expect to find biochemical indicators such as monoamine oxidase differentials in schizophrenics and their relatives.

Accepting the neurophysiological model, we would expect to find deviant patterns in the processing of information input reflecting deviation in attention and arousal. These hypotheses have been tested by such techniques as reaction time, sensory integration, pupillography, skin conductance, and evoked potentials.

The recent discoveries in brain structure and function arising from the use of X-ray transmission scanning (CAT scans), positron emission tomography (PET), and nuclear magnetic resonance (NMR) have given neuropathology a new lease on life. It is to be expected that differences between patients and normals would be found in the anatomy and physiology of the brain by means of recent advances in the technology of brain scanning (Buchsbaum & Haier, 1983).

Each of these scientific models would require some modification of our diagnostic procedures in order to provide data for the construct validity of the diagnosis. Thus, the genetic model would require more careful interviewing methods of blood relatives to determine family incidence of mental disorder. The ecological model would require a more careful examination of the ecological niche the person occupies, stressing not only the generally accepted parameters such as socioeconomic status and crowding, but also the more subtle aspects of available opportunities for growth, privacy, and so forth, and their frustration. The developmental model would place more emphasis on premorbid history, and the learning theory model would require more careful surveys of reinforcement contingencies in the family, at work, and in leisure situations. The internal environment model would require a careful survey of body chemistry and metabolism along the lines dictated by recent findings, while the neurophysiological model would require the application of information processing theory with the specific laboratory techniques found to be differential between patients and normals as well as between patient groups. The application of brain scanning techniques would provide a more reliable method for detecting organicity as well as provide differential diagnosis between various categories of mental disorder (Zubin, 1985).

While these studies are still in status nascendi, it would be well to include an appendix to DSM-IV which would present the results of such studies in the form of an additional axis—a vulnerability axis. If this is done, it may be possible that DSM-X or some earlier version eventually will have included in its main body the results of this axis. These results, however, cannot come from large-scale studies, but must depend upon carefully conducted small-scale studies before they can become part of our corpus of certitude.

Vulnerability Model

That the various etiological models do not exist in isolation is so apparent that it hardly needs mention, despite the fact that many researchers as well as laboratories often ignore this fact. In order to provide an integrating model that would include the seven etiological models, a supraordinate vulnerability model has been suggested (Zubin & Spring, 1977). It consists of the following assumptions:

1. Schizophrenia occurs in vulnerable individuals when they are subjected to sufficient stress and strain environmentally through their life events or endogenously through their biochemistry, which may also be triggered by environmental life events.

2. When the stress induced by the life events surpasses the threshold of vulnerability, an episode develops, unless certain moderating variables absorb the stress and protect the individual, thus preventing the episode from developing. Notable among these moderating variables are the social network, ecological niche, and premorbid personality.

3. The episode ends when the stress subsides and the person returns to his premorbid level of adjustment, or nearly so. Since the occurrence of an episode is an overwhelming experience, there is a great likelihood that certain residual effects may persist. Whether these effects are to be attributed to schizophrenia itself or to iatrogenic, nosocomial, or ecogenic influences independent of schizophrenia is still unknown. Such factors as inability to find a job or loss of friends because of being labeled schizophrenic may be tangential rather than direct influences of the disorder.

4. If the premorbid level was satisfactory, the person is regarded as recovered—this is why good premorbids tend to do well.

5. If the premorbid level of adjustment was precarious (but not psychotic), the person may be regarded erroneously as still unrecovered—this may be the reason why poor premorbids tend to be regarded as doing poorly.

To summarize, the only permanent characteristic of the schizophrenics is their vulnerability; their episodes are transient.

Chronic Schizophrenia

One of the most controversial aspects of the new view regarding the vulnerability approach to mental disorders, especially schizophrenia, is the question of chronicity. If schizophrenia is an episodic disorder, how can we explain the apparent frequency of chronic schizophrenics? Is chronicity an artifact, or is it a natural sequence in the course of the disorder?

Though the incidence of chronics is relatively small, they accumulate over time to yield a high prevalence. Even of those appearing to be chronic, some 30%, according to Bleuler's (1978) data, remain needlessly in the hospital because they have nowhere else to go. Is it possible that chronic schizophrenia could be a psychosocial artifact caused by the psychosocial consequences of acute attacks of illness rather than a natural sequence in the development of the illness? The symptomatology of schizophrenia can be classified into positive and negative categories (Cromwell, 1982; Crow, 1980, 1981; Strauss, Carpenter, & Bartko, 1974; Wing, 1978).

The acute schizophrenics are characterized by largely positive symptoms and the chronics by mostly negative symptoms even though some patients possess both types of symptoms. Positive symptoms refer to the presence of overtly deviant characteristics, for example, hallucinations, delusions, thought disorder, incoherent speech, and other florid symptoms. Negative symptoms refer to the absence of behavior expected in a normal individual: capacity for emotional involvement, activity, drive, speech, social interaction, clarity of thought and movement, attention to personal appearance, self-support, psychosexual inclinations, and other socially expected responses. Deviations in these normally expected behaviors constitute the clinical poverty syndrome. But are these negative symptoms necessarily the result of schizophrenia? First, these negative symptoms may have characterized some of the individuals in their premorbid status, and it is no surprise to find these traits still present after the episode ends. About 70% of the schizophrenics in Bleuler's (1978) data fall into this category. Some of these negative symptoms may be prodromal, appearing in the incipient stages of an already developing episode. It is often difficult to differentiate between premorbid characteristics and prodromal characteristics. From the point of view of vulnerability theory, there is no need to make this differentiation, since it is likely that the prodromal symptoms would disappear with the end of the episode and only the premorbidly based characteristic would remain.

Furthermore, there is a group of patients whose deviant behavior may have developed while in the hospital. If such behavior persists after their discharge, it is mistakenly regarded as the residual consequence of the disorder rather than merely of incarceration.

We had thought that we were alone in regarding chronic schizophrenia as an artifact and perhaps as a temporary aberration which may eventually disappear if proper preventive methods are applied. To our surprise, Luc Ciompi (1980) contends, as we do, that chronic schizophrenia could be mainly a psychosocial artifact caused by the psychosocial consequences of acute attacks of illness.

Ciompi argues as follows: Most of the negative symptoms reflect hospitalism and institutionalism. They occur not only in mental hospitals, but in prisons, understaffed nursing homes, and wherever monotony and stimulus deprivation obtain, and often disappear under stimulation. These negative symptoms are not limited to schizophrenics, and it is often difficult to tell in the long-term wards what the diagnosis of the ward residents originally was.

A more detailed analysis of the nature of negative symptoms leads to the problem of the etiology and fate of negative symptoms. The most generally accepted notion about negative symptoms is their persistence, that is, why they have tended to become associated with chronic schizophrenia. But has the permanency of negative symptoms been established?

One strategy, advocated by Will Carpenter and others (1985) is to try out a variety of strategies to eliminate, if possible, the negative symptoms, since they seem to be the big stumbling block in the recovery from chronicity.

Depending upon the probable source of the negative symptoms, the following strategies are proposed:

1. If the positive symptoms are a response to the psychosis resulting from self-preoccupation or from a defense maneuver to dampen its impact, they should generally disappear with the recovery from the episode provided they have not been stamped in by nosocomial and/or iatrogenic influences.

2. If they are induced by drug treatment (akinesia, sedation), a change in the treatment regime seems indicated.

3. If they reflect the understimulation which Wing and Brown (1970) found to be the case in many instances, they can be eliminated by environmental manipulation.

4. If they are induced by the acute psychotic episode or postepisodically, proper therapeutic intervention should be found by clinical trial and error.

5. If these strategies fail to eliminate the negative symptoms, they could be regarded as genuine aspects of the schizophrenic process which gives schizophrenia its chronic characteristics. However, before accepting this conclusion, it would be of interest to determine whether these negative symptoms are not a reflection of the premorbid personality characteristics.

The data from the three European follow-up studies (Bleuler, 1978; Ciompi, 1980; Huber, Gross, Schüttler, & Linz, 1980) indicate that the general trend for schizophrenia is improvement rather than deteriorative chronicity, and if there is a true course for schizophrenia, it is an open life process rather than a unidirectional disease process, with general improvement and even in some instances eventual cure rather than deterioration: Witness the sporadic recovery of patients even after a lifetime of chronicity.

The long-term outcome of schizophrenia is often independent of genetic influence as measured by the presence or absence of family history of schizophrenia. This is in contrast to the acute onset of the illness which shows a relationship to family history, though not invariably. Since genetics does not relate to chronicity, environmental factors must be operative.

There is evidence for the association of chronicity and relapse with such psychosocial factors as life events, labeling, and highly critical families, but very little association with psychopathology and diagnosis. The iatrogenic, ecogenic, and nosocomial aspects of psychosocial factors have sufficient influence to maintain the state of chronicity or produce relapse. Modern family research, despite the heterogeneity of its methodological approaches, consistently shows that family-dynamic factors play a role in the prolongation and resumption of schizophrenic states (Zubin, in press).

There is still no generally accepted evidence today of any type of somatic,[1] biochemical, or other organic basis for the chronicity of schizophrenia, though there seems to be preliminary tentative evidence of such etiology for the acute, albeit, transient characteristics of the early phase of the illness.

After presenting the arguments in favor of considering chronicity as an artifact, Ciompi proceeds to list the counterarguments of those who regard chronicity as an essential element in the schizophrenic disorder and not an artifact. He doubts the validity of these counterarguments and gives his reasons for their invalidity. First, the existence of irreversible residual states or negative symptoms would argue for chronicity. In response, Ciompi points out that irreversibility may develop as a result of environmental influences and not necessarily as a result of persistent, functional, or organic disorder. The sporadic recovery from long-enduring chronicity contradicts the irreversibility hypothesis.

Second, the possibility of the biochemical or organic basis for chronic schizophrenia has to be considered. This argument is negated by the fact that chemical intervention is effective in acute schizophrenia with its positive symptoms, yet seems to be ineffective in the negative symptoms. These may require psychosocial intervention. This raises the question of whether the negative symptoms are an essential part of the schizophrenic disorders. There is a possibility that the negative symptoms may not be a reflection of the morbid state of schizophrenia, but may instead reflect the premorbid characteristics of the individual or his postmorbid or residual symptoms induced not by the disorder, but by the side effects of the disorder—labeling, self-derogation, inability to obtain jobs, and so on.

Third, it is sometimes difficult to differentiate between chronic and acute schizophrenia, since the former sometimes retains the positive symptoms alongside the negative ones. This counterargument is not easily resolved, and until the differential diagnostic problem of separating acute from chronic schizophrenia is solved, no conclusion can be reached. It has occurred to the present writer that there is a great likelihood that there exists a small group of patients [estimated at no more than 10% in Bleuler's (1978) data]

---

1. The evidence from CAT scans and PET scans is still not specific to schizophrenia.

who appear to be continuously in an episode and are continuously hospital-ized. These may be individuals who are so vulnerable that even the usual everyday stress that the human condition is subject to is sufficient to trigger a series of rapid episodes, with only brief, perhaps unnoticed, intervals of normality between them. These may be the individuals in whom the positive and negative symptoms comingle; the positive items reflect the onset, and the negative, the aftereffect of the brief episode. There is, of course, the possibility that a small proportion of this 10% is permanently chronic due to excess internal secretions or some other causal agents.

The fourth and final counterargument concerns the ubiquity of chronic-ity. Does this mean that chronicity is independent of the environmental influences that have been postulated? It is difficult to answer this question, but until it can be demonstrated that all the psychosocial factors can be dismissed as ineffective, the ubiquity argument cannot be decisive. Further-more, this ubiquity is not uniformly distributed across cultures and, hence, is most likely subject to environmental influences.

In summary, Ciompi's arguments and counterarguments as well as those of the author lead to the conclusion that the hypothesis that chronicity is an artifact is not negated and may be a tenable view to take. All in all, these arguments help buttress the claims that chronicity is not a natural, inevitable outcome of schizophrenia anymore than that poverty is a natural outcome of physical disorders.

It will become necessary to develop methods for ensuring that the small group of possible chronic schizophrenics satisfies the criteria for the continu-ous presence of the episode and are not pseudochronic. In other words, we need not only markers of vulnerability, but also markers that determine the boundaries of episodes. How this is to be accomplished is a matter for further research.

Treatment

Another problem that is not yet within the framework of DSM-III is the role of treatment in diagnosis. Since one of the chief purposes of diagnosis is selection of treatment, the role of diagnosis in the selection of a specific therapy from the ever-increasing number of options is a crucial aspect of the classification system and may require a special axis.

Perhaps the most prevalent treatment is the chemotherapeutic ap-proach, and it is well recognized that neuroleptics and chemotherapy in general are not a "cure" in the sense that, say, antibiotics cure infections. If the function of neuroleptic treatment is not cure, but mitigation by raising the threshold for the impact of life event stressors (or for the impact of the drop-off in the reinforcements required to maintain homeostatic coping ability) (Salzinger, 1980), it becomes clear why relapse occurs even under complete compliance with the drug regime. The blood level of the neuroleptic corresponding to the prescribed dosage may become too low to provide the protection against the impact of stress, or the traumatic impact of the stress (or drop in reinforcement frequency) may become so excessive that the protective nature of the dosage is no longer adequate.

The point to be stressed is not that the drug is needed to reduce psychotic manifestations, which are assumed to be continuously present and require continued suppression. Quite to the contrary. It is suggested that psychotic manifestations are *not* always present. These manifestations appear only in response to life event stressors, and it is the consequent stress which they produce that is being contained by the drug treatment or other types of treatment. The view that psychotic manifestations fluctuate spontaneously or randomly may be a reflection of an older concept that schizophrenia has a natural course of its own which has to play itself out. A more careful monitoring of the course of illness may reveal the existence of ministressors of everyday existence as well as the more dramatic maxistressors which account for exacerbation or relapse. Among these stressors are probably the side effects of the neuroleptic treatment itself, which also needs monitoring.

It is likely that just as chemotherapy can suppress or eliminate acute positive symptoms, psychosocial treatment can be utilized in the suppression, prevention, or elimination of the chronic negative symptoms. This may lend additional evidence for considering chronicity an artifact rather than a natural aspect of the schizophrenic disorder.

Difficulties in Diagnosing Mental Disorder

Aside from a lack of specified criteria, which is being corrected by RDC, there is an inherent weakness in diagnosing mental disorders, especially schizophrenia, because it is behaviorally or cognitively based and has no palpable somatic accompaniment as is often the case in physical disorders.

The behavior of mental patients is determined not only by their mental disorder, but also by their underlying premorbid personality and the conditions under which they function, and it is this combination of effects which is the presenting picture at the time of admission. If we could separate the behavior due to the mental disorder from the behavior due to the premorbid personality and to their interaction, we could recognize the focal disorder (schizophrenia) in isolation and probably find this factor characteristic of all similarly afflicted patients. What we perceive, however, is not the effect of the focal disorder, but the effect of the illness, which reflects the premorbid personality itself and its interaction with the disorder. This is why no two schizophrenics are alike—their focal disorder may be the same, but their illness is different. The relation between premorbid personality and psychopathology is still moot and involves such thorny issues as the distinction between "trait" and "state," but it might be valuable to adopt the null hypothesis and study premorbid personality as an independent variable or set of variables. In fact, studies in Lund, Sweden (Hagnell, 1966), have found that the premorbid personality, as measured by the Sjöbring method, does not relate to occurrence of mental disorder, but does color it once it appears. This is somewhat at loggerheads with the data on the same population when "lesional" aspects of personality were considered. Perhaps the Sjöbring personality variants lie essentially in the normal sphere and do not show the greater deviances that the lesional factors show.

It should be noted, however, that Gottesman and Shields (1972) found that 13 of 33 schizophrenics in their study of twins, or nearly 40%, were judged schizoid in their premorbid personality, and nine more were regarded as otherwise abnormal, bringing the total of deviant personalities to two-thirds. This is in agreement with the proportions of premorbidly deviant personalities in Bleuler's (1978) study. It is of interest that the concordance in Gottesman and Shield's twin study of monozygotic twins (1972) was highest in the pairs of monozygotic twins when the proband twin was schizoid and lowest when the proband was normal. It would be interesting to examine these data or see if when concordance versus discordance are the independent variables, the difference in the proportion of schizoids is still significant where the proband twin was schizoid and lowest when he or she was normal.

However, a comparison of Bleuler's (1978) premorbid personality data for his schizophrenics with the distribution of primary personality (normal vs. lesional) in the Lundby study (Zubin, Magaziner, & Steinhauer, 1983) has shown that although there is a relationship in the general population between premorbid personality and the occurrence of an episode, it is rather weak. The risk for schizophrenia in the deviant primary personalities in the general population is 9% compared to the risk of only 0.7% in the nondeviant. There must be other factors besides poor premorbid personality that facilitate the development of an episode in a presumably vulnerable individual, since only 9% of the deviant primary personalities develop episodes while 91% do not. Thus, even if we limit ourselves to genotypes only for the etiology of schizophrenia and accept the estimate for penetrance at .25, we would expect 36% of the deviant personalities to be vulnerable, that is, have the genotype, but only 9% developed the phenotype. What protects the remaining unaffected 27%?

Moderating Variables

It is clear that vulnerability alone does not ensure the occurrence of an episode. In order for an episode to occur in a vulnerable person, there is first a need for a sufficient amount of stress to exceed the coping ability of the person or to overcome his capacity for homeostatic containment of the stress. Once the stress threshold is breached, there are several more protective mechanisms that have to be overcome before the episode sets in. First is the social network surrounding the person. If it is sufficiently strong and supportive, the episode may be stillborn. Then there is the ecological niche the person occupies which provides physical, social, and economic facilities that may abort an episode. Third is the premorbid personality which, if it is sufficiently well developed, may provide the coping ability to ward off the episode. There are probably other factors that may also serve as moderating variables which may prevent or enhance the risk of the episode, depending upon their strengths.

Heterogeneity of Diagnostic Categories

The method of classification in DSM-III is polythetic rather than monothetic, since the RDC do not provide a homogeneous group for each diagnostic category. It is not unlikely that individuals in the same category may have no single criterion in common. This heterogeneity has led many workers to wonder whether schizophrenia is a unitary entity or is composed of several subgroups. The advent of the drug era has also brought a search for subtypes of the various diagnostic categories based on similarity in responses to specific drugs. This has opened up a demand for clustering techniques which would identify the individuals belonging to each of the various homogeneous subtypes. The frequent failure to replicate such findings has resulted in the conclusion that blind empirical search for such subtypes without any underlying testable hypotheses was a vain attempt at lifting oneself by one's own bootstraps. Fleiss and Zubin (1969) have pointed out that we need better mathematical models for typology before wasting our time in unchartered courses.

Furthermore, the differences between the dimensional approach and the typological approach are often vitiated by the factor analytic approach used in determining the dimensions used in clustering, since factor analysis makes assumptions which nullify typological assumptions (Fleiss & Zubin, 1969). For example, typology thrives on nonlinear relationships between variables and on discontinuous nonnormal distributions, assumptions that are incompatible with factor analysis. Consequently, it is foolhardy to expect to find types when the assumptions they are based on are not compatible with the techniques used to find the types.

There is another point of view, however, which would indicate that the conflict between dimensionality and typology is ephemeral. It can best be illustrated by an incident during a prior conference in diagnosis (Katz, Cole, & Barton, 1965). The same question had been raised then, 20 years ago, and the discussion had lasted till late in the evening. I couldn't fall asleep that night and, waking at 4:00 A.M., I turned on the TV only to discover that I had tuned into the Farmer's Hour and was listening to a lecture on pomology—how to tell good from bad apples! Apparently, the earlier method was to have an apple knocker tap the apple with his knuckles to determine whether it had too much water core and whether it was immature. Today, the reporter indicated, the method consists of conveying the apples on a conveyer belt under two sets of monochromatic lights. The amount of light absorbed is read off a dial which automatically determines the fate of the apple. Apparently, the typology of the apple knocker has been converted to a dimensional measure for classifying the apples. Upon further thought, I concluded that actually this dimensionality is probably the reflection of the genetic makeup of the apple seed—again a typological classification into good and bad genes. But genes accomplish their work by secreting certain biochemical substances (amino acids) in smaller or larger quantities. Again, the typological genetic classification has been altered to a continuous dimensionality. And so on. . . . Apparently the state of the art determines whether typology or dimensionality is to be preferred for classification. Furthermore, mathematical techniques can probably be developed for converting a typological classification into a dimensional one, and vice versa. Thus, the taxonomy depends upon the state of the art, and until we are forced to do otherwise by the weight of the evidence, we can hold on to a unitary concept of schizophrenia, despite its heterogeneity.

Metamorphosis of Schizophrenia

In addition to the impact of the new discoveries in etiology, there has also been a growing, though not yet generally accepted, change in attitude toward some mental disorders, especially schizophrenia and the affective disorder. Among these changes are the following (Zubin *et al.*, 1983):

1. Schizophrenia is becoming more benign in its outcome when compared to the outcome during the first third of this century—only about 10% of schizophrenics remain chronic, 30% recover and return to the community, and 60% oscillate back and forth in their episodes.

2. Schizophrenics with good premorbid personalities tend to have good outcomes, while the poor premorbids have poor outcomes. This is one of the most stable generalizations in psychopathology and has held true since Kraepelin's days.

3. Sudden onset leads to good outcome while gradual insidious onset leads to poor outcome is another stable generalization.

4. Schizophrenics are not schizophrenic all the time and a good number have but one episode, and even those who have more than one episode are only intermittently sick, often returning to a well state between episodes.

5. The contrast between the medical model for mental disorders and the vulnerability model can be epitomized as follows: The medical model regards the patient as a sick person who has intermittent well periods. The vulnerability model, on the other hand, regards the patient as an essentially healthy individual who has intermittent episodes.

These five factors have led to a veritable Kuhnian paradigmatic revolution in our thinking about schizophrenia. "Once a schizophrenic, always a schizophrenic," no longer is tenable, but what does differentiate the schizophrenic from others?

Markers of Mental Disorders

To test the validity of the vulnerability model, it becomes necessary to develop markers that would identify vulnerable individuals. In order to make such identification, it is necessary to discover certain characteristics that would serve as earmarks of vulnerability.

As used here, "markers" refers to specific types of performance or characteristics that identify individuals who either had a schizophrenic episode in the past, are having one presently, or have a high risk of developing an episode in the future. Ideally such a marker should be present only in those vulnerable to schizophrenia and not to any other mental disorder.

Table 23-1 shows the status of the various types of markers by their preepisode, episode, and postepisode status (Zubin & Steinhauer, 1981). Three types of markers are presented.

1. Vulnerability Markers (A, AA, D). In order to qualify as a vulnerability marker, it should be present in the preepisode, episode, and postepisode periods, and should also be present in greater frequency than chance in unaffected siblings. There are several types of vulnerability markers. "A" satisfies all the requirements for a vulnerability marker. "AA" is a marker that is present during all the three specified periods, but is not characteristic of siblings, and hence is probably nonfamilial. "D" is a vulnerability marker that disappears after the episode ends, but nevertheless is found in siblings. Apparently the episode extinguishes the marker.[2]

2. Episode Markers (B). This marker is present only during the episode and does not characterize unaffected siblings. The starting point in the search for episode markers is to assess the individuals who have already exhibited their vulnerability by having had or are presently having an episode. Once the marker is found, it may be applied to the general population to identify those who are undergoing an undetected episode or in the case of a vulnerability marker, those who are vulnerable (possess the marker) but have not yet, or never will, develop an episode. The episode marker can also

2. This is hypothetical since no such marker has yet been observed.

Table 23-1

Types of Markers by Preepisode, Episode, and Postepisode Status, and Presence in Sibling[a]

Marker	Preepisode	Episode	Postepisode	Sibling	Type of marker
A	+[b]	+	+	+	Vulnerability
AA	+	+	+	−	Vulnerability, nonfamilial
B	−	+	−	−	Episode
BB	−	+	−	+	?
C	+	−	+	+	Vulnerability
CC	+	−	+	−	Vulnerability, nonfamilial
D	+	−	−	+	Vulnerability, normalized by episode
DD	+	−	−	−	Vulnerability (nonfamilial), normalized by episode
E	−	+	+	−	Residual effect of episode
EE	−	+	+	+	?
F	+	+	−	+	Vulnerability, normalized by episode
FF	+	+	−	−	Vulnerability (nonfamilial), normalized by episode
G	−	−	+	−	Residual effect of episode
GG	−	−	+	+	?
H	−	−	−	−	Nondifferential for schizophrenia
HH	−	−	−	+	?Invulnerability, nonfamilial

[a]From Zubin and Steinhauer (1981, p. 486).

[b]+, marker present; −, marker absent; ?, uncertainty whether pattern occurs in nature.

be useful in patients undergoing an episode to determine whether the episode is still active or has terminated, since the episode marker waxes and wanes with the episode.

Since the starting point is usually a patient in the hospital with an episode, it is difficult to determine without suitable follow-up or follow-back, whether the marker under investigation is an episode marker or a vulnerability marker. To differentiate between the two types of markers, the status of the marker must be known in the preepisode period, during the episode, and postepisode.

3. Residual Markers (E, G). These markers may make their appearance during the episode, but persist after the episode. Whether they are indigenous to the disorder or are the result of iatrogenic, nosocomial, or ecogenic factors is still unknown.

In addition to these three types of markers, there are certain prodromal characteristics which usually appear when an episode is imminent. However, these prodromal characteristics are not always followed by an episode and, hence, cannot serve as markers, but as predictors of a possibly approaching episode.

4. Invulnerability Markers. The "HH" marker, which is present in sib-

lings of schizophrenics but absent in the probands themselves, presents an interesting possibility. Perhaps an HH marker is an indicator of invulnerability, a characteristic which is antithetical to schizophrenia, even as Meduna thought epilepsy was. Similarly, the AA marker that is absent in siblings in a proportion significantly below the general population, but is present in the probands in preepisode, episode, and postepisode intervals, may identify by its absence the individuals who are resistant to schizophrenia. A search for such markers would indeed be a worthwhile endeavor.

Markers and Information Processing

The search for markers of psychopathology had previously been erratic and unsystematic, based primarily on hoped for serendipity. For a more productive approach, the search should be guided by an overall rational strategy rather than by trial and error. Although there are no criteria for selecting the most suitable strategy, the information processing approach has found favor in many laboratories. The reason for this choice is based on the assumption that the deviant behavior observed in psychopathology may arise as a result of impairment or deviation in the information processing capacities of an individual (Kietzman, Zubin, & Steinhauer, 1983). Now, in the preinformation processing days, I would have been delighted to find a differential between patients and normals and add this differential to the repertoire of previous findings. From the point of view of information processing, the finding of a difference is now only the starting point. It becomes important to know just where, when, and how the differences developed in the pathway between the input of the stimulus and the emergence of the response.

Information processing consists of the manipulation of symbols and patterns (Simon, 1979), generated either endogenously (by, e.g., attention) or exogenously (from stimulation by the environment), which are stored and subsequently built into more complex structures. While the basic elementary operations underlying the global manipulation of symbols and patterns are not yet well understood (Posner & Boies, 1971), it is becoming clear that such processes as pattern recognition and comparison, preattentive processes, and primary automatic processes constitute important examples of information processing. Since one of the prevalent theories about the nature of schizophrenia and other mental disorders is that they are based on a cognitive dysfunction, or failure, at least in part, to deal normatively with symbols and patterns, it is understandable why we turn to information processing in our search for markers for schizophrenia.

The information processing approach delineates different stages in the pathway between stimulus and response. The basic notion is that all behaviors, even the simplest, pass through these different steps or stages and that by focusing upon specific stages, one is actually emphasizing different types of behaviors, for example, perception and memory. Occurring simultaneously with the behaviors of the different stages are other endogenous events or processes which are viewed as controlling the ongoing processing activities, for example, attentional factors which are known to have an influence on behavior.

Since mental activity must somehow be based on or related to brain activity, it becomes necessary to build a bridge between the two if we are ever to fully understand information processing. For this reason, we deal separately in our search for markers with, on the one hand, the manipulation of symbols and patterns which constitutes the flow of information and, on the other, with some of the possible parallel metabolic or neurophysiological correlates of the symbols and patterns. This approach which has developed in normal cognitive psychology has now begun to be applied to psychopathology. It is similar to the analogy that has been made between computer processing and behavioral processing, with a strong emphasis upon delineating various stages of processing, identifying the components presumed to be operating at these various stages, and exploring the role that endogenous events and processes (called control processes) have upon the stages and components of processing. The purpose of information processing research is to elucidate the various stages and control processes. Once it is possible to systematically describe and explain behavior in terms of stages and processes, one can consider how the different stages and processes are interrelated. Such knowledge could be used to explain complex behavioral reactions and responses in psychopathology.

Psychoses versus Personality Disorders

Another problem that the vulnerability model addresses is that of the difference between the precision in the definition of DSM-III categories in the functional disorders as compared to the more diffuse imprecision in the neurotic and personality disorders.

The functional disorders are characterized as states (episodes) which wax and wane. The only persistent trait in such cases is vulnerability, which is more or less a permanent characteristic of the individual. In the personality disorders, we deal with a persistent behavioral trait which is a permanent characteristic of the individual, and though it may be exacerbated or mitigated by life events and contingencies, the disorder itself is a persistent trait of the individual. The same probably holds true of neurosis. For this reason, these three conditions cannot be treated in the same way. Thus, we can expect complete recoveries in the functional disorders when the episode ends, but not to the same extent in personality and neurotic disorders, unless these long-lasting imbedded traits can be eliminated.

Implications of the Vulnerability Model for DSM-IV

With regard to predictive validity, the differentiation between the more narrow concept of schizophrenia in DSM-III and the previously held wider
concept has led to a more severe outcome for the narrower definitions.
Furthermore, the outcome in developing countries (World Health Organization, 1979) seems to be better than in developed countries. However, not all
the narrowly defined schizophrenics fail to improve, and not all the schizophreniform patients tend to improve. Furthermore, not all the patients in
developing countries do well on follow-up. The vulnerability model, in contrast with the medical model, introduces the concept of triggering life events
as a necessary precursor of an episode in a vulnerable person and further
provides for moderating variables to abort an episode even if it is incited by
life event stressors. These factors may explain the recurrence of episodes or
their nonrecurrence on follow-up. Thus, by considering the disorder as
episodic, to be triggered by external or internal stressors, and by considering
the role of moderating variables in the production or abortion of new
episodes, the contradictions in outcome do not appear as imponderable. This
model also explains why not all the good premorbid personalities fare well in
outcome and not all the poor premorbid personalities fare poorly. Other
moderating variables such as social networks and ecological niches need to be
considered.

The implication of the vulnerability hypothesis is that our diagnostic
studies need to regard schizophrenia as some type of allergy and try to
discover the contingencies that elicit it. In fact, a study of these contingencies
could become the basis for a new type of diagnosis based on a behavioral
analysis as Kanfer and Saslow (1965) have done. To this end, we need
measures of vulnerability to schizophrenia as well as markers for the beginnings and ends of episodes. Armed with such indicators, we may be able to
take the next giant step—that of preventing the vulnerable from developing
even a first episode. To this end, we need to develop criteria that would serve
for screening markers in the general population. Only in this way can we
find the vulnerable, and once detected, afford them preventive guidance.

Potential Vulnerability and Episode Markers

The potential markers for mental disorders were recently reviewed by
several authors (Usdin & Hanin, 1982; Zubin, 1979; Zubin & Steinhauer,
1981). There seems, therefore, no need to add another review at this time,
especially since progress in this field is not very rapid.

A dispassionate view of the marker field leads one to the conclusion that,
at the present time, there are no markers specific to a given category of
disorder, but there seem to be markers that occur more frequently in the
mentally ill during their episode, and some of them also occur in a significant

proportion of unaffected relatives. In developing a vulnerability axis, it becomes necessary to suggest which are the most promising markers at this time. In a previous publication (Zubin & Steinhauer, 1981), it was suggested that a useful classification of markers is provided by the etiological models from which they spring. Thus, the etiotype of the genetic model is the genotype, and each of the other models give rise to their specific etiotypes. Table 23-2 shows the distribution of potential vulnerability markers by etiotype.

Since the publication of Table 23-2, several additional markers have come to the fore. Among these are the Continuous Performance Task (CPT) (Kornetsky & Orzack, 1978), Span of Apprehension (Asarnow, Steffy, MacCrimmon, & Cleghorn, 1978), and Dichotic Listening with distraction (B. Spring, personal communication).

In connection with episode markers, it is important to note that in addition to utilizing follow-up studies to monitor the waxing and waning of episode markers, there is also a more direct route for determining immediately the presence or absence of an episode. This consists of challenging the individual with either a biochemical or a behavioral challenge, even as the presence of diabetes can be determined by the challenge of the glucose tolerance test. Janowsky, Davis, Huey, and Judd (1979) have proposed the

Table 23-2
Potential Vulnerability or Episode Markers by Etiotype

Model type	Etiotype	Potential vulnerability or episode markers
Genetic	Genotype	Consanguinity, HLA (human leukocyte antigen typing)
Ecological	Ecotype	Migration, social marginality, socioeconomic status, social isolation, emotional milieu of home, deviant social network
Developmental	Auxanotype	Season of birth (winter), postnatal cerebral damage, opthalmological defects in probands and relatives, absence of intimacy in adolescence
Learning theory	Mathetotype	Severe communication disorder, inability to develop adaptive behavior or benefit from past experience, inappropriate reinforcement, reaction time crossover index, cross-modality index
Internal environment	Chemotype	Levels of monomaine oxidase, dopamine β-hydroxylase, red blood cell catechol-*o*-methyltransferase, serum creatinine phosphokinase, platelet monoamine oxidase activity
Neurophysiological	Neurophysiotype	Pupillary response, smooth pursuit eye movements, event-related potentials
Neuroanatomical	Neuroanatomotype	Dilated ventricles, muscle anomalies, cerebral blood flow anomalies

Ritalin challenge test for this purpose and van Kammen and his colleagues (1982) have utilized the amphetamine challenge test. These challenges tend to exacerbate the clinical manifestations if the patient is still in his episode, but fail to do so if the episode is over.

The dexamethosone challenge test for depression is another way of probing for the presence of an episode. It is to be hoped that the tremendous effort now being exerted in the validation of these techniques will result in a useful group of reliable and valid instruments which could provide the basis of the vulnerability axis.

One type of behavioral challenge for probing the presence or absence of an episode, suggested by Alex Zautra (personal communication), can be useful not only in probing, but also in therapeutic strategies. Zautra divided schizophrenic patients into two task groups. One group was given the task of behaving in such a manner that the ward personnel would tend to favor their release from the hospital, while the other was given the task of behaving in such a manner that the staff would not countenance release. Some of the patients in the latter group reported when instructed to be ornery that they were in fact already behaving in a way which was likely to keep them in the hospital. Having become aware of their ornery behavior, to their own surprise as well as to the surprise of the staff, they turned about face and began to demonstrate their release worthiness. Apparently, many patients automatically continue their maladaptive behavior even after their episode has ended. A challenge of the type described here might serve to disturb and disrupt the maladaptive routine and indicate that the episode has passed (i.e., an episode marker) in addition to providing a therapeutic strategy.

Summary

The purpose of this chapter has been to provide the tentative beginnings of an additional axis for DSM-IV. As Rue Cromwell (1982) has pointed out, eight decades of exclusive devotion to symptomatology-based diagnoses is enough! We need to add the evidence for markers stemming from etiological investigations as an independent basis for making diagnoses. The search for markers which the vulnerability hypothesis has set into motion may provide the underpinnings of the vulnerability axis. The introduction of a systematic approach for discovering these markers under the general paradigm underlying information processing may yield a series of markers of the vulnerability, episode, residual, or prodromal type which may provide the cutting edge for more homogeneous categories in our nosology. Furthermore, by epidemiologic studies of the general population, the vulnerable individual may be detected even before the first episode strikes. Cases of undetected disorders may be found by the testing for episode markers, and evidence for past episodes can be revealed by testing for residual markers. The imminence of an episode may be detectable by the search for prognostic as well as prodromal factors. Thus, the proposed new axis, when fully developed, ought to provide a new systematic approach which may buttress present nosology by more objective evidence or provide new categories or subtypes that describe new but more homogeneous entities.

To accomplish this goal, a veritable academy of interdisciplinary colleagues is mandatory. One way of hastening the accomplishment of this approach is to convoke an academy of scientists covering the entire range of sciences dealing with the classification of human behavior, both normal and abnormal, to provide a taxonomy of behavior. Nearly all scientific fields deal with the problem of classification, but most prominent in this area, in addition to taxonomy, are philosophy of science, anthropology, psychiatry, psychology, sociology, statistics, and computer science. An academy of this type could serve the field of taxonomy even as the Academie Francaise serves the French language. It is clear that classification of mental disorders cannot be left to psychiatrists alone, even as ichthyology cannot be left to fishermen or navigation science to sea captains!

REFERENCES

Asarnow, R. F., Steffy, R. A., MacCrimmon, D. J., & Cleghorn, J. M. (1978). An attentional assessment of foster children at risk for schizophrenia. In L. C. Wynne, R. L. Cromwell, & S. Matthysse (Eds.), *The nature of schizophrenia: New approaches to research and treatment* (pp. 339–358). New York: Wiley.

Bleuler, M. (1978). *The schizophrenic disorders: Long-term patient and family studies.* New Haven, CT: Yale University Press. [Die Schizophrenen Geisstesstörungen im Lichte Langjähriger Kranken. Stuttgart: Thieme, 1972.]

Buchsbaum, M. S., & Haier, R. J. (1983). Psychopathology: Biological approaches. *Annual Review of Psychology, 34,* 401–430.

Carpenter, W. T., Jr., Heinrichs, D. W., & Alphs, L. D. (1985). Treatment of negative symptoms. *Schizophrenia Bulletin, 11,* 440–452.

Ciompi, L. (in press). Is chronic schizophrenia an artifact? Arguments and counterarguments. *Fortschritte der Neurologie und Psychiatrie,* 237–248.

Cromwell, R. (1982). Eight decades focused on symptom classification is enough: A discussion. In M. J. Goldstein (Ed.), *Preventive intervention in psychopathology: Are we ready?* (pp. 114–125). Washington, DC: U.S. Government Printing Office.

Cronbach, L. J., & Meehl, P. E. Construct validity in psychological tests. *Psychological Bulletin,* 1955, *52,* 281–302.

Crow, T. J. (1980). Molecular pathology of schizophrenia: More than one disease process? *British Medical Journal, 280,* 66–68.

Crow, T. J. (1981). Riposte: positive and negative schizophrenic symptoms and the role of dopamine. *British Journal of Psychiatry, 139,* 251–254.

Fleiss, J. L., & Zubin, J. (1969). On the methods and theory of clustering. *Multivariate Behavioral Research, 4,* 235–250.

Gottesman, I. I., & Shields, J. (1972). *Schizophrenia and genetics.* New York: Academic Press.

Hagnell, O. (1966). *A prospective study of the incidence of mental disorder.* Stockholm: Svenska Bokforlaget.

Huber, G., Gross, G., Schüttler, R., & Linz, M. (1980). Longitudinal studies of schizophrenic patients. *Schizophrenia Bulletin, 6,* 592–605.

Huxley, J. S. (1940). Introductory: Towards the new systematics. In J. S. Huxley (Ed.), *The new systematics*. (p. 11). London: Oxford University Press (Clarendon).

Janowsky, D. S., Davis, J. M., Huey, L., & Judd, L. L. (1979). Adrenergic and cholinergic drugs as episode and vulnerability markers of affective disorders and schizophrenia. *Psychopharmacology Bulletin, 15*, 33–34.

Kanfer, F. H., & Saslow, G. (1965). Behavioral diagnosis. *Archives of General Psychiatry, 12*, 529–538.

Katz, M., Cole, J. O., & Barton, W. E. (1965). *Classification in psychiatry and psychopathology*. Chevy Chase, MD: U.S. Department of Health, Education and Welfare.

Kietzman, M. L., Zubin, J., & Steinhauer, S. (1983). Information processing in psychopathology. In V. Sarris & A. Parducci (Eds.), *Perspectives in psychological experimentation: Towards the year 2000* (pp. 291–309). Hillsdale, NJ: Erlbaum.

Kornetsky, C., & Orzack, M. H. (1978). Physiological and behavioral correlates of attention dysfunction in schizophrenic patients. *Journal of Psychiatric Research, 14*, 69–79.

Kreisman, D. (1970). Social interaction and intimacy in preschizophrenic adolescence. In J. Zubin & A. M. Freedman (Eds.), *The psychopathology of adolescence* (pp. 299–318). New York: Grune & Stratton.

MacCorquodale, K., & Meehl, P. E. (1948). On a distinction between hypothetical constructs and intervening variables. *Psychological Review, 55*, 95–107.

Posner, M., & Boies, S. (1971). Components of attention. *Psychological Review, 78*, 391.

Salzinger, K. (1980). Behavioral mechanisms to explain abnormal behavior. *Annals of the New York Academy of Sciences, 340*, 66–87.

Simon, H. A. (1979). Information models of cognition. *Annual Review of Psychology, 30*, 369.

Strauss, J. S., Carpenter, W. T., Jr., & Bartko, J. J. (1974). The diagnosis and understanding of schizophrenia: Part III. Speculations on the processes that underlie schizophrenic symptoms and signs. *Schizophrenia Bulletin, 11*, 61–76.

Usdin, E., & Hanin, I. (1982). *Biological markers in psychiatry and neurology*. Oxford: Pergamon Press.

van Kammen, D. P., Bunney, W. E., Jr., Docherty, J. P., Marder, S. R., Ebert, M. H., Rosenblatt, J. E., & Rayner, J. N. (1982). d-Amphetamine-induced heterogeneous changes in psychotic behavior in schizophrenia. *American Journal of Psychiatry, 139*, 991–997.

Wing, J. K. (1978). The social context of schizophrenia. *American Journal of Psychiatry, 135*, 1333–1339.

Wing, J. K., & Brown, G. W. (1970). *Institutionalism and schizophrenia*. London: Oxford University Press.

Wing, J. K., Cooper, J. E., & Sartorius, N. (1974). *The description and classification of Psychiatric Symptoms*. London & New York: Cambridge University Press.

World Health Organization. (1979). *Schizophrenia—An international follow-up study*. New York: Wiley.

Zubin, J. (1972). Scientific models for psychopathology in the '70's. *Seminars in Psychiatry, 4*, 183–196.

Zubin, J. (1979). Chairman markers of vulnerability to mental disorders. *Psychopharmacological Bulletin, 15*, 7–49.

Zubin, J. (1985). Psychobiological markers for schizophrenia: State of the art and future perspectives. *Psychopharmacology Bulletin, 21*, 490–496.

Zubin, J. (in press). Possible Implications of the Vulnerability Hypothesis for the Psychosocial Management of Schizophrenia. In W. Boeker, & H. D. Brenner (Eds.). *Management of schizophrenia: Multidimensional concepts, psychosocial and cognitive treatments, work with relatives and autoprotective strategies*. Bern: Huber.

Zubin, J., Magaziner, J., & Steinhauer, S. (1983). The metamorphosis of schizophrenia: From chronicity to vulnerability. *Psychological Medicine, 13*, 551–571.

Zubin, J., & Spring, B. (1977). Vulnerability: A new view of schizophrenia. *Journal of Abnormal Psychology, 86*, 103–126.

Zubin, J., & Steinhauer, S. (1981). How to break the logjam in schizophrenia: A look beyond genetics. *Journal of Nervous and Mental Disease, 169*, 477–492.

CHAPTER 24

Biochemical Concepts of Schizophrenia

Craig N. Karson, Joel E. Kleinman, and Richard Jed Wyatt

Introduction

The notion that mental illness has its origin in neurochemical events has been embraced by leading neuropsychiatrists for over a century. An early, careful study at McLean Hospital of the biochemical constituents in urine of psychiatric patients was performed by Otto Folin. Folin (1904) states ". . . numerous publications on these subjects furnish abundant evidence of the existence of a widespread hope that chemical investigations will, perhaps, sooner or later yield a clearer understanding of these diseases than can be looked for from the other sciences that have been brought to bear on them." The successful pharmacological treatment of mental illness has subsequently lent support to the hypothesized link between biochemistry and psychiatric illness. A noteworthy example is the dopamine hypothesis of schizophrenia, which is based, in part, on the antipsychotic and antidopaminergic properties of the neuroleptic medications.

Although the pharmacological approach has yielded numerous hypotheses and therapeutic benefits, the biochemical basis of the schizophrenic syndrome remains elusive. This chapter reviews several biochemical hypotheses of schizophrenia which involve the following neurochemicals: dopamine, norepinephrine, serotonin, phenethylamine (PEA), L-γ-aminobutyric acid (GABA), endogenous opiates, and other peptides.

Craig N. Karson, Joel E. Kleinman, and Richard Jed Wyatt. Neuropsychiatry Branch, IRP, National Institute of Mental Health, Washington, DC.

Schizophrenia: Subtyping the Syndrome

Over the years the schizophrenic syndrome has been subdivided into many subtypes. This penchant for subtyping stems from the belief that subtypes may represent critical dimensions of schizophrenia or even different disorders. Unfortunately, problems with subtype validity, interrater reliability, and stability over time have led to some disenchantment with this notion.

One subtyping system that has been widely used has been the division of the schizophrenic syndrome into paranoid and nonparanoid subtypes. It is thought that the paranoid subtype is characterized by a relative absence of both thought disorder and affectual blunting (Kraepelin, 1919). Individuals with paranoid schizophrenia often have well-formed delusions and a later onset of illness.

Another phenomenological distinction has been drawn between certain types of signs and symptoms of schizophrenia. Those typical of the acutely psychotic state, such as hallucinations, delusions, and incoherent speech, have been termed "positive" symptoms. The crippling apathy, desocialization, and emotional blunting are often grouped together as "negative" or "defect" symptoms. Positive symptoms are said to be more responsive to neuroleptic treatment. Negative symptoms may be more resistant to neuroleptic treatment and are associated with chronicity, features of intellectual impairment, and evidence of structural brain abnormalities (reviewed by Crow, 1980). Hence, schizophrenic patients with few negative symptoms are thought to have a more favorable prognosis than those with more negative symptomatology. Most studies of the biochemical aspects of schizophrenia have concentrated on positive symptoms. With the current emphasis on negative symptomatology, including the development of rating scales (Andreasen & Olsen, 1982), it may become possible to study the biochemistry associated with these symptoms.

Brain imaging techniques can provide another method for subdividing the schizophrenic syndrome. The clearest example of this is provided by computerized axial tomography (CAT scan). Early studies with pneumoencephalograms had shown that a substantial number of schizophrenic patients had enlarged cerebral ventricles. This work was, however, not widely recognized. Nearly half a century later, Johnstone, Frith, Crow, Husband, and Kreel (1976) obtained CAT scans from 17 elderly schizophrenic patients to search for abnormalities of brain structure, such as those seen in dementias. What they found was that a significant proportion of the patients studied had large cerebral ventricles. Patients with large ventricles also did poorly on neuropsychological testing and had a tendency toward less positive and more negative symptomatology (Johnstone et al., 1976). Weinberger, Torrey, Neophytides, and Wyatt (1979) as well as others confirmed these findings in rigorous studies employing a substantial number of younger patients.

In summary, there are many concepts about subtypes of schizophrenia. In this chapter we will concentrate on the three systems often used in biochemical investigations of this disorder. These include the distinction between paranoid and nonparanoid schizophrenic patients, patients with and without large cerebral ventricular size, and positive or negative schizophrenic symptoms.

Monoamines in Schizophrenia

Dopamine, norepinephrine, serotonin, and phenylethylamine (PEA) are monoamines, also termed biogenic amines. Whereas dopamine and norepinephrine are metabolic products of the amino acid tyrosine, serotonin is produced by an analogous metabolic pathway from tryptophan. PEA is produced by the decarboxylation of phenylalanine. These monoamines and their enzymes of formation and degradation have been examined in many biochemical studies of schizophrenia. This section reviews the current status of the monoamine hypotheses of schizophrenia.

Dopamine

Ten years after the introduction of neuroleptic medications into the clinical practice of psychiatry, Carlsson and Lindqvist (1963) demonstrated the dopamine blocking properties of these agents. As receptor binding techniques developed, it was found that neuroleptics blocked dopamine receptors in direct proportion to their clinical potency (Creese, Burt, & Synder, 1976). Together this evidence suggests that the antipsychotic properties of neuroleptics result from blockade of dopamine receptors. Neuroleptic dopamine receptor blockade and the psychotogenic properties of amphetamine, which is an indirect dopamine agonist, form the evidentiary crux of the "dopamine hypothesis" of schizophrenia. This hypothesis states that increased dopaminergic activity in the brain accounts for the psychotic symptoms of the schizophrenic syndrome. Among the problems with this hypothesis, however, is that neuroleptics are effective in the treatment of many psychoses, not just schizophrenia. As a consequence, perhaps a "dopamine hypothesis of psychosis" might be a more appropriate term.

Since there are a number of brain dopamine systems (i.e., nigrostriatal, mesolimbic, mesocortical, hypothalamic, and retinal), the question arises as to which might be relevant to schizophrenia. Thus far, the mesolimbic system has been considered the most interesting because of preclinical studies indicating its relevance to motivation and affect (Stevens, 1973). Interest has also begun to focus on the mesocortical system for similar reasons, though the lack of standardized dissections and low concentrations of dopamine present in the cortex have presented some practical problems for researchers.

The question also arises as to which dopaminergic neuronal events may be relevant to schizophrenia. Is the putative abnormality in the dopamine system a problem of synthesis, degradation, release, or reuptake? Is it in the postsynaptic receptor or somewhere else? Recent research has focused on the dopamine receptor, but discoveries of dopamine receptor subtypes have complicated matters considerably. For instance, it has been shown that there are dopamine binding sites that activate adenylate cyclase (D_1 receptors) and those that do not (D_2 receptors) (Kebabian & Calne, 1976). It now appears, however, that D_2 receptors may actually inhibit dopamine-linked adenylate cyclase production (Table 24-1) (Stoof & Kebabian, 1981).

This examination of the complexities of studying human brain dopamine activity reveals the oversimplified and nonspecific nature of the dopamine hypothesis. If one line of investigation proves negative, another brain region, synaptic event, or receptor subtype opens up, making the hypothesis irrefutable. Consequently, the parameters of dopaminergic involvement in relation to the hypothesis should be specified a priori for each study. This same rigor should, in fact, apply to each biochemical hypothesis of schizophrenia, as the complexities outlined for dopamine exist for other neurochemicals as well.

PROLACTIN

Prolactin is a neurohormone secreted from the anterior pituitary having important effects on the female reproductive system and responding rapidly to stress in both men and women. Its secretion is inhibited by dopamine released from neurons with their cell bodies in the arcuate nucleus of the hypothalamus. The dopamine receptors of the anterior pituitary system seem to be comprised exclusively of D_2 receptors (Kebabian & Caine, 1976). Consequently there was hope that serum or plasma prolactin concentration could serve as an indicator of elevated brain D_2 activity in schizophrenia. Decreased serum or plasma prolactin concentrations would be expected if there is increased dopamine activity in the hypothalamic–pituitary axis. Three immediate problems arise:

Table 24-1
Properties of Putative Dopamine Receptor Subtypes

Property	D_1 receptor	D_2 receptor
Cyclase linkage	(+)	(−)
Affinity for dopamine	High	Low
Affinity for spiperone	Low	High
Effect of stimulation	↑ cAMP (adenylate cyclase) formation[a]	↓ cAMP formation

1. The pituitary gland is not sequestered within the blood–brain barrier, so dopamine activity related to events in the periphery may affect prolactin.

2. Nonspecific factors such as stress and hypotension can increase prolactin concentrations.

3. The arcuate nucleus may not be representative of other brain dopamine cells.

With the above limitations in mind, it is not surprising that prolactin concentrations in medication-free schizophrenic patients have been normal in an overwhelming majority of studies. Two findings involving prolactin, however, continue to be of interest. First, serum prolactin concentration inversely correlates with the degree of positive symptomatology (Johnstone, Crow, & Mashiter, 1977) which could indicate a relationship between D_2 receptors and positive symptomatology. This finding has been replicated in schizophrenic subjects with normal cerebral ventricles in our laboratory. Second, schizophrenic patients whose serum prolactin concentrations remain low (<6 ng/ml) on neuroleptic treatment show more clinical deterioration when they are subsequently withdrawn from neuroleptics (Brown & Laughren, 1981). Since neuroleptics usually increase prolactin concentrations, patients whose prolactins remain low in the face of neuroleptic treatment may have a greater degree of dopaminergic system hyperactivity. This could have potential applications in predicting relapse or the dosage of neuroleptic medication.

CEREBROSPINAL FLUID (CSF)

Another method of studying schizophrenic brain biochemistry is the measurement of dopamine and its metabolites in the CSF. One study of CSF dopamine concentrations in schizophrenia found normal concentrations in schizophrenic patients (Gattaz, Riederer, Reynolds, Gattaz, & Beckman, 1983). All patients were paranoid schizophrenic patients. Of 28 patients, 13 were free of medication for 4 or more weeks. The relatively low number of medication-free subjects and the fact that all patients were of one subtype indicates the need for further studies. Preliminary results from our laboratory using a larger, more heterogeneous group of medication-free patients indicate that concentrations of dopamine may, in fact, be low (Kaufmann, unpublished data).

Homovanillic acid (HVA), an important metabolite of dopamine, has been found in normal concentration in the CSF (Bowers, 1973). Separate studies have found low HVA concentration in patients with relatively more Schneiderian symptoms (Post, Fink, Carpenter, & Goodwin, 1975).

POSTMORTEM STUDIES

Decreased concentrations of nigrostriatal dopamine in Parkinson's disease were discovered by examining the brains of deceased victims. Postmortem brain studies have been undertaken in schizophrenia as well with hopes for a better neurochemical understanding of this disorder. While postmortem studies are potentially extremely powerful because of the direct nature of the measurements, they have limitations. First, most schizophrenic patients have received neuroleptic medications on a chronic basis. Hence, in postmortem studies it is extremely difficult to sort out lasting effects of chronic neuroleptic treatment on parameters such as the concentrations and binding site numbers of putative neurotransmitters. Second, there is a variable interval between death and autopsy. During this "postmortem interval" (PMI), the concentrations of many compounds of interest are apt to change.

The most consistent finding from postmortem investigations has been increased numbers of D_2 receptors in the caudate, putamen, and nucleus accumbens in the brains of schizophrenic patients. At least four groups of investigators are in agreement about this. Each, unfortunately, has sampled only a small number of drug-free patients (reviewed by Kleinman et al., 1982). MacKay et al. (1982) reported a threefold elevation in binding sites in patients receiving neuroleptics until their death ($N = 16$) in contrast with no increase in four patients drug-free for the month prior to death. Their finding, suggests the increase in D_2 receptor numbers is produced by neuroleptic treatment. This issue may be resolved with future studies including more patients free of medication at the time of death. One important ancillary finding is that the number of D_2 sites positively correlates with premortem ratings of positive symptomatology (Crow et al., 1981). Unfortunately, this may also be a drug effect, as patients with more positive symptoms probably receive more neuroleptics.

D_1 receptors have received less attention than D_2 receptors, probably because they are more difficult to study, and initial studies found no alteration in brain dopamine adenylate cyclase activity in schizophrenia. Increased dopamine-sensitive adenylate cyclase activity in response to the powerful stimulus of either NaF or SKF 38393 has been recently demonstrated, however, in the brains of patients with schizophrenia (Memo, Kleinman, & Hanbauer, 1983). If replicated, this may indicate a functional overactivity of D_1 receptors in schizophrenia, although the potential problem of chronic neuroleptic treatment must again be considered.

Several early reports indicated that there were normal concentrations of the dopamine metabolites, HVA and dihydroxyphenylacetic acid (DOPAC), in the nucleus accumbens of schizophrenic brains (reviewed by Kleinman et al., 1982). In the most recent report about brain dopamine, Reynolds (1983) found increased concentrations of dopamine in the left but not the right amygdala of patients with schizophrenia. Future studies of cortical dopamine and its metabolites will be of interest, although methodological problems can be expected due to the relatively low concentrations.

SPONTANEOUS EYE-BLINK RATE

Decreased blink rates are found in Parkinson's disease along with decreased concentrations of dopamine in the nigrostriatum. Monkeys given the dopamine agonist apomorphine show a dose-related increase in blink rate (Karson, 1983). Both pieces of evidence support the hypothesis that spontaneous eye-blink rate reflects central dopamine activity and is useful as a noninvasive indicator of dopaminergic activity. Because sulpiride, a specific D_2 antagonist, blocks the apomorphine-induced increase in blink rate, D_2 receptors may be specifically involved in blink rate modulation. If blink rate positively correlates with central dopamine activity, one test of the dopamine hypothesis of schizophrenia should be to determine if spontaneous eye blinks are increased in schizophrenic patients.

The mean blink rate of 44 medication-free chronic schizophrenic patients was 30 blinks/minute compared with 24 blinks/minute in 54 normal controls ($p < .05$) (Karson, 1983). Three other groups of investigators have also found elevated blink rates in schizophrenic patients. Moreover, in our patients, neuroleptic-produced dopamine receptor blockade normalized the elevated rate. As with increased D_2 receptor numbers in postmortem schizophrenic brains, an unanswered question for blink rate is the degree to which former neuroleptic treatment contributed to the increased rate in schizophrenic patients. Another question is the diagnostic specificity of increased blink rates.

PSYCHOPHARMACOLOGICAL STUDIES

If certain signs and symptoms of schizophrenia are related to elevated central nervous system (CNS) dopamine activity, then drugs that are dopamine agonists should intensify symptoms in individuals who are schizophrenic and perhaps cause schizophrenic symptoms in nonschizophrenic individuals. Two pieces of evidence support this notion. First, amphetamine, an indirect dopamine agonist, supposedly intensifies schizophrenic symptomatology. Moreover, amphetamine can cause a syndrome similar to paranoid schizophrenia in otherwise normal individuals when taken chronically in high doses. Second, L-dopa, which is metabolized to dopamine in the CNS, sometimes causes hallucinations and delusions in previously psychiatrically normal individuals with Parkinson's disease.

Several serious problems have become apparent with these notions. Amphetamine stimulates the release of norepinephrine presynaptically and L-dopa can be metabolized to norepinephrine. Hence, both pieces of evidence could also be interpreted to support a hypothesis of norepinephrine hyperactivity in schizophrenia. In fact, there is evidence, reviewed later, that paranoid schizophrenia may be related to noradrenergic and not dopaminergic hyperactivity. Another blow to the amphetamine story is the failure to find

amphetamine-produced exacerbations in the signs and symptoms of schizophrenia in a majority of patients (Kornetsky, 1976).

The effects of more specific dopamine receptor agonists have been
studied. Such agonists include bromocriptine, a putative D_2 receptor agonist,
and other similar ergot alkaloids (pergolide and lisuride) as well as apomorphine. The dose of agonists is also of interest because some investigators
have found that low doses of certain dopamine agonists appear to selectively
stimulate a putative autoreceptor which in turn "down-regulates" the dopamine system. Hence, it is conceivable that a low dose of a dopamine
receptor agonist might reduce psychotic symptoms.

A different psychopharmacological strategy involves the study of agents
that deplete dopamine. One such drug is the antipsychotic drug reserpine,
which depletes dopamine presynaptically. Another dopamine-depleting
agent is α-methyl-*para*-tyrosine (AMPT), which competitively inhibits tyrosine hydroxylase, the rate-limiting enzymatic step in catecholamine formation. AMPT has been reported to have antipsychotic effects, but this has
been difficult to replicate (reviewed by Wyatt et al., 1982). Reserpine depletes
norepinephrine and serotonin as well as dopamine, while AMPT depletes
norepinephrine, complicating the interpretation of these results.

With regard to neuroleptics, most recent studies tend to concentrate on
the factors predicting response to these medications. For example, a preliminary report from our laboratory found diminished neuroleptic responsiveness in schizophrenic patients with large cerebral ventricles (Weinberger
et al., 1980). Such patients were also less responsive to subcutaneous injec-
tions of the dopamine agonist apomorphine, indicating that patients with
large ventricles are relatively resistant to both dopamine agonism and antag-
onism.

We have recently undertaken a replication of the neuroleptic response
study with a similar group of patients who were perhaps slightly less resistant to neuroleptic therapy (Weinberger, Karson, Bigelow, & Wyatt, 1982).
Twenty-seven chronic schizophrenic inpatients (RDC) were able to complete
a drug-free period lasting 6 weeks. Afterward they received haloperidol
(0.4 mg/kg) daily for 6 weeks. Nine other patients with chronic schizophrenia were unable to complete the medication-free period for clinical reasons.
With this small number of patients, there were no differences in the neuroleptic responsiveness of patients who completed the study with respect to
normal and large cerebral ventricles. However, the mean ventricular size of
the patients who did not complete the drug-free period was significantly less
than those who did. This implies that patients with smaller ventricles are
more sensitive to neuroleptic withdrawal, consistent but not identical with
our previous results.

CONCLUSIONS

During the past decade tools such as receptor binding techniques, CAT
scans, more specific dopamine receptor agonists, and measurement of pro-

lactin and blink rates have lent some support to the dopamine hypothesis. Nevertheless, a clear-cut demonstration of noniatrogenic elevations in dopaminergic activity of schizophrenic patients has proved elusive. Permanent biochemical changes due to chronic neuroleptic treatment may be responsible for the elevated D_2 receptor numbers, increased stimulation of the D_1 receptors in the brains of schizophrenic patients, as well as increased blink rates. Our current findings are summarized in Table 24-2.

Crow (1980) has attempted to synthesize much of what has been presented in this review of dopamine in the concepts of Type I and Type II syndromes. Schizophrenic patients with the Type I syndrome demonstrate positive symptoms, elevations in D_2 receptor numbers, and a lack of intellectual impairment. Type II patients have negative symptoms, impaired neuropsychological functioning, a greater incidence of large cerebral ventricles, and other subtle CAT scan abnormalities, and may not have dopaminergic hyperactivity.

Table 24-2
Dopamine in Schizoprhenia: Positive Findings

Type of study	Findings	Have findings been replicated?	Problems in terms of dopamine hypothesis
Postmortem	1. Increased numbers of D_2 receptors	Yes	Neuroleptic effect?
	2. Increase sensitivity of D_1 receptors	No	1. Not yet replicated 2. Inconsistent with the activity of haloperidol, a relatively weak D_1 antagonist
	3. D_2 receptor numbers correlate to premortem positive symptoms	No	Not yet replicated
CSF	1. Low HVA in patients with Schreiderian symptoms	Once	More replications needed
Prolactin	1. Positive correlation with positive symptoms	Once	More replications needed
Blink rate	1. Increased	Yes	1. Neuroleptic effect 2. May be found in other psychiatric disorders
Pharmacological studies	1. Neuroleptics exert therapeutic effect	Yes	Not specific to schizophrenia
	2. Amphetamine and L-dopa can induce psychoses	Yes	May relate to norepinephrine effects

In terms of phenomenology, increased D_2 receptor numbers may be associated with positive symptoms. This is demonstrated by the correlation between the degree of positive symptomatology and D_2 receptor numbers in postmortem brains and with serum prolactin concentrations. Since Schneiderian symptoms are forms of positive symptoms, the CSF decrease in HVA in schizophrenic patients with more of these symptoms may also be relevant. If these patients have "down-regulated" the production and turnover of dopamine because of overactivity at or increased numbers of dopamine receptor sites, then this evidence could also be consistent with a relationship between D_2 receptors and positive symptoms.

FUTURE DIRECTIONS

Positron emission tomography (PET scan) holds promise because of the possibility that the metabolism of radiolabeled dopamine agonists and neuroleptics can be studied. Hence, dynamic differences in the metabolism of dopaminergic drugs between normals and schizophrenic patients could be quantitated. The recent success using radiolabeled L-dopa (Wagner *et al.*, 1983) and haloperidol and spiroperidol (Welch, Kilbourn, Mathias, Mintun, & Raichle, 1983) is certainly an important step forward. One note of caution is necessary. PET scans are highly state dependent, even to such subtle external stimuli as music, and undoubtedly internal stimuli as well. It is questionable whether schizophrenic patients can control their internal mental environment to a degree remotely comparable with normals. Hence, the "resting" images from awake patients with schizophrenia may never be comparable to normal controls who are awake. Since these resting images constitute the PET scan "baseline," it may be difficult to interpret changes from baseline in schizophrenia. A possible solution to this problem may lie in scanning subjects who are sleeping and comparing records obtained from comparable sleep stages.

Interest has been generated by neurophysiological techniques which, though not necessarily novel, have recently been shown to have dopaminergic correlates. One of these techniques is evoked potentials. It now appears that the latency of the early and late components of visual evoked potentials may be inversely correlated with central dopamine activity, whereas their amplitude is positively correlated. Of further interest may be the P300, a late event-related potential with cognitive determinants.

Until recently the electroretinogram (ERG), an evoked potential from the retina, was used only to study degeneration of retinal function. It now appears that the amplitude of the major component of the ERG, the b wave, may be inhibited by haloperidol, and hence positively correlated to dopamine activity in the retina. Studies demonstrating the link of retinal dopamine systems to adenylate cyclase make this system even more enticing, since it may mean that the ERG is a noninvasive, direct indicator of D_1 activity in at least one brain dopamine system (Spano, Govoni, Hofman, Kumakura, & Trabucci, 1977).

Although the dopamine hypothesis of schizophrenia remains one of the most extensively tested biochemical concepts of this disorder, the evidence in its favor is unconvincing. Even if abnormalities of central dopaminergic systems are clearly demonstrated, we will still have to account for their etiology.

Norepinephrine

Interest in norepinephrine in schizophrenia has waxed and waned. In general, it has been relegated to a "bit" role in the biochemical hypotheses of schizophrenia. Ten years ago there was a focus on possible hypoactivity of the noradrenergic system and its relationship to disruptions of central reinforcement mechanisms in schizophrenic patients. Recent emphasis has been on noradrenergic hyperactivity, either as a general phenomenon in schizophrenia or one restricted to the paranoid subtype. Current findings are summarized in Table 24-3.

Table 24-3

Norepinephrine in Schizoprhenia: Positive Findings

Method of study	Findings	Replication of findings?	Problems with findings
Postmortem	1. Increased norepinephrine concentrations in the nucleus accumbens of paranoid schizophrenic patients	Yes, but only once	Small sample sizes, need further replication
CSF	1. Increased concentration of norepinephrine, particularly in paranoid schizophrenic patients	Yes	1. Small number of medication-free studies, needs further replication 2. Medication-free schizophrenic patients are often hyperactive and uncooperative, which raises the question of the role of these factors
Pharmacology	1. Amphetamines cause paranoid schizophrenic-like syndrome	Yes	May relate to actions on dopamine
	2. Reserpine is an effective antipsychotic	Yes	May relate to actions on dopamine
	3. A possible antipsychotic role for propranolol	Yes and no	More recent studies are negative

BLOOD STUDIES

Studies of the norepinephrine system in blood appear promising, although the relevance of peripheral events to brain events remains uncertain. Plasma norepinephrine in sitting drug-free acute patients is increased compared with normals. Another recent report found a greater increase in plasma norepinephrine concentrations upon standing in schizophrenic patients than controls. Two plasma studies of 3-methoxy, 4-hydroxyphenylglycol (MHPG), the major metabolite of norepinephrine in the CNS, have too few schizophrenic subjects (two and seven, respectively). To be considered definitive Noradrenergic binding sites are decreased on platelets in schizophrenic subjects, while the prostaglandin E_1 (PGE-stimulated adenylate cyclase activity is reduced (Kafka & van Kammen, 1983). Since neuroleptics have α-blocking actions, this could be a drug effect. Plasma studies involving norepinephrine and related substances have not examined subtypes such as paranoia.

URINE

Urinary norepinephrine and MHPG concentrations are normal in schizophrenia (reviewed by Kleinman, Reid, Lake, & Wyatt, 1985). One study did report an inverse correlation between schizophrenic psychopathology and urinary MHPG concentrations. This finding could be due to the increased difficulty of urine collections in very ill schizophrenic patients.

CSF

A number of studies have found increased concentrations of norepinephrine in the CSF of schizophrenic patients. Lake et al. (1980) examined patients 2-4 weeks after medication withdrawal. The increase was more characteristic of paranoid patients. Encouragingly, in a recent study of drug-free paranoid schizophrenic patients, a trend toward increased norepinephrine concentration was also found (Gattaz et al., 1983). MHPG is not found in increased concentrations in the CSF in schizophrenia in general or paranoid schizophrenics in particular.

POSTMORTEM STUDIES

Increased norepinephrine concentrations have been reported in a number of limbic nuclei including the nucleus accumbens of four paranoid schizophrenic patients (Farley, Sharnak, & Hornykiewicz, 1980). This latter has been replicated in our laboratory. In addition, the major brain metabolite of norepinephrine, MHPG, is increased in the nucleus accumbens of paranoid schizophrenic patients also. Noradrenergic receptor numbers, including α-receptor and β-receptor binding sites, as measured by [3H]WB-4101 and [3H]dihydroalprenolol, respectively, do not appear to be elevated in the brains of schizophrenic patients, though this question has not been examined thoroughly either in terms of multiple brain regions or paranoid subtype.

PHARMACOLOGICAL STUDIES

In the previous section, the problem of catecholamine nonspecificity in the interpretation of the results of pharmacological studies of amphetamine and reserpine was discussed. On the face of it, neuroleptics, which have α-blocking as well as dopamine-blocking properties, appear to present the same problem. But the α-blocking properties of neuroleptics do not appear to correlate with their clinical potency (Creese et al., 1976).

Moreover, there are specific noradrenergic agonists and antagonists which can be used. For instance, phenoxybenzamine, a mixed α blocker, is ineffective in schizophrenia. But, like dopamine receptors, noradrenergic receptors can also be subdivided. Three groups of noradrenergic receptors have been discovered, α_1, α_2, and β. Hence, it is desirable to look at the clinical effects of even more specific agonists and antagonists.

Of the more specific agents, propranolol, a β blocker, has received the most attention. A number of early studies reported that at very high doses (up to 2 g), propranolol was an effective antipsychotic agent in schizophrenia. More recently, several large well-controlled studies have not demonstrated therapeutic efficacy, diminishing the initial optimism surrounding this drug. These studies have not systematically studied the specific question of paranoia.

Clonidine, a specific α_2 agonist, did not have a therapeutic effect in three initial studies. One recent report, however, found that clonidine was as effective as trifluoperazine (R. Freedman et al., 1982).

SUMMARY

There is a small body of evidence that supports a role for noradrenergic hyperactivity in schizophrenia, and work needs to be done to substantiate and enlarge previous findings. One problem in studying plasma norepinephrine clinically is that it increases with movement to an upright position and with motor hyperactivity in general. Investigators familiar with the behavior of medication-free chronic schizophrenic patients realize that there is often a practical problem of keeping such patients at rest and in a prone position, thus making such studies difficult.

Serotonin and Other Indoles

Increases and decreases in the concentrations of serotonin have been hypothesized in schizophrenia. Other metabolites of tryptophan have received attention as possible endogenous psychotogens. Unfortunately, the findings are often in conflict or are negative, and a role has not emerged for the indoles in schizophrenia.

BLOOD

Until recently, an equal number of studies found increased or normal concentrations of whole blood serotonin. Two recent studies have at least temporarily tipped the balance toward an increase. DeLisi, Neckers, Weinberger, and Wyatt (1981) found a mean increase of serotonin in blood of 33 schizophrenic patients, with the increase largely restricted to the patients with large cerebral ventricles. D. X. Freedman, Belendiuk, Belendiuk, and Crayton (1981) showed an elevation of the mean platelet serotonin levels in a group of 33 schizophrenic patients. Unfortunately, almost all the patients in both these studies were receiving neuroleptic medications, though in the former study blood concentrations of serotonin in six patients withdrawn from medication were unchanged by neuroleptic treatment. A medication effect could account for the apparently contradictory results with a CSF study involving ventricular size (Potkin, Weinberger, Linnoila, & Wyatt, 1983) in medication-free subjects. It is also possible that there is a reciprocal relationship between blood and CSF serotonin concentrations.

One series of investigations examined the rate of uptake of serotonin in the platelets of medication-free schizophrenic patients. With one exception, these studies show reduced serotonin uptake in schizophrenic patients. While the reduction is not pronounced in most family members, almost 25% of family members do have a comparable reduction (Rotman, Zemishlany, Munitz, & Wijsenbeek, 1982). If follow-up of these family members demonstrates a more than expected incidence of schizophrenia, then reduced reuptake could serve as a potential marker for vulnerable individuals. Unfortunately, depressed patients also demonstrate reduced serotonin reuptake. Hence, the interpretation of this finding is unclear.

URINE

An early subject of investigation was urinary tryptamine, the product of the direct metabolism of tryptophan by monoamine oxidase (MAO). Increased concentrations were found in all groups of psychotic subjects and appeared to occur at the time of psychotic exacerbations. These findings have not been vigorously pursued in the past decade.

Another line of investigations was the attempt to find increased urinary concentrations of the products of abnormal methylation of the indoles such as bufotenine and 5-methoxy-N,N-dimethyltryptamine. These attempts have not been successful thus far (reviewed by Wyatt et al., 1982).

CSF

In general, schizophrenic patients appear to have normal CSF concentrations of 5-hydroxyindoleacetic acid (5-HIAA), the major metabolite of serotonin. One study, however, in which 21 of 24 of the patients were medication-free, found markedly decreased concentrations of CSF 5-HIAA in patients with large cerebral ventricles (Potkin et al., 1983).

POSTMORTEM STUDIES

Farley et al. (1980) reported increased concentrations of serotonin and its metabolite 5-HIAA in the limbic system and striatum of chronic paranoid schizophrenic patients. This has been reproduced in our laboratory in the putamen and globus pallidus of a larger group of schizophrenic patients (Korpi *et al.*, in press).

PHARMACOLOGICAL STUDIES

Interestingly, the antipsychotic potencies of the neuroleptics correlate with their ability to block serotonin receptors ($r = .4$), though not nearly to the degree of dopamine receptor blockade ($r = .9$) (Creese *et al.*, 1976). Apart from this, pharmacological manipulations of the serotonergic system have been largely fruitless in schizophrenia. Drugs that increase central serotonin concentrations, such as its metabolic precursor L-5-hydroxytryptophan, are without benefit. The serotonin antagonist *p*-chlorphenylalanine (PCPA), which blocks tryptophan hydroxylase, an enzyme of serotonin formation, is also ineffective. Lysergic acid diethylamide (LSD), a serotonin receptor blocker, is psychotomimetic, but schizophrenic patients can usually differentiate the effect of this drug from exacerbations of their illness. Fenfluramine, an agent which depletes brain serotonin, is undergoing a therapeutic trial.

SUMMARY

Both the notions and findings about serotonergic involvement in schizophrenia are in conflict and difficult to synthesize. Of particular interest are the findings of increased serotonin concentrations in the brain and reduced platelet reuptake. Future blood studies should be performed on medication-free patients.

Phenylethylamine (PEA)

Due to its structural similarities to amphetamine and its amphetamine-like actions in animals, PEA has been postulated to be an endogenous psychotogen. Hence, its concentration in urine, where it is usually measured, has been hypothesized to be increased in schizophrenic patients.

The initial report of elevated urinary PEA concentrations in schizophrenia consisted of only seven subjects. Two negative studies had five and four subjects, respectively. Later it was reported that 16 paranoid patients had increased urinary PEA concentrations compared with 15 nonparanoid patients (Potkin *et al.*, 1979). This finding was replicated in a study performed in India. Unfortunately, many of the subjects in Potkin's report were receiving neuroleptics. Our attempts to further replicate this finding in medication-free patients has not been successful. Moreover, a recent report found normal concentrations of CSF PEA in nine paranoid patients who were not receiving medications (Beckman, Waldmeir, Lambert, & Gataz, 1983).

Monoamine Metabolizing Enzymes

Monoamine Oxidase (MAO)

MAO is a crucial degradative enzyme for monoamines. A lowering of the activity of this enzyme could conceivably lead to increased concentrations of each. Hence, the finding of lowered MAO activity in the platelets of patients with chronic schizophrenia (Murphy & Wyatt, 1972) sparked enormous research interest. There is increasing evidence, however, that at least part of the low platelet MAO activity in schizophrenia results from neuroleptic treatment. Negative postmortem studies of brain MAO (reviewed by Wyatt et al., 1982) also call into question the role of this enzyme in schizophrenia.

But platelet MAO may still be of interest in schizophrenia. Two recent findings indicate that platelet MAO may be linked to central dopamine activity and may be abnormally regulated in schizophrenia. First, there is a significant inverse correlation between the putative dopaminergic marker, blink rate, and platelet MAO in chronic schizophrenic patients, but not normal individuals (Karson et al., 1983). Second, a high dose of oral glucose decreases platelet MAO activity in schizophrenic patients, but not normal individuals (Karson et al., 1982).

Dopamine β-Hydroxylase (DBH)

DBH catalyzes the conversion of dopamine to norepinephrine. Decreased activity of this enzyme would lead to a relative decrease in norepinephrine and an increase in dopamine concentration in noradrenergic neurons.

Despite initial reports of decreased DBH activity in schizophrenic brains, it now appears that there is normal activity of this enzyme in brain, CSF, and plasma (reviewed by Wyatt et al., 1982). Drugs such as fusaric acid and disulfiram, which block DBH, can cause psychosis in nonpsychotic individuals and exacerbate schizophrenic symptomatology, a finding opposing the noradrenergic hyperactivity notion of schizophrenia.

Catechol-O-Methyltransferase (COMT)

COMT provides the major extraneuronal route of catecholamine degradation. It is not decreased in the brain of patients with schizophrenia, and studies of erythrocyte COMT are conflicting.

L-γ-Aminobutyric Acid (GABA) and Benzodiazepines

GABA is a relatively unbiquitous neurotransmitter in the CNS which is generally considered to have an inhibitory function. In particular, GABA seems to exert an inhibitory influence on nigrostriatal dopaminergic activity (Hökfelt et al., 1977), which, in light of the dopamine hypothesis, makes this neurochemical system of great interest in schizophrenia. It also appears that there is a functional and perhaps physical coupling of receptor sites for the benzodiazepines and GABA, with the benzodiazepines exhibiting GABA agonistic properties. Hence, the benzodiazepines are also of conceptual interest in schizophrenia.

Once again theory clashes with the reality of the scientific endeavor. Postmortem studies in schizophrenia include one which has found normal brain GABA concentrations and one which has found low concentrations. Brain glutamic acid decarboxylase (GAD) activity, an enzyme of GABA synthesis, is normal in schizophrenia, as is GABA receptor binding. Most CSF studies of GABA in medication-free schizophrenic patients are also normal, though one recent study does suggest lower GABA levels early in the illness (van Kammen, Sternberg, Hare, Water, & Bunney, 1982).

One of the controversies in the psychopharmacology of schizophrenia involves the possible antipsychotic properties of the benzodiazepines. Given at normal doses (daily equivalent of 40 mg of diazepam), these drugs are not effective as an adjunct to neuroleptic therapy. In fact, they may increase violent thoughts and behavior. At megadoses (250 mg of Valium daily), claims of antipsychotic efficacy have been made in several studies but refuted in one well-controlled study (Jimeson, van Kammen, Post, Docherty, & Bunney, 1982). Other GABA agonists such as muscimol and valproic acid are ineffective or have adverse effects on schizophrenic patients.

In conclusion, there is little evidence that abnormalities of the GABA-benzodiazepine system are involved in schizophrenia. A question remains about the antipsychotic efficacy of megadoses of the benzodiazepines.

Endogenous Opiates

Opiates constitute one of the oldest classes of psychopharmacological agents. But until the recent discovery of brain opiate receptors and their endogenous ligands, they were of little interest to schizophrenia researchers. Two reports involving endogenous opiates heightened interest in the involvement of endogenous opiates in schizophrenia. One claimed therapeutic efficacy of the opiate receptor ligand β-endorphin. The other involved hemodialysis and the claim that a leuenkephalin found in the dialysate of schizophrenics might be an endogenous schizophrenogenic compound. We now review the disappointing course of events for these compounds in schizophrenia.

CSF

In the best study to date, Pickar, Cohen, Naber, and Cohen (1982) have found low overall CSF opiate activity in schizophrenic patients, correlating only with anxiety–depression scores of the Brief Psychiatric Rating Scale (BPRS).

Postmortem Studies

One study found significantly decreased concentrations of met-enkephalin in the caudate nucleus of paranoid but not undifferentiated schizophrenic patients (Kleinman *et al.*, 1982). It was not found in other areas of the brain. Neuroleptics cause increases in met-enkephalin in rats which makes this finding difficult to ascribe to neuroleptic treatment. Moreover, neuroleptic-treated human controls had normal concentrations of met-enkephalin in their caudate nuclei.

Hemodialysis

Hemodialysis is included in this section because of an initial report of isolation of a leu-enkephalin from the dialysate of schizophrenic patients. Subsequent groups have not been able to isolate the abnormal peptides from the dialysate (reviewed by Wyatt *et al.*, 1982). And, unfortunately, most controlled studies of hemodialysis have not shown a therapeutic effect in schizophrenia.

Psychopharmacological Studies

To explore a possible role for endogenous opioid system hyperactivity in schizophrenia, patients have been given opiate receptor agonists. Initial uncontrolled studies found significant improvement with β-endorphin, a finding not replicated in three controlled studies (reviewed by Pickar *et al.*, 1982). A group of related compounds is the γ-endorphines [des-tyrosine-γ-endorphin (DTyE) and des-enkephalin-γ-endorphin (DEyE)]. A beneficial effect has been reported for DTyE, but not substantiated by other studies (Meltzer, Busch, Tricou, & Robertson, 1982). One study has reported an antipsychotic effect for DEyE (Verhoeven, van Ree, Heezium-van Boutum, de Weid, & van Praag, 1982). If these compounds do exert an antipsychotic effect, it is possibly due to a neuroleptic-like effect on dopamine receptors.

To reduce postulated opiate system hyperactivity in schizophrenia, many investigators have given opiate antagonists, most notably naloxone. Large well-controlled studies have shown no effect of this drug in medication-free chronic schizophrenic patients (Pickar *et al.*, 1982). Several have found a statistically significant but clinically inapparent improvement in patients receiving neuroleptics.

Summary

Despite encouraging initial reports, no clear evidence has emerged that abnormalities of the endogenous opioid system are involved in schizophrenia. A more specific hypothesis is needed (i.e., hypo- or hyperactivity, a specific brain area, and a specific ligand) as well as more systematic studies, particularly of postmortem changes.

Other Peptides

Advancements in biochemical techniques, particularly the radioimmune assay (RIA), have made it possible to explore the concentrations of the almost limitless number of neuropeptides in the postmortem brains and CSF of schizophrenic patients. These include somatostatin (SLI), bombesin, cholecystokinin (CCK), neurotensin (NT), thyrotropin-releasing hormone (TRH), substance P, and vasoactive intestinal polypeptide (VIP). One of the most interesting compounds is CCK, because it is found in anatomical proximity to dopamine in the brain. A preliminary report focused on reduced CCK in the amygdala and hippocampus of schizophrenic patients with negative symptoms (Owen *et al.*, 1983). Another study from our laboratory found normal CCK in both these structures of schizophrenic patients who were not subtyped according to negative symptoms. In separate single preliminary studies, reduced NT and bombesin in CSF have been reported. Similarly, in one or two brain areas schizophrenics have been reported to have increases in NT and VIP concentrations.

Other Compounds

The possible role of nutrients such as vitamins, minerals, and glutens in schizophrenia has been reviewed elsewhere and the evidence is not convincing (Wyatt *et al.*, 1982).

Conclusions

Integrating biochemistry and schizophrenia is a difficult endeavor. One possible explanation for this difficulty is that schizophrenia is a heterogeneous disorder, with some subgroups of patients that are biochemically deviant. This notion has been most thoroughly applied to the neurochemical dopamine. It has been suggested that patients whose illness is characterized by positive symptoms are most likely to have dopaminergic hyperactivity, while patients with social and intellectual deterioration (negative symptoms or defect state) as the prominent clinical problems may not have dopaminergic hyperactivity. The finding that the latter type of patients may have structural brain abnormalities has raised speculation regarding the cause of these structural changes (i.e., viral infection). Animals with dopaminergic tract lesions or receiving neuroleptic medications as well as humans with Parkinson's disease demonstrate defects that could be construed as negative symptoms, raising the possibility that these symptoms could result from a hypodopaminergic state as well (Wyatt, 1983).

Another facet of the catecholamine hyperactivity hypothesis of schizophrenia is evidence from both brain and CSF that patients with paranoid schizophrenia have noradrenergic hyperactivity. Insofar as patients with paranoid schizophrenia classically demonstrate many positive and few negative symptoms (Type I patients), it would have been predicted that they demonstrate dopaminergic hyperactivity.

Such inconsistencies might be explained by invoking one set of mechanisms for the proposed dopamine hyperactivity (i.e., increased numbers of postsynaptic dopamine receptors) and another for noradrenergic hyperactivity (i.e., increased norepinephrine synthesis). This lack of specificity of proposed mechanisms exemplifies one difficulty which makes biochemical hypotheses difficult to refute. With the paucity of biochemical findings in schizophrenia, however, it becomes difficult to further refine a particular hypothesis. We present a series of guidelines developed to assess the status of current hypotheses in order to evaluate which may have reached a more refinable stage.

1. A hypothesis for a particular biochemical system should clearly predict hyper- and hypoactivity so that the evidence garnered can be readily applied and interpreted.

2. Whenever possible, the hypothesis should be supported by findings in the brain which have been repeatedly replicated.

3. If examinations from CSF, blood, or urine on neurophysiological measurements are to be done, then they should be performed in a relatively large number of patients ($N>15$?) who have been medication-free for long enough to reduce the likelihood of medication artifact. Studies with young patients who have not been chronically institutionalized or treated chronically with neuroleptics should be emphasized.

4. Neuropharmacological agents of a particular neurochemical system should definitely effect schizophrenic symptomatology in the direction predicted by the hypothesis which concerns the neurochemical system unless a destruction of the system is proposed. It is preferable that an antischizophrenic effect be demonstrated. According to these guidelines, the dopamine and norepinephrine hyperactivity theories of schizophrenia remain the most promising (Table 24-4).

These conclusions may make one guarded about the future of biochemistry in schizophrenia research. It should be borne in mind, however, that most of the neurochemicals of the human brain probably remain unknown. Perhaps the future rests with an approach that integrates biochemical, morphological, immunological, or viral concepts. A clear association with biochemical abnormalities and schizophrenia has not yet been found.

Table 24-4

Biochemical Conceptions of Schizophrenia: Current Status

Biochemical system	Undirectional hypothesis	Replicated postmortem brain findings	Replicated CSF, blood, or urine findings performed in large numbers of medication-free subjects	Neuropharmacological agents of the biochemical system clearly affect the disorder in the direction predicted by the hypothesis	Overall status of biochemical hypothesis
Dopamine	Yes, hyperactivity (perhaps a subgroup with normal or low dopaminergic activity)	Yes (artifact?)	No	Yes (neuroleptics)	Equivocal but promising
Norepinephrine	Yes, hyperactivity (earlier hypothesis proposed hypoactivity)	Yes?	Yes	? (Are propranolol or clonidine effective antipsychotics?)	Equivocal but promising
Serotonin	No	No	No	No	Poor
GABA	Yes, hyperactivity	No	No	? (Are megadose benzodiazepines effective antipsychotics?)	Poor
Endogenous opiate	No	No? (increased met-encephalin in paranoid schizophrenic patients, neuroleptic effect?)	No	? (Are DEyE and DTyE effective antipsychotics)	Poor

REFERENCES

Andreasen, N. C., & Olsen, S. (1982). Negative symptoms in schizophrenia. *Archives of General Psychiatry, 39,* 784–788.

Beckman, H., Waldmeir, P., Lambert, J., & Gataz, W. F. (1983). Phenethylamine and monoamine metabolites in CSF of schizophrenics: Effect of neuroleptic treatment. *Journal of Neural Transmission, 52,* 103–110.

Bowers, M. B. (1973). 5-Hydroxyindoleacetic acid (5-HIAA) and homovanillic acid following probenicid in acute psychotic patients treated with phenothiazines. *Psychopharmacologia, 28,* 309–318.

Brown, W. A., & Laughren, T. (1981). Low serum prolactin and early relapse following neuroleptic withdrawal. *American Journal of Psychiatry, 138,* 237–239.

Carlsson, A., & Lindqvist, R. (1963). The effect of chlorpromazine and haloperidol on formation of 3-methoxytyramine and normetanephrine in mouse brain. *Acta Pharmacologica et Toxicologica, 20,* 140–144.

Creese, I., Burt, D. R., Snyder, S. H. (1976). Dopamine receptor binding predicts clinical and pharmacological potencies of antischizophrenic drugs. *Science, 192,* 481–483.

Crow, T. J. (1980). Molecular pathology of schizophrenia: More than one disease process? *British Medical Journal, 280,* 66–68.

Crow, T. J., Owen, F., Cross, H. J., Ferrier, N., Johnstone, E. C., McCreddie, R. M., Owens, D. G. C., & Poulter, M. (1981). Type I and type II schizophrenia defined by morphological and biochemical criteria: Response to neuroleptics. In P. Reiderer & E. Usdin (Eds.), *Transmitter biochemistry of human post-mortem brain tissue.* New York: Macmillan.

DeLisi, L. E., Neckers, L. M., Weinberger, D. R., & Wyatt, R. J. (1981). Increased whole blood serotonin concentrations in chronic schizophrenic patients. *Archives of General Psychiatry, 38,* 647–650.

Farley, I. J., Sharnak, K. S., & Hornykiewicz, O. (1980). Brain monoamine changes in chronic paranoid schizophrenic and their possible relation to increased dopamine receptor sensitivity. In G. Pepeu, M. J. Kuhan, & S. J. Enna (Eds.), *Receptors for neurotransmitters and peptide hormones.* New York: Raven Press.

Folin, O. (1904). Some metabolism studies: With special reference to mental disorders. *American Journal of Insanity, 60,* 702.

Freedman, D. X., Belendiuk, K., Belendiuk, G. W., & Crayton, J. W. (1981). Blood tryptophan metabolism in chronic schizophrenia. *Archives of General Psychiatry, 38,* 655–659.

Freedman, R., Kirch, D., Bell, J., Adler, L. E., Pecevitch, M., Pachtman, E., & Denver, P. (1982). Clonidine treatment of schizophrenia: Double-blind comparison to placebo and neuroleptic drugs. *Acta Psychiatrica Scandinavica, 65,* 35–45.

Gattaz, W. F., Riederer, P., Reynolds, G. P., Gattaz, D., & Beckman, H. (1983). Dopamine in the cerebrospinal fluid of schizophrenia patients. *Psychiatry Research, 8,* 243–250.

Hökfelt, T., Ljungdahl, A., Fuxe, K., Johansson, O., Perez de la Mora, M., & Agnati, L. (1977). Some attempts to explore possible central gabaergic mechanisms with special reference to control of dopamine neurons. In E. Usdin, D. A. Hamburg, & J. D. Barchas (Eds.), *Neuroregulators and psychiatric disorders* (pp. 358–367). New York: Oxford University Press.

Jimeson, D. C., van Kammen, D. P., Post, R. M., Docherty, J. R., & Bunney, W. E. (1982). Diazepam in schizophrenia: A preliminary double blind trial. *American Journal of Psychiatry, 139,* 489–491.

Johnstone, E. C., Frith, C. D., Crow, T. J., Husband, J., & Kreel, L. (1976). Cerebral ventricular size and cognitive impairment in chronic schizophrenia. *Lancet, 2,* 924–926.

Johnstone, E. C., Crow, T. J., & Mashiter, K. (1977). Anterior pituitary hormone secretion in chronic schizophrenia: An approach to neurochemical mechanism. *Psychological Medicine, 7,* 223–228.

Kafka, M. S., & van Kammen, D. P. (1983). α-Adrenergic receptor function in schizophrenia. *Archives of General Psychiatry, 40,* 264–270.

Karson, C. N. (1983). Spontaneous eye blinks rates and dopaminergic systems. *Brain, 106*, 643–653.

Karson, C. N., Bridge, T. P., Phelps, B. H., Wise, C. D., Potkin, S. G., Apostoles, P. S., & Wyatt, R. J. (1982). The effect of oral glucose on platelet monoamine oxidase. *Biological Psychiatry, 17*, 1011–1015.

Karson, C. N., Kleinman, J. E., Berman, K. F., Phelps, B. H., Wise, C. D., DeLisi, L. E., & Jeste, D. V. (1983). An inverse correlation between spontaneous eye blink rate and platelet monoamine oxidase activity. *British Journal of Psychiatry, 142*, 43–46.

Kebabian, J. W., & Calne, D. B. (1976). Multiple receptors for dopamine. *Nature (London), 277*, 993–996.

Kleinman, J. E., Karoum, F., Rosenblatt, J. E., Gillin, J. C., Hong, J., Bridge, T. P., Zalcman, S., Storch, F., del Carmen, R., & Wyatt, R. J. (1982). Postmortem neurochemical studies in chronic schizophrenia. In E. Usdin & I. Handin (Eds.), *Biological markers in psychiatry and neurology* (pp. 67–76). Oxford: Pergamon.

Kleinman, J. E., Reid, A., Lake, C. R., & Wyatt, R. J. (1985). Studies of norepinephrine in schizophrenia. In M. C. Ziegler & C. R. Lake (Eds.), *The catecholamines in psychiatric and neurologic disorders* (pp. 285–311). Boston, MA: Butterworth.

Kornetsky, C. (1976). Hyporesponsivity of chronic schizophrenic patients to dextroamphetamine. *Archives of General Psychiatry, 33*, 1425–1428.

Korpi, E. R., Kleinman, J. E., Goodman, F. I., Phillips, I., DeLisi, L. E., Linnoila, M., & Wyatt, R. J. (in press) Serotonin and 5-hydroxyindoleacetic acid concentrations in different regions of suicide victims: Comparison with chronic schizophrenic subjects with or without suicide as cause of death. *Archives of General Psychiatry*.

Kraepelin, E. (1919). *Dementia praecox* (R. M. Barclay, Trans.). Edinburgh: E. & S. Livingstone.

Lake, C. R., Sternberg, D. E., van Kammen, D. P., Ballenger, J. C., Ziegler, M. C., Post, R. M., Kopin, I. J., & Bunney, W. E. (1980). Schizophrenia: Elevated cerebrospinal fluid norepinephrine. *Science, 207*, 331–333.

MacKay, A. N. P., Iverson, L., Rossor, M., Spokes, E., Bird, E., Arregui, A., Creese, I., & Snyder, S. H. (1982). Increased brain dopamine and dopamine receptors in schizophrenia. *Archives of General Psychiatry, 39*, 991–997.

Meltzer, H. Y., Busch, D. A., Tricou, B. J., & Robertson, A. (1982). Effect of (des-tyr)-gamma-endorphin in schizophrenia. *Psychiatry Research, 6*, 313–326.

Memo, M., Kleinman, J. E., & Hanbauer, I. (1983). Coupling of dopamine D_1 recognition sights with adenylate cyclase in nuclei accumbens and caudatus of schizophrenics. *Science, 202*, 1304–1307.

Murphy, D. M., & Wyatt, R. J. (1972). Reduced monoamine oxidase activity in blood platelets from schizophrenic patients. *Nature (London), 23*, 225–226.

Pickar, D., Cohen, M.-R., Naber, P., & Cohen, R. M. (1982). Clinical studies of the opioid system. *Biological Psychiatry, 17*, 1243–1276.

Post, R. M., Fink, E., Carpenter, W. T., & Goodwin, F. K. (1975). Cerebrospinal fluid amine metabolites in acute schizophrenia. *Archives of General Psychiatry, 32*, 1063–1069.

Potkin, S. G., Karoum, F., Chuang, L.-W., Cannon-Spoor, H. E., Phillips, I., & Wyatt, R. J. (1979). Phenethylamine in paranoid chronic schizophrenia. *Science, 206*, 470–471.

Potkin, S. G., Weinberger, D. R., Linnoila, M., & Wyatt, R. J. (1983). Low CSF 5-hydroxyindoleacetic acid in schizophrenic patients with enlarged cerebral ventricles. *American Journal of Psychiatry, 140*, 21–25.

Reynolds, G. P. (1983). Increased concentrations and lateral asymmetry of amygdala dopamine in schizophrenia. *Nature (London), 306*, 527–529.

Rotman, A., Zemishlany, Z., Munitz, H., & Wijsenbeek, H. (1982). The active uptake of serotonin by platelets of schizophrenic patients and their families: Possibility of a genetic marker. *Psychopharmacology, 77*, 171–174.

Spano, P. F., Govoni, S., Hofman, M., Kamakura, K., & Trabucci, M. (1977). Physiological and pharmacological influences on dopaminergic receptors in the retina. *Advances in Biochemical Pharmacology, 16,* 307–310.

Stevens, J. R. (1973). An anatomy of schizophrenia. *Archives of General Psychiatry, 29,* 177–189.

Stoof, J. C., & Kebabian, J. W. (1981). Opposing roles for D_1 and D_2 dopamine receptors in efflax of cyclic AMP from rat neostriatum. *Nature (London), 294,* 366–368.

Van Kammen, D. P., Sternberg, D. E., Hare, T. A., Water, R. N., & Bunney, W. E. (1982). CSF levels of gamma-aminobutyric acid in schizophrenia. *Archives of General Psychiatry, 39,* 91–97.

Verhoeven, W. M. A., van Ree, J. M., Heezium-van Boutum, A., de Weid, D., & van Praag, H. M. (1982). Antipsychotic properties of des-enkephalin-gamma-endorphin in treatment of schizophrenic patients. *Archives of General Psychiatry, 39,* 648–652.

Wagner, H. N., Burns, D., Dannals, R. F., Wong, D. F., Langstrom, B., Duelfer, T., Frost, J. J., Ravert, H. T., Links, J. M., Rosenbloom, S. B., Lukas, S. E., Kramer, A. V., & Kuhar, M. J. (1983). Imaging dopamine receptors in the human brain by positron tomography. *Science, 221,* 1264–1266.

Weinberger, D. R., Torrey, E. F., Neophytides, A. N., & Wyatt, R. J. (1979). Lateral cerebral ventricular enlargement in chronic schizophrenia. *Archives of General Psychiatry, 36,* 735–739.

Weinberger, D. R., Bigelow, L. B., Kleinman, J. E., Klein, S. T., Rosenblatt, J. E., & Wyatt, R. J. (1980). Cerebral ventricular enlargement in chronic schizophrenia: An association with poor response to treatment. *Archives of General Psychiatry, 37,* 11–14.

Weinberger, D. R., Karson, C. N., Bigelow, L. B., & Wyatt, R. J. (1982). *Cerebral ventricular size and response to neuroleptic treatment.* Presented at the annual meeting of the American College of Neuropsychopharmacology, Nashville, TN.

Welch, M. J., Kilbourn, M. R., Mathias, C. J., Mintun, M. A., & Raichle, M. E. (1983). Comparison in animal modes of ^{18}F-haloperidol: Potential agents from imaging the dopamine receptor. *Life Science, 33,* 1687–1693.

Wyatt, R. J. (1983). *The dopamine hypothesis: Variations on a theme.* Presented at the annual meeting of the American College of Psychiatry, New Orleans, LA.

Wyatt, R. J., Cutler, N. R., DeLisi, L. E., Jeste, D. V., Kleinman, J. E., Luchins, D. J., Potkin, S. G., & Weinberger, D. R. (1982). Biochemical and morphological factors in the etiology of the schizophrenic disorders. In L. Grinspoon (Ed.), *The American Psychiatric Association annual review, Psychiatry 1982* (pp. 112–153). Washington, DC: American Psychiatric Press.

CHAPTER 25

Somatoform Disorders

Eugene H. Rubin, Charles F. Zorumski, and Samuel B. Guze

Introduction

Unexplained somatic complaints have long been associated with psychiatric disorders. The DSM-III category of somatoform disorders represents an attempt to clarify the issues surrounding the disorders in which symptoms suggest physical illness but for which no "organic" cause can be found. This category includes somatization disorder, conversion disorder, psychogenic pain disorder, hypochondriasis, and atypical somatoform disorder. Since the spirit of DSM-III is to provide specific inclusion and exclusion criteria by which the reliability and validity of psychiatric disorders can be studied, the following review of somatoform disorders will focus on research examining these features. Diagnostic reliability implies that different examiners can agree on the presence or absence of the essential features of the illness(es). Field trials of DSM-III diagnoses indicate that acceptable reliability is obtainable for many disorders (Hyler, Williams, & Spitzer, 1982). Establishing whether particular criteria define a valid disease entity remains more problematic, since independent correlates of validity, such as laboratory tests or biopsies, do not yet exist. Current attempts at establishing validity therefore are based upon less independent approaches, including clinical description and delimitation from other disorders, establishment of familial illness patterns by pedigree studies, and establishment of characteristic natural history patterns by long-term follow-up (Guze, 1978; E. Robins & Guze, 1970). Several psychiatric syndromes have been shown to be diagnostically discrete by these methods (Goodwin & Guze, 1979).

Eugene H. Rubin, Charles F. Zorumski, and Samuel B. Guze. Department of Psychiatry, Washington University School of Medicine, St. Louis, Missouri.

All DSM-III categories may not prove valid in the above sense. It is of value, of course, to establish which syndromes are valid, since this allows greater confidence in predicting natural history and prognosis, thus aiding in treatment planning and long-term management. Some DSM-III syndromes may not have predictive validity by themselves, but could be useful as adjectival descriptors modifying other syndromes. It will be important to establish how such descriptors influence the course and management of the underlying disorder. As an example, psychotic symptoms accompanying major depression may affect course and influence treatment, but may not necessarily change the overall diagnosis. Similarly, certain personality features may influence clinical presentations of established syndromes but not change the long-term outcome or genetics.

When data are not available that bear on validity, research approaches to obtain such information will be suggested.

Somatization Disorder

Of the four syndromes listed under somatoform disorders, somatization disorder has been the best studied. Specific criteria defining Briquet's syndrome, the forerunner of somatization disorder, have been available for over 20 years and have been the basis for a series of clinical studies evaluating the usefulness of this diagnosis (Guze, 1967, 1975). In the following overview, the terms somatization disorder and Briquet's syndrome are used interchangeably; however, while the criteria for somatization disorder were derived from those defining Briquet's syndrome, there are definitional differences, and the overlap may not be complete (Stoltzman, Helzer, Robins, Croughan, & Singerman, 1981). Both definitions describe patients with a long history of multiple, medically unexplained somatic complaints that involve many organ systems. These symptoms frequently lead to hospitalizations, surgical operations, and drug trials, as well as social complications. The major difference between somatization disorder and Briquet's syndrome involves the specific number of somatic complaints required for diagnosis (Stoltzman et al., 1981).

When a patient satisfies criteria for Briquet's syndrome, the course of the illness can be predicted with considerable confidence. For instance, even though these patients have multiple somatic complaints, in 90% of cases no other disease will develop that in retrospect will explain the initial symptoms (Perley & Guze, 1962). The clinician can, therefore, be conservative about many diagnostic and therapeutic procedures. Somatization disorder usually runs a chronic course and clinicians can expect repetitive complaints and disruptive behavior over the years (Coryell & Norten, 1981). At the same time, recent studies have not found an increased mortality, and patients and their families can be reassured that their symptoms will not prove prematurely fatal (Coryell, 1981).

Although suicidal thoughts and attempts are frequent (Coryell, 1981; G. Murphy, 1977), patients with somatization disorder, unlike patients with major affective disorder, do not have an increased incidence of completed suicides (Coryell, 1981). The knowledge that suicide is unlikely allows for a circumspect approach to appropriate management.

Briquet's syndrome occurs mostly in women, and family studies indicate an increased incidence in female relatives (Coryell, 1980; Woerner & Guze, 1968). At the same time, male relatives have an increased incidence of antisocial personality disorder. These observations led to the hypothesis that somatization disorder and antisocial personality disorder are different phenotypic manifestations of a similar genetic process (Cloninger, 1978; Cloninger & Guze, 1970). In addition, females with Briquet's syndrome and males with antisocial personality disorder and/or alcoholism often marry one another, thus further enhancing the familial linkage of these conditions (Woerner & Guze, 1968). This knowledge has practical as well as theoretical implications. Knowing that a patient with Briquet's disorder often lives in an environment containing other cases as well as individuals with alcoholism and antisocial personality disorder can help the clinician evaluate the patient and plan appropriate intervention.

There are currently a few laboratory parameters that may correlate with somatization disorder. Meares and Horvath (1972) and Horvath, Friedman, and Meares (1980) reported marked differences in habituation of skin resistance in patients with chronic hysteria (similar to somatization disorder) compared to patients with acute hysteria (conversion symptoms) or patients with anxiety. It would be interesting to know if this abnormality correlates with the severity of the illness or response to treatment. Confirmation and extension of this laboratory finding is awaited. Such an abnormality in patients whose major subjective symptoms may involve sensory interpretation is also theoretically intriguing.

Flor-Henry, Fromm-Auch, Tapper, and Schopflocher (1981) have demonstrated that patients with somatization disorder perform poorly on a variety of neuropsychological tests. Of their 10 patients with Briquet's syndrome, 9 had abnormal performances compared to no abnormal scores in the control group. Their 8-hour test battery was designed to localize pathology to the anterior or posterior regions of either the dominant or nondominant hemisphere. Patients with Briquet's syndrome showed bilateral anterior deficits, with the nondominant hemisphere dysfunction usually being more severe. Anterior functions were usually more severely affected than posterior functions. This work provides further evidence of central nervous system involvement associated with this illness. Further refinements of this approach could prove useful in understanding the extent and localization of such pathology.

In summary, data exist suggesting that Briquet's syndrome is a clinically valid and useful concept. Knowledge of natural history, morbidity, mortality, and associated family illness pattern enables the clinician to better understand the illness and provide the best treatment (G. E. Murphy, 1982). The preliminary neurophysiological and neuropsychological findings need replication and further study. It is necessary, however, to show that the criteria for somatization disorder and those for Briquet's syndrome define essentially the same population.

Conversion Disorder

The DSM-III category of conversion disorder describes patients in whom the predominant disturbance is a loss or alteration in physical functioning, other than sexual dysfunction or pain states, and in whom psychological factors are thought to be of etiological importance. Conversion symptoms, thus described, are common and occur in a wide range of psychiatric and medical illnesses (Guze, Woodruff, & Clayton, 1971; Lazare, 1981). In order to fulfill DSM-III criteria for conversion disorder, these symptoms should not be under voluntary control and should not be due to a physical disorder, schizophrenia, or somatization disorder. Thus, conversion disorder represents a diagnosis of exclusion consisting of conversion symptoms unassociated with major medical or psychiatric illness. In the following, data examining the natural history, family studies, and laboratory evaluations of conversion symptoms will be overviewed. In addition, an attempt will be made to determine whether a syndrome of primary conversion disorder exists or whether conversion symptoms should be considered in an adjectival sense only.

In examining the natural history of conversion symptoms, the population studied as well as the definition of conversion symptoms used have major influences on the data. As defined in DSM-III, conversion symptoms refer to *all* unexplained physical symptoms exclusive of pain and sexual dysfunction. This may be too broad a definition, and some investigators feel that these symptoms have specificity only when used to describe pseudoneurological findings (Goodwin & Guze, 1979).

Among psychiatric patients pseudoneurological symptoms are most often seen in subjects with somatization disorder, but are also commonly associated with drug addiction, alcoholism, sociopathy, or schizophrenia (Gatfield & Guze, 1962). In addition, these symptoms occur in patients with medical and neurological illnesses, and subjects with coexisting "organic" illness constitute a sizable percentage of index cases, especially among older subjects (Stefansson, Messina, & Meyerowitz, 1976). Follow-up studies of patients with conversion symptoms show that 20–30% eventually develop a physical disorder that was likely to have been etiologically related to the prior unexplained symptom (Gatfield & Guze, 1962; Slater & Glithero, 1965). Therefore, in populations presenting for medical care, the vast majority of subjects with pseudoneurological symptoms have or will develop symptoms of major psychiatric disorders or organic illnesses. Consistent with this, follow-up studies indicate increased mortality and morbidity in patients with these specific conversion symptoms, the outcome being related to the underlying associated illness (Gatfield & Guze, 1962; Slater & Glithero, 1965).

A number of investigators believe that isolated conversion symptoms are rare and that such a clinical presentation should prompt a careful evaluation and close follow-up. There are other data indicating that conversion symptoms may occur in some populations unassociated with underlying illnesses. In a group of postpartum women, histories of isolated pseudoneurological symptoms were common (Farley, Woodruff, & Guze, 1968). Similarly, in a population of soldiers, pseudoneurological symptoms may not be associated with other psychiatric syndromes (Carden & Schramel, 1966). Certainly a relationship between stress and conversion symptoms is suggested in this population. Unfortunately, the study reporting this finding did not specify the details of differential diagnosis or the criteria for diagnosis. Community epidemiologic studies with reliable instruments for diagnosing DSM-III disorders would be required to clarify the issues surrounding the existence of isolated conversion disorder in the general population. The identification of a population of primary conversion disorder would provide the basis for natural history and family studies to determine if such a diagnosis is valid and remains stable over time.

In addition to problems with population selection, another difficulty with the diagnosis of conversion disorder is shown in a recent study examining the specificity of the DSM-III criteria. Bishop and Torch (1979) could not differentiate conversion disorder from psychogenic pain disorder on a variety of clinical variables. Thus, with use of the broad DSM-III definition of conversion symptom, there is a lack of diagnostic specificity among the somatoform disorders. Further studies examining questions of reliability and validity of conversion disorder are needed before definite conclusions can be made regarding whether this syndrome exists as a separate entity or as a symptom of other syndromes. Pedigree studies can be useful in helping to clarify these issues. Slater (1961) found no evidence of concordance in monozygotic or dizygotic twins, but did find that the symptomatic twin usually had a lower birth weight, poorer health, and increased incidence of being left-handed. Unfortunately, there are no other family studies.

Some attempts have been made to study psychological and physiological parameters in subjects with conversion symptoms. Personality inventories such as the Minnesota Multiphasic Personality Inventory (MMPI) have been of limited value in identifying these patients with conversion symptoms who will develop organic illness at follow-up (Watson & Buranen, 1979). Features such as primary or secondary gain, la belle indifference, and disturbed sexuality have also been of limited utility (Bishop & Torch, 1979; Lazare, 1981). Neuropsychological tests indicate that subjects with conversion symptoms are suggestible and give field-dependent responses, that is, their answers are dependent on the surroundings (Bendefeldt, Miller, & Ludwig,

1976). In addition, these patients exhibit poor recent memory and decreased attentional skills. Ludwig (1972) has hypothesized that these deficits represent abnormalities in processing of afferent stimuli. As already mentioned, Meares and Horvath (1972) and Horvath et al. (1980) compared habituation of skin resistance in patients with acute conversion symptoms, chronic somatic difficulties, and anxious controls. They found that the chronic patients showed marked differences in habituation of skin resistance responses to repeated stimulation compared to both the patients with acute conversion symptoms and the anxious controls. There was no evidence that conversion symptoms alone were related to any abnormality in this type of testing. Difficulties exist in these studies. No attempt was made to determine which psychiatric or medical diseases were associated with the conversion symptoms. It is likely that the populations studied were heterogeneous.

In summary, conversion symptoms occur in a wide range of medical, neurological, and psychiatric disorders. During follow-up, most patients with conversion symptoms show diagnosable psychiatric or medical disorders. Subjects may exist in the community who do not seek medical attention but fulfill the DSM-III criteria for conversion disorder; however, direct data supporting this possibility are not available. In addition, it is unknown whether the presence of conversion symptoms associated with another disorder provides useful information concerning the outcome of the primary illness. For example, no data exist indicating that patients with sociopathy and conversion symptoms differ in outcome or treatment response to patients with sociopathy and no conversion symptoms. Finally, there is evidence that the DSM-III definition of conversion symptom lacks specificity. Based on the available literature, a narrow definition of pseudoneurological symptom may lead to better diagnostic discreteness and allow more confidence in predicting natural history.

Hypochondriasis

Unlike the diagnosis of somatization disorder, the DSM-III diagnosis of hypochondriasis is based on little systematic data. The criteria for this diagnosis include (a) a preoccupation with having a serious illness in the absence of medical confirmation, (b) lack of reassurance by discussion of negative medical findings, and (c) impaired functioning as a result of these beliefs. In addition, DSM-III stipulates that this diagnosis should not be made if other psychiatric syndromes such as affective disorder, somatization disorder, or schizophrenia are present. The few data available concerning hypochondriasis suggest that most patients are ill with other psychiatric disorders and that primary hypochondriasis is rare. In the following discussion, Kenyon's work (1964) as well as recent studies examining the relationship of hypochondriasis and affective disorder will be reviewed.

Kenyon (1964, 1976) studied psychiatric patients with chart diagnoses of hypochondriasis. He classified these patients into primary or secondary hypochondriasis, depending on whether somatic symptoms were the major problem or only one among other more striking psychiatric manifestations. The major disorder associated with secondary hypochondriasis was depression. Of the patients with primary hypochondriasis approximately one-third had associated psychiatric disorders even though the hypochondriasis was the major focus. In addition, the mental status examination of patients with primary hypochondriasis revealed that 40% had current depressive symptoms and 40% had current symptoms of anxiety. Unfortunately, no formal diagnostic criteria were used in determining the presence or absence of concurrent psychiatric disorders. Interestingly, over 30% of these patients with primary hypochondriasis had previously been diagnosed as having affective disorder. Follow-up of the patients with primary hypochondriasis demonstrated that over 20% developed other psychiatric syndromes, two-thirds being affective disorder and one-fifth schizophrenia. Over 40% of patients with either primary or secondary hypochondriasis had a positive family history of unspecified psychiatric disorders. Kenyon (1964, 1976) concluded that true hypochondriasis is rare or nonexistent and suggested that hypochondriasis usually exists as part of other psychiatric syndromes and when present usually implies a poor prognosis. Kenyon's work provides most of the epidemiologic data concerning this symptom complex.

Depression and medically unexplained somatic complaints are frequently related, and several studies examined this relationship. Cadoret, Widmer, and Troughton (1980) have shown that in a primary care setting, depressions frequently present with somatic complaints. These complaints are present before other symptoms of depression and decrease within a year after the other symptoms abate. This suggests that somatic complaints are frequent presenting and persisting symptoms of depression. Their course is linked to the natural history of the depressive episode. Unfortunately, the percentage of patients with somatic complaints who also fulfill the criteria for hypochondriasis was not specified in this study. We suspect that the relationship between depression and somatic complaints also applies to hypochondriacal complaints, but specific data addressing this are lacking.

Kreitman, Sainsbury, Pearce, and Costain (1965) compared depressed patients with and without hypochondriacal complaints. Those with such complaints had an increased incidence of "psychosomatic" illness, marital disharmony, and sexual maladjustment. Unfortunately, this work does not specify diagnostic criteria and does not exclude patients with Briquet's syndrome or other psychiatric disorders.

The approach used by Cadoret and Kreitman in studying the relationship of somatic symptoms to affective disorder may yield information with practical utility. Kreitman's work suggests that treatment of depression with somatic complaints may require particular attention to the psychosocial environment. Cadoret's work showing that somatic complaints often precede other symptoms of depression suggests that patients with a prior history of depression who present with unexplained somatic symptoms should be watched closely for a depressive relapse and early pharmacologic and/or psychotherapeutic intervention should be considered.

Though the available evidence suggests that hypochondriasis is best considered as a part of other psychiatric syndromes, caution is indicated because the available data are mainly from psychiatric patients. As Mayou (1976) points out, hypochondriasis may be common in nonpsychiatric populations. This could be determined by studying medical outpatients or general community populations, using a reliable diagnostic interview (L. N. Robins, Helzer, Croughan, & Ratcliff, 1981) in conjunction with a reliable instrument for hypochondriasis. Medical students offer an interesting population in which to study hypochondriasis (Idzorek, 1975; Woods, Natterson, & Silverman, 1966); many of them develop symptoms of hypochondriasis during medical school (Woods *et al.*, 1966).

Psychogenic Pain Disorder

The predominant feature of psychogenic pain disorder is pain that is unexplained by physical findings and that is thought to be associated with psychological factors. In addition, the pain must not be associated with another psychiatric disorder. This means that psychogenic pain disorder is a diagnosis of exclusion. The validity and clinical utility of this diagnosis and the recent proposal of Williams and Spitzer (1982) to alter the criteria for this disorder will be examined.

Most publications about psychogenic pain do not refer to the exclusion criteria used in DSM-III. The association of psychogenic pain with other psychiatric illnesses has been recognized by several investigators. Engel (1959) described pain syndromes as common among hysterics, depressives, hypochondriacs, and schizophrenics. Engel also referred to a group of patients who apparently did not have diagnosable psychiatric illnesses, but who did manifest psychological patterns similar to pain patients with other psychiatric disorders. Other investigators also have found that many chronic pain subjects have coexisting psychiatric disorders. Large (1980) reported that 145 of 172 subjects seen in a pain clinic had a coexisting psychiatric disorder, with the majority suffering from depression, hysteria, personality disorder, or drug dependence. Unfortunately, diagnostic criteria were not specified, thus limiting the conclusions that can be drawn from this study.

Besides the association of psychogenic pain with a variety of psychiatric syndromes, Bishop and Torch (1979) indicate further difficulties with the diagnosis. These authors, using criteria similar to DSM-III, were unable to differentiate psychogenic pain patients from subjects with conversion disorder, using a variety of clinical variables. They concluded that these two disorders are not diagnostically discrete. In addition, an overlap between somatization disorder and psychogenic pain is apparent. Among other symptoms, the criteria for somatization disorder include a category of unexplained pains, and it is likely that many patients studied as representing psychogenic pain in fact suffered from somatization disorder. Systematic studies evaluating the overlap among the somatoform disorders have not been reported to date, exclusive of the study of Bishop and Torch (1979).

A relationship between psychogenic pain and affective disorder has been evaluated in recent studies. Blumer and Heilbronn (1982) report that subjects with the "pain prone disorder" are usually depressed with characteristic clinical and psychosocial features. These authors conclude that chronic pain of psychological origin is a variant of depressive disease. Lindsay and Wyckoff (1981) provide support for this contention by reporting that 87% of patients in their pain center meet research criteria for depression. Further strengthening a relationship between pain and depression, these authors found that 59% of depressed subjects in a private psychiatric practice had a significant complaint of persistent pain. Cadoret et al. (1980) report that the presentation of depression as vague somatic symptoms (often pain) is a function of the clinical setting, being particularly common in general medical practice. In a general practice setting, such presenting complaints (back pain, headache, etc.) may not obviously suggest depression, so the clinician must be alert and make specific inquiries concerning other depressive symptoms.

The few available studies examining the families of psychogenic pain patients also point to a link with affective disorder. Blumer and Heilbronn (1982) reported significantly more depression in the families of psychogenic pain patients than in families of chronic medical patients. An increased incidence of alcohol abuse also occurred in the index families, but this difference was not significant. Based on these findings, the authors postulate that chronic pain disorder is a form of "depressive spectrum disorder," that is, primary depression in families with alcoholism and sociopathy (Winokur, Behar, & van Valkenburg, 1978). In a separate study, Schaffer, Donlon, and Bittle (1980) reported that 65% of chronic pain patients met criteria for depressive spectrum disorder. Furthermore, among subjects lacking "organic" pathology, 86% had positive family histories of psychiatric disorder, supporting a conclusion that there may be a difference between chronic pain patients with and without organic findings.

Although definitive biological markers do not exist for psychiatric disorders, the dexamethasone suppression test and REM latency have been reported to have considerable specificity for depression (Carroll et al., 1980; Kupfer, 1976). Blumer, Zorick, Heilbronn, and Roth (1982) applied these tests to 20 patients with psychogenic pain and found 40% exhibited dexamethasone nonsuppression and 40% exhibited shortened REM latency, suggesting a possible link between depression and chronic pain in some patients. Recent evidence, however, suggests that other psychiatric illnesses as well as physiological alterations (e.g., weight loss) may be associated with abnormalities of the dexamethasone suppression test (Berger, Doerr, Lund, Bronisch, & von Zerssen, 1982), limiting the conclusions that can be drawn using this approach to indicate a pain–depression relationship. Other psychological and physiological tests have not proved definitive in the differential diagnosis of pain patients. For example, the MMPI does not differentiate "organic" from "functional" complaints (Rosen, Frymoyer, & Clements, 1980).

The treatment response of chronic pain patients has produced a number of interesting findings suggesting a relationship between psychogenic pain and depression. It is known that psychotropic medications may prove beneficial in patients with chronic pain (Hendler, 1982). Blumer et al. (1982) indicate that the response of pain patients to antidepressants strengthens the association between pain syndromes and affective disorder, particularly in subjects with abnormal dexemethasone suppression or shortened REM latency. It is not clear, however, that such a conclusion ought to be drawn, since psychotropic agents have a variety of effects, including direct influences on neurochemical pathways involved in pain perception (Basbaum & Fields, 1978). Furthermore, antidepressants can be useful in doses lower than those used to treat depression, arguing for a mode of action separate from that involved in the treatment of affective disorder.

Based on the observations outlined in this review and the need for a systematic definition of psychogenic pain to advance research in this area, Williams and Spitzer (1982) have proposed a revision of the criteria for this disorder. The revised criteria, renaming the syndrome "idiopathic pain disorder," would require preoccupation with severe pain for greater than 6 months as the predominant disturbance. The pain must be inconsistent with known anatomic distribution, without organic cause or out of proportion to organic pathology, and specifically not due to somatization disorder, schizophrenia, or major depression. These criteria are as yet untested, but appear to be a step forward in that the requirement of 6 months of symptoms may select a more homogeneous population, eliminating more acute unexplained pain states. Furthermore, the exclusion criteria are more explicit, emphasizing the disorders most often seen in chronic pain patients. These proposed criteria would be even more restrictive and perhaps more useful if the exclusion criteria were expanded to include subjects with sociopathy, drug abuse, alcoholism, and severe anxiety states in whom the response to pain may be exaggerated (Large, 1980; Pilowsky & Spence, 1976).

Evidence to date, however, showing the existence of an independent primary pain syndrome is lacking. Questions must be raised whether the DSM-III criteria for psychogenic pain disorder describe a discrete nosological category or a mixed collection of psychiatric syndromes. As currently defined, the disorder cannot be easily distinguished from a variety of psychiatric illnesses, including other somatoform disorders. Data also indicate that a sizable subgroup of patients with psychogenic pain suffer from depression. These patients show clinical pictures, family histories, and laboratory test results consistent with this diagnosis. Another group of subjects meet criteria for sociopathy, drug dependence, alcoholism, schizophrenia, or anxiety states. One approach to the study of psychiatric disorders among chronic pain patients would be to apply a reliable psychiatric interview, such as the Diagnostic Interview Schedule (L. N. Robins *et al.*, 1981), to a series of patients meeting the proposed criteria of Williams and Spitzer (1982). In this way, the prevalence of major psychiatric disorders among the population of pain subjects could be ascertained. It is possible that a residual group of subjects with psychogenic pain as a primary diagnosis would be identified. This group might constitute a relatively homogeneous sample in which to study outcome, genetics, laboratory tests, and treatment response. Furthermore, subjects meeting criteria for other psychiatric diagnoses could also be studied to evaluate the effect of the pain syndrome on the outcome of their underlying disorder. Another important question is whether the presence of organic pathology influences the course of psychogenic pain. One approach in studying this would be to select subjects using the criteria of Williams and Spitzer (1982) and to evaluate differences in the prevalence of psychiatric disorders between those subjects without organic pathology and those in whom the pain is an "exaggerated" response to existing pathology. It is conceivable that differences in prevalence of psychiatric disorders, familial illness patterns, and outcome exist between these groups and that such differences could suggest hypotheses concerning the pathophysiology of disorders of pain perception.

Atypical Somatoform Disorders

This category classifies syndromes that have characteristics of somatoform disorders yet do not fit the criteria for any of the four disorders previously discussed. Since there are no specific criteria for this residual category, there are no studies of reliability or validity. Among the disorders classified as "atypical somatoform" are the syndromes of monosymptomatic hypochondriasis. Bishop (1980) recently reviewed three such syndromes: delusions of parasitosis, dysmorphophobia, and olfactory reference syndrome. These symptom complexes are usually associated with other psychiatric disorders, such as affective illness or schizophrenia (Bishop, 1980), but are not clearly related to any of the "typical" somatoform disorders. Since no criteria exist, it is difficult to know if yet other syndromes should be classified as atypical somatoform disorders.

A word of caution regarding the DSM-III atypical categories should be noted. A specific relationship between the atypical and typical categories of somatoform disorders is implied by the common classification as somatoform disorders. This, however, may be misleading, since systematic evidence does not exist supporting such a relationship. An alternate way of classifying atypical cases would be to use the more general category of "undiagnosed psychiatric illness," as described by Feighner *et al.* (1972). The advantage of an undiagnosed category is that it allows for unbiased systematic follow-up. Over time many of these patients will meet criteria for specific diagnoses, and the nature of their illnesses will become clearer (Liss, Welner, & Robins, 1972; Welner, Liss, Robins, & Richardson, 1972). Some may feel that it is a disadvantage to lump all atypical patients into one category; however, at the current state of psychiatric knowledge, it is our opinion that this approach best serves research endeavors as well as patient care by avoiding premature and possibly inappropriate classification.

Conclusions

In reviewing somatoform disorders from the perspective of systematic studies, it is evident that much research is required before we can accept the validity of the four DSM-III disorders. The DSM-III criteria, however, provide a framework for the needed studies. Current evidence indicates that a variety of psychiatric disorders often have vague, unexplained somatic complaints as prominent manifestations and that these psychiatric conditions can be recognized using specific diagnostic criteria and careful follow-up. Of the four syndromes classified in DSM-III under somatoform disorders, somatization disorder has been studied the best, with data available supporting the use of this category as a specific, separate entity. The other three categories lack such data. It is evident that conversion symptoms, though relatively common, are usually associated with other psychiatric and medical illnesses. The same can be said for hypochondriasis, that is, most patients with such symptoms have or will develop associated psychiatric syndromes. The practitioner is best advised to ask the appropriate diagnostic questions and to be especially alert for affective disorder. Psychogenic pain disorder probably represents a heterogeneous group of patients, some suffering from chronic medical illnesses with or without superimposed psychiatric disorders and others suffering primarily from psychiatric conditions. Some evidence suggests that there may exist a psychogenic pain syndrome which resembles depressive spectrum disorder.

Patients with complaints that lead to a diagnosis of somatoform disorder are frequently difficult for the primary care physician to manage. These patients are often demanding and manipulative, requiring a great deal of time and effort. From the evidence reviewed concerning conversion symptoms, hypochondriacal complaints, and unexplained pain, it is clear that a careful search for treatable medical and psychiatric illnesses is indicated. The psychiatrist can help with both differential diagnosis and recommendations for management. In patients with somatization disorder, the primary physician needs to be conservative about invasive procedures and medication, and the psychiatrist can frequently aid in the management of this very difficult condition (G. E. Murphy, 1982). For all these disorders, good management requires careful diagnosis and consistent sympathetic follow-up.

REFERENCES

American Psychiatric Association. (1980). *Diagnostic and statistical manual of mental disorders* (3rd ed.). Washington, DC: Author.

Basbaum, A. I., & Fields, H. L. (1978). Endogenous pain control mechanisms: Review and hypothesis. *Annals of Neurology, 4*, 451–462.

Bendefeldt, F., Miller, L. L., & Ludwig, A. M. (1976). Cognitive performance in conversion hysteria. *Archives of General Psychiatry, 33*, 1250–1254.

Berger, M., Doerr, P., Lund, R., Bronisch, T., & von Zerssen, D. (1982). Neuroendocrinological and neurophysiological studies in major depressive disorders: Are there biological markers for the endogenous subtype? *Biological Psychiatry, 17*, 1217–1241.

Bishop, E. R. (1980). Monosymptomatic hypochondriasis. *Psychosomatics, 21*, 731–741.

Bishop, E. R., & Torch, E. M. (1979). Dividing "hysteria": A preliminary investigation of conversion disorder and psychalgia. *Journal of Nervous and Mental Disease, 167*, 348–356.

Blumer, D., & Heilbronn, M. (1982). Chronic pain as a variant of depressive disease: the pain prone disorder. *Journal of Nervous and Mental Disease, 170*, 381–406.

Blumer, D., Zorick, F., Heilbronn, M., & Roth, T. (1982). Biological markers for depression in chronic pain. *Journal of Nervous and Mental Disease, 170*, 425–428.

Cadoret, R. J., Widmer, R. B., & Troughton, E. P. (1980). Somatic complaints: Harbinger of depression in primary care. *Journal of Affective Disorders, 2*, 61–70.

Carden, N. L., & Schramel, D. J. (1966). Observations of conversion reactions seen in troups involved in the Viet Nam conflict. *American Journal of Psychiatry, 123*, 21–31.

Carroll, B. J., Feinberg, M., Greden, J. F., Tarika, J., Albala, A. A., Haskett, R. F., James, N. McI., Kronfol, Z., Lohr, N., Steiner, M., de Vigne, J. P., & Young, E. (1980). A specific laboratory test for the diagnosis of melancholia. Standardization, validation and clinical utility. *Archives of General Psychiatry, 38*, 15–22.

Cloninger, C. R. (1978). The link between hysteria and sociopathy: An integrative model of pathogenesis based on clinical, genetic and neurophysiological observations. In H. S. Akiskal & W. L. Webb (Eds.), *Psychiatric diagnosis: Exploration of biologic predictors*. New York: Spectrum.

Cloninger, C. R., & Guze, S. B. (1970). Psychiatric illness and female criminality: The role of sociopathy and hysteria in the antisocial woman. *American Journal of Psychiatry, 127*, 303–311.

Coryell, W. (1980). A blind family history study of Briquet's syndrome: Further validity of the diagnosis. *Archives of General Psychiatry, 37*, 1266–1269.

Coryell, W. (1981). Diagnosis-specific mortality, primary unipolar depression and Briquet's syndrome (somatization disorder). *Archives of General Psychiatry, 38*, 939–942.

Coryell, W., & Norten, S. G. (1981). Briquet's syndrome (somatization disorder) and primary depression: Comparison of background and outcome. *Comprehensive Psychiatry, 22*, 249–256.

Engel, G. L. (1959). "Psychogenic" pain and the pain-prone patient. *American Journal of Medicine, 26*, 899–918.

Farley, J., Woodruff, R. A., & Guze, S. B. (1968). The prevalence of hysteria and conversion reactions. *British Journal of Psychiatry, 114*, 1121–1125.

Feighner, J. P., Robins, E., Guze, S. B., Woodruff, R. A., Winokur, G., & Muñoz, R. (1972). Diagnostic criteria for use in psychiatric research. *Archives of General Psychiatry, 26*, 57–63.

Flor-Henry, P., Fromm-Auch, D., Tapper, M., & Schopflocher, D. (1981). A neuropsychological study of the stable syndrome of hysteria. *Biological Psychiatry, 16*, 601–626.

Gatfield, P. D., & Guze, S. B. (1962). The prognosis and differential diagnosis of conversion reactions: A follow-up study. *Diseases of the Nervous System, 23*, 623–631.

Goodwin, D. W., & Guze, S. B. (1979). *Psychiatric diagnosis* (2nd ed.). New York: Oxford University Press.

Guze, S. B. (1967). The diagnosis of hysteria: What are we trying to do? *American Journal of Psychiatry, 124*, 77–84.

Guze, S. B. (1975). The validity and significance of the clinical diagnosis of hysteria (Briquet's syndrome). *American Journal of Psychiatry, 132*, 138–141.

Guze, S. B. (1978). Validating criteria for psychiatric diagnosis: The Washington University approach. In H. S. Akiskal & W. L. Webb (Eds.), *Psychiatric diagnosis: Exploration of biologic predictors.* New York: Spectrum Publications.

Guze, S. B., Woodruff, R. A., & Clayton, P. J. (1971). A study of conversion symptoms in psychiatric outpatients. *American Journal of Psychiatry, 128*, 643–646.

Hendler, N. (1982). The anatomy and psychopharmacology of chronic pain. *Journal of Clinical Psychiatry, 43*, 15–20 (3,Sec.2).

Horvath, T., Friedman, J., & Meares, R. (1980). Attention in hysteria: A study of Janet's hypothesis by means of habituation and arousal measures. *American Journal of Psychiatry, 137*, 217–220.

Hyler, S. E., Williams, J. B. W., & Spitzer, R. L. (1982). Reliability in the DSM-III field trials. *Archives of General Psychiatry, 39*, 1275–1278.

Idzorek, S. (1975). A functional classification for hypochondriasis with specific recommendations for treatment. *Southern Medical Journal, 68*, 1326–1332.

Kenyon, F. E. (1964). Hypochondriasis: A clinical study. *British Journal of Psychiatry, 110*, 478–488.

Kenyon, F. E. (1976). Hypochondriacal states. *British Journal of Psychiatry, 129*, 1–14.

Kreitman, N., Sainsbury, P., Pearce, K., & Costain, W. (1965). Hypochondriasis and depression in outpatients at a general hospital. *British Journal of Psychiatry, 111*, 607–615.

Kupfer, D. J. (1976). REM latency: A psychobiologic marker for primary depressive disease. *Biological Psychiatry, 11*, 159–174.

Large, R. G. (1980). The psychiatrist and the chronic pain patient: 172 anecdotes. *Pain, 9*, 253–263.

Lazare, A. (1981). Conversion symptoms. *New England Journal of Medicine, 305*, 745–748.

Lindsay, P. G., & Wyckoff, M. (1981). The depression-pain syndrome and its response to antidepressants. *Psychosomatics, 22*, 571–577.

Liss, J. L., Welner, A., & Robins, E. (1972). Undiagnosed psychiatric patients. Part 2: Follow up study. *British Journal of Psychiatry, 121*, 647–651.

Ludwig, A. M. (1972). Hysteria: A neurobiological theory. *Archives of General Psychiatry, 27*, 771–777.

Mayou, R. (1976). The nature of bodily symptoms. *British Journal of Psychiatry, 129*, 55–60.

Meares, R., & Horvath, T. (1972). "Acute" and "chronic" hysteria. *British Journal of Psychiatry, 121*, 653–657.

Murphy, G. E. (1977). Suicide and attempted suicide. *Hospital Practice, 12*, 73–81 (No. 11).

Murphy, G. E. (1982). The clinical management of hysteria. *Journal of the American Medical Association, 247*, 2559–2564.

Perley, M. J., & Guze, S. B. (1962). Hysteria: The stability and usefulness of clinical criteria. *New England Journal of Medicine, 266*, 421–426.

Pilowsky, I., & Spence, N. D. (1976). Illness behavioral syndromes associated with intractable pain. *Pain, 2*, 61–71.

Robins, E., & Guze, S. B. (1970). Establishment of diagnostic validity in psychiatric illness: Its application to schizophrenia. *American Journal of Psychiatry, 126*, 107–111.

Robins, L. N., Helzer, J. E., Croughan, J., & Ratcliff, K. S. (1981). National Institute of Mental Health diagnostic interview schedule. *Archives of General Psychiatry, 38*, 381–389.

Rosen, J. C., Frymoyer, J. W., & Clements, J. H. (1980). A further look at validity of the MMPI with low back patients. *Journal of Clinical Psychology, 36*, 994–1000.

Schaffer, C. B., Donlon, P. T., & Bittle, R. M. (1980). Chronic pain and depression: A clinical and family history survey. *American Journal of Psychiatry, 137*, 118–120.

Slater, E. (1961). Hysteria 311. *Journal of Mental Science, 107*, 359–381, 1961.

Slater, E., & Glithero, E. (1965). A follow-up of patients diagnosed as suffering from "hysteria." *Journal of Psychosomatic Research, 9*, 9–13.

Stefansson, J. G., Messina, J. A., & Meyerowitz, S. (1976). Hysterical neuroses, conversion type: Clinical and epidemiological considerations. *Acta Psychiatrica Scandinavica, 53*, 119–138.

Stoltzman, R. K., Helzer, J. E., Robins, L. N., Croughan, J. L., & Singerman, B. (1981). How does DSM-III differ from the systems on which it was built? *Journal of Clinical Psychiatry, 42*, 411–421.

Watson, C. G., & Buranen, C. (1979). The frequency and identification of false positive conversion reactions. *Journal of Nervous and Mental Disease, 167*, 243–247.

Welner, A., Liss, J. L., Robins, E., & Richardson, M. (1972). Undiagnosed psychiatric patients. Part 1. Record study. *British Journal of Psychiatry, 120*, 315–319.

Williams, J. B. W., & Spitzer, R. L. (1982). Idiopathic pain disorder: A critique of pain-prone disorder and a proposal for a revision of the DSM-III category of psychogenic pain disorder. *Journal of Nervous and Mental Disease, 170*, 415–419.

Winokur, G., Behar, D., & van Valkenburg, M. D. (1978). Is a familial definition of depression both feasible and valid? *Journal of Nervous and Mental Disease, 166*, 764–768.

Woerner, P. I., & Guze, S. B. (1968). A family and marital study of hysteria. *British Journal of Psychiatry, 114*, 161–168.

Woods, S. M., Natterson, J., & Silverman, J. (1966). Medical students' disease: Hypochondriasis in medical education. *Journal of Medical Education, 41*, 785–790.

CHAPTER 26

A Biopsychosocial Analysis of Psychosomatic Disease

George S. Everly, Jr.

For decades the notion that psychosomatic diseases were "caused" primarily by psychogenic variables such as personality constellations, specific attitudes, or various intrapsychic conflicts has not only persisted, but has inevitably influenced diagnostic classifications and therapeutic interventions as well. Weiner (1977) cogently argues that such perspectives are still being maintained today despite the fact that they no longer seem justifiable. The purpose of this chapter is to offer a biopsychosocial analysis of psychosomatic disease states. The purpose of such an analysis is to underscore, from an interactive system's perspective, the multifactorial configuration and intrafactor variability of psychosomatic etiology and pathogenesis, as in Weiner's (1977) terms, the "heterogeneity" of the psychosomatic phenomenon. Implications for classification and treatment will be discussed.

Epistemological Consideration

The epistemological importance of experimental design is well understood by empiricists. Through the simultaneous manipulation of one or more independent variables, while controlling for other sources of effect, the experimenter may isolate and measure the impact of an independent variable upon some dependent variable. Blalock (1964) suggests that the primary goal of rigorous experimental design is to more clearly understand the relation-

George S. Everly, Jr. Psychophysiological and Health Psychology Laboratory, Loyola College, Baltimore, Maryland.

ship between associated variables, thereby minimizing the tendency to employ "simplifying assumptions" about the relationship between those variables. He cogently argues that such simplifying inferences, while intended to
fill the gaps of knowledge that may exist in understanding the associated
variables, actually tend to oversimplify and thereby distort the relationship
between the variables of interest.

In the case of nonexperimentally generated, observational evidence
(such as in the case of psychosomatic disease), there is a far greater tendency
on the part of the observer to employ simplifying inferences concerning the
nature of the observed phenomenon (Blalock, 1964). This is particularly true
when the phenomenon being observed is not effectively isolated. This condition prohibits the observer from ruling out, on an empirical basis, the
influence of a large number of variables that are potentially operating in the
observed phenomenon.

To summarize so far, the experimentalist can reduce the number of
simplifying inferences made about the relationship between associated variables on the basis of design manipulations (e.g., blocking). The consumer of
nonexperimentally generated, observational evidence lacks this luxury and
must resort to the cognitive strategies of theory development for organizing
the evidence which has been observed. This condition potentiates the increased utilization of relatively less plausible simplifying inferences, depending upon the manner in which the evidence is cognitively formulated into
theory (Blalock, 1964; Pepper, 1942).

In Pepper's (1942) treatise on evidence, he describes two styles of theory
formulation that have particular relevance to the study of psychosomatic
medicine: (a) analytic theory development, and (b) synthetic theory development. The analytic and synthetic styles of theory development are best
viewed as opposite ends of a continuum rather than as nominal categories.

Analytic theory development (not to be confused with psychoanalytic
theory) tends to be mechanistic, categorical, and assume a linear cause and
effect relationship among variables. In general, it is a reductionistic perspective built upon a quantum of simplifying inferences. Schwartz (1982)
describes such a system as "concrete, relatively binary, single-category, sin-
gle-cause" (pp. 1042–1043). Interaction effects are overlooked, while linear,
single cause–effect models are promoted.

Synthetic theory development, on the other hand, attempts to integrate
and synthesize associated variables, focusing upon interactions and relationships. Schwartz (1982) describes such a system as a "more dynamic, relatively continuous, multicategory, multicause" approach (p. 1043). It is an
open system of theory development recognizing interactions among variables and the need for a model which accepts multiple causes for similar
effects.

In his useful application of Pepper's styles of theory formulation to
biopsychosocial research, Schwartz (1982) states that to this point research
in health and illness has been dominated by an analytic-like approach to

evidence. "It is clear that much progress has been made to date using this paradigm. However, this paradigm is turning out to be insufficient at both theoretical and research levels in accounting for multiple variables that interact and thereby affect health and illness" (Schwartz, 1982, p. 1043).

Schwartz's comments have particular relevance in the area of psychosomatic research. In the case of psychosomatic disease states, psychosomatic theory formulation serves as the basis for understanding and acting upon the disease. The following example should illustrate this point.

When an unexplained phenomenon (e.g., a psychosomatic disease) is first observed, it is a common practice to scrutinize the phenomenon as to offer a theory that attempts to explain the phenomenon (in this case, a theory of psychosomatic disease). The theory is usually expressed in terms familiar to the observers and that will bring the phenomenon into a realm of general understanding (e.g., traditionally accepted principles of psychology and pathophysiology). On the basis of the theory, some form of classification system (e.g., diagnostic categories) may then emerge. The classification system is usually employed to provide greater clarity to and understanding of the observed phenomenon. The classification system also inadvertently serves to perpetuate the theory used to explain the phenomenon, this to the exclusion of other theoretical formulations. Finally, a technology (i.e., a treatment intervention which is built on the theory and perhaps refined by the classification system) is then designed to provide the observers with some control over the phenomenon.

Theory formulation, then, literally provides the foundation for understanding and acting upon the observed phenomenon. In the case of psychosomatic disease states, the theory of psychosomatic disease may serve as the basis for not only diagnostic classification, but for therapeutic intervention as well.

Historically, psychosomatic theorists have tended to utilize theoretical formulations which have clustered toward the analytic end of the theoretical continuum. These theories have been burdened with "simplifying assumptions" about psychosomatic processes. It may be predicted, in congruence with Schwartz's perspective, that such theoretical formulations would prove inadequate and generally deficient when applied to complex multifactorial phenomena such as psychosomatic disease processes (Weiner, 1982). This prediction has been borne out as evidenced by decades of psychosomatic research which has followed analytic theoretical formulations and has failed to suitably explain the etiology and pathogenesis of psychosomatic diseases (see Weiner, 1977, for a review). In the case of multifactorial, interactive phenomena such as psychosomatic disease (Grinker, 1973; Weiner, 1977, 1982), a synthetic process of theory formulation is clearly indicated (Everly & Rosenfeld, 1981; Girdano & Everly, 1979; Grinker, 1973; Schwartz, 1982; Weiner, 1977, 1982). The adoption of such a theoretical perspective will have implications for not only our understanding of psychosomatic disease processes, but for classification and treatment as well.

In summarizing this initial section, it has been suggested that the process of psychosomatic theory formulation is a critical step in the epistemological process as it relates to understanding, classifying, and treating psychosomatic disease. Drawing upon the work of Pepper (1942), Schwartz (1982) argues that medical theory has traditionally adopted an analytic-like theoretical framework which has proved insufficient when applied to multifactorial health phenomena. The section concludes by advocating the adoption of a synthetic theoretical framework upon which to better understand multifactorial, interactive phenomena such as psychosomatic disease states.

Historical Background

In direct contrast to the synthetic, multifactorial orientation for psychosomatic phenomena proposed in this chapter, historically the major psychosomatic theorists employed a far more analytic and highly specific theoretical framework.

Among the earliest of the attempts at formulating a coherent psychosomatic theory was that of Dunbar (1943). She described specific personality profiles which seemed highly correlated with selected psychosomatic diseases. For example, she described the hypertensive patient as being shy, reserved, rigid, yet possessing the tendency for "volcanic eruptions of feelings." On the other hand, the highly achievement-oriented perfectionist would be more likely to develop migraine headaches. Dunbar's analyses, while noteworthy as a pioneering effort, represented a classic example of linear, unidimensional theory formulation. As such, the theory failed to consider the roles of environmental factors, physiological mechanisms of mediation, and target organ vulnerabilities as other important aspects of the psychosomatic process.

Subsequent theorists such as Grace and Graham (1952), Wolff (1953), Alexander (1950), Alexander, French, and Pollock (1968), and G. Engel (1967) began to include such factors into the overall psychosomatic schema, but failed to do so in a clearly integrative and comprehensive manner (Weiner, 1977).

According to Weiner (1977), there now exists "three major psychosomatic theories of the initiation of disease—the specific conflict theory, the situational theory, and the stress theory. . . . None of these theories is completely satisfactory" (p. 611).

The specific conflict theory was first postulated by Alexander as early as 1950. He implied that specific psychosomatic diseases were produced by specific unconscious emotional conflicts congruent with a psychoanalytic interpretation. For example, peptic duodenal ulcers may be viewed as the symptomatic manifestation of frustrated dependence desires originally oral in character. Although Alexander and his co-workers expressed an appreciation for physiological mechanisms of mediation and target organ vulnerabilities as intervening factors, they failed to express an appreciation for the multivariate potential which exists within each of those factors. According to Weiner (1977), "Alexander assumed that the pathogenetic mechanism in each disease is always the same. In light of our present knowledge this assumption is probably incorrect" (p. 611).

The situational theory of psychosomatic disease directly contradicts the specific conflict theory. Rather than attempting to correlate specific attitudes or conflicts with subsequent psychosomatic diseases, the situational theory examines the broader context within which a host of emotions and attitudes may occur. G. Engel and Schmale (1967; G. Engel, 1967; Schmale & Engel, 1967) examine situational contexts such as Cannon's (1914) "fight or flight" response as well as Engel's "conversation withdrawal" response, the former consisting of fear, anger, or other related psychological states coupled with various catabolic physiological responses, while the latter consisting of helplessness, hopelessness, and other associated states of psychological impotence coupled with a potentially wide spectrum of anabolic physiological responses. Therefore, this theory postulates that many emotions and attitudes may share the same basic situational context, and it is this context that acts as the basis for the psychosomatic disease process, not the specific emotions or conflicts.

The postulations of G. Engel and his co-workers appear to be valid for certain patient populations (e.g., ulcerative colitis, peptic duodenal ulcer, and rheumatoid arthritis), but not for others (Knapp & Nemetz, 1960). Weiner (1977) concludes that the situational theory of psychosomatic disease has simply not been borne out by the empirical evidence currently available. While the theory addresses heretofore neglected aspects of psychosomatic disease, the perspective fails to explain adequate variation to provide sufficient viability.

The stress theory of psychosomatic disease is based primarily upon the work of Selye (1956). The major focus of Selye's research has been the nonspecific activation of the hypothalamic–anterior pituitary–adrenal cortical physiological response axis during exposure to noxious stimuli. Selye hypothesized that chronic activation of this axis led to psychosomatic disease states, though he failed to delineate exactly why. Beginning in the 1960s Selye's work began to be criticized for an apparent lack of appreciation for idiosyncratic cognitive/affective variables in the initiation of a stress response (Everly & Rosenfeld, 1981; Lazarus, 1966) and for an overemphasis on the nonspecific nature of the physiological response mechanisms of mediation (Levi, 1972; Mason, 1971). In effect, the stress theory of psychosomatic disease seems to lack the comprehensive nature that appears to be needed to unify this field (refer to Schwartz, 1982).

Each one of the major theories of psychosomatic disease reviewed here and elsewhere (see Everly & Rosenfeld, 1981; Lachman, 1972; Weiner, 1977) tends to emphasize one factor in the psychosomatic disease process. Although they may often mention other factors in their theoretical formulation, they still emphasize one component as the main source of effect. Such an approach violates a truly multifactorial, integrative model, as has been postulated as being necessary to better understand the psychosomatic disease process. That is not to say that these theories of psychosomatic disease have not contributed to the field—they have. Each major theory, in its own way, has seemed to account for some heretofore unexplained portion of the variance in the psychosomatic disease process. This fact in itself gives further theoretical and empirical support to the notion postulated in the beginning of this chapter that what is needed to better explain psychosomatic disease is a truly multifactorial, interactive model. It now remains for the next section to present such a model.

An Interactive Biopsychosocial Model of Psychosomatic Disease

A key premise upon which this chapter is built is the belief that psychosomatic disease represents a dynamic, interactive "biopsychosocial" phenomenon, that is, psychosomatic diseases result from a complex interaction of biological, psychological, and social factors, with no single factor generally assuming a prepotent role to the exclusion of other factors across individuals. Such a belief underscores the role of dynamic, interacting individual differences in the psychosomatic disease process.

Weiner (1977, 1982) has cogently described the inadequacies of traditional models of psychosomatic disease. He advocates the development of a new theoretical model which is more comprehensive and which reflects the "heterogeneity" of factors that play a role in the psychosomatic disease process. In his review of psychosomatic theories, Reiser (1977) states, "To formulate a psychosomatic theory, we must see man as existing in a 'bio-psycho-social' field. With intracellular processes at one end and a panoply of social, cultural, and even historical influences at the other, this open transactional system allows constant bidirectional flow of information and energy" (p. 214).

The basic tenets for such an interactive biopsychosocial model of psychosomatic disease can be traced back to the work of the general systems theorists in the late 1940s and early 1950s (see von Bertalanffy, 1968; Miller, 1978). These tenets were later incorporated into the work of theorists such as Williams (1967) and Millon (1969). G. Engel (1977) advanced a biopsychosocial model relevant to the general understanding of health and disease. Girdano and Everly (1979) applied such a model to health education. Levi (1979) applied a similar model to preventive medicine. Leigh and Reiser (1980) refined the model and applied it to general medical practice, while Schwartz (1982) discussed such a model's relevance to behavioral medicine research. But it was Roy Grinker (1973), writing in the early 1950s, who first applied systems theory directly to psychosomatic medicine. He wrote that since psychosomatic etiology "is not a linear cause and effect, a direct and monistic relationship between graded hierarchical levels of complexity, we should study circular, transactional, and corrective processes with the greatest effort towards inclusiveness; at least, excluded processes should be defined" (pp. 181–182).

The core principle undergirding systems theory is that the behavior of any living organism is best understood as a function of a dynamic interaction of its parts. According to von Bertalanffy (1968) then, any organism (system) should be viewed as an integrated whole and its behavior should be viewed as a function of its interacting parts (i.e., the integrated whole) rather than as the simple mechanistic sum of compartmentalized linear processes. Attempts, based upon analytic theoretical formulations, to reductionistically dissect the whole as to discover the nature of its functional parts (as has been the case in the study of psychosomatic disease for close to 30 years) run the risk of yielding a distorted perspective of the whole. Such attempts usually fail to recognize the role of functional interactions among parts. Indeed, the very processes that we have historically used to try to better understand phenomena such as psychosomatic diseases may actually have distorted our perspective of the nature of the phenomenon that we have attempted to understand in the first place.

The biopsychosocial model described below is not intended to fill all of the gaps in psychosomatic theory, but rather is merely designed to demonstrate the interactive, multifactorial configuration of the psychosomatic disease process, with an emphasis on the potential for intrafactor variability. Therefore, rather than proposing a reductionistic or rigidly linear model of psychosomatic disease, this chapter will describe an interactive, multifactorial model designed to underscore the importance of individual differences in the etiology and pathogenesis of psychosomatic diseases. The model draws heavily upon the work of Levi (1972, 1979), Weiner (1977, 1982), Everly (1978), and Everly and Rosenfeld (1981).

The biopsychosocial model of psychosomatic disease presented below has three major components acting and interacting within it: (*a*) environmental factors, (*b*) psychological factors, and (*c*) biological factors (see Figure 26-1). Let us briefly review these three components and the variables active within each.

Environmental factors, particularly social "life events" factors, have been shown to play a significant role in human health and disease. According to Weiner (1982), "Until recently, psychosomatic medicine had . . . failed to incorporate into its research and theory the role of the social (not only the human) environment. Social factors clearly play a role in every aspect of health care and of disease" (p. 35).

Early research by Wolff (1953) had indicated that stressful life events play a significant role in the etiology of psychosomatic disease states through the initiation of various neurophysiological response mechanisms. Holmes

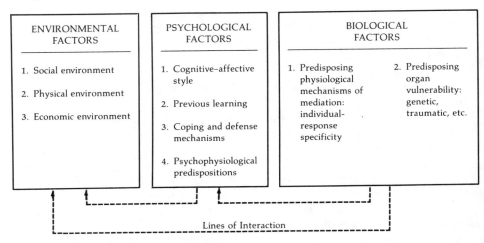

Figure 26-1. *An interactive biopsychosocial model of psychosomatic disease.*

and Rahe and their colleagues conducted a series of retrospective and prospective studies that found that environmental changes were indeed highly correlated with subsequent psychosomatic disease manifestations (Holmes & Rahe, 1967; Rahe, 1973; Rahe, McKean, & Arthur, 1966).

While the list of environmental variables which may play a role in the initiation of the psychosomatic disease process seems inexhaustible, the pathogenetic mechanism underlying virtually all environmental variables in the psychosomatic process can be identified as a stimulus-dependent insult to the organism's homeostatic functioning. This notion that certain environmental stimuli can affect a somewhat reliable psychophysiological alteration (usually hyperarousal or hypoarousal) across individuals is well known to psychophysiologists as "stimulus response specificity" (B. Engel, 1972; Rosseler & Engel, 1977). Gellhorn (1957) has noted that response patterning can indeed occur to situationally dependent conditions. Rosseler and Engel (1977) remark that this tendency is so great that "Some stimuli are apparently almost universal in their effects" (p. 55).

Despite evidence that suggests environmental variables can indeed affect significant psychophysiological alterations, it is simply not warranted to assign a prepotent etiological role to such variables to the exclusion of other factors in the psychosomatic disease process. Henry and Stephens (1977) argue that environmental variables are best viewed as psychosomatic "triggers" which serve to initiate many psychosomatic events. Clearly, the impact of environmental variables is not causally linear, but rather is subject to mitigation or amplification by intervening variables such as cognitive appraisal and cognitive/behavioral coping responses (Weiner, 1982). This brings us to the second major component in the biopsychosocial model of psychosomatic disease: psychological variables.

Psychological variables are clearly the oldest of the proposed etiological factors in the psychosomatic disease process. Dunbar (1943) correlated "personality profiles" with psychosomatic diseases. Alexander (1950) correlated specific intrapsychic conflicts with the development of psychosomatic diseases. Friedman and Rosenman (1974) correlated behavior patterns with coronary heart disease, while Yunik (1980) correlated coping patterns with overall illness susceptibility. Research by Ax (1953), Schachter (1957), Averill (1969), Rosseler (1973), and Henry and Stephens (1977) even identified emotion-specific patterns of psychophysiologic responsiveness with implications for subsequent development of psychosomatic disease states.

In attempting to integrate psychological factors into environmental factors, theorists such as Arnold (1960), Lazarus (1966), and Wolf (1981) place primary etiological importance upon the "cognitive appraisal" of the environmental factor. In other words, it may be argued that much of the environmental stimulus's psychophysiological potency may be determined by the individual's cognitive interpretation of that stimulus. As was the case with the environmental factors, the psychological factors possess significant potential for variability. Potential variability may be due to a myriad of individual psychological differences such as the overall cognitive–affective style, previous learning, coping and defense mechanisms, and psychophysiological predispositions (e.g., an ergotropically "tuned" response predisposition predisposes an individual to hyperaroused reactions to environmental stimulation (see Gellhorn, 1957).

We see so far in this biopsychosocial model of psychosomatic disease that the major role of the environmental variables is to initiate the psychosomatic chain of events. The environmental variables, while clearly potent unto themselves, are also subject to subsequent mitigation or amplification by a host of psychological variables such as personality constellations (Gellhorn, 1957; Rosseler & Engel, 1977) before they impact biological substrata. This brings us to the final major factor in this model of psychosomatic disease: biological variables.

The major biological variables in the psychosomatic disease process fall under the headings of physiological mechanisms of mediation and predisposing organ vulnerabilities.

The term "physiological mechanisms of mediation" refers to the underlying physiological response axes responsible for transducing environmental and psychological variables into psychosomatic symptomatology. There are three major physiological response axes: (a) the neural (autonomic), (b) the neuroendocrine, and (c) the endocrine. Furthermore, within each of these major axes exist other response pathways (Everly & Rosenfeld, 1981).

The neural response axis consists of the sympathetic and parasympathetic nervous systems. The effect of activation of this neural axis is thought to be the immediate and generalized arousal of the ergotropic or trophotropic systems (dual activation has been noted by Gellhorn, 1957).

The role of the neuroendocrine response axis appears to be the continuation of the ergotropic response by way of the sympathoadrenomedullary hormones—epinephrine and norepinephrine. The increased release of these hormones can stimulate additional mediational mechanisms such as increased cardiac output; reduction of arterial lumen at the vascular beds in the skin; reduced blood flow to the kidneys and aspects of the gastrointestinal system; increased plasma levels of free fatty acids, triglycerides, and total cholesterol; induction of myocardial ischemia and necrosis; facilitation of deposition, calcification, and rupture of thromboembolitic components of the blood; and increased tension within the striated musculature (Everly & Rosenfeld, 1981; Mason, 1968b; McCabe & Schneiderman, 1983).

End organ outcome related to the mediational mechanisms just enumerated include increased arterial blood pressure, atherosclerosis, angina pectoris, myocardial infarction, arrhythmias, subjective report of anxiety, thrombosis, striated muscle contraction syndromes, and vasospastic syndromes (Everly & Rosenfeld, 1981; Henry & Stephens, 1977).

Finally, the endocrine axis is another potential mechanism of mediation in psychosomatic disease states. Most coherently described by Selye (1956) and Mason (1968a), the endocrine response axis actually consists of numerous and diverse endocrinological pathways.

One of these pathways, the hypothalamic–anterior pituitary–adrenal cortical system, is receiving considerable attention in recent psychosomatic research efforts. Stimulation of this pathway may lead to the release of the glucocorticoid and/or mineralocorticoid hormones. Their effects are thought to include the stimulation of subsequent mediational mechanisms, including suppression of aspects of the immune system; increased levels of plasma free fatty acids, triglycerides, and total cholesterol; increased sodium retention; increased serum glucose levels; and thymicolymphatic retardation (in animals). These processes have been correlated with subsequent end organ outcome such as immunosuppression, clinical depression, peptic ulceration, increased arterial blood pressure, and numerous cardiovascular disorders (Everly & Rosenfeld, 1981; Henry & Stephens, 1977; Mason, 1968a; Selye, 1956).

It is important to keep in mind that the adrenal cortical pathway, while important, is not the only endocrine pathway. Other endocrine pathways have been shown to exist and be responsive to stressful stimulus conditions. These pathways may manifest themselves by the release of somatotropic hormone, thyroid stimulating hormone, gonadotropic hormones, vasopressin, and oxytocin (Makara, Palkovits, & Szentagothai, 1980). The roles that these hormones play in the psychosomatic process are extremely complex and not clearly understood at this time. What does seem clear, however, is that the stimulation of these pathways as well as those described earlier can occur individually, collectively, or in countless combinations. Furthermore, many of what appear to be similar or identical end organ outcomes, for example, hypertension, may be caused by numerous and very dissimilar mechanisms of mediation (see Everly & Rosenfeld, 1981; Henry & Stephens, 1977; McCabe & Schneiderman, 1983; Weiner, 1977).

To summarize this discussion of mechanisms of mediation, earlier in this section it was indicated that certain stimulus conditions and various emotions appear to reliably activate discrete psychophysiological response patterns across individuals. This phenomenon has been called stimulus-response specificity. In addition to stimulus-response specificity, researchers have identified another form of response patterning—"individual-response specificity" (B. Engel, 1972; Rosseler & Engel, 1977). Individual-response specificity refers to a patient's idiosyncratic tendency to respond to a variety of stressful stimuli with the same physiological response pattern, such as those enumerated earlier. It has been suggested (Everly & Rosenfeld, 1981; Rosseler & Engel, 1977) that such response patterning itself may be pathogenetic. Thus, we see that the potential for physiological response variability within and between individuals is rather staggering and serves to further underscore the interactive multifactorial process underlying psychosomatic phenomena.

A final consideration under the heading of biological factors in the psychosomatic disease process would be preexisting organ vulnerabilities. It is clear that the range of limits for "normal" human anatomy and physiological functioning is broad indeed. The size of various endocrine glands may vary up to 1200% and hormonal function may vary up to 600% across normal, healthy adults (Williams, 1956). While benign in their own right, under certain conditions, or in combination, extreme anatomical or physiological variations may serve to predispose an individual to various psychosomatic diseases. Called the "weak-organ" hypothesis by some, there is considerable evidence that through genetic programming, trauma, or learning history some individuals may indeed possess a biological predisposition within a specific organ system for the development of some psychosomatic disease (Farber, 1982; Lachman, 1972; Rosseler & Engel, 1977; Weiner, 1977).

In the present biopsychosocial model of psychosomatic disease, environmental factors, psychological factors, and biological factors have been shown, singularly and through interaction, to possess pathogenetic qualities relevant to a model of psychosomatic disease. The fact that the research has shown each one of these factors capable of explaining some degree of pathogenetic variance stands in support of the adoption of a multifactorial, interactive model rather than continuing to pursue single cause–effect models. Environmental factors have been shown to possess some degree of pathogenetic potency in their own right. However, they have also been shown to be affected by psychological factors which themselves have been shown to possess some degree of pathogenetic potency. Finally, the pathophysiological mechanisms of mediation and predisposing organ vulnerabilities have been shown to be numerous and complex. All of these conditions support the notion that the psychosomatic disease process represents a complex multifactorial interactive process which may be uniquely different for not only different diseases, but for different individuals as well.

Implications for Classification

If, as suggested in this chapter, the psychosomatic disease phenomenon is indeed multifactorial, then this fact should somehow be reflected in the way we classify such diseases.

The notion of the psychosomatic disease as a multifactorial phenomenon failed to appear in the *Diagnostic and Statistical Manual of Mental Disorders*, 2nd Edition (DSM-II) (American Psychiatric Association, 1968). In this manual, the term psychosomatic was replaced by psychophysiologic and defined as a "group of disorders characterized by physical symptoms that are caused by emotional factors and involve a single organ system" (p. 46). Diseases were then grouped according to the organ system involved. This classification schema had clear shortcomings based on what we now know. It failed to provide for multiple organ involvement, it failed to consider the role that emotional processes may play to exacerbate existing medical conditions, and it became enmeshed in the notion of emotional "causality" which is impossible to demonstrate on the basis of observational data.

The revision of the DSM-II, the DSM-III (American Psychiatric Association, 1980), attempted to remedy some of the problems inherent in the DSM-II's classification schema for psychosomatic diseases. The DSM-III offers a multiaxial diagnostic system which includes "Clinical Syndromes" (Axis I), "Personality Disorders" (Axis II), "Physical Disorders and Conditions" (Axis III), "Severity of Psychosocial Stressors" (Axis IV), and "Highest Level of Adaptive Functioning Past Year" (Axis V). The Axis I category of "Psychological Factors Affecting Physical Condition" (316.00) still allows for the listing of disorders thought to be psychosomatic or psychophysiologic in nature. However, the concept of psychosomatic has been broadened to include psychological factors which initiate or exacerbate a physical condition. The additional axes (III, IV, and V) allow the clinician to more fully describe the nature of the psychosomatic disease condition. This system allows for consideration of multiple organ involvement in psychosomatic diseases, avoids the trap of assuming emotional causality, and more readily accepts the potential for multifactorial influences in psychosomatic disease states. Disorders traditionally known as hysterical syndromes or conversion disorders are now classified under the Axis I category of "Somatoform Disorders" so as not to confuse them with psychosomatic disorders.

The DSM-III, while a significant improvement over the DSM-II in relation to the classification of psychosomatic diseases, still possesses significant shortcomings when scrutinized from a synthetic systems perspective, however. Although the DSM-III's multiaxial format allows the clinician to more fully describe any psychosomatic manifestation diagnosed on Axis I (316.00) through the use of Axis IV (psychosocial stressors) and Axis V (highest level of adaptive functioning), it fails to provide a more clinically complete biopsychosocial description of that psychosomatic manifestation. Even when the options of using Axes IV and V are selected in describing psychosomatic manifestations, the clinician is asked to employ ordinal scaling procedures, almost exclusively reflective of environmental considerations, on both axes. Axis IV consists of grossly simplified approximations of life events factors which have been criticized even in their more complete empirically derived format (Weiner, 1977, 1982). Axis V asks the clinician to consider adaptive functioning in terms of global factcors such as social relations, occupational functioning, and the use of leisure time. To summarize, the options now available to the clinician in the DSM-III for classifying psychosomatic diseases, even when Axis IV and Axis V are both employed, clearly neglect clinically relevant factors in the biopsychosocial model such as mitigating or amplifying psychological variables and biological variables that may directly or indirectly contribute to the psychosomatic disease process. Therefore, the classification system for psychosomatic diseases, in its present state, fails to show any meaningful appreciation for the role of individual differences and multifactorial biopsychosocial interaction in the psychosomatic disease process.

For future classificatory consideration, the psychosomatic disease is best conceived of as any disease in which psychological factors serve to predispose, initiate, or exacerbate organic pathology. This perspective, by definition, includes illnesses that range from acute but recurrent viral infections to chronic degenerative diseases, as well as the traditional psychosomatic disease entities. Any classification schema built upon this premise must be sensitive enough to reflect individual differences in the environmental, psychological, and biological factors which constitute the psychomatic disease process.

A biopsychosocial classification system for psychosomatic diseases could easily be integrated within a multiaxial format, similar to the DSM-III's format, beginning with the identification of the physical condition presumably affected by psychological factors. This designation would occur on Axis I (Clinical Syndromes). Greater clarification and appreciation for individual differences would then be added to the Axis I classification through the addition of a formalized multiaxial biopsychosocial subclassification format which entails three subclassifications: (a) the contribution that environmental factors may have played in the initiation or facilitation of the psychosomatic chain of events; (b) the role that psychological factors may have played in the mitigation or amplification of those environmental factors; and (c) the role that existing biological factors (such as anatomical or physiological variations, preexisting trauma, infections, risk factors, and genetic endowments) may have played in the psychosomatic disease process. For example:

Axis I: Physical Conditions Affected by Psychological Factors—Migraine
Headaches

1. Environmental Factors	a. Undesirable change in working conditions
	b. Unexpected pregnancy
2. Psychological Factors	a. Environmental factors viewed as a loss of control
	b. Obsessive tendencies
3. Biological Factors	a. Mother and grandmother with history of migraine headaches

The multiaxial subclassifications provide greater clinical insight into patient idiosyncracies which help define the psychosomatic process. These subclassifications can be effectively presented solely in a descriptive format (as above) without the need for the rather arbitrary ordinal scaling procedure now used with the DSM-III on Axes IV and V. This multiaxial subclassification format need only be used in conjunction with psychosomatic diagnoses. Use of the proposed biopsychosocial classification system in no way restricts the use of Axes III, IV, or V within the existing DSM-III; it merely serves to augment the clinical description regarding psychosomatic diseases. What were traditionally considered hysterical syndromes and conversion reactions (now called somatoform disorders) would, of course, be classified separately on Axis I.

The proposed biopsychosocial classification model is not only more clinically descriptive, but is more readily inclined to reflect an appreciation for the heterogeneous nature of the psychosomatic disease process. Furthermore, such a classification model may well lead to a better understanding of the complexities of psychosomatic diseases. Improved understanding may then serve as the basis for improved treatment as well.

Implications for Treatment

The acceptance of a synthetically derived, interactive biopsychosocial model of psychosomatic disease carries with it certain implications for not only classificatory schema, but treatment paradigms as well. It seems reasonable to assume that accepting a biopsychosocial model of psychosomatic disease includes the recognition that such diseases not only can be, but probably should be treated using a biopsychosocial treatment model. As Levi (1979) states: "To be effective a program should be based on . . . a holistic (overall) view of man and environment; that is, equal and integral consideration for physical, mental, social and economic aspects" (p. 28). Many of the issues relevant to utilizing such a treatment model have been discussed elsewhere (see Everly & Rosenfeld, 1981; Leigh & Reiser, 1980; Levi, 1979; Weiner, 1977, 1982) and therefore will be described only briefly here.

A biopsychosocial treatment model would ideally combine interventions directed toward the patient's environmental, psychological, and biological domains and rendered from a concomitant temporal perspective when feasible.

Interventions into the patient's environmental domain would include any and all strategies designed to promote a positive change in the patient's overall ecosystem. Such interventions might include family therapy, the building of social and economic support networks, career counseling, and even dietary management, along with other related strategies.

Interventions into the patient's psychological domain might include, but not be limited to psychoanalysis, psychotherapy, behavior therapy, relaxation training, and other interventions designed to initiate a health-promoting change in the patient's personality structure or behavior pattern. Psychotropic pharmacotherapy might be employed to temporarily reduce the patient's pathognomonic propensity for excessive psychophysiological reactivity.

Finally, interventions into the patient's biological domain might include, but not be limited to the following: the medical management of the biological risk factors and the symptomatic manifestations of the psychosomatic disease process; psychotropic pharmacotherapy directed at the reduction of excessive psychophysiological arousal; relaxation training with the intent of having the patient develop skill in the autogenic initiation of the trophotropic state (see Everly & Rosenfeld, 1981, for a rationale); and physical exercise (see Everly & Rosenfeld, 1981, and Martin & Dubert, 1982, for a rationale).

Because this intervention schema is theoretically derived using a synthetic analysis, it possesses the cybernetic qualities of ongoing interaction and modification based upon the progress and needs of the patient.

Summary

It seems unjustifiable to assume that psychosomatic diseases are caused by invariant pathogenetic processes. Furthermore, similar psychosomatic diseases may be caused by dissimilar processes across individuals. In Weiner's (1982) words, "every disease is multifactorially determined *and* heterogeneous in nature" (p. 36). The biopsychosocial model of psychosomatic disease described in this chapter attempts to point out the multifactorial configuration and variability potential that exists within psychosomatic disease states along with the need to appreciate the role of individual differences in understanding, classifying, and treating such diseases.

It is apparent that theories of human health and disease that are derived using analytic theory formulation are no longer tenable. Rather, synthetic theoretical perspectives are needed to understand such conditions, psychosomatic diseases being the case in point. As Williams (1967) notes, "It seems indefensible to assume that people are built in separate compartments, one

anatomical, one physiological, one biochemical, one psychological, and that
these compartments are unrelated or only distantly related to each other.
Each human being possesses and exhibits unity" (p. 17).

By viewing humankind from a dynamic multifactorial interactive biopsychosocial perspective (Pepper's synthetic perspective), we should be better
able to understand, classify, and treat psychosomatic diseases.

REFERENCES

Alexander, F. (1950). *Psychosomatic medicine.* New York: Norton.
Alexander, F., French, T., & Pollock, G. (1968). *Psychosomatic specificity.* Chicago, IL: University of
    Chicago Press.
American Psychiatric Association. (1968). *Diagnostic and statistical manual of mental disorders* (2nd
    ed.). Washington, DC: Author.
American Psychiatric Association. (1980). *Diagnostic and statistical manual of mental disorders* (3rd ed.).
    Washington, DC: Author.
Arnold, M. (1960). *Emotion and personality.* New York: Columbia University Press.
Averill, J. (1969). Autonomic response patterns during sadness and mirth. *Psychophysiology, 5,*
    399–414.
Ax, A. (1953). The psychophysiological differentiation between fear and anger in humans.
    Psychosomatic Medicine, 15, 433–442.
Blalock, H. (1964). *Causal inferences in nonexperimental research.* Chapel Hill: University of North
    Carolina Press.
Cannon, W. B. (1914). The emergency function of the adrenal medulla in pain and in the major
    emotions. *American Journal of Physiology, 33,* 356–372.
Dunbar, H. F. (1943). *Psychosomatic diagnosis.* New York: Harper (Hoeber).
Engel, B. (1972). Response specificity. In N. Greenfield & R. Sternbach (Eds.), *Handbook of
    psychophysiology* (pp. 571–576). New York: Holt, Rinehart, & Winston.
Engel, G. (1967). A psychological setting of somatic disease: The "giving up–given up" complex.
    Proceedings of the Royal Society of Medicine, 50, 553.
Engel, G. (1977). The need for a new medical model: A challenge for biomedicine. *Science, 196,*
    129–136.
Engel, G., & Schmale, A. (1967). Psychoanalytic theory of psychosomatic disorder. *Journal of the
    American Psychoanalytic Association, 15,* 344–363.
Everly, G. (1978). *The organ specificity score as a measure of psychophysiological stress reactivity.* Unpub-
    lished doctoral dissertation, University of Maryland, College Park.
Everly, G., & Rosenfeld, R. (1981). *The nature and treatment of the stress response.* New York: Plenum
    Press.
Farber, S. (1982). Genetic diversity and differing reactions to stress. In L. Goldberger &
    S. Breznitz (Eds.), *Handbook of stress* (pp. 123–133). New York: Free Press.
Friedman, M., & Rosenman, R. (1974). *Type A behavior and your heart.* New York: Knopf.
Gellhorn, E. (1957). *Autonomic balance and the hypothalamus.* Minneapolis: University of Minnesota.
Girdano, D., & Everly, G. (1979). *Controlling stress and tension: A holistic approach.* Englewood Cliffs,
    NJ: Prentice-Hall.
Grace, W., & Graham, D. (1952). Relationship of specific attitudes and emotions to certain
    bodily diseases. *Psychosomatic Medicine, 14,* 243–251.
Grinker, R. (1973). *Psychosomatic concepts.* New York: Jason Aronson.
Henry, J. P., & Stephens, P. (1977). *Stress, health, and the social environment.* New York: Springer-
    Verlag.
Holmes, T., & Rahe, R. (1967). The social readjustment rating scale. *Journal of Psychosomatic
    Research, 11,* 213–218.
Knapp, P., & Nemetz, S. (1960). Acute bronchial asthma—concomitant depression with excite-
    ment and varied antecedent patterns in 406 attacks. *Psychosomatic Medicine, 22,* 42–46.

Lachman, S. (1972). *Psychosomatic disorders.* New York: Wiley.

Lazarus, R. (1966a). *Psychological stress and the coping process.* New York: McGraw-Hill.

Lazarus, R. (1966b). *Stress and coping.* New York: McGraw-Hill.

Leigh, H., & Reiser, M. (1980). *Biological, psychological, and social dimensions of medical practice.* New York: Plenum Press.

Levi, L. (1972). Psychosocial stimuli, psychophysiological reactions and disease. *Acta Medica Scandinavia, Supplementum 528.*

Levi, L. (1979). *Psychosocial factors in preventive medicine.* Washington, DC: Public Health Service.

Makara, G., Palkovits, M., & Szentagothai, J. (1980). The endocrine hypothalamus and the hormonal response to stress. In H. Selye (Ed.), *Selye's guide to stress research* (pp. 280–337). Princeton, NJ: Van Nostrand-Reinhold.

Martin, J., & Dubert, P. (1982). Exercise applications and promotion in behavioral medicine. *Journal of Consulting and Clinical Psychology, 50,* 1004–1017.

Mason, J. W. (1971). A re-evaluation of the concept of "non-specificity" in stress theory. *Journal of Psychiatric Research, 8,* 323–333.

Mason, J. W. (1968a). A review of psychoendocrine research on the pituitary–adrenal cortical system. *Psychosomatic Medicine, 30,* 576–607.

Mason, J. W. (1968b). A review of psychoendocrine research on the sympathetic–adrenal medullary system. *Psychosomatic Medicine, 30,* 631–653.

McCabe, P., & Schneiderman, N. (1983). Psychophysiologic reactions to stress. In N. Schneiderman & J. Tapp (Eds.), *Behavioral medicine.* Hillsdale, NJ: Erlbaum.

Miller, J. G. (1978). *The living system.* New York: McGraw-Hill.

Millon, T. (1969). *Modern psychopathology: A biosocial approach to maladaptive learning and functioning.* Philadelphia, PA: Saunders.

Pepper, S. (1942). *World hypotheses.* Berkeley: University of California Press.

Rahe, R. (1973). Life change measurement as a predictor of illness. *Proceedings of the Royal Society of Medicine, 61,* 1124–1126.

Rahe, R., McKean, J., & Arthur, R. (1966). A longitudinal study of life change and illness patterns. *Journal of Psychosomatic Research, 10,* 355–360.

Reiser, M. (1977). The challenge of newer research findings for psychosomatic theories. In G. Usdin (Ed.), *Psychiatric medicine* (pp. 195–227). New York: Brunner/Mazel.

Rosseler, R. (1973). Personality, psychophysiology, and performance. *Psychophysiology, 10,* 315–327.

Rosseler, R., & Engel, B. (1977). The current status of the concepts of physiological response specificity and activation. In Z. Lipowski, D. Lipsitt, & P. Whybrow (Eds.), *Psychosomatic medicine* (pp. 50–57). London & New York: Oxford University Press.

Schachter, J. (1957). Pain, fear, and anger in hypertensives and normotensives. *Psychosomatic Medicine, 19,* 17–29.

Schmale, A., & Engel, G. (1967). The "giving up–given up" complex illustrated on film. *Archives of General Psychiatry, 17,* 135.

Schwartz, G. (1982). Testing the biopsychosocial model: The ultimate challenge facing behavioral medicine. *Journal of Clinical and Consulting Psychology, 50,* 1040–1053.

Selye, H. (1956). *The stress of life.* New York: McGraw-Hill.

von Bertalanffy, L. (1968). *General systems theory.* New York: Braziller.

Weiner, H. (1977). *Psychobiology and human disease.* New York: Elsevier/North-Holland.

Weiner, H. (1982). Psychobiological factors in bodily disease. In T. Millon, C. Green, & R. Meagher (Eds.), *Handbook of clinical health psychology* (pp. 31–52). New York: Plenum Press.

Williams, R. (1956). *Biochemical individuality.* New York: Wiley.

Williams, R. (1967). The biological approach to the study of personality. In T. Millon (Ed.), *Theories of personality and psychopathology* (pp. 14–24). New York: Holt, Rinehart, Winston.

Wolf, S. (1981). The role of the brain in bodily disease. In H. Weiner, M. Hofer, & A. Stunkard (Eds.), *Brain, behavior, and bodily disease* (pp. 1–9). New York: Raven Press.

Wolff, H. G. (1953). *Stress and disease.* Springfield, IL: Charles C Thomas.

Yunik, S. (1980). *The relationship of personality variables and stressful life events to the onset of physical illness.* Unpublished doctoral dissertation, University of Miami, Coral Gables, FL.

CHAPTER 27

The Relationship between Personality Disorder and Psychiatric Illness

H. J. Walton

Introduction

The relationship described in this chapter between personality and psychiatric illness emerged from a series of investigations. The early studies (Presly & Walton, 1973; Walton, Foulds, Littmann, & Presly, 1970; Walton & Presly, 1973) explored the reliability of psychiatric diagnosis of personality disorder; the later studies were concerned with the relationship between illness and disorder and explored how personality disorder influences the outcome of psychiatric illness. The evidence presented, therefore, deals with the interaction between personality and illness, and focuses on changes in the state of the patient during the course of time.

The psychiatric literature has long reflected that there are good grounds for a distinction between "personality disorders," on one hand, and neurotic and psychotic illnesses, on the other. In the United States, this differentiation has been made formal by providing Axis II for separate diagnosis of personality disorders in the revision of the diagnostic classification system, DSM-III (American Psychiatric Association, 1980). The diagnostic system used in Britain, the *International Classification of Diseases* (ICD-9) (World Health Organization, 1975), now also emphasizes the need to diagnose illness and personality disorder separately.

Clinicians have often acted to the contrary in their diagnostic practice, as if there is a relationship of mutual exclusiveness between the diagnosis of illness, on one hand, and personality disorder, on the other. This was reflected in former ICD and American Psychiatric Association DSM classifi-

H. J. Walton. Department of Psychiatry, University of Edinburgh, Edinburgh, United Kingdom.

cations. Many psychiatrists still continue to view the two diagnoses as mutually exclusive, focusing primarily on a patient's illness and on the condition of the personality secondarily, if at all.

Despite the new systems of diagnostic classification (ICD-9 and DSM-III), the patient's personality and whether or not personality disorder is present is still largely neglected in contemporary psychiatric practice.

Our Diagnostic Practice

Our practice and the basis of the clinical research described here has been to diagnose both the illness and personality status of every patient (i.e., symptoms and traits, respectively). While differentiation within the "personality disorder" axis is by type of traits (e.g., aggressive, overdemonstrative, aloof, fixed and rigid, etc.), differentiation within the illness axis is by type of symptom (e.g., phobia, depression, thought disorder, etc.). Differentiation between illnesses is by constellations of symptoms or syndromes, for example, phobic state or schizophrenia. Differentiation within the personality disorders is by constellations of traits, for example, those constituting paranoid personality disorder or hysterical personality disorder.

Various Approaches to the Study of Personality

The concepts most appropriately used for studying personality will vary with the main purpose of any investigation. To focus on traits is, of course, not the only way in which to study personality. Various approaches can be taken in the clinical study of personality, each one the more appropriate for particular purposes:

1. Personality disorder can be studied in terms of traits shown by patients, an approach which may be especially fruitful for descriptive or diagnostic purposes.

2. Another approach is to focus on disturbed personal relationships. Abnormal personality is then categorized and studied by exploring the recurrent difficulties in the patient's mode of associating with other people, for example, aggressive and domineering or submissive and dependent. Personality obtains its meaning from the patient's personal relationships.

3. Focusing on concrete repetitive acts illuminates the investigation of personality disorder. This approach also contributes to the devising of treatment strategies. Stressed by some authors is emphasis on acts, on items of abnormal behavior, such as criminal behavior, alcohol misuse, or marital violence.

Detailed information relevant to all three aspects is available for all patients in the present investigation.

Psychiatric Illness

The cohort of patients studied was a consecutively admitted group of inpatients, as specified below, suffering from psychiatric illnesses. Psychiatric illness was assumed to be present when there had been a change (i.e., the occurrence of one of the generally described syndromes) which occasioned distress to the individual or to his associates, which had no clearly evident organic basis, and which resulted in some limitation or distortion of previous functioning. Illness is usually described in terms of symptoms and signs. A symptom is a qualitative change from a previous condition, about which the individual complains, and which is found rarely in the general population. A sign is a qualitative change in mental or bodily functioning which the skilled observer recognizes as a characteristic feature of a given illness.

States are defined as those milder quasi-neurotic conditions, intermediate between normality and neurosis, with symptoms not greatly different qualitatively from normal conditions. Experiences of anxiety and depression come into this category; for example, it is often debated whether mild anxiety, such as occurs over world events, such as international strife, is pathological. (Existential psychiatrists would say no.) It is also sometimes difficult to decide when a bereavement response has become a depressive illness.

The Differentiation of Personality and Illness

While the importance of separate consideration of personality disorder and illness has been accepted by many other writers (e.g., Lewis, 1974; Shepherd & Sartorius, 1974; Zubin, 1967), numerous others have argued against such a distinction, at least as regards the personality disorders and the neuroses. For example, Jaspers (1963) included the neuroses under the term "Personality Disorders," and Schneider (1958) in turn had subsumed both the neuroses and the personality disorders under "Psychopathic Personalities." Such writers do not consider the distinction between personality and illness as important. Thus, Slater and Roth (1969) state:

> Tachycardia, sweating, feelings of fear, insomnia, depression, faints, fugues and the other phenomena which we call neurotic symptoms, are easily thought of as manifestations of a given personality and constitution in circumstances favourable to their development. We could also consider tendencies to seek relief in alcohol, outbursts of temper, wandering, dereliction of duty, lying and thieving, and acts of ruthless cruelty in the same light. There can be no fundamental distinction; and such distinction as there is depends on their social effects and their liability to be dealt with by doctors or by other agents of society. (p. 97)

Authors taking this position postulate that personality disorder is merely a less severe form of neurotic illness. We do not accept these views.

The major theoretical differences between traits and symptoms (or signs) can be described as follows:

1. Traits are universal, while symptoms are not. Traits are regarded as present throughout the general population. Differences among people are quantitative, and "abnormality" as it refers to personality refers only to an extreme degree of a characteristic (i.e., present to an extent rarely found in the general population). Symptoms and signs in contrast affect only a subgroup of the general population. Most people do not have symptoms and signs which are outside their personal or behavioral repertoire.

2. Traits describe the "normal" continuities of behavior and are relatively enduring. Symptoms and signs, on the other hand, signify a disruption of this continuity of behavior and are relatively transient.

3. Traits are relatively ego-syntonic; in contrast, symptoms are ego-dystonic, that is, experienced as alien or a change in the person.

Categorical and Dimensional Approaches to Personality Disorder

Both of these approaches are employed in this research.

A Category Diagnostic Approach

In the present investigation, a system of personality diagnoses previously developed was used (Walton *et al.*, 1970). The psychiatrists rating the patients were asked to judge the severity of the personality disorder if present. Mild degrees of personality disorder are present in those who subjectively identify their impairment (Table 27-1).

Table 27-1
Categories of Personality Disorder

0. No abnormality	
1. Mild:	Character disorder (usually complained of by the patient himself)
	a. Withdrawn
	b. Dependent
	c. Overassertive
2. Moderate:	Personality disorder (usually identified clinically)
	a. Schizoid
	b. Hysterical
	c. Paranoid
	d. Cycloid
	e. Obsessional
3. Severe:	Sociopathy (usually identified socially)
	a. Passive
	b. Aggressive

Personality disorder of moderate degree (e.g., hysterical, schizoid, obsessional) is usually readily identified by the clinically informed, often on the basis of the patient's social difficulties or disturbed personal relationships.

Severe abnormality of personality is recognized in those who harm others by aggressive acts or are a gross liability because of their fecklessness.

The mild and severe forms are described in terms of the patient's predominant impairment in relationships with other persons, while the intermediate class bears classical labels signifying well-known personality dispositions often thought to be related to psychiatric illnesses for which similar terms are employed. The weaknesses in this diagnostic system have been pointed out (Walton et al., 1970).

The traditional diagnostic categorical system calls on psychiatrists to employ single labels and treats each type of disorder, for example, obsessional, schizoid, as mutually exclusive categories. The use of a category approach results in diagnostic disagreement among clinicians assessing the same patients; it also causes much relevant information to be discarded, resulting in a simplistic clinical perspective. A person can obviously have a complex personality disorder with mixed abnormal personality types, for example, both psychopathy and hysterical features.

A Dimensional Diagnostic Approach

The alternative to a category diagnostic approach is the development of a dimensional diagnostic system of personality disorders, each patient evaluated for each of the components of personality represented. The diagnostic result is then not a single category attribution, but a profile taking into account numerous dimensions.

While debate continues whether a dimensional approach is preferable, it must be obvious that this will be so for certain purposes (as the work of Eysenck and Cattell illustrates). For other purposes a category approach is to be preferred; for example, in the present state of clinical recognition of personality disorder, psychiatrists may be persuaded to attempt category diagnoses (as ICD-9 and DSM-III advocate), but may find a dimensional approach too complex to adopt.

Sample of Patients Studied

Our sample consisted of consecutive admissions to Ward 1 in the Professorial Unit of the Royal Edinburgh Hospital. Every patient admitted over a period of 27 months was considered for inclusion. Patients were included if they met the following criteria:

1. First admission
2. Aged 18–55 years

3. Not with a primary diagnosis of organic psychiatric illness

4. If schizophrenic, with an illness of less than 2 years' duration

The age limits were set to correspond to those of the normative samples of the psychometric tests used and to exclude possible changes due to aging in older patients. Chronic schizophrenic patients were excluded because of likely personality deterioration as a result of the illness.

Of all 192 patients admitted during the study period, 52 were excluded by these defined criteria, leaving a sample of 140 patients in the original 1971 study sample (55 men and 85 women), with a mean age of 30.2 years ($SD = 9.9$ years). Complete initial data were collected on all patients. The retested sample for whom full follow-up data were collected numbered 134 patients. Five patients from the 1971 cohort were excluded from this retested sample because they did not complete all the psychological tests, and another patient who was in Britain only transiently was also excluded.

The subjects were listed in chronological order of their admission to hospital at the time of the 1971 study. In the follow-up study, they were contacted in the same order so as to minimize differences in the length of the follow-up period.

A comparison of our study sample with Royal Edinburgh Hospital admissions as a whole during the same period showed that our sample contained more sociopathic patients and patients with neurosis, and fewer with schizophrenia. Our patients were younger, and there was a higher proportion of women.

The Investigative Method

The investigation was collaborative, many colleagues of different professional disciplines taking part. It was done in Ward 1, Professorial Unit, Royal Edinburgh Hospital, which is run on therapeutic community lines under my direction.

The investigations, in progress over a decade, were carried out mainly by psychiatrists and clinical psychologists. However, the clinical setting being a therapeutic community, the work was feasible only with the full participation of nursing staff, occupational therapists, and psychiatric social workers.

Assessment at First Admission

Four methods of assessment were undertaken during each patient's first admission (T_1).

PSYCHIATRIC ILLNESS DIAGNOSIS

Psychiatrists rated illness and psychologists administered psychometric tests. Psychiatric diagnoses of illness (and personality disorders) were made independently for each patient by three (out of five) psychiatrists at the patient's first admission conference between 4 and 11 days of admission.

The categories into which the illness diagnoses were sorted were as follows: psychotic depression; other psychoses; neurotic depression and/or anxiety; phobic, conversion, dissociative or obsessional neurosis; and other.

PERSONALITY DIAGNOSIS, CATEGORICAL

The psychiatrists making clinical assessments of personality were provided with a system of categories including those contained in the *International Classification of Diseases* (ICD-8) (World Health Organization, 1974) and in the American Psychiatric Association classification (DSM-II) (American Psychiatric Association, 1968). Both DSM-II and ICD-8 went into effect in 1968.

The earlier study (Walton *et al.*, 1970) of this system has been mentioned above. The category method was used by having three psychiatrists (out of a pool of five raters) independently rate each of the patients at the time of first admission, in terms of (*a*) the category of abnormal personality judged to be present and (*b*) its severity. The five psychiatrists taking part as raters knew the patients well, having seen them in group therapy sessions or in individual interviews, and were all present at a key ward round when the patient was interviewed. The basis on which the rating was done was that one psychiatrist carried out the clinical interview while the other two raters were present. The three psychiatrists then diagnosed the personality of each patient independently, choosing the diagnosis most applicable to the patient from the 12 possible personality categories listed in Table 27-1.

PERSONALITY DIAGNOSIS, DIMENSIONAL

An inventory was designed to cover all traits commonly recognized as relevant to personality disorders (Table 27-2). Every patient in the series was then rated on all these traits. (The raters also entered their overall personality disorder diagnoses as item 47.) The rating inventory, the rating procedure, and the analysis of the data has been reported previously (Presly & Walton, 1973).

Four-point scales were constructed for each of the 35 items, from anxiety (item 2 above) to suggestibility (item 36), with the criteria for each point operationally defined ranging from normality to extreme pathology (Table 27-3 presents an example).

The rating form also allowed for some abnormal behaviors (e.g., alcoholism, antisocial acts, suicidal behavior, and sexual dysfunction) to be recorded (items 37–45), as well as the severity of personality disorder (item 1).

The psychiatrists rated all patients in the sample during the first admission. The resulting dimensional profiles were then subjected to further statistical treatment (see below). The dimensional system developed in this way allows for the identification of more than one prominent set of traits in an individual patient, and for quantitative variations among individual patients to be specified on any given set of traits.

Table 27-2
Personality Trait Relating Inventory

None: Mild:
Moderate: Severe:

1. Severity of disorder
2. Anxiety
3. Guilt processes
4. Officiousness
5. Unlikability
6. Meekness, submissiveness
7. Impulsiveness
8. Dependency on others
9. Overindependence
10. Cyclothymic tendency
11. Ability to profit from experience
12. Lack of regard or consequence of acts
13. Indecisiveness
14. Detachment from others
15. Suspiciousness
16. Irresponsibility

17. Ingratiation
18. Avoidance of competition
19. Irritability
20. Avoidance of close relationships
21. Need for attention
22. Insincerity
23. Timidity
24. Insensitivity
25. Conscience defect
26. Sexual provocativeness
27. Egocentricity
28. Extrapunitiveness
29. Intropunitiveness
30. Physical aggression
31. Superficiality in personal relationships
32. Exploitativeness of others

33. Excessive display of emotion
34. Meticulousness
35. Stubbornness
36. Suggestibility
37. Disturbance in personal relationships
38. Drug dependence
39. Sexual deviation
40. Degree of associated psychiatric illness
41. Alcoholism
42. Antisocial acts
43. Suicidal behavior
44. Sexual dysfunction
45. Work impairment
46. Personality disorder dominant over illness
47. Personality diagnosis: specify

PSYCHOMETRIC ASSESSMENT AT FIRST ADMISSION

Psychometric tests were administered by one clinical psychologist within a mean period of 3.5 days ($SD = 2.14$ days) of admission. In some cases the patient's mental state necessitated a delay, but only twice did this exceed 1 week.

The tests used were (1) the Symptom–Sign Inventory (SSI); (2) the Hostility–Direction of Hostility Questionnaire (HDHQ); (3) the 16 PF Inventory (Presly, 1971). Three psychometric measures of "sociopathy" emerged from the initial stages of the investigation (McIver & Presley, 1974): the Extrapunitiveness scale of the HDHQ; the G ("Expediency vs. Conscien-

Table 27-3
Scale of Ability to Profit from Experience

0. Usual capacity to learn from experience
1. Rather unable to alter unsuccessful behavior patterns
2. Marked inability to learn from any but drastic setbacks
3. Does not show any ability to modify self-destructive or maladaptive behavior as a result of setbacks or disasters.

tiousness") of the 16 PF; and the Q_3 ("Undisciplined vs. Controlled") scale of the 16 PF. These will be referred to subsequently.

The SSI Personal Disturbance (PD) Scale is a measure derived from the patient's self-reporting about his illness status on an inventory devised by Foulds (1962) containing only items that refer to symptoms and signs of neurotic and psychotic illness. The range of test scores was ranked in three categories: (1) patient's scoring on the PD illness scale as not ill ($\overline{PD}$); (2) those scoring as borderline (?PD); and (3) those with high scores indicating current illness symptoms (PD). The SSI was administered first, followed by the HDHQ which was completed in the examiner's presence. The 16 PF was then explained in detail and the examples worked through. Most patients were then allowed to take the form away for completion and were instructed to return it the following day. The psychometric findings were then correlated with the psychiatric clinical assessments.

Follow-up after 3 Years

The patients were contacted in the order of their admission some 3 years later.

Two follow-up investigations were done: (*a*) A psychiatrist, Mark Aveline, assessed the degree of psychiatric illness at the end of 3 years since the first admission to hospital. He also assessed the patient's degree of social disability in five areas (work—including housework, leisure activity, sexual satisfaction, in the family, and in social relationships outside the family): Scores on each social adjustment item were summed. From these assessments the stability and predictive value of clinical measures of illness and personality could be examined in relation to outcome of illness. (*b*) A clinical psychologist, David McIver (1979), concurrently repeated the psychometric test procedures described above.

Evidence was obtained by these investigations about the stability of initial assessments of personality and illness in 134 patients. The main findings will now be reported.

Results of First Study

The Category System of Diagnosis of Personality Disorder

BETWEEN-RATER DIFFERENCES IN THE USE OF DIAGNOSTIC CATEGORIES

There were marked differences in the category diagnosis of personality disorder by different psychiatrists at the first admission. Rater A used the category "schizoid" twice as often as the other two psychiatrists carrying out ratings of the same patients. Rater B overused the label "hysterical" as compared with his two colleagues, who were equal in the frequency with which they employed this diagnostic category. Rater C was liberal in his diagnosis of the "dependent" personality type, a category used only half as often by Rater A and hardly at all by Rater B. It was thus not possible for the trio of psychiatrists to assign patients satisfactorily to a diagnostic category using only a single personality label. It is evident that a categorical diagnostic approach could not be applied reliably.

DIFFERENCES IN THE ASSIGNMENT OF DIAGNOSES TO MEN AND WOMEN

There were marked differences in the frequency with which personality disorder categories were assigned to male and female patients. The greatest differences were found in the use of the categories of "hysterical" and "sociopathy, passive." This discrepancy had also been found in an earlier investigation of another sample of patients (Walton *et al.*, 1970). For all five raters, the label "hysterical personality disorder" was applied only 8 times in 165 ratings of male patients compared with 73 times for 255 female patient ratings. All psychiatrists more commonly diagnosed passive sociopathy in men than in women. Finally, schizoid personality disorder was twice as commonly diagnosed in men.

The Dimensional Approach to Diagnosis of Personality Disorder

RELIABILITY OF TRAIT RATINGS

This system of rating was found to be considerably more reliable, psychiatrists agreeing in their rating of patients' personalities on the basis of their specific traits.

A principal components analysis of the trait ratings by clinicians yielded five dimensions. Each dimension was labeled descriptively according to its item content, as shown in Table 27-4.

Each patient thus had a score on each of the five scales derived from the principal components analysis. A profile for each patient can be constructed with the relevant value for all five components of personality disorder. This procedure was then subsequently successfully replicated in a different sample of patients. A method was thus devised enabling clinicians reliably to assess at least some of the dimensions of abnormal personality.

Table 27-4
Dimensions of Personality

1. Sociopathy (31% of the variance)
2. Submissiveness (15% of the variance)
3. Hysterical ⎫
4. Obsessional ⎬   The three dimensions together accounting for 18% of the variance
5. Schizoid ⎭

Results of the Follow-up Study

Change over Time of Categorical Diagnosis of Personality

The stability or otherwise of the categorical diagnosis of the subjects' personality was investigated. Approximately 60% of patients were given the same personality diagnosis at T_1 and again at T_2. The changes in category diagnosis in those patients not rediagnosed as they had been 3 years previously involved all the categories of personality diagnosis.

At the follow-up psychiatric assessment, therefore, the category diagnosis of the personalities of 60% of the patients remained the same, despite very considerable illness changes. It was interesting to note that the diagnostic shift applied to all diagnoses. It has therefore not been shown that some and not other of the personality categories retain stability over the 3 years of follow-up investigation.

Change in Dimensional Diagnosis of Personality

After the follow-up interval of approximately 3 years, the changes over time of the dimensional personality profiles were examined. At T_2, subjects were rated mainly by only one clinician (R1) but, in order to assess the reliability of his ratings, two random subgroups ($N = 13$, $N = 11$, respectively) were rated by two clinicians (i.e., R1 × R2 and R1 × R3). Agreement between clinicians at T_2 was broadly similar to that which had been found at T_1.

The test–retest correlations for 102 patients whose profiles were compared after 3 years are as shown in Table 27-5.

Table 27-5 shows that test–retest correlations for the 102 patients compared at T_1 and T_2 were high for the Sociopathy scale and, to a lesser extent, for the Hysterical and Submissiveness scales. The Schizoid scale gave lower, but still significant test–retest correlations. The Obsessional scale correlated less closely but still significantly at the two points in time, T_1 and T_2. On the Sociopathy, Submissiveness, Schizoid, and Hysterical scales,

Table 27-5
Dimensions of Personality: Test-Retest Correlations

1. Sociopathy	$r = .62^{***}$
2. Submissiveness	$r = .41^{***}$
3. Hysterical	$r = .50^{***}$
4. Obsessional	$r = .24^{*}$
5. Schizoid	$r = .33^{***}$

$^{*}p = .05.$
$^{***}p = .001.$

subjects were rated as more "normal" at T_2 than at T_1. Changes in personality profile ratings were equally likely among men and women patients. These changes were clearly related to recovery from illness [as assessed at T_2 by the psychiatrist and independently by the psychometric test (SSI) administered by the clinical psychologist].

We have therefore shown that although the personality dimensions have satisfactory interrater reliability, they do change, and this mutability appears a function of recovery from accompanying psychiatric illness.

Changes in Illness Status

Over half of the patients recovered satisfactorily from their psychiatric illness in the course of 3 years: 56% were diagnosed by the psychiatrist at T_2 as having no symptoms or only minimal symptoms (Table 27-6). Men fared better than women.

A quarter of the patients had a further psychiatric hospitalization during the 3 years of the follow-up period. A third of the subjects were currently in regular treatment contact at the time of follow-up, and 40% were taking psychotropic medication at that time. Men and women were equally likely to be taking psychotropic medication. Women were more likely than men to be hospitalized again and also to be in treatment at follow-up. Of those with symptoms, 65% had symptoms similar to those at the first admission. Illness diagnosis at the first admission (T_1) was not predictive of illness outcome after 3 years (T_2).

Initial Personality Diagnosis and Illness Outcome

Category diagnosis of personality at the key admission was not predictive of illness outcome. However, an association was found between the category personality diagnosis and the patient's subsequent social adjustment, the degree of social disability as rated by the psychiatrist at follow-up (T_2).

Personality trait ratings (dimensional diagnosis) at the first admission did not predict illness outcome. There was again an association, however, with the psychiatric rating of the amount of disability present at T_2.

Table 27-6
Follow-up Illness Assessment (By Independent Psychiatrist at T_2)

Continuously symptom-free	9[a]
Residual symptoms only	19
Interim breakdown with complete remission	28
Interim breakdown with partial or no remission	30
Continuously ill since T_2	14

[a]Percentage.

Psychometric Test Finding and Outcome

A variety of personality attributes tested psychologically at the first admission were found to be associated with illness outcome. But most of the apparently predictive personality attributes were so only because of their association with illness.

The tested personality attributes relating to "sociopathy" measured at the first admission, as described above (Extrapunitiveness, G, and Q_3), were independently predictive of outcome. The predictive relationships between illness and the traits associated with sociopathy were as follows: (a) Those subjects who were less severely ill usually had a good illness outcome, regardless of the presence or absence of sociopathy; (b) for those subjects who had been more severely ill, poor outcome was significantly related to the presence of sociopathy. It is thus important to make psychometric assessments of both personality and of illness separately when investigating illness outcome.

Important findings emerged about the patient's illness state at follow-up after 3 years, using the SSI Personal Disturbance Scale as an index of illness outcome. Psychiatric assessment of the clinical severity of illness at follow-up showed that patients who were symptom-free and those with mild symptoms comprise 61% of the sample. This corresponds closely to the 59% also identified as similarly well by the PD scale. The psychiatrist carrying out the follow-up evaluation found that 22% of patients had moderately severe symptoms, an exactly similar proportion having borderline PD scores (PD?).

Psychiatric assessment at follow-up showed 18% of patients to have a severe degree of symptoms, corresponding to the 20% identified by the PD scale of the SSI (Table 27-7).

Independent psychological test corroboration was thus obtained of the psychiatrist's rating of the severity of the illness state at T_2. The psychometric classification of subjects by the Personal Disturbance Scale therefore predicted illness outcome at the time of retest (and also during the course of 3 years).

The categories of the Symptom–Sign Inventory administered at T_2 were found to be consistently related to a number of clinical indices of illness

Table 27-7

Relation between Clinical and Psychometric Test Assessment of Outcome

Clinical severity of illness T_2 (%)	SSI PD scale T_2 (%)
Nil (39) }	
Mild (22)	PD (59)
Moderate (22)	?PD (22)
Severe (18)	PD (20)

status at T_2 and during the course of the 3 years preceding T_2 (e.g., the number of psychiatric hospital admissions during the follow-up period). The different groups at outcome varied in (a) the probability of having greater severity of symptoms as rated clinically at follow-up; (b) greater social disability; and (c) unsatisfactory illness status throughout the follow-up period. In addition, the psychometric classification was associated with (d) differences in the probability of having current psychiatric treatment contact; and (e) current psychotropic medication. (f) The other significant but least strong relationship was with repeated psychiatric admissions during the 3-year follow-up period.

Conclusions

All the patients in the investigation received their treatment and subsequent outpatient management in a ward conducted as a therapeutic milieu, the treatment intentionally devised to foster personality change. Thus, intended treatment effects, the course of the psychiatric illness, and the extent to which personality disorder is modifiable are all components in the outcome perceived over time.

The investigation of personality disorder in relation to psychiatric illness thus proves to be a complex undertaking. The findings of the investigations reported here carry a number of far-reaching theoretical implications. Of particular interest is the evidence obtained about the mutability of personality, in contradiction to the established view that personality is relatively fixed. It has long been known that many so-called measures of personality do change. Examples which may be cited are measures of the trait of Extraversion, as developed by Eysenck; the Intropunitiveness Scale of Foulds also changes, for example, over a matter of weeks in patients recovering from depressive illness.

This work shows that attributes not previously regarded as mutable do in fact alter considerably. We demonstrate that when patients are followed up for long enough, attributes of personality previously regarded as stable are found to change profoundly. Moreover, a complex interaction of illness with personality is demonstrated. The relationship between illness outcome and personality change, furthermore, is interactive. Of particular importance are attributes characterizing sociopathy. Sociopathic patients with less severe illnesses do as well prognostically as those not personally deviant, but those with sociopathic traits who have serious illnesses recover less well.

The method most acceptable clinically for diagnosing personality disorder, the category approach advocated in both DSM-III and ICD-9, is not employed reliably by psychiatrists independently assessing personality disorder when patients are first admitted to hospital with psychiatric illness.

Although psychiatrists do not use a category system for diagnosing personality disorder at all reliably, it does not follow in the least that category diagnostic systems of personality disorder have to be abandoned. Rather, the conclusion must be that psychiatrists need to be conscious of the pitfalls presenting when a single lable is applied to categorize so complex an entity as a patient's personality. About two-thirds of patients were assigned the same category diagnosis of personality when first admitted and again when rediagnosed by a different psychiatrist 3 years later. Those diagnosed differently were in all categories of personality disorder; that is, some diagnoses are not more stable than others.

The unsatisfactory reliability of a category system for the diagnosis of personality disorder also has research implications. The relationship previously reported betweeen specific personality types and psychiatric illness is thrown into question. Many earlier studies purporting to relate psychiatric illnesses with particular personality types (such as those of Holmboe & Astrup, 1957; Kringlen, 1965; Odegaard, 1964) depended on classification of personality into single descriptive categories (often assigned by a single clinician), an approach we have shown to be unreliable even under favorable circumstances. It is evident that replication studies using a different approach to the diagnosis of personality disorder are clearly needed.

The dimensional personality disorder system, on the other hand, based on trait ratings was satisfactorily stable. Patients' personality profiles (in all five dimensions derived by the statistical analysis) were similar on admission and again 5 years later to a statistically significant degree. On all but the Obsessional dimension, the patients' profiles were significantly less disordered after the passage of 3 years, and the degree of improvement was similar for both sexes.

The Sociopathy dimension was the most unchanging, a well-established and unfortunate clinical reality. Next most fixed were the Submissiveness and the Hysterical dimensions. The Schizoid and the Obsessional dimensions changed most during the course of 3 years, but were still significantly similar.

Over 3 years, the Sociopathy, Submissiveness, Schizoid, and Hysterical dimensions all changed in the direction of greater normality. Changes in personality disorder dimensions over time were similar for men and for women.

The personality change in the direction of greater normality is shown to be related to improvement of the associated psychiatric illness. This is highly variable. Over half the patients recovered from their psychiatric illness. A third became ill again during the 3 years and did not recover satisfactorily from the relapse. A small but important 14% of patients remained ill after their initial admission. In the majority, those with symptoms after 3 years were ill in the same way as initially. One type of illness did not carry a better prognosis than another for subsequent freedom from symptoms.

The personality diagnosis on first admission, both the category diagnosis and the dimensional profile, had predictive implications for the adequacy of the patient's subsequent social adjustment. Personality diagnosis has therefore not emerged as useful for predicting outcome from illness, but it was useful for predicting, whether ill or not, the person will be socially adjusted 3 years later at work, in the family, and in other relationships.

The psychometric tests of personality are equally informative. Patients who function on the relevant psychological tests as "sociopathic" do not recover from serious psychiatric illness as satisfactorily; in contrast, those subjects measured as sociopathic do as well as subjects not socially deviant when the associated psychiatric illness was not severe.

Psychometrically measured illness state at the first admission (by the Personal Disturbance scale) correlated very well with the independent psychiatric assessment of severity of illness. The PD scale scores were associated with a patient's chances of being readmitted to hospital during the period of observation, of being more socially disabled and consistently ill, with being still in treatment at follow-up, and with being on medication. Recovery from illness was thus a major component in personality change in the direction of great normality, whether the improvement from illness was as assessed clinically by the psychiatrist at follow-up or by psychometric retesting (the PD scale).

REFERENCES

American Psychiatric Association. (1968). *Diagnostic and statistical manual of mental disorders* (2nd ed.). Washington, DC: Author.

American Psychiatric Association. (1980). *Diagnostic and statistical manual of mental disorders* (3rd ed.). Washington, DC: Author.

Foulds, G. A. (1962). *Personality and personal illness*. London: Tavistock.

Holmboe, R., & Astrup, C. (1957). A follow-up study of 255 patients with acute schizophrenic and schizophreniform psychoses. *Acta Psychiatrica Scandinavica, Supplementum, 115*.

Jaspers, K. (1963). *General psychopathology* (7th ed.). (J. Hoenig & M. Hamilton, Trans.). Manchester: Manchester University Press.

Kringlen, E. (1965). Obsessional neurotics: A longterm follow-up. *British Journal of Psychiatry, 111*, 709–722.

Lewis, A. (1974). Psychopathic personality: A most elusive category. *Psychological Medicine, 4*, 133–140.

McIver, D. (1979). *Personality and psychiatric illness*. Ph.D. thesis, University of Edinburgh.

McIver, D., & Presly, A. S. (1974). Towards the investigation of personality deviance. *British Journal of Social and Clinical Psychology, 13*, 397–404.

Odegaard, O. (1964). Personality and mental illness. *Acta Psychiatrica Scandinavica, 40*, Suppl. 180, 5–13.

Presly, A. S. (1971). *The classification of deviant personalities and their relationship to personal illness in a psychiatric unit*. Ph.D. thesis, University of Edinburgh.

Presly, A. S., & Walton, H. J. (1973). Dimensions of abnormal personality. *British Journal of Psychiatry, 122*, 269–767.

Schneider, K. (1958). *Psychopathic personality* (9th ed.) (M. Hamilton, Trans.). London: Cassell.

Shepherd, M., & Sartorius, N. (1974). Personality disorder and the international classification of diseases. *Psychological Medicine, 4,* 141–146.

Slater, E., & Roth, M. (1969), *Clinical psychiatry* (3rd ed.). London: Baillière, Tindall & Cassell.

Walton, H. J., Foulds, G. A., Littmann, S. K., & Presly, A. S. (1970). Abnormal personality. *British Journal of Psychiatry, 116,* 497–510.

Walton, H. J., & Presly, A. S. (1973). Use of a category system in the diagnosis of abnormal personality. *British Journal of Psychiatry, 122,* 259–268.

World Health Organization (1974). *Glossary of mental disorders and guide to their classification, for use in conjunction with the International Classification of Diseases,* 8th revision, Geneva, 1974.

World Health Organization (1975). *Manual of the International Statistical Classification of Diseases, Injuries and Causes of Death,* 1975 (Ninth) Revision, Geneva, Volumes 1 and 2, 1977 and 1978.

Zubin, J. (1967). Classification of the behaviour disorders. *Annals of Developmental Psychology, 18,* 373–406.

CHAPTER 28

The 1982 Interpersonal Circle: An Analysis of DSM-III Personality Disorders

Donald J. Kiesler

DSM-III (American Psychiatric Association, 1980) represents a marked improvement over previous systems of psychiatric classification. Nevertheless, continued modifications and improvements are both desirable and expected. This is particularly the case for the DSM-III group of the Personality Disorders which, in contrast to other major diagnostic categories, still is characterized by distressingly low interobserver reliabilities.

It seems clear, as Davidson (1982) documents, that as a class the DSM-III Personality Disorders are the weakest members of the nosological network. Their descriptions

> appear to represent a "mixed bag" of descriptive categories including interpersonal, behavioral, symptomatic, anemastic and physiological features. The extent to which these features are consistently set forth is undetermined. . . . Since no unifying theoretical structures served as a frame of reference for deducing the components of the category, the various kinds of descriptors associated with these components [are] unsystematically scattered across the eleven identified personality disorders. (pp. 59–60)

This conceptual state of affairs is unfortunate, especially since two major internally consistent approaches to the Personality Disorders have been and are available to the scientific and clinical communities. One, from a biosocial learning viewpoint, was articulated by Millon as long ago as 1969 and has been systematically updated in a recent volume (Millon, 1981) and in Chapter 30 of this volume. The second comes from interpersonal theory in the

Donald J. Kiesler. Department of Psychology, Virginia Commonwealth University, Richmond, Virginia.

Sullivan (1953) and Leary (1957) tradition and incorporates as a central feature Interpersonal Circle assessment measures.

The present chapter attempts a systematic presentation of the second (interpersonal) tradition as an alternative conceptualization of the Personality Disorders. The interpersonal approach, in contrast to the DSM-III "mixed bag," exclusively uses descriptors of overt interpersonal behaviors derived systematically from interpersonal theory for personality and psychotherapy (Anchin & Kiesler, 1982; Carson, 1969; Kiesler, 1983, in press; Leary, 1957; Sullivan, 1953). This chapter therefore attempts a more concrete translation of the argument by others (Adams, 1964; Leary, 1957; McLemore & Benjamin, 1979; Wiggins, 1982) that interpersonal theory offers a scientifically and clinically viable alternative to DSM psychiatric diagnosis.

More specifically, I will attempt to show how the Interpersonal Circle (Kiesler, 1982, 1983; Leary, 1957; Wiggins, 1979, 1982) provides a theoretically derived and operationally anchored taxonomy which can provide both reliable diagnosis and differential therapy for the Personality Disorders. In contrast to Benjamin's (Chap. 29 of this volume) ongoing National Institutes of Mental Health research project, which applies her interpersonally derived Structural Analysis of Social Behavior (SASB) to the full range of DSM diagnosis, the present chapter both restricts its focus to the Personality Disorders and concentrates exclusively on a two-dimensional (in contrast to Benjamin's three-dimensional) interpersonal model.

Interpersonal Infrastructure of the DSM-III Personality Disorders

In interpersonal theory, abnormal behavior is defined as inappropriate or inadequate interpersonal communication. It consists of a rigid, constricted, and extreme pattern of interpersonal behaviors by which the abnormal person, without any clear awareness, engages others who are important in his or her life. The abnormal person, rather than possessing the flexibility of the normal individual to use the broad range of interpersonal behaviors warranted by different social situations, is locked into a rigid and extreme use of limited classes of interpersonal actions. As a result, the abnormal individual, through verbal and nonverbal messages, continually elicits or pulls from others a rigidly constricted range of intense and predominantly aversive responses. Finally, the abnormal person assumes little responsibility for continuing rejections by others, since he or she does not understand how these aversive effects occur and does not "intend" them.

DSM-III discussion of the Personality Disorders contains remarkably similar statements. DSM-III Personality Disorders occur "when personality traits are inflexible and maladjustive and cause either significant impairment in social or occupational functioning or subjective distress." These maladaptive traits represent "enduring patterns of perceiving, relating to, and thinking about the environment and oneself, and are exhibited in a wide range of important social and personal contexts." The disorders begin in childhood or adolescence and are characteristic of most of adult life. In contrast to the psychoses and neuroses, psychiatric signs and symptoms need not be clinically prominent at all. Finally, "frequently the individual with a Personality Disorder is dissatisfied with the impact his or her behavior is having on others or with his or her inability to function effectively."

These DSM definitions clearly reveal an interpersonal conceptual bias. In addition, findings from several studies (Davidson, 1982; Lorr, Bishop, & McNair, 1965; Tryer & Alexander, 1979; Walton, Foulds, Littman, & Presly, 1970) reveal strong empirical relationships between DSM descriptors for the Personality Disorders and the taxonomic structure of interpersonal measures. The upshot is that interpersonal theory, besides construing abnormal behavior in terms highly similar to those used by DSM-III, also offers an empirically based, internally consistent taxonomy for classification of interpersonal behavior in its normal and abnormal ranges.

Basic to this taxonomy is the notion that interactants continually are negotiating two major interpersonal issues: affiliation (love–hate, friendliness–hostility) and control (dominance–submission, higher–lower status). At an early developmental stage, a person settles on a distinctive interpersonal style, role, and/or self-definition which leads the person repeatedly to make interpersonal claims on others in terms of how close or intimate and how much in charge or dominant the person wants to be with others. In subsequent interactions, this relatively constant self-presentation is reciprocally reinforced or validated by responses the person pulls from interactants. In short, interpersonal theory asserts that each of us continually exudes a "force field" which pushes others to respond to us with constricted classes of control and affiliation actions; thereby we pull from others "complementary" responses designed to affirm and validate our chosen style of living and being.

The Kaiser Research Group (Freedman, Leary, Ossorio, & Coffey, 1951; LaForge & Suczek, 1955; Leary, 1957) was the first to operationalize the domain of interpersonal behavior on the "Interpersonal Circle" around the axes of Control and Affiliation. Their and subsequent other interpersonal circles (Wiggins, 1982) define an array of categories of interpersonal behaviors, usually numbering 16 (labeled A–P), that operationalizes individual differences in interpersonal behavior. On the circle perimeter, the 16 "segments" (located at polar ends of the eight circle diameters) are defined as classes of interpersonal actions representing behavioral contrasts and/or semantic opposites. Each of the segments is a blend of the two axis dimensions reflecting mathematically weighted combinations of Control (-4 submission, through 0, to $+4$ dominance) and Affiliation (-4 hostile, through 0, to $+4$ friendly).

For each of the 16 segments the radius of the circle represents the intensity or extremeness of corresponding interpersonal behaviors. The degree of abnormality of a particular interpersonal behavior is represented precisely by its distance from the midpoint of the circle. To permit assessment of the entire continuum of mild to extreme, normal to abnormal interpersonal behavior, some circles provide two "levels" of definitions and operationalization for each of the 16 segments. In sum, on the Interpersonal Circle a person's behavior is characterized as abnormal if across a variety of interactional situations it exhibits (a) rigid adherence to one or a few of the 16 segments, and/or (b) actions at extreme levels of one or a few circle segments.

Since 1955 several adult measures of the Interpersonal Circle have been developed, including LaForge and Suczek's (1955) Interpersonal Check List, Lorr and McNair's (1965, 1967) Interpersonal Behavior Inventory, Wiggins's (1979, 1981) Interpersonal Adjective Scales, and Kiesler et al.'s (1976) Impact Message Inventory. These and other interpersonal measures have been excellently reviewed and critiqued by Wiggins (1982). I will focus the remainder of this chapter on the latest version of the Interpersonal Circle (Kiesler, 1982, 1983), which provides a theoretical and empirical integration of the earlier two-dimensional circle measures in the form of an Interpersonal Circle taxonomy. Figure 28-1 presents the 1982 Interpersonal Circle.[1]

Basically the 1982 Circle is a taxonomy which defines a large item sample of the universe of possible two-dimensional (Control and Affiliation) interpersonal behaviors. The complete classification system (Kiesler, 1982) contains 350 bipolar interpersonal items, 3 to 9 of which define one of 64 segment-pair subclasses at the mild-moderate or extreme level of each of the 16 segments. Each of the two levels of each segment is defined by 3 to 5 subclasses, with the number of items defining each of the 32 levels ranging from 17 to 28, with a median of 21.5. Each of the 16 segments (including both levels) is defined by 37 to 53 items, with a median of 42.5. The reader is referred to Kiesler (1982) for more detail.

Inspection of Figure 28-1 shows that each of the 16 segments of the 1982 Circle is assigned three separate labels. One designates the entire continuum (the circle radius) of interpersonal behaviors constituting a particular segment (e.g., A: Dominant, E: Hostile, I: Submissive, M: Friendly). A second label designates the mild–moderate (more normal) level of a particular segment continuum (e.g., A_1: Controlling, E_1: Antagonistic/Harmful, I_1: Docile, M_1: Cooperative/Helpful). A third names the extreme (more abnormal) level of a particular segment (e.g., A_2: Dictatorial, E_2: Rancorous/Sadistic, I_2: Subservient, M_2: Devoted/Indulgent). Hence, the entire continuum of segment A is designated Dominant, the mild–moderate (more normal) level is called Controlling, and the extreme (more abnormal) level is named Dictatorial.

---

1. The complete version of the 1982 Circle (Kiesler, 1982), including segment and subclass definitions and defining items as well as a content analysis of ICL, IAS, IBI, and IMI items, is available from the author.

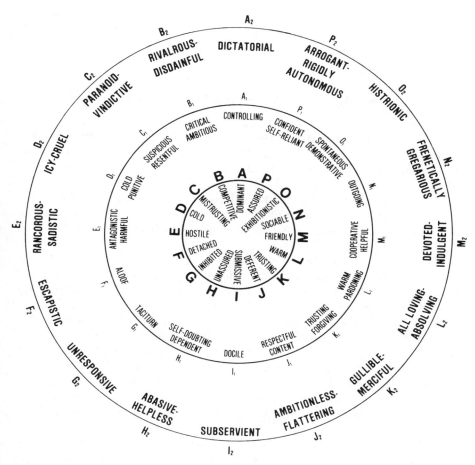

Figure 28-1. *The 1982 Interpersonal Circle.*

In characterizing a particular person's interpersonal behaviors in terms of Circle position, it is important to understand that behaviors at any one segment (e.g., C) can blend with behaviors of the highly correlated adjacent segment on either side (i.e., B as well as D). Each of the 16 segments represents a conceptually "pure" class of interpersonal behaviors that rarely, if ever, occur alone in the actual behavior of a particular person. At a minimum, a person's behavior seems to be a blend of two adjacent segments (an octant) and may combine a triad of segments. Further, according to the interpersonal "rigidity" definition of maladjustment, the Circle slice is of necessity smaller for the maladjusted than for the more normal individual. Interpersonal researchers disagree among themselves as to the most heuristic tack for subject or behavior classification and data analysis, with some arguing for analysis of segments (Kiesler, 1983; LaForge, 1977), some for octants (Leary, 1957; Wiggins, 1982), and others for quadrants (Carson, 1969).

Interpersonal Diagnosis of the Personality Disorders

Having briefly introduced the 1982 Circle, I will now turn to a detailed discussion of its use for diagnosis of the Personality Disorders. The final section will discuss differential treatment strategies inherent in and theoretically derivable from the 1982 Circle.

Mere inspection of Figure 28-1 will undoubtedly suggest to the reader corresponding locations at various Circle octants of the 11 DSM-III Personality Disorders. However, we shall see shortly that exact location is, and should be, a more complex issue.

Before addressing these complexities, let us first review briefly the manner in which previous interpersonal investigators, namely, Leary (1957) and Wiggins (1982), have interfaced their versions of the Interpersonal Circle with the psychiatric group of the Personality Disorders. In proceeding, it is important to realize that neither investigator used a Circle measure that satisfies the full structure defined by the 1982 Circle taxonomy, although Wiggins's Interpersonal Adjective Scales are clearly superior to other available measures. Since I have documented elsewhere (Kiesler, 1982, 1983) how earlier interpersonal measures, especially Leary's, have important segment omissions, misdefinitions, and misplacements, I will also translate Leary and Wiggins's proposed Circle locations for the Personality Disorders into 1982 equivalents.

Table 28-1 lists the 11 DSM-III Personality Disorders and the corresponding Circle octant locations which Leary (1957) and Wiggins (1982) assigned. As one example, we can see from Table 28-1 that both Leary and Wiggins diagnose the Dependent personality as falling in the JK octant of the Circle. Leary's Circle defines the two Dependent classes of interpersonal behavior as J: Docile and K: Dependent; Wiggins lables them J: Unassuming and K: Ingenuous; and the equivalent 1982 Circle segments are H: Unassured and K: Trusting. Hence, if we use for the moment 1982 Circle descriptors (Kiesler, 1982), a person exhibiting more normal levels of Dependent behavior engages others as H_1: Self-Doubting/Dependent (i.e., self-doubting, dependent, unassured, awkward, glum) and K_1: Trusting/Forgiving (i.e., unguarded, trusting, innocent, forgiving, generous). A more abnormal Dependent person engages others as H_2: Abasive/Helpless (i.e., abasive, helpless, immobilized, bumbling, depressed) and K_2: Gullible/Merciful (i.e., totally unwary, gullible, guileless, merciful, prodigal). More detailed defintions and item descriptors of these H and K as well as other 1982 Circle segments can be found in Kiesler (1982).

Table 28-1

Leary's (1957) and Wiggins's (1982) Placements of the DSM Personality Disorders on the Interpersonal Circle (and 1982 Circle Equivalent Segments for Each Placement)

DSM-III Personality Disorder	Leary (1957) Circle location	1982 Circle equivalent segments	Wiggins (1982) Circle location	1982 Circle equivalent segments
Paranoid	No designation		DE: Cold-Quarrelsome	DE: Cold-Hostile
Schizoid	FG: Rebellious-Distrustful	EC: Hostile-Mistrusting	FG: Aloof-Introverted	FG: Detached-Inhibited
Schizotypal	No designation		No designation	
Histrionic	LM: Cooperative-Overconventional	ML: Friendly-Warm	LM: Warm-Agreeable	LM: Warm-Friendly
Narcissistic	BC: Narcissistic-Competitive	PC: Assured-Mistrusting	BC: Arrogant-Calculating	PC: Assured-Mistrusting
Antisocial	DE: Sadistic-Aggressive	DE: Cold-Hostile	No designation	
Borderline	No designation		No designation	
Avoidant	No designation		No designation	
Dependent	JK: Docile-Dependent	JK: Deferent-Trusting	JK: Unassuming-Ingenuous	HK: Unassured-Trusting
Compulsive (obsessive)	PA: Autocratic-Managerial HI: Self-Effacing-Masochistic	BA: Competitive-Dominant HI: Unassured-Submissive	PA: Ambitious-Dominant	BA: Competitive-Dominant
Passive-aggressive	No designation		HI: Lazy-Submissive	JI: Deferent-Submissive

From Table 28-1 we also can already see some problems with previous DSM interpersonal translations. First, neither Leary nor Wiggins articulated Circle equivalents for three of the DSM-III Personality Disorders: Schizotypal, Borderline, and Avoidant. Second, Leary designates no explicit equivalent for Paranoid and Passive–Aggressive personalities, while Wiggins offers no octant anchoring for the Antisocial personality. Third, both investigators completely agree on placement of only four DSM disorders: Histrionic at LM, Narcissistic at BC, Dependent at JK, and Compulsive at PA—yet, when even these four octants are relocated to fit the definitions of the 1982 Circle taxonomy, there actually is agreement for only one disorder, LM: Histrionic. Finally, although the octant label (FG) ascribed by Leary to the Schizoid personality suggests agreement with Wiggins, content analysis of Leary's FG items (Kiesler, 1982) actually shows these behaviors to fall at 1982 Circle Segments EC—hence, Leary's actual placement of the Schizoid personality differs from that of Wiggins.

It seems we can conclude from Table 28-1 that the two previous interpersonal translations of the DSM Personality Disorders (a) have not succeeded in locating all 11 disorders on the Interpersonal Circle, (b) at best agree on Circle location for only 4 of the 11 disorders, and (c) at worst agree on Circle location for only 1 of the 11 disorders. Finally, it seems we must conclude that available interpersonal explications of the Personality Disorders are not impressive in terms of interobserver agreement.

However, we must keep in mind that Leary (1957) interfaced his Circle with an earlier DSM version, while Wiggins (1982) targeted the current DSM-III disorders. Also, as I have documented in detail elsewhere (Kiesler, 1982, 1983), the measure (Interpersonal Check List) which Leary used to define his Circle contains significant measurement gaps and segment mislocations that can easily explain many of his differences with Wiggins's placements.

In the remainder of this section I will attempt another Circle translation of the DSM-III Personality Disorders using the more comprehensive 1982 Circle, which was explicitly designed to integrate the strengths and avoid the weaknesses of previous Circles. By using this latest taxonomy, I believe we can arrive at explications of the DSM Personality Disorders which, over time, will demonstrate much higher levels of interobserver agreement.

Before proceeding, however, we first have to question the validity of the translation task itself; that is, is it more useful to accept on an a priori basis the clinical validity and "real" existence of the DSM-III Personality Disorders and then to focus our efforts on translating DSM disorders onto corresponding segments or octants of the 1982 Circle? Or might it be much more useful in the long run, in light of the internally consistent theoretical structure of the Circle, to first derive Personality Disorder possibilities from the Circle and then to search for clinical verification of these theoretical types? In the latter case, launching our efforts from the solid structure of interpersonal theory would avoid the atheoretical and descriptive "mixed bag" deficiencies of DSM-III (McLemore & Benjamin, 1979). In the former, starting from the base of observed, albeit unsystematically, "live" clinical disorders seems to ensure a continual anchoring of our efforts in existent patient problems in living.

In my opinion, solid advantages exist for both directions of attack. Hence, while this section will focus on translation of DSM disorders onto the 1982 Circle, we need to keep in mind the alternative possibility of empirical attack.

Another caution is necessary since some Personality Disorders derivable from the 1982 Circle seem rarely to be found in clinical populations. Apparently, as a manifestation of their characteristic interpersonal pattern, some theoretically definable Circle disorders avoid seeking help from others and, as a result, show up very infrequently in clinical treatment settings. For example, persons whose behaviors fall in the strongly dominant octants of the Circle may be infrequent clinical patrons, since "the very essence of these maladjustments is a compulsive maintenance of autonomy, independence and domination—social techniques which preclude the role of psychiatric patient" (Leary & Coffey, 1955, p. 119). In similar fashion, more extreme deferent and trusting styles in the bottom right quadrant of the Circle may also be underrepresented clinically, since their rigid patterns may fit more easily and subtly into traditionally acceptable societal roles. Generally these and similar possibilities imply strongly that our analysis starting from clinical populations will necessarily overlook some persons possessing extreme and rigid interpersonal patterns, but who confine the scope of their abnormality within everyday life situations in such a way that they seldom come to the attention of mental health practitioners.

Having stated these cautions, I will now articulate some principles that seem necessary as guides for our task of translating DSM-III Personality Disorders onto the 1982 Interpersonal Circle.

Principle 1. *Circle diagnosis focuses exclusively on assessment of overt social–interpersonal behaviors of abnormal persons. These observable actions include both verbal and nonverbal behaviors.*

One of the major uses of interpersonal measures is by interactants or observers who characterize or rate the interpersonal behavior of subjects. For this rating task the focus is on the external behaviors of subjects; hence there is no proper place for respondents to rely on inferences about subjects' motives, feeling states, cognitions, or other covert events.

It is this restricted focus on overt behavior that provides a clear advantage of interpersonal diagnosis over DSM-III descriptions of the Personality Disorders, since DSM-III unsystematically combines descriptions of overt interpersonal behaviors with symptomatic, anemastic, physiological, affective, and cognitive events. The exclusive focus of the Interpersonal Circle on observable behavior in and of itself promises superior interobserver reliability for Circle assessments.

In the long run, however, it's also clear that interpersonal diagnosis will remain incomplete and inadequate until it incorporates independent systematic assessments of the covert behavioral domain—including distinctive affective, perceptual, cognitive, and other important internal experiences—which correlate with the various overt styles described by the 1982 Circle (Carson, 1982; Golding, 1977; Golding, Valone, & Foster, 1980).

Principle 2. *To provide reliable and valid characterizations, Circle diagnosis must assess an abnormal person's behaviors by identifying (a) the exact Circle segments which define the person's transactions with others, and (b) the exact level (mild vs. moderate vs. extreme) on each segment that defines the extremeness and/or rigidity of the abnormal pattern.*

For example, it is insufficient merely to locate behaviors of the Dependent personality on 1982 segments IJ: Submissive–Deferent without specifying further whether the pattern falls at I_1: Docile or the more extreme I_2: Subservient, and whether at J_1: Respectful/Content or at the more extreme J_2: Ambitionless/Flattering.

Although it is theoretically possible that an abnormal person's interpersonal behaviors could be "rigid" (i.e., restricted to one or a few segments only) and also at "mild" levels, this does not seem a likely or frequent condition. What seems more probable is that any rigid pattern would be expressed by behaviors characterized at least at the "moderate" level and often at the "extreme" level. Further, it is entirely possible that an abnormal person's behaviors can be extreme on one segment and moderate to mild on adjacent segments. Hence, valid characterization of a particular Personality Disorder necessitates a profile statement which subsumes not only a given number of Circle segments, but also the exact level of each constituent segment.

Principle 3. *Interpersonal diagnosis combines both dimensional and typological assessment of interpersonal behaviors toward the goal of Roschian categorical descriptions of each Personality Disorders.*

What this means, as Wiggins (1982) documents, is that Circle diagnosis will never be able to classify the Personality Disorders at mutually exclusive Circle segments or octants. From a Roschian perspective (Rosch, 1978; Rosch & Mervis, 1975), the taxonomic descriptions of the Circle segments do not identify sets of critical or categorically necessary defining elements, all of which must be present for a person's behavior to be classified at a particular segment. Rather, it is assumed instead that Circle segments operate as Roschian categories wherein the interpersonal behaviors defining a particular segment cluster around a "prototype" or exemplar, with less prototypic elements merging into the "fuzzy" boundaries of related adjacent segments.

Hence, as Wiggins (1982) emphasizes, the Interpersonal Circle provides a geometric representation of relationships between "fuzzy sets" in which membership is probabilistic and continuous rather than determinate and discrete. As a result, it is more valid to conceptualize interpersonal diagnostic categories as "wedge-shaped segments of a circle, in which elements of a category (segment) are organized with reference to a prototype that falls near the center of the perimeter of a given wedge" (p. 204).

When we speak, for example, of a Compulsive Personality, we are using a prototype construct representing a category whose members collectively have a large number of attributes, no single set of which is definitive in the sense that all members exhibit that set of attributes. There is no set of Circle segment behaviors that is necessarily exhibited by each Compulsive individual. Nevertheless, some attributes are typical in that on the average many Compulsives show them. It is the profile of average or representative characteristics that constitutes the prototype of the Compulsive person. Thus, when we call a patient Compulsive, we do so not with respect to a small set of necessary and sufficient attributes, but rather with respect to the patient's comparison or degree of fit with the prototype of Circle segments defining the Compulsive Personality.

It follows then, as Wiggins (1982) concludes, that there is no reason to expect a one-to-one correspondence between DSM categories and Circle segments, since psychiatric categories function as Roschian fuzzy sets, as recent studies demonstrate (Cantor, Smith, French, & Mezzich, 1980; Horowitz, French, Lapid, & Weckler, 1982; Plutchik, 1967, 1980; Plutchik & Platman, 1977; Schaefer & Plutchik, 1966; Wiggins, 1980). Instead, what we can expect is that a characteristic or prototypic profile of interpersonal variables or Circle segments will be associated with each diagnostic category.

In sum, the 1982 Circle offers the advantages of the combined dimensional and categorical approach which Millon (1981), among others, advocates. The major diagnostic utility of the Circle resides in designating "prototypic" possibilities that various Personality Disorders may assume, keeping in mind that no particular patient will ever match exactly the definitional exemplar. It becomes the task of interpersonal assessment, then, using its battery of interpersonal measures (Wiggins, 1982), to establish the empirical profile of Circle segments which validly defines the distinctive behavioral prototype for each of the Personality Disorders. Having established each prototype, any individual patient's manifestation of a particular Personality Disorder can be summarized as the empirical degree of fit between his or her behavior pattern and a particular prototype.

Principle 4.   *It seems highly probable that the various Personality Disorders will not be described by Circle prototypes which contain isomorphic segmental structure.*

The prototype for one Personality Disorder may subsume elements from a single Circle octant, while that for another may subsume a wider band of segments. Similarly, one disorder's profile might include the extreme level of one segment with moderate-level behaviors from an adjacent segment, while another disorder might peak at the extreme level of each of two adjacent segments. Further, for those more extreme Personality Disorders which show more complexity in their interpersonal patterns, valid diagnosis may require characterizations of behaviors from octants highly dissimilar to one another, indeed falling in different Circle quadrants. These possibilities are consistent with recent research which shows that individuals differ in the degree to which their behaviors show cross-situational consistency (Bem & Allen, 1974; Epstein, 1979; Mischel & Peake, 1982).

In a similar vein, Millon (1981), in his creative presentation of the Personality Disorders from a biosocial learning framework, differentiates disorders that show distinct and consistent interpersonal styles from those that show ambivalent behavioral patterns. For example, in Millon's analysis individuals exhibiting either the Dependent or Independent personality patterns show distinct and consistent preferences as to whether to turn to others or to themselves to gain security and comfort. In contrast, such clear-cut behavioral commitments are not made by Millon's more ambivalent personalities such as the Obsessive–Compulsive and Passive–Aggressive. The latter individuals remain unsure as to which way to turn to gain security and comfort, and continue to experience conflict as to whether to depend on themselves or on others for reinforcements. In terms of Circle diagnosis, then, it seems likely that Millon's ambivalent personalities each would be defined by a prototype which subsumes octants from more than one Circle quadrant and, hence, would present more complex assessment problems.

In sum, it seems quite probable that in order to capture the varying complexity of the various clinical Personality Disorders, interpersonal prototypic diagnosis will need multiple patternings of Circle segments and levels. Indeed, much of the work ahead of us is to validate the distinct concrete pattern or profile of Circle segments for each of the Personality Disorders.

Principle 5.   *To accomplish reliable and valid diagnosis of the DSM Personality Disorders using the Interpersonal Circle, relevant correlated situations need to be specified and interfaced with the Circle segments defining each particular prototype.*

This principle states that interpersonal diagnosis must incorporate the well-established interactional position (Endler & Magnusson, 1976) wherein interacting situation and person factors that are operative for a particular disorder are clearly articulated.

An important interpersonal tenet is that the more abnormal a person, the more likely it is that his or her interpersonal behaviors will override environmental influences, remaining rigidly consistent across situations and interactants. As Leary (1957) notes, the abnormal person "tends to overdevelop a narrow range of one or two interpersonal responses. They are expressed intensively and often, whether appropriate to the situation or not. . . . The more extreme and rigid the person, the greater his interpersonal 'pull'—the stronger his ability to shape the relationship with others" (p. 126). What Principle 5 asserts, however, is that the degree and limits of the transsituational consistency operative for each of the Personality Disorders need to be carefully determined.

Valid interpersonal diagnosis, then, would not only express in empirical terms the degree of fit of a particular patient to a defining prototype for that disorder (expressed as a distinctive profile of Circle segments), but would also explicitly designate distinctive classes of situations and interpersonal contexts in which the prototypical behavior pattern is most likely to be expressed. The distinctive situational bandwidth most relevant to a particular Personality Disorder must be clearly specified as an essential part of the diagnostic prototype.

For diagnostic purposes, for example, it may be sufficient to assess Millon's (1981) distinct and consistent Dependent personality in almost any interpersonal or situational context. Yet for valid diagnosis of his more ambivalent Obsessive–Compulsive personality, it may be crucial to look for "compulsive" patterns in occupational settings or in those where the person's role is defined as more dominant (e.g., as a parent or supervisor), while "obsessive" patterns may be evident only in situations where role expectations are ambiguous, as in social or interpersonally intimate encounters.

Another aspect of this issue is that it has become increasingly evident, as Bem and Allen (1974) and Millon (1981) argue, that not all personality traits or dimensions apply to all people, that each of us displays consistency only in those behaviors central to our style in living, and, therefore, that valid description of individual differences resides in designation of those interpersonal behaviors that are most important, central, or salient for an individual. Classes of these central behaviors, then, are likely to be more resistant to situational influences, while other more peripheral behaviors may be more readily influenced by environmental factors.

As one possibility it may be the case that when the control–status or affiliation–intimacy demands in their life change, some of the Personality Disorders may adjust to the new situational demands by expressing more peripheral interpersonal patterns (e.g., behaviors from a less characteristic quadrant). For example, a Compulsive Personality, if thrust into a paternal or maternal role, might exhibit transactions with his or her children characteristic of the top-left rather than the more prototypical bottom-left quadrant. Or a Histrionic individual, who more typically shows gregarious and exhibitionistic behavior from the top-right quadrant, may shift to behavior from the bottom-right quadrant (deferent and trusting) when confronted with a competitive job situation with subtle or obvious hostile overtones.

Another possibility is that some Personality Disorders may reveal their central stylistic patterns only over successive transactions. A maladaptive pattern may not be immediately evident from a one-time interaction, regardless of the situation. For example, the Sociopathic individual rarely affects others as manipulative during a single encounter; rather it is from instances of interaction over time that the maladaptive pattern begins to emerge clearly to interactants. Likewise, some Personality Disorders such as the Borderline seem to be defined by extreme shifts from one maladaptive pattern to another—in the case of the Borderline shifting over time between icy paranoia and oppositional behavior in the top-left quadrant and trusting, adoring, and compliant behavior in the bottom-right quadrant.

In sum, if Circle diagnosis is to contribute to full understanding of the

DSM-III Personality Disorders, its assessment must systematically incorporate the important situational and temporal factors relevant to expression of each's maladaptive interpersonal pattern, including both central and peripheral components. An important move in this direction is the recent work of Buss and Craik (1981, 1983), which emphasizes interpersonal "acts" in contrast to dispositions. Their "act-in-context" interpersonal descriptors anchor interpersonal assessment simultaneously in both overt behaviors and situations. One outcome of this creative research may be that the next version of the Interpersonal Circle will be based upon a taxonomy constituted from items of an "act-in-context" form.

Principle 6. For optimally useful interpersonal diagnosis, the prototypical pattern of interpersonal behavior defining a particular Personality Disorder needs to be related specifically to the distinctive situational influence of the therapist and therapeutic context.

To be ultimately useful, interpersonal diagnosis needs to relate directly to the treatment situation. It can accomplish this by specifying precisely how behaviors typical of the therapist role are likely to influence expression of a particular patient's prototypical behavior as well as by specifying the distinctive complementary covert engagements the therapist can expect to experience with that patient in their sessions.

Further, it seems likely that some facets of the interpersonal style of a disordered individual may be more available and apparent to the therapist, while they remain much less evident or rarely seen by others in the patient's life. For example, as Chewning (1982) describes, in interacting with an Avoidant personality, the therapist may see self-doubting components that are carefully kept hidden from others: "The therapist, being in the 'helper' position, is more likely than others to be the object of at least a mild degree of self-dissatisfaction concerning negative self-worth. . . . This moderate disclosure may temper the cold, aloof, disengaged impact that is 'generally' experienced by other interactants" (p. 12).

In interpersonal theory, the rigid and extreme interpersonal behavior prototypical of a specific disordered personality itself represents the problem. Accordingly, the prototypical pattern will be experienced "live" by the therapist in the treatment situation. This pattern needs to be targeted for intervention both as it operates maladjustively with the therapist and with other persons in the patient's life.

As we shall see shortly, once a patient's interpersonal behavior has been diagnosed as showing good fit to the defining prototype for a particular Personality Disorder (in terms of a distinctive profile of Circle segments and designated situations), then precise intervention possibilities are derivable from the Circle which can be sequentially staged across the course of therapy using the principles of "complementarity," "acomplementarity," and "anticomplementarity," described in detail by Kiesler (1983).

To accomplish all this, however, it is vital that the therapeutic situation be included specifically among the range of situational contexts interacting with the patient's prototypical style of functioning. The expected "counter-pull" of the therapy situation as it influences expression of the patient's style needs to be articulated clearly, since it defines for the therapist the first stage of a series of interventions designed to progressively alter the patient's behavior toward less extreme and rigid presentations.

We can now summarize the diagnostic principles that need to guide our search for associations between the 1982 Circle and the DSM-III Personality Disorders.

1. As one aspect of interpersonal diagnosis, Circle diagnosis focuses exclusively on assessment of overt, observable interpersonal behaviors of abnormal persons. It thereby avoids inferences about patients' motives, feeling states, cognitions, or other covert events.

2. Circle diagnosis of the DSM-III Personality Disorders needs to designate both the exact Circle segments as well as the exact level on each segment which characterize the maladaptive behavior for each disorder.

3. The task of interpersonal diagnosis is to establish the empirical profile of Circle segments that represents the distinctive prototype of exemplary behaviors for each of the Personality Disorders. Since diagnostic categories represent fuzzy sets, there is no reason to expect an exact one-to-one correspondence between Personality Disorder categories and Circle segments.

4. There is no compelling reason to assume that the Circle structure of the prototypes defining each of the various disorders will be identical or isomorphic. Prototypic descriptions of the Personality Disorders may incorporate different levels and segment bands, may subsume more than one Circle octant, and, in some cases, may include octants from different quadrants.

5. For comprehensive interpersonal diagnosis of the Personality Disorders, classes of situations associated with and most relevant to each defining prototype need to be clearly specified so that assessment can target these environmental contexts. The distinctive situational bandwidth most relevant to a particular prototype must be specified as an essential component of the assessment procedure.

6. The therapeutic situation must be distinctively included in this situational specification. The expected counterpulls of the therapy situation as it influences each prototypical disorder need to be designated, since, employing Circle principles, it defines for the therapist the first stage of sequential interventions designed to progressively alter the patient's style toward less extreme and rigid self-presentations.

At this point in our discussion it should be evident that considerable conceptual and empirical work remains to be done before interpersonal diagnosis will compile anything like a sophisticated body of knowledge regarding the Personality Disorders. This is the case even if we ignore entirely the longer range issue of how these Personality Disorders might interface with Axis I symptomatic disorders. In my opinion, elaboration of in-depth formulations of interpersonal diagnosis and therapy will result primarily from intensive and restricted targeting by investigators of one or two Personality Disorders at a time—in contrast to attempts at wide-band coups.

Having stated this, it seems we might nevertheless profit from a "first-step" wide-band attempt, incorporating the diagnostic principles just detailed, to characterize the 11 DSM-III Personality Disorders on the 1982 Circle. Table 28-2 summarizes the DSM-III descriptors for each of the Personality Disorders as well as their corresponding 1982 Circle segment levels as determined by my own content analysis.[2]

We can draw several important conclusions from the content analysis presented in Table 28-2.

1. The translations confirm Principle 4 above, that the prototypes ultimately defining the clinical Personality Disorders will exhibit structures that are nonisomorphic in terms of number of Circle segments, segment levels, and quadrant range. We find only 5 of the 11 DSM-III disorders which can be located at a particular octant of the 1982 Circle: Histrionic (N_2O_2), Narcissistic (O_2P_2), Dependent (HI, levels unspecified), Compulsive (F_1G, G level unspecified), and Passive–Aggressive (E_1F_1). We find 2 of the 11 disorders whose DSM-III descriptors locate them at only one segment: Schizoid (F_2, but with no evidence of F_{2c}: Eccentric) and Antisocial (E, unspecified level). We find two disorders characterized by a triad of Circle segments: Paranoid ($C_2D_1E_1$) and Avoidant ($F_1G_1H_1$). Finally, we find each of the remaining two disorders characterized by segments from different quadrants: Schizotypal (C_1F, F level unspecified) and Borderline (showing dramatic shifts in behavior between segments in opposite quadrants: B_2 to J_2, E_2 to M_2). Table 28-3 summarizes the 1982 Circle translations for the 11 disorders.

2. Also present in these Circle translations is clear evidence that the DSM-III descriptors for the various disorders target abnormal interpersonal behaviors of varying levels of intensity. Some disorders fall at mild–moderate levels of segment intensity (e.g., Avoidant: $F_1G_1H_1$), others show mixed-level patterns (e.g., Paranoid: $C_2D_1E_1$), while others define segment behaviors all at the extreme level (e.g., Narcissistic: O_2P_2).

3. Circle diagnosis of the Personality Disorders reveals no patterns that would directly support the three "clusters" outlined in DSM-III, namely, (a) "odd or eccentric" disorders (Paranoid, Schizoid, Schizotypal), (b) "dramatic, emotional, or erratic" disorders (Histrionic, Narcissistic, Antisocial, Borderline), and (c) "anxious or fearful" disorders (Avoidant, Dependent, Compulsive, Passive–Aggressive). Instead, the clustering of the Personality Disorders shown in Table 28-3 seems to express the degree of complexity (segment and level structure) present in the various prototypes. This results

---

2. My content analysis is based on the segment subclass definitions and items detailed in the complete version of the 1982 Circle (Kiesler, 1982), a copy of which, as mentioned earlier, may be obtained from the author.

Table 28-2

Translation of DSM-III Descriptors for the 11 Personality Disorders
into Corresponding 1982 Circle Segment Behaviors[a]

DSM-III descriptors	Corresponding 1982 Circle segment behaviors
301.00 Paranoid	
A. Pervasive, unwarranted suspiciousness and mistrust of people (ignores contradictory evidence, hypervigilant, avoids blame, devious/scheming, transient ideas of reference), pathological jealousy, expectation of tricking or harm, searching for confirmation of bias	C 　2a Hypervigilant 　2b Paranoid/blindly jealous 　1c Cunning 　1d Resentful
B. Hypersensitivity (quick to take offense, argumentative, exaggerates difficulties, ready to counterattack, inability to relax—tense)	E 　1a Antagonistic 　1b Quarrelsome
C. Restricted affectivity (appearing serious, cold, and unemotional, pride in being objective/rational, lack of sense of humor, absence of soft, tender, sentimental feelings)	D 　1a Cold 　1b Stern 　1c Strict/Punitive
301.20 Schizoid	
A. Absence of warm, tender feelings for others	
B. Indifference to praise or criticism or to the feelings of others	F 　1a–2a Disinterested-Disengaged
C. Close friendships with no more than one or two persons including family members (prefers to be loner, appears reserved and seclusive, pursues solitary interests)	F 　1b–2b Distant–Hermetic
D. Appears cold and aloof (humorless, dull, without appropriate affect)	F 　1c Preoccupied
E. No eccentricities of speech, behavior, or thought	No F 　2c Autistic/eccentric
301.22 Schizotypal	
A. Magical thinking (superstitiousness, clairvoyance, telepathy, etc.)	
B. Ideas of reference (paranoid ideation)	
C. Social isolation (no close friends, social contacts limited to essential everyday task)	F 　1b–2b Distant–Hermetic
D. Recurrent illusions, depersonalization, derealization	
E. Odd or peculiar speech (digressive, overelaborate, circumstantial, metaphorical, words used deviantly)	F 　1c–2c Preoccupied–Autistic/Eccentric
F. Constricted or inappropriate affect and inadequate rapport in face-to-face interaction	F 　1a–2a Disinterested-Disengaged
G. Suspiciousness, guardedness	C 　1a Vigilant 　1b Suspicious/Jealous

Table 28-2

(*Continued*)

DSM-III descriptors	Corresponding 1982 Circle segment behaviors
H. Anxiety and hypersensitivity to real or imagined criticism	
301.50 Histrionic	

A. Behavior that is overly dramatic, reactive, and intensely expressed (self-dramatization, drawing attention to self, craving activity and excitement, overreaction to minor events, irrational angry outbursts or tantrums)	O
	  2a Loquacious/Divulging
	  2b Histrionic
	  2c Impulsive

B. Characteristic disturbances in interpersonal relationships (superficially warm and charming but perceived as shallow; quick to form friendships but can become very demanding, egocentric, and inconsiderate of others; dependent, helpless, constantly seeking reassurance; prone to manipulate suicidal threats, gestures, or attempts; impressionable and easily influenced by others or by fads)	O
	  2d Hypersuggestible
	N
	  2a Intrusive
	  2b Monophobic
	  2c Hyperactive/Hyperconventional

301.81 Narcissistic	

A. Grandiose sense of importance or ungenuineness (exaggeration of achievements and talents, having special problems)	F
	  2a Egotistical
	  2c Cocky

B. Preoccupation with fantasies of unlimited success, power, brilliance, beauty, or ideal love (driven, pleasureless pursuit of these goals)	P 2c Euphoric

C. Exhibitionism; requires constant attention and admiration	O
	  2a Loquacious/divulging
	  2b Histrionic

D. Cool indifference or marked feelings of rage, inferiority, shame, humiliation, or emptiness in response to criticism, defeat, or indifference of others	P 2b Rigidly autonomous

E. Characteristic disturbances in interpersonal relationships (entitlement; interpersonal exploitativeness; alternating between overidealization and devaluation of others; lack of empathy)	O
	  2c Impulsive
	  2d Hypersuggestible

301.70 Antisocial	
A. Current age at least 18	

B. Onset before age 15 of truancy, expulsion from school, delinquency, running away from home, persistent lying, casual sexual intercourse, drunkenness or substance abuse, thefts, vandalism, fights)	E
	  1a–2a Antagonistic–Rancorous
	  1b–2b Quarrelsome–Belligerent
	  1c–2c Impolite–Rude
	  1d–2d Harmful–Sadistic

Table 28-2
(*Continued*)

DSM-III descriptors	Corresponding 1982 Circle segment behaviors
C. Since age 18, inability to sustain consistent work behavior, inability to function as responsible parent, illegal behaviors, two or more divorces/separation, repeated physical fights or assaults, defaulting on financial obligations, failure to plan ahead or impulsivity, lying to or conning others, vehicular recklessness)	

301.83   Borderline

A. Impulsivity or unpredictability in self-damaging areas such as sex, gambling, substance use, shoplifting, overeating	
B. A pattern of unstable and intense relationships (idealization, devaluation, manipulation)	M E 2a Devoted ⟷ 2a Rancorous 2b Concurring ⟷ 2b Belligerant J B 2d Flattering ⟷ 2d Disdainful
C. Inappropriate, intense anger or lack of control of anger	E 2b Belligerent
D. Identity disturbance and uncertainty about self-image, gender identity, career choice, friendship patterns	
D. Affective instability, marked shifts from normal mood to depression, irritability, or anxiety	
F. Intolerance of being alone	
G. Physically self-damaging acts (suicidal gestures, self-mutilation, recurrent accidents, or physical fights)	
H. Chronic feelings of emptiness or boredom	J 2a Listless

301.82   Avoidant

A. Hypersensitivity to rejection, humiliation, or shame; hypervigilant to social derogation	G 1a Silent/private
B. Unwillingness to enter into relationships without strong guarantees of uncritical accdeptance	
C. Social withdrawal (distances from close personal attachments, engages in peripheral social and vocational roles)	F 1b–2b Distant–Hermetic
D. Desire for affection and acceptance	
E. Low self-esteem (devalues self-achievements, overly dismayed by personal shortcomings)	H 1a Self-doubting

Table 28-2
(*Continued*)

DSM-III descriptors	Corresponding 1982 Circle segment behaviors
301.60 Dependent	
A. Passively allows others to assume responsibility for major areas of life; leaves major decisions to others	I 1a–2a Following/Complying–Servile 1b–2b Passive/Acquiescent–Spineless
B. Subordinates own needs to those of persons on whom he or she depends to avoid any possibility of having to rely on self; unwilling to make demands of people they depend on to avoid jeapordizing the relationship	I 1c–2c Weak/Yielding–Submissive 1d–2d Obedient–Slavish/Fawning
C. Lacks self-confidence (belittles own abilities or assets; sees self as helpless, stupid)	H 1a–2a Self-doubting–Abasive 1b–2b Dependent–Helpless 1c–2c Unassured–Immobilized 1d–2d Awkward–Bumbling 1e–2e Glum–Depressed
301.40 Compulsive	
A. Restricted ability to express warm and tender emotions (stingy with emotions and material possessions; perceived as stilted, stiff, formal, serious)	G 1a Silent/Private 1b Undemonstrative 1c Stiff/Controlled F 1a Disinterested
B. Perfectionism that interferes with ability to grasp "the big picture" (preoccupation with rules, efficiency, trivial details, procedures, order, schedules, lists); time poorly allocated; although efficiency and perfection are idealized, they are rarely obtained)	G 1c Stiff/Controlled
C. Insistence that others submit to his or her way off doing things and lack of awareness of the feelings elicited by this behavior (sensitive to their relative status in relationships and resists the authority of others)	G 1d–2d Opinionated–Obstinate
D. Excessive devotion to work and productivity to the exclusion of pleasure and the value of relationships with others (frequently postpones pleasurable activities)	F 1b Distant 1c Preoccupied
E. Indecisiveness; decision making is either avoided, postponed, or protracted (ruminates about priorities, inordinate fear of making mistakes)	H 1c Unassured

Table 28-2

(*Continued*)

DSM-III descriptors	Corresponding 1982 Circle segment behaviors
301.84 Passive–Aggressive	
A. Resistance to demands for adequate performance in both occupational and social functioning (opposes demands to increase or maintain a given level of functioning)	E 1a Antagonistic 1b Quarrelsome
B. Resistance expressed indirectly through procrastination, dawdling, stubbornness, intentional inefficiency, "forgetfulness"	E 1c Impolite F 1b Distant 1c Preoccupied
C. Pervasive and long-standing social and occupational ineffectiveness (leading to not being promoted on job)	
D. Persistence of the behavior pattern even under circumstances in which more self-assertive and effective behavior is possible (occurs in a variety of contexts)	

[a] A–P = segments; subscripts 1 and 2 = levels; subscripts a–e = segment subclasses.

in four clusters: "clear-cut octant" prototypes, "clear-cut segment," "triadic," and "mixed quadrant" prototypes.

4. Inspection of Table 28-2 reveals that some DSM-III descriptors target behaviors that do not fall in the Circle domain of overt interpersonal behaviors. Among these are descriptors targeting inferred motivational states (e.g., Avoidant: B and D), inferred affective events (e.g., Borderline: E and F), inferred cognitive events (e.g., Schizotypal: A and B), and anemastic events (e.g., Borderline: G). Further, some disorders are defined almost exclusively by interpersonal descriptors (e.g., Paranoid, Histrionic), others provide a mix of interpersonal and other descriptors (e.g., Passive–Aggressive), while still others provide few, if any, interpersonal descriptors (e.g., Antisocial). These observations underline Principle 1 of Circle diagnosis that, in contrast to DSM-III, Circle diagnosis focuses exclusively on assessment of overt, observable interpersonal behaviors exhibited by abnormal persons.

5. From Table 28-3, it is apparent that DSM-III disorders are classified predominantly in the hostile left-half of the 1982 Circle. Among these a few disorders show behaviors from the top-left (hostile–dominant) quadrant, but most fall in the bottom-left (hostile–submissive) quadrant. Two exceptions (Narcissistic and Histrionic) are found in the top-right (friendly–dominant) quadrant. Finally, DSM-III offers no definitions of disorders classifiable in

Table 28-3
Placement of DSM-III Personality Disorders on the 1982 Circle[a]

A. "Octant" prototypes
    1. Histrionic N_2O_2: Frenetically Gregarious–Histrionic
    2. Narcissistic O_2P_2: Histrionic–Arrogant/Rigidly Autonomous
    3. Dependent   HI: Unassured–Submissive (levels unspecified)
    4. Compulsive F_2G: Aloof–Inhibited (G level unspecified)
    5. Passive–Aggressive E_2F_2: Antagonistic/Harmful–Aloof

B. "Triad" prototypes
    6. Paranoid $C_2D_1E_1$: Rivalrous/Disdainful–Cold/Punitive–Antago-
                                         nistic/Harmful
    7. Avoidant $F_1G_1H_1$: Aloof–Taciturn–Self-Doubting/Dependent

C. "Segment" prototypes
    8. Antisocial   E: Hostile (level unspecified)
    9. Schizoid F_2: Escapistic (without F_{2c}: Autistic/Eccentric

D. "Mixed quadrant" prototypes
    10. Schizotypal C_2F: Suspicious/Resentful–Detached (F level un-
                                         specified)
    11. Borderline $B_2 \leftrightarrow J_2$: Rivalrous/Disdainful $\leftrightarrow$ Ambitionless/Flatter-
                                         ing
                                    $E_2 \leftrightarrow M_2$: Rancorous/Sadistic $\leftrightarrow$ Devoted/Indulgent

[a]A–P = segments; subscripts 1 and 2 = segment levels.

the bottom-right (friendly–submissive) quadrant, nor at the dramtically dominant octants (AB or AP). As discussed earlier, for various reasons these abnormal persons missing from DSM-III, but theoretically and empirically identifiable on the Circle, seldom appear in psychiatric treatment settings.

6. Finally, from Table 28-2 it is evident that DSM-III descriptions of the Personality Disorders completely ignore Principles 5 and 6 of Circle diagnosis. Nowhere among the DSM-III section on the Personality Disorders can one find any discussion, much less specification, of either (*a*) the important classes of situations in which the various dysfunctional patterns will and will not be evident, or (*b*) the specific manner in which patients will present their respective abnormal patterns within the context of the therapy session itself. If future versions of DSM continue to ignore these vital contextual issues, users will continue to find it difficult to arrive at reliable diagnostic assessments or to derive differential treatment programs.

Circle Diagnosis and Differential Psychotherapy

So far I have tried to show how remarkable overlap exists between DSM-III and Interpersonal Circle conceptualizations of the Personality Disorders, how Circle diagnosis is embedded in an internally consistent and empirically anchored theoretical structure, how, through use of interpersonal measures, Circle diagnosis can provide more reliable and valid assessment of the Personality Disorders, and how Circle diagnosis can provide empirical profiles for prototypical classification of the Personality Disorders.

The important remaining task of this chapter is to demonstrate, albeit briefly, the ultimate predictive power of the Interpersonal Circle for therapeutic intervention with the Personality Disorders. Indeed, the real promise of the Circle is that, having identified prototypic segments which define a particular disorder, theoretically derivable interventions can be systematically designated! Although the comprehensive specifics of these intervention packages are far from being articulated, basic skeletal principles have been described in detail (Kiesler, 1983, in press).

This final section will briefly illustrate these basic principles of interpersonal therapy by applying them to one of the DSM-III disorders, the Compulsive Personality. This category represents a long-term personal interest (Kiesler, 1973, 1977) and also provides an apparent "clear-cut octant" (F_1G, G level unspecified) prototype, which simplifies my translation task. The reader is referred again to Table 28-2 for the DSM-III and 1982 Circle descriptors which define the Compulsive Personality. More extensive clinical descriptions of the disorder can be found also in Salzman (1973, 1979) and Shapiro (1965).

Unfortunately, none of these sources designates the situational components needed for interpersonal diagnosis of the Compulsive Personality. Nevertheless, let's assume that, by use of one or more of the interpersonal measures reviewed by Wiggins (1982), we can reliably diagnose a particular patient as precisely fitting the F_1G prototype of the Compulsive Personality. From interpersonal theory and from the 1982 Interpersonal Circle, we can now make four crucial predictions which form the skeleton of a differential treatment package for that patient.

1. We can predict precisely the goal of therapy for our Compulsive patient. The therapeutic goal is to facilitate an increased frequency and intensity of interpersonal behaviors from the octant NO which is directly opposite on the Circle to FG. The prediction follows from the principle that optimal change in interpersonal behavior results from helping the patient interact with others in a manner more like that of a person whose behaviors fall at the octant directly opposite on the Circle—in the case of our Compulsive, to behave more like a normal "histrionic" (N_1O_1) individual.

The goal of interpersonal therapy is to interrupt a patient's rigid presentation of constricted classes of more extreme interpersonal acts which constitute aversive stimuli to significant others prodding them to avoid or escape from the patient or to be trapped into incongruent transactions. In order to experience a wider range of transactional experiences having more positive consequences, the patient needs to learn to emit acts of less intensity from his or her constricted octant and to emit acts from a broader range of Circle segments. In the case of our Compulsive, more frequent occurrence of NO interpersonal acts—since they demand behaviors weighted exactly oppositely on the Control and Affiliation dimensions (FG = $-3,-2$ Affiliation, $-1,-2$ Control; NO = $+3,+2$ Affiliation, $+1,+2$ Control)—has the greatest likelihood of pulling the Compulsive patient's FG interpersonal behaviors away from the perimeter of the Circle toward the midpoint (from more to less extreme intensity), and the greatest likelihood of "spreading" or expanding the patient's interpersonal repertoire to include other Circle segments.

2. We can predict the precise overt and covert reactions that will be "pulled" from the therapist in early transactions with the Compulsive patient. A basic tenet of interpersonal theory is that a person's interpersonal actions tend, with a probability greater than chance, to initiate, invite, or evoke from an interactant "complementary" responses that lead to a repetition of the person's actions—in turn protecting and validating the person's valued style of self-definition and self-presentation. Complementarity occurs on the basis of "reciprocity" in respect to the Control dimension or axis of the Circle (dominance pulls submission, submission pulls dominance) and on the basis of "correspondence" in respect to the Affiliation dimension (hostility pulls hostility, friendliness pulls friendliness). Further, it is axiomatic in interpersonal theory that an abnormal person exerts more influence on the nature of the transaction than does a more normal interactant.

From these principles we can predict that in their earlier sessions a Compulsive patient inevitably will "pull" overt responses from the therapist characterized at the complementary D_1C: Cold–Mistrusting octant of the Circle. In addition, we can predict the complementary covert engagements of "impact messages" that will be "pulled" from the therapist and can measure them directly through use of the Impact Message Inventory (Kiesler et al., 1976; Perkins et al., 1979). In short, we can predict that the "objective countertransference" of the therapist in the first or "hooked" stage of therapy with a Compulsive patient will be from the DC: Cold–Mistrusting octant.

3. We can predict that the therapist is able to effect cognitive ambiguity and uncertainty for the Compulsive patient, as the first step toward disrupting the patient's maladaptive style, by shifting to therapeutic "asocial" responses (Beier, 1966). The therapist responds to the patient in an asocial and disengaged way whenever the therapist withholds the customary, preferred, or expected complementary response. In turn, this permits the patient to experience, often for the first time, new consequences for his or her maladaptive behaviors. Examples of commonly used therapeutic asocial responses include delay responses, reflection of content or feeling, labeling of the patient's interaction style, interpersonal metacommunication, and use of therapeutic paradox. In the case of our Compulsive patient, asocial therapist responses would require that (a) the therapist in no way provide the DC: Cold–Mistrusting complementary response "bid for" so rigidly by the Compulsive patient, and (b) that any therapist response have ambiguous meaning

in the sense that the patient cannot pinpoint at all a position on the Circle from which the therapist is responding.

4. Finally, we can predict that in later sessions the therapist can exert greatest pressure for positive change in the Compulsive by offering therapeutic responses "anticomplementary" on the Circle to the patient's maladaptive style. For our Compulsive patient the therapist provides anticomplementary responses when the therapist responds from the KL: Trusting–Warm octant. Segments K (−2 Control, +2 Affiliation) and L (−1 Control, +3 Affiliation) are exact anticomplementaries to segments G (−2 Control, −2 Affiliation) and F (−1 Control, −3 Affiliation), respectively.

The therapist stance that exerts maximum pressure for patient improvement—for moving a patient toward the opposite octant on the Circle, the goal of therapy—is the complement of the opposite octant. The therapist pulls for greatest improvement in the FG: Compulsive patient when the therapist responds from octant KL: Trusting–Warm (which is complementary to octant NO), or, said differently, when the therapist provides, instead of the CD: Mistrusting–Cold complementary response, the (KL) opposite of the complementary response. In sum, maximum elicitation or enhancement of the desired NO: Sociable–Exhibitionistic behaviors from the Compulsive patient results from therapist interventions which exhibit anticomplementary KL: Trusting–Warm features.

Obviously these four predictions from the Interpersonal Circle provide only the skeleton of an ultimately comprehensive treatment package for a patient diagnosed as a Compulsive Personality. Many additional components are necessary, including guidelines for analysis of situational manifestations of the Compulsive's maladaptive pattern; specification of interventions which target cognitive, affective, and other covert events lawfully associated with the patient's overt FG interpersonal style; specific rules that would guide the therapist's metacommunicative use of covert complementary responses or impact messages; and rules that would govern optimal sequencing over sessions of asocial, acomplementary, and anticomplementary therapist responses.

However, it should also be obvious that even these four predictions represent a significant advance when compared to what is predictively available in other discussions of the Personality Disorders, and especially when compared to the absence in DSM-III of anything like differential treatment prescriptions.

In conclusion, I hope I have been able to convince the reader of the potential power provided by interpersonal theory and the Interpersonal Circle for diagnosis and differential treatment of the Personality Disorders. I hope I have presented "a case" which might impress future revisionists of DSM-III that the Interpersonal Circle offers considerable advantages to psychiatric classification of the Personality Disorders and should be adopted as a theoretical and empirical base for future versions.

REFERENCES

Adams, H. B. (1964). "Mental illness" or interpersonal behavior? *American Psychologist, 19*, 191–197.

American Psychiatric Association. (1980). *Diagnostic and statistical manual of mental disorders* (3rd ed.). Washington, DC: Author.

Anchin, J. C., & Kiesler, D. J. (Eds.). (1982). *Handbook of interpersonal psychotherapy*. Elmsford, NY: Pergamon Press.

Beier, E. G. (1966). *The silent language of psychotherapy: Social reinforcement of unconscious processes*. Chicago, IL: Aldine.

Bem, D., & Allen, A. (1974). On predicting some of the people some of the time: The search for cross-situational consistencies in behavior. *Psychological Review, 81,* 506–520.

Buss, D. M., & Craik, K. H. (1981). The act frequency analysis of interpersonal dispositions: Aloofness, gregarious, dominance, and submissiveness. *Journal of Personality, 49*, 175–192.

Buss, D. M., & Craik, K. H. (1983). The act frequency approach to personality. *Psychological Review, 90*, 105–126.

Cantor, N., Smith, E. E., French, R. D., & Mezzich, J. (1980). Psychiatric diagnosis as prototype categorization. *Journal of Abnormal Psychology, 89*, 181–193.

Carson, R. C. (1969). *Interaction concepts of personality*. Chicago, IL: Aldine.

Carson, R. C. (1982). Self-fulfilling prophecy, maladaptive behavior, and psychotherapy. In J. C. Anchin & D. J. Kiesler (Eds.), *Handbook of interpersonal psychotherapy*. Elmsford, NY: Pergamon Press.

Chewning, M. F. (1982). *Interpersonal diagnosis and treatment of the avoidant personality*. Unpublished manuscript, Virginia Commonwealth University, Richmond.

Davidson, K. M. (1982). *Personality disorders: Examination of the descriptive features relevant to diagnosis*. Doctcoral dissertation, Virginia Commonwealth University, Richmond.

Endler, N. S., & Magnusson, D. (Eds.). (1976). *Interactional psychology and personality*. Washington, DC: Hemisphere Press.

Epstein, S. (1979). The stability of behavior. I. On predicting most of the people much of the time. *Journal of Personality and Social Psychology, 37*, 1097–1126.

Freedman, M. B., Leary, T. F., Ossorio, A. G., & Coffey, H. S. (1951). The interpersonal dimension of personality. *Journal of Personality, 20*, 143–161.

Golding, S. L. (1977). Individual differences in the construal of interpersonal interactions. In D. Magnusson & N. Endler (Eds.), *Personality at the cross-roads: Current issues in interactional psychology*. New York: Wiley.

Golding, S. L., Valone, K., & Foster, S. W. (1980). Interpersonal construal: An individual differences framework. In N. Hirschberg (Ed.), *Multivariate methods in the social sciences: Applications*. Hillsdale, NJ: Erlbaum.

Horowitz, L. M., French, R. D., Lapid, J. S., & Weckler, D. A. (1982). Symptoms and interpersonal problems: The prototype as an integrating concept. In J. C. Anchin & D. J. Kiesler (Eds.), *Handbook of interpersonal psychotherapy*. Elmsford, NY: Pergamon Press.

Kiesler, D. J. (1973). *A communications approach to modification of the obsessive personality: An initial formulation*. Unpublished manuscript, Emory University, Atlanta, GA.

Kiesler, D. J. (1977). *Communications assessment of interview behavior of the "obsessive" personality*. Unpublished manuscript, Virginia Commonwealth University, Richmond.

Kiesler, D. J. (1982). *The 1982 interpersonal circle: A taxonomy for complementarity in human transactions*. Richmond: Virginia Commonwealth University.

Kiesler, D. J. (1983). The 1982 interpersonal circle: A taxonomy for complementarity in human transactions. *Psychological Review, 90*, 185–214.

Kiesler, D. J. (in press). Interpersonal methods of diagnosis and treatment. In R. Michaels & J. Cavenar (Eds.), *Psychiatry*. Philadelphia, PA: Lippincott.

Kiesler, D. J., Anchin, J. C., Perkins, M. J., Chirico, B. M., Kyle, E. M., & Federman, E. J. (1976). *The imapct message inventory*. Richmond: Virginia Commonwealth University.

LaForge, R. (1977). *Using the ICL: 1976.* Unpublished manuscript, Mill Valley, CA.

LaForge, R., & Suczek, R. F. (1955). The interpersonal dimension of personality. III. An interpersonal check list. *Journal of Personality, 24,* 94–112.

Leary, T. (1957). *Interpersonal diagnosis of personality.* New York: Ronald Press.

Leary, T., & Coffey, H. S. (1955). Interpersonal diagnosis: Some problems of methodology and validation. *Journal of Abnormal and Social Psychology, 50,* 110–124.

Lorr, M., Bishop, P. F., & McNair, D. M. (1965). Interpersonal types among psychiatric patients. *Journal of Abnormal and Social Psychology, 70,* 468–472.

Lorr, M., & McNair, D. M. (1965). Expansion of the interpersonal behavior circle. *Journal of Personality and Social Psychology, 2,* 823–830.

Lorr, M., & McNair, D. M. (1967). *The interpersonal behavior inventory, form 4.* Washington, DC: Catholic University of America.

McLemore, C. W., & Benjamin, L. S. (1979). Whatever happened to interpersonal diagnosis? A psychosocial alternative to DSM-III. *American Psychologist, 34,* 17–34.

Millon, T. (1969). *Modern psychopathology: A biosocial approach to maladaptive learning and functioning.* Philadelphia, PA: Saunders.

Millon, T. (1981). *Disorders of personality: DSM-III: Axis II.* New York: Wiley.

Mischel, W., & Peake, P. K. (1982). Beyond déjà vu in the search for cross-situational consistency. *Psychological Review, 89,* 730–755.

Perkins, M. J., Kiesler, D. J., Anchin, J. C., Chirico, B. M., Kyle, E. M., & Federman, E. J. (1979). The impact message inventory: A new measure of relationship in counseling/psychotherapy and other dyads. *Journal of Counseling Psychology, 26,* 363–367.

Plutchik, R. (1967). The affective differential: Emotion profiles implied by diagnostic concepts. *Psychological Reports, 20,* 19–25.

Plutchik, R. (1980). *Emotion: A psychoevolutionary synthesis.* New York: Harper & Row.

Plutchik, R., & Platman, S. R. (1977). Personality connotations of psychiatric diagnosis: Implications for a similarity model. *Journal of Nervous and Mental Disease, 165,* 418–422.

Rosch, E. (1978). Principles of categorization. In E. Rosch & D. B. Lloyd (Eds.), *Cognition and categorization.* Hillsdale, NJ: Erlbaum.

Rosch, E., & Mervis, C. B. (1975). Family resemblances: Studies in the internal structure of categories. *Cognitive Psychology, 7,* 573–605.

Salzman, L. (1973). *The obsessive personality: Origins, dynamics and therapy.* New York: Jason Aronson.

Salzman, L. (1979). Psychotherapy of the obsessional. *American Journal of Psychotherapy, 33,* 32–40.

Schaefer, E. S., & Plutchik, R. (1966). Interrelationships of emotions, traits, and diagnostic constructs. *Psychological Reports, 18,* 399–410.

Shapiro, D. (1965). *Neurotic styles.* New York: Basic Books.

Sullivan, H. S. (1953). *The interpersonal theory of psychiatry.* New York: Norton.

Tryer, P., & Alexander, J. (1979). Classification of personality disorders. *British Journal of Psychiatry, 135,* 163–167.

Walton, H. J., Foulds, G. A., Littman, S. K., & Presly, A. S. (1970). Abnormal personality. *British Journal of Psychiatry, 116,* 497–510.

Wiggins, J. S. (1979). A psychological taxonomy of trait-descriptive terms: The interpersonal domain. *Journal of Personality and Social Psychology, 37,* 395–412.

Wiggins, J. S. (1980). Circumplex models of interpersonal behavior. In L. Wheeler (Ed.), *Review of personality and social psychology* (Vol. 1). Beverly Hills, CA: Sage.

Wiggins, J. S. (1981). *Revised interpersonal adjective scales.* Unpublished manuscript, University of British Columbia, Vancouver.

Wiggins, J. S. (1982). Circumplex models of interpersonal behavior in clinical psychology. In P. C. Kendall & J. N. Butcher (Eds.), *Handbook of research methods in clinical psychology.* New York: Wiley.

CHAPTER 29

Adding Social and Intrapsychic Descriptors to Axis I of DSM-III

Lorna Smith Benjamin

There is little question that the DSM-III has increased the reliability of psychiatric nomenclature. Indeed, objectification and operationalization of diagnostic decision making was one of the major goals set forth for DSM-III (Spitzer, Williams, & Skodol, 1980; p. 154). One of the costs of increasing reliability by operationalizing and objectifying diagnostic criteria was the loss of some psychodynamic concepts which had been included in DSM-II such as unconscious conflict. Among providers of psychotherapy, the omission of concepts such as conflict, defenses, and object relations has been regarded as a serious shortcoming. One of the more balanced commentaries on the absence of psychodynamics in DSM-III was offered by Karasu and Skodol (1980), who suggested that a sixth axis be added to cover some of the psychodynamic phenomena after there has been a response to a call "for psychotherapy researchers . . . to develop a valid and reliable method that would lend itself to systematic evaluation of the patient's conflicts, object relations, defenses, coping mechanisms and mental structure" (p. 610).

Social Variables Are Biological Too

Traditional psychodynamics have been omitted from the DSM-III, but social variables in the form of personality or character traits are included on Axis II. Theoretically, personality disorders can stand alone on Axis II, but in practice an Axis II disorder usually is seen as an add-on, as a complication of the basic

Lorna Smith Benjamin. Department of Psychiatry, University of Wisconsin Medical School, Madison, Wisconsin.

Axis I "clinical syndrome." Besides being "second," Axis II has poor reliability
(Frances, 1980): "The personality disorders as a group still attain the lowest
reliability of any major category in the classification. There are at least two
inherent reasons for this: (1) Most of the personality disorders are probably
no more than severe variants of normally occurring personality traits that
are distributed continuously and without clear boundaries to indicate pathology, and (2) personality assessment is inevitably confounded by intercurrent
state and role factors" (p. 1050). However, if the Millon Clinical Multiaxial
Inventory (MCMI) is used to assist the interview method, the reliability of
Axis II classifications should increase dramatically. The test-retest reliabilities for the 11 scales of the MCMI which bear the names of Axis II classifications range from .77 to .91 (Millon, 1982, p. 47). Descriptions of Axis II
classifications in terms of the 1982 version of the Leary Interpersonal Circle
(Kiesler, Chapter 28 of this volume) probably also will improve the problematic status of Axis II described by Frances (1980). Benjamin (in press) also has
proposed a dimensional approach to Axis II.

Despite the improving status of Axis II personality trait descriptions,
DSM-III still neglects major intrapsychic dynamic factors traditionally of
significant concern to practitioners of psychotherapy. Belief in the existence
of social and intrapsychic correlates with Axis I phenomena (such as anxiety
and depression) is the cornerstone of psychodynamic theory and therapy.
The so-called "character disorders" described by Axis II, though clinically
important, are by no means the main concern of psychodynamicists. DSM-
III, then, neglects major intrapsychic dynamic factors traditionally of significant concern to practitioners of psychotherapy. DSM-III does not adequately
address concerns of health care providers and researchers who consider
social interaction and intrapsychic factors to be equal in importance to
symptoms when diagnosing and treating major psychiatric illness.

Within mainline psychiatry, relatively few believe that social variables
have primary (not secondary add-on) relevance to major psychiatric illness.
Generally, the more serious the disturbance, the wider the belief that the
patient's problems are primarily due to a biochemical, genetically based
mechanism. Biochemical factors have scientific respectability, and they have
become emphasized increasingly in psychiatric theory, research, and practice. Probably the factor of scientific respectability accounts for the increasing trend toward the so-called biological psychiatry, while the relative lack of
scientific respectability for dynamic approaches accounts for the decrease in
the importance of psychosocial psychiatry.

But this view of social factors as fundamentally "unbiological" is not
appropriate. The eminent biologists, Tinbergin and Lorenz, received the
Nobel Prize for their scientific work describing regularities in the behavior of
animals. Tinbergin noted (1951) that a zoological taxonomy for animals
would be just as reliable if it were based upon behavioral rather than
structural attributes. The argument is simple: Behavior and structure
evolved together under the principle of the survival of the fittest. If aided by
patient, careful observation, behavior patterns can show astonishing regu-

larity and predictability. If behavior did not show order, then genetically selected behavioral propensities wouldn't be adaptive, and the organism— including its biochemistry—wouldn't survive. To be more consistent with evolutionary theory, the so-called biological psychiatrists might better call themselves biochemical psychiatrists. Behavior is as biological as biochemistry, and behavior belongs in psychiatry and psychology as a truly legitimate biological phenomenon. The addition of social patterns to the formal biological psychiatric nosology awaits the ability to describe them adequately in scientific terms. When the addition is made, social variables should be linked directly to the biochemical and symptomatic presentation. They should not be "second class" either in diagnosis or in treatment.

This plea for restoration of social and intrapsychic variables to mainline psychiatric thinking is not based on a wish to attack and/or displace biochemical approaches. Both biochemical and environmental factors are important. Evolutionary theory suggests there are strong genetic components to any observed behavior, and behavior clearly is greatly affected by biochemical mechanisms. A scientific biological behaviorism would integrate the biochemical and the behavioral approaches by holding that the unfolding of genetic plans is affected greatly by interaction with environment. The nature, sequence, intensity, and duration of the environmental experiences can have a profound impact on the unfolding of behavioral propensities. Models for this interactional philosophy of nature and nurture are easy to find: Consider intelligence, or consider learning to play a musical instrument or learning a complicated athletic sport. All are acknowledged to have major and significant genetic input, and all are profoundly affected by environmental input. Why not also accept such an interactional interpretation of the unfolding of social interaction and intrapsychic tendencies? Why not postulate, for example, that some people are born with a greater propensity for dominance or for attachment, but that dominance and bonding also will be affected greatly by interaction with the environment? Why not admit behavior to mainstream scientific psychiatry and to the domain of biology? Promising beginnings of the effort systematically to connect social behavior and psychiatric syndromes have been made by Lorr, Bishop, and McNair (1965) and Plutchik and Platman (1977). An effective clinical presentation of the direct connection between personality style and psychopathology was presented by Shapiro (1965) and by Millon (1969, 1981). The present chapter demonstrates a means to expand upon these vital additions to scientific psychiatry.

Goals of the Interpersonal Diagnostic Research Project

As a co-author, I have been critical of the DSM-III (McLemore & Benjamin, 1979) and have suggested that an interpersonal behavioral taxonomy might have a number of scientific advantages over the traditional psychiatric nomenclature. In 1980 I began work on an interpersonal diagnostic research project called Diagnosis Using Structural Analysis of Social Behavior (SASB), funded by the National Institute of Mental Health (NIMH). The goals of the project were (a) the addition of social descriptors to the DSM-III and/or (b) the creation of an alternative interpersonal nosology. That research project expired in its fourth year, and the present chapter is the first formal written report involving the first goal: actual description of Axis I DSM-III categories in terms of social and intrapsychic variables as defined and measured by SASB. Results to date are strongly supportive of the idea that SASB can provide a scientific description of dynamic and social variables involved in primary Axis I as well as Axis II syndromes.

Sampling Patients for the Interpersonal Diagnostic Research Project

The Interpersonal Diagnostic Project undertook as its first task the unexpectedly difficult task of locating and reliably defining psychiatric inpatients who clearly fall into one of selected DSM-III Axis I categories. To ensure maximal relevance, Axis I diagnostic categories common on inpatient services had been selected for study: They were Major Depression, Major Depression with Psychosis, Paranoid Schizophrenia, Bipolar Disorder–Manic, Bipolar Disorder–Depressed, Schizoaffective, and Undifferentiated Schizophrenia. The two Axis II categories, Borderline Personality and Antisocial Personality, also were included because they are found in psychiatric inpatient settings quite often and present major management and treatment problems for the health care provider. By early 1983, relatively complete protocols had been obtained from 108 subjects and those data files are the basis of the present chapter. Data from 96 additional subjects accumulated, and if future funds permit, eventually will be used to cross-validate present findings.

Making the DSM-III Diagnoses on Psychiatric Inpatients

After receiving appropriate training from qualified personnel at Washington University, our procedure for obtaining research-quality diagnoses was to follow the Diagnostic Interview Schedule, DIS, which is the current NIMH Structured Diagnostic Interview. The NIMH computer algorithm for processing and interpreting the DIS interview was used to obtain DSM-III labels. In addition, interview data were processed by the University of Wisconsin Physician Interview Program (PIP), which presents the diagnostician with DSM-III questions and branches on the decision trees exactly as specified by the DSM-III itself (Greist, Klein, & Erdman, 1976). When symptoms were surveyed systematically in the highly structured DIS interview and processed exactly according to the logic specified in the DSM-III using either the NIMH or the PIP algorithms, multiple diagnoses nearly always emerged. For example, with the NIMH program analyzing the DIS results, 4 out of the first 28 inpatients had the following combination of diagnoses: Major Depression—Definite plus Mania—Definite plus Schizophrenia—Definite. One of the four also had the Axis II label, Antisocial Personality. In other words, 14% of our initial sampling was multiply labeled on major pathological branches: unipolar and bipolar affective disorders and schizophrenic disorders. Without question, there is such extensive overlapping of symptoms that differential diagnoses among major discrete branches of the DSM-III diagnostic system cannot routinely be made.

The problem of multiple diagnoses is described by the DIS constructors as a problem of hierarchy. The DIS program leaves the investigator room to specify his or her own preference for hierarchy. One suggested rule is to use first-appearing symptoms. The PIP program solves the hierarchy problem as does the DSM-III: by simply asking for clinician judgment. For example, if a cluster of symptoms is identified, the clinician is asked to say whether he or she thinks it is clinically significant, whether it is a derivative or a primary presentation. The diagnosis is made in the direction of the primary and most significant aspects of the clinical presentation.

Rejecting the solution of "expert clinician judgment" to deal with the hierarchy problem, we ultimately were able to operationalize some methods for making the hierarchical decisions. The result was a manual, the LIDR, which exhaustively examines each frame in the DSM-III/PIP interview and operationalizes for the interviewer how to find the answer to every DSM-III hierarchical diagnostic judgment. For example, if DSM-III logic requires an answer to the question, "(Are the) patient's symptoms clinically significant?", the LIDR manual says to determine clinical significance by whether the patient has reported that she or he has told a doctor about the symptoms, whether he or she has taken medication for the symptoms, or whether the patient has indicated in the DIS interview that the symptoms have upset his or her life a lot. The DIS pages and question numbers are then listed for the diagnostician to review the original interview record to find the answers. The LIDR manual is a major contribution to the research diagnostic project, and the work of operationalizing each of the frames was accomplished by Patricia Hanson and by Paula Machtinger.

Because patients often would not tell us important information in the DIS, we added to the diagnostic chain a formal chart checklist. A systematic scan of the admission and discharge chart notes is controlled by the LIDR.

Independent, primary diagnoses for the selected nine inpatient categories using the NIMH Structured Interview, the PIP implementation of DSM-III logic, and the chart checklist, all controlled by the LIDR manual, yielded kappa = .861 for 41 subjects. This kappa compares very favorably with kappas reported for DSM-III itself (Axis I diagnoses for adults, Phase 1, kappa = .68; Phase 2, kappa = .72; Axis II, Phase 1, kappa = .56; Phase 2, kappa = .64). Very tight criteria for coder agreement were used in the present study; we counted a disagreement if one coder said paranoid schizophrenic and the other said chronic undifferentiated schizophrenic, and we only counted agreements if both judges in fact agreed upon the primary diagnoses. If one judge gave a specific category as primary and the other judge gave that same category as secondary, we recoded a disagreement. Patients were entered in the study on the basis of their primary category. Details of our diagnostic procedure appear in P. Hanson, P. Machtinger, and L.S. Benjamin (unpublished) and in Greist, et al. (1984).

A Special Subsample: Affective "versus" Schizophrenic Symptomatology

The idea of scientifically relating social variables and dynamic concepts to major Axis I psychiatric illness is challenging. An even greater challenge would be to see what social parameters could specifically add to the classification of Axis I illnesses simultaneously involving psychotic thought disorder and affective disorder. Some biochemical psychiatrists postulate that affective symptoms and psychotic disturbances in thinking represent theoretically different illnesses (review by Stone, 1980). Under this belief system, illnesses presenting both affective symptoms and thought disorders are anomalies. Two such Axis I categories in the present project which include both affective and psychotic symptoms are (a) major depression with psychotic features and (b) schizoaffective disorder. Although the 1978 draft of the DSM-III subdivided schizoaffective into three categories, namely, manic, depressed, and mixed (295.7X), the final version of DSM-III does not subdivide the category schizoaffective. However, we were able to identify a subgroup of schizoaffectives who reported only "blues" as affective symptoms. For purposes of exploring the potential of SASB social parameters to enrich the understanding of major psychiatric illness on Axis I, the present chapter will concentrate primarily on the two groups showing thought disorder plus depressed affective symptoms, namely, major depression with psychotic features and schizoaffective–depressed. Of course, the diagnoses were made completely independently of knowledge of patient responses to the SASB social measures.

From the initial sample of 108 inpatients having clear DIS–PIP–LIDR diagnoses plus completed protocols, we obtained 11 schizoaffectives and 8 major depressions with psychotic features. Of the 11 schizoaffectives, 5 reported only "blues" as affective symptoms. Although the Ns of 8 and 5 are small for the subsample, it is important to note that a trend must be quite robust to reach significance with small N. Because of the loss of power with a small sample, nearly every subject must show essentially the same tendencies to achieve the .05 level. During the 17 years SASB technology has been under development, trends identified as significant with initial samples typically are strengthened as the samples are expanded in size. The trends to be reported here comparing these small but interesting diagnostic subgroups are statistically and clinically significant. They will be subject to replication, and confirmation is expected.

Measures

Shortly after admission, patients' charts were scanned for chief complaints consistent with symptoms for the nine categories under study. After obtaining appropriate permissions and consents, patients were given the DIS interview, and if the DIS–LIDR–PIP chain yielded a primary diagnosis in one of the nine categories included, patients were asked to participate in the study. If they consented, they were given a lengthy series of SASB questionnaires about their social perceptions of themselves, their family, the staff, and other patients. In addition, they were given the Minnesota Multiphasic Personality Inventory (MMPI), the SCL-90, the Wiggins Interpersonal Checklist, the Paykel Life Stress Scale, and the Shipley–Hartford Vocabulary Test. Staff rated the patient on the Brief Psychiatric Rating Scale (BPRS) and on the SASB social scales. Student "handholders" unacquainted with SASB were available to keep the patients company while they worked on the lengthy protocols. Initially, the number of completed protocols was relatively small, but after the introduction of the handholders, there was a 96% completion rate. Subjects were paid $17 for participating and were offered computer-generated, clinician-assisted interpretation of their SASB ratings. Almost universally, patients said they learned a lot from the SASB social feedback and that they were glad they participated in the study.

The SASB parameters are called pattern coefficients and positive values of these coefficients provide a measure of attack, control (or submission), and power conflict for each relationship. Negative values suggest friendliness, autonomy, and attachment conflict. Pattern coefficients can be tested for statistical significance, and the high degree of order in most individuals' ratings usually permits the conclusion that a specific relationship is seen as controlling, submissive, autonomous, friendly, hostile, or conflicted. Different conflict coefficients define double binding, ambivalence, and intrapsychic conflict. Using SASB questionnaires, patients rated themselves, their families, the staff, and other patients. Staff rated patients with staff and with other patients.

What Is Structural Analysis of Social Behavior?

The Model

SASB is a model that classifies social interactions and intrapsychic events in terms of three basic underlying dimensions. By assigning a value on each of the three dimensions, the logic of the model then yields 108 qualitatively different classifications. In other words, by making only three judgments, 108 different social and intrapsychic descriptions can be generated. Categories in the model can be collapsed to reduce the system to as few as 12 categories (quadrants) if a simpler description is desired. The full version of the SASB model with all 108 categories is presented in Figure 29-1. The SASB model can be used both formally and informally for research, teaching, and clinical practice. For measuring the social perceptions of patients, staff, family members, and others, there is a psychometric available named the INTREX questionnaire. Responses to the INTREX questionnaires can be interpreted by software which yields research parameters and/or a clinically useful text addressed to the patients themselves (Benjamin, 1974, 1977, 1981, 1982).

The SASB model also can be used by objective observers to code videotapes or audiotapes of psychotherapy, or of family, group, or other social interactions. Available software for analyzing the behavioral observations can provide estimates of probabilities that any given person will make transitions from one social state to another when interacting with specific other persons. This software promises to be quite useful in studying pathological family interactions (Benjamin, Foster, Giat-Roberto, and Estroff, 1986; Humphrey, 1983; Humphrey, Apple, & Kirshenbaum, in press).

The three different parts of the SASB model shown in Figure 29-1 describe three different types of focus. The top part of Figure 29-1 describes focus on other and technically represents a transitive action from one person to another. A nonverbal representation of transitive action is shown in Figure 29-2 by the stick figure directing its energy and attention outward. Prototypically, transitive action is characteristic of parents in relation to children and describes what is to be done to, for, or about the other person. The middle section of Figure 29-1 describes focus on self and represents an intransitive state. Focus on self is prototypically characteristic of children and is represented nonverbally in Figure 29-2 by the stick figure which is in a reactive, relatively inactive posture.

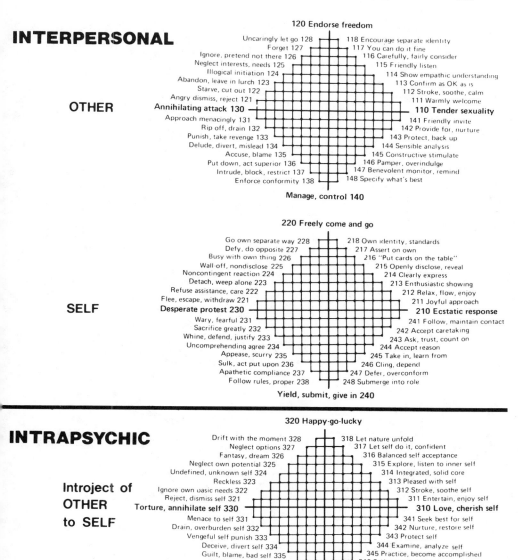

Figure 29-1. *Full version of the SASB model. A total of 108 classifications of interpersonal and intrapsychic behavior can be made on the basis of only three decisions: focus, amount of affiliation, and amount of interdependence (see text). Identifying the three underlying dimensions and arranging them according to the structure shown in this figure also permits a number of inferences. Examples include predictions of what will go with what (complementarity), what will draw out the opposite of what you have now (antitheses), and the connection between the social milieu and the self-concept (introjection). From Benjamin (1979). Copyright 1979, William Alanson White Psychiatric Foundation. Reprinted by permission.*

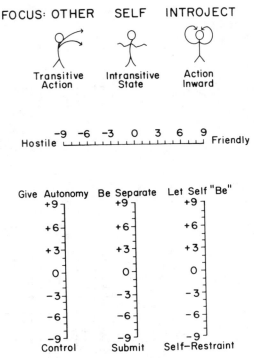

Figure 29-2. *Key for making the three decisions necessary to make classifications on the SASB model of Figure 29-1. The first decision is focus, and the possibilities are presented nonverbally by the three stick figures. The second decision is affiliation and ranges on the horizontal axis from extremely hostile to extremely friendly. The third decision is interdependence and is represented on the vertical axis; poles of the scale are different for each type of focus. If transitive action is the focus, interdependence ranges from controlling to giving autonomy; if an intransitive state is the focus, interdependence ranges from submission to autonomy. If transitive action directed inward is the focus, interdependence ranges from self-restraining to letting the self go. Classifications in the control–submit regions of the model describe enmeshment, and classifications in the give–take autonomy region describe differentiation. Transitive action directed inward upon the self ranges from self-restraint to letting the self be as is.*

The third part of the SASB model shown in Figure 29-1 describes introjected or intrapsychic behaviors, and these detail what happens if transitive action is turned inward upon the self. Introjection was described at length by Harry Stack Sullivan (1953) and represents the idea that we treat ourselves as important others have treated us. The theory of introjection connects the social milieu with the intrapsychic and uses logic characteristic of object relations theorists.

The need for distinguishing different types of focus in the SASB model has been challenged by Wiggins (1982) and by Kiesler (1983), both of whom are advocates of the Leary Interpersonal Circle. The Leary Circle, like the SASB model, is based on circumplex logic, but does not include focus, and consequently appears in one rather than three planes. Focus is a concept unfamiliar to psychiatry and psychology, but it is relatively well known by sociologists and by linguists who study deep structure of language. The identification of focus requires far more than the presence of the word "you" to describe focus on other or the presence of the word "I" to describe interpersonal focus on self or of intrapsychic events. Focus is best described by the grammatical concepts of transitivity and intransitivity; these ideas are evolved by folk wisdom and identify very different important types of interpersonal transaction. The identification of the three types of focus (transitivity, intransitivity, transitivity turned inward) provides enormous discriminative power among diagnostic groups, as will be shown in the analyses below. Once clinicians learn to identify focus, the accuracy of their clinical perceptions and interventions is markedly improved (personal communications, postgraduate clinical trainees in the University of Wisconsin Department of Psychiatry). An illustrative example of the contribution of focus to accurate clinical perception is the wife who is enraged when her husband comes home and reads the paper rather than talk to her. He is mystified by her "crazy" behavior, and she is outraged by his "density." The rage is fueled by the wife's assumption he is focusing on her (I don't want to be with you), whereas his view is that he is focusing on himself (I need rest and quiet integrative time alone). The discrepancy in perception of focus largely accounts for the misunderstanding between them.

For each of the types of focus, the SASB model describes the varying degrees of friendliness shown on the horizontal scale in Figure 29-2. Friendliness ranges from −9 units, representing extreme hostility, to +9 units, representing extreme friendliness. The horizontal scales on all three parts of the SASB model are the same. All of the points on the right-hand side of Figure 29-1 represent behaviors that are friendly and all of the points on the left-hand side represent behaviors that are hostile. Degrees of hostility and friendliness vary with the distance on the horizontal axis from the origin.

For the three types of focus, the vertical axes have different poles, and the different poles are named in the bottom part of Figure 29-2. If there is a transitive action, the vertical scale ranges from extreme control (−9) to complete giving of autonomy (+9). If there is an intransitive state, the vertical scale ranges from submit (−9) to being completely separate or differentiated (+9). If focus is introjected, the vertical scale ranges from self-restraint (−9 = control directed inward) to letting the self be as it is (+9 = the giving of autonomy turned inward). The vertical axes operationally define individuals' positions on a continuum ranging from complete enmeshment on the lower poles to complete differentiation on the upper poles. The enmeshment and differentiation are friendly or unfriendly, depending on whether they are classified on the right- or left-hand side of the model.

Once an event has been classified in terms of focus and given a number (−9 to +9) on the horizontal or the affiliation dimension as well as a number

(−9 to +9) on the vertical or the interdependence dimension, the coding decisions have been completed and the logic of the SASB model will yield one of the 108 categories as the classification. Coding in terms of the SASB model will be illustrated using an example that contains inherent contradictions characteristic of a double bind and thought to be important in major psychiatric illness by many psychosocial clinicians. The example to be coded is from a psychiatric inpatient who had a severe lead phobia, which failed to respond to antidepressants or antipsychotics, or to a well-planned behavior therapy desensitization program. Over and over again, the patient stated that lead and lead derivatives were present everywhere; therefore she reasoned that she was contaminated and could not touch her baby. The baby languished and the mother–infant bond was gravely threatened. The patient (a college graduate) became nonfunctional both as a wife and a mother, all under the delusional belief that she was, in fact, protecting her baby by not touching her with her contaminated body.

In contrast to research codings which meticulously address every word present (see Benjamin, 1986) clinical codings using the SASB model permit coding of paraphrases. A reasonable paraphrase for this woman's problem would be, "I can't touch my baby in order to protect her from my contamination." Not touching the baby is a transitive action, focus on other. The failure to perform as a mother is hostile. Using the horizontal scale on Figure 29-2, the coding of the hostility might be located as a bit more than halfway between neutrality and murder (−6). The poles on the vertical or interdependence dimension for focus on other are shown in Figure 29-2 to be dominance versus the giving of autonomy. Not touching the baby would represent leaving the baby separate or differentiated to a moderate degree; the giving of autonomy might be about +3 on the vertical axis for focus on other shown in Figure 29-2. The numbers assigned for the horizontal and vertical axes are −6, +3, respectively, and they can be counted out on a 19 × 19 grid, like the one in Figure 29-1, with the origin in the middle. Six steps leftward on the horizontal axis and three steps upward on the vertical axis determine the coding point, and then a line drawn through the origin and the coding point would determine the vector describing not touching the baby. If a transparency of Figure 29-1 drawn to scale is superimposed over the grid, the classification is made at the point at which the vector intersects the edge of the diamond defining focus on other. Alternatively on Figure 29-1 itself, a line can be drawn from the origin to the coding point and then be projected outward until the line crosses the edge of the diamond. For the coding point values (−6, +3), the classification is 123, Abandon, leave in lurch. In other words, the coding of not touching the baby in terms of transitive action, −6 units of hostility and +3 units of autonomy, yields the classification: Abandonment. The distance of the coding point from the origin represents the intensity of the abandonment. Judgments about how far out on the hostile axis and how far out on the autonomy axis the event should be located can vary from individual to individual. However, the disagreements usually are about intensity, not about category: Almost always, disagreements about the correct codings on one axis are compensated by disagreements about the correct coding on the other axis, so that the classification still is made on the same vector. To illustrate, an individual who thought not touching the baby was extremely attacking and coded it as murderous, -9, would be the same individual who would want to call not touching the baby as quite encouraging of separateness, say $+5$. The point $(-9, +5)$ lies on the same vector as $(-6, +3)$, but it lies further out from the origin. This second judge would code abandonment too, but the abandonment is seen as more intense.

Not touching the baby has been coded as abandoning. But SASB also permits coding the additional complication that from the patient's view, the behavior is intended to protect the infant. Protection is a transitive action (focus on other), and it is friendly, say $+6$. Protectiveness is influencing rather than giving of autonomy; protecting the baby can be given a score of -3 on the vertical dimension. The resultant vector $(+6, -3)$ yields the category 143, Protect, back-up on Figure 29-1. The judgments for not touching plus protecting the baby yield the two SASB model points 123, Abandon, leave in lurch, and 143, Protect, back-up. On Figure 29-1, these classifications are opposites in the geometric sense, and they also are psychological opposites. The classifications have operationally defined the interpersonal contradictoriness inherent in the chief complaint. The patient's method of protecting her baby actually gives the opposite effect, namely, abandonment. During an SASB-guided interview (see Benjamin, 1982), the patient accepted the interpretation that in so doing she was replicating what her own mother had done: Her biological mother (the grandmother) had given the patient up for adoption "for her own good." The protectiveness was the part about the baby's own good, and the abandonment was self-evident. This interpretation led to a very meaningful uncovering of rage at and confusion about the biological mother. The resulting treatment plan involved attempting to locate the patient's biological mother in order to work through the conflict about whether the patient had been given up for "selfish" reasons (not be bothered with a baby while in college) or for the patient (to make sure she could be in a good home where she could be properly cared for). The precise identification of the psychosocial contradiction in the chief complaint led directly to a precise identification of the contradictions in the psychosocial history, and it had specific psychosocial treatment implications. The double coding shows how a dynamic conflict can be operationally defined by the SASB method. Such codings have been shown in research contexts to be quite reliable (Humphrey, 1983; Humphrey & Benjamin, submitted).

Including the conflict just described, there are 18 contradictory points located opposite each other on the SASB model for each of the three types of focus shown in Figure 29-1. The geometric and psychological definition of 54 sets of opposites permits the operational definition of clinical concepts such as double bind (contradictory transitive actions), ambivalence (contradictory intransitive states or reactions), and intrapsychic conflict (contradictory transitive actions directed inward upon the self).

In addition to defining opposites, the structural organization of Figure 29-1 permits a number of other interpersonal and intrapsychic inferences. Among these are the principles of complementarity (a prediction of what behavior can be expected from a second member of a dyad) and introjection (a prediction of the impact of a transitive action toward another on that person's self-concept). Still other interpersonal and intrapsychic inferences can be made using the internal logic of the SASB model. Definition and discussion of some of these features can be found in Benjamin (1974, 1977, 1981, 1982, 1984).

The INTREX Questionnaires

Questionnaire items carefully honed to represent the theoretically prescribed types of focus, affiliation, and interdependence for each of the 108 model points have been developed in six major revisions over a period of 17 years. Validity of the INTREX items has been tested by factor analyses, dimensional ratings, and autocorrelation procedures. For clinical use, the respondent rates each INTREX item on a scale marked at 10-point intervals ranging from 0 to 100, with 50 serving as the boundary between "true and false." Different versions of the questionnaires substitute He/She/I/They as appropriate, and ratings of other people (He/She/They) are called the "See the World" set (STW), whereas ratings of the rater (I forms) are called the "Meet the World" set (MTW). As Frances noted (1980) in a discussion of problems with measuring personality, interpersonal behaviors and perceptions are expected to be different in different situations and moods. The INTREX solution to the problem is to ask raters repeatedly to rate themselves in different situations (with spouse, mother, etc.) and moods (best-worst). The Trait × State × Situation philosophy distinguishes INTREX from the trait theory inherent in interpersonal checklists and in DSM-III Axis II wherein a person has a categorical trait such as submissiveness or withdrawal.

The Pattern Coefficients

Analyses of the INTREX questionnaires are accomplished by an array of software, most of which is available at cost to qualified researchers and teachers. Of major research interest are the pattern coefficients from program FIG, described in detail in Benjamin (1984).

Examples of pattern coefficients from program Figure, FIG, are shown in Figures 29-3 and 29-4. The open circles in Figure 29-3 present the average cluster scores for eight psychiatric inpatients diagnosed as major depression with psychotic features rating their introject at its worst. Clusters are successive groups of 4 or 5 points on the SASB model (Figure 29-1), starting at 12 o'clock and proceeding clockwise. The successive names for the clusters on the introject surface rated for Figure 29-3 are as follows: 1 = spontane-

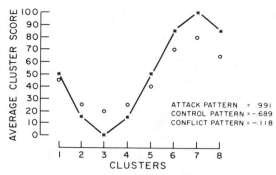

Figure 29-3. *Average cluster scores for a group of 8 inpatients having major depression with psychotic features. Clusters, represented on the abscissa, represent successive small groups of points on the SASB model (Figure 29-1), starting with the positions at "12 o'clock" and proceeding in a clockwise direction. The successive names for the clusters on the introject surface rated for Figure 29-3 are as follows: 1 = spontaneous self; 2 = self-accepting and exploring; 3 = self-nourishing and cherishing; 4 = self-protecting and enhancing; 5 = self-monitoring and restraining; 6 = self-indicting and oppressing; 7 = self-rejecting and destroying; 8 = daydreaming and neglecting of self. The data points represented by open circles show the orderly progression predicted by the structure of the SASB model, with the peak endorsements occurring at cluster 7, which represents the five points around the suicidal pole (9 o'clock) of the introject surface of Figure 29-1. The correlation between data points for these patients (circles) and theoretical points representing consistent organization around the suicidal pole (asterisks) was .991.*

ous self; 2 = self-accepting and exploring; 3 = self-nourishing and cherishing; 4 = self-protecting and enhancing; 5 = self-monitoring and restraining; 6 = self-indicting and oppressing; 7 = self-rejecting and destroying; 8 = daydreaming and neglecting of self. Inspection of Figure 29-3 shows an orderly arrangement among data points, suggesting maximal endorsement at the suicidal pole (cluster 7) and minimal endorsement at the opposite of suicide, namely, self-nourishing and cherishing (cluster 3). This orderly data pattern has a correlation of .991, with a cosine curve which peaks on the suicidal pole, and is shown in Figure 29-3 as a solid line connecting asterisks. With six degrees of freedom for eight pairs of points, a correlation greater than .71 is significant at the .05 level. Therefore, the major depressive (with psychotic features) inpatients as a group show a significant and maximal level of suicidality = .991.

Program FIG compares the profiles defined by cluster scores to 21 possible theoretical patterns generated by the logic of cosine and of orthogonal polynomials; most of the mathematically defined curves in program FIG have reasonable psychological names (see Benjamin, 1984).

A very different pattern coefficient is shown in Figure 29-4, which presents data from a schizoaffective patient's rating of his significant other focusing on him at her worst. Successive clusters for focus on other are named as follows: 1 = freeing and forgetting; 2 = affirming and understanding; 3 = nurturing and comforting; 4 = helping and protecting; 5 = watch-

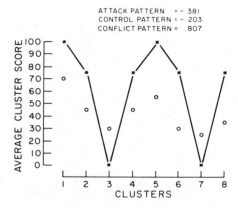

Figure 29-4. *Average cluster scores for a schizoaffective-depressed inpatient's perception of his signifi-cant other at her worst focusing on him. Successive cluster names are as follows: 1 = freeing and forgetting; 2 = affirming and understanding; 3 = nurturing and comforting; 4 = helping and protecting; 5 = watching and managing; 6 = belittling and blaming; 7 = attacking and rejecting; 8 = ignoring and neglecting. The data points represented by open circles show an organized tendency for higher endorsements to occur at the autonomy pole (cluster 1) and at its opposite, the control pole (cluster 5). The correlation was .807 between the data points (circles) and the theoretical points (asterisks) describing conflict at these two opposite poles. When this conflict involves transitive actions, it measures double bind; if it occurs when the ratings are of intransitive states, this conflict pattern represents ambivalence; and if the pattern appears in ratings of the introject, it represents a conflict between restraining the self and letting the self go. Negative conflict coefficients measure attachment (love–hate) conflicts in which case the maximal endorsements occur at clusters 3 and 7, the poles around the horizontal axis of the model in Figure 29-1.*

ing and managing; 6 = belittling and blaming; 7 = attacking and rejecting; 8 = ignoring and neglecting. Peak ratings for the spouse of the schizoaffec-tive occurred at contradictory poles of autonomy-giving (clusters 1 and 8) and control (cluster 5). This contradiction is described by a conflict coeffi-cient from Program FIG of .807 and is said to represent a double bind. The trend in this case is significant at the .05 level.

Figure 29-3 shows an attack pattern, and Figure 29-4 shows a conflict pattern. A third set of coefficients describes a control pattern and is repre-sented by an inverted U shape, indicating progressively greater endorsement as the clusters describing maximal interdependence (4, 5, 6) are approached. If, for example, there is a significant control coefficient for data describing the focus on self surface (middle part of Figure 29-1), the successive cluster names would be as follows: 1 = asserting and separating; 2 = disclosing and expressing; 3 = approaching and enjoying; 4 = trusting and relying; 5 = deferring and submitting; 6 = sulking and appeasing; 7 = protesting and withdrawing; 8 = walling off and avoiding. Peaking at clusters 4, 5, and 6 would describe a consistent submissiveness (the complement of control).

The attack (ATK), control (CON), and conflict (CFL) coefficients repre-sent three parameters to describe three orthogonal types of order in the obtained data and are accompanied by meaningful clinical names which differ depending on which type of focus has been rated. For transitive action, ATK = attack; CON = control; and CFL = double bind. For intransitive reaction, ATK = hateful withdrawal; CON = submission; and CFL = ambivalence (intimacy-distance). For introjection of transitive action, ATK = suicide; CON = self-restraint; and CFL = intrapsychic conflict. Significant negative values of the respective coefficients suggest the opposite: for focus on other, -ATK = friendly initiation; -CON = give autonomy; and -CFL = attachment conflict; for focus on self: -ATK = love; -CON = take autonomy; and -CFL = ambivalence (love-hate); for introject: -ATK = self-love; -CON = let self be; and -CFL = self-love–hate conflict.

The pattern coefficients from program FIG can be used to compare DSM-III diagnostic groups to see if object relations terms such as ambivalence, double-bind, or attachment, are relevant descriptors. In addition to providing the three-dimensional measure of ATK, CON, and CFL, Program FIG also yields a single best-fit coefficient to characterize specific relationships in terms of the pattern coefficients as friendly, controlling, autonomy, conflicted, and so on. The SASB technology provides a scientific means to apply clinical object-relations concepts to social perceptions.

Results

Description of Discriminant Function Analysis Using a Traditional Symptom Measure to Compare All Nine Diagnostic Groups

Stepwise discriminant function analysis (BMDP Program P7M) was used to separate the nine diagnostic groups on the symptomatic measures (SCL-90, MMPI, BPRS) as well as the social measures (the SASB, the Wiggins). First, the discriminant function program identifies all variables in the set which show significant differences by an F test. (Users familiar with the BMDP program will know that the program arbitrarily uses an F of 4, but does allow for the user to specify exact values appropriate to define the .05 level for different sample sizes. We elected to use the flexible exact F option.) Next, the variable with the largest significant F, the one identifying the most variance between the diagnostic groups, is removed to be used in the discriminant function. Then each of the remaining variables is made independent of the removed variable by the analysis of covariance. The idea of the covariance correction is to make all the remaining potential candidates for the discriminant function equation independent of the variable that has already been selected. The diagnostic groups are compared again by an F test on each of the remaining covariance-corrected variables. If any of the remaining variables shows a significant F, it too is removed and saved for the discriminant function. This process of identifying good discriminators and making the remaining set independent of those that have already been selected is repeated until no more covariance-corrected variables can be found which will yield a significant F. Once the program has run its course and identified as many variables as it can to serve in the discriminant function, the function itself is computed. Selected variables are weighted to maximize the differences among groups. Classification functions are constructed for each group, and an individual is classified in the group associated with his or her highest classification function value.

The stepwise nature of this process means that the order of variables in the data files can affect the variables that are entered in the final equations because of possible intercorrelations among sets. For example, suppose there is a high correlation between raters' tendencies to submit to mother and tendencies to submit to father and that submission to parents is characteristic of some of the groups to be discriminated. Then if one of the parents is selected for the discriminant function analysis, and the covariance between parents is partialed out, the remaining parent "doesn't have a chance" to appear in the final equation. Multivariate analysis is somewhat "tricky" in this regard, and one must be extremely cautious in interpreting the psychological meaning of particular variables selected and of their weights in discriminant function equation. A successful discriminant function analysis will show that diagnostic groups can be separated using a particular variable set and that individuals can be classified with X% accuracy, but it is by no means clear that the selected subset is the only subset of variables that could do so. Interpretation of differences in discriminant function weights among diagnostic groups is best tempered by referral to simple mean differences between groups.

Discriminant function analysis was able correctly to classify 26.1% of the sample of 92 inpatients who completed the SCL-90 forms; the canonical correlation was .66. Discriminant function based on MMPI correctly identified 40.9% of 93 inpatients completing MMPI forms, with a canonical $R = .72$. The BPRSFS scores generated by nurses' ratings of 55 patients correctly identified 50% of the sample, with a canonical $R = .80$. The BPRSIS scores were the best of all ratings; these nurse-generated measures of symptoms, such as somatic concerns, conceptual disorganization, hallucination behavior, and mannerisms and posturing, correctly identified 70.9% of the sample of 55 rated by the nurses, with a canonical R of .83. No discriminant function could be constructed using epidemiologic variables. However, the epidemiologic variables sex and educational level showed significant differences among the nine diagnostic groups by ANOVA. There were no significant differences associated with socioeconomic status, age, estimated IQ, vocabulary scores, life stress scores, or number of children.

Clearly discriminant function analysis is able to identify patient groups based on these symptomatic measures, and the best measures were not patient-generated, but rather those based on primary nurse ratings of classical symptoms using the well-validated symptomatic measure, BPRS.

Comparison of Nine Groups of Inpatients Using
Discriminant Function on Social Measures

Discriminant function analysis of the Wiggins Interpersonal Checklist correctly classified 21.9% of 103 patients, with a canonical R of .56. When using the INTREX questionnaires to separate nine diagnostic groups, the discriminant function technique was more successful than with any other patient-generated measure, but not as successful as the nurses' ratings of classical symptoms on the BPRSIS. Table 29-1 shows the frequencies of incorrect as well as correct classifications by diagnostic group. Classifications using the "I" (MTW) set of SASB variables for the 84 patients having completed protocols had an accuracy rate of 48.8%.

Inspection of Table 29-1 shows that the SASB MTW set was most accurate for the major depression group (86.7%). Classification was poorest for the antisocial group (18.2%). Some of the errors of classification are similar to common clinical errors. For example, 37% of the misclassified paranoids were called manic. Of the misclassified bipolar depressed, 66% were called major depression. Classification of major depression with psychosis was 57.1% accurate, and errors went to major depression (66%) and schizoaffective (33%).

The classification functions themselves appear in the center of Table 29-1. Of the seven variables used in the discriminant function, five also showed significant differences among the groups by simple ANOVA. Six additional variables showed significant differences by ANOVA of diagnostic groups, but were not included in the discriminant function. Frequently—but not always—the weights in the classification functions had the same implications as the simple mean differences used by ANOVA. For example, both mean differences and classification weights suggested submission to mother (CON8) was greater for the groups with affective disorders: major depression with or without psychosis, bipolar manic, and bipolar depressed.

In the lower part of Table 29-1, the distance among diagnostic groups on the covariance-corrected discriminant function variables is presented. These Fs show which groups were more similar and which more different according to the covariance-corrected variables used in the discriminant function. For example, major depression was significantly different from borderlines, paranoid schizophrenics, bipolar manics, schizoaffectives, and antisocial.

For nine-group comparison, discriminant function analysis based on patients' view of the social milieu (STW) was less successful than patients' descriptions of themselves (MTW). Of the 95 patients having complete protocols for the STW set, 31% were correctly cast into the nine groups.

SASB measures of patients were more successful when data were provided by RN observers than by the patients themselves. In fact, the success rate of the INTREX measures completed by nurses approached that of the BPRSIS nurse-generated measures. Whereas the BPRSIS was 70.9% suc-

Table 29-1

Comparison of Nine Diagnostic Groups on SASB Pattern Coefficients[a]

Classification matrix	Percent Correct	1	2	3	4	5	6	7	8	9
1 = Major depression uncomplicated	86.7	13	1	0	0	1	0	0	0	0
2 = Major depression with psychosis	57.1	2	4	0	0	0	1	0	0	0
3 = Borderline	58.3	1	2	7	0	0	0	0	2	0
4 = Paranoid schizophrenic	27.3	0	1	0	3	3	0	1	2	1
5 = Bipolar-manic	60.0	0	0	0	0	6	1	1	2	0
6 = Schizoaffective	25.0	1	1	1	2	0	2	1	0	0
7 = Antisocial	18.2	0	0	1	1	4	1	2	0	2
8 = Bipolar-depressed	50.0	2	0	0	0	1	0	0	3	0
9 = Chronic undiff. schizophrenia	25.0	1	0	1	0	0	0	1	0	1
Total	*48.8*	*20*	*9*	*10*	*6*	*15*	*5*	*6*	*9*	*4*

Classification functions	1	2	3	4	5	6	7	8	9
ATK2 = My suicidality at worst	7.16	6.22	5.71	3.44	2.82	3.94	2.72	6.15	4.87
ATK4 = I protest and withdraw, SO worst	−7.59	−8.55	−10.09	−3.91	−6.93	−7.94	−5.58	−7.25	−3.76
ATK11 = I attack staff	−18.60	−19.65	−18.19	−13.79	−13.73	−17.59	−8.31	−17.61	−11.43
CON8 = I submitted to mother	9.73	7.76	4.22	5.24	7.04	4.81	3.93	8.52	5.61

	1	2	3	4	5	6	7	8	9
ATK12 = I protest and withdraw, staff	1.32	5.18	6.41	2.41	1.17	5.14	1.12	1.14	1.82
CON13 = I control other patients	-4.90	-5.49	-2.09	-2.46	-2.28	-3.63	-.81	-3.88	-.59
CON11 = I control staff	-.16	2.98	1.83	1.46	-.70	2.16	-1.76	2.26	-2.04
Constant	-20.71	-17.23	-14.69	-8.35	-12.55	-12.29	-6.98	-16.94	-9.17

F tests between groups	1	2	3	4	5	6	7	8	9
1 = Major depression									
2 = Major depression, psychotic	1.76								
3 = Borderline	6.89*	1.92							
4 = Paranoid schizophrenic	7.22*	3.16	4.54*						
5 = Bipolar manic	4.75*	3.29	5.54*	2.46					
6 = Schizoaffective	4.55*	1.15	1.40	1.45	2.07				
7 = Antisocial	9.47*	5.22*	5.09*	2.23	2.43	2.89			
8 = Bipolar depressed	1.18	1.26	3.38	2.39	1.99	2.01	4.58*		
9 = Chronic undifferentiated schz.	3.48	2.50	2.33	1.21	2.34	2.05	.96	2.34	

[a]The top part of the table shows the accuracy by diagnostic group; overall accuracy was 48.8%, and this was the best performance of all patient rated measures. The middle section shows the classification weights, and all were also significant by ANOVA except for CON13 and CON11. The bottom third tests the distance between diagnostic groups on the discriminant functions. Differences on SASB social measures behave like differences on symptoms; for example, there is small distance between paranoid schizophrenics and bipolar manics; a very large distance between major depression and antisocial personality.

cessful, the SASB nurse ratings correctly identified 63.3% of the 49 patients rated, with the canonical $R = .81$. Variables used (maximal weight indicated in parentheses) were: Patient submits to staff (major depression), patient attacks other patients (borderline), patient controls other patients (antisocial), and patient power-binds other patients (antisocial).

It is remarkable that the social variables, especially the patient-rated social perceptions, were effective in distinquishing among the nine diagnostic groups. Clearly, it is appropriate to compare psychiatric inpatients in terms of social concepts such as hostile, submissive, or ambivalent. The performance of the social variables will be more closely examined by comparing two groups very difficult to distinguish diagnostically: major depression with psychosis and schizoaffective depressed. Other difficult diagnostic comparisons such as paranoids versus manics will be presented elsewhere.

Comparison of Major Depression with Psychotic Features to Schizoaffective Depressed

The sample sizes available for comparing these selected patients having both affective and psychotic symptomatology are woefully small (maximum $N = 15$). However, the validity of the exercise is supported by the fact that the findings make clinical sense. Replication, of course, is highly desirable.

For a sample of 8 patients having psychotic depression and 4 having schizoaffective-depressed illness who completed the MMPI, the result was 84.6% successful. The BPRSIS ratings were completed on only 4 depressions and 1 schizoaffective, but the schizoaffective was correctly identified. The SCL-90 failed on a sample of 15 subjects; also failing to create a successful discriminant function were the epidemiologic variables and the Wiggins Interpersonal Checklist.

All of the (7 psychotic depressed and 4 schizoaffective depressed) subjects were correctly identified using the SASB MTW variable set (cannonical $R = .86$), and 100% of the (8 psychotic depressed and 3 schizoaffective) subjects were correctly identified using the SASB STW set (cannonical $R = .997$). Variables used for the classification in the MTW set were: I control my significant other at my best (CON3), and I power-bind other patients (CFL13). The MTW classification function for schizoaffective depressed put much greater weight on both these variables than did the classification function for psychotic depression. The STW classification function used the variables: I am suicidal when at my best (ATK1); Father power-bound me (CFL9); Father power-bound mother (CFL13); Other patients control me (CON17); and Other patients power-bind me (CFL17). The STW classification function gave much greater weights to schizoaffective-depressed classification for all of these variables except for Other patients control me.

Using analysis of variance (ANOVA), significant differences between the two groups were found for the variable Other patients power bind me (CFL17), with the schizoaffective-depressed group having a much greater mean (.67) than the psychotic depression group (.01). In addition, psychotic depressives perceived significantly more control in the family of origin: The variable, Mother controlled father (CON11), had a much greater mean (.56) for this group than for the schizoaffective-depressed group (−.16). And from the MTW set, the psychotic depressives reported strong tendencies to submit to mother (CON8 = .64), whereas the schizoaffectives did not (CON8 = .16); the differences were significant. Patients' descriptions of themselves power-binding other patients were significantly greater for the schizoaffective depressed group (.41 v. −.01). Other variables differentiating the two groups at a significant level by ANOVA suggested schizoaffectives perceive less friendliness in others and in themselves than the psychotic depressions: Other patients attack me had a mean value of −.81 for the psychotic depressions and −.55 for schizoaffective depressions. I attack other patients was −.90 for psychotic depressions and −.76 for schizoaffective. One attack coefficient reversed the trend for the schizoaffectives to be less friendly: The protest and withdrawal from significant other when in the best state was −.77 for major depression with psychosis, and −.89 for schizoaffective depression.

Variables that showed significant difference by ANOVA and that also were selected for the discriminant function were: I power-bind other patients, and Other patients power-bind me. For these measures, schizoaffectives had far higher conflict coefficients; the combined ANOVA and discriminant function fingings suggest that a good interpersonal diagnostic indicator for making a differential between these two very similar diagnostic groups would be to inquire in interview about the patient's perception of other patients and of him or herself with other patients. Schizoaffective depressed should show some conflict over trying to tell other patients what to do versus letting others go their own separate ways. Schizoaffective depressed also should be concerned that other patients are trying to boss them around contradicted by worries that other patients also are not paying much attention.

The ANOVAs and discriminant function analyses just discussed were performed on individual patients' pattern coefficients. Procedures that test for significance of differences between groups use the average of the individuals' attack, control, and conflict coefficients as the estimate for the group attack, control, and conflict coefficients. An alternative method for identifying patterns in the diagnostic groups is to average the individual patient's cluster scores and then compute the single set of pattern coefficients (attack, control, conflict) characterizing the group profile. This group profile method was used to construct Figure 29-3, whereas an individual profile was shown in Figure 29-4. Usually the individual coefficients method and the group profile method yield similar conclusions, but the group profile method emphasizes trends. For example, the psychotic depression group and the schizoaffective-depressed group were very different from the other diagnostic groups by the fact their suicidality was noticeable in the introject ratings even in the best state. All other groups showed marked friendliness toward themselves in the best state, whether measured by group profiles or by averaging individual pattern scales. The average of individual introjected attack coefficients was .51 for psychotic depressives and −.02 for the schizo-affective-depressed group. By the group profile method, however, the suicidality pattern in the best state was .81 for the psychotic depressions and .85 for the schizoaffective-depressed group. In short, the group profile method emphasizes or magnifies the tendency for these patients to feel suicidal even when at their best. The group profile method has the advantage of damping individual "noise" and amplifying trends characteristic of the group; the group profile method has the disadvantage that it cannot be used to test the significance of differences between groups. With the group profile method, there can only be a test of the significance of the goodness of fit of a given pattern coefficient to the group profile (see Benjamin, 1984).

Tables 29-2 and 29-3 present the pattern coefficients for the group profiles for the psychotic depressions, the schizoaffective depressed. Group profiles for 19 inpatients with relatively uncomplicated major depressive disorder are added to provide a frame of reference. The major depressive individuals do not have other disorders and are the type for whom there is no "obvious" life stress. Table 29-2 shows the complementary patterns described by considering the perception of the other person's transitive actions (e.g., he controls me) and the rater's intransitive reactions (e.g., I submit to him). SASB complementarity is defined by SASB model points at the same topological location (e.g., "6 o'clock" on Figure 29-1) on the inter-personal surfaces of the model (see Benjamin, 1974). Table 29-3 shows the reciprocal type of complementary relating: the rater's transitive actions (I control him) and the other person's intransitive reactions (He submits to me).

The large number of significant negative attack coefficients in both tables shows that patients in these three diagnostic groups see others and themselves as quite friendly. The only exception to the friendly trend is the comparatively hostile withdrawal of the psychotic depressives from the significant other at worst.

Although not shown in Tables 29-2 and 29-3, there is another important similarity among the three groups: All three show extremely high degrees of self-attack at their worst (though the pure major depressives are reasonably friendly toward themselves when at their best). And when suicidal, all three groups are not only self-attacking, but they also are self-neglecting. The self-restraint shown in the best states by a positive control coefficient becomes self-neglect in the worst states and is measured by a substantial negative control coefficient. In other words, the worst state—suicidality—is accompanied by self-attack AND a letting go. This probably corresponds to the clinical observation of hopelessness (as distinct from helplessness) seen in dangerously suicidal individuals.

The control sections of Tables 29-2 and 29-3 are also noteworthy. Table 29-3 shows that the three groups generally have large negative control

Table 29-2

Pattern Coefficients for the Group Profiles: Complementary sets of the Form "He/She/They Initiate—I React[a]

	Psychotic Depression	Schizo-Affective Depressed	Pure Major Depression
Attack			
My SO attacks me—best	−.96*	−.84*	−.95*
My SO attacks me—worst	.39	−.81*	−.78*
My mother attacked me	−.67	−.61	−.82*
My father attacked me	−.73*	.42	−.90*
Staff attacks me	−.59	−.72*	−.87*
Other patients attack me	−.90*	−.77*	−.91*
I protest with SO—best	−.92*	−.88*	−.96*
I protest with SO—worst	.63	−.71*	−.21
I protested with mother	−.71*	−.31	−.68
I protested with father	−.68	.63	−.73*
I protest with staff	−.55	−.72*	−.82*
I protest with other patients	−.87*	−.93*	−.83*
Control			
My SO controls me—best	.57	.48	.53
My SO controls me—worst	−.68	−.51	.39
My mother controlled me	.84*	.49	.85*
My father controlled me	.77*	.80*	.75*
Staff controls me	.61	.55	.57
Other patients control me	−.40	−.53	−.63
I submit to SO—best	.78*	−.37	.69
I submit to SO—worst	−.75*	.41	.32
I submitted to mother	.95*	.59	.95*
I submitted to father	.99*	.86*	.96*
I submit to staff	.62	.49	.65
I submit to other patients	−.42	−.58	−.41
Conflict			
My SO power binds me—best	.18	.44	.17
My SO power binds me—worst	.76*	.42	.54
My mother power bound me	.57	.83*	.34
My father power bound me	.41	.43	.36
Staff power binds me	.66	.63	.32
Other patients power bind me	.14	.55	.30
I am ambivalent with SO—best	.26	.21	.21
I am ambivalent with SO—worst	.44	.42	.84*
I was ambivalent with mother	.28	.73*	.36
I was ambivalent with father	.24	.53	.36
I am ambivalent with staff	.60	.53	.46
I am ambivalent with patients	.31	.15	.42

[a]Data for major depressive disorder are for comparative purposes. Asterisks indicate significant trends. The negative of attack is friendliness, and the negative of control or submission is autonomy.

Table 29-3

Pattern Coefficients for the Group Profiles: Complementary sets of the Form "I Initiate—He/She/They React[a]

	Psychotic Depression	Schizo-Affective Depressed	Major Depressive Disorder
Attack			
I attack my SO—best	−.92*	−.88*	−.86*
I attack my SO—worst	−.77*	−.82*	−.83*
I attacked mother	−.88*	−.61	−.92*
I attacked father	−.90*	−.58	−.90*
I attack staff	−.81*	−.85*	−.87*
I attack other patients	−.95*	−.88*	−.91*
My SO protests—best	−.92*	−.90*	−.92*
My SO protests—worst	−.61	−.89*	−.87*
My mother protested	−.95*	−.87*	−.92*
My father protested	−.89*	−.64	−.91*
Staff protests	−.85*	−.88*	−.88*
Other patients protest	−.94*	−.93*	−.93*
Control			
I control my SO—best	.41	−.37	−.37
I control my SO—worst	−.93	−.60	−.78*
I controlled mother	.39	−.49	−.50
I controlled father	−.41	−.67	−.56
I control staff	−.63	−.63	−.66
I control other patients	−.53	−.55	−.64
My SO submits to me—best	−.45	−.39	−.43
My SO submits to me—worst	−.88*	−.87*	−.66
My mother submitted to me	−.66	−.66	−.40
My father submitted to me	−.48	−.78*	−.58
Staff submits to me	−.69	−.66	−.53
Other patients submit to me	−.42	−.54	−.61
Conflict			
I power bind my SO—best	−.08	.21	−.12
I power bind my SO—worst	.18	.24	.31
I power bound my mother	.08	.45	.15
I power bound my father	−.24	.31	.17
I power bind staff	.29	.39	.24
I power bind other patients	.08	.28	.17
My SO is ambivalent—best	.10	.07	.13
My SO is ambivalent—worst	.25	−.19	.29
My mother was ambivalent	.21	−.22	.14
My father was ambivalent	.27	.48	.27
Staff is ambivalent	.44	.34	.27
Other patients are ambivalent	.17	.12	.23

[a]Asterisks indicate significant trends. The negative of attack is friendliness and the negative of control/submission is autonomy. A positive conflict coefficient represents interdependence conflict and a negative one indicates attachment conflict.

coefficients when describing themselves in transitive action toward spouses, parents, staff, and other patients. Negative control coefficients indicate strong autonomy-giving, and are complemented by perceived autonomy-taking by the significant other in the intransitive state (negative submission coefficients). Conversely, control coefficients are mostly large and positive when describing other's control directed toward the patient, when describing the patient's perceived submission to that control (Table 29-2). All three groups saw both mother and father as highly controlling and themselves as very submissive in relation to parents (and staff). In other words, these depressed patients do not see themselves as exerting influence upon significant others or parents, yet they see themselves very much as the recipients of and compliers with strong influence coming from these important others.

In the worst state, significant others are seen as less controlling and more giving of autonomy (backing off). The observation introduces the possibility that the depressive illness is at least in part an interpersonal defense against overcontrol. Relations with peers (other patients) are characterized by friendly autonomy, not by control or submission. The differences among ratings of parents, spouses, staff, and peers demonstrate the importance of the SASB Trait $\times$ State $\times$ Situation philosophy, as contrasted to categorical interpersonal trait measures.

Finally, the conflict sections of Tables 29-2 and 29-3 demonstrate how the circumplex theory of SASB permits a very useful operational definition of difficult clinical concepts such as double bind and ambivalence. Double bind is measured by the conflict coefficient for focus on other. If it is positive, there is a power-bind (control vs. let go), and if it is negative, there is an attachment bind (love vs. hate). The conflict coefficient for the schizoaffective group rating their mothers suggests significant perceived double power binds (.83). These double binds were complemented by significant ambivalence in relation to mother (.73). The presence of strong trends toward double binds and ambivalence have long been believed by clinicians to be necessary conditions for schizophrenia, and it is noteworthy that the presence of both trends at a significant level occurred only in the schizoaffective group. The psychotic depressions also perceived significant double binding, but theirs was of the significant other at his or her worst. Developmental theory would hold the perception of the contradiction inherent in the power bind (do it your way as long as it is mine) in a spouse would be very destructive, but less destructive than if given by parents during childhood before identity is well formed. Dynamically speaking, psychotic depressives could be expected to have more ego strength (e.g., better prognosis) than the schizoaffective depression because their "crazy-making" experience power binds came after some self-definition had occurred. Clinically, schizoaffectives have a worse prognosis than do psychotic depressives.

Finally, the pure major depressions showed a significant ambivalence coefficient in relation to significant other at worst (.84). The uncomplicated major depression shows a strong tendency to be conflicted about whether to just give in or whether to leave (take a walk, read a book) when having interpersonal difficulty. This contrasts to the psychotic depressives who clearly take autonomy from the significant other at worst. Note that the conflict of the major depressive is in the reaction, the focus on self, and is different from the schizoaffective's tendencies to perceive contradictory transitive action coming their way (other patients power-bind me) or to engage in such power-binding transitive actions themselves (I power-bind other patients, mother, staff, etc.). In Table 29-3, six of the six measures of the rater power-binding others show the schizoaffective to have the strongest tendencies to this type of transaction. The questionnaire ratings showing that persons on the schizophrenic continuum not only perceive double binds coming from others, but also return them demonstrate a finding that is being confirmed in the SASB behavioral codings of videotapes of actual family interactions (Benjamin et al., 1986). This newly documented "parent abuse" by patients "doing onto others as (they perceive) has been done to them" will be elaborated upon elsewhere.

An alternative format for the data in Table 29-2 and 29-3 is offered by the three-dimensional displays of Figures 29-5 and 29-6; Figure 29-5 presents the group profiles for the psychotic depressions and Figure 29-6 for the schizoaffective-depressed patients. The three dimensional graphs in Figures 29-5 and 29-6 were constructed by a subroutine called SURGEN available at the Madison Academic Computing Center. To conform to the SASB model, attack coefficients were plotted with friendliness to the right and hostility to the left of the X axis. Interdependence was plotted with autonomy or differentiation on the top and interdependence or symbiosis on the bottom of the Y axis. The third dimension, the Z axis, plotted the magnitude of the conflict coefficient. If the data point is high in the upward direction on the Z axis, it represents a positive conflict coefficient and means the conflict was on the interdependence axis of the SASB model. If the projection in the three-dimensional plot is in a downward direction, it represents negative conflict coefficient and suggests a conflict described by the attachment (horizontal) axis of the SASB model.

Figures in the three-dimensional format permit an overview of all the ratings and allow comprehension of similarities and differences among groups at a glance. For example, the self-attack of the psychotic depressives and of the schizoaffective-depressed patients in both their best and worst states is apparent by the location of the introject plots (labels 1 and 2) near the end of the attack scale. The letting go during the suicidal worst state is made clear by the fact that introjects at the worst are in the quadrant showing hostile letting go, whereas introjects at best are in the quadrant showing (hostile) self-control. The schizoaffective's compliant but hostile reactions to fathers contrasts with the compliant but relatively friendly reaction to fathers by the psychotic depressions (see different locations of label 10, I react to father, in Figures 29-5 and 29-6). Similarly, the hostile

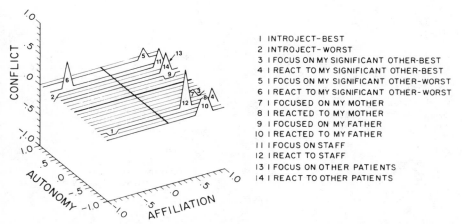

I INTROJECT–BEST
2 INTROJECT–WORST
3 I FOCUS ON MY SIGNIFICANT OTHER-BEST
4 I REACT TO MY SIGNIFICANT OTHER-BEST
5 I FOCUS ON MY SIGNIFICANT OTHER-WORST
6 I REACT TO MY SIGNIFICANT OTHER-WORST
7 I FOCUSED ON MY MOTHER
8 I REACTED TO MY MOTHER
9 I FOCUSED ON MY FATHER
10 I REACTED TO MY FATHER
11 I FOCUS ON STAFF
12 I REACT TO STAFF
13 I FOCUS ON OTHER PATIENTS
14 I REACT TO OTHER PATIENTS

Figure 29-5. *Three-dimensional presentation of group profiles for the psychotic depressive patients using the "I" form of the INTREX questionnaires. The striped plane has the same axes as the SASB model of Figure 29-1: The horizontal runs from hostility on the left to friendliness on the right. Points are plotted in the horizontal dimension on the basis of the magnitude of the attack coefficient. Orthogonal to the affiliation axis is the interdependence axis, and it runs from maximal enmeshment at the bottom to maximal autonomy at the top. Points are located on this axis on the basis of the control coefficient values. The vertical axis in the figure presents the magnitude of the conflict coefficient (see Figure 29-4). The labels numbered 1–14 each were sampled by 36 items from the INTREX questionnaire. The 14 different labels represent the different types of focus of the SASB model applied to different situations (mother, staff) and different states (best, worst). For example, label 12 is measured by the 36 items describing the focus on self surface when the patient was rating him or herself in relation to staff. For this group of 36 items, the attack coefficient showed moderate friendliness (located midway on the horizontal axis), substantial submissiveness (located near the bottom of the submission pole), and much ambivalence (represented by the relatively high peaking on the third axis).*

withdrawal of the psychotic depressives from the significant other at worst can be contrasted with the submissive and still friendly self-description of schizoaffective depressed by comparing the locations of label 10 (I react to SO at worst) in the two figures. Again, the psychotic depressives show more difficulty with significant others, whereas the schizoaffectives show more difficulties with family of origin. The generally friendly perceptions of and by both groups are shown by the preponderance of plots at the far right-hand side of Figures 29-5 and 29-6 near the top of the friendliness scale. The general tendency to be submissive to parents and to staff is shown by the location of labels 8, 10, and 12 in the submissiveness regions of both figures.

A casual scan of such three-dimensional figures for the other diagnostic groups in the study reveals distinctly different patterns and demonstrates in a graphic manner that social descriptors of the inpatients are meaningful. There is no reason to believe that these social and intrapsychic differences are secondary to the psychiatric presentation. For example, most of the patients are incapacitated to some degree or other by their psychiatric

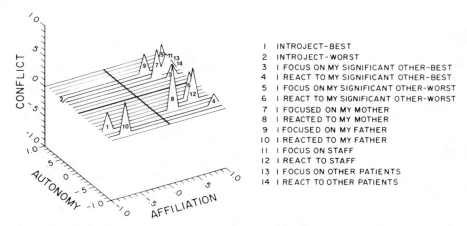

	INTROJECT-BEST
1	INTROJECT-BEST
2	INTROJECT-WORST
3	I FOCUS ON MY SIGNIFICANT OTHER-BEST
4	I REACT TO MY SIGNIFICANT OTHER-BEST
5	I FOCUS ON MY SIGNIFICANT OTHER-WORST
6	I REACT TO MY SIGNIFICANT OTHER-WORST
7	I FOCUSED ON MY MOTHER
8	I REACTED TO MY MOTHER
9	I FOCUSED ON MY FATHER
10	I REACTED TO MY FATHER
11	I FOCUS ON STAFF
12	I REACT TO STAFF
13	I FOCUS ON OTHER PATIENTS
14	I REACT TO OTHER PATIENTS

Figure 29-6. *Three-dimensional display for the group profiles of the schizoaffective-depressed inpatients rating themselves in various states and situations.*

patient status, but only the diagnostic groups with affective disorder (major depression with and without psychosis, schizoaffective disorder–depressed, bipolar illnesss–depressed) show the extreme submissiveness (helplessness) plotted in Figures 29-5 and 29-6. Similarly, other types of conflict shown by the different groups make "dynamic" sense and will be presented in detail elsewhere. The general conclusion here is that social and intrapsychic parameters as operationally defined by SASB are meaningful descriptors for major (Axis I) psychiatric illness. There is the potential in this technology for deepening the scientific understanding of the environmental contribution to the psychiatric illness. The specific conclusions about psychotic depression compared to schizoaffective depression are that psychotic depressives are more likely to perceive control coming from others, whereas the schizoaffectives are more likely to perceive themselves and others engaged in double power binds. This is not categorically true in every instance and the findings require replication, but the interpretations are completely consistent with clinical belief systems to the effect double binds are more characteristic of the schizophrenias. Further, helplessness (submission) is clinically believed to be more characteristic of the pure affective disorders. The present additional finding of ambivalence in depressives also has recently been reported by Raulin (1984). It is easy to observe clinically once it has been called to one's attention. The treatment implication is that depressed people can be helped if they can become more assertive. In the SASB model, assertiveness is the opposite of submission, but is not the same as dominance. Depressives are more responsive to the idea of asserting by self-defining ("I'd rather not") as distinct from asserting by dominating and pushing others around ("Why do we always have to do it your way?"). The differences obtained for ratings of best and worst states within diagnostic groups, the differences between diagnostic groups, and the confirmation of trends by staff ratings assure that the interpersonal postures described as dynamically important for the different diagnoses are not mere artifacts of the clinical state of the patient during hospitalization (e.g., Hirshfield *et al.*, 1982).

Using Social Variables to Predict Discharge Medication

Under the belief that behavior and biochemistry or structure move in parallel, it would follow that homogeneous groupings of patients on the basis of biochemical measures should yield homogeneous clusters of patients based on social variables too, provided the linkage between the biochemistry and social behavior is direct enough. It has just been demonstrated that diagnostic groupings based on traditional symptomatology do have meaningful social characteristics. Pursuing the logic of parallelism, there also should be a correspondence between the social parameters and the medications which prove most effective in relieving presenting symptoms. It is, of course, very difficult to define exactly what an effective medication is or has been, but for present preliminary purposes, a very pratical measure has been selected: It is presumed that the medications prescribed at the time of discharge represent the best clinical estimate of the medication most likely to be effective. Any trends identified by this preliminary procedure would, of course, have ultimately to be confirmed by appropriate double-bind placebo studies, by careful control of drug interaction effects, by careful selection of measures of response to treatment, and by adequate follow-up.

Using the selected preliminary measure of most effective medication on the sample of major depressions with psychosis and schizoaffective depressed led nowhere because very few of these individuals were discharged on any medication other than antidepressant medication. However, if the present sample is expanded by adding the other patients who also had a primary diagnosis of schizoaffective disorder, but who did not show a purely depressive form, three other medication groups can be defined in addition to those discharged on antidepressants: those discharged on antipsychotics, those discharged on lithium, and those discharged on antipsychotics plus lithium.

Using the MTW set and requiring that each medication group have at least two members, a sample of 11 patients was identified which had completed SASB profiles. These included 4 patients discharged on antidepressants, 2 discharged on antipsychotics, 2 discharged on lithium, and 3 discharged on antipsychotics plus lithium. The discriminant function among these four groups was 100% successful and used the variables: (1) I control myself at best (highest for those discharged on antipsychotics); (2) I attack my significant other at my worst (lowest for those discharged on antipsychotics); (3) I am ambivalent in reaction to my significant other at my worst (highest for those discharged on antidepressants); (4) I controlled my mother (lowest for those discharged on antipsychotics); and (5) I controlled my father (highest for those discharged on antipsychotics). In the preceding list, groups having weights with the greatest absolute value are named. Again, intercorrelations make interpretation of classification functions equivocal, but some of the weights do make "sense." Most noteworthy is the repetition of the observation that pure depressions (antidepressant only) are characterized by ambivalent reaction to significant other at worst. The discriminant function 2 space for the MTW set defining medications groups is shown in Figure 29-7.

Using the STW set and requiring that each medication group have at least two members, a sample of 11 patients was identified which had complete SASB profiles. These included 5 patients discharged on antidepressants, 2 discharged on antipsychotics, and 4 discharged on antipsychotics plus lithium. The discriminant function among these three groups was 100% successful, and the variables used were as follows: My significant other

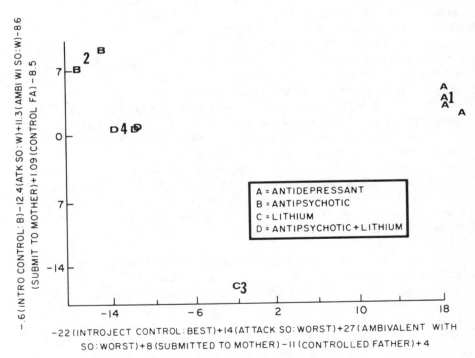

Figure 29-7. *Discriminant function analysis using INTREX questionnaire scores to classify 10 patients having diagnoses either of schizoaffective disorder or major depression with psychotic features. Patients are grouped according to the medication on which they were discharged. Classifications using social variables were 100% accurate and provide support for the hypothesis that social variables, if conceived and measured precisely, will show direct parallel with biochemical variables.*

power-binds me; My father protests and withdraws from me; and Other patients protest and withdraw from me.

The four medication groups also were successfully defined by discriminant functions constructed using other measures: MMPI, 86.7%; Wiggins Interpersonal Trait Checklist, 56.3%; BPRS Individual Scores, 100%; and SCL-90, 50%. The symptomatic measures did better at identifying medication groups than diagnostic groups. Because of space limitations, these results will not be examined in detail. They are highly supportive of the general hypothesis that if social parameters can be scientifically defined, they will correlate strongly, directly, and clearly with the biochemical and/or structural and/or genetic groupings.

Parallel Models for Affect and for Cognition

Another necessary consequence of the logic of parallelism is that if social behavior is orderly and runs in parallel with biochemical and physical attributes, and if there can be a model describing order in social behavior, then it also must be possible to contruct a model for affective behavior and a model for cognitive style. Affect and cognitive style relate directly to DSM-III Axis I emphasis on affective disturbances and thought disorders. There is an evolutionary logic for also looking at affect and cognition. Cognitive style has to do with how the organism perceives the world, and how the organism perceives the world is a major determinant of whether he or she can behave adaptively. Affect also is important in understanding and predicting behavior because affects represent the experiential mechanisms by which adaptive social behaviors are implemented. For example, the sexual affect is very compelling and assures the survival of the species. Less broadly recognized, but probably equally important, is an affect that goes with being dominant; most people find dominant affects to be more comfortable than the complementary affect associated with the submissive position. If dominance has been evolved to control the use of space, time, and supplies, and that in turn optimizes survival, then evolutionary purposes would be best served if it was affectively "desirable" to be dominant (and have access to the best supplies), and unpleasant or undersirable to be submissive (thereby creating a pressure to move somewhere else where it might feel better and provide more access to materials needed for survival).

Figures 29-8 and 29-9, respectively, present first drafts of the proposed models for Structural Analysis of Affective Behavior (SAAB) and for Structural Analysis of Cognitive Behavior (SACB). A verbal description of these models previously appeared in Benjamin (1981). An example of a prior circumplex model for affects was proposed by Plutchik (1980). In the center of Figures 29-8 and 29-9 is the quadrant version of the SASB model; the quadrant version of the social model is to provide easy comparison of the

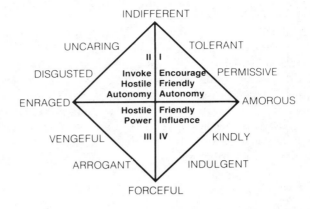

Figure 29-8. *First-draft model for Structural Analysis of Affective Behavior (SAAB). The quadrant version of the model for social behavior (Figure 29-1) appears in the center. The affective model shows affects expected to accompany social behaviors located at the same positions on the SASB model of Figure 29-1. Principles of opposition, complementarity, and antithesis apply for the affects as well as for the social behaviors.*

affective and cognitive domains with the social. The social, affect, and cognitive models show many interesting parallels. Parallels among the three models on the axes of the focus on other surfaces are as follows: Dominant behavior is paralleled by a forceful affect and a cognitive style of sharp focusing on detail. The opposite of dominance is giving of autonomy which is paralleled by an indifferent affect and a broad scanning cognitive style. Loving behaviors are paralleled by an amorous affect and by a cognitive style of openness and extension. These are opposed on the other pole of the horizontal axes by murderous behavior accompanied by enraged affect and a terminating, narrowing cognitive style.

For the domain of transitive action or focus on other, the affects paralleling the friendly giving of autonomy are those combining amorousness and indifference; they are named (Figure 29-8) tolerance and permissiveness. Parallel cognitive styles (Figure 29-9) are balanced give and take, and encouragingness; these combine extension and broad scan.

Affects paralleling friendly influencing behavior are kindliness and indulgence; these are a combination of amorousness and forcefulness. Parallel

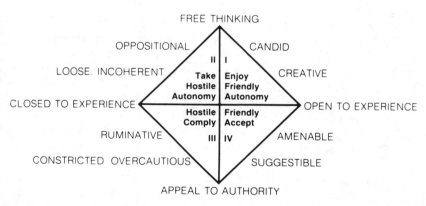

Figure 29-9. *First draft of the model for Structural Analysis of Cognitive Behavior (SACB). The hypothesis is that there is order to cognitive style as well as to affect and social behavior and that the three have evolved in parallel. The model presents cognitive styles expected to accompany the social behaviors shown at the same positions in Figure 29-1. For example, the dominating, controlling person (plotted at the lower pole of the focus on other surface) involves sharp focusing on details. If that cognitive style moves leftward in a hostile direction, it becomes judgmental and parallels blaming, superior actions (same location, Figure 29-1). Principles of opposition, complementarity, and antithesis apply to the cognitive as well as the affective and social models.*

cognitive styles are rationality and persuasiveness which combine sharp focus on detail and extension.

Hostile control is paralleled by the affects of vengefulness and arrogance; these are a combination of forcefulness and rage. Associative cognitive styles are judgmentalism and nihilism; they represent a combination of sharp focus on detail and termination.

Hostile invocation of autonomy is paralleled by the affects of uncaringness and disgust; they represent a combination of indifference and rage. Associated cognitive styles are tuning out and illogic. These styles combine termination and broad scanning.

For the domain of intransitive states, or focus on self, submissive behavior is paralled by the affect of helplessness and the cognitive style of appeal to authority. Submissiveness is opposed by taking of autonomy, and the associated affect is unconcern; the autonomous cognitive style is free thinking. Reactive affiliation is a loving affect associated with a cognitive style of openness to experience. The opposite of lovingness is hatefulness and its associated cognitive style is closed to experience.

The affects paralleling the taking of friendly autonomy are exuberance and relaxation. They are associated with cognitive styles of creativeness and candor. Affects paralleling friendly acceptance are trust and hopefulness, and the associated cognitive styles are amenability and suggestibility. Affects paralleling hostile compliance are humiliation and fearfulness, and they are associated with cognitive styles of constriction, overcautiousness, and rumination. Affects paralleling the taking of hostile autonomy are pessimism and bitterness, and they are associated with the cognitive styles of loose incoherence and oppositionalism.

The affective and cognitive models have structural attributes like those of the model for social behavior. Opposites are defined, complements are possible, and the introjective theory also would hold. For example, the person engaged in hostile power would have the affect of vengeful arrogance, and the person who complemented that hostile power with hostile compliance would have the affect of fearfulness and humiliation. Similarly, the nihilistic judgmental person would be complemented by a person who was constricted, overcautious, and ruminative. Complementarity for the other quadrants in Figures 29-8 and 29-9 can be determined by the reader by inspection.

Opposites too are perfectly apparent. For example, in Figure 29-8, the opposite of fearfulness and humiliation is relaxed exuberance, and the opposite of hopefulness and trustingness is bitterness and pessimism. In the cognitive domain, the opposite of amenability and suggestibility is loose incoherence and oppositionalism. The opposite of the constricted, ruminative approach is the creative and candid approach.

The models proposed in Figures 29-8 and 29-9 are provisional and compare developmentally in validation to the SASB model 17 years ago. Items have not been written that rigorously define and test the proposed points and relations among them. A very small sample of psychiatric residents has been used to begin to test the construct validity of the model in this very preliminary form. Those results were supportive of the hypothesized structure, but suggest extensive refinement and revision needs to be done before Figures 29-8 and 29-9 would approach the substantial construct validity of the SASB social model, Figure 29-1.

Nevertheless, the hypothesis of parallel structure for affect and cognition is consistent with the present finding of tight parallels between social behavior in diagnostic groups and parallels between social behavior and effectiveness of medication. In addition, clinical observation supports the idea of parallels among these three models. For example, the person who is suggestible appeals to authority and is quite constricted and overcautious; this same person can be expected to show behaviors in the submissive regions of the SASB model and to have the affects of hopefulness when feeling good, but helplessness and humiliation or even fearfulness when feeling less friendly. The diagnostic label of depression usually applies to these three sets: submissiveness, appeal to authority, constriction, suggestibility (cognitive styles), and helplessness (affect).

A formal comparison of correspondence between symptoms as measured by SCL-90, MMPI, BPRS, and social behaviors as measured by INTREX will be presented elsewhere. The Millon Clinical Multiaxial Inventory (MCMI; Millon, 1981) yields reliable and meaningful computer-generated interpersonal trait descriptions directly related to DSM-III Axis II categories such as schizoid, avoidant, dependent, histrionic, or narcissistic personality. The MCMI was developed from a structural model involving focus, friendliness, and dominance. When the INTREX method is applied to outpatient samples, it will be important to compare results to the MCMI. It is expected that SASB descriptions of attachment, control, ambivalence, and so on will correspond to the MCMI Axis II trait descriptions sensibly. For example, a patient scoring high on the compulsive scale of the MCMI perhaps will have very high SASB control and submission coefficients, with only moderately large friendliness scores (negative attack coefficients). The parallel with the cognitive model would describe the compulsive personality as judgmental and having sharp focus on detail, and as constricted, overcautious, with a "contradictory" (complementary) tendency to appeal to authority. The affects of the compulsive would be arrogance and forcefulness alternating with humiliation and helplessness.

Conclusion

In conclusion, the present data suggest that social parameters as defined by the SASB model, questionnaires, and software do indeed describe many "dynamic" object-relations concepts in an operational, highly replicable fashion. The trait $\times$ state $\times$ situation philosophy of SASB controls the variance associated with changes in role or situation and mood or state. By comparing observer ratings with self-descriptions and by comparing patient perceptions of current self with memory of early family experiences, it is possible scientifically to define defenses such as projection, reaction formation, and denial (see Benjamin, 1981, and 1984, for discussions of coping mechanisms and defenses). The SASB model defines connections between object relations and internal mental structure (introject). The SASB quantification of social and intrapsychic phenomena permits statistical comparison of diagnostic groups with each other and with normals. Strengths, or coping mechanisms, as well as weaknesses are assessed.

Many classical clinical beliefs can be scientifically validated using the SASB approach. In the present analysis, validated clinical beliefs include the finding of double binding and ambivalence in a schizoaffective-depressed sample, and excessive submissiveness (helplessness) in a psychotically depressed sample. There also has been a documentation of the belief that vicious self-attack combined with hopelessness (letting go) definitely is more characteristic of the dangerously suicidal state, whatever the diagnosis. Another (albeit not classical) finding is that the major depressive syndrome is characterized by the intransitive reaction of conflict between submitting and walking away or withdrawing peaceably. Findings confirm the clinical belief that depressed people need help in becoming more assertive.

It is hypothesized that there are structural parallels among social behavior, cognition, and affect. For example, it is hypothesized that an associated biochemistry goes with the submissive, helpless state. A patient could be helped to change the behaviors associated with the helpless state either by changing the biochemistry (affect and/or cognition) and/or by changing the parallel behaviors. Similarly, it is reasonable to expect that a biochemistry exists which sensibly parallels a confused state naturally accompanying double-binding behaviors. It is time to stop imagining social behaviors are not related to symptoms. Let Axis II join Axis I in an integrated manner, and let dynamic concepts rejoin the mainstream of psychiatric diagnosis and treatment.

ACKNOWLEDGMENTS

This work was supported in part by Grant MH33604-04 from the National Institutes of Mental Health. Appreciation also is expressed to Warren Olson, chief of the University of Wisconsin Psychiatry Inpatient Service, for facilitating the participation of staff and patients in this project. Other psychiatry service chiefs who were vital to our project are Charles Hodulik of Madison General Hospital, Thomas Pfaehler of Methodist Hospital, and Gary Meyers and Virginia Sincaban of Mendota Mental Health Institute. The replication so important to validating the present somewhat revolutionary findings will be abbreviated because the grant renewal received only a "good" priority in times when "excellent" is needed actually to be funded. Extreme gratitude is expressed to the Wisconsin Alumni Research Foundation and to the

Department of Psychiatry Research and Development Fund which supplied supplementary funding for 6 months so that the project could terminate in an orderly fashion and obtain at least a minimal replication sample. I would like to thank members of the research project staff for their dedication to precision and hard work while also keeping a sense of humor: Dee Jones, Patricia Hanson, Paula Machtinger, and Hu Hshieo-Yun.

REFERENCES

Benjamin, L. S. (1974). Structural analysis of social behavior. *Psychological Review, 81*, 392–425.

Benjamin, L. S. (1977) Structural analysis of a family in therapy. *Journal of Consulting and Clinical Psychology, 45*, 391–406.

Benjamin, L. S. (1979). Structural analysis of differentiation failure. *Psychiatry: Journal for the Study of Interpersonal Process, 42*, 1–23.

Benjamin, L. S. (1981). A psychosocial competence classification system. In J. D. Wine & M. D. Smye (Eds.), *Social competence* New York: Guilford Press.

Benjamin, L. S. (1982). Use of structural analysis of social behavior (SASB) to guide interventions in psychotherapy. In J. Anchin & D. Kiesler (Eds.), *Handbook of interpersonal psychotherapy.* Oxford: Pergamon Press.

Benjamin L. S. (1984). Principles of prediction using structural analysis of social behavior (SASB). In R. A. Zucker, J. Aronoff, & A. I. Rabin (Eds.), *Personality and the prediction of behavior* (Vol. 1). New York: Academic Press.

Benjamin, L. S. (in press). Use of the SASB dimensional model to develop treatment plans, I: Narcissism. *Journal of Personality Disorders.*

Benjamin, L. S. (1986). Use of structural analysis of social behavior (SASB) for operational definition and measurement of some dynamic concepts. *Psychiatry, Journal for the study of interpersonal process, 47.*

Benjamin, L. S., Foster, S. W., Giat-Roberto, L., & Estroff, S. E. (1986). Breaking the family code: Analyzing videotapes of family interactions by structural analysis of social behavior. In L. S. Greenberg & W. M. Pinsof (Eds), *Psychotherapeutic process: A research handbook,* New York: Guilford Press.

Derogatis, L. R. (1977). *SCL-90 administration, scoring and procedures manuals for the revised version.* Baltimore, MD: Leonard R. Derogatis.

Derogatis, L. R., & Cleary, P. A. (1977). Confirmation of the dimensional structure of the SCL-90: A study in construct validation. *Journal of Clinical Psychology, 33*, 981–989.

Frances, A. (1980). The DSM-III personality disorders section: A commentary. *American Journal of Psychiatry, 137*, 1050–1054.

Greist, J. H., Klein, M. H., & Erdman, H. P. (1976). Routine on-line psychiatric diagnosis by computer. *American Journal of Psychiatry, 133*, 1405–1407.

Greist, J. H., Mathisen, K. S., Klein, M. H., Benjamin, L. S., Erdman, H. P., & Evans, F. J. (1984). Psychiatric diagnosis: What role for the computer. *Hospital and Community Psychiatry, 35*, 1089–1093.

Hirschfeld, R. M. A., Klerman, G. L., Clayton, P. J., Keller, M. B., McDonald-Scott, P., & Larkin, B. H. (1982). *Assessing personality: Effects of the depressive state on trait measurement.* Bethesda, MD: National Institute of Mental Health—Clinical Research Branch, Colloborative Program on the Psychobiology of Depression.

Humphrey, L. L. (1983). A sequential analysis of family processes in Anorexia and Bulimia. In *New directions in anorexia nervosa. Proceedings of the fourth Ross conferene on medical research.* Columbus, OH: Ross Laboratories.

Humphrey, L. L., Apple, R. F., & Kirshenbaum, D. S. (in press). Differentiating bulimic-anorexic from normal families using an interpersonal and a behavioral observation system. *Journal of Consulting and Clinical Psychology.*

Humphrey, L. L., & Benjamin L. S. (1986). Using structural analysis of social behavior to assess critical but elusive family processes: A new solution to an old problem. Manuscript submitted for publication.

Karasu, T. B., & Skodol, A. E. (1980). VIth axis for DSM-III: Psychodynamic evaluation. *American Journal of Psychiatry, 137*, 607–610.

Kiesler, D. J. (1983). The 1982 interpersonal circle: A taxonomy for complementarity in human transactions. *Psychological Review. 90*, 185–214.

Lorr, M., Bishop, P. F., & McNair, D. M. (1965). Interpersoanl types among psychiatric patients. *Journal of Abnormal Psychology, 70*, 468–472.

McLemore, C., & Benjamin, L. S. (1979). Whatever happened to interpersonal diagonisis: A psychosocial alternative to DSM-III. *American Psychologist, 34*, 17–34.

Millon, T. (1969). *Modern psychopathology: A biosocial approach to maladaptive learning and functioning.* Philadelphia, PA: Saunders.

Millon, T. (1981). *Disorders of personality. DSM-III: Axis II.* New York: Wiley.

Millon, T. (1982) *Millon clinical multiaxial inventory manual.* Minneapolis, MN: National Computer Systems.

Overall, J. E., & Gorham, D. P. (1962). The brief psychiatric rating scale. *Psychological Reports, 10*, 799–812.

Paykel, E. S., Prusoff, B. A., & Uhlenhuth, E. H. (1971). Scaling of life events. *Archives of General domain. Journal of Personality and Social Psychology, 37*, 395–412.

Plutchik, R. (1980) *Emotion: A psychoevolutionary synthesis.* New York: Harper & Row, 1980.

Plutchik, R., & Platman, S. R. (1977). Personality connotations of psychiatric diagnoses. *Journal of Nervous and Mental Disease, 165*, 418–422.

Raulin, M. L. (1984). Development of a scale to measure intense ambivalence. *Journal of Consulting and Clinical Psychology, 52*, 63–72.

Shapiro, D. (1965). *Neurotic styles.* New York: Basic Books.

Spitzer, R. L., Williams, J. B. W., & Skodol, A. E. (1980). DSM-III: The major achievements and an overview. *American Journal of Psychiatry, 137*, 151–164.

Stone, M. H. (1980). *The borderline syndromes.* New York: McGraw-Hill.

Sullivan, H. S. (1953). *The interpersonal theory of psychiatry.* New York: Norton.

Tinbergin, N. (1981). *The study of instinct.* London & New York: Oxford University Press.

Wiggins, J. S. (1979). A psychological taxonomy of trait descriptive terms: The interpersonal domain. *Journal of Personality and Social Psychology, 37*, 395–412.

Wiggins, J. S. (1984). Circumplex models of interpersonal behavior in clinical psychology. In P. C. Kendall & J. N. Butcher (Eds.), *Handbook of research methods in clinical psychology.* New York: Wiley.

CHAPTER 30

A Theoretical Derivation of Pathological Personalities

Theodore Millon

Scholars often find it useful to step back from their intense and close involvement in their subject, disengage themselves from its current themes and assumptions, and reflect on a series of philosophically naive yet fundamental questions, such as:

What is essential to the subject?

What distinguishes it from others?

What are the questions for which I should find answers?

What observations and concepts have given the field its legitimacy as a science?

Do these data and ideas limit or distort my thinking?

Can the empirical elements of the subject be identified in a more efficient and reliable manner than previously?

Can its central notions be defined more relevantly or articulated more insightfully than heretofore?

Might I formulate relationships among its elements in a more productive and coherent way than has been done in the past?

The content of this and the following chapter reflects efforts to answer questions such as these. It also provides the rationale for a theory, as well as the clinical prototypes and diagnostic criteria generated by that theory. The subject matter to which the theory applies—personality disorders—encompasses the several, relatively distinct ways in which individuals persistently and pervasively function in an interpersonally and intrapsychically pathogenic manner.

Theodore Millon. Departments of Psychology and Psychiatry, University of Miami, Coral Gables, Florida.

Before presenting the theory and its derivations, it may be useful to briefly note a number of issues relevant to the concept of personality itself as well as its disorders.

General Issues

The vast majority of empirical discoveries and theoretical constructs that have occupied the attention of psychologists and psychiatrists have suffered the fate that General Douglas MacArthur thought unique to old generals, that is, they never die, they just fade away. As Meehl (1978) has put it:

> There is a period of enthusiasm about a new theory, a period of attempted application to several fact domains, a period of disillusionment as the negative data come in, a growing bafflement about inconsistent and unreplicable empirical results, multiple resort to ad hoc excuses, and then finally people just sort of lose interest in the thing and pursue other endeavors. (p. 807)

Theories, constructs, and findings of such fortune are legion, a sad comment on the "scientific" status of our subject, no less our naive eagerness to follow one evanescent or insubstantial fad after another. Although most conceptual pursuits in the softer psychologies have come and gone, justly or otherwise (as others have remained immutably entrenched despite impressive rebuttals or incompatible evidence), there are encouraging signs that cumulative knowledge and a refining process may be under way in the study of personality.

Especially promising is the observation that the essential elements that give substance to personality—the fact that people exhibit distinctive and abiding characteristics—have survived through the ages, albeit under diverse rubrics and labels. This durability attests, at the very least, either to personality's intuitive consonance with authentic observation, its intrinsic, if naive human interest, or its decided and convincing utility. The apparent viability of the concept as well as its invulnerability in academic circles is all the more noteworthy when one considers the number of spirited, if misguided, efforts in recent years to undo it. This achievement is even more impressive when one considers the number of recently popular constructs that have faded to a status more consonant with their trivial character, or have, under the weight of their scientific inefficacy, succumbed to scholarly weariness or boredom. By contrast, personality and its disorders appear not only to have weathered mettlesome assaults, witness the position reversals of its most ardent critics (e.g., Mischel, 1973, 1979), but appear to be undergoing a wide-ranging renaissance in both professional and scientific circles. This resurgence may be worth elaborating briefly, for it signifies the coalescence of powerful, if disparate trends.

First, from a rather mundane and practical viewpoint, most mental health practitioners employ their professional skills today in outpatient rather than inpatient settings. Their "clients" are no longer the severely disturbed "State Hospital" psychotic, but ambulatory individuals seen in private offices or community clinics, beset with personal stressors, social inadequacies, or interpersonal conflicts, typically reported in symptoms such as anxiety, depression, or alcoholism, but which signify the outcroppings of longstanding patterns of maladaptive behaving, feeling, thinking, and relating: in other words, their "personality style."

Second, there has been a marked shift in the focus of dynamic therapies from that of "surface" neurotic symptoms to that of "underlying" personality functions. This reorientation reflects the intriguing evolution of psychoanalytic theory since the turn of the century. Auchincloss and Michels (1983) describe this progression in an illuminating review of the psychoanalytic concept of "character." They write, "Today it is generally accepted that character disorders, not neurotic symptoms, are the primary indication for analysis. . . . Psychoanalysis (as a technique) and character analysis have become synonymous" (p. 2).

As character theory progressed from the ideas of Abraham on libidinal development to those of Reich on defensive armor, personality (character) changed from being a developmentally phase-specific cluster of symptoms to a system of intrapsychic resistances that blocked the treatment of these symptoms. Recent contributions of ego, self, and object-relations theorists have extended our awareness of the highly varied consequences of early psychic deprivations. Today, character structure is seen not only as a system of defensive operations, but a complex organization of structures that are the focus of therapeutic attention and intervention.

It is not only the changing patient population of clinical practice or the recently evolved role given "character" and "personality organization" in analytic theory that signifies the growing prominence of the construct. In the realms of "hard science," that of quantitative clinical assessment and psychometrics, psychologists and psychiatrists alike have turned their skills toward the reliable identification and valid measurement, not of "traits" of personality, a well-worn subject of diminished scientific merit, but of the new "disorders" of personality (Reich, 1984). This change in focus may be seen most clearly in the content of recently developed clinical instruments. These assessment tools contrast in scope and intent with both the historically important projective techniques, such as the Rorschach, and the well-established, if nondynamic objective inventories, such as the Minnesota Multiphasic Personality Inventory (MMPI). Newly minted are a group of impressively constructed clinical interview schedules, such as the DIB (Gunderson, Kolb, & Austin, 1981), which seek to build a composite picture of a single, comprehensive entity, in this case the "borderline personality," or the broadly based self-report inventory, the MCMI (Millon, 1983a), with its psychometrically validated series of scales designed to identify and describe the dynamics of all 11 DSM-III, Axis II disorders.

A few words should be said concerning the special role of the DSM-III (American Psychiatric Association, 1980) in giving prominence to the personality disorders. With the advent of this official system, personality not only gained a place of consequence among syndromal categories, but became central to its multiaxial schema. The logic for assigning personality its own axis is more than a matter of differentiating syndromes of a more acute and dramatic form from those that may be overlooked by virtue of their long-standing and prosaic character, a position assumed by Kendell (1983). More relevant to this partitioning decision was the assertion that personality can serve usefully as a dynamic substrate of affective, cognitive, and behavioral dispositions from which clinicians can better grasp the "meaning" of their patients' more transient or florid disorders. In the DSM-III, then, personality disorders have not only attained a nosological status of prominence in their own right, but they have been assigned a contextual role that makes them fundamental to the understanding of other psychopathologies.

Personality as a System

Opinions differ concerning how best to define personality. There is general agreement, however, that it is an inferred abstraction rather than a tangible phenomenon with material existence. Problems inevitably arise, however, when professionals reify these conceptual constructs into substantive entities. To paraphrase Kendell (1975), "familiarity leads us to forget their origins in human imagination." Certainly, personality should not be construed as a palpable "disease." It is a man-made construction invented to facilitate scientific understanding and professional communication. Should constructs fail in these aims, they should be recast or discarded. Unfortunately, most are likely to fade slowly, as do old generals, receding ever deeper into the dustbins of history.

What should the construct "personality" represent?

It may best be conceived as the psychological equivalent of the body's biological system of structures and functions. To elaborate: Our body as a whole comprises a well-organized, yet open system of relatively stable structures that interconnect functionally as they process a wide range of both internal and external events in a coherent and efficient manner. The diversity of functions carried out by the body is awesome in its complexity and efficacy, as is the internal organization of structures impressively elaborate in its intricacy and articulation. The distinctive configuration of structures and functions that have evolved ensures that the system as a whole remains both viable and stable. This is achieved by processes that maintain internal cohesion and by actions that utilize, control, or adapt to external forces. A biological disorder arises when one or several of the following occurs: The balance and synchrony among internal components go awry; a particular structure is traumatized or deteriorates, with the result that it repetitively or persistently malfunctions; foreign entities such as bacteria or viruses intrude themselves, either overwhelming or insidiously undermining the system's integrity.

The construct "personality" represents a psychic system of structures and functions which parallel those of the body. It is not a potpourri of unrelated traits and miscellaneous behaviors, but a tightly knit organization of stable structures (e.g., internalized memories and self-images) and coordinated functions (e.g., unconscious mechanisms and cognitive processes). Given continuity in one's constitutional equipment and a narrow band of experiences for learning behavioral alternatives, this "system" develops an integrated pattern of characteristics and inclinations that are deeply etched, cannot be easily eradicated, and pervade every facet of life experience. The system *is* the sum and substance of what is meant by personality. Mirroring the body's organization, it is a distinctive configuration of interlocking perceptions, feelings, thoughts, and behaviors that provide a template and disposition for maintaining psychic viability and stability. From this perspective, mental disorders are best conceived as stemming from failures in the personality system's dynamic pattern of adaptive competencies. Just as physical ill health is never a simple matter of an intrusive alien virus, but reflects also deficiencies in the body's capacity to cope with particular physical environments, so too is psychological ill health not merely a product of psychic stress alone, but represents deficiencies in the personality system's capacity to cope with particular psychosocial environments.

Implied in the preceding paragraph is the assertion that adequate clinical analyses of both physical and mental disorders require data beyond those which inhere in the individual alone. In the biological realm, it must encompass knowledge of relevant features of the physical environment; in the psychological domain, it calls for an awareness of the character of the psychological environment. Kendell points to the reciprocal nature of this person–environment field in the following illustration (1975):

> A characteristic which is a disadvantage in one environment may be beneficial in another. The sickle cell trait is a deviation from the norm which in most environments produces a slight but definite biological disadvantage. In an environment in which malaria is endemic, however, it is positively beneficial. . . . This is a particularly serious matter where mental illness is concerned because here the environment, and especially its social aspects, is often of paramount importance. Qualities like recklessness and aggressiveness, for example, may lead a man to be regarded as a psychopath in one environment and to be admired in another. (p. 15)

For the greater part of our psychodiagnostic history, attention has focused on the patient's internal characteristics alone. When one moves to a systems perspective, external social and interpersonal dynamics are given equal status. As noted in Kendell's illustration, it may be clinically impossible to disentangle these elements when appraising the clinical consequences of an internal characteristic, for example, whether the sickle cell trait is advantageous or disadvantageous. For diagnostic purposes, internal and external factors are inextricably linked elements. Intrapsychic structures and dispositions are essential, but they will prove functional or dysfunctional depending on their efficacy in specific interpersonal, familial, or social contexts. (It should be noted parenthetically that to assert that internal and external factors are interdependent and reciprocal is *not* to say that they contribute equal shares to the variance or prevalence of a particular pathology.)

The rationale for broadening the notion of a "disorder" to include the interplay of both internal and external systems is especially appropriate when evaluating personality syndromes. Not only does personality express itself in everyday, routine interactions within group and familial settings, but the ordinary characteristics that comprise the patient's personality will elicit reactions that feed back to shape the future course of whatever impairments the person may already have. Thus, the behaviors, mechanisms, and self-attitudes that individuals exhibit with others will evoke reciprocal responses that influence whether their problems will improve, stabilize, or intensify. It is not only how experiences are processed intrapsychically, therefore, but also how social and familial dynamics unfold that will determine whether the patient functions in an adaptive or maladaptive manner.

Figures 30-1, 30-2, and 30-3 may be useful in illustrating the preceding concept of personality and environmental systems (adapted from G. Murphy, 1947).

Systems versus Disorders and Reactions

The use of quotes around the term "disorder" reflects a recognition that nosological classifications can go awry if their categories encompass too wide a range of clinical conditions; there is need to subdivide the subject of psychopathology along critical points of distinction. As discussed in Millon (in press), the ideal framework for a taxonomy of mental disorders should be based on dimensions such as space and time. Translated into nosological terms, space means the degree to which the manifestation of a pathological process falls on a continuum from "circumscribed" (focal) to "pervasive" (systemic). Time represents the duration of the psychopathology, that is,

Figure 30-1. *Personalities A, B. C, and D are distinguishable individuals that may be identified by their manifest likenesses and differences.*

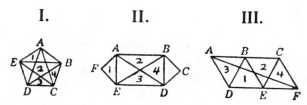

Figure 30-2. *Personalities I, II, and III are distinguishable in their manifest features, in the relationships that exist among these features, and also in the pattern of their internal structure and functions.*

where it falls on a continuum from "transient" (acute) to "enduring" (chronic). It is largely on these grounds that an attempt is made here to differentiate among personality systems, symptom disorders, and behavior reactions (Millon, 1969).

In addition to the two dimensions of circumscribed-pervasive and transient-enduring, the primary basis for distinguishing the concepts of system, disorder, and reaction is the extent to which the observed pathology can be attributed to ingrained or internal characteristics versus external psychosocial stressors or precipitants. We recognize, as previously discussed, that pathology always reflects a person–environment interaction. Nevertheless, it will be useful to distinguish types of pathology in terms of the extent to which their determinants derive from personological versus situational sources.

Personality systems are best conceived as those syndromes that are "activated" primarily by internally embedded structures and pervasive ways of functioning. At the opposite end of this person–situation or internal-external continuum are the behavior reactions, best construed as specific pathological responses attributable largely to circumscribed environmental precipitants. Between these two polar extremes lie what we have termed the symptom disorders, categories of psychopathology that are anchored more

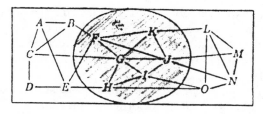

Figure 30-3. *The personality system (shaded area) is set within an environmental system (boxed area). Each stands in a dynamic relation to the other. It is the personality–environment field that is analyzed for diagnostic purposes.*

or less equally and simultaneously to internal personal attributes and external situational events. Exhibited as intensifications of a patient's characteristic style of functioning or as disruptions in his or her underlying psychic structures, symptom disorders are conceived as reactions to situations for which the individual's personality system is notably vulnerable.

Viewed from a different perspective, the structural and functional attributes that comprise personality have an inner momentum and autonomy; they are expressed with minimal inducement or external provocation. In contrast, the responses comprising behavior reactions are conceived as stimulus specific. They not only operate independent of the individual's personality, but are elicited by events that are apt to be judged consensually as "objectively" troublesome. Symptom disorders are similar to behavior reactions in that they are prompted also by external events, but their close connection to inner personality dynamics results in the intrusion of memories and affects that complicate what might otherwise be a simple reaction to the environment. Hence, they often fail to "make objective sense," appearing irrational and strangely complicated. To the knowledgeable clinician, however, a disorder signifies the presence of an unusual vulnerability on the part of the patient; in effect, a seemingly neutral stimulus has reactivated a painful hidden memory or emotion. Viewed in this manner, symptom disorders arise in individuals who are encumbered with notably adverse past experiences. The upsurge of deeply rooted feelings presses to the surface, overrides present realities, and becomes the prime stimulus to which the individual responds. It is this flooding into the present of the reactivated past that gives symptom disorders much of their symbolic, bizarre, and hidden meaning.

In contrast to symptom disorders, behavior reactions are simple and straightforward. They do not "pass through" a chain of complicated internal structures and circuitous functional transformations before emerging in manifest form. Uncontaminated by the intrusion of distant memories and intrapsychic processes, behavior reactions tend to be rational and understandable in terms of precipitating stimuli. Isolated from past emotions and defensive manipulations, they are expressed in an uncomplicated and consistent fashion, unlike symptom disorders, whose features are highly fluid, wax and wane, and take different forms at different times.

The terminology and categories of the DSM-III have not been differentiated in accord with the preceding discussion; the label "disorder" is applied to all pathological syndromes, including those termed "personality disorders." There may be good reason to reflect further on these distinctions as we plan the DSM-IV.

It will suffice for the present to translate these distinctions into DSM-III terms. Axis II, personality (trait or disorder), represents a system of deeply ingrained structures and broadly exhibited functions that persist and endure over extended periods and have come to characterize the individual's distinctive manner of relating to his environmental system. Both symptom disorders and behavior reactions closely correspond to the categories comprising the clinical syndromes of Axis I. And with reference to the preceding section, we might consider Axis IV, psychosocial stressors, to be a somewhat foreshortened representation of the environmental (social and familial) system. Framed in this schema, symptom disorders (Axis I) may best be conceived as the upshot of a dynamic interaction between Axis II (personality) and Axis IV (stressors).

Personality Continua

No sharp line divides normal from pathological behavior; they are relative concepts representing arbitrary points on a continuum or gradient. Not only is the personality system so complex that certain areas of psychological functioning operate normally while others do not, but environmental circumstances change such that behaviors and strategies that prove adaptive at one time fail to do so at another. Moreover, features differentiating normal from abnormal functioning must be extracted from a complex of signs that not only wax and wane, but often develop in an insidious and unpredictable manner.

Pathology results from the same forces that are involved in the development of normal functioning. Important differences in the character, timing, and intensity of these influences will lead some individuals to acquire pathological structures and functions, whereas others develop adaptive ones. When an individual displays an ability to cope with the environment in a flexible manner, and when his or her typical perceptions and behaviors foster increments in personal satisfaction, then the person may be said to possess a normal or healthy personality. Conversely, when average or everyday responsibilities are responded to inflexibly or defectively, or when the individual's perceptions and behaviors result in increments in personal discomfort or curtail opportunities to learn and to grow, then we may speak of a pathological or maladaptive pattern.

Despite the tenuous and fluctuating nature of this normality–pathology continuum, three features may be abstracted to serve as differentiating criteria; they are a functional inflexibility, a tendency to foster vicious or self-defeating circles, and a tenuous structural stability under conditions of stress (Millon, 1969).

In the case of *functional inflexibility*, the alternative strategies the individual employs for relating to others, for expressing feelings, and for resolving conflict and stress are not only few in number, but appear to be practiced rigidly, that is, imposed upon conditions for which they are ill-suited. The individual is not only unable to adapt effectively to the circumstances of life, but arranges his environment to avoid neutral events that are experienced as conflictful or stressful. As a consequence, opportunities for learning new, more adaptive behaviors are reduced, and life becomes ever more narrowly circumscribed.

What distinguishes pathological from normal personality functioning is not only its rigidity and inflexibility, but its tendency to *foster vicious circles*. What this means is that the person's habitual cognitions, mechanisms, and behaviors perpetuate and intensify preexisting difficulties. Maneuvers such as reaction formation, cognitive constriction, and behavioral arrogance are processes by which individuals restrict their opportunities for new learning, misconstrue essentially benign events, and provoke reactions from others that reactivate earlier problems. In effect, *pathological personality systems are themselves pathogenic*; that is, they generate and perpetuate existent dilemmas, provoke new predicaments, and set into motion self-defeating sequences which cause their already established difficulties not only to persist, but to be further aggravated.

The third feature that distinguishes the pathological from the normal end of the continuum is what we term *structural instability*, that is, a fragility or lack or resilience under conditions of subjective stress. Given the ease with which troubled personalities are vulnerable to the reactivated past, and given their paucity of alternative coping mechanisms, they are extremely susceptible to the impact of new difficulties. Faced with recurrent failures, anxious lest old, unresolved conflicts reemerge, and unable to recruit new functional strategies, these persons are likely to revert to increasingly pathological coping, to less adequate cognitive and emotional controls, to a loss of psychic cohesion, and, ultimately, to confused and erratic transactions with "reality."

An Integrative Theory

The DSM-III was developed intentionally and explicitly to be atheoretical. This stance was taken not from an antipathy to theory per se, but rather to maximize acceptance of the document by clinicians of diverse viewpoints. Extolling the tenets in the DSM-III of one or another theoretical school would, it was believed, alienate those holding dissimilar perspectives and thereby disincline them from adopting and utilizing the manual.

Those whose conceptual models were well established in the DSM-II, but were subsequently expunged from DSM-III, registered bitter complaints about their deletion. Questions were raised also as to whether the atheoretical position taken by the DSM Task Force was at all logical or sound. Some voiced shock and dismay over the shedding of a specific conceptual model, for example, psychoanalysis, whereas others expressed their qualms over ostensive negative consequences of the lack of any theoretical framework that could coordinate or provide thematic unity to the DSM-III.

Central to questions such as these is an assumption that much is to be gained by bringing the unifying and explanatory powers of a theory to bear on classifications such as the DSM-III. Given the competing, if not contradictory perspectives among current theories, problems arise as to which propositions and which concepts should be the chosen ones. This chapter is not the place to elaborate a reasoned position on matters such as these. A few words may be useful, however, as a precis of the author's "biosocial-learning" theory of personality pathology (Millon, 1969, 1981, 1983b).

It is unfortunate that the number of theories that have been advanced to "explain" psychopathology is directly proportional to the internecine squabbling found in the literature. Paroxysms of "scientific virtue" and pieties of "methodological purity" rarely are exclaimed by theorists themselves, but are by their less creative disciples. As the author has previously commented (Millon, 1969):

> Theories arise typically from the perceptive observation and imaginative speculation of a creative scientist. This innovator is usually quite aware of the limits and deficiencies of his "invention" and is disposed in the early stages of his speculation to modify it as he develops new observations and insights. Unfortunately, after its utility has been proven in a modest and limited way, the theory frequently acquires a specious stature. Having clarified certain ambiguities and survived initial criticisms, it begins to accumulate to a coterie of disciples. These less creative thinkers tend to accept the theory wholeheartedly and espouse its superior explanatory powers and terminology throughout the scientific market place. They hold to its propositions tenaciously and defend it blindly and unequivocally against opposition. In time it becomes a rigid and sacred dogma and, as a result, authority replaces the test of utility and empirical validity. Intelligent men become religious disciples; their theory is a doctrine of "truth," not a guide to the unknown. (p. 41)

Ostensibly toward the end of pragmatic sobriety, those of an antitheory bias have sought to persuade the profession of the failings of premature formalization, warning us that we cannot arrive at the future we yearn for by lifting our science by its own bootstraps. To them, there is no way to traverse the road other sciences have traveled without paying the dues of an arduous program of empirical research. Formalized axiomatics, they say, must await the accumulation of "hard" evidence that is simply not yet in. Shortcutting the route with ill-timed theoretical systematics will lead us down primrose paths, preoccupying our attentions as we wend fruitlessly through endless detours, each of which could be averted by holding fast to an empirical philosophy and methodology.

No one argues against the view that theories that float, so to speak, on their own, unconcerned with the empirical domain of clinical knowledge, should be seen as the fatuous achievements they are and the travesty they make of the virtues of a truly coherent conceptual system. Formal theory should not be "pushed" far beyond the data, and its derivations should be linked at all points to established clinical observations. Given the vast scope of psychopathology as well as the extent of knowledge still to be gathered, diagnostic theories are best kept limited today both in their focus and specificity. At this stage in our science, a "general theory of psychopathology" may be no more feasible a goal than would a truly unified field theory of physics. On the other hand, the psychoanalytically based model of the classical "psychoneuroses" may be as commendable as is the theory of classical "electromagnetics." Each theory may ultimately be subsumed under a more comprehensive formulation, but for the present, given extant knowledge in their respective domains, they refer to an appropriate range of empirical referents.

A theoretical framework can be a compelling instrument for coordinating and giving consonance to complex and diverse clinical observations—if its concepts are linked to relevant facts in the empirical world. By probing "beneath" surface impressions to inner structures and processes, previously isolated facts and difficult to fathom data may yield new relationships and expose clearer meanings. As Meehl has noted (1978), theoretical systems comprise related assertions, shared terms, and coordinated propositions that provide fertile grounds for deducing and deriving new empirical and clinical observations. Scientific progress occurs, then, when observations and concepts elaborate and refine previous work. This progression does not advance by "brute empiricism" alone, however, that is, by merely piling up more descriptive and more experimental data. What is elaborated and refined in theory is understanding, an ability to see relationships more plainly, to conceptualize categories more accurately, and to create greater overall coherence in a subject, that is, to integrate its elements in a more logical, consistent, and intelligible fashion.

A problem arises when introducing theory into the study of psychopathology. Given our intuitive ability to "sense" the correctness of a psychological insight or speculation, theoretical efforts that impose structure or formalize these insights into a scientific system will be perceived not only as cumbersome and intrusive, but alien as well. This discomfiture and resistance does not arise in fields such as nuclear physics, where everyday observations are not readily available and where perceptive insights are few and far between. In such subject domains, scientists are not only quite comfortable, but turn readily to deductive theory as a means of helping them explicate and coordinate knowledge. It is paradoxical, but true and unfortunate that psychopathologists learn their subject quite well merely by observing the ordinary events of life. As a consequence of their ease in this regard, clinicians appear to shy from and hesitate placing their trust in the "obscure and complicating," yet often fertile and systematizing powers inherent in formal theory, especially theories that are new or that differ from those learned in their student days.

Adding to these hesitations is the fact that the formal structure of most theories is haphazard and unsystematic; concepts often are vague, and procedures by which empirical consequences may be derived are tenuous. Instead of presenting an orderly arrangement of concepts and propositions by which hypotheses may be clearly derived, most theorists present a loosely formulated pastiche of opinions, analogies, and speculations. Brilliant as many of these speculations may be, they often leave the reader dazzled rather than illuminated.

As the author has written elsewhere (Millon, in press), ambiguous concepts in structurally weak theories make it impossible to derive systematic and logical hypotheses; this results in conflicting derivations and circular reasoning. Most theories of psychopathology have generated brilliant deductions and insights, but few of these ideas can be attributed to their structure, the precision of their concepts, or their formal procedures for hypothesis derivation.

Despite the shortcomings of both historic and contemporary concepts of psychopathology, abstract principles and theories can "facilitate a deeper seeing, a more penetrating vision that goes beyond superficial appearances to the order underlying them" (Bowers, 1977). For example, pre-Darwinian taxonomists such as Linnaeus limited themselves to "apparent" similarities and differences among animals as a means of constructing their categories. Darwin was not "seduced" by appearances. Rather, he sought to understand the principles by which overt features came about. His classifications were based not only on descriptive qualities, but on explanatory ones. It is in the spirit of such "explanatory principles" that we hope the reader will approach the theoretical proposals that follow.

A Framework of Three Polarities

An attempt will be made in the following pages to formulate a schema that is neither doctrinaire nor loosely eclectic in its approach. Rather, the theory presented is intended to be both relevantly focused in scope and sufficiently systematic in its application of principles to enable the major varieties of personality pathology to be derived logically and coherently. The full range of this schema has been published by the author in earlier texts (Millon, 1969, 1981) and is extended to include several new elements and disorders for the first time in this chapter. Identified as a biosocial-learning theory, it attempts to generate the established and recognized personality categories through formal deduction and to show their relationships and covariations with other mental disorders.

In reviewing the many theories that have been formulated through the centuries (Millon, 1983b), a reader cannot help but be impressed by both the number and diversity of personality concepts and types that have been proposed. In fact, one might well be inclined to ask, first, where the catalog of possibilities will end and, second, whether these different frameworks overlap sufficiently to enable the identification of common trends or themes. In response to this second question, we find that a number of theorists, going back to the turn of this century, proposed a set of three polarities that were used time and again as the raw materials for constructing personality configurations.

For example, S. Freud wrote in 1915 (1915/1925) what many consider to be among his most seminal papers, those on metapsychology and, in particular, the section entitled "Instincts and Their Vicissitudes." Speculations that foreshadowed several concepts developed more fully later, both by himself and others, were presented in preliminary form in these papers. Particularly notable is a framework that Freud advanced as central to understanding the mind; unfortunately, his basic scaffolding of three polarities was never developed by him as a system for conceptualizing personality structures and functions, as he may ultimately have intended. It was framed as follows:

> . . . Our mental life as a whole is governed by three polarities, namely, the following antitheses:
>> Subject (ego)–Object (external world)
>> Pleasure–Pain
>> Active–Passive
>
> The three polarities within the mind are connected with one another in various highly significant ways. (1915, pp. 76–77)
>
> We may sum up by saying that the essential feature in the vicissitudes undergone by instincts is *their subjection to the influences of the three great polarities that govern mental life.* Of these three polarities we might describe that of activity–passivity as the *biological,* that of the ego–external world as the *real,* and finally that of pleasure–pain as the *economic,* respectively. (1915, p. 83)

Freud's three polarities were "discovered" and employed by theorists both earlier and later than he—in France, Germany, Russia, and other European nations, as well as in the United States. The three dimensions of *active–passive, subject–object,* and *pleasure–pain* were identified either in part or in all their components by Heymans and Wiersma, McDougall, Meumann, Kollarits, Kahn, and others.

Despite the central role Freud assigned these polarities, he failed to capitalize on them as a basis for formulating character types. Preoccupied with discovering the symptom derivatives of instincts as they unfold during psychosexual development, Freud showed little interest at the time in constructing a typology of character structures. Although he may have failed to pursue their potentials for a psychoanalytic characterology, the ingredients he chose were drawn upon by an unusual number of pre-World War I personality typologists. Since forgotten as turn-of-the-century clinical speculation, the scaffolding built from these polarities was "created" and refashioned anew by the author (Millon, 1969). Unacquainted with this early literature at the time, and employing a contemporary social learning model for building a personality nosology, the author constructed a framework essentially identical to that proposed by Freud as the "great polarities that govern all of mental life"; phrased in the terminology of learning concepts, they comprised the following three polar dimensions: (reinforcement nature): positive–negative; (reinforcement source): self–other; and (instrumental behavior): active–passive.

The concepts of the first polarity, that of positive and negative reinforcements, are synonymous with those of pleasure and pain; the opposition between self and other as the primary sources of reinforcement corresponds directly to Freud's distinction between subject (ego) and object (external world); both schemas select identical terms, active and passive, as the third polarity. When the parallels between the polarities I proposed and those of Freud were brought to my attention at the conclusion of a paper I delivered at an analytic meeting a decade or so ago, I expressed an unsureness as whether "to cry or to laugh," the former owing to the recognition that conceptions I thought originated afresh in my own work were far less original than I would have liked, the latter owing to the realization that my ideas were neither idiosyncratic nor illusory. The historic company who shared this formulation was distinguished indeed, adding to a conviction that the three polarities were a sturdy foundation upon which to build a classification schema.

This encouraging, if retrospective, consensus on the theoretic value of the polarities secures but a first step toward a personality nosology. Convincing professionals of the validity of the schema requires detailed explications, on the one hand, and unequivocal evidence of utility, on the other. We must not only clarify what is meant by each term comprising the polarities, for example, identify or illustrate their empirical referents, but also specify ways in which they combine and manifest themselves clinically.

Before detailing the clinical features that derive from the schema, let us briefly note certain very broad aspects of relating the three polarities to personality. First, personality may be conceived as a complex of structures and functions designed to essentially maximize comfort and minimize discomfort (pleasure–pain). Beyond this, these structures and functions reflect where the individual looks to achieve these aims (self–others) and how he or she behaves in doing so (active–passive). Pathological deficits or imbalances that occur in the *nature* (pleasure vs. pain), *source* (self vs. others), or *instrumental behaviors* (active vs. passive) that individuals employ will result in any of ten clinically-relevant, *basic* personality patterns, as well as three, usually more severe variants.

THE PLEASURE–PAIN POLARITY: PATHOLOGY IN THE NATURE OF REINFORCEMENT

This distinction recognizes that energies, drives, motivations, feelings, emotions and affects can ultimately be placed on a dimension between two opposing or polar extremes—events that are experienced as attractive, pleasurable, or positively reinforcing versus those that are aversive, painful, or negatively reinforcing. Efforts to identify specific kinds of reinforcements that fall on this polarity are likely to distract from or blur the essential distinction being made. Thus, the particular events or objects which people find pleasurable (e.g., sex, sports, art, or money) are legion, and for every patient who experiences a certain event as rewarding, one can find another, possessing a similar pathological pattern, who experiences that same event as distasteful or painful; for example, some patients who are driven to seek attention are sexually promiscuous, whereas others are repelled by sexuality in any form. In short, categorizations based on the specific properties of reinforcing objects will prove not only futile and cumbersome, but misguiding as well.

The author shares with several forerunners the belief that a fundamental separation can be drawn between two contrasting, if not opposing motivational domains: pain and pleasure. For example, this polar distinction has been given strong empirical support in recent research by Gray (1972, 1975, 1982) and Fowles (1980, 1983). Proposing anatomical loci of a need gratification "reward" system and a punishment avoidance "behavioral inhibition" system, these theorists have sought to provide an empirical basis for a relationship between these motivational systems and different types of personality and psychopathology.

Going beyond the experimental data of Gray and Fowles, we may ask: On what basis can pathology in the *nature* or capacity of either the pain and pleasure systems be seen as relevant to personality disorders? Three possibilities present themselves. First, there may be patients in which both motivational systems are deficient, that is, they lack the capacity, relatively speaking, to experience life's events either as painful or pleasurable. Second, there may be patients in which only *one* motivational system is present or is abnormally prominent, the more clinically significant of the two possibilities here being that of intense pain-vulnerability, with a corresponding diminished pleasure reactivity, that is, they experience most of life's events as painful and few as pleasurable. And third, there may be patients in which the usual or "normal" properties associated with pain and pleasure are confused or reversed, that is, they seek out or create what would be objectively aversive events and experience them as "pleasurable." Elaborating the clinical consequences of these possibilities will be useful.

Let us turn to the *first* possibility, those patients who are characterized by a diminished capacity to experience *both* pleasure and pain; they seem neither interested in personal enjoyment or social satisfaction, nor do they evidence much discomfort with personal difficulties or social discord. Deficits such as these across the entire pain-pleasure polarity underlie what has been termed in the DSM-III as the *schizoid personality*.

The *second* clinically meaningful combinations to be derived from this polarity comprises those who exhibit a diminished ability to experience pleasure, but are unusually sensitive or responsive to psychic pain; to them, life is vexatious, possessing few rewards and much anguish. This pattern of heightened psychic pain and diminished psychic pleasure lies at the heart of what has been termed in the DSM-III as the *avoidant personality*. Both schizoids and avoidants share a minimal sense of joy and contentment; only one, the avoidant, is disposed also to feel sad or tormented. The theory groups these two personalities, referring to them as the *detached* patterns, the former, schizoid, noted as the passive-detached, the latter, avoidant, as the active-detached. Unable to experience pleasure either from self or others, both detached types tend to drift into increasingly isolated and self-alienated behaviors.

The *third* possibility, stemming from reversals in the attributes of pain and pleasure, leads to two other, well-known personality types. Both variants interpret events and engage in relationships in a manner that is not only at variance with the biologically-based pleasure and pain motivational systems, but that runs contrary to the associations these life events usually acquire through learning. To one group, the *self-defeating (masochistic) personality*, pain is the preferred experience, passively or "receptively" accepted, if not sought for in both intimate and ordinary social relationships, intensified by purposeful self-denial and blame acceptance, aggravated by acts that engender difficulties, and by thoughts that exaggerate past misfortunes and anticipate future ones. The second variant of this reversal of the pain–pleasure polarity, what we prefer to term the *aggressive (sadistic)* personality, considers pain (stress, fear, cruelty) rather than pleasure to be the preferred mode of life; that is, the individual assumes an active role in dominating, controlling and competing with others. Toward that end, acts that humiliate, demean, if not brutalize others are experienced as pleasurable, as are opportunities for engaging in socially provocative, personally demanding or risk-taking experiences. We have grouped these two personalities under the label "discordant patterns" to reflect, on the one hand, the dissonant structure of their pain–pleasure systems and, on the other, the conflictive character of their interpersonal relations. The self-defeating (masochistic) type, being on the receiving end of these fractious relationships, is referred to as the passive-discordant, whereas the latter, more expressive aggressive (sadistic) type, is termed the active-discordant.

Aspects of the developmental background and clinical features of these theory-derived personalities may provide the reader with a sense of how abstract concepts such as pain and pleasure can be conceived as relevant etiologic attributes.

Schizoid patients are characterized best by a pathology in their capacity to experience *both* positive and negative reinforcements; they neither strive for rewards nor do they seek to avoid punishment (relatively speaking). Deficiencies such as these may arise from several etiological sources. Some may lack the constitutional makeup requisite for seeking, sensing, or discriminating reinforcing events. Others may have been deprived of the stimulus nourishment necessary for the maturation of motivational or emotional capacities. A third group may have been exposed to irrational and confusing family communications or to contradictory patterns of reinforcement, both of which may result in cognitive perplexities or motivational apathies. Whatever the complex of causes may have been, schizoid patients acquire little or no body of either pleasurable of painful objects to motivate their behaviors. For example, a pathetic 8-year-old boy, who may have begun life deficient in the capacity to experience reinforcements and who was reared by a withdrawn, psychotic mother, exhibited no interest in people or objects, seemed content to sit and stare at a wall, was unmoved by events that surrounded him, and appeared indifferent both to threats of pain and to its experience at moderate intensities.

The second "detached" group, those labeled *avoidant* personalities, gets little gratification but considerable pain from both self and others. Although they experience few pleasures in life, they do feel and react strongly to discomfort and punishment. Developmentally, we may speculate that the neurological or physiochemical makeup of these avoidant individuals was constructed to dispose them maximally to pain and minimally to pleasure; for example, centers of the limbic system may have been unequally dense or may have been disadvantageously wired to other brain regions. Equally possible, if not more probable in these cases, is a history of harsh and rejecting early experiences which may have oversensitized these individuals to psychic pain and anxiety. Exposed repeatedly to such events, they may have learned not only to anticipate an omnipresent threat, but to devise a widespread protective strategy of avoidance to minimize its recurrence. To illustrate, a 14-year-old girl was described as having been extremely tense and fearful "almost from the moment she was born." This temperamental disposition was aggravated by repeated parental intimidation and humiliation; by the time she was 7, she hid in closets to avoid people, covered her face when asked questions by her teachers, and cried whenever she thought someone was making fun of her. Such avoidant types usually are deprived of experiences that might strengthen feelings of competence and self-worth; moreover, having a low opinion of themselves, they cannot turn to themselves as a source of positive reinforcement. Ultimately, they seek rewards neither from themselves nor from others, seem perpetually on guard and are oriented solely to the avoidance of painful rejection and humiliation.

The background of the two "discordant" types, the *self-defeating* (*masochistic*) and *aggressive* (*sadistic*) personalities, has been a topic of considerable speculation for decades, most prominently in the psychoanalytic literature (Brenner, 1959; Loewenstein, 1957; Menaker, 1953). This chapter is not the place to summarize this body of circuitously reasoned hypotheses. Although the role of biological anomalies in the inherent wiring of these personalities, another domain of speculation, cannot be totally dismissed, it too stretches the imagination beyond the usual range of self-evident plausibility. Not so incredulous are hypotheses generated via a social-learning or developmental paradigm. Thus, by virtue of circumstantial association, elements normally evocative of pain and pleasure could very well become transposed or interconnected; for example, among future masochists the pain of physical brutality or the anguish of verbal conflict may have been followed repetitively by sexual intimacy, leading to the learned assumption that fractious provocations are a necessary precursor to ultimate acceptance and tenderness. Similarly, among future aggressive (sadistic) personalities, competitive ambition and social brutality can readily be reinforced as a means to security, status and pleasure by demonstrably resulting in personal achievements and dominance over others. In a more complicated sequence, guilt absolution may have been successfully achieved by repeated self-abasement, acts that generalize over time into a broad masochistic pattern (self-denial, servility) that preventively "undoes" the possibility of future misbehaviors.

THE OTHER-SELF POLARITY: PATHOLOGY IN THE SOURCE OF REINFORCEMENT

The polarity of object–subject or, as I prefer to term it, other–self is central to contemporary psychoanalytic thought. A year prior to outlining his concept of three polarities, Freud (1914) formulated two directions of early libidinal object choice, the so-called anaclitic and narcissistic. The former undergirds the development of affectionate and need-satisfying relationships with the external world or "objects," whereas the latter refers to the focusing on ego or "subject" as object choice. Those whose early experiences are "healthy" progress developmentally through a dialectic balance between the two; problematic consequences, however, can follow either progression. For Anna Freud (1965), a troubled anaclitic course leads to poorly integrated or unstable object relations. Failures in what she terms the introjective (narcissistic) developmental line result in an unconsolidated or undifferentiated sense of self or identity.

The importance of "object–relations" theory (Fairbairn, 1954; Kernberg, 1975; Klein, 1952; Mahler, Pine, & Bergman, 1975) in expanding the frontiers of modern psychoanalytic thought cannot be overstated. Nor can the recent emergence of "self" theory (Gedo, 1979; Goldberg, 1978; Jacobson, 1964; Kohut, 1971) be underestimated as a reinvigorating perspective. As Blatt and Shichman have put it (1983): "Self-definition and interpersonal relatedness are part of the processes often discussed as the development of the concept of the self and the object world. . . . Disruptions of (their) developmental lines . . . define two primary configurations of personality and psychopathology" (p. 200).

Also of note is the recently popular views of erstwhile behaviorists who have broken from their former exclusive focus on external reinforcers (objects, stimuli, others) to that of self-reinforcers. For example, Bandura (1977) now places primary emphasis on the role of self-reinforcement as the major agent of behavior change.

Anticipating this line of thought, the author wrote as follows (Millon, 1969):

> Most people experience a wide range of both positive and negative reinforcers. However, some individuals acquire these reinforcements from a narrow band of events and objects; as a consequence, their behaviors and strategies are oriented toward these few prepotent highly rewarding and highly punishing sources.
>
> How can patients be characterized in terms of the *sources* from which they experience their positive and negative reinforcements?
>
> A listing of the varied and sundry places where reinforcements can be acquired will prove fruitless. But one distinction seems relevant and useful.

It represents the observation that some patients turn to others as their source of reinforcement, whereas some turn primarily to themselves. (p. 194)

The distinction of object-subject, or *other-self*, recognizes that among all matters and entities in the environment there are two domains that stand out above all others in their power to affect us: our own selves and others.

Following the polarity model, we must ask whether particular clinical consequences occur among individuals who turn almost exclusively *either* toward others *or* toward themselves as a means of experiencing pleasure and avoiding pain. Such persons differ from the two detached and the two discordant types we discussed previously; for example, neither detached type experienced pleasure from self or others. Personalities whose difficulties are traceable to the pathology of choosing one or the other polar end of the other–self dimension do experience both pain and pleasure, and do experience them in a consonant, nonreversed manner; their pathology arises from the fact that they are tied almost exclusively *either* to others *or* to themselves as the *source* of these experiences. The distinction between these two contrasting sources of reinforcement underlies what we have termed the "dependent" and the "independent" personality orientations. In later paragraphs we will describe the ambivalent orientation, those who are in conflict between turning toward self or toward others as their source of pain/pleasure reinforcement. For the present, however, let us turn to the dependent and independent types and describe how they look clinically.

Those with a *dependency* pathology have learned that feeling good, secure, confident, and so on—that is, those feelings associated with pleasure or the avoidance of pain—is provided almost exclusively by *others*. Behaviorally, these persons display a strong need for external support and attention; should they be deprived of affection and nurturance they will experience marked discomfort, if not sadness and anxiety. Any number of early experiences may set the stage for dependency pathology. For example, in one major group, those termed the *dependent personality* in DSM-III, we see individuals who have been exposed to an overprotective training regimen and, therefore, fail to acquire competencies for autonomy and initiative; experiencing competitive peer failures leads them to forego further attempts at self-assertion and self-gratification. They learn early that rewarding experiences are not readily achieved by themselves but are secured better by leaning on others. This personality demonstrates what the theory terms a "passive" dependency pathology. Also turning to others as their primary source of reinforcement are a group of personalities that take an "active" dependency stance. They achieve their ends by engaging busily in a series of manipulative, seductive, gregarious and attention-getting maneuvers. It is this active style of dependent pathology that characterizes the behavior of the DSM-III *histrionic personality*, according to the theory.

Patients falling into what we have termed the "independent" personality pattern also exhibit a pathology in their source of reinforcement; however, they demonstrate a primary reliance on *self* rather than others. They have learned that maximum pleasure and minimum pain is achieved by turning exclusively to themselves as its source. The tendency to draw upon self as the primary reinforcement source follows two major lines of development. In the first, the *narcissistic personality*, it reflects the acquisition of a self-image of superior worth, learned largely in response to admiring the doting parents. Providing self-rewards are highly gratifying if one values oneself or possesses either a "real" or inflated sense of self-worth. Displaying manifest confidence, arrogance, and an exploitive egocentricity in social contexts, this self-orientation is termed the "passive" independent style in the theory, since the individual "already" has all that is important—himself. The second pattern of self-orientation develops initially as a form of protection and counteraction. These "actively" independent types, labeled the *antisocial personality* in DSM-III, turn to themselves to avoid the pain they anticipate from others and to compensate by furnishing themselves with self-generated rewards in their stead. Learning that they cannot depend on others these patients counterbalance this loss not only by trusting themselves alone, but by seeking retribution for what they see as past humiliations. Turning to self and seeking increased strength and power to gain revenge, they are irresponsible and duplicitous, exploiting and usurping what others possess as sweet reprisal indeed; further, their security is now "assured," having aggrandized themselves beyond their lesser origins.

In both dependent and independent orientations, patients are seen as demonstrating pathology in that their preference for obtaining their reinforcements *either* from others or from themselves is unbalanced, grossly one-sided. Clear-cut distinctions toward self or other are not made by all patients. "Normal" individuals, of course, exhibit a comfortable balance between both self and others. Certain pathological personality orientations, those whom we shall speak of as "ambivalent," also draw upon both reinforcement sources, but are in intense conflict as whether to turn to themselves *or* to others. A number of these patients, those represented in the DSM-III *passive-aggressive personality*, vacillate between others and self, behaving obediently one time, and reacting defiantly the next. Feeling intensely, yet unable to resolve their ambivalence, they weave an erratic course from voicing self-deprecation and guilt for failing to meet the expectations of others to expressing stubborn negativism and resistance over having submitted to their wishes rather than following their own desires. These patients, whose conflicts are overt, worn on their sleeves, so to speak, are characterized in the theory as "actively" ambivalent, a richer and more varied lot than the manual portrayal of the passive-aggressive. The other major ambivalent pattern, the DSM-III *compulsive personality* disorder, displays a picture of distinct other-directness, a consistency in social compliance and interpersonal respect; their histories usually indicate their having been subjected to constraint and discipline, but *only* when they transgressed parental strictures and expectations. Beneath the conforming veneer they exhibit are intense desires to rebel and assert their own independent feelings and impulses. They are trapped in conflict; to avoid intimidation and punishment they have learned to deny the validity of their own wishes and emotions and, in their stead, have adopted as "true" the values and precepts set forth by others. The disparity they sense between their own urges and the behaviors they must display to avoid the condemnation of others has led to omnipresent physical tensions and to rigid psychological controls. Termed in the theory as "passive" ambivalents, they correspond to the DSM-III compulsive personality.

THE PASSIVE–ACTIVE POLARITY: PATHOLOGY IN INSTRUMENTAL COPING STYLE

We have referred often to this dimension in prior characterizations, but it will be useful nevertheless to clarify and elaborate briefly on the features they represent.

In speaking of the active–passive dimension, we mean that the vast range of behaviors engaged in by patients may fundamentally be grouped in terms of whether they take the initiative in altering and shaping life's events or whether their behaviors are reactive and accomodate to those events.

Those who are passively oriented engage in few overtly manipulative strategies to gain their ends. They display a seeming inertness, a lack of ambition or persistence, an acquiescence, and a resigned attitude in which they initiate little to shape events, waiting for the circumstances of their environment to take their course before making adaptations. They may be temperamentally ill-equipped to assert themselves; perhaps past experience has deprived them of opportunities to acquire a sense of competence, a confidence in their ability to master the events of their environment; equally possible is a naive confidence that things will come their way with little or no effort on their part. From a variety of diverse sources, then, these individuals engage in few overt instrumental activities to intercede in events or produce the effects they desire. Passivity is their strategy. They seem suspended, immobile, restrained, or listless, waiting for things to happen and reacting to them only after they occur.

Descriptively, those who are actively oriented are best characterized by their alertness, vigilance, persistence, decisiveness, and ambition in goal-directed behaviors. They plan strategies, scan alternatives, manipulate events, and circumvent obstacles, all to the end of eliciting pleasures and rewards, or avoiding the distress of punishment, rejection, and anxiety. Although specific goals may change from time to time, these individuals intrude upon passing events and are energetically and busily intent on controlling the circumstances of their environment, if not the course of their lives.

Lest it appear that the active–passive polarity stands only as a speculative construct, brief note should be made of the growing empirical literature that provides a strong biological undergirding to the clinical relevance of this distinction. Most pertinent in this regard is the work on temperament, personality, and psychopathology by Buss and Plomin (1975), Escalona and Heider (1959), Fiske and Maddi (1961), L. B. Murphy and Moriarty (1976), and Thomas and Chess (1977).

Concordance Between Theory and DSM-III

Using the theoretical model as a basis, the author has recently elaborated and extended his personality classification schema into one that combined in a five-by-two matrix the dependent, independent, ambivalent, discordant, and detached orientations with the activity–passivity polarity. This produced 10 basic types, with 3 dysfunctional variants, for a total of 13 theory-derived personality configurations (see Table 30–1). Despite their close correspondence to the official DSM-III Axis II disorders, these personalities should be conceived as heuristic prototypes, not as reified diagnostic entities (see Chapter 2 of this volume).

1. The *passive-detached* orientation is akin to the DSM-III Schizoid personality disorder. These patients are noted by their lack of desire and their incapacity to experience depth in either pleasure or pain. They tend to be apathetic, listless, distant, and asocial. Affectionate needs and emotional feelings are minimal and the individual functions as a passive observer detached from the rewards and affections as well as from the demands of human relationships.

2. The *active-detached* orientation is much the same as the DSM-III Avoidant personality disorder. These patients experience few positive reinforcers from either self or others, are vigilant, perennially on guard, and are ever ready to distance themselves from an anxious anticipation of life's painful or negatively reinforcing experiences. Their adaptive strategy reflects a fear and mistrust of others. They maintain a constant vigil lest their impulses and longing for affection result in a repetition of the pain and anguish they previously had experienced with others. Only by active withdrawal can they protect themselves. Despite desires to relate, they have learned that it is best to deny these feelings and keep a good measure of interpersonal distance.

3. The theoretically generated *passive-dependent* orientation corresponds to the DSM-III Dependent personality disorder. These individuals have learned not only to turn to others as their source of nurturance and security, but to wait passively for their leadership in providing them. They are characterized by a search for relationships in which they can lean upon others for affection, security, and leadership. This personality's lack of both initiative and autonomy is often a consequence of parental overprotection.

Table 30-1
Theory-Based Framework for Personality Pathology

Pathology domain	Self–Other			Pain–Pleasure	
Reinforcement source	Other + Self –	Self + Other –	Self ↔ Other	Pain → Pleasure	Pleasure – Pain ±
Interpersonal pattern / Instrumental coping style	Dependent	Independent	Ambivalent	Discordant	Detached
Passive variant	Dependent	Narcissistic	Compulsive	Self-Defeating (masochistic)	Schizoid
Active variant	Histrionic	Antisocial	Passive–Aggressive	Aggressive (sadistic)	Avoidant
Dysfunctional variant	Borderline	Paranoid	Borderline or Paranoid		Schizotypal

As a function of these experiences, they have simply learned to comforts of assuming a passive role in interpersonal relations, accepting what kindness and support they may find, and willingly submitting to the wishes of others in order to maintain their affection.

4. The derived *active-dependent* orientation matches the DSM-III Histrionic personality disorder. Although they turn toward others to no lesser extent than do passive-dependents, these individuals appear on the surface to be quite dissimilar from their passive counterparts; this difference in overt style owes to the active-dependent's facile and enterprising manipulation of events, which maximizes the receipt of attention and favors as well as avoids social disinterest and disapproval. These patients often show an insatiable, if not indiscriminate search for stimulation and affection. Their clever and often artful social behaviors give the appearance of an inner confidence and independent self-assurance; beneath this guise, however, lies a fear of genuine autonomy and a need for repeated signs of acceptance and approval. Tribute and affection must constantly be replenished and is sought from every interpersonal source and in every social context.

5. The *passive-independent* orientation parallels the DSM-III Narcissistic personality disorder. These individuals are noted by their egotistic self-involvement, experiencing primary pleasure simply by passively being or focusing on themselves. Early experience has taught them to overvalue their self-worth; this confidence and superiority may be founded on false premises, that is, be unsustainable by real or mature achievements. Nevertheless, they blithely assume that others will recognize their specialness. Hence, they maintain an air of arrogant self-assurance and, without much thought or even conscious intent, benignly exploit others to their own advantage. Although the tributes of others are both welcome and encouraged, their air of snobbish and pretentious superiority requires little confirmation either through genuine accomplishment or social approval. Their sublime confidence that things will work out well provides them with little incentive to engage in the reciprocal give and take of social life.

6A. The *active-independent* orientation resembles the outlook, temperament, and socially unacceptable behaviors of the DSM-III Antisocial personality disorder. These individuals act to counter the expectation of pain and depredation at the hand of others; this is done by engaging in duplicitous and illegal behaviors designed to exploit the environment for self-gain. Their orientation reflects their skepticism concerning the motives of others, a desire for autonomy, and a wish for revenge over what are felt as past injustices. They are irresponsible and impulsive, actions they see as justified because others are judged unreliable and disloyal. Insensitivity and ruthlessness are the only means to head off abuse and victimization.

6B. The *active-discordant* orientation extends the boundaries of the DSM-III in a new and important direction, one that recognizes individuals who are not judged publicly to be antisocial, but whose actions signify personal pleasure and satisfaction in behaviors that humiliate others and violate their rights and feelings. Depending on social class and other moderating factors, they may parallel the clinical features of what is known in the literature as the sadistic character or, on the other hand, display character styles akin to the competitively striving "type A" personality. Termed aggressive personalities in the author's theory, they are generally hostile, pervasively combative, and appear indifferent to, if not pleased, by the destructive consequences of their contentious, if not abusive and brutal behaviors. Although many cloak their more malicious and power-oriented tendencies in publicly approved roles and vocations, they give themselves away in their dominating, antagonistic, and frequent persecutory actions.

7. The *passive-ambivalent* orientation coincides with the DSM-III Compulsive personality disorder. These individuals have been intimidated and coerced into accepting the reinforcements imposed on them by others. Their prudent, controlled, and perfectionistic ways derive from a conflict between hostility toward others and a fear of social disapproval. They resolve this ambivalence not only by suppressing resentment, but by overconforming and by placing high demands on themselves and others. Their disciplined self-restraint serves to control intense, though hidden oppositional feelings, resulting in an overt passivity and seeming public compliance. Lurking behind this front of propriety and restraint, however, are intense anger and oppositional feelings that occasionally break through their controls.

8A. The *active-ambivalent* orientation approximates, but is more extensive in the number and diversity of traits it encompasses than the DSM-III Passive-Aggressive personality disorder. Here the individual struggles between following the reinforcements offered by others as opposed to those desired by himself. This struggle represents an inability to resolve conflicts similar to those of the passive-ambivalent (compulsives); however, the conflicts of actively ambivalent personalities remain close to consciousness and intrude into everyday life. These patients get themselves into endless wrangles and disappointments as they vacillate between deference and obedience one time, and defiance and aggressive negativism the next. Their behavior displays an erratic pattern of explosive anger or stubbornness intermingled with periods of guilt and shame.

8B. The *passive-discordant* orientation corresponds to the newly introduced DSM-III-R self-defeating (masochistic) personality disorder, a character type well described in the literature. Relating to others in an obsequious and self-sacrificing manner, these persons allow, if not encourage others to exploit or take advantage of them. Focusing on their very worst features, many assert that they deserve being shamed and humbled. To compound their pain and anguish, states they experience as comforting and which they strive to achieve, they actively and repetitively recall their past misfortunes as well as transform otherwise fortunate circumstances into their potentially most problematic outcomes. Typically acting in an unpresuming and self-effacing way, they will often intensify their deficits and place themselves in an inferior light or abject position.

Three additional pathological personality orientations are formulated in the theory to represent severe dysfunctional levels. They differ from the

first 10 configurations by several criteria, notably deficits in social competence and frequent (but readily reversible) psychotic episodes. Less integrated in terms of personality organization and less effective in coping than
their 10 milder counterparts, they are especially vulnerable to the everyday
strains of life. Their major features and similarities to DSM-III personality
disorders are summarized next.

S: The DSM-III Schizotypal personality disorder represents the poorly
integrated dysfunctional detached orientation in the theory. These persons
prefer social isolation with minimal personal attachments and obligations.
Inclined to be either autistic or confused cognitively, they think tangentially
and often appear self-absorbed and ruminative. Behavioral eccentricities are
notable, and the individual is often perceived by others as strange or different. Depending on whether their pattern has basically been active or passive,
there will be either an anxious wariness and hypersensitivity or an emotional
flattening and deficiency of affect.

C: The DSM-III Borderline personality disorder corresponds in part to
the theory's dysfunctional dependent, dysfunctional discordant, and dysfunctional ambivalent orientations. Each of these personalities experiences
intense endogenous moods, with recurring periods of dejection and apathy,
often interspersed with spells of anger, anxiety, or euphoria. What distinguishes them most clearly from the two other dysfunctional patterns, the
schizotypal and the paranoid, is the dysregulation of their affects, seen most
clearly in the instability and lability of their moods. Additionally, many reveal
recurring self-mutilating and suicidal thoughts, appear overly preoccupied
with securing affection, have difficulty maintaining a clear sense of identity,
and display a cognitive-affective ambivalence, evident in simultaneous feelings of rage, love, and guilt toward others.

P: The DSM-III Paranoid personality disorder matches aspects of three
of the theory's types most clearly, primarily the dysfunctional independent
orientation, but also, to a somewhat lesser extent, the dysfunctional discor-
dants and ambivalents. Here are seen a vigilant mistrust of others and an
edgy defensiveness against anticipated criticism and deception. There is an
abrasive irritability and a tendency to precipitate exasperation and anger in
others. Expressed often is a fear of losing independence, leading this patient
to vigorously resist external influence and control. Whereas the other two
dysfunctional patterns are noted either by the instability of their affect
(borderline) or the dysregulation of their cognitions (schizotypal), paranoids
are distinctive by virtue of the immutability of their feelings and the inflexibility of their thoughts.

On Personality Severity

With a few exceptions, we sequenced the previous list of personality orientations in terms of levels of severity. A question that should be asked concerns
the criteria we employed for considering one personality as more severe than
another. A full rationale will not be elaborated here (see Millon, 1981). We

merely note that a perspective including the interplay of intrapsychic and interpersonal dynamics was taken to group the 13 Axis II personalities into three broad categories. Essentially, severity was gauged by estimating the probability that a particular personality orientation would fit in one or another of the several, typical sociocultural niches available in contemporary Western society; stated differently, we sought to gauge the likelihood, in a culture such as ours, that the personality style would be able to maintain its structural coherence and would be able to function in a rewarding manner.

1. The first category, and the least likely to become severe, includes the DSM-III dependent, histrionic, narcissistic, and antisocial personality disorders. These four patterns are either dependent or independent in their style of interpersonal functioning. Also, their intrapsychic structures enable them to conceive of themselves and to deal with others in a relatively coherent, "nonsplit," or nonconflictful manner, that is, in a reasonably consistent and focused rather than diffused or divided way. Moreover, because their needs and traits dispose these patients to keep up their interpersonal relationships, they are able to manage their social environment so as to be cognitively sustained and emotionally nourished, and thereby increase the likelihood that they can maintain their psychic cohesion.

2. The second group, that viewed at a midlevel of personality severity, includes the compulsive, passive-aggressive, aggressive (sadistic), self-defeating (masochistic), schizoid, and avoidant disorders. These represent a lower level of structural cohesion and psychological functioning than the first group for several reasons. In the two ambivalent types, the compulsive and passive-aggressive personalities, there is a split within both their interpersonal and their intrapsychic orientations; they are unable to maintain an inner structural coherence, a nonconflictual direction in their personal relationships, or consistency in their defensive operations. There is a fundamental intrapsychic dissension, a core split between taking an independent *or* taking a dependent stance; as a consequence, they repeatedly undo or reverse the actions they previously took, thereby embedding further their feeling of being internally divided. Along similar lines, the two discordant types are not only trapped in an intrapsychic reversal of their motivational systems, but they are also driven to create problematic interpersonal relations. They seek, if not provoke, social conflicts and fractious circumstances as a means of gratifying their perverse and confused pain–pleasure experiences. Their actions perpetuate their pathology; not only do they sustain them, but increase them, as in a vicious circle. The third pair of these six personality types, the two detached types, labeled schizoid and avoidant personalities in the DSM-III, are judged also at a midlevel of severity. Both are disengaged or estranged from external support systems. As a consequence, they are likely to have few subliminatory channels and fewer still sources of emotional nurturance and cognitive stability, the lack of which will dispose them increasingly to social regressions and autistic preoccupations.

3. The third set, reflecting still lower levels of structural integration and psychic functioning, includes the DSM-III borderline, paranoid, and schizo-

typal disorders. All three are functionally problematic, difficult to relate to socially, and often isolated, hostile, or confused; hence, they are not likely to elicit the interpersonal support that could bolster their flagging defenses and orient them to a more effective and satisfying life-style. Moreover, a clear breakdown in the cohesion of personality organization is seen in both schizotypal and borderline disorders. The converse is evident in the paranoid, where there is an overly rigid and narrow focus to the personality structure. In the former pair, there has been a dissolution or diffusion of ego capacities; in the latter paranoid pattern, there is an inelasticity and constriction of personality, giving rise to a fragility and inadaptability of functions.

Concluding Comment

As noted earlier, diagnosticians and nosologists must take care not to be beguiled by the oversimplifications of a classification schema, including the one presented in this chapter. What has been proposed in the theory is merely a heuristic tool, a systematic way of organizing our thinking about the complicated and diverse orientations of patient personalities. The tool we have proposed should sharpen our perceptions and our understanding. But, let us not "put the cart before the horse." Labels appended to patients are abstractions designed to facilitate our thinking and communication. They should not create illusions that a patient's "essence" or "disease" has been uncovered. Constructs such as "passive-dependent" do not represent tangible entities. With these caveats in mind, it may be useful to turn to the next chapter, that relating to personality prototypes and their diagnostic criteria.

REFERENCES

American Psychiatric Association. (1980). *Diagnostic and statistical manual of mental disorders.* Washington, DC: Author.

Auchincloss, E. L., & Michels, R. (1983). Psychoanalytic theory of character. In J. P. Frosch (Ed.), *Current perspectives on personality disorders.* Washington, DC: American Psychiatric Press.

Bandura, A. (1977). Self-efficacy: Toward a unifying theory of behavior change. *Psychological Review, 84,* 191–215.

Blatt, S. J., & Shichman, S. (1983). Two primary configurations of psychopathology. *Psychoanalysis and Contemporary Thought, 6,* 187–254.

Bowers, K. S. (1977). There's more to Iago than meets the eye: A clinical account of personal consistency. In D. Magnusson & N. S. Endler (Eds.), *Personality at the crossroads.* Hillsdale, NJ: Erlbaum.

Brenner, C. (1959). The masochistic character: Genesis and treatment. *Journal of the American Psychoanalytic Association, 7,* 197–226.

Buss, A. H., & Plomin, R. (1975). *A temperament theory of personality development.* New York: Wiley.

Escalona, S., & Heider, G. (1959). *Prediction and outcome.* New York: Basic Books.

Fairbairn, W. R. D. (1954). *An object relations theory of personality.* New York: Basic Books.

Fiske, D. W., & Maddi, S. R. (Eds.). (1961). *Functions of varied experience*. Homewood, IL: Dorsey Press.

Fowles, D. C. (1980). The three arousal model: Implications of Gray's two-factor learning theory for heart rate, electrodermal activity, and psychopathy, *Psychophysiology, 17*, 87–104.

Fowles, D. C. (1983). Motivational effects on heart rate and electrodermal activity: Implications for research on personality and psychopathology. *Journal of Research in Personality, 17*, 48–71.

Freud, A. (1965). *Normality and pathology of childhood: Assessments of development*. New York: International Universities Press.

Freud, S. (1925). On narcissism: An introduction. In J. Strachey (Ed. and Trans.), *Collected papers* (Vol. 4). London: Hogarth Press. (Original work published 1914)

Freud, S. (1925). The instincts and their vicissitudes. In J. Strachey (Ed. and Trans.), *Collected papers* (Vol. 4). London: Hogarth Press. (Original work published 1915)

Gedo, J. (1979). *Beyond interpretation: Toward a revised theory for psychoanalysis*. New York: International Universities Press.

Goldberg, A. (Ed.). (1978). *The psychology of the self: A casebook*. New York: International Universities Press.

Gray, J. A. (1972). Learning theory, the conceptual nervous system and personality. In V. D. Nebylitsyn & J. A. Gray (Eds.), *Biological bases of individual behavior*. New York: Academic Press.

Gray, J. A. (1975). *Elements of a two-process theory of learning*. New York: Academic Press.

Gray, J. A. (1982). *The neuropsychology of anxiety*. New York: Oxford University Press.

Gunderson, J. G., Kolb, J. E., & Austin, V. (1981). The diagnostic interview for borderline patients. *American Journal of Psychiatry, 138*, 896–903.

Jacobson, E. (1964). *The self and the object world*. New York: International Universities Press.

Kendell, R. E. (1975). *The role of diagnosis in psychology*. Oxford: Blackwell Scientific Publications.

Kendell, R. E. (1983). DSM-III: A major advance in psychiatric nosology. In R. Spitzer, J. B. W. Williams, & A. E. Skodol (Eds.), *International perspectives on DSM-III*. Washington, DC: American Psychiatric Press.

Kernberg, O. (1975). *Borderline conditions and pathological narcissism*. New York: Jason Aronson.

Klein, M. (1952). *Developments in psychoanalysis*. London: Hogarth.

Kohut, H. (1971). *The analysis of the self*. New York: International Universities Press.

Loewenstein, R. (1957). A contribution to the psychoanalytic theory of masochism. *Journal of the American Psychoanalytic Association, 5*, 197–234.

Mahler, M. S., Pine, F., & Bergman, A. (1975). *The psychological birth of the human infant*. New York: Basic Books.

Meehl, P. E. (1978). Theoretical risks and tabular asterisks: Sir Kasl, Sir Ronald, and the slow progress of soft psychology. *Journal of Consulting and Clinical Psychology, 46*, 806–834.

Menaker, E. (1953). Masochism—A defense reaction of the ego. *Psychoanalytic Quarterly, 22*, 205–220.

Millon, T. (1969). *Modern psychopathology: A biosocial approach to maladaptive learning and functioning*. Philadelphia, PA: Saunders.

Millon, T. (1981). *Disorders of personality: DSM-III, Axis II*. New York: Wiley.

Millon, T. (1983a). *Millon clinical multiaxial inventory, manual* (3rd ed.). Minneapolis, MN: National Computer Systems.

Millon, T. (Ed.). (1983b). *Theories of personality and psychopathology* (3rd ed.). New York: Holt, Rinehart, & Winston.

Millon, T. (in press). On taxonomic models in psychopathology. In C. G. Last & M. Hersen (Eds), *Issues in diagnostic research*. New York: Plenum Press.

Mischel, W. (1973). Toward a cognitive social reconceptualization of personality. *Psychological Review, 80*, 252–283.

Mischel, W. (1979). On the interface of cognition and personality. *American Psychologist, 34*, 740–754.

Murphy, G. (1947). *Personality: A biosocial approach to origins and functions*. New York: Harper.

Murphy, L. B., & Moriarty, A. E. (1976). *Vulnerability, coping and growth.* New Haven, CT: Yale University Press.

Reich, J. (1984). Instruments measuring Axis II of DSM-III: A review. In *DSM-III: A continuing review.* Symposium presented at the meeting of the American Psychiatric Association, Los Angeles, May.

Thomas, A., & Chess, S. (1977). *Temperament and development.* New York: Brunner/Mazell.

CHAPTER 31

Personality Prototypes and Their Diagnostic Criteria

Theodore Millon

This chapter will address the issue of whether the construct "prototype" can usefully be conceived as paralleling the medical concept of "syndrome." In so doing, we must ask whether "psychological" syndromes, either in fact or logic, exist in the same sense as do biological syndromes. Prior to providing a rationale for the reality of psychological syndromes, especially as they apply to personality pathology, we will outline the manner in which the concept of prototypes, borrowed from cognitive psychology and recently introduced as a formulation for construing and categorizing mental disorders, can be adopted meaningfully as the psychological equivalent of medical syndromes; if it proves apt in this regard, DSM-IV might properly retitle its Axis II section to read "Personality Prototypes."

Syndromes, Types, and Prototypes

To refresh our memories and make our definitions more explicit, the medical terms "signs" and "symptoms" represent either objectively recorded or subjectively reported changes in state or function that often arise in conjunction with known pathological processes; these changes not only serve to alert the diagnostician that a pathological process may be under way, but often help identify both its location and character.

The concept "syndrome" represents the clustering of a set of signs or symptoms that frequently co-occur or covary. Not all of the signs and

Theodore Millon. Departments of Psychology and Psychiatry, University of Miami, Coral Gables, Florida.

symptoms of a disease are likely to be immediately observed, but the presence of a subset of a syndromic pattern often suggests that other features that typify it might be uncovered upon closer examination. This searching and diagnostically confirming procedure is described well by Dahlström (1972):

> Some pattern of complaints, clinical findings, and signs is tentatively identified. Study of individuals manifesting this syndromic pattern proceeds retrospectively in an effort to identify both antecedent conditions and precipitating events (etiology), concurrently in an effort to identify additional signs or symptoms that may be part of the syndrome and possibly enhance differential diagnostic accuracy (nosology or diagnostics), and prospectively to plot the subsequent course of the disorder (prognosis) or evaluate the impact of various ameliorative interventions (therapeusis). The aims of these investigations are of course to develop some formulation of the nature of the disorder and to be able to prevent future manifestations in the afflicted individual and in others (prophylaxis) or at least ameliorate the condition when it does appear. (p. 8)

By convention, syndromes do not identify a person, but define a disorder; that is, they represent pathological processes that affect particular and limited structures or functions of the individual, but are neither synonymous nor coterminous with the individual as a whole. As a result of their restricted nature, several syndromes may coexist in the same person. Not only do they occupy less "space," so to speak, than does the entire individual, but syndromes are usually time-limited, that is, both impermanent and possessing a circumscribed temporal course. Variations in quantitative severity from person to person and from time to time within a single person also characterize syndromes. Not only is there a waxing and waning in the salience of its component signs and symptoms, but only a few of its typical indices are likely to be manifest at any one time. Owing both to its changeability and partial expression, definitive assignments of a syndrome often require the presence of certain necessary or joint criteria. Rarely, however, are the signs and symptoms comprising these criteria syndromically exclusive, that is, never found in other syndromes.

Whereas the term syndrome represents a cluster or set of covarying symptoms, the term "type" designates a group of individuals who exhibit in common a single, preeminent characteristic that distinguishes them from other individuals. Among other points of differentiation, types usually are conceived as holistic, that is, to represent or synthesize the individual's total psychological functioning. Further, the singular feature that sets the concept of type apart from other similar concepts is that its referents are usually assumed to be both durable and pervasive, that is, stable over time and consistent across situations. The qualities of holism, stability, and consistency have made the notion of "types" especially attractive to theorists as a framework for categorizing personalities.

The construct "prototype" has a long history, but only recently has it been introduced as a potentially useful option for classifying psychopathology. As presently formulated it appears to meld several attributes of both syndrome and type. It may prove especially apt as we seek to develop a schema for representing both the composite of diverse elements that comprise personality (the syndrome aspect) as well as the features that distinguish personality from other forms of psychopathology, namely, holism, durability, and pervasiveness (the type aspect).

How has the concept of prototype been defined?

Horowitz, Post, French, Wallis, and Siegelman (1981) describe the construct succinctly:

> A prototype consists of the most common features or properties of members of a category and thus describes a theoretical ideal or standard against which real people can be evaluated. All of the prototype's properties are assumed to characterize at least some members of the category, but no one property is necessary or sufficient for membership in the category. Therefore, it is possible that no actual person would match the theoretical prototype perfectly. Instead, different people would approximate it to different degrees. The more closely a person approximates the ideal, the more the person typifies the concept. (p. 575)

Mischel (1984) characterizes the prototypal approach as useful in recognizing the

> especially "fuzzy" nature of natural categories along the lines articulated by Wittgenstein. Category knowledge about persons and situations is represented by a loose set of features that are correlated, but only imperfectly, with membership in that category. The approach implies that categorization decisions (e.g., about who is a prototypic extrovert or used car salesman type) will be probabalistic and that the members of a category will vary in degree of membership. There will be many ambiguous borderline cases that yield overlapping, fuzzy boundaries between the categories. To study such fuzzy sets, one seeks the clearest and best exemplars (the most prototypic members), omitting the less prototypic, borderline instances. The prototype approach both to persons and to situations lends itself readily to the construction of orderly taxonomies containing categories at different levels of abstraction or inclusiveness. (p. 356)

Cantor, Smith, French, and Mezzich (1980) note that the "classical" approach to diagnosis depends on the identification of singly necessary or jointly sufficient features. By contrast, the prototypal view merely requires that sets be comprised of correlated features. As a result of this conceptual openness,

> prototypes permit extensive heterogeneity of category instances. Thus, one instance may contain most of the correlated features of the prototype and another may contain hardly any at all . . . prototypes make sense out of variations in typicality, where typical instances are simply those that share

many correlated features with the category prototype. . . . The higher the overlap, the faster, more accurately, and more confidently the instance can be classified. An immediate consequence of this prototype-matching process is that typical instances will be categorized more efficiently than atypical ones, because typical instances have greater featural overlap with their prototypes. . . . To the degree that the prototypes for two categories have many common features and few distinctive ones, the categorizer may have difficulty distinguishing between members of these categories. . . . There is one more factor that must be considered in a prototype-matching process. This factor reflects the degree of richness of a category prototype (as measured by the total number of its features) as well as the distinctiveness of the prototype (as measured by the number of its features that are not shared by rival categories). (pp. 184–185)

It is evident that the prototype approach shares many of the attributes associated with the syndrome concept, notably the diversity of choices among its correlated signs and symptoms, and hence the heterogeneity found among similarly diagnosed patients. Albeit implicitly, the prototype model guided the thinking of several DSM-III Task Force members who formulated both the rules and diagnostic criteria of the manual, for example, the opportunity to select only a subset of the criteria that composed a category, the presence of "mixed" syndromes, even the encouragement of multiple diagnoses. Cantor *et al.* (1980) record that these DSM-III changes

help to emphasize, rather than obscure, the probabalistic nature of diagnostic categorizations. On the basis of the new manual, clinicians can now be trained to expect heterogeneity among patients and to recognize the probabalistic nature of diagnostic categorizations. Also, utilization of confidence/ typicality ratings in diagnosis can be encouraged, and diagnoses can be made on the basis of degree of fit between the patient's cluster of symptoms and the prototypes for various different categories. (p. 192)

Although diverging from the single, overarching attribute that characterizes a "typology" (e.g., extraversion or introversion), the prototype concept is well suited to represent the "typical," pervasive, durable, and holistic features that distinguish personality categories from the more symptomatic, less widespread, frequently transient, and narrowly circumscribed clinical syndromes.

Development of Personality "Prototypes"

There is a logic to the syndrome concept in medical disorders. Bodily changes wrought by infectious diseases and structural deteriorations repeatedly display themselves in a reasonably uniform pattern of signs and symptoms that "make sense" in terms of how anatomic structures and physiological processes are altered and dysfunction. Moreover, these biological changes provide a foundation for identifying the etiology of these disorders as well as for recognizing their pathogenesis, course, and prognosis. Logic and fact together enable us to construct a rationale to explain why most medical syndromes express themselves in the signs and symptoms they do.

Can the same be said for psychological syndromes, specifically "personality prototypes"? Is there a logic, perhaps even evidence, for believing that certain signs and symptoms (e.g., behaviors, cognitions, affects, mechanisms) cluster together as do medical syndromes, that is, not only covary frequently, but make sense as a coherently organized and reasonably distinctive group of clinical characteristics? Are there theoretical and empirical justifications for believing that the varied features of personality display a configurational unity and expressive consistency over time? Will the careful study of individuals reveal congruency among attributes such as overt behavior, intrapsychic functioning, and biophysical disposition? Is this coherence and stability of psychological functioning a valid phenomenon, that is, not merely imposed upon observed data by virtue of clinical expectation or theoretical bias?

We contend that the answer to each of the preceding questions is yes. Stated simply, the observation of prototypic personality patterns by clinicians may be connected to the fact that people possess relatively enduring biophysical dispositions which give a consistent coloration to their experiences, and that the range of experiences to which people are exposed throughout their lives is both limited and repetitive (Millon, 1969, 1981). Given the limiting and shaping character of biological and psychological factors, it should not be surprising that individuals develop clusters of prepotent and deeply ingrained behaviors, cognitions, and affects that clearly distinguish them from others of dissimilar backgrounds. Once several of the components of a particular cluster are identified, knowledgeable observers should be able to infer the likely presence of other, unobserved, but frequently correlated features comprising that cluster.

If we accept the assumption that most people do display a cluster of internally consistent characteristics, we are led next to the question of whether groups of patients evidence commonality in the clusters they display. The concepts of clinical syndrome and personality prototype rest on the assumption that there are a limited number of such shared clusters, that is, diagnostic signs and symptoms, pathognomonic or not, which can confidently be used to distinguish certain groups or classes of patients. The fact that patients can profitably be classified into such syndromes or prototypes does not, of course, negate the fact that patients, so categorized, display considerable differences as well, a fact observed, of course, with medical diseases quite routinely. The philosopher, Grünbaum (1952), illustrates this point in the following:

> Every individual is unique by virtue of being a distinctive assemblage of characteristics not precisely duplicated in any other individual. Neverthe-

less, it is quite conceivable that the following . . . might hold: If a male child having specifiable characteristics is subjected to maternal hostility and has a strong paternal attachment at a certain stage of his development, he will develop paranoia during adult life. If this . . . holds, then children who are subjected to the stipulated conditions in fact become paranoiacs, however much they may have differed in other respects in childhood and whatever their other differences may be once they are already insane. (p. 672)

What are the "specifiable characteristics" and what are the life experiences that give rise to clusters of clinical behavior that comprise identifiable syndromes or prototypes? If we review our literature in psychopathology, we will see that much of it addresses this specific question. Although this chapter is not the place to review so vast a body of theory, knowledge, and speculation, a few paragraphs indicating how personality prototype clusters are acquired may be useful.

The question to be addressed may best be phrased as follows: Why does the possession of characteristic A increase the probability, appreciably beyond chance, of also possessing characteristics B, C, and so on? Less abstractly, why do particular behaviors, attitudes, mechanisms, and so on covary in repetitive and recognizable ways rather than exhibit themselves in a more or less haphazard fashion? And, even more concretely, why do each of the following: behavioral defensiveness, interpersonal provocativeness, cognitive suspicion, affective irascibility, and excessive use of the projection mechanism, co-occur in the same individual rather than be uncorrelated and randomly distributed among different individuals?

The "answers," to be elaborated shortly, are, first, that temperament and early experience simultaneously affect the development and nature of several emerging psychological structures and functions; that is, a wide range of behaviors, attitudes, affects, and mechanisms can be traced to the same origins, leading thereby to their frequently observed covariance. Second, once an individual possesses these initial characteristics, they will, in turn, set in motion a series of derivative life experiences that will shape the acquisition of new psychological attributes causally related to the characteristics that preceded them in the sequential chain.

The following sections provide but a few of the many common origins and successive linkages that alter the probability that particular psychological characteristics will be found frequently to pair with specific others, resulting thereby in what we observe and term clinical syndromes and personality prototypes. Additional illustrations of these reciprocal covariances and serially unfolding concatenations may be found in Millon (1969, 1981).

BIOLOGICAL DISPOSITIONS

The child's constitutional temperament is important because it strengthens the probability that certain kinds of behavior will be learned. For example, highly active and responsive children relate to and learn about their environment quickly. Their liveliness, zest, and power may lead them to a high measure of personal gratification. Conversely, their energy and exploratory behavior may result in excess frustration if they overaspire or run into insuperable barriers; unable to gratify their activity needs effectively, they may grope and strike out in erratic and maladaptive ways. Adaptive learning in constitutionally passive children also is shaped by their biological equipment. Ill-disposed to deal with their environment assertively and little inclined to discharge their tensions physically, they may learn to avoid conflicts and step aside when difficulties arise. They are less likely to develop guilt feelings about misbehavior than active youngsters who more frequently get into trouble, receive more punishment, and are therefore inclined to develop aggressive feelings toward others. But in their passivity, these youngsters may deprive themselves of rewarding experiences and relationships; they may feel "left out of things" and become dependent on others to fight their battles and to protect them from experiences they are ill-equipped to handle on their own.

Constitutional tendencies also evoke counteractions from others which accentuate these initial dispositions. For example, the child's biological endowment shapes not only his behavior, but that of his parents as well. If the child's primary disposition is cheerful and adaptable and has made his care easy, the mother will tend quickly to display a positive reciprocal attitude; conversely, if the child is tense and wound up, or if his care is difficult and time-consuming, the mother will react with dismay, fatigue, or hostility. Through his own behavioral disposition then, the child elicits a series of parental behaviors which reinforce his initial pattern.

In both active and passive illustrations, the presence of specific temperamental inclinations sets into motion a series of secondary experiences that lead to an increased probability that particular self and interpersonal attitudes will be acquired. The personality prototype of youngsters with these initial dispositions and consequent experience is likely to include correlated features, including attributes relating to self-perception, affective expression, and interpersonal conduct.

EARLY EXPERIENCE

The concept of "stimulus nutriment" (Rapaport, 1958) suggests that the simple impingement of environmental stimuli upon the maturing organism has a direct bearing on the chemical composition, ultimate size, and patterns of neural branching within the brain. Stated simply, the sheer *amount* of stimulation to which the child is exposed has a determinant effect on the maturation of his neural capacities. The belief that the maturing organism must receive periodic stimulus nutriments for proper development has led some theorists to suggest that the organism actively seeks an optimum level of stimulation. Thus, just as the infant cries out in search of food when deprived or wails in response to pain, so too may it display behaviors which provide it with sensory stimulation requisite to maturation. Although infants are restricted largely to stimulation supplied by environmental agents, they often engage in what appear to be random exercises, exercises which, in effect, furnish them with the stimulation they require. Thus, in the first months of life, infants can be seen to track auditory and visual stimuli; as they mature further, they grasp incidental objects, and then mouth, rotate, and fondle them. Furthermore, we observe that the young of all species engage in more exploratory and frolicsome behavior than adults. These seemingly "functionless" play activities may not be functionless at all; they may be essential to growth, an instrumental means of self-stimulation that is indispensable to the maturation and maintenance of biological capacities.

Implicit in the preceding is the view that the organism's partly matured capacities enable it to provide for itself sources of stimulation necessary for further maturation; according to this thesis, each stage of maturational development establishes a foundation of capacities which are prerequisites for and conducive to the development of more advanced stages of maturation. For example, a child with deficient sensory capacities such as vision may be unable to maneuver within its environment, and consequently may be delayed in the development of motor capacities such as walking and running.

Constitutionally insensitive and underresponsive children are likely to evoke little attention, cuddling, and affection from their parents; as a consequence, they are deprived of the social and emotional cues requisite to learning affectionate and attachment behaviors. Soon characterized as reserved, indifferent, and formal, the youngster is increasingly surrounded by a cold, if not bleak social atmosphere, and finds himself relating to others in an evermore unemotional, remote, and disaffiliated way. The consequences of the child's initial proclivities have now had double- and triple-barreled effects. Not only has he been hampered by specific initial deficiencies, but they have yielded progressive and long-range consequences that have retarded the development of a complex set of diverse competencies. Early deficits have precipitated a whole series of secondarily stunted and distorted capacities which have sequentially unfolded into a "prototypical" pattern of personality characteristics, notably behavioral lethargy, interpersonal aloofness or indifference, impoverished cognitive processes, flat affectivity, self-complacency, and so on.

PARENTAL RELATIONSHIPS

The training procedures that are used to control a child's behavior may have far more profound and wide-ranging effects than the parents intended. For example, overcontrolling parents, disposed to keep their offspring in line via intimidation and restrictive measures, set the stage for the development of a complex of behaviors, attitudes, and feelings that often cohere into an identifiable and subsequently troublesome personality prototype. Such overly trained and overly disciplined youngsters will be given little opportunity to shape their destiny. Whether by coercion or enticement, they are led, too early, to control their emergent feelings, to focus their thoughts along narrowly defined paths, and to follow the prescriptions of parental demands.

They have been subverted into adopting the identities of others. Whatever individuality they may have acquired is drowned in models of adult orderliness, propriety, and virtue. Such oversocialized and rigid youngsters lack the spontaneity, flexibility, and creativeness we expect of the young; they have been trained to be old men and women before their time, too narrow in perspective to respond to the excitement, variety, and challenge of new events. Parental overcontrol has fixed them on a restrictive course and has deprived them of the rewards of being themselves. Moreover, should these youngsters fail to satisfy parental demands and thereby be subject to harassment and punishment, they are likely to develop pervasive anticipatory anxieties about fulfilling the expectations of authorities in general, learn to cover up failures and inadequacies, limit themselves to activities that are "safe" or easily achieved, and so on.

If the child submits and succeeds in fulfilling parental expectations, he or she is apt to become an overly obedient and circumspect person. Quite typically, these individuals learn not only to keep their impulses and contrary thoughts in check, but, by vicarious observation and imitation, to adopt the parental behavior model, becoming perfectionistic, inflexible, rule-bound, harsh, and demanding of others. This configuration of characteristics corresponds to a well-known personality prototype, notably one comprised of rigidly organized behaviors, interpersonal respectfulness, constricted and indecisive cognitive processes, solemn affect, and a self-image of efficiency and conscientiousness.

SOCIAL AND SELF-PERPETUATION

The dominant features of a child's early behavior form a distinct impression upon others. Once this early impression is established, people expect that the child will continue to behave in his or her distinctive manner; in time, they develop a fixed and simplified image of "what kind of person the child is." The term "stereotype," borrowed from social psychology, represents this tendency to simplify and categorize the attributes of others. People no longer view a child passively and objectively once they having formed a stereotype of him or her; they now are sensitized to the distinctive features they have learned to expect. The stereotype begins to take on a life of its own; it operates as a screen through which the child's behaviors are selectively perceived to fit the characteristics attributed to him or her. Once cast in this mold, the child will experience a consistency in the way in which others react to him or her, one that fails to take cognizance of the varieties and complexities of his or her behaviors. No matter what the child does, he or she finds that his or her behavior is interpreted in the same fixed and rigid manner. Exposed time and again to the same reactions and attitudes of others, the child may give up efforts to convince them that he or she can change.

For example, if a "defiant" child displays the slightest degree of resentment in response to unfair treatment, he or she will be jumped on as hopelessly recalcitrant; should the child do nothing objectionable, questions will be raised as to the sincerity of his or her motives. Faced with repeated negative appraisals and unable to break the stereotype into which he or she has been cast, the youngster will relapse after every effort to change, ultimately learning to expect others to be unfair, cynical, and derogating, regardless of his or her actions. The importance of such expectancies lies in the fact that they distort objective realities. Thus, this youngster may transform what may have been a perfectly neutral or supportive comment into one that is seen as humiliating or threatening. Instead of interpreting events as they objectively exist, then, the child, too, selectively distorts them to fit his or her expectancies. These anticipations channel the child's attentions and magnify his or her awareness of insignificant features of his or her environment; they intrude constantly to obscure and warp an accurate perception of reality. Distortions of this kind have an insidiously cumulative and spiraling effect. By misconstruing reality in such ways as to make it corroborate his or her expectancies, the individual will, in time, intensify his or her initial mistrust and suspicions. Ordinary, even rewarding events may come to be seen as signs of deception. Neutral events are experienced "as if" they were, in fact, conspiratorial. The individual creates and accumulates threatening possibilities where none exist in reality. Insidiously, step by step, a cluster of diverse personality attributes has been acquired, unfolding into a prototypical configuration of correlated characteristics, notably behavioral defensiveness, provocative interpersonal conduct, cognitive suspiciousness, inviolability of self, and irascible affect.

The preceding illustrations are just a few of the factors and sequences that can create linkages among characteristics that ultimately comprise and give shape to what we have termed "personality prototypes."

Clinical Attributes

Individuals differ in the degree to which their behaviors are enduring and pervasive. Moreover, each individual displays this durability and pervasiveness only in certain of his or her characteristics; that is, each of us possesses a limited number of attributes that are resistant to changing times and situational influences, whereas other of our attributes are readily modified. Furthermore, it should be noted that the features which exhibit this consistency and stability in one person may not be the same features exhibited by others. These core qualities of persistence and extensiveness appear only in characteristics that have become crucial in maintaining the individual's structural balance and functional style, for example, passive-dependent, active-detached. To illustrate: The "interpersonal" attribute of significance for some is being agreeable, never differing or having conflict; for another, it may be interpersonally critical to keep one's distance from people so as to avoid rejection or the feeling of being humiliated; for a third, the influential interpersonal characteristic may be that of asserting one's will and dominating others.

Each personality prototype should comprise a small and distinct group of primary attributes that persist over time and exhibit a high degree of consistency across situations (Mischel, 1984). These enduring (stable) and pervasive (consistent) characteristics are what we search for when we "diagnose" personality.

In the following paragraphs, we will identify a number of the major attributes of personality that possess clinical significance. More specifically, we will outline a set of structural and functional characteristics that not only will aid us in differentiating among the pathological personalities, but will provide us with diagnostic criteria for identifying each personality prototype.

Many of the signs, symptoms, and characteristics that patients exhibit can usefully be categorized and dimensionalized for purposes of clinical analysis (see Chapter 3 in both Leary, 1957, and Millon, 1969). One set of distinctions, that differentiating diagnostic features in accord with biophysical, intrapsychic, phenomenological, and behavioral data levels, reflects the focus of the four classical and doctrinaire approaches that characterize the study of psychopathology, namely, the biological, the psychoanalytic, the cognitive, and the behavioral (Millon, 1983b).

Valuable though it may be to organize a schema which represents these historic models, it may be more useful to put them aside in favor of an arrangement that represents the personality system in a manner similar to that of the body system, that is, dividing its components into *structural* and *functional* attributes. The biological subjects of anatomy and physiology, respectively, investigate embedded and essentially permanent structures, which serve as mechanisms for action, and functions, which regulate internal changes and external transactions.

Dividing the characteristics of the psychological world into structural and functional realms is by no means a novel notion. Psychoanalytic theory has dealt since its inception with topographic constructs such as conscious, preconscious, and unconscious, and later with structural concepts such as id, ego, and superego; likewise, a host of "quasi-stationary" functional processes, such as the so-called ego apparatuses, notably motility, attention, perception, and cognition, have been posited and studied (Gill, 1963; Rapaport, 1959).

There are several benefits to differentiating the more-or-less stable and organized clinical attributes (structures) from those that represent processing and modulating features (functions). For the present, it will suffice simply to define the terms "function" and "structure" as they apply to clinical matters; we may then proceed to identify those attributes that are most relevant to personality diagnosis.

Functional Attributes

Functional characteristics represent dynamic processes that transpire within the intrapsychic world and between the individual and his psychosocial environment. For definitional purposes, we might say that functional clinical attributes represent "expressive modes of regulatory action," that is, behaviors, cognitions, perceptions, affect, and mechanisms which manage, adjust, transform, coordinate, balance, discharge, and control the give and take of inner and outer life.

Not only are there several modes of regulatory action (e.g., behavioral, cognitive, affective), but there are numerous variations in the way each of these functional modalities are manifested or expressed (e.g., affectively flat, affectively hostile, affectively labile). Every individual employs every modality in the course of his life, but individuals differ with respect to the modalities they enact most frequently and, even more so, diverge in which of the expressive variations of these functions they typically manifest. As Bowers has put it (1977): "The way a person performs a common behavior is sometimes quite revealing. One person ordinarily eats and makes love fastidiously; another person is given to gluttony in both circumstances. The more idiosyncratically expressive a common behavior is . . . (the more it is) attributable to a relatively stable personality and behavioral organization" (p. 75).

Particular modalities and expressive variations characterize certain personalities best, but even the most distinctive of personalities will display several variations of a modality. Dissimilar individuals differ in which modality variations they express most often, but these differences are largely a matter of *quantitative frequency* (dimensionality) and not *qualitative distinctness* (categorality).

Five functional clinical attributes relevant to personality will be briefly described. Thirteen expressive variations, one associated with each personality prototype, will be specified later in detailed tables.

1. Behavioral Presentation. These relate to the observables of physical and verbal behavior, usually recorded by noting what the patient does and how he does it. Through inference, observations of overt behavior enable us to deduce either what the patient unknowingly reveals about him or herself or, often conversely, what he or she wishes us to think or to know about him or her. The range and character of behavioral functions are not only wide and diverse, but they convey both distinctive and worthwhile clinical information, from communicating a sense of personal incompetence to exhibiting general defensiveness to demonstrating a disciplined self-control, and so on.

2. Interpersonal Conduct. A patient's style of relating to others may be captured in a number of ways, such as the manner in which his or her actions impact on others, intended or otherwise, the attitudes that underlie, prompt, and give shape to these actions, the methods by which he or she engages others to meet his or her needs, or his or her way of coping with social tensions and conflicts. Extrapolating from these observations, the

clinician may construct an image of how the patient functions in relation to others, be it antagonistically, respectfully, aversively, secretively, and so on.

3. Cognitive Style. How the patient perceives events, focuses his or her attention, processes information, organizes thoughts, and communicates his or her reactions and ideas to others are among the most useful indices to the clinician of the patient's distinctive way of functioning. By synthesizing these signs and symptoms, it may be possible to identify indications of what may be termed an impoverished style, or distracted thinking, or cognitive flightiness, or constricted thought, and so on.

4. Expressive Mood. Few observables are more relevant to clinical analysis than the predominant character of an individual's affect and the intensity and frequency with which he or she expresses it. The "meaning" of extreme emotions is easy to decode. This is not so with the more subtle moods and feelings that insidiously and repetitively pervade the patient's ongoing relationships and experiences. Not only are the expressive features of mood conveyed by terms such as distraught, labile, fickle, or hostile communicated via self-report, but they are revealed as well, albeit indirectly, in the patient's level of activity, speech quality, and physical appearance.

5. Unconscious Mechanism. Although "mechanisms" of self-protection, need gratification, and conflict resolution are consciously recognized at times, those that remain unconscious and thereby avoid reflective appraisal often begin a sequence of events that intensifies the very problems they were intended to circumvent. Mechanisms usually represent internal processes and, hence, are more difficult to discern and describe than processes anchored closer to the observable world. Despite the methodological problems they present, the task of identifying which mechanisms are chosen (e.g., rationalization, displacement, reaction-formation) and the extent to which they are employed is central to a comprehensive personality assessment.

Structural Attributes

These attributes represent a deeply embedded and relatively enduring template of imprinted memories, attitudes, needs, fears, conflicts, and so on, which guide the experience and transform the nature of ongoing life events. Psychic structures have an orienting and preemptive effect in that they alter the character of action and the impact of subsequent experiences in line with preformed inclinations and expectancies. By selectively lowering thresholds for transactions that are consonant with either constitutional proclivities or early learnings, future events are often experienced as variations of the past. The following describes both the character and persistence of these structural residues of early experience (Millon, 1969).

> Significant experiences of early life may never recur again, but their effects remain and leave their mark. Physiologically, we may say they have etched a neurochemical change; psychologically, they are registered as memories, a

permanent trace and an embedded internal stimulus. In contrast to the fleeting stimuli of the external world, these memory traces become part and parcel of every stimulus complex which activates behavior. Once registered, the effects of the past are indelible, incessant and inescapable. They now are intrinsic elements of the individual's makeup; they latch on and intrude into the current events of life, coloring, transforming and distorting the passing scene. Although the residuals of subsequent experiences may override them, becoming more dominant internal stimuli, the presence of earlier memory traces remains in one form or another. In every thought and action, the individual cannot help but carry these remnants into the present. Every current behavior is a perpetuation, then, of the past, a continuation and intrusion of these inner stimulus traces.

The residuals of the past do more than passively contribute their share to the present. By temporal precedence, if nothing else, they guide, shape or distort the character of current events. Not only are they ever present, then, but they operate insidiously to transform new stimulus experiences in line with past. (p. 200)

For purposes of definition, structural attributes might be described as "cognitive-affective substrates and action dispositions of a quasi-permanent nature." Possessing a network of interconnecting pathways, these structures contain the internalized residues of the past in the form of memories and affects that are associated intrapsychically with conceptions of self and others.

Three structural attributes relevant to personality will be briefly described. Thirteen variations, one for each personality prototype, will be specified in later tables.

1. Self-image. As the inner world of symbols is mastered through development, the "swirl" of events that buffet the young child gives way to a growing sense of order and continuity. One major configuration emerges to impose a measure of sameness upon an otherwise fluid environment, the perception of self-as-object, a distinct, ever-present, and identifiable "I" or "me." Self-identity provides a stable anchor to serve as a guidepost and to give continuity to changing experience. Most persons have an implicit sense of who they are, but differ greatly in the clarity and accuracy of their self-introspections. Few can articulate the psychic elements that comprise this image, such as stating knowingly whether they view themselves as primarily alienated, or inept, or complacent, or conscientious, and so on.

2. Internalized Content. As noted previously, significant experiences from the past leave an inner imprint, a structural residue composed of memories, attitudes, and affects that serve as a substrate of dispositions for perceiving and reacting to life's ongoing events. Analogous to the various organ systems of which the body is composed, both the character and substance of these internalized representations of the past can be differentiated and analyzed for clinical purposes. Variations in the nature and content of this inner world can be associated with one or another personality and lead us to employ descriptive terms to represent them, such as shallow, vexatious, undifferentiated, concealed, and irreconcilable.

3. Intrapsychic Organization. The overall architecture that serves as a framework for an individual's psychic interior may display weakness in its structural cohesion, exhibit deficient coordination among its components, and possess few mechanisms to maintain balance and harmony, regulate internal conflicts, or mediate external pressures. The concept of intrapsychic organization refers to the structural strength, interior congruity, and functional efficacy of the personality system. "Organization" is a concept akin to and employed in conjunction with current psychoanalytic notions such as borderline and psychotic levels, but this usage tends to be limited, relating essentially to quantitative degrees of integrative pathology, not to variations either in integrative character or configuration. In a table presented later in the chapter, "stylistic" variants of this structural attribute will be associated with each of the 13 personality prototypes; their distinctive organizational qualities will be represented with descriptors such as "inchoate," "disjoined," and "compartmentalized."

Diagnostic Criteria

The purpose of this section is to make more explicit and tangible, to operationalize, so to speak, the concepts that have been presented in this and the previous chapter. Although true operational definitions call for the specification of precise methods of quantifying theoretical constructs, these will not be addressed here; readers interested in "operational" psychometric techniques relevant to the personality concepts presented here might find it of value to read the manual for the Millon Clinical Multiaxial Inventory (Millon, 1983a), a self-report inventory anchored both to the author's theory and to the syndromes of DSM-III.

Termed "operational criteria" in the early stages of DSM-III development, the outline of specified signs and symptoms comprising the basis of assigning each of the manual's syndromes was subsequently and more properly retitled "diagnostic criteria."

MERITS OF DIAGNOSTIC CRITERIA

In his excellent review of issues associated with psychiatric diagnosis, Kendell (1975) writes of the following all-too-common problem: "The information that the subjects of a particular study had all been diagnosed as schizophrenics or hysterics often tells us remarkably little about them, certainly not enough for us to be able to assemble another group of patients with any confidence that they would be comparable" (p. 137).

In an earlier chapter on the history of the DSM-III that the author has written for this volume (Chapter 2), the virtues of specifying clear criteria for defining the common characteristics of patients assigned the same diagnostic label are noted as follows:

It is this very precision in articulating specific and uniform rules of definition, originally and significantly termed "operational criteria," that makes the DSM-III so serviceable and potentially fruitful also as a research tool. Not only do the criteria delineate the components that will enable reasonably homogeneous group assignments, but its application as a standard national (and it is hoped, international) gauge will ensure at least a modicum of reliability and comparability among studies undertaken at diverse research settings.

It is not only when contradictory findings occur that one wonders whether the problem can be traced to the assignment of the same diagnostic label to intrinsically dissimilar patients. Common also are communication confusions and disagreements among practicing clinicians. Unless they agree on the criteria they employ for a diagnostic entity, it may be impossible to determine whether the conflicting parties are talking about the same syndrome.

COMPARABILITY OF CRITERIA

It seems reasonable to assume that greater clarity in clinical communications as well as greater research reliability will follow the systematic use of diagnostic criteria. However, as noted in Chapter 2 of this volume, "Most of the criteria (in the DSM-III) lack empirical support. Some are inadequately explicit or, conversely, are overly concrete in their operational referents. Many are redundant both within and with other diagnostic classes. Others are insufficiently comprehensive in syndromal scope or display a lack of parallelism and symmetry among corresponding categories."

Part of the difficulty in specifying more definitive or explicit criteria lies in the intrinsic nature of psychopathology itself, or as Meehl (1978) has put it, "from the organism's real compositional nature and structure and the causal texture of its environment." Nevertheless, diagnostic criteria for personality prototypes will enable us to be, to quote Meehl again, "quasi-exact about the inherently inexact." And to quote again from Chapter 2 of this volume, "Syndromes of the DSM-III are conceptual prototypes, and not tangible entities. . . . Given that these syndromes are, in the main, only theoretical constructs, it will more than suffice for both clinical and research purposes to employ what has been devised—a standardized, reliable, and internally coherent mosaic of criterion descriptors."

Despite the inherent limitations that are built into syndromic and prototypic categories, several shortcomings among the DSM-III diagnostic criteria should and can be remedied. In Chapter 19 of this volume, Frances and Widiger record a number of factors that undermine the homogeneity of Axis II class membership requirements. These difficulties arise in part from a lack of comparability among diagnostic criteria: for example some categories require all defining features to be present (e.g., dependent personality), whereas others allow choice among the criteria (e.g., borderline personality). According to Frances and Widiger, Axis II is "inconsistent in the extent to which the members of each category are assumed to be homogeneous with respect to the definitional features." The authors indicate that this heterogeneity in diagnostic requirements will bear directly on the efficiency and utility of each definitional feature as well as possibly compromise the validity of the covariates that ostensibly comprise each syndrome.

Heterogeneous requirements are especially problematic in classically structured syndromes, that is, those requiring singly necessary or jointly sufficient diagnostic criteria. Prototypic categories, by contrast, are composed intentionally in a heterogeneous manner, that is, they accept the legitimacy of syndromic diversity and overlap. Nevertheless, there still is need to reduce the "fuzziness" between boundaries so as to eliminate excessive numbers of unclassifiable and borderline cases. One step toward the goal of sharpening diagnostic discriminations is to spell out a distinctive criterion for every diagnostically relevant clinical attribute aligned with every prototypal category. For example, if the attribute "interpersonal conduct" is deemed of clinical value in assessing personality, then singular diagnostic criteria should be specified to represent *the* characteristic or distinctive manner in which *each* personality "conducts its interpersonal life."

By composing a taxonomic schema that includes all relevant clinical attributes (e.g., behavior, affect, cognitive), and specifies a defining feature on every attribute for each of the 13 personalities, the proposed prototypal model would both be fully comprehensive in its clinical scope and possess parallel and directly comparable criteria among all Axis II categories. A format of this nature will not only furnish logic and symmetry to the DSM taxonomy, but will enable investigators to be systematic in determining the relative diagnostic efficacy of presumed prototypal covariates. Moreover, clinicians would be able to appraise both typical and unusual syndromal patterns as well as establish the coherence, if not the "validity" of both recently developed and classically established diagnostic entities. These goals are being carried out in a current nationwide study by the author and his colleagues in which some 100 participating clinicians are assessing the personality attributes of approximately 1,000 patients. The investigation has set out to obtain data not only on each of the preceding matters, but also to determine the conditional probabilities of various hypothesized criteria combinations, to calculate "specificity" and "selectivity" measures employing independent clinical and psychometric criterion gauges, to attempt to specify the optimum number of criteria for assigning each personality diagnosis, and so on.

QUALITATIVE AND QUANTITATIVE NATURE OF CRITERIA

In the study to which we have just referred, clinical judges are asked not only to identify which criterion (e.g., distraught, hostile, labile) of an attribute (e.g., expressive mood) best characterizes a particular patient, but to record a number (from 1 to 10) to represent the degree of prominence or pervasiveness of that attribute's criterion. Moreover, judges are encouraged, where appropriate, to record *and* quantify more than one criterion per clinical attribute (e.g., if suitable, to note both "distraught" mood and "labile" mood).

The purpose of this procedure is to affirm the view that categorical (qualitative distinction) and dimensional (quantitative distinction) models of classification need not be framed in opposition, no less be considered mutually exclusive (Millon, 1981; Widiger & Kelso, 1983). Assessments can be formulated, first, to recognize qualitative (categorical) distinctions in *what* behavior best characterizes a patient, permitting the multiple listing of several such behaviors, and , second, to differentiate these behaviors quantitatively (dimensionally) so as to represent their relative degrees of clinical prominence or pervasiveness. For example, on the "interpersonal conduct" attribute, patient A may be appraised as deserving quantitative ratings of 10 on the "aversive" criterion, 6 on the "ambivalent" criterion, and 4 on the "secretive" criterion. Patient B may be assigned a rating of 9 on the "ambivalent" criterion, 7 on "aversive," and 2 on "paradoxical." Both patients are characterized by the "aversive" and "ambivalent" criteria, but to differing extents; they are not only distinguishable quantitatively (dimensionally) on two of the same qualitative or categorical criteria, but differ as well on qualitative grounds, one have exhibited "secretive," the other "paradoxical" interpersonal conduct.

Cumulative "scores" across multiple clinical attributes obtained via such assessment procedures will result in personality configurations composed of mixed diagnostic assignments. These diagnostic profiles are highly informative and can be especially useful, for example, in identifying which attribute should serve as the initial focus of therapy, for example, deciding to address that criterion of interpersonal conduct that may benefit by "group or family techniques," or pinpointing a feature of mood expression that may be especially responsive to "psychopharmacologic treatment," or discerning the character and level of intrapsychic organization that may be conducive to "psychodynamically oriented therapy," and so on.

Clinical Attribute Criteria

Each of tables, 31-1–31-8, presents a set of diagnostic features for each of the clinical attributes. Reference to earlier paragraphs will refresh the reader's memory of the nature and scope of these attributes. The criteria within each table are aligned with the personality prototype they characterize. Reading horizontally, there is a single "defining" term recorded for each criterion (e.g., "lethargic" is the term that portrays the schizoid's "behavioral presentation" attribute); also furnished is a brief descriptive text that elaborates or illustrates a number of each criterion's typical signs and symptoms.

Personality Prototype Criteria

Tables 31-9–31-21 present the same criterion information as do Tables 31-1–31-8. However, the arrangement in these tables aligns criteria according to

Table 31-1

Personality	A. Behavioral Presentation
1. Schizoid	Lethargic: Appears to be in a state of fatigue, low energy and lack of vitality; is phlegmatic, sluggish, displaying deficits in activation, motoric expressiveness and spontaneity.
2. Avoidant	Guarded: Warily scans environment for potential threats; overreacts to innocuous events and anxiously judges them to signify personal ridicule and threat.
3. Dependent	Incompetent: Ill-equipped to assume mature and independent roles; is docile and passive, lacking functional competencies, avoiding self-assertion and withdrawing from adult responsibilities.
4. Histrionic	Affected: Is over-reactive, stimulus-seeking and intolerant of inactivity, resulting in impulsive, unreflected and theatrical responsiveness; describes penchant for momentary excitements, fleeting adventures and short-sighted hedonism.
5. Narcissistic	Arrogant: Flouts conventional rules of shared social living, viewing them as naive or inapplicable to self; reveals a careless disregard for personal integrity and an indifference to the rights of others.
6A. Antisocial	Impulsive: Is impetuous and irrepressible, acting hastily and spontaneously in a restless, spur-of-the-moment manner; is shortsighted, incautious and imprudent, failing to plan ahead or consider alternatives, no less heed consequences.
6B. Aggressive (Sadistic)	Fearless: Is unflinching, recklessly daring, thick-skinned and seemingly undeterred by pain; is attracted to challenge, risk and harm, as well as undaunted by danger and punishment.
7. Compulsive	Disciplined: Maintains a regulated, repetitively structured and highly-organized life pattern; is perfectionistic, insisting that subordinates adhere to personally established rules and methods.
8A. Passive-Aggressive	Stubborn: Resists fulfilling expectancies of others, frequently exhibiting procrastination, inefficiency and erratic, as well as other contrary and irksome behaviors; reveals gratification in demoralizing and undermining the pleasures and aspirations of others.
8B. Self-Defeating (Masochistic)	Abstinent: Presents self as nonindulgent, frugal and chaste, refraining from exhibiting signs of pleasure or attractiveness; acts in an unpresuming and self-effacing manner, preferring to place self in an inferior light or abject position.
S. Schizotypal	Aberrant: Exhibits socially gauche habits and pecular mannerisms; is perceived by others as eccentric, disposed to behave in an unobtrusively odd, aloof, curious or bizarre manner.
C. Borderline	Precipitate: Displays a desultory energy level with sudden, unexpected and impulsive outbursts; abrupt, endogenous shifts in drive state and in inhibitory control, places activation equilibrium in constant jeopardy.
P. Paranoid	Defensive: Is vigilantly alert to anticipate and ward off expected derogation and deception; is tenacious and firmly resistant to sources of external influence and control.

Table 31-2

Personality	B. Interpersonal Conduct
1. Schizoid	Aloof: Seems indifferent and remote, rarely responsive to the actions or feelings of others, possessing minimal "human" interests; fades into the background, is unobtrusive, has few close relationships and prefers a peripheral role in social, work and family settings.
2. Avoidant	Aversive: Reports extensive history of social pan-anxiety and distrust; seeks acceptance, but maintains distance and privacy to avoid anticipated humiliation and derogation.
3. Dependent	Submissive: Subordinates needs to stronger, nurturing figure, without whom feels anxiously helpless; is compliant, conciliatory, placating, and self-sacrificing.
4. Histrionic	Flirtatious: Actively solicits praise and manipulates others to gain needed reassurance, attention, and approval; is demanding, self-dramatizing, vain and seductively exhibitionistic.
5. Narcissistic	Exploitive: Feels entitled, is unempathic and expects special favors without assuming reciprocal responsibilities; shamelessly takes others for granted and uses them to enhance self and indulge desires.
6A. Antisocial	Irresponsible: Is untrustworthy and unreliable, failing to meet or intentionally negating personal obligations of a marital, parental, employment or financial nature; actively violates established social codes through duplicitous or illegal behaviors.
6B. Aggressive (Sadistic)	Intimidating: Reveals satisfaction in competing with, dominating and humiliating others; regularly expresses verbally abusive and derisive social commentary, as well as exhibiting vicious, if not physically brutal behavior.
7. Compulsive	Respectful: Exhibits unusual adherence to social conventions and proprieties; prefers polite, formal and correct personal relationships.
8A. Passive-Aggressive	Contrary: Assumes conflicting and changing roles in social relationships, particularly dependent acquiescence and assertive independence; is concurrently or sequentially obstructive and intolerant of others, expressing either negative or incompatible attitudes.
8B. Self-Defeating (Masochistic)	Deferential: Relates to others in a self-sacrificing, servile and obsequious manner, allowing, if not encouraging others to exploit or take advantage; is self-abasing and solicits condemnation by accepting undeserved blame and courting unjust criticism.
S. Schizotypal	Secretive: Prefers privacy and isolation, with few, highly tentative attachments and personal obligations; has drifted over time into increasingly peripheral vocational roles and clandestine social activities.
C. Borderline	Paradoxical: Although needing attention and affection, is unpredictably contrary, manipulative and volatile, frequently eliciting rejection rather than support; reacts to fears of separation and isolation in angry, mercurial and often self-damaging ways.
P. Paranoid	Provocative: Displays a quarrelsome, fractious and abrasive attitude; precipitates exasperation and anger by a testing of loyalties and a searching preoccupation with hidden motives.

Table 31-3

Personality	C. Cognitive style
1. Schizoid	Impoverished: Seems deficient across broad spheres of knowledge and evidences vague and obscure thought processes that are below intellectual level; communication is easily derailed, loses its sequence of thought or is conveyed via a circuitous logic.
2. Avoidant	Distracted: Is preoccupied and bothered by disruptive and often perplexing inner thoughts; the upsurge from within of irrelevant and digressive ideation upsets thought continuity and interferes with social communications.
3. Dependent	Naive: Is easily persuaded, unsuspicious and gullible; reveals a Pollyanna attitude toward interpersonal difficulties, watering down objective problems and smoothing over troubling events.
4. Histrionic	Flighty: Avoids introspective thought and is overly attentive to superficial and fleeting external events; integrates experiences poorly, resulting in scattered learning and thoughtless judgments.
5. Narcissistic	Expansive: Has an undisciplined imagination and exhibits a preoccupation with immature fantasies of success, beauty or love; is minimally constrained by objective reality, takes liberties with facts and often lies to redeem self-illusions.
6A. Antisocial	Deviant: Construes events and relationships in accord with socially unorthodox beliefs and morals; is disdainful of traditional ideals and contemptuous of conventional rules.
6B. Aggressive (Sadistic)	Dogmatic: Is strongly opinionated and close-minded, as well as unbending and obstinate in holding to one's preconceptions; exhibits a broad-ranging authoritarianism, social intolerance and prejudice.
7. Compulsive	Constricted: Constructs world in terms of rules, regulations, time schedules and social hierarchies; is unimaginative, indecisive and notably upset by unfamiliar or novel ideas and customs.
8A. Passive-Aggressive	Negativistic: is cynical, skeptical and untrusting, approaching positive events with disbelief, and future possibilities with trepidation; has a misanthropic view of life, expressing disdain and caustic comments toward those experiencing good fortune.
8B. Self-Defeating (Masochistic)	Inconsistent: Thinks and repeatedly expresses attitudes contrary to inner feelings; experiences contrasting emotions and conflicting thoughts toward self and others, notably love, rage and guilt.
S. Schizotypal	Autistic: Mixes social communication with personal irrelevancies, circumstantial speech, ideas of reference and metaphorical asides; is ruminative, appears self-absorbed and lost in daydreams with occasional magical thinking, obscure suspicious and a blurring of fantasy and reality.
C. Borderline	Capricious: Experiences rapidly changing, fluctuating and antithetical perceptions or thoughts concerning passing events; vacillating and contradictory reactions are evoked in others by virtue of ones behaviors, creating, in turn, conflicting and confusing social feedback.
P. Paranoid	Suspicious: Is skeptical, cynical and mistrustful of the motives of others, construing innocuous events as signifying hidden or conspiratorial intent; reveals tendency to magnify tangential or minor social difficulties into proofs of duplicity, malice and treachery.

Table 31-4

Personality	D. Expressive Mood
1. Schizoid	Flat: is emotionally impassive, exhibiting an intrinsic unfeeling, cold and stark quality; reports weak affectionate or erotic needs, rarely displaying warm or intense feelings, and apparently unable to experience either pleasure, sadness or anger in any depth.
2. Avoidant	Anguished: describes constant and confusing undercurrents of tension, sadness and anger; vacillates between desire for affection, fear of rebuff and numbness of feeling.
3. Dependent	Pacific: is characteristically warm, tender and noncompetitive; timidly avoids social tension and interpersonal conflicts.
4. Histrionic	Fickle: displays short-lived dramatic and superficial emotions; is overreactive, impetuous and exhibits tendencies to be easily enthused and as easily angered or bored.
5. Narcissistic	Insouciant: manifests a general air of nonchalance and imperturbability; appears cooly unimpressionable or buoyantly optimistic, except when narcissistic confidence is shaken, at which time either rage, shame or emptiness is briefly displayed.
6A. Antisocial	Callous: is insensitive, unempathetic and coldblooded, as expressed in a wide ranging deficit in social charitableness, human compassion or personal remorse; exhibits a coarse uncivility, as well as an offensive, if not ruthless indifference to the welfare of others.
6B. Aggressive (Sadistic)	Hostile: has an excitable and pugnacious temper which flares readily into contentious argument and physical belligerance; is mean-spirited and fractious, willing to do harm, even persecute others to get one's way.
7. Compulsive	Solemn: is unrelaxed, tense, joyless and grim; restrains warm feelings and keeps most emotions under tight control.
8A. Passive-Aggressive	Irritable: frequently touchy, obstinate and resentful, followed in turn by sulky and moody withdrawal; is often fretful and impatient, reporting being easily annoyed or frustrated by others.
8B. Self-Defeating (Masochistic)	Doleful: is frequently forlorn and mournful; will intentionally display a plaintive and gloomy appearance, occasionally to induce guilt and discomfort in others.
S. Schizotypal	Distraught or Insentient: reports being apprehensive and ill-at-ease, particularly in social encounters; is agitated and anxiously watchful, distrustful of others and wary of their motives; or manifests drab, apathetic, sluggish, joyless, and spiritless appearance; reveals marked deficiencies in face-to-face rapport and emotional expression.
C. Borderline	Labile: fails to accord unstable mood level with external reality; has either marked shifts from normality to depression to excitement, or has extended periods of dejection and apathy, interspersed with brief spells of anger, anxiety, or euphoria.
P. Paranoid	Irascible: displays a cold, sullen, churlish and humorless demeanor; attempts to appear unemotional and objective, but is edgy, envious, jealous, quick to react angrily or take personal offense.

Table 31-5

Personality	E. Unconscious Mechanism
1. Schizoid	Intellectualization: describes interpersonal and affective experiences in a matter of fact, abstract, impersonal or mechanical manner; pays primary attention to formal and objective aspects of social and emotional events.
2. Avoidant	Fantasy: depends excessively on imagination to achieve need gratification and conflict resolution; withdraws into reveries as a means of safely discharging affectionate, as well as aggressive impulses.
3. Dependent	Introjection: is firmly devoted to another to strengthen the belief that an inseparable bond exists between them; jettisons any independent views in favor of those of another to preclude conflicts and threats to the relationship.
4. Histrionic	Dissociation: regularly alters self presentations to create a succession of socially attractive but changing facades; engages in self-distracting activities to avoid reflecting on and integrating unpleasant thoughts and emotions.
5. Narcissistic	Rationalization: is self-deceptive and facile in devising plausible reasons to justify self-centered and socially inconsiderate behaviors; offers alibis to place onself in the best possible light, despite evident shortcomings or failures.
6A. Antisocial	Acting Out: inner tensions that might accrue by postponing the expression of offensive thoughts and malevolent actions are rarely constrained; socially repugnant impulses are not refashioned in sublimated forms, but are discharged directly in precipitous ways, usually without guilt.
6B. Aggressive (Sadistic)	Isolation: can be coldblooded and remarkably detached from an awareness of the impact of one's destructive acts; views objects of violation impersonally, as symbols of devalued groups devoid of human sensibilities.
7. Compulsive	Reaction Formation: repeatedly presents positive thoughts and socially commendable behaviors that are diametrically opposite ones deeper, contrary and forbidden feelings; displays reasonableness and maturity when faced with circumstances that evoke anger or dismay in others.
8A. Passive-Aggressive	Displacement: discharges anger and other troublesome emotions either indirectly or by shifting them from their instigator to settings or persons of lesser significance; expresses resentments by substitute or passive means, such as acting inept or perplexed, or behaving in a forgetful or indolent manner.
8B. Self-Defeating (Masochistic)	Devaluation: repetitively recalls past injustices and anticipates future disappointments as a means of raising distress to homeostatic levels; misconstrues, if not sabotages good fortune so as to enhance or maintain preferred suffering and pain.
S. Schizotypal	Undoing: bizarre mannerisms and idiosyncratic thoughts appear to reflect a retraction or reversal of previous acts or ideas that have stirred feelings of anxiety, conflict or guilt; ritualistic or "magical" behaviors serve to repent for or nullify assumed misdeeds or "evil" thoughts.
C. Borderline	Regression: retreats under stress to developmentally earlier levels of anxiety tolerance, impulse control and social adaptation; among adolescents, is unable to cope with adult demands and conflicts, as evident in immature, if not increasingly infantile behaviors.
P. Paranoid	Projection: actively disowns undesirable personal traits and motives, and attributes them to others; remains blind to ones own unattractive behaviors and characteristics, yet is overalert to, and hypercritical of, similar features in others.

Table 31-6

Personality	F. Self-Image
1. Schizoid	Complacent: reveals minimal introspection and awareness of self; seems impervious to the emotional and personal implications of everyday social life.
2. Avoidant	Alienated: sees self as a person who is socially isolated and rejected by others; devalues self-achievements and reports feelings of aloneness and emptiness, if not depersonalization.
3. Dependent	Inept: views self as weak, fragile and inadequate; exhibits lack of self-confidence by belittling own aptitudes and competencies.
4. Histrionic	Sociable: views self as gregarious, stimulating and charming; enjoys the image of attracting acquaintances and pursuing a busy and pleasure-oriented social life.
5. Narcissistic	Admirable: confidently exhibits self, acting in a self-assured manner and displaying achievements; has a sense of high self-worth, despite being seen by others as egotistic, inconsiderate and arrogant.
6A. Antisocial	Autonomous: sees self as unfettered by the restrictions of social customs and the restraints of personal loyalties; values the image and enjoys the sense of being free, unencumbered and unconfined by persons, places, obligations or routines.
6B. Aggressive (Sadistic)	Competitive: is proud to characterize self as assertively independent, vigorously energetic and realistically hardheaded; values aspects of self that present tough, domineering and power-oriented image.
7. Compulsive	Conscientious: sees self as industrious, reliable, meticulous and efficient; fearful of error or misjudgment and, hence, overvalues aspects of self that exhibit discipline, perfection, prudence and loyalty.
8A. Passive-Aggressive	Discontented: sees self as misunderstood, unappreciated and demeaned by others; recognizes being characteristically resentful, disgruntled and disillusioned with life.
8B. Self-Defeating (Masochistic)	Undeserving: focuses on the very worst features of self, asserting thereby that one is worthy of being shamed, humbled and debased; feels that one has failed to live up to the expectations of others and, hence, deserves to suffer painful consequences.
S. Schizotypal	Estranged: possesses permeable ego-boundaries, exhibiting recurrent social perplexities and illusions as well as experiences of depersonalization, derealization and dissociation; sees self as forlorn, with repetitive thoughts of life's emptiness and meaninglessness.
C. Borderline	Uncertain: experiences the confusions of an immature, nebulous or wavering sense of identity; seeks to redeem precipitate actions and changing self-presentations with expressions of contrition and self-punitive behaviors.
P. Paranoid	Inviolable: has persistent ideas of self-importance and self-reference, asserting as personally derogatory and scurrilous, if not libelous, entirely innocuous actions and events; is pridefully independent and highly insular, experiencing intense fears, however, of losing identity, status and powers of self-determination.

Table 31-7

Personality	G. Internalized Content
1. Schizoid	Meager: inner representations are few in number and minimally articulated, largely devoid of the manifold percepts and memories, nor the dynamic interplay among drives and conflicts that typify even well-adjusted persons.
2. Avoidant	Vexatious: inner representations are composed of readily reactivated, intense and conflict-ridden memories, limited avenues of gratification, and few mechanisms to channel needs, bind impulses, resolve conlficts or deflect external stressors.
3. Dependent	Immature: inner representations are composed of unsophisticated ideas and incomplete memories, rudimentary drives and childlike impulses, as well as minimal competencies to manage and resolve stressors.
4. Histrionic	Shallow: inner representations are composed largely of superficial and segregated affects, memories and conflicts, as well as facile drives and insubstantial mechanisms.
5. Narcissistic	Contrived: inner representations are composed far more than usual of illusory ideas and memories, synthetic drives and conflicts, and pretentious, if not simulated, percepts and attitudes, all of which are readily refashioned as the need arises.
6A. Antisocial	Rebellious: inner representations comprise an ungovernable mix revengeful attitudes and restive impulses driven to subvert established cultural ideals and mores, as well as to debase personal sentiments and material attainments of society which were denied them.
6B. Aggressive (Sadistic)	Pernicious: inner representations are best distinguished by the presence of strongly driven aggressive energies and malicious attitudes, as well as by a contrasting paucity of sentimental memories, tender affects, internal conflicts, shame or guilt feelings.
7. Compulsive	Concealed: only those inner affects, attitudes and actions which are socially approved are allowed conscious awareness or behavioral expression, resulting in gratification being highly regulated, forbidden impulses sequestered and tightly bound, personal and social conflicts defensively denied, kept from awareness, and all maintained under stringent control.
8A. Passive-Aggressive	Oppositional: inner representations comprise a complex of countervailing inclinations and incompatible memories that are driven pervasively by strong dissident impulses designed to nullify the achievements and pleasures of others.
8B. Self-Defeating (Masochistic)	Debased: inner representations are composed of disparaged past memories and discredited achievements, of positive feelings and erotic drives transposed onto their least attractive opposites, of internal conflicts intentionally aggravated, of mechanisms of anxiety reduction subverted by processes which intensify discomfort.
S. Schizotypal	Chaotic: inner representations consist of a jumble of piecemeal memories and percepts, random drives and impulses, and uncoordinated channels of regulation that are only fitfully competent for binding tensions, accomodating needs and mediating conflicts.
C. Borderline	Incompatible: rudimentary and expediently devised, but repetitively aborted, learnings have led to perplexing memories, enigmatic attitudes, contradictory needs, antithetical emotions, erratic impulses, and opposing strategies for conflict reduction.
P. Paranoid	Unalterable: inner representations are precisely arranged in an unusual configuration of deeply held attitudes, unyielding percepts and implacable drives which, in turn, are aligned in an idiosyncratic and fixed hierarchy of tenacious memories, immutable cognitions and irrevocable beliefs.

Table 31-8

Personality	H. Intrapsychic Organization
1. Schizoid	Undifferentiated: given an inner barrenness, a feeble drive to fulfill needs, and minimal pressures to defend against or resolve internal conflicts, nor to cope with external demands, internal structures may best be characterized by their limited coordination and sterile order.
2. Avoidant	Fragile: a precarious complex of tortuous emotions depend almost exclusively on a single modality for its resolution and discharge, that of avoidance, escape and fantasy and, hence, when faced with unanticipated stress, there are few resources available to deploy and few positions to revert to, short of a regressive decompensation.
3. Dependent	Inchoate: owing to entrusting others with the responsibility to fulfill needs and to cope with adult tasks, there is both a deficit and a lack of diversity in internal mechanisms and regulatory controls, leaving a miscellany of relatively undeveloped and undifferentiated adaptive abilities, as well as an elementary system for functioning independently.
4. Histrionic	Disjoined: there exists a loosely knit and carelessly united conglomerate in which processes of internal regulation and control are scattered and unintegrated, with few methods for restraining impulses, coordinating defenses, and resolving conflicts, leading to mechanisms that must of necessity, be broad and sweeping to maintain psychic cohesion and stability, and, when successful, only further isolate and disconnect thoughts, feelings and actions.
5. Narcissistic	Spurious: coping and defensive strategies tend to be flimsy and transparent, appear more substantial and dynamically orchestrated than they are, regulating impulses only marginally, channeling needs with minimal restraint, and creating an inner world in which conflicts are dismissed, failures are quickly redeemed, and self-pride is effortlessly reasserted.
6A. Antisocial	Unbounded: inner defensive operations are noted by their paucity, as are efforts to curb refractory drives and attitudes, leading to easily transgressed controls, low thresholds for impulse discharge, few subliminatory channels, unfettered self-expression and a marked intolerance of delay or frustration.
6B. Aggressive (Sadistic)	Eruptive: despite a generally cohesive structure composed of routinely adequate modulating controls, defenses and expressive channels, surging, powerful and explosive energies of an aggressive and sexual nature produce precipitous outbursts that periodically overwhelm and overrun otherwise competent restraints.
7. Compulsive	Compartmentalized: psychic structures are rigidly organized in a tightly consolidated system that is clearly partitioned into numerous, distinct and segregated constellations of drive, memory and cognition, with few open channels to permit interplay among these components.
8A. Passive-Aggressive	Divergent: there is a clear division in the pattern of internal elements such that coping and defensive maneuvers are often directed toward incompatible goals, leaving major conflicts unresolved and psychic cohesion impossible by virtue of the fact that fulfillment of one drive or need inevitably nullifies or reverses another.

Table 31-8 (*Continued*)

Personality	H. Intrapsychic Organization
8B. Self-Defeating (Masochistic)	Inverted: owing to a signficiant reversal of the pain-pleasure polarity, structures have a dual quality—one more-or-less conventional, the other its obverse—resulting in a repetitive undoing of affect and intention, of a transposing of channels of need gratification with those leading to frustration, and of engaging in actions which produce antithetical, if not self-sabotaging consequences.
S. Schizotypal	Fragmented: coping and defensive operations are haphazardly ordered in a loose assemblage, leading to spasmodic and desultory actions in which primitive thoughts and affects are discharged directly, with few reality-based sublimations, and significant further disintegrations of structure likely under even modest stress.
C. Borderline	Diffused: inner structures exist in a dedifferentiated configuration in which a marked lack of clarity and distinctness is seen among elements, levels of consciousness occasionally blur and an easy flow occurs across boundaries that usually separate unrelated percepts, memories, and affects, all of which results in periodic dissolutions of what limited psychic order and cohesion is normally present.
P. Paranoid	Inelastic: systemic constriction and inflexibility of coping and defensive methods, as well as rigidly fixed channles of conflict mediation and need gratification, creates an overstrung and taut frame that is so uncompromising in its accomodation to changing circumstances that unanticipated stressors are likely to precipitate either explosive outbursts or inner shatterings.

Table 31-9
1. Schizoid Personality

Functional Processes

(a) BEHAVIORALLY LETHARGIC (e.g., appears to be in a state of fatigue, low energy and lack of vitality; is phlegmatic, sluggish, displaying deficits in activation, motoric expressiveness, and spontaneity).

(b) INTERPERSONALLY ALOOF (e.g., seems indifferent and remote, rarely responsive to the actions or feelings of others, possessing minimal "human" interests; fades into the background, is unobtrusive, has few close relationships and prefers a peripheral role in social, work, and family settings).

(c) COGNITIVELY IMPOVERISHED (e.g., seems deficient across broad spheres of knowledge and evidences vague and obscure thought processes that are below intellectual level; communication is easily derailed, loses its sequence of thought or is conveyed via a circuitous logic).

(d) FLAT MOOD (e.g., is emotionally impassive, exhibiting an intrinsic unfeeling, cold and stark quality; reports weak affectionate or erotic needs, rarely displaying warm or intense feelings, and apparently unable to experience pleasure, sadness, or anger in any depth).

(e) INTELLECTUALIZATION MECHANISM (e.g., describes interpersonal and affective experiences in a matter-of-fact, abstract, impersonal, or mechanical manner; pays primary attention to formal and objective aspects of social and emotional events).

Structural Attributes

(f) COMPLACENT SELF-IMAGE (e.g., reveals minimal introspection and awareness of self; seems impervious to the emotional and personal implications of everyday social life).

(g) MEAGER INTERNALIZATIONS (e.g., inner representations are few in number and minimally articulated, largely devoid of the manifold percepts and memories, nor the dynamic interplay among drives and conflicts that typify even well-adjusted persons).

(h) UNDIFFERENTIATED INTRAPSYCHIC ORGANIZATION (e.g., given an inner barrenness, a feeble drive to fulfill needs, and minimal pressures to defend against or resolve internal conflicts, nor to cope with external demands, internal structures may best be characterized by their limited coordination and sterile order).

Table 31-10
2. Avoidant Personality

Functional Processes

(a) BEHAVIORALLY GUARDED (e.g., warily scans environment for potential threats; overreacts to innocuous events and anxiously judges them to signify personal ridicule and threat).

(b) INTERPERSONALLY AVERSIVE (e.g., reports extensive history of social pan-anxiety and distrust; seeks acceptance, but maintains distance and privacy to avoid anticipated humiliation and derogation).

(c) COGNITIVELY DISTRACTED (e.g., is preoccupied and bothered by disruptive and often perplexing inner thoughts; the upsurge from within of irrelevant and digressive ideation upsets thought continuity and interferes with social communications).

(d) ANGUISHED MOOD (e.g., describes constant and confusing undercurrents of tension, sadness and anger; vacillates between desire for affection, fear of rebuff and numbness of feeling).

(e) FANTASY MECHANISM (e.g., depends excessively on imagination to achieve need gratification and conflict resolution; withdraws into reveries as a means of safely discharging affectionate, as well as aggressive impulses.

Structural Attributes

(f) ALIENATED SELF-IMAGE (e.g., sees self as a person who is socially isolated and rejected by others; devalues self-achievements and reports feelings of aloneness and emptiness, if not depersonalization).

(g) VEXATIOUS INTERNALIZATIONS (e.g., inner representations are composed of readily reactivated, intense and conflict-ridden memories, limited avenues of gratification, and few mechanisms to channel needs, bind impulses, resolve conflicts, or deflect external stressors).

(h) FRAGILE INTRAPSYCHIC ORGANIZATION (e.g., a precarious complex of tortuous emotions depend almost exclusively on a single modality for its resolution and discharge, that of avoidance, escape, and fantasy and, hence, when faced with unanticipated stress, there are few resources available to deploy and few positions to revert to, short of a regressive decompensation).

Table 31-11
3. Dependent Personality

Functional Processes

(a) BEHAVIORALLY INCOMPETENT (e.g., ill-equipped to assume mature and independent roles; is docile and passive, lacking functional competencies, avoiding self-assertion, and withdrawing from adult responsibilities).

(b) INTERPERSONALLY SUBMISSIVE (e.g., subordinates needs to stronger, nurturing figure, without whom feels anxiously helpless; is compliant, conciliatory, placating, and self-sacrificing).

(c) COGNITIVELY NAIVE (e.g., is easily persuaded, unsuspicious, and gullible; reveals a Pollyanna attitude toward interpersonal difficulties, watering down objective problems and smoothing over troubling events).

(d) PACIFIC MOOD (e.g., is characteristically warm, tender and noncompetitive; timidly avoids social tension and interpersonal conflicts).

(e) INTROJECTION MECHANISM (e.g., is firmly devoted to another to strengthen the belief that an inseparable bond exists between them; jettisons any independent views in favor of those of another to preclude conflicts and threats to the relationship).

Structural Attributes

(f) INEPT SELF-IMAGE (e.g., views self as weak, fragile, and inadequate; exhibits lack of self-confidence by belittling own aptitudes and competencies).

(g) IMMATURE INTERNALIZATIONS (e.g., inner representations are composed of unsophisticated ideas and incomplete memories, rudimentary drives, and childlike impulses, as well as minimal competencies to manage and resolve stressors).

(h) INCHOATE INTRAPSYCHIC ORGANIZATION (e.g., entrusts others with the responsibility to fulfill needs and to cope with adult tasks, thus there is both a deficit and a lack of diversity in internal mechanisms and regulatory controls, leaving a miscellany of relatively undeveloped and undifferentiated adaptive abilities, as well as an elementary system for functioning independently).

Table 31-12
4. Histrionic Personality

Functional Processes

(a) BEHAVIORALLY AFFECTED (e.g., is overreactive, stimulus-seeking, and intolerant of inactivity, resulting in impulsive, unreflected, and theatrical responsiveness; describes penchant for momentary excitements, fleeting adventures, and short-sighted hedonism).

(b) INTERPERSONALLY FLIRTATIOUS (e.g., actively solicits praise and manipulates others to gain needed reassurance, attention, and approval; is demanding, self-dramatizing, vain, and seductively exhibitionistic).

(c) COGNITIVELY FLIGHTY (e.g., avoids introspective thought and is overly attentive to superficial and fleeting external events; integrates experiences poorly, resulting in scattered learning and thoughtless judgments).

(d) FICKLE MOOD (e.g., displays short-lived dramatic and superficial emotions; is overreactive, impetuous and exhibits tendencies to be easily enthused and as easily angered or bored).

(e) DISSOCIATION MECHANISM (e.g., regularly alters self presentations to create a succession of socially attractive but changing facades; engages in self-distracting activities to avoid reflecting on and integrating unpleasant thoughts and emotions).

Structural Attributes

(f) SOCIABLE SELF-IMAGE (e.g., views self as gregarious, stimulating, and charming; enjoys the image of attracting acquaintances and pursuing a busy and pleasure-oriented social life).

(g) SHALLOW INTERNALIZATIONS (e.g., inner representations are composed largely of superficial and segregated affects, memories, and conflicts, as well as facile drives and insubstantial mechanisms).

(h) DISJOINED INTRAPSYCHIC ORGANIZATION (e.g., there exists a loosely knit and carelessly united conglomerate in which processes of internal regulation and control are scattered and unintegrated, with few methods for restraining impulses, coordinating defenses, and resolving conflicts, leading to mechanisms that must, of necessity, be broad and sweeping to maintain psychic cohesion and stability, and, when successful, only further isolate and disconnect thoughts, feelings, and actions).

Table 31-13
5. Narcissistic Personality

Functional Processes

(a) BEHAVIORALLY ARROGANT (e.g., flouts conventional rules of shared social living, viewing them as naive or inapplicable to self; reveals a careless disregard for personal integrity and an indifference to the rights of others).

(b) INTERPERSONALLY EXPLOITIVE (e.g., feels entitled, is unempathic, and expects special favors without assuming reciprocal responsibilities; shamelessly takes others for granted and uses them to enhance self and indulge desires).

(c) COGNITIVELY EXPANSIVE (e.g., has an undisciplined imagination and exhibits a preoccupation with immature fantasies of success, beauty, or love; is minimally constrained by objective reality, takes liberties with facts, and often lies to redeem self-illusions.

(d) INSOUCIANT MOOD (e.g., manifests a general air of nonchalance and imperturbability; appears cooly unimpressionable or buoyantly optimistic, except when narcissistic confidence is shaken, at which time either rage, shame or emptiness is briefly displayed).

(e) RATIONALIZATION MECHANISM (e.g., is self-deceptive and facile in devising plausible reasons to justify self-centered and socially inconsiderate behaviors; offers alibis to place oneself in the best possible light, despite evident shortcomings or failures).

Structural Attributes

(f) ADMIRABLE SELF-IMAGE (e.g., confidently exhibits self, acting in a self-assured manner and displaying achievements; has a sense of high self-worth, despite being seen by others as egotistic, inconsiderate, and arrogant).

(g) CONTRIVED INTERNALIZATIONS (e.g., inner representations are composed far more than usual of illusory ideas and memories, synthetic drives, conflicts, and pretentious, if not simulated, percepts and attitude; all of which are readily refashioned as the need arises).

(h) SPURIOUS INTRAPSYCHIC ORGANIZATION (e.g., coping and defensive strategies tend to be flimsy and transparent, appear more substantial and dynamically orchestrated than they are, regulating impulses only marginally, channeling needs with minimal restraint, and creating an inner world in which conflicts are dismissed, failures are quickly redeemed, and self-pride is effortlessly reasserted).

Table 31-14
6A. Antisocial Personality

Functional Processes

(a) BEHAVIORALLY IMPULSIVE (e.g., is impetuous and irrepressible, acting hastily and spontaneously in a restless, spur-of-the-moment manner; is short-sighted, incautious, and imprudent, failing to plan ahead or to consider alternatives, no less heed consequences).

(b) INTERPERSONALLY IRRESPONSIBLE (e.g., is untrustworthy and unreliable, failing to meet or intentionally negating personal obligations of a marital, parental, employment or financial nature; actively violates established social codes through duplicitous or illegal behaviors).

(c) COGNITIVELY DEVIANT (e.g., construes events and relationships in accord with socially unorthodox beliefs and morals; is disdainful of traditional ideals and contemptuous of conventional values).

(d) CALLOUS MOOD (e.g., is insensitive, unempathic, and coldblooded, as expressed in a wide ranging deficit in social charitableness, human compassion or personal remorse; exhibits a coarse uncivility, as well as an offensive, if not ruthless indifference to the welfare of others.)

(e) ACTING OUT MECHANISM (e.g., inner tensions that might accrue by postponing the expression of offensive thoughts and malevolent actions are rarely constrained; socially repugnant impulses are not refashioned in sublimated forms, but are discharged directly in precipitous ways, usually without guilt).

Structural Attributes

(f) AUTONOMOUS SELF-IMAGE (e.g., sees self as unfettered by the restrictions of social customs and the restraints of personal loyalties; values the image and enjoys the sense of being free, unencumbered, and unconfined by persons, places, obligations, or routines).

(g) REBELLIOUS INTERNALIZATIONS (e.g., inner representations comprise an ungovernable mix of revengeful attitudes and restive impulses driven to subvert established cultural ideals and mores, as well as to debase personal sentiments and material attainments of society which were denied them).

(h) UNBOUNDED INTRAPSYCHIC ORGANIZATION (e.g., inner defensive operations are noted by their paucity, as are efforts to curb refractory drives and attitudes, leading to easily transgressed controls, low thresholds for impulse discharge, few subliminatory channels, unfettered self-expression, and a marked intolerance of delay or frustration).

Table 31-15
6B. Aggressive (Sadistic) Personality

Functional Processes

(a) BEHAVIORALLY FEARLESS (e.g., is unflinching, recklessly daring, thick-skinned, and seemingly undeterred by pain; is attracted to challenge, risk, and harm, as well as undaunted by danger and punishment).

(b) INTERPERSONALLY INTIMIDATING (e.g., reveals satisfaction in competing with, dominating and humiliating others; regularly expresses verbally abusive and derisive social commentary, as well as exhibiting vicious, if not physically brutal behavior).

(c) COGNITIVELY DOGMATIC (e.g., is strongly opinionated and close-minded, as well as unbending and obstinate in holding to one's preconceptions; exhibits a broadranging authoritarianism, social intolerance, and prejudice).

(d) HOSTILE MOOD (e.g., has an excitable and pugnacious temper which flares readily into contentious argument and physical belligerance; is mean-spirited and fractious, willing to do harm, even persecute others to get one's way).

(e) ISOLATION MECHANISM (e.g., can be coldblooded and remarkably detached from an awareness of the impact of one's destructive acts; views objects of violation impersonally, as symbols of devalued groups devoid of human sensibilities).

Structural Attributes

(f) COMPETITIVE SELF-IMAGE (e.g., is proud to characterize self as assertively independent, vigorously energetic, and realistically hardheaded; values aspects of self that present tough, domineering and power-oriented image).

(g) PERNICIOUS INTERNALIZATIONS (e.g., inner representations are best distinguished by the presence of strongly driven aggressive energies and malicious attitudes, as well as by a contrasting paucity of sentimental memories, tender affects, internal conflicts, shame, or guilt feelings).

(h) ERUPTIVE INTRAPSYCHIC ORGANIZATION (e.g., despite a generally cohesive structure composed of routinely adequate modulating controls, defenses, and expressive channels, surging, powerful, and explosive energies of an aggressive and sexual nature produce precipitous outbursts that periodically overwhelm and overrun otherwise competent restraints).

Table 31-16
7. Compulsive Personality

Functional Processes

(a) BEHAVIORALLY DISCIPLINED (e.g., maintains a regulated, repetitively structured, and highly organized life pattern; is perfectionistic, insisting that subordinates adhere to personally established rules and methods).

(b) INTERPERSONALLY RESPECTFUL (e.g., exhibits unusual adherence to social conventions and proprieties; prefers polite, formal, and correct personal relationships).

(c) COGNITIVELY CONSTRICTED (e.g., constructs world in terms of rules, regulations, time schedules and social hierarchies; is unimaginative, indecisive, and notably upset by unfamiliar or novel ideas and customs).

(d) SOLEMN MOOD (e.g., is unrelaxed, tense, joyless, and grim; restrains warm feelings and keeps most emotions under tight control).

(e) REACTION FORMATION MECHANISM (e.g., repeatedly presents positive thoughts and socially commendable behaviors that are diametrically opposite ones deeper, contrary and forbidden feelings; displays reasonableness and maturity when faced with circumstances that evoke anger or dismay in others).

Structural Attributes

(f) CONSCIENTIOUS SELF-IMAGE (e.g., sees self as industrious, reliable, meticulous and efficient; fearful of error or misjudgment and, hence overvalues aspects of self that exhibit discipline, perfection, prudence, and loyalty).

(g) CONCEALED INTERNALIZATIONS (e.g., only those inner affects, attitudes and actions which are socially approved are allowed conscious awareness or behavioral expression, resulting in gratification being highly regulated, forbidden impulses sequestered and tightly bound, personal and social conflicts defensively denied, kept from awareness, and all maintained under stringent control).

(h) COMPARTMENTALIZED INTRAPSYCHIC ORGANIZATION (e.g., psychic structures are rigidly organized in a tightly consolidated system that is clearly partitioned into numerous, distinct, and segregated constellations of drive, memory, and cognition, with few open channels to permit interplay among these components).

Table 31-17
8A. Passive–Aggressive Personality

Functional Processes

(a) BEHAVIORALLY STUBBORN (e.g., resists fulfilling expectancies of others, frequently exhibiting procrastination, inefficiency, and erratic, as well as other contrary and irksome behaviors; reveals gratification in demoralizing and undermining the pleasures and aspirations of others).

(b) INTERPERSONALLY CONTRARY (e.g., assumes conflicting and changing roles in social relationships, particularly dependent acquiescence and assertive independence; is concurrently or sequentially obstructive and intolerant of others, expressing either negative or incompatible attitudes).

(c) COGNITIVELY NEGATIVISTIC (e.g., is cynical, skeptical, and untrusting, approaching positive events with disbelief, and future possibilities with trepidation; has a misanthropic view of life, expressing disdain and caustic comments toward those experiencing good fortune).

(d) IRRITABLE MOOD (e.g., frequently touchy, obstinate, and resentful, followed in turn by sulky and moody withdrawal; is often fretful and impatient, reporting being easily annoyed or frustrated by others).

(e) DISPLACEMENT MECHANISM (e.g., discharges anger and other troublesome emotions either indirectly or by shifting them from their instigator to settings or persons of lesser significance; expresses resentments by substitute or passive means, such as acting inept or perplexed, or behaving in a forgetful or indolent manner).

Structural Attributes

(f) DISCONTENTED SELF-IMAGE (e.g., sees self as misunderstood, unappreciated and demeaned by others; recognizes being characteristically resentful, disgruntled and disillusioned with life).

(g) OPPOSITIONAL INTERNALIZATIONS (e.g., inner representations comprise a complex of countervailing inclinations and incompatible memories that are driven pervasively by strong dissident impulses designed to nullify the achievements and pleasures of others).

(h) DIVERGENT INTRAPSYCHIC ORGANIZATION (e.g., there is a clear division in the pattern of internal elements such that coping and defensive maneuvers are often directed toward incompatible goals, leaving major conflicts unresolved and psychic cohesion impossible by virtue of the fact that fulfillment of one drive or need inevitably nullifies or reverses another).

Table 31-18
8B. Self-Defeating (Masochistic) Personality

Functional Processes

(a) BEHAVIORALLY ABSTINENT (e.g., presents self as nonindulgent, frugal and chaste, refraining from exhibiting signs of pleasure of attractiveness; acts in an unpresuming and self-effacing manner, preferring to place self in an inferior light or abject position).

(b) INTERPERSONALLY DEFERENTIAL (e.g., relates to others in a self-sacrificing, servile and obsequious manner, allowing, if not encouraging others to exploit or take advantage; is self-abasing and solicits condemnation by accepting undeserved blame and courting unjust criticism).

(c) COGNITIVELY INCONSISTENT (e.g., thinks and repeatedly expresses attitudes contrary to inner feelings; experiences contrasting emotions and conflicting thoughts toward self and others, notably love, rage and guilt).

(d) DOLEFUL MOOD (e.g., is frequently forlorn and mournful; will intentionally display a plaintive and gloomy appearance, occasionally to induce guilt and discomfort in others).

(e) DEVALUATION MECHANISM (e.g., repetitively recalls past injustices and anticipates future disappointments as a means of raising distress to homeostatic levels; misconstrues, if not sabotages good fortune so as to enhance or maintain preferred suffering and pain).

Structural Attributes

(f) UNDESERVING SELF-IMAGE (e.g., focuses on the very worst features of self, asserting thereby that one is worthy of being shamed, humbled, and debased; feels that one has failed to live up to the expectations of others and, hence, deserves to suffer painful consequences).

(g) DEBASED INTERNALIZATIONS (e.g., inner representations are composed of disparaged past memories and discredited achievements, of positive feelings and erotic drives transposed into their least attractive opposites, of internal conflicts intentionally aggravated, of mechanisms of anxiety reduction subverted by processes which intensify discomfort).

(h) INVERTED INTRAPSYCHIC ORGANIZATION (e.g., owing to a significant reversal of the pain–pleasure polarity, structures have a dual quality—one more-or-less conventional, the other its obverse—resulting in a repetitive undoing of affect and intention, of a transposing of channels of need gratification with those leading to frustration, and of engaging in actions which produce antithetical, if not self-sabotaging consequences).

Table 31-19
S. *Schizotypal Personality*

Functional Processes

(a) BEHAVIORALLY ABERRANT (e.g., exhibits socially gauche habits and pecular mannerisms; is perceived by others as eccentric, disposed to behave in an unobtrusively odd, aloof, curious, or bizarre manner).

(b) INTERPERSONALLY SECRETIVE (e.g., prefers privacy and isolation, with few, highly tentative attachments and personal obligations; has drifted over time into increasingly peripheral vocational roles and clandestine social activities).

(c) COGNITIVELY AUTISTIC (e.g., mixes social communication with personal irrelevancies, circumstantial speech, ideas of reference and metaphorical asides; is ruminative, appears self-absorbed and lost in daydreams with occasional magical thinking, obscure suspicious and a blurring of fantasy and reality).

(d) DISTRAUGHT OR INSENTIENT MOOD (e.g., reports being apprehensive and ill-at-ease, particularly in social encounters; is agitated and anxiously watchful, distrustful of others and wary of their motives); *or* (e.g., manifests drab, apathetic, sluggish, joyless, and spiritless appearance; reveals marked deficiencies in face-to-face rapport and emotional expression).

(e) UNDOING MECHANISM (e.g., bizarre mannerisms and idiosyncratic thoughts appear to reflect a retraction or reversal of previous acts or ideas that have stirred feelings of anxiety, conflict or guilt; ritualistic or "magical" behaviors serve to repent for or nullify assumed misdeeds or "evil" thoughts).

Structural Attributes

(f) ESTRANGED SELF-IMAGE (e.g., possesses permeable ego-boundaries, exhibiting recurrent social perplexities and illusions as well as experiences of depersonalization, derealization and dissociation; sees self as forlorn, with repetitive thoughts of life's emptiness and meaninglessness).

(g) CHAOTIC INTERNALIZATIONS (e.g., inner representations consist of a jumble of piecemeal memories and percepts, random drives and impulses, and uncoordinated channels of regulation that are only fitfully competent for binding tensions, accommodating needs and mediating conflicts).

(h) FRAGMENTED INTRAPSYCHIC ORGANIZATION (e.g., coping and defensive operations are haphazardly ordered in a loose assemblage, leading to spasmodic and desultory actions in which primitive thoughts and affects are discharged directly, with few reality-based sublimations, and significant further disintegrations of structure likely under even modest stress).

Table 31-20
C. Borderline Personality

Functional Processes

(a) BEHAVIORALLY PRECIPITATE (e.g., displays a desultory energy level with sudden, unexpected and impulsive outbursts; abrupt, endogenous shifts in drive state and in inhibitory control, places activation equilibrium in constant jeopardy).

(b) INTERPERSONALLY PARADOXICAL (e.g., although needing attention and affection, is unpredictably contrary, manipulative, and volatile, frequently eliciting rejection rather than support; reacts to fears of separation and isolation in angry, mercurial and often self-damaging ways).

(c) COGNITIVELY CAPRICIOUS (e.g., experiences rapidly changing, fluctuating and antithetical perceptions or thoughts concerning passing events; vacillating and contradictory reactions are evoked in others by virtue of ones behaviors, creating, in turn, conflicting and confusing social feedback).

(d) LABILE MOOD (e.g., fails to accord unstable mood level with external reality; has either marked shifts from normality to depression to excitement, or has extended periods of dejection and apathy, interspersed with brief spells of anger, anxiety, or euphoria).

(e) REGRESSION MECHANISM (e.g., retreats under stress to developmentally earlier levels of anxiety tolerance, impulse control and social adaptation; among adolescents, is unable to cope with adult demands and conflicts, as evident in immature, if not increasingly infantile behaviors).

Structural Attributes

(f) UNCERTAIN SELF-IMAGE (e.g., experiences the confusions of an immature, nebulous or wavering sense of identity; seeks to redeem precipitate actions and changing self-presentations with expressions of contrition and self-punitive behaviors).

(g) INCOMPATIBLE INTERNALIZATIONS (e.g., rudimentary and expediently devised, but repetitively aborted, learnings have led to perplexing memories, enigmatic attitudes, contradictory needs, antithetical emotions, erratic impulses, and opposing strategies for conflict reduction).

(h) DIFFUSED INTRAPSYCHIC ORGANIZATION (e.g., inner structures exist in a dedifferentiated configuration in which a marked lack of clarity and distinctness is seen among elements, levels of consciousness occasionally blur and an easy flow occurs across boundaries that usually separate unrelated percepts, memories, and affects, all of which results in periodic dissolutions of what limited psychic order and cohesion is normally present).

Table 31-21
P. Paranoid Personality

Functional Processes

(a) BEHAVIORALLY DEFENSIVE (e.g., is vigilantly alert to anticipate and ward off expected derogation and deception; is tenacious and firmly resistant to sources of external influence and control).

(b) INTERPERSONALLY PROVOCATIVE (e.g., displays a quarrelsome, fractious and abrasive attitude; precipitates exasperation and anger by a testing of loyalties and a searching preoccupation with hidden motives).

(c) COGNITIVELY SUSPICIOUS (e.g., is skeptical, cynical, and mistrustful of the motives of others, construing innocuous events as signifying hidden or conspiratorial intent; reveals tendency to magnify tangential or minor social difficulties into proofs of duplicity, malice and treachery).

(d) IRASCIBLE MOOD (e.g., displays a cold, sullen, churlish, and humorless demeanor; attempts to appear unemotional and objective, but is edgy, envious, jealous, quick to react angrily or take personal offense).

(e) PROJECTION MECHANISM (e.g., actively disowns undesirable personal traits and motives, and attributes them to others; remains blind to ones own unattractive behaviors and characteristics, yet is over-alert to, and hypercritical of, similar features in others).

Structural Attributes

(f) INVIOLABLE SELF-IMAGE (e.g., has persistent ideas of self-importance and self-reference, asserting as personally derogatory and scurrilous, if not libelous, entirely innocuous actions and events; is pridefully independent and highly insular, experiencing intense fears, however, of losing identity, status and powers of self-determination).

(g) UNALTERABLE INTERNALIZATIONS (e.g., inner representations are precisely arranged in an unusual configuration of deeply held attitudes, unyielding percepts and implacable drives which, in turn, are aligned in an idiosyncratic and fixed hierarchy of tenacious memories, immutable cognitions and irrevocable beliefs).

(h) INELASTIC INTRAPSYCHIC ORGANIZATION (e.g., systemic constriction and inflexibility of coping and defensive methods, as well as rigidly fixed channels of conflict mediation and need gratification, creates an overstrung and taut frame that is so uncompromising in its accommodation to changing circumstances that unanticipated stressors are likely to precipitate either explosive outbursts or inner shatterings).

personality prototype. The defining features of each personality are listed in a standard order, with "functional" attributes preceding the "structural" ones.

Concluding Comment

This and the previous chapter are themselves summaries, brief synopses of the rationale and products of a theory. Although a number of conceptual issues were discussed, their philosophical complexities were minimized or condensed in the service of highlighting the theory's more innovative proposals.

Central to the line of development of both chapters was the belief that psychological theory can provide fruitful pathways for exposing, selecting, or deriving productive concepts. Thus, the polarity framework enabled us to generate a series of personality prototypes that correspond unusually well to the clinically derived DSM-III, Axis II disorders. The configuration of clinical attributes associated with these personality prototypes also furnished a basis for developing lists of comprehensive and parallel diagnostic criteria. The theory fulfilled two major taxonomic goals: First, its derivations match the clinical categories of a preexisting and useful classification system, and, second, it extended the range of and clarified distinctions among pretheory categories. Most personality theories of the past have formulated concepts that fail to parallel and, hence, call for substantial revisions in established clinical nosologies. The theory proposed in these chapters discards none of our personality categories, but does provide a framework and logic to coordinate, refine, and extend them.

REFERENCES

Bowers, K. S. (1977). There's more to Iago than meets the eye: A clinical account of personal consistency. In D. Magnusson & N. S. Endler (Ed.), *Personality at the crossroads*. Hillsdale, NJ: Erlbaum.

Cantor, N., Smith, E. E., French, R. D., & Mezzich, J. (1980). Psychiatric diagnoses as prototype categorization. *Journal of Abnormal Psychology, 89*, 181–193.

Dahlström, W. G. (1972). *Personality systematics and the problem of types*. Morristown, NJ: General Learning Press.

Gill, M. M. (1963). *Topography and systems in psychoanalytic theory*. New York: International Universities Press.

Grünbaum, A. (1952). Causality and the science of human behavior. *American Scientist, 4*, 665–676.

Horowitz, L. M., Post, D. L., French, R. D., Wallis, K. D., & Sieglman, E. Y. (1981). The prototype as a construct in abnormal psychology. 2. Classifying disagreement in psychiatric judgment. *Journal of Abnormal Psychology, 90*, 575–585.

Kendell, R. E. (1975). *The role of diagnosis in psychology*. Oxford: Blackwell Scientific Publications.

Leary, T. (1957). *Interpersonal diagnosis of personality*. New York: Ronald Press.

Meehl, P. E. (1978). Theoretical risks and tabular asterisks: Sir Karl, Sir Ronald, and the slow progress of soft psychology. *Journal of Consulting and Clinical Psychology, 46,* 806–834.

Millon, T. (1969). *Modern psychopathology: A biosocial approach to maladaptive learning and functioning.* Philadelphia, PA: Saunders.

Millon, T. (1981). *Disorders of personality: DSM-III, Axis II.* New York: Wiley.

Millon, T. (1983a). *Millon clinical multiaxial inventory, manual* (3rd ed.). Minneapolis, MN: National Computer Systems.

Millon, T. (Ed.)., (1983b). *Theories of personality and psychopathology* (3rd ed.). New York: Holt, Rinehart, & Winston.

Mischel, W. (1984). Convergences and challenges in the search for consistency. *American Psychologist, 39,* 351–364.

Rapaport, D. (1958). The theory of ego autonomy: A generalization. *Bulletin of the Menninger Clinic, 22,* 13–35.

Rapaport, D. (1959). The structure of psychoanalytic theory: A systematizing attempt. In S. Koch (Ed.), *Psychology: A study of a science* (Vol. 3). New York: McGraw-Hill.

Reich, J. (1984). Instruments measuring Axis II of DSM-III: A review. In *DSM-III: A continuing review.* Symposium presented at the meeting of the American Psychiatric Association, Los Angeles, May.

Widiger, T., & Kelso, K. (1983). Psychodiagnosis of Axis II. *Clinical Psychology Review, 3,* 491–510.

Author Index

713

Subject Index